Optimum Vitamin Nutrition

in the production of quality animal foods

Published by 5M Publishing
Benchmark House
8 Smithy Wood Drive
Sheffield, S35 1QN
United Kingdom
www.5mpublishing.com
books@5mpublishing.com

ISBN: 978-0-9555011-4-2

Printed in the United Kingdom February 2013.

A CIP catalogue record for this book is available from the British Library.

DSM Nutritional Products Ltd
Animal Nutrition & Health
PO Box 2676
4002 Basel, Switzerland
Phone: +41 61 815 8888
Fax: +41 61 815 8270
www.dsmnutritionalproducts.com

Requests for permission to reproduce or translate DSM Nutritional Products publications should be submitted to the address above.

CONTENTS

TABLE OF CONTENTS

FOREWORD

The vital importance of vitamins for the health of humans and other animals was established in the early and mid-20th century. Their specific roles in metabolism were investigated and a great deal of research was carried out to set the minimum requirement for each vitamin by each class and age of farm livestock. The main aim in those times was to find the minimum amounts to avoid deficiency symptoms. This work was carried out around the middle of the 20th century, and a number of highly respected organisations, such as the National Research Council of the US, Agricultural Research Council of the UK and France's Institut National de Recherche Agronomique based their estimates of vitamin requirements on the substantial body of research and published these around 20 years ago.

In the meantime, our food-producing animals - particularly poultry and pigs but cattle too - have changed fundamentally in terms of their productivity, and the systems under which they are kept have been modernised for greater efficiency. The impact of these changes on an animal's requirement for a particular vitamin today can be little better than educated guesswork, since hardly any research has been conducted into the needs of modern genotypes in the intervening years.

The last two decades have also seen significant changes in societal attitudes, including a greater interest by consumers in how their food is produced, which has raised concerns, among others, related to animal welfare, the developments of antibiotic resistance in pathogens (in both human and veterinary medicine) and greater demands on food quality, both as a source of nutrients and a lifestyle choice.

To help update our knowledge of these complexities of 21st century life, DSM Nutrition has invited recognised experts in their respective fields to review the vitamin requirements of the various classes of farm livestock for maintenance, growth, breeding and production. They have also addressed aspects of animal health and welfare, as well as product (meat, milk egg) quality, where appropriate.

The resulting book, Optimum Vitamin Nutrition – in the Production of Quality Animal Foods, comprises seven chapters that will provide a valuable reference for the many nutritionists, veterinarians and other technicians around the world involved in animal production.

The book will also provide a useful basis for future research into the as-yet undiscovered ways in which vitamins can play a role in providing a growing global human population with adequate quantities of nutritious and safe food in a sustainable way, respecting both animal welfare and the environment.

Jackie Linden
Senior Editor, *ThePoultrySite.com*
Sheffield, UK
July 2012

THE IMPORTANCE OF OPTIMUM VITAMIN NUTRITION FOR THE FOOD CHAIN

J. M. Hernández, G. Weber and M. F. Soto-Salanova
DSM, Switzerland

UPDATING THE NUTRITIONAL STANDARDS OF VITAMINS IN A CONSTANTLY EVOLVING WORLD

Today, well into the 21st century, the crucial issues relating to the production of food are changing. Key concepts such as productivity and efficiency continue to be of vital importance. But more and more the emphasis is on the quality of food, health and animal welfare. Indicators point to the need for continuous development in the field of animal nutrition to meet future challenges posed by the livestock industry in our times and environment.

Vitamins play crucial roles in both human and animal nutrition. As organic catalysts present in small quantities in the majority of foods, they are essential for the normal functioning of metabolic and physiological processes such as growth, development, health and reproduction. The requirements for vitamins in animals are not fixed: they vary according to new genotypes, levels of yield and production systems. Vitamin functions and requirements are increasingly better understood.

The new concept of **optimum vitamin nutrition** is essential today. Its object is

to develop a new standard for vitamin supplementation in the diet of livestock, aimed not only at preventing the initial phases of some diseases, but also improving an animal's productive growth rate, given a healthier environment.

What we are talking about is optimum vitamin supplementation in the diet of animals, over and above the established minimum requirements, and adapted to the specific conditions of each animal species, permitting an improvement in the animal's state of health and well-being, thus optimizing its productive potential at the same time as ensuring the production of high-quality and nutritionally balanced foods.

Vitamin requirements in animals are affected by a multitude of factors. The inclusion of a nutritional program with appropriate levels of vitamins in an animal's diet not only allows it to completely realise its genetic potential, but at the same time improves various aspects related to health and well-being, its productivity and the quality of the

Figure 1. Reduction in the time needed for a broiler to achieve 1.5 kg of live weight

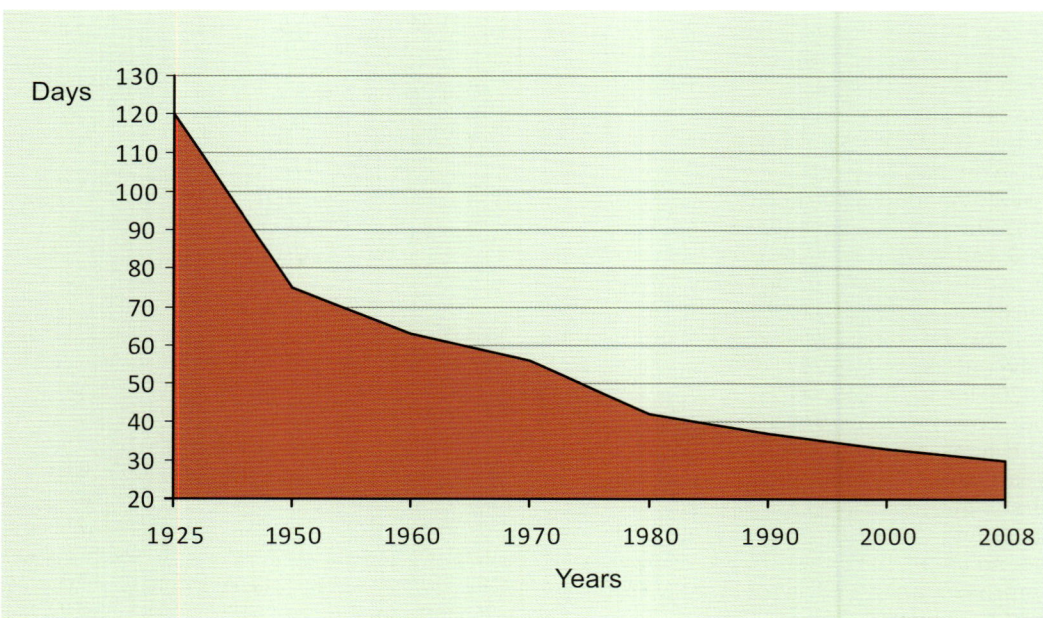

Figure 2. Development of consumption/bird and feed conversion in broilers (1955-2008).
(Source: Broiler management guides)

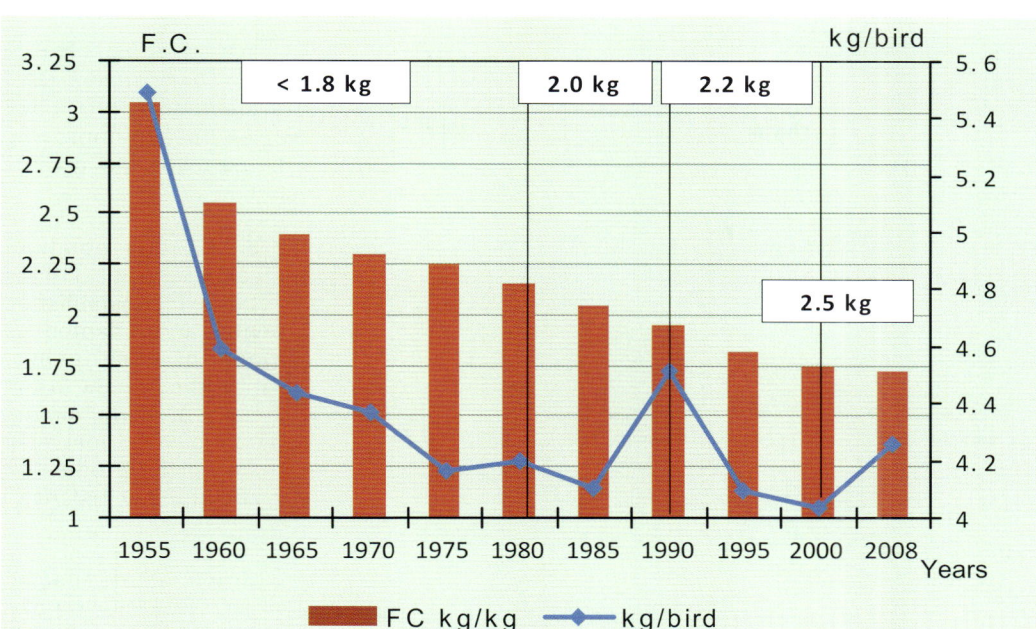

food it produces, be it meat, milk or eggs. Healthier animals will produce healthier foods.

Historically, the recommendations on vitamins suggested by various international scientific organs such as the NRC, ARC, INRA *(National Research Council, Agriculture Research Council, Institut National de Recherche Agronomique)*, etc. were given with the objective of preventing nutritional deficiencies, and some of the studies on which they are based are more than 10, 20 or even 30 years old. We all know that the livestock industry today has little in common with the industry of 30 years ago. **Figures 1, 2, 3 and 4** show a comparison where it can be seen that key performance parameters such as average daily weight gain, feed conversion rate, carcass yield in poultry have increased by 50-100% compared to 1970. In parallel, average milk production per cow per year has more than doubled and hens produce 35% more eggs than 30 years ago. It is logical to assume, therefore, that nutrition programs for farm animals, including vitamin supplements, need to be adjusted in a manner consistent with improved animal management techniques and genetic makeup.

Figure 3. Improvements in chicken carcass yield and composition
(Havenstein *et al.*, 1994, 2003)

Characteristic	1957	1991	2003
Age, days	84	42	42
Live weight, kg	1.41	2.13	2.67
Carcass weight, kg	0.91	1.39	1.93
Carcass yield, %	65.1	67.7	72.3
% breast	13.0	15.0	20.0
% carcass fat	12.3	14.2	13.7
% abdominal fat	1.1	1.5	1.4

Likewise, in recent times there have been important legislative changes in the European Union (EU) which have put an end to the use of animal by-product meal, growth promoters and a great majority of antibiotics, substances which until recently were routinely used in animals' feed. At the same time the EU is developing new rules on animal welfare which, in the short to medium term, will entail less intensive methods in the livestock industry, with the

13

Figure 4. Improvements in turkey carcass yield and composition (Herendy *et al.*, 2004)

Characteristic	Males 1967 rate	Males 1999 rate	Females 1967 rate	Females 1999 rate
Live weight, kg				
6 weeks	0.91	2.59	0.74	1.60
10 weeks	2.42	6.72	1.71	5.24
16 weeks	4.64	13.90	3.17	10.19
20 weeks	6.12	19.14	3.89	12.62
% carcass yield, 20 weeks	62.5	77.3	65.0	83.4
% breast/live weight 20 weeks	13.6	24.9	13.8	26.2
% abdominal fat/l.w., 20 weeks	0.9	0.9	1.8	2.5

aim of improving the health and well-being of the animals. Although these changes have started in Europe, other countries are moving into that direction e.g. new legislation to ban battery cages for laying hens in California in 2010; banning antibiotics in ruminants in Uruguay in 2011. Additionally, European retailers and wholesalers are demanding EU specifications when importing meat and eggs from third countries such as Brazil, Argentina, India, etc. which is making the global industry move in the same direction.

Meanwhile, farmers need to be competitive with regard to livestock productivity (weight gain, conversion indices, final weight of the animal, etc.) to face strong international competition where free trade is an ever-more tangible reality **(Figure 5)**.

From the nutritional point of view, in these fast-changing circumstances so different than those we have become accustomed to in the last few years, it is time to re-evaluate

Figure 5. Update on current broiler issues on the poultry farm

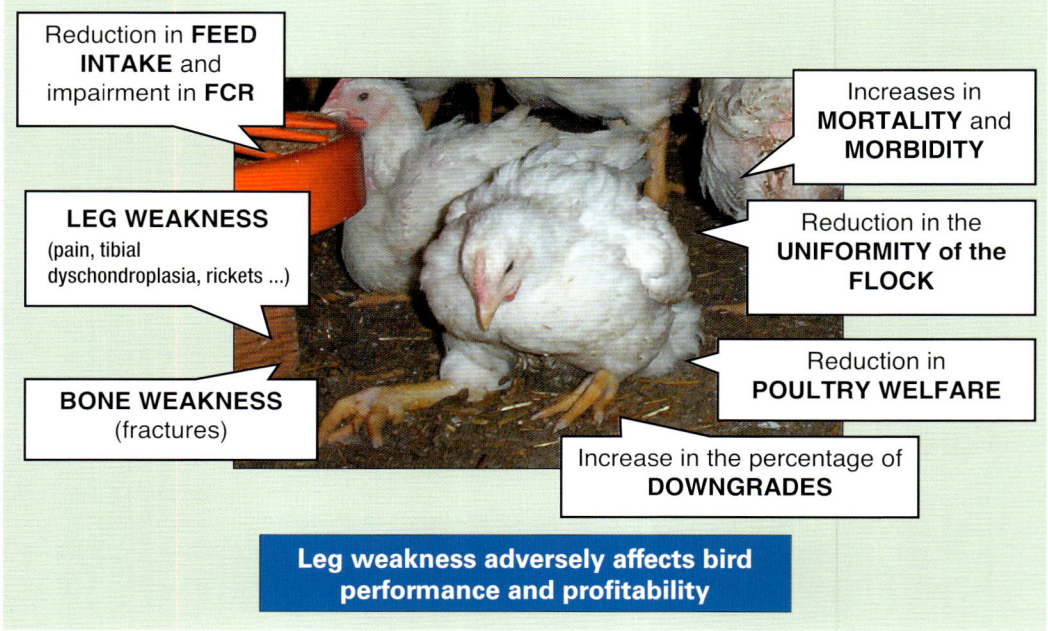

Reduction in **FEED INTAKE** and impairment in **FCR**

Increases in **MORTALITY** and **MORBIDITY**

LEG WEAKNESS (pain, tibial dyschondroplasia, rickets ...)

Reduction in the **UNIFORMITY of the FLOCK**

BONE WEAKNESS (fractures)

Reduction in **POULTRY WELFARE**

Increase in the percentage of **DOWNGRADES**

Leg weakness adversely affects bird performance and profitability

the vitamin requirements of animals with the aim of safely and efficiently producing healthy and nourishing food which meets consumer expectations.

ESSENTIAL MICRONUTRIENTS IN THE ANIMAL (ORGANISM)

Vitamins are unique and essential nutrients in the diet of both humans and animals. They are key elements in each and every one of the organism's vital functions: maintenance, growth, development, health and reproduction. They also combine two characteristics:

- the daily requirement for each of the vitamins is very small, an aspect in which they differ from macronutrients such as carbohydrates, fats and proteins;

- vitamins are organic compounds, unlike other essential nutrients such as minerals (iron, iodine, zinc, etc.).

Vitamins are particularly important because they allow optimum metabolism of other nutrients in the animal diet.

In general, humans and animals need to derive vitamins from their diet as they do not have the capacity to produce sufficient quantities by themselves. The discovery of vitamins and their function in preventing the classical deficiency diseases are among the most important achievements of the last century. Vitamins are essential for growth, health, reproduction and survival. They are present in numerous reactions of the cellular metabolism and play a critical role in the Krebs or citric acid cycles.

Vitamins may only represent less than 1% of the cost of animal feed **(Figure 6)** but they are present in 100% of metabolic functions, a fact which gives them the status of micronutrients of "macro-importance". They are found in minimal quantities in most compound feeds and their absence from the diet gives rise to specific deficiency diseases

Figure 6. Impact of vitamin cost in feed and eggs

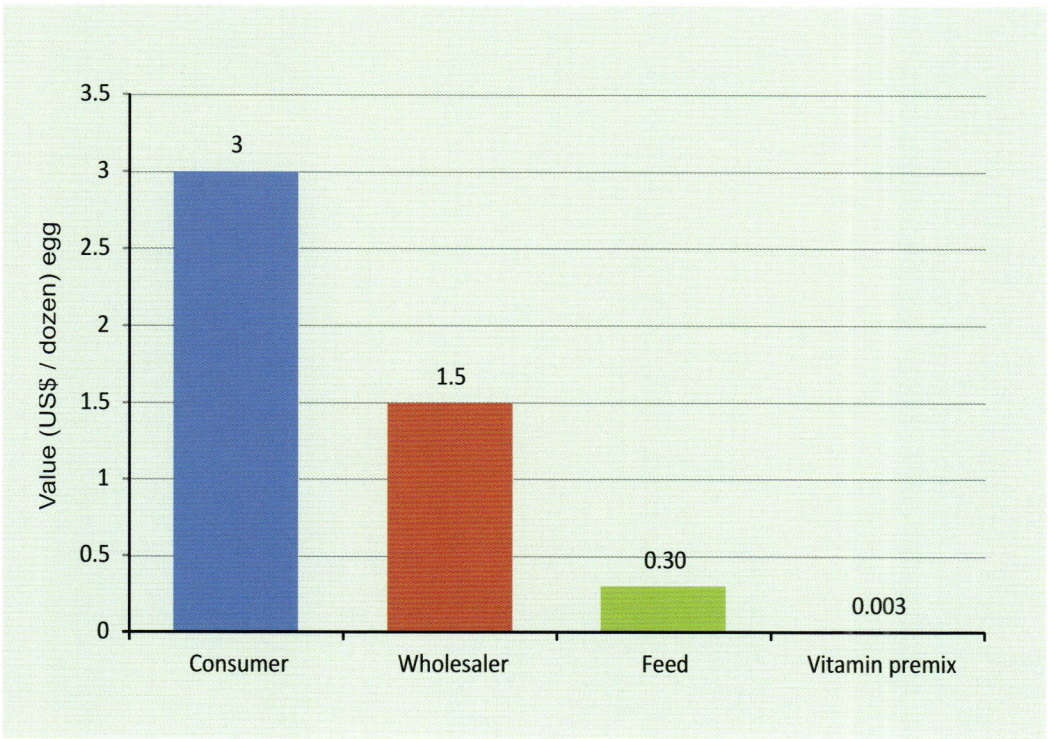

Table I. Vitamins: Active forms, summary of their functions and signs of deficiency

	Natural forms	Commercial forms	Function	Deficiency symptoms
Vitamin A	A_1 = Retinol or Retinal	Vitamin A_1 acetate and palmitate	Vision Steroid synthesis Epithelialization	Severely retarded growth Blindness Skin problems Higher susceptibility to infections
	A_2 = 3-Dehydroretinal	Retinal on protective/ hydrodispersible support		
Vitamin D	D_2 = Ergocalciferol	Vitamin D_2	Absorption and fixing of calcium D_2 shows no activity in birds	Rickets Osteomalacia
	D_3 = Cholecalciferol	Vitamin D_3 free or fixed on protective/ hydrodispersible support		
Vitamin E	α-Tocopherol	dl-α-tocopherol	Antioxidant Stimulates defenses at 20 times its minimum requirements	Muscular dystrophy Exudative diathesis Encephalomalacia
	α-Tocopherol	dl-α-tocopherol acetate		
Vitamin K	K_1 = Phylloquinone	K_1	Anticoagulant	Hemorrhages Anemia
	K_2 = Menaquinone	K_3 = menadione		
Vitamin B_1	Thiamine (aneurine)	Thiamine hydrochloride	Sugar degradation	Chick polyneuritis
		Thiamine mononitrate		
Vitamin B_2	Riboflavin	Riboflavin	H_2 transport Respiratory chain	Retarded growth leg weakness and paralysis
		Riboflavin-5-sodium phosphate		
Vitamin B_6	Pyridoxine Pyridoxal Pyridoxamine	Pyridoxine hydrochloride	In enzymes which control amino acid metabolism	Low appetite Low growth Skin disorders
Vitamin B_{12}	Cyanocobalamin	Cyanocobalamin	Co-factor in the synthesis of nucleic acids	Low growth
	Methylcobalamin	Hydroxycobalamin		
Pantothenic acid	Co-enzyme A	Ca and Na pantothenate	Interconversions between fatty acids, carbohydrates and amino acids	Loss of weight Skin disorders Nervous system disorders
		Pantothenol		
Niacin (PP)	Nicotinic acid	Nicotinic acid	Group active in enzymes of the respiratory chain	Low growth Dermatitis Leg weakness
	Nicotinamide	Nicotinamide		
Folic acid	Pteroylmonoglutamate	Folic acid (pteroylmonoglutamic)	Nucleic acid biosynthesis	Low growth Anemia Leg weakness
	Pteroylpolyglutamate			
Biotin	Free and combined D-biotin	D-biotin	Coenzyme in synthesis of fatty acids, amino acids and purines	Skin lesions Retarded growth Foot problems
Choline	Choline (ester)	Choline chloride	Transmethylations Phospholipid component	Low growth Perosis Fatty liver
Vitamin C	Ascorbic acid Dehydroascorbic acid	Ascorbic acid Ca or Na ascorbate	Corticosteroid hormone genesis	Lower resistance to stress

because of their importance for normal functioning of the metabolism. While the need to provide additional vitamins in feed is unquestioned, there are doubts about the levels of supplementation needed to achieve an optimum economic return under field conditions. As a general rule, the optimum economic supplementation level is that which allows achievements of the best rate of growth, feed conversion, state of health (including the animal's immunological status) and which in addition provides the reserves appropriate for the animal.

Nutrition is optimal when an animal efficiently utilises the nutrients provided in the feed for survival, health, growth, and reproduction **(Table I)**. Although all the nutrients, including proteins, fats, carbohydrates, minerals and water, are essential for carrying out these vital functions, vitamins play a key role in basic functions such as an appropriate

immune response in the animals.

The performance of farm animals continues to improve thanks to modern rearing and breeding systems, improvements or adjustments to housing and zootechnical advances. Intensive farming systems, though, may increase metabolic rate and lead to diseases caused by stress, increasing susceptibility to vitamin deficiencies and to suboptimal yields. A great majority of nutritionists and investigators recognize that the minimum vitamin requirements needed to prevent clinical deficiency symptoms may not be sufficient to achieve an optimum state of health and production.

The following chapters will review in greater depth the multiple metabolic functions specific to each of the vitamins in different animal species.

VITAMIN LEVELS IN ANIMAL DIET: THE NUTRITIONIST'S GREAT UNKNOWN QUANTITY

Establishing the right levels of vitamin supplementation is of great concern for animal nutritionists. Economic cost and benefit must be an essential driver for revising

and determining vitamin supplements in feed. The cost of supplementing feed with essential vitamins must be assessed taking into account the risk of suffering

Figure 7. Vitamin E levels (ppm in feed) in pigs according to different sources

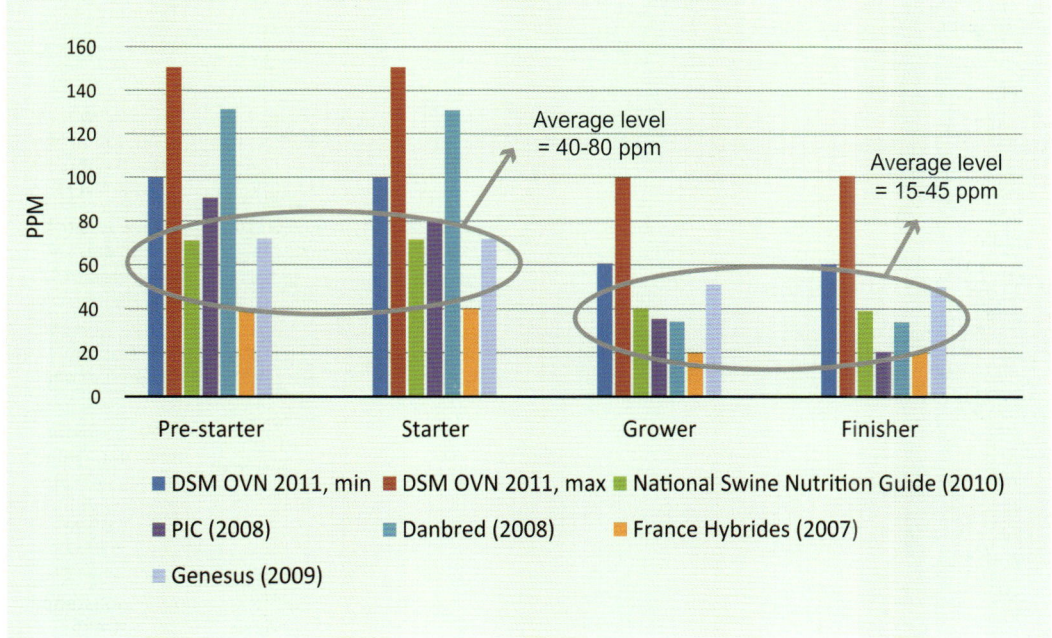

losses from deficiency symptoms and sub-optimal production. The great challenge for nutritionists, then, is to choose a particular level from the numerous recommendation tables available.

There are currently different recommendations for vitamins in feed originating from industries in the animal feed sector, research institutes, animal genetics companies and from vitamin manufacturers themselves. **Figure 7** contains an example of the use of vitamin E in swine. Here, important differences can be observed in the form in which the studies have been produced.

The Agriculture Research Council (ARC) in the UK and the National Research Council (NRC) in the USA periodically publish nutritional recommendations for different species, which generally constitute reference sources of limited value from the viewpoint of commercial feed formulation. The recommendations mentioned are based on the establishment of feed vitamin levels needed to prevent the occurrence of clinical deficiency symptoms. The recommendations of the NRC, for example, are revisions which are usually carried out on the basis of studies done in experimental conditions which are perfectly controlled but far away, in most cases, from the reality of production, and do not take into account the stress factor which is such a frequent part of livestock rearing. Stress in animals is a common fact of animal farming which can drastically influence nutritional needs, and yet the great majority of recommendations made by various research centers do not consider vitamin levels for such situations.

It is advisable to take into account the following aspects to make more efficient use of the NRC's vitamin recommendations:

1. The levels indicated have been established with the object of preventing deficiencies in the animal.

2. They do not include any kind of safety margin to cover loss of vitamin activity stemming from usual feed storage conditions or feed processing. In other words, the recommended NRC levels must be those present in the feed which the animal consumes and at the time it is eating it.

3. They do not include safety margins for the eventuality that the animals are subjected to some sort of stress (such as intensive farming) or sub-clinical disease.

4. They do not take into account possible adverse environmental conditions, such as high temperatures, which may reduce feed consumption

5. In most cases, they are not specific to the new animal genotypes which are now being produced with the aim of optimizing livestock farming.

In practice, nutritionists usually consider stress and other economically important variables in their formulations. There is a great disparity between the levels of supplementation prescribed by the industry and by the NRC or the ARC. While the industry continues to adjust vitamin supplements in feed with the object of achieving an optimum yield and state of health in the animal, the NRC has introduced only a few minor changes for the majority of animal species in the last few decades. It is unlikely that the vitamin needs established some decades ago apply to today's animals. The majority of nutritionists agree on this aspect, and in fact supplements of many vitamins are given at levels 5 or 10 times higher than those recommended by the NRC. The greatest differences are in the vitamins A, D_3, E, B_{12}, riboflavin and folic acid, while variations are minimal with K_3, pantothenic acid, niacin and B_6.

Tables II, III and IV show some examples of different vitamin recommendations for different species of animals.

Table II. Recommended vitamin levels (IU or mg/kg air-dry feed) by principal broiler genetic companies and DSM Optimum Vitamin Nutrition (OVN) levels

Grow-out phase	Source / Units	Starter				Grower				Finisher			
		Cobb (2008)*	Ross (2007)*	Hubbard (2006)	DSM OVN (2011)	Cobb (2008)*	Ross (2007)*	Hubbard (2006)	DSM OVN (2011)	Cobb (2008)*	Ross (2007)*	Hubbard (2006)	DSM OVN (2011)
Vitamin A	IU	13000-14000	11000-12000	15000	11000-15000	11000-12000	9000-10000	12500	10000-12500	11000	9000-10000	10000	10000-12500
Vitamin D3	IU	5000	5000	3000	3000-5000	5000	5000	3000	3000-5000	5000	4000	2000	3000-5000
25-OH-D3 (HyD)	mg	-	-	0.0625	0.069	-	-	-	0.069	-	-	-	0.069
Vitamin E	IU	80	75	50-100	150-300 [1][2]	60	50	30-100	50-100 [3]	50	50	30-100	50-100 [4]
Vitamin K	mg	4	3	3	3-4	4	3	3	3-4	3	2	2	3-4
Vitamin B1	mg	4	3	3	3-4	4	3	3	2-3	2	2	2	2-3
Vitamin B2	mg	9	8	8	8-10	9	8	9	7-9	8	5	6	6-8
Vitamin B6	mg	4	4-5	4	4-6	4	4-5	3	4-6	3	2-3	3	4-6
Vitamin B12	mg	0.02	0.016	0.03	0.02-0.04	0.015	0.016	0.016	0.02-0.03	0.015	0.01	0.01	0.02-0.03
Niacin	mg	60	60-55	60	60-80	50	60-55	50	60-80	50	40-35	50	50-80
D-Panthothenic acid	mg	15	15-13	15	15-20	12	15-13	10	12-18	12	15-13	10	10-15
Folic acid	mg	2	2	1.5	2.0-2.5	2	2	1.5	2.0-2.5	1.5	1.5	1	2.0-2.5
Biotin	mg	0.15-0.2	0.15-0.2	0.2	0.2-0.4	0.15-0.2	0.15-0.2	0.2	0.2-0.3	0.12-0.18	0.1	0.1	0.2-0.3
Vitamin C	mg	-	-	200	100-200 [5]	-	-	200	100-200 [5]	-	-	200	100-200 [5]
Choline	mg	400	1600	700	400-700	400	1500	600	400-700	350	1400	600	400-600

* Range for some vitamins is referred to maize (lower) or wheat (higher) diets
(1) Add 5 mg/kg for each 1% dietary fat when fat is higher than 3%;
(2) Higher level for optimum immune function
(3) Under heat stress conditions increase level up to 200 mg/kg
(4) For optimum meat quality increase level up to 200 mg/kg
(5) Recommended under heat stress conditions; use phosphorylated form in heat treated feeds

19

Table II. Recommended vitamin levels (IU or mg kg air-dry feed) for laying hens by principal genetic companies and other sources

	Source / Units	ISA Brown (2010)	Hy-Line (2010)	Lohman (2009)	Villamide and Fraga (1999)[1]	FEDNA (2008)	Leeson and Summers (2005)	DSM OVN (2011)	Maximum level in literature	Reference
Vitamin A	IU	10000	8800	10000	9300	8000-10000	8000	8000-12000	12000	Lin et al., 2002: better immune response in heat stress
Vitamin D3	IU	2500	3300	2500	2160	2000-3000	35000	3000-4000	3500; 6000; 15000	Faria et al., 1999; Mattila 2004: improved bone strenght in laying hens
25-OH-D3 (HyD)	mg	-	0.055	-	-	-	-	0.069	0.069	Terry et al., 1999: improved egg production
Vitamin E	IU	20	16.5	10-30	7.6	8-20	50	20-30 [2]	500	Bollingier et al., 1998: reduced effect of chronic heat stress
Vitamin K	mg	3.0	2.2	3.0	1.4	1.4-2.1	3	2.5-3	10	Fleming et al., 1998 and 2003: improved bone strenght in layers and pullets
Vitamin B1	mg	2.0	1.7	1.0	0.9	0.4-1.5	2	2-2.5	1.25	Padhi and Combs 1965: better productive performance
Vitamin B2	mg	5.0	5.5	4.0	3.9	4-6	5	5-7	8.8	Squires and Naber,1993b: improved production and reduced blood spots in breeders
Vitamin B6	mg	5.0	3.3	3.0	1.6	1.5-3	3	3.5-5	6	Weiser et al., 1991: prevention of bone deformities
Vitamin B12	mg	0.015	0.022	0.015	0.012	0.009-0.015	0.01	0.015-0.025	0.036	Akhmeddkanove et al., 1997: optimal production in hheat stress
Niacin	mg	40	28	30	21.4	18-35	40	30-50	250-1550	Dikicioglu et al., 2000: better shell quality and feed conversion; lower cholesterol in yolk
D-Panthothenic acid	mg	12	6.5	8	7.45	7-10	10	8-12	-	-
Folic acid	mg	0.75	0.6	0.5	0.31	0.2-0.6	1	1-1.5	1.5	Liu and feng, 1992: improved performance in old hens
Biotin	mg	0.05	0.055	0.025	0.02	0.035-0.08	0.1	0.1-0.15	-	-
Vitamin C	mg	100	-	-	-	-	-	100-200 [3]	2000	Orban et al.,1993: improved bone and shell mineralization
Choline	mg	1400	110	400	247	150-250	400	300-500	1500-2000	Mendoca et al., 1989: reduced fat deposition in liver

(1) Average vitamin supplementation in laying hens by Spanish industry
(2) Under heat stress conditions increase level up to 200 mg/kg
(3) Recommended under heat stress conditions; use phosphorylated form in heat treated feeds
References are located at the end of the Laying Hens Chapter

Table IV. Recommended vitamin levels (IU or mg/kg air-dry feed) for growing-finishing pigs by principal genetic companies and other sources

Source /Units		NRC (1998)			Average industry levels in Spain (2000)*		Average industry levels in USA (2000)**				PIC		DanBred	DSM OVN (2011)	
		20-50 kg	50-80 kg	80-120 kg	Grower/ Finisher		Grower		Finisher		25-70 kg	>70 kg	30-100 kg	30-70 kg	> 70 kg
					Average	CV%	Average	CV%	Average	CV%					
Vitamin A	IU	13000	13000	13000	7800	18	7500	27	5700	40	6500	5000	4000	7000-10000	5000-8000
Vitamin D3	IU	150	150	150	1650	22	1110	48	841	47	1200	1000	400	1500-2000	1000-1500
25-OH-D3 (HyD)	mg	-	-	-	-	-	-	-	-	-	-	-	-	0.05	0.05
Vitamin E	IU	11.0	11.0	11.0	9.5	50	27.7	35	20.0	37	35.0	20.0	36.0	60-100 [1]	60-100 [1][2]
Vitamin K	mg	0.5	0.5	0.5	0.7	130	2.3	48	1.7	59	3.5	2.0	2.0	2-4	2-4
Vitamin B1	mg	1.0	1.0	1.0	0.8	94	0.4	163	0.6	169	-	-	2.0	2-3	1-2
Vitamin B2	mg	2.5	2.0	2.0	3.35	39	5.4	26	3.8	37	6.0	4.0	2.0	7-10	6-10
Vitamin B6	mg	1.0	1.0	1.0	1.0	82	0.4	179	0.9	171	-	-	3.0	2.5-4.5	2-3.5
Vitamin B12	mg	0.010	0.005	0.005	0.02	18	0.024	32	0.019	48	0.03	0.02	0.02	0.03-0.05	0.03-0.05
Niacin	mg	10.0	7.0	7.0	15.5	30	29	28	22.0	41	25.0	20.0	20.0	20-40	20-40
D-Panthothenic acid	mg	8.0	7.0	7.0	9.00	27	18.0	31	15.0	45	20.0	15.0	10.0	25-45	25-45
Folic acid	mg	0.3	0.3	0.3	0.04	317	0.19	182	0.3	186	-	-	-	1.0-1.5	0.5-1
Biotin	mg	0.05	0.05	0.05	0.007	257	0.046	149	0.06	153	-	-	0.1	0.15-0.30	0.10-0.20
Choline	mg	-	-	-	-	-	-	-	-	-	-	-	-	150-300	100-200

* Villamide and Fraga, 2000; ** Coelho, 2000
(1) Add 5 mg/kg for each 1% dietary fat when fat is higher than 3%;
(2) For optimum meat quality additional 150 mg/kg
References are located at the end of the Pigs Chapter

BIOAVAILABILITY OF VITAMINS IN ANIMALS

Many of the raw materials used in animal feeding contain variable quantities of vitamins. The amounts of vitamins available in the feed are limited by the nutritional requirements of these materials. In practice, the vitamin amounts in feed deriving from raw materials vary considerably. The overall content is low and in any case, their presence in the feed does not guarantee their bioavailability or that the animal will indeed benefit from them.

It is common knowledge that vitamin levels in raw materials vary significantly from one geographical region to another; they also depend on the time of harvesting and the climatic conditions at each harvest. Long storage periods and the use of preservatives, fungicides, etc. negatively affect the vitamin levels in raw materials. Some of the factors which most adversely affect the level of vitamins in feed ingredients are:

- the harvest location
- the use of fertilizers
- genetic modifications which increase productive yield
- climate
- agricultural practices such as crop rotation
- harvesting conditions
- storage conditions and the use of preservatives
- bioavailability

The real content of vitamins in feed is determined by chemical and microbiological analyses in authorized laboratories, which provide the real value at a given time for a certain sample or batch of the respective ingredient. But given the great number of factors which affect the stability of vitamins (temperature, humidity, light, etc.), it would be necessary to undertake periodic costly analyses of the main raw materials to be able to use those values reliably in the formulation – at a minimum cost – of the feed, with continuous adaptation of the values to avoid potential variations of the expected level.

In many cases, vitamins derived from feed raw materials are present in complex forms, not completely released during the animal's digestive process, and therefore, cannot be absorbed by the animal, thus contributing nothing to its needs. In practice, only the content of the vitamin in its free form is taken into account when calculating the total vitamin content in feed.

The term **bioavailability** refers exclusively to the vitamin content in an ingredient which is available to be absorbed and participate in the animal's physiological and metabolic processes.

Various substances are used to protect the vitamins in commercial vitamin preparations during feed production processes and from aggressive environmental agents during storage. It is therefore essential to take into account the bioavailability of these substances when determining the vitamin content of any type of feed ingredient.

On the other hand there are in nature, both in plant and animal products, a great number of substances which can effectively limit the bioavailability of certain vitamins for the animal. These anti-nutritional agents can also be released by certain types of bacteria or fungi as by-products of their metabolic activity, as well as being present in the normal environment of the production facilities. Their most frequent mechanism of action consists of deactivating the free form of the vitamin in question or preventing its absorption. Among the most common cases we can find are:

- deactivation of thiamine (B1) by thiaminase,

- formation of an inactive compound, as in the case of the deactivation of biotin by avidin,

- blocking the site of absorption or an independent chemical reaction, as in the case of dicumarol and vitamin K.

The addition of fats and oils as energy sources is a common practice in feed manufacturing. Attention should be paid to the total content of unsaturated fatty acids, since they increase the likelihood of oils and fats becoming rancid. This would affect the absorption of fat-soluble vitamins such as A, E and D. Likewise, oxidation of the fats also contributed to biotin deactivation.

STABILITY OF VITAMINS IN ANIMAL FEED

Different factors can affect the stability of substances as unstable as vitamins, whether in their pure commercial form, in vitamin-mineral premixes (**Figure 8**) or after feed manufacturing and storage. Some of these factors are connected with the catalytic activity of the molecules themselves, the handling of commercial forms and their premixes, the characteristics of the mix, the presence of various antagonistic substances and the conditions of storage.

The vitamins present in raw materials are very susceptible to the adverse conditions mentioned above and a considerable loss of vitamin activity is a common occurrence in these macroingredients. In contrast, the highest-quality commercial forms of vitamins are generated in industrial processes which stabilise and protect the active molecules during manufacturing and storage, both in premixes and in feed. It is important that stabilisation of the vitamin must not compromize its bioavailability.

Some of the most methods in stabilising compounds are described below:.

Use of antioxidants

Antioxidants are included in the formulation of commercial vitamin products to prevent the oxidation of fat-soluble vitamins and prolong the shelf life of these compounds. The period, during which vitamin content is guaranteed, will depend to a great extent on storage conditions. In general those commercial forms which have an appropriate quantity of antioxidant substances have a longer effective shelf life.

Mechanical methods

In this case, the process consists of covering the active substance with a stabilising coat. This coating protects the vitamin molecule inside from the adverse effect of aggressive external agents such as oxygen, ultraviolet

Figure 8. Stability of different sources of canthaxanthin in a broiler breeder premix (Gadient *et al.*, 2010)

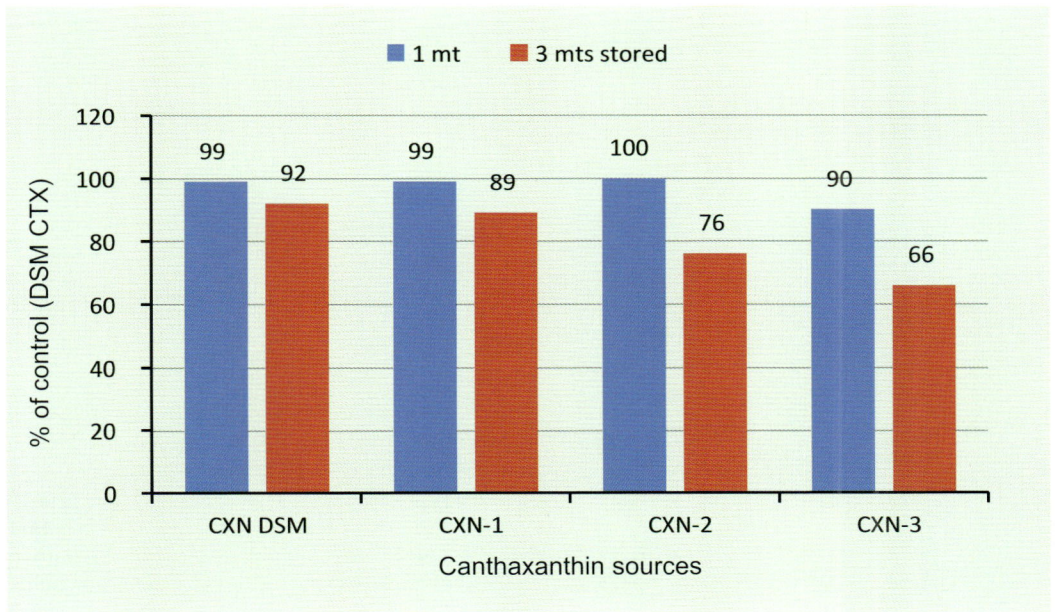

Table V. Factors which influence vitamin stability

Vitamin	Temp.	O_2	H_2O	Light	Acid pH	Alkaline pH
A	xx	xx	x	xx	x	0
D3	x	xx	x	x	x	0
E	0	0	x	x	0	xx
K3	x	x	xx	0	xx	0
B1	x	x	xx	0	0	xx
B2	0	0	x	xx	0	0
B6	xx	0	x	x	x	0
B12	xx	x	x	x	0	0
Cal. pan.	x	0	x	0	x	0
Niacin	0	0	0	0	0	0
Biotin	x	0	0	0	0	0
Folic acid	xx	0	xx	xx	xx	0

0: Stable   x: Sensitive to...   xx: Very sensitive to...

radiation from sunlight, humidity, extreme temperatures, etc. **(Table V)**.

On a practical level this method has proven highly effective for protecting these substances and, depending on their characteristics, can be combined with a process of spray drying which provides a large number of active particles (all with the active form of the vitamin) thus facilitating a subsequent homogenous mixture in the animal's feed.

In any case, the factors just mentioned will affect vitamins in different ways as shown below.

Vitamins A, D and carotenoids
- Prone to oxidation when exposed to air
- Sensitive to oxidizing agents
- Isomerise in acid pH
- Sensitive to prolonged heat
- Sensitive to the catalytic effect of minerals

Vitamin E
- Prone to oxidation in the presence of air
- Sensitive to alkaline environment
- The ester is more stable

Vitamin K
- Sensitive to heat
- Prone to oxidation in the presence of oxygen

Vitamin B_1 (thiamine)
- Stable at low pH, loss of activity when pH increases
- Sensitive to the presence of oxygen and other oxidizing agents in neutral or alkaline solutions
- Splits on reacting with sulphites, with immediate separation at pH 6
- Sensitive to metallic ions such as copper
- The thiaminases present in some animal and vegetable products are known antagonists of this vitamin

Vitamin B_2 (riboflavin)
- Sensitive to light, especially in alkaline solutions
- Stable in acid and neutral media
- Unstable in alkaline solutions
- Sensitive to reducing agents

Vitamin B_6 (pyridoxine)
- Sensitive to light
- Relatively stable in acid solutions and dry mixes

Vitamin B_{12} (cobalamin)
- Poor stability in alkaline or slightly acid environment
- Sensitive to oxidizing reactions and reducing agents
- Ascorbic acid, thiamine and nicotinamide metabolites accelerate this vitamin's decomposition
- Sensitive to light in very dilute solutions

Biotin
- Stable in air, acids and at neutral pH
- Slightly unstable in alkaline solutions

Niacin
- Relatively stable under practical conditions

Pantothenic acid
- Poor stability in alkaline or acid environment
- Very hygroscopic, especially in its dl-calcium pantothenate form
- Decomposes through hydrolysis, especially at low and high pH values

Folic acid
- Poor stability in acid solutions below pH 5
- Sensitive to oxidizing reactions and reducing agents
- Decomposes in sunlight
- Poor stability in hygroscopic environments and in the presence of minerals

Ascorbic acid
- Sensitive to radiation
- Oxidizes rapidly in all types of solution
- Catalysed by metallic ions, such as copper and iron
- Degrades rapidly at high temperatures

THE CONCEPT OF OPTIMUM VITAMIN NUTRITION IN PRACTICE

The object of this concept is to supplement animal feed with the amounts of each water-soluble and fat-soluble vitamin considered as most appropriate (the "optimum") to optimize the state of health and the productivity of farm animals while guaranteeing the efficacy (desired effect at minimum cost) of the recommended levels. The levels of supplementation required for optimum vitamin nutrition are generally higher than those necessary to prevent clinical deficiency symptoms. These optimum supplementation levels should likewise compensate for the stress factors affecting the animal or the feed, thus guaranteeing they do not limit its performance or health.

Figure 9 describes the concept of a *cost-effective window* for vitamin supplementation, in which vitamin levels must satisfy but not exceed the aim of achieving optimum health and productivity. Below, some definitions of terms applicable to the concept of optimum vitamin nutrition (OVN) shown in **Figure 9** are highlighted.

Figure 9. The Optimum Vitamin Nutrition (OVN) concept

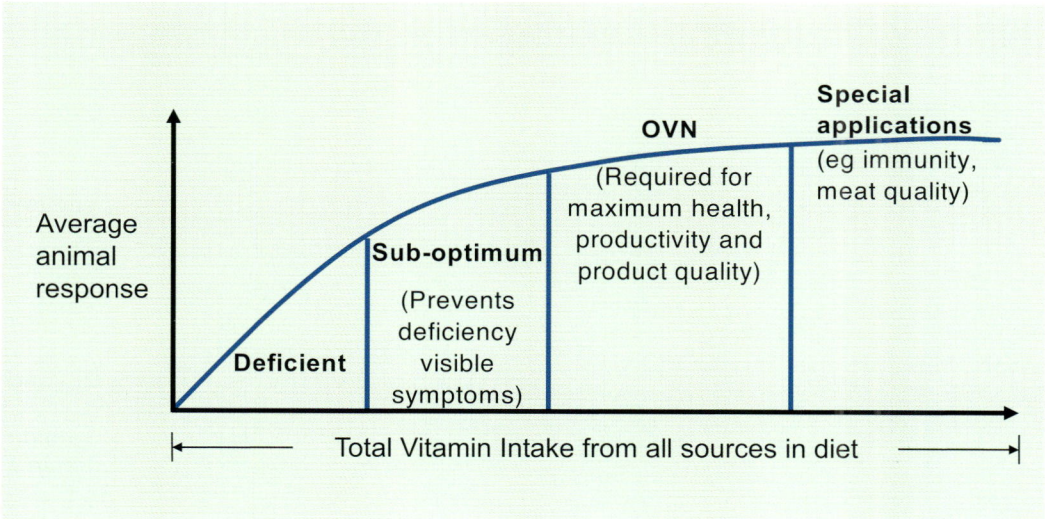

Special applications (eg immunity, meat quality)

OVN (Required for maximum health, productivity and product quality)

Sub-optimum (Prevents deficiency visible symptoms)

Deficient

Average animal response

Total Vitamin Intake from all sources in diet

1. *Animal response* refers to productivity results (feed conversion, growth rate, reproductive or immunity status, the animal's state of health, etc.) as a consequence of the ingestion of vitamins.

2. *Total vitamin intake* describes the total level of vitamins, irrespective of source, which is provided in the diet, i.e. supplemented plus bioavailable vitamins which may be present in raw materials.

3. *Deficient or minimum vitamin intake* refers to the level of supplementation which places the animal in danger of showing clinical deficiency symptoms or metabolic disorders due to a lack of nutrients and where the level of vitamins falls short of the guidelines published by the NRC.

4. *A sub-optimum intake* prevents the appearance of clinical deficiency symptoms. Supplementation levels comply with or exceed the NRC's guidelines but are not adequate to maintain an optimum state of health and productivity.

5. *An optimum intake* compensates for the negative factors influencing animal performance and therefore contributes to achieving an optimum state of well-being, health and productivity.

6. *Excessive levels of vitamin supplementation* are vitamin levels which, although still safe, impact on the cost of feed to such an extent that they are not economically justified from the productive point of view. With respect to the safety of vitamins, only very large quantities (between 10 and 100 times the levels used in practice) of some vitamins such as A and D in feed might occasionally cause some sort of disorder in animals.

Recently, consumers have been demanding food with a greater added value, such as vitamin-rich eggs or milk, the occasional consumption of which contributes to a balanced human diet. This would imply a vitamin content for feed in the range described in point 6 above, with the aim, not only to optimize the animal's productive response but also to produce an "enriched" food, according to the legislation currently in force in most countries, and with a greater added value for the final consumer.

There are different factors affecting vitamin requirements, some of them directly influencing dietary vitamin intake/supplemention and its utilization by the animal. For instance, the assessment of vitamin content in raw materials, the harvesting of these raw materials, as well as processing and storage conditions of feed ingredients, and the inherent variability and bioavailability of the vitamins can be considered of utmost importance.

Other factors affecting vitamin requirements are: the type of production, housing (especially whether or not animals are kept under cover), causes of stress, illnesses and other environmental conditions (for example, a hot environment or contamination by mycotoxins), vitamin antagonists and the use of medicaments which may limit or even block the action of certain vitamins. Requirements will therefore vary depending on the extent of these factors.

In summary, it can be stated that the implementation of a nutritional program with the most appropriate levels of all the vitamins in animal feed has a main objective of offering the following benefits to the food chain:

- *Optimum health and well-being* of animals, as a prerequisite for production of safe and healthy meat, milk and eggs.

- *Optimum productivity*, given better sanitary conditions, and greater efficiency in animal farming, considering performance parameters such as feed conversion, final body weight, weight gain, etc.

- *Optimum food quality* to provide consumers with a balanced nutrion.

OPTIMIZING ANIMAL'S HEALTH AND WELL-BEING

Improving animal health and well-being constitutes a crucial aspect in the production of food of animal origin (from the various types of meat through milk to eggs). Therefore, a primary objective for nutrition and management programs is to minimize the incidence of diseases and their debilitating effect on animals. It is common knowledge that there is a close relationship between nutrition, health and well-being.

Supplementing an animal's diet with optimum quantities of vitamins at times of greatest vulnerability to infection reduces the risk of contracting a disease.

Health and immunity

Vitamins, when given in adequate quantities, play an essential role in the ability of an animal to develop an effective immune response to disease.

Since the onset of a disease cannot be predicted, the immune system needs to be prepared long before the infection occurs.

Korver and Saunder-Blades (2006) observed

that white blood cells of chicks coming from breeders fed vitamin D_3 consistently inactivated more *E. coli* than those from the control group. The ability of the immune cells of chicks from the maternal 25-OH-D3 had a greater ability to kill pathogenic bacteria. **(Figure 10)**

Numerous studies done in swine, poultry and cattle have demonstrated a close relationship between low levels of vitamin E in the tissues and a decrease in immunocompetence (the immune system's response) long before the appearance of any clinical signs of disease. Vitamins E and C are powerful antioxidants which protect cells from free radicals and other types of by-products harmful to an animal's metabolism. The same studies proved that high levels of vitamin E in feed during the first three weeks of an animal's life resulted in:

- improvement in the immune response to infection and vaccination

- improvement in flocks affected by sub-clinical infections

Figure 10. Chick immunity improvement with 25-OH-D3 (ROVIMIX® Hy•D®) in breeder feed (chicks d1 and d4 from 31-week-old breeders, similar results at 45 & 63 weeks) (Korver and Saunder-Blades, 2006)

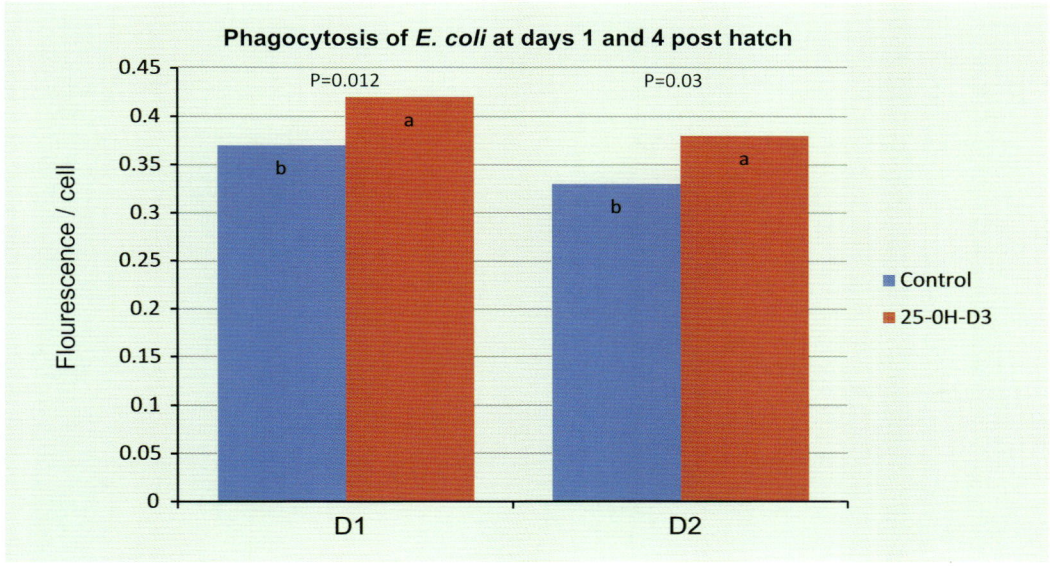

(Values with different letters are significantly different)

- fewer relapses due to secondary infections

More specifically, in pigs, the following effects were documented.

- Optimum levels of vitamin E in the diet significantly reduce mastitis-metritis-agalactia syndrome (MMA) in sows, as well as diarrhoea in piglets.

- Providing an optimum level of vitamins in the diet of sows in gestation and lactation improves the nutrient content of colostrum and milk, decreasing the immune challenges and increasing the viability of newborn piglets.

- Several studies have demonstrated beneficial effects in the health and growth of recently weaned piglets which received a vitamin C supplement in their diet.

Reproduction

When breeding animals were fed diets rich in vitamin E during growth and production, the results were:

- improved response in the production of antibodies during vaccination

- a clear association between high levels of vitamin E in the liver and more viable offspring

Increasing the vitamin E levels during embryogenesis will further enhance the immune system.

A study with 1,100 BUT turkey hens and 270 toms (Soto-Salanova et al., 2011) revealed that a combination of 25-OH-D3 and canthaxanthin improved the percentage of first grade poults from 79.5% to 81.4%. This was related to improved egg production, hatchability and fertility (**Figure 11**).

Well-being

It is well known that infections are a cause of pain and suffering in animals. In general, farmers, genetics companies, integrators, etc. involved in animal care have the utmost interest in assuming responsibility for ensuring satisfactory standards of well-being.

In the food sector too there is an increasing number of retailers, wholesale distributors, and even fast food chains which have incorporated high standards of animal welfare in their codes of best practice, with

Figure 11. Infertile eggs (%) in turkey breeders (Soto-Salanova et al., 2011) (P< 0.01)

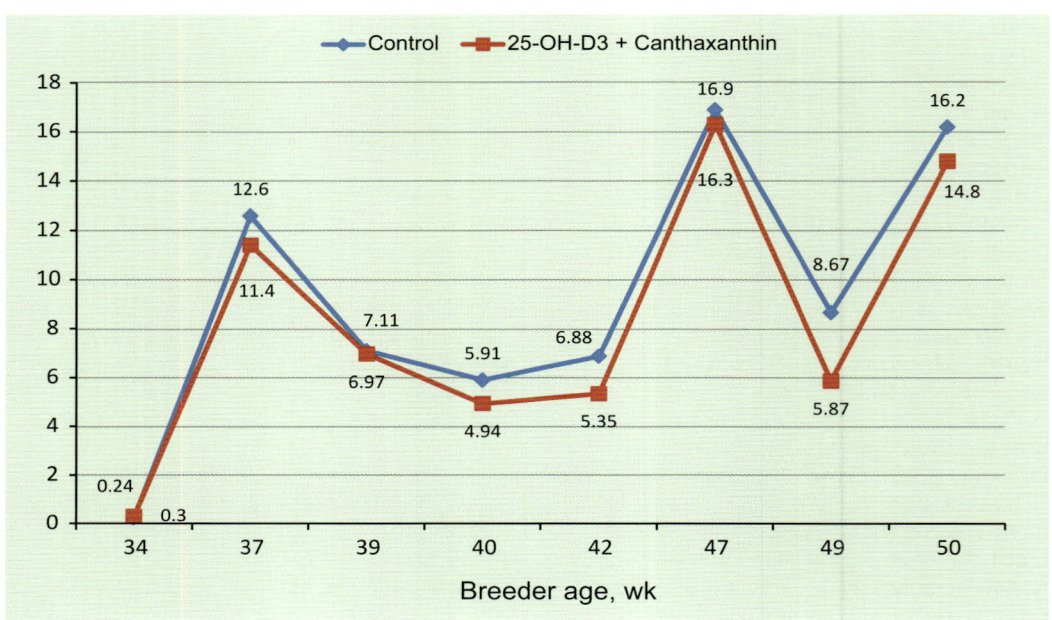

the aim of giving animals a healthy life which will contribute to ensuring healthier food for their consumers.

Optimum vitamin supplementation in an animal's diet will contribute to improving its well-being because:
• optimum vitamin levels contribute to improving the metabolism, nutrition and well-being of farm animals
• improving immunity increases resistance to diseases
• some vitamins, such as biotin, contribute to reducing the incidence of foot problems, thus preventing certain types of lameness, while others, such as vitamin C, alleviate the negative effects of stress on health

OPTIMIZING PRODUCTIVITY

In pigs, advances have been achieved over decades through genetic selection, accelerating growth rates and favoring certain genotypes to increase the production of lean meat. These advances have changed the nutritional requirements of pigs because of improvements in the utilization of feed.

Recently published data have demonstrated that pigs grow faster, under experimental and commercial conditions, when the supplementation of B-group vitamins in the diet is increased. From an economical stand point, the improvement in performance parameters after optimizing dietary vitamin supply significantly improved the cost: benefit ratio, with the consequent benefit for the farmer.

Under practical conditions, stress can represent a serious threat to achieving optimum performance. Stress reduces feed intake, and, as a consequence, vitamin concentration in the feed should be increased to satisfy the animal's needs. Stress also increases the animal's metabolic needs–so, in most cases, an initial nutritionally balanced meal will result in a diet with potential nutritional deficiencies. Recent results from pigs indicate that an appropriate supplement of vitamin C in the feed can alleviate the harmful effects of the stress caused by heat on the quality of semen, thus satisfying the nutritional requirements of boars in such demanding conditions.

Breeding sows have been selected to produce large litters with the greatest possible number of healthy and viable piglets. Several studies have clearly shown that optimum levels of biotin, folic acid, riboflavin, vitamin E, vitamin A and/or beta-carotene in an animal's diet produce excellent results in the performance of sows, such as a greater number of piglets born alive and weaned, and a decrease in the interval between weaning and estrus.

In growing poultry, several recently published North American studies suggest that a diet with high levels of vitamins of the B-group can improve the performance and the productivity of broilers. In turkeys, a multitude of studies show that high levels of biotin can improve feed efficiency, weight gain, while also reducing mortality. Likewise, trials carried out with increasing levels of biotin in wheat-based diets showed an improvement in the live weight and in the feed conversion of broilers.

In breeding birds it has been shown that high levels of vitamins are needed for the production of viable chicks. The embryo is very sensitive, not only to changes in environment, but also to insufficient supplies of most vitamins, and embryonic malformations and mortality are some of the main visible symptoms of deficiency in one or several vitamins.

In recent years, numerous tests, both experimental and in the field, have been carried out to evaluate the potential synergistic effects of feeding an optimum vitamin nutrition level on the main performance parameters, compared with the average level used by the industry. Some of these results in pig and poultry farming show a considerable economic benefit.

• +0.11-0.79 €/piglet, **(Table VI)**
• +0.03 €/kg pig live weight, López and Muñoz, 2002
• Diets with an optimum vitamin level increased the final weight of chickens by 2.7%, Pérez-Vendrell et al. 2002 **(Fig. 12)**.

29

Table VI. Cost/benefit of OVN diet for piglets
(Data not published).

		Low vit. level	Average vit level	High OVN level
Cost of feed	€/kg feed	0.187	0.189	0.191
Consumption of feed	kg/piglet	24.28	24.39	24.44
Cost of feed per piglet	€/piglet	4.54	4.61	4.67
Average daily gain (ADG)	g/piglet per day	564	568	584
Weight gain in 28 days	kg/piglet	15.792	15.904	16.352
Sale price of piglet	€/kg	1.65	1.65	1.65
Value of weight gain	€/piglet	26.06	26.24	26.98
Meat value – feeding costs	€/piglet	21.52	21.63	22.31
Net benefit OVN	€/piglet	-	0.11	0.79

Figure 12. Live weight of chicken (40 days) with control diet (c; average level of vitamins) and OVN diet, with different density of animals (28 kg/m² vs 37 kg/m²).
(Perez-Vendrell *et al.*, 2002)

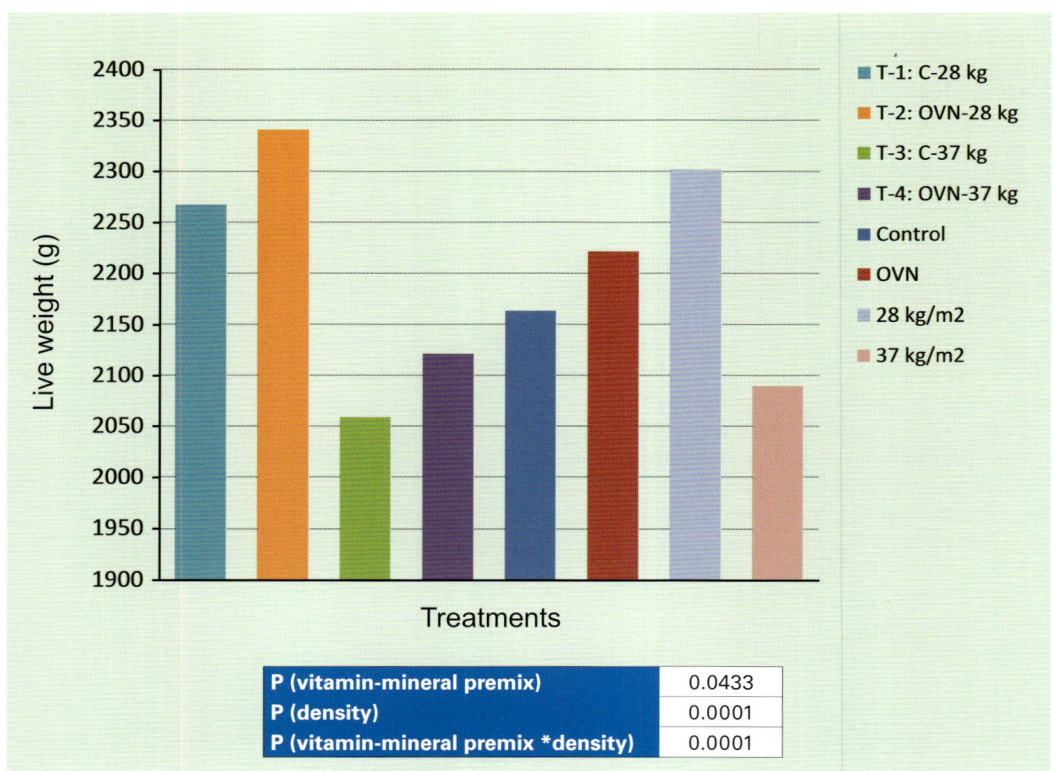

P (vitamin-mineral premix)	0.0433
P (density)	0.0001
P (vitamin-mineral premix *density)	0.0001

OPTIMIZING THE QUALITY OF FOOD FOR THE CONSUMER

Meat and eggs are sources of protein in the human diet. A gradual and continuous increase can be observed in the demand for meat and egg products, a fact which should be taken into account when defining the nutritional strategy that should be developed in animal diets.

Lipid oxidation constitutes a problem for the conservation of meat since it can lead to undesirable smells and flavors associated with rancidity, a fact of major relevance in processed meat which is particularly susceptible to this oxidation process.

Feeding animals a diet rich in unsaturated vegetable fats can considerably increase levels of monounsaturated and polyunsaturated fatty acids in meat. There are a number of polyunsaturated fatty acids which react with oxygen yielding undesirable short-chain compounds responsible for the deterioration of the organoleptic characteristics of the meat. This, in consequence, will reduce the acceptance of the meat by the consumer.

Animals fed diets with high levels of vitamin E can counteract this effect and so improve the final quality of the meat:

• by protecting the meat's lipids from oxidation, thus reducing the formation of undesirable smells and flavors,

• by reducing drip loss and improving the texture of the meat.

In the same way, inadequate supplies of vitamin E in the diet increase the probability of spontaneous oxidation of milk fat, which negatively affects its flavor, giving rise to a characteristic metallic or cardboard taste. Increasing the level of vitamin E in the cow's diet will correct the problem of oxidized milk fat, which is more frequent during the winter when cows are fed silage and/or hay.

With regards to other food of animal origin, levels of vitamins present in eggs have a direct relationship with the vitamin levels in the diet of the hen. Thus a hen feeding program based on higher vitamin levels will increase the vitamin content of eggs, and in this way contribute to giving the eggs a higher and more balanced nutritional value, as can be seen in **Figures 13,14,15, 16 and 17.**

Similar investigations by the same authors on 40-day chickens (Pérez-Vendrell *et al.,* 2002) showed that breast meat of broilers fed a diet containing optimum level of vitamins will contain more of some nutrients such as vitamins E, B_1 and pantothenic acid. This breast meat can be considered as having a more balanced nutritional value (**Figures 18, 19 and 20**).

A Europe-wide survey carried out in 1996, analyzing different samples of pork chops from a number of European countries, showed that the meat contributed four times more to a consumer's diet in Denmark, Belgium and Germany than in Spain (**Figure 21**). The lower content of an essential nutrient such as vitamin E in pork is a reflection of a lower level of vitamin E in the diet of the animals produced in Spain compared to those of other countries.

Figure 13. Vitamin A content in liquid egg (µg retinol/100g egg) with control diet (average vitamin level in industry) and OVN diet, in hens housed in sheds with poor ventilation; compared with average level in eggs
(Inst. Estudios del Huevo; Pérez-Vendrel *et al.*, 2002)

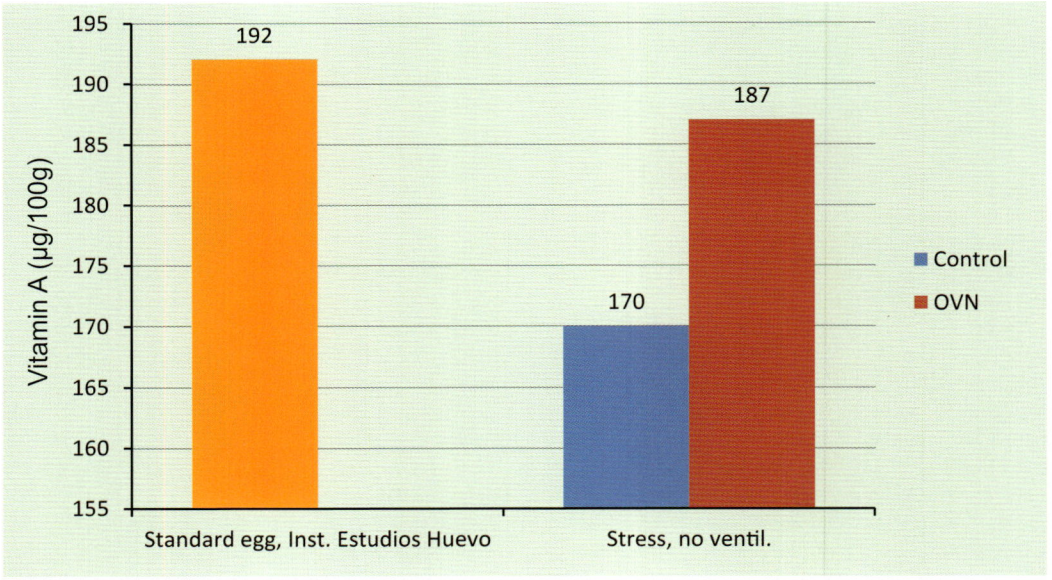

Figure 14. Vitamin B$_2$ content in liquid egg (µg/100g egg) with control diet (average vitamin level in industry) and OVN diet, in hens housed in sheds with poor ventilation; compared with average level in eggs
(Inst. Estudios del Huevo; Pérez-Vendrel *et al.*, 2002)

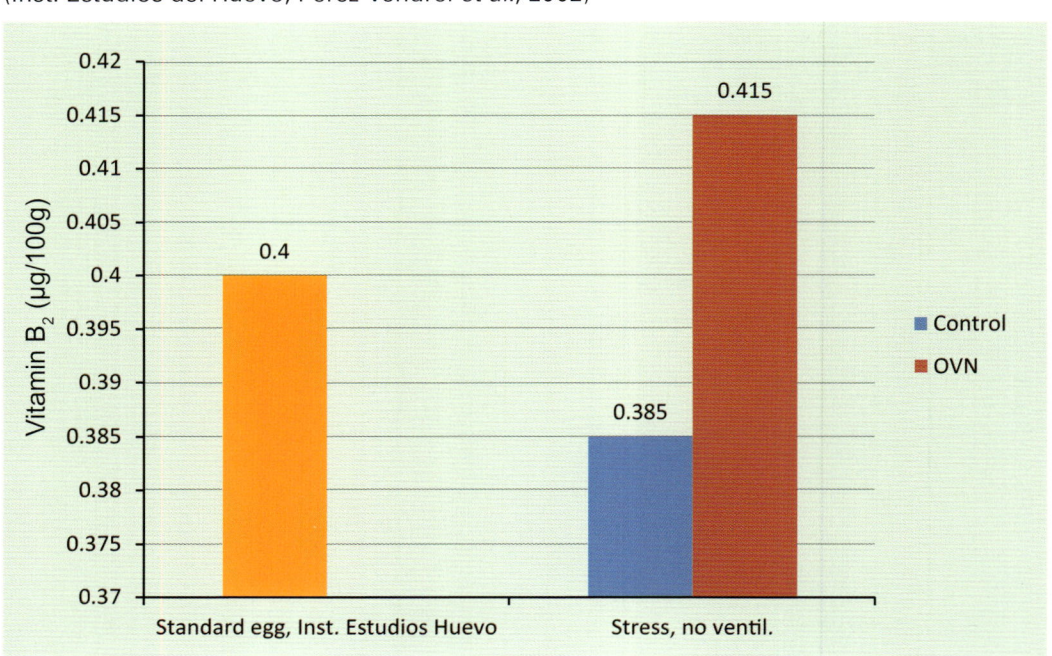

Figure 15. Vitamin B$_{12}$ content in liquid egg (µg/100g egg) with control diet (average vitamin level in industry) and OVN diet, in hens housed in sheds with poor ventilation; compared with average level in eggs
(Inst. Estudios del Huevo; Pérez-Vendrel *et al.*, 2002)

Figure 16. Pantothenic acid content in liquid egg (mg/100g egg) with control diet (average vitamin level in industry) and OVN diet, in hens housed in sheds with poor ventilation; compared with average level in eggs
(Inst. Estudios del Huevo; Pérez-Vendrel *et al.*, 2002)

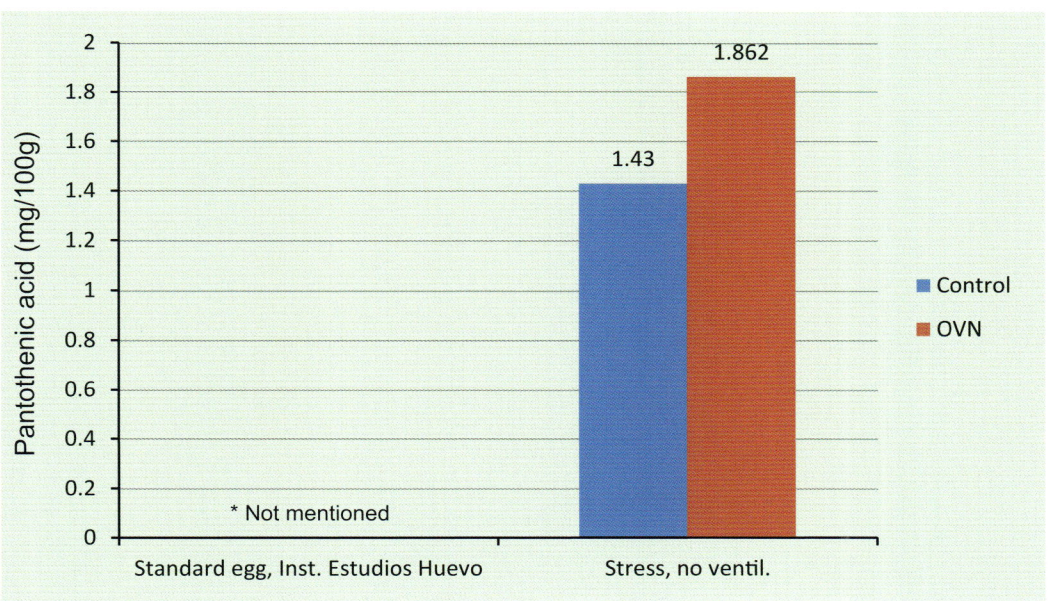

Figure 17. Biotin content in liquid egg (µg/100 g egg) with control diet (average vitamin level in industry) and OVN diet, in hens housed in sheds with poor ventilation; compared with average level in eggs
(Inst. Estudios del Huevo; Pérez-Vendrel *et al.*, 2002)

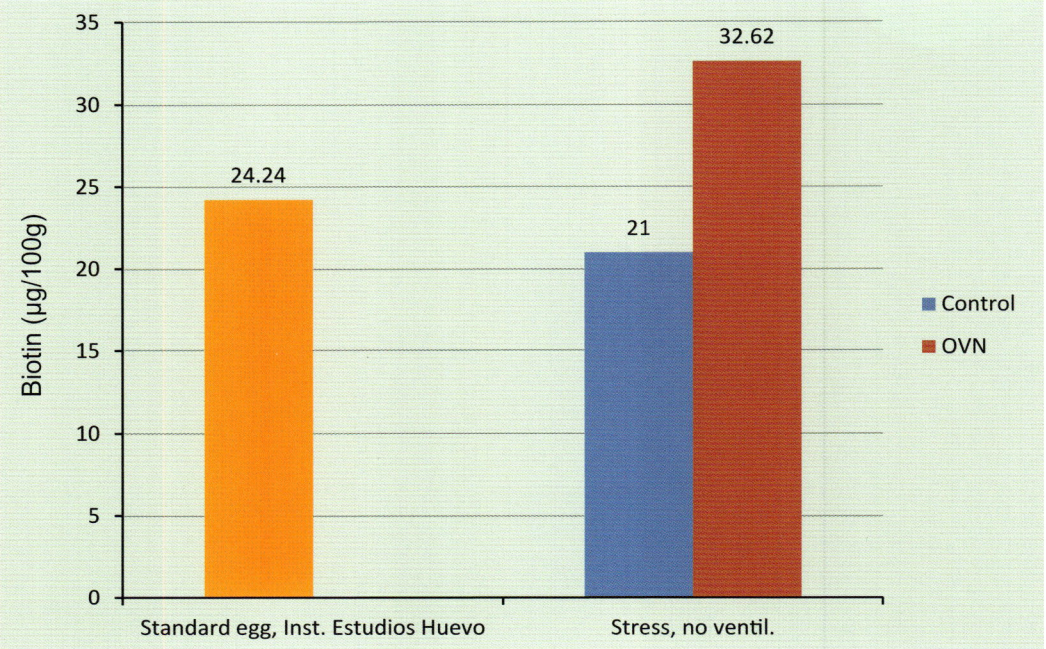

Figure 18. Vitamin E content in chicken breast (40 days) fed on control diet (average vitamin level) and OVN diet, with different density of animals (28 kg/m² vs 37 kg/m²).
(Pérez-Vendrel *et al.*, 2002)

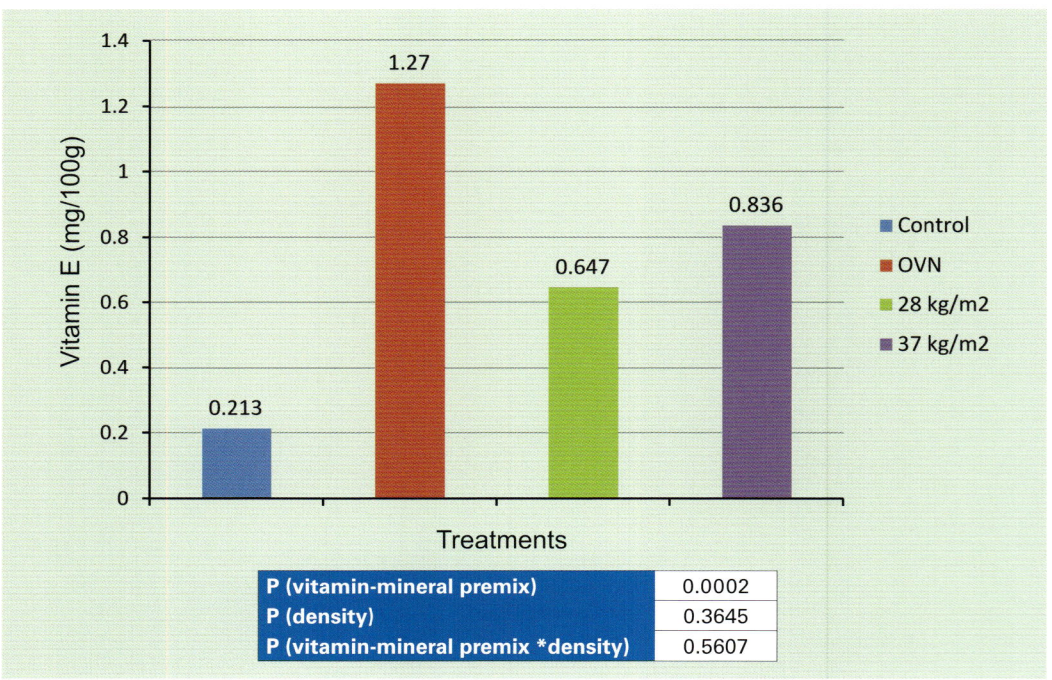

P (vitamin-mineral premix)	0.0002
P (density)	0.3645
P (vitamin-mineral premix *density)	0.5607

Figure 19. Vitamin B_1 content in chicken breast (40 days) fed on control diet (average vitamin level) and OVN diet, with different density of animals (28 kg/m² vs 37 kg/m²). (Pérez-Vendrel *et al.*, 2002)

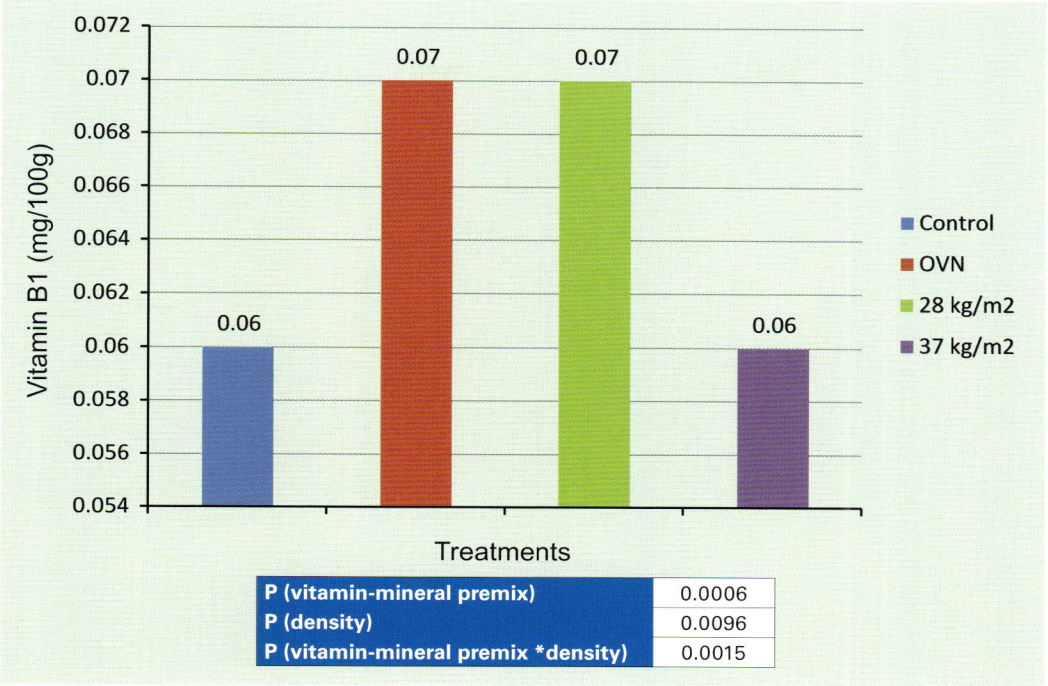

P (vitamin-mineral premix)	0.0006
P (density)	0.0096
P (vitamin-mineral premix *density)	0.0015

Figure 20. B_{12} acid content in chicken breast (40 days) fed on control diet (average vitamin level) and OVN diet, with different density of animals (28 kg/m² vs 37 kg/m²). (Pérez-Vendrel *et al.*, 2002)

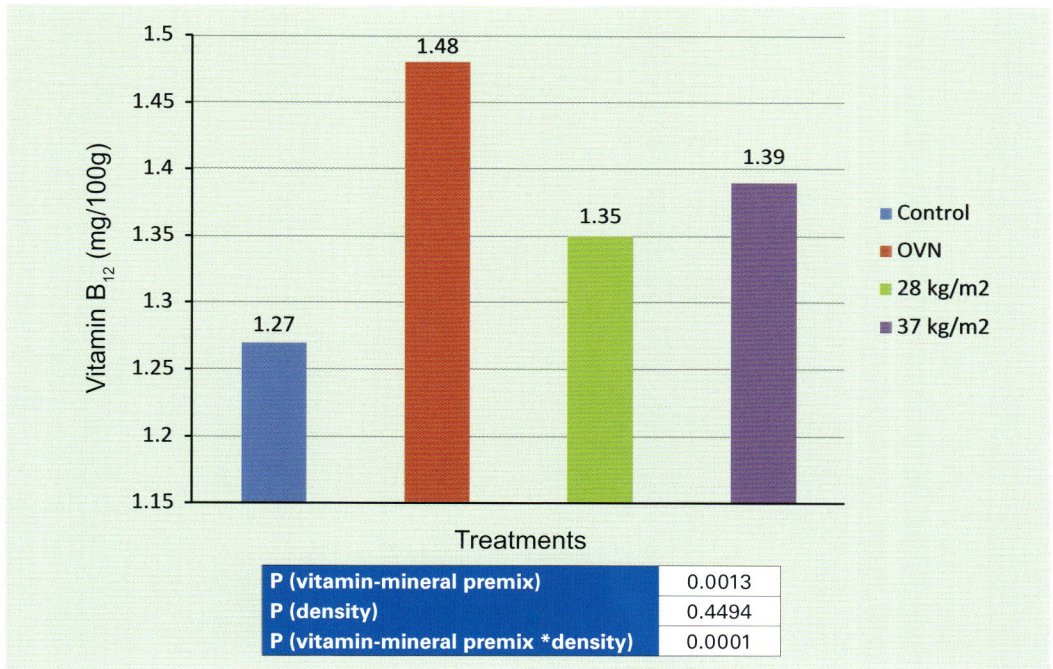

P (vitamin-mineral premix)	0.0013
P (density)	0.4494
P (vitamin-mineral premix *density)	0.0001

Figure 21. Vitamin E levels in fresh pork in Europe (Roche survey 1996)

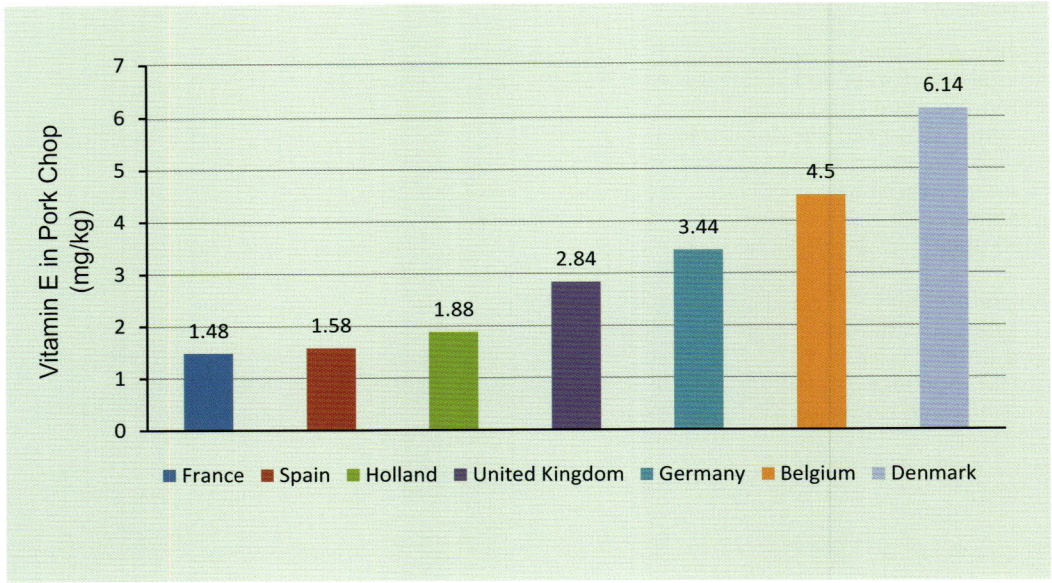

OPTIMUM VITAMIN NUTRITION: A DYNAMIC PROCESS IN CONSTANT EVOLUTION

Optimum vitamin supplementation in an animal's diet, over and above the established minimum needs and adapted to the specific conditions of each species, will improve the state of health and well-being of the animal, thus optimizing its productive potential and promoting the production of high-quality food that is nutritionally balanced.

These optimum levels are based on a large number of studies carried out in university and industrial centers, on the requirements so far published by different associations and leading animal breeding companies and vitamin manufacturers, and on the wide experience of the worldwide livestock industry.

The concept guarantees farmers minimum risk of negative nutritional factors, such as variability in the natural content of feed ingredients, the existence of anti-nutritional factors, different levels of stress, etc. Although these vitamin recommendations for feed allow for the majority of the factors which influence an animal's vitamin needs, in extreme conditions where the processing of feed is very aggressive (use of feed expanders or extruded feed), further supplementation with some vitamins may be necessary. The negative effects on the stability of vitamins can be reduced by using more appropriate commercial vitamin forms where their coating and the bioavailability of the active substance are key elements to be taken into account.

In the following chapters some of the leading professors from various Spanish veterinary faculties review the studies carried out worldwide on the impact of vitamins on the main species of food-producing animals. These studies emphasize the beneficial effects optimum vitamin levels have on the animal, both on health and well-being, and on production parameters, and likewise to bring out those aspects where there is currently insufficient information available, with the intention of filling these gaps in future updates of this work.

Given that animal farming is a dynamic, constantly changing process – a change demanded, in the majority of cases, by society, for economic reasons related to the productivity of animals, and by farming systems – levels of vitamin supplementation need to be reassessed more frequently.

The concept of optimum vitamin nutrition always considers the costs of vitamin supplementation in an animal's diet – in many cases less than 1% of the cost of feed – against the risk of suffering losses through vitamin deficiencies and through working with yield indices below the optimum. Those nutritionists who follow the recommended guidelines based on the OVN concept are ensuring that vitamins are not limiting an animal's genetic potential.

REFERENCES

Casals R., Calsamiglia S. 2002. Uso de niveles óptimos de vitaminas en vacuno de carne. *Mundo Ganadero* June 2002.

Calsamiglia S., Casals R. 2002. Necesidad y uso de niveles óptimos de vitaminas en nutrición del vacuno de leche. *Producci ón Animal* June 2002.

Cepero R. 2002. Actualización de las necesidades vitamínicas de broilers y pavos. *Producción Animal* Sept. 2002.

Gadient, M., Schierle, J., and Hernandez, J.M., 2010. Stability of red carotenoids in stored poultry premix. XIII European Poultry Conference. Tours, France. August 23-27, 2010.

Havenstein, G.B., Ferket, P.R., and Qureshi, M.A. (2003). Carcass composition and yield of 1957 vs 2001 broilers when fed representative 1957 and 2001 broiler diets. Poultry Sci., 82:1509-1518.

Havenstein, G.B., Ferket, P.R., Scheideler, S., and Larson, B.T. (1994). Carcass composition and yield of 1957 vs 1991 broilers when fed "typical" 1957 and 1991 broiler diets. Poultry Sci., 73:1785-1804.

Herendy, V., Süto, Z., and Horn, P. (2004). Comparison of turkey strains and feeding management of the 1967´s and the 1999's regarding growth and slaughter characteristics. Proc. XXII World's Poultry Congress, Istanbul 2004, CD-rom.

Hernandez J.M. 2002. Importancia de una óptima nutrición vitamínica. *Nuestra Cabaña* June 2002.

Korver, D., and Saunders-Blades, J., 2006. HyD and poultry: Bones and beyond. DSM Presymposium Seminar at the WPSA XII European Poultry Conference. Verona, Italy. September 10-14, 2006.

López-Bote C. *et al.*, 2002. Óptima nutrición vitamínica en ganado porcino. *Anaporc* June 2002.

López J.A., Muñoz A. 2002. Resultados prácticos de mejoras productivas en dietas de cerdos con una óptima nutrición vitamínica. *Anaporc* Oct. 2002.

Monográfico Óptima Nutrición Vitamínica en ganado porcino. *Jornadas Técnicas SEPOR* Sept. 2002.

Pérez-Vendrell A.M. *et al.*, 2002. Effect of optimum vitamin levels in broiler diets on performance and meat quality parameters. *European Conference Poultry Nutrition* Sept. 2002.

Soto-Salanova, M.F., Hamelin, C, Brière, S; Lévêque, G; Hernandez, J.M. 2011. Effect of 25-hydroxy-cholecalciferol and canthaxanthin (MaxiChick™) supplementation on turkey breeder performance and on the quality of the day-old-poult . 2011 International Poultry Scientific Forum 24-25 January 2011 Atlanta GA, USA

Anon. 2001. Special Vitamins. *World Poultry* Nov. 2001.

OPTIMUM VITAMIN NUTRITION IN POULTRY BREEDERS

A. C. Barroeta[2], G. Gonzalez[2],
J. Sanz[1] and R. Cepero Briz[1]
[1]Dept. of Animal Production and Food Science
Faculty of Veterinary Science. University of Zaragoza, Spain
[2] Animal Nutrition and Welfare Service
Department of Animal and Food Science
Universitat Autònoma de Barcelona. 08193 Bellaterra, Spain
ana.barroeta@uab.es

INTRODUCTION

The process of reproduction in birds is a crucial stage with great repercussions for productivity, food quality and economic performance of poultry companies. The animals selected for breeding purposes require specialized attention, precise management practices, a good state of health and a diet of high nutritional quality which should be strictly controlled. An adequate and continuous supply of nutrients is necessary for good breeding performance. In particular vitamins are essential nutrients for the development of the reproductive organs, the maintenance of their functional capacity and the development of zygotes and embryos. More detailed information on the importance of vitamins in the feeding of breeder birds is available in the reviews by Whitehead (1988), Larbier and Leclerq (1994), Klasing (1998), Mc Dowell (2000 and 2004), Kidd (2003), Surai (2003), Leeson and Summers (2008) Calini and Sirri (2006).

An appropriate and specific vitamin supply in each of an animal's physiological phases has positive consequences which go beyond the initial objective of preventing deficiency symptoms. Under practical conditions, an optimum supply of vitamins in addition to the minimum requirements is recommended to obtain advantages at different levels. Optimum vitamin supplementation allows better nutrient utilization, a higher growth rate accompanied by an appropriate physical condition as well as a good state of health including an effective immune response. Furthermore, in the specific case of breeders, it also has a positive effect on the development and functionality of the reproductive system as well as on the quality and viability of the embryo, with an influence on the weight, vitality, nutritional reserves, immunological status and subsequent development of the chicken. To achieve this, it needs to be ensured that the animal receives the quantity of essential vitamins that allows it to achieve its genetic and productive potential. In general, and as has already been shown for other species and production phases, the appropriate ingestion and availability of vitamins on the part of the animal may be compromised for numerous reasons such as variability in raw materials,

bioavailability, the presence of antagonists, interactions between nutrients, and the processing and storage of feed. Furthermore, in the specific case of birds selected for breeding, the following situations must be taken into account.

Only a few studies have been carried out on poultry breeder strains to evaluate the nutritional and still less on the vitamin requirements of these birds. Thus the majority of official tables are based on estimates or extrapolations from other types of birds and on data proposed some decades ago. It is evident that these values are not appropriate for the current situation in the poultry sector and that those recommendations should be increased. As a matter of fact, the NRC in 1994 gives vitamin requirements for light breeder strains producing white eggs based on results with hens producing white table eggs obtained before 1987. In the case of heavy breeders it only indicates the requirements of biotin documented in work by Whitehead *et al.* (1985). No studies are shown on meat breeder males and in consequence no minimum vitamin requirement levels were proposed.

Genetic selection is continually advancing and breeder strains are changing continuously. Growth rate and reproduction indicators are improving progressively, which results in parallel increases in the nutritional and vitamin requirements of these animals.

Furthermore, these greater rates of production and reproduction in current strains tend to compromize the metabolic capacity of the bird. In consequence we have more delicate animals which are more susceptible to suffering stress due to different physiological, immunological and environmental causes. For this reason the availability and activity of vitamins related to the metabolism and antioxidant defense is of great importance. The studies by Rebel *et al.* (2004) demonstrate that supplementing breeder feed with vitamin doses above the minimum requirements benefits the immune system of both mother and progeny.

The supply of micronutrients, and especially

of vitamins, is fundamental for breeder males. Vitamins have clear repercussions on the growth and size of the male reproductive organs and, in consequence, both on the quantity of semen produced and on the motility and viability of the spermatozoa. Furthermore, vitamins participate in metabolic aspects such as the synthesis and activity of hormones which have an influence on the reproductive system, with vital importance for libido and fertility.

It is known that the vitamin requirements for the production of hatchling eggs are higher than for table eggs. In other words the vitamin supply in rations for breeder birds, whether male or female, should be higher than in the feed for the production of non-hatchling eggs. Adequate vitamin intake has positive repercussions not only on the laying of eggs but also on their fertility and hatchability and on the subsequent embryonic and post-hatch development of the chick (Fisher and Kemp, 2000). It has been indicated that the vitamin level supplied in the ration has an inverse correlation with the incidence of embryo mortality during the intermediary phase of incubation (between 7 and 14 days). It must be remembered that a fertile egg should contain all the nutrients necessary for the development and viability of the chick. During the incubation process there is no continuous external supply of nutrients; this depends solely on the composition of the egg produced. It is evident that the hen's nutrition has very important repercussions on the health and development of her progeny, and out of the various nutrients, vitamins play a fundamental role. It has been clearly demonstrated that there is a direct relationship between the vitamin content of a produced egg and the hen's intake of these essential nutrients. One especially important and topical issue is that through providing nutrients, and especially vitamins, to breeders, aspects related to the well-being of the chickens and the quality of the final product can be modified. More investigations into this possibility are needed.

Vitamins as micronutrients represent a minimal fraction of the ration (around 0.05%) and represent 2–3% of the total cost of the feed. However, the absence or inadequate intake of a single vitamin has damaging effects on health, growth and reproduction.

When feed intake is reduced, vitamin supplementation should be adjusted with the aim of ensuring that the quantity of vitamins ingested permits the maximum potential for production. The specific situation of restricted feeding of breeder hens entails the risk of a marginal ingestion of vitamins which can be avoided by fortifying the vitamin content of the feed. Furthermore, stress situations such as higher temperatures in the summer months represent a challenge to the birds' immunological system, which provokes a fall in the consumption of feed, compromizing the intake of vitamins.

Given all this, it would be advisable to apply a balanced vitamin supplementation program, over and above the minimum requirements, which would allow the best cost/benefit ratio to be maintained. This involves applying safety margins which compensate for the variation in feed ingredients, strains and production systems found in the market. In practice, the feed industry includes vitamin levels in feeds for meat chicken breeders which are around twice as high as for commercial egg laying hens. Likewise, commercial rations for breeders are formulated with vitamin levels above the minimum requirements set by the NRC (1994) and by applying high safety margins, above all, for vitamins A, E, D, K and niacin (Villamide and Fraga, 1999) (**Table I**).

We will now go on to describe the most relevant aspects of each vitamin, especially in relation to the breeding environment. We will describe the results of optimum supplementation, in other words between the minimum and maximum recommended, of the different vitamins in feed for breeders, and their repercussions on aspects of fertility, hatchability, quality and viability of the chicks, but also in aspects of the well-being and health of the animals. Lastly, we will indicate the vitamin levels used in practice and the recommendations made by the various official bodies, genetics companies and feed additive firms for female and male breeders of the heavy strains that produce meat chickens and for breeder turkeys.

Table I. Range of vitamin supplementation in commercial feeds for meat chicken breeders in Spain. (adapted from Villamide and Fraga, 1999)

	Maximum	Minimum	Mean
Vitamin A (IU)	15,000	10,000	13,500
Vitamin D (IU)	3,200	2,400	2,952
Vitamin E (IU)	67.0	7.5	30.7
Menadione (mg)	6.00	1.00	2.85
Thiamine (mg)	5.00	0.00	2.12
Riboflavin (mg)	10.0	5.00	8.83
Vit. B6 (mg)	5.00	1.00	3.82
Vit. B12 (mg)	0.03	0.01	0.02
Niacin (mg)	50.0	20.0	34.9
Pantothenic acid (mg)	18.0	8.5	14.7
Folic acid (mg)	3	0.5	1.41
Biotin (mg)	0.25	0	0.14
Choline (mg)	600	240	348

VITAMIN A AND CAROTENOIDS

Vitamin A includes all the non-carotenoid beta-ionone derivatives with biological activity similar to all-trans-retinol. Vegetables contain a variety of carotenoids which can be transformed into vitamin A, with greater or lesser efficacy, by specific enzymes located in the animals' intestinal wall. However, less than 10% of carotenoids can be converted into vitamin A, and, in birds, only alpha- and beta-carotene and cryptoxanthin found in natural feed materials are capable of contributing to the supply of this vitamin (Surai et al 2001). Poultry diets are supplemented with synthetic retinol, the contribution of carotenoids from feed in the formation of vitamin A is minimal (Surai *et al.*, 2003). In animal tissues they exist predominantly as retinal, retinol, retinaldehyde, retinoic and retinyl esters.

Vitamin A and beta-carotene become dispersed in micelles from prior to absorption from the intestine. These micelles are composed of mixtures of bile salts, monoglycerides, and long chain fatty acids, together with vitamins D, E and K, all of which influence the transfer of vitamin A and beta-carotene to the intestinal cell. Here most of the beta-carotene is converted to vitamin A, which in turn, is converted to various esters depending to a great extent upon the type of fatty acid being absorbed with the vitamin A. In plasma, vitamin A can be transported both as the free alcohol as well as in the esterified form. The esters are transported to the liver with the portomicrons which are derived from absorbed lipids. Throughout the blood, these molecules arrive at the liver and can be effective by different pathways. (Leeson and Summers, 2001).

Vitamin A has a fundamental importance in several metabolic processes (**Figure 1**). If vitamin A binds to proteins in the cytosol, forms the visual pigment rhodopsin that is important for sight, especially in poultry adapting to low intensity light in intensive production. In the nucleus, vitamin A binds to completely different retinoic acid binding proteins. This new complex binds specific regions of chromatin and causes changes in the rate of transcription of specific genes. Vitamin A has important effects on bone growth and thus the development of young animals, the quantity and quality of semen produced, the growth and differentiation of epithelial tissues of the reproductive system, and the embryo, among others. In this respect it has been observed that vitamin A has a morphogenetic activity, with responsibility for the differentiation of cells during the embryonic development of the chicken (Klasing, 1998, McDowell 2004). Finally, vitamin A contributes to maintain lysozyme stability inside the cells.

Among the first symptoms of vitamin A deficiency to appear is the decrease of sexual activity in males and failure of spermatogenesis, accompanied by a reduction in fertility and in the number of hatched eggs. Breeder cocks need to receive sufficient vitamins for high sexual activity during the breeding period, as they usually copulate 20 to 30 times a day, which makes a high rate of sperm synthesis necessary. Supplies of vitamin A above requirements permit an adequate rate of growth in breeder males, with an optimum development of the organs and systems involved in reproduction (Damjanov *et al.*, 1980).

Hepatic reserves of vitamin A are usually enough to maintain the production of several eggs with adequate concentrations of this vitamin. In this case the dietary supply is important during the pre-laying phase to achieve a good reserve level in the hen to carry it through the subsequent breeding phase (Surai *et al.*, 1998b). During laying, it is recommended to supply doses of vitamin A above the minimum requirements, not only to avert deficiency symptoms, but also with a view to preventing problems due to reduced absorption or insufficient reserves, and to ensure an adequate content in the fertile egg. Retinol is the initial form of vitamin A transferred to the egg, as it is the form of vitamin A which unites with the binding protein of retinol. Vitamin A is mainly in the aqueous part of the yolk and is gradually transferred to the embryo during incubation (Vieira *et al.*, 1995). (**Figure 1**)

It has been observed that when breeders consume marginal quantities of vitamin A, their progeny have lower reserves of the vitamin and disorders are manifested after hatching (Hill *et al.*, 1961). The study conducted by Surai *et al.* (1998b) demonstrated a direct relationship between the quantity of vitamin A in the ration of the breeders and that deposited in the egg, and in the liver both of the hen and her embryos. Adequate vitamin A content in

Figure 1. Main sources and types of the precursors of vitamin A. Schematic illustration of the absorption and the purpose of the metabolites and main functions developed.

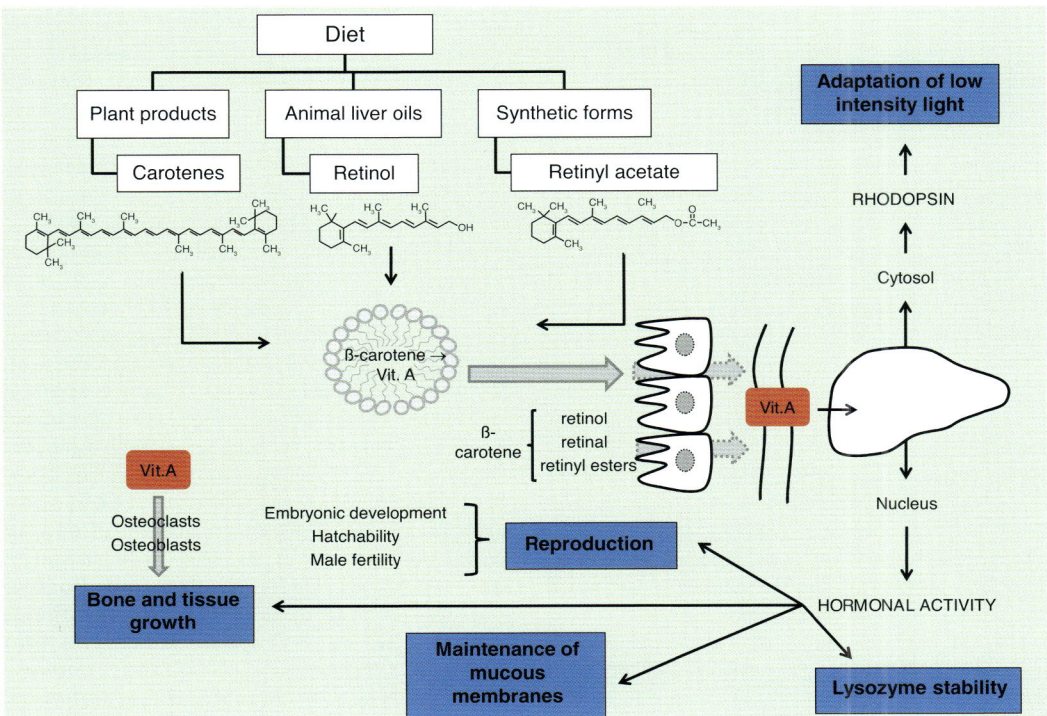

the hatching egg results in better growth rate, greater capacity for immune response and prevents pigmentation problems in the chicken. During its development, the embryo uses a relatively small and constant quantity of vitamin A; the rest will remain accessible to nourish the chick in the days after hatching. The work by Squires and Naber (1993a) demonstrates that after 25–27 weeks of administering feed with different doses of vitamin A, the eggs of the breeders supplemented with 16,000 IU/kg contained 10 times more vitamin A (24 IU vitamin A per gram of yolk) than the fertile eggs of the hens without additional vitamin A. Similarly, more eggs were laid and hatched.

It has also been demonstrated that supplying vitamin A has an influence on the immune response of chicks and consequently on their susceptibility to disease (Haq et al., 1996). Vitamin A is also involved in the antioxidant defense of the developing embryo (Gaal et al., 1995). In addition, carotenoids are known to form precursors of vitamin A by cleavage and reduction of beta-carotene, which also has an important antioxidant role (Rocha et al., 2010). The presence of other antioxidants and the negative interaction with vitamin E demonstrated by Surai et al., 1998 should be taken into account in this respect.

One IU of vitamin A activity is equivalent to the activity of 0.3 µg of retinol or 0.6 µ g of ß-carotene, that is to say 1 mg of ß-carotene is equivalent to 1,667 IU of vitamin A. The minimum requirements recommended by the NRC (1994) are 3,000 IU/kg and are based on studies from 1961 and 1965 on hens producing white table eggs. An excess can provoke pigmentation problems and deficiencies in other fat-soluble vitamins. For this reason and because of its capacity for storage, the maximum tolerance level is set at 40,000 IU/kg (National Research Council, 1987).

The majority of recommendations published by recognized bodies, based on the scientific results of recent years, indicate inclusion quantities between 8,000 and 12,000 IU/kg of vitamin A for breeder feeds (Tables II and III).

Carotenoids are bioactive molecules present in the bird diets. There exist over 600 forms that differ in the molecular structure and biological function (Goodwin, 1984). In birds, carotenoids function as pigments in feathers and skin, as antioxidants, as precursors of vitamin A, and they play various roles in the endocrine and immune systems (Surai, 2003; Bortolotti et al., 2003). The most important carotenoid is ß-carotene which is transformed into vitamin A in the animal body but which has no pigmenting activity. Pigmenting carotenoids are mainly molecules that have no vitamin A activity at all; they are transferred unchanged to the yolk or to the skin (Braeunlich et al., 1974). The color of the avian products is a valuable aspect for the consumer. In poultry, a single yolk may contain about 40-45 % of the total carotenoids found in the liver (Surai and Speake, 2000; Surai et al., 1999b), which is the main site of carotenoid accumulation (Surai et al., 2001), and consequently more than 50 % of total carotenoid reserves in the body are in the ovary (Surai unpublished data; see Nys, 2000). It is well documented that supplementation of the diet of chickens increases yolk carotenoids (**Figure 2**).

Moreover, the deposition level of carotenoids in tissues (plasma and yolk) is indicative of variation in availability (i.e. diet) and physiological demands (i.e. reproduction) and can be used as indicators of the animal's health status. Bortolotti et al. (2003) demonstrated that plasma carotenoids at the end of the laying period were strongly correlated with number of eggs laid. Souza et al. (2008) added 6 mg of canthaxanthin/kg of feed in the broiler breeder diet and observed a reduction in the number of infertile eggs and embryonic mortality and an improvement in hatchability.

Some authors have concluded that carotenoids can modulate the antioxidant system of the embryo and hatched chick and help to maintain its efficiency. Embryonic tissues are characterised by high concentrations of polyunsaturated fatty acids; thus, it is necessary to add vitamins and minerals with antioxidant activity to broiler breeder diets to improve the oxidative protection of the newly hatched chick (Rocha et al., 2010). The high concentration of polyunsaturated fatty acids in embryonic tissues (Surai et al., 1997a) is associated with increased oxygen

Figure 2. Scatterplot of toal cartonoid concentration (μg/g) in diet versus in egg yolks in poultry and red-legged partridges in this study on diets containing relatively high (H) and low (L) concentrations of carotenoids (adapted from Bortolotti *et al.*, 2003).

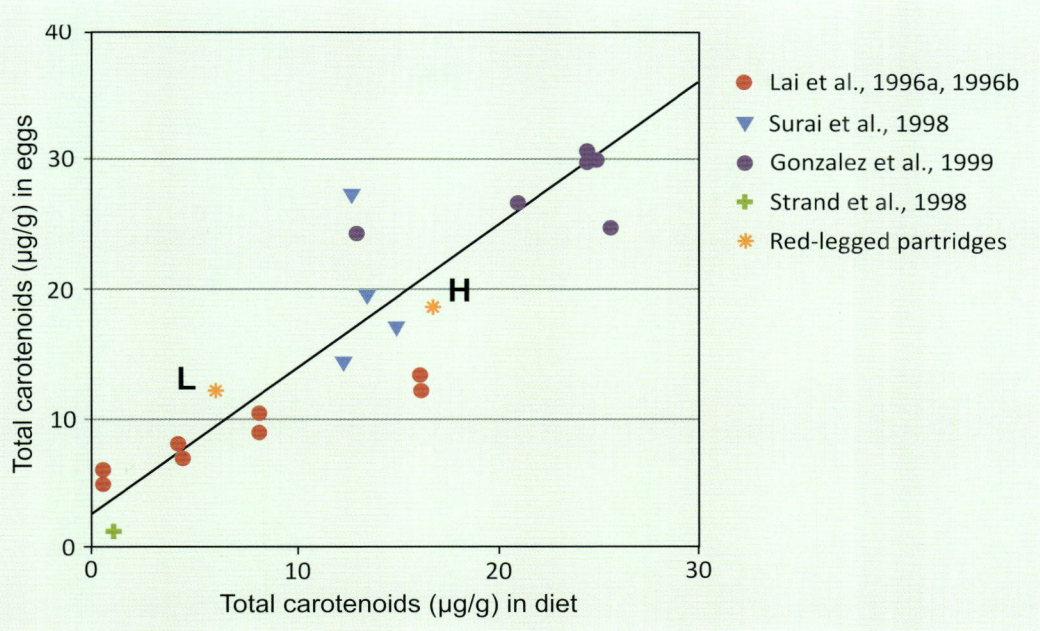

consumption and respiration towards the end of the incubation period (Wilson *et al.*, 1992), which are accompanied by changes in the concentration of antioxidant enzymes in the embryonic tissues (Surai, 1999). The antioxidant enzymes SOD, GSH-Px and catalase protect embryonic tissues against lipid peroxidation during incubation and act as the principal antioxidant defense system at hatch (Surai *et al.*, 1999b). Surai and Sparks (2001) confirmed that maternal diet has an important role in the formation of antioxidant systems during embryonic development and confirmed that the antioxidant potential of the egg yolk and embryonic tissues were increased with a diet based on corn (11.8 mg carotenoids/kg diet) compared to a diet based on wheat (5.6 mg carotenoids/kg diet). It has been demonstrated that the enrichment of broiler breeder diets with carotenoids is the main factor influencing the carotenoid concentration in chicken tissues during the first weeks of life (Koutsos *et al.*, 2003 and Karadas *et al.*, 2005).

Canthaxanthin supplementation has shown a positive effect on vitamin E concentration in three ways (Surai,*et al.*, 2003):

1) Increased assimilation of gamma-tocopherol in the diet and its transfer to the egg yolk, increasing concentrations of this substance in the liver of the embryo and hatching chick.

2) Increased alpha-tocopherol concentrations in tissues and plasma of hatched chicks, because canthaxanthin acts as an antioxidant during the embryonic development leaving less free radicals available to react with vitamin E. Thus, vitamin E is conserved and its concentration is increased.

3) Possibly contributed to the regeneration of vitamin E through electron transfer from the carotenoids to the alpha-tocopheroxyl radical.

Based on the important role of carotenoids as antioxidants and immune-stimulating agents immediately after hatching, the authors concluded that the consumption of carotenoids by broiler breeders, in addition to influencing the incorporation of these substances by progeny tissues, may increase chicken viability.

VITAMIN D

Sterols with vitamin D activity have a common steroid nucleus and differ in the nature of the lateral chain attached to carbon 17. Of these, the principal natural provitamins are ergocalciferol (vitamin D_2, found predominantly in plants) and cholecalciferol (vitamin D_3, found mainly in animals). It is assumed that birds utilize vitamin D_2 with a relative efficiency to vitamin D_3 of less than 10%.

Vitamin D requirements can be covered in two ways: by ingestion and/or via the endogenous synthesis of vitamin D_3 from cholesterol, a process which requires the animals to be exposed to sunlight. In the case of breeders of heavy strains, which for both rearing and breeding purposes are generally kept indoors without exposure to sunlight, vitamin D_3 synthesis is insufficient to cover requirements and they should receive an external supply in their feed.

Vitamin D is an essential component in the bird's endocrine system, participating in the regulation of calcium and phosphorus homeostasis with an involvement in bone mineralization and eggshell formation. There is also evidence in different species that vitamin D plays a regulatory role in the immune system. The active form of vitamin D, $1,25\text{-}(OH)_2\text{-}D_3$, acts as a steroid hormone. In **Figure 3** the main functions of calcitriol in poultry are highlighted

Cholecalciferol must be activated through hydroxymethylation. More than 30 metabolites of vitamin D can be formed, among which $1,25\text{-}(OH)_2\text{-}D_3$ is the principal active form. The formation of this metabolite requires two hydroxylations, the first of which is catalyzed by hepatic enzymes and is based on the transformation to $25\text{-}(OH)\text{-}D_3$, which is the circulating and storage form of vitamin D. The second hydroxylation takes place in the kidney and is regulated by the parathyroid hormone according to the concentrations of calcium and phosphorus present. Subsequently the $1,25\text{-}(OH)_2\text{-}D_3$ is transported to the intestine, to the bones or to another part of the kidney where it participates in the metabolism of calcium and phosphorus (**Figure 4**). The level of $1,25\text{-}(OH)_2\text{-}D_3$ in the plasma of a hen in the egg production phase is double that before the start of laying.

It should be remembered that the formation of an egg entails the deposition of some 2 g of calcium. The calcium deposited in the shell of the egg can be of two origins: from the ration or from the mobilization of the calcium reserves stored in the medullary bone, which is clearly affected by the union of the parathyroid hormone and the $1,25\text{-}(OH)_2\text{-}D_3$ to the bone cells. Vitamin D and its metabolites circulate through the organism bound to a vitamin D-binding protein. This protein is an essential component in the maintenance of an adequate level of vitamin D in the organism. Vitamin D binding protein has a greater affinity for $25\text{-}(OH)\text{-}D_3$, the principal circulating form, then cholecalciferol and $1,25\text{-}(OH)_2\text{-}D_3$. (**Figure 4**)

However, laying hens, have a unique vitamin D_3 binding protein which has an affinity mainly for cholecalciferol, this binds phosvitin and liberates vitamin D_3 to the ovarian follicles which will constitute the future egg yolk (Fraser and Emtage,

Figure 3. Main functions of calcitriol ($1α,25\text{–}(OH)_2\text{–}D_3$) in poultry

$1α,25\text{-}(OH)_2\text{-}D_3$ Calcitriol

- Calcium absorption from the intestines and kidneys
- Phosphorus absorption from the intestines
- Mobilization of calcium from the bones in times of higher demand
- Regulation of synthesis of calcium absorption from the intestines and calcium transport via blood circulation
- Regulate calcification processes such as egg shell formation and skeletal development
- Regulation of immune cells

Figure 4. Metabolic transformation of vitamin D2 and vitamin D3
(adapted from Leeson and Summers, 2001)

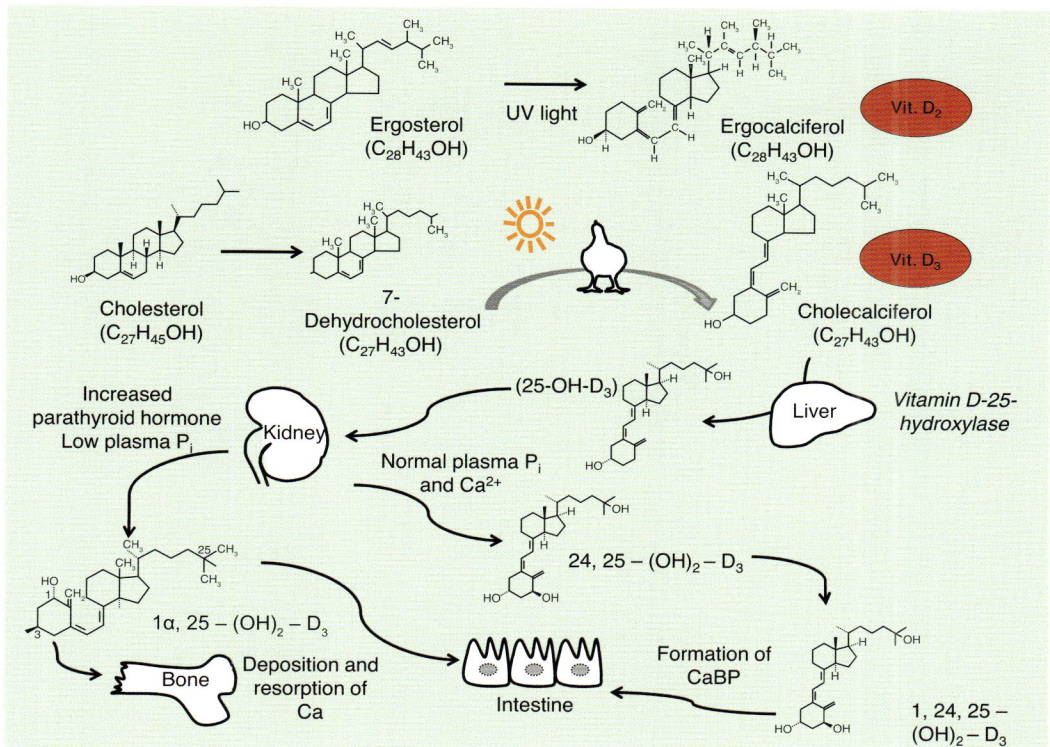

1976, Norman and Hurwitz, 1993). There is a positive correlation between the vitamin D_3 content in hen feed and the content of vitamin D_3 and 25-(OH)-D_3 in the egg (Mattila *et al.*, 1999). The vitamin D_3 within the egg yolk is used by the embryo during its development. The embryo's enzymes start to be competent from one to two weeks of incubation, when they become capable of converting cholecalciferol to 25-(OH)-D_3 in the liver and 25-(OH)-D_3 to $1,25$-(OH)$_2$-D_3 in the kidney (Moriuchi and Deluca, 1974; Kubota *et al.*, 1981). Having reached this stage the $1,25$-(OH)$_2$-D_3 regulates the homeostasis of calcium, activating the absorption of calcium from the yolk membrane, where vitamin D-dependent calcium binding protein, calbindin, is present (Tuan and Suyama, 1996). As the embryo's calcium requirements increase, the $1,25$-(OH)$_2$-D_3 also facilitates the absorption of calcium from the shell via the chorioallantoic membrane (Hart and Deluca, 1985, Narbaitz, 1987, Clark *et al.*, 1990, Elaroussi *et al.*, 1994).

In some species of birds when the yolk has low vitamin D content, the incubation process is disrupted from the 5th day (Millar *et al.*, 1977, Scott *et al.*, 1982). In this case, there is disruption to the transport of calcium from the eggshell via the chorioallantoic membrane and consequently the embryo's bones are poorly calcified. When the lack of vitamin D is widespread, a large proportion of the chicks die at the end of incubation as they are incapable of completing the hatching process. The chicks that are hatched tend to be weak and present ossification problems (Shen *et al.*, 1981, Narbaitz, 1987). The greater the reserve of vitamin D in the yolk sac, the better prepared the future chick will be for development of the bone tissue, a process that requires high mobilization of calcium.

The work of Edwards (1995) and Driver *et al.* (2004 and 2006) demonstrated that chickens from breeders more than 50 weeks old fed diets containing 2,000 IU/kg of vitamin D_3, had higher growth rates and better bone formation than those from breeders fed diets with marginal supplies of this vitamin (250–500 IU/kg). Other authors have indicated increases in the production and hatchability of eggs as well as a reduction in embryo mortality by increasing vitamin D levels in the feed of breeders (Bethke *et al.*, 1936, Sunde *et al.*, 1978, Abdulrahim *et al.*, 1979). Better bone development and density have been observed in the progeny and a lower incidence of tibial dyschondroplasia by Grimminger, 1966, and Ameenuddin *et al.*, 1986. These effects also have been described in turkeys (Bethke *et al.*, 1936, Murphy *et al.*,1936). Atencio *et al.* (2005a, 2005b, 2005c and 2006) carried out several experiments aimed at elucidating the requirements of breeders of heavy strains and they determined that the requirements increase with age and depend on the parameter used. Between 27 and 36 weeks of age maximum egg production and maximum hatchability were obtained with levels of vitamin D_3 between 1,390 and 1,424 IU/kg. Between weeks 37 and 66, the vitamin D_3 requirements rose to approximately 2,800 IU/kg. These authors also demonstrated that chicks from breeders that consumed high levels of vitamin D_3 (2,000–4,000 IU/kg) and fed with different levels of calcium presented the highest live weights, a higher level of ash in the tibia and fewer leg problems. Similar results have been described in female breeder turkeys which on consuming rations with 2,700 IU/kg of vitamin D_3 produced heavier poults with a higher tibia ash content (Stevens *et al.*, 1984). Inoculation of 25-(OH)-D_3 *in ovo* entailed an increase in the weight gain of progeny at 10 days of age (Gonzales *et al.*, 2003).

Vitamin D supplementation is especially important in the final phases of the laying period, when there is a decrease in hatchability associated with the lower quality of the shell deposited on the egg. Dietary supplementation of 25-(OH)-D_3 resulted in better quality egg shells and lower embryo mortality at the second week of development from hens more than 60 weeks of age (Torres *et al.*, 2009). The absorption and metabolism of calcium are regulated by calcitriol, the biosynthesis of which requires vitamin D_3 and vitamin C.

In the majority of tables of nutritional value of feedstuffs, vitamin D levels are calculated based on the equivalent bioactivity of vitamin D_2 plus D_3. However, vitamin D_2 is a poor source of vitamin D for birds due to its low bioavailability. Supplementation with adequate levels of vitamin D_3 or of metabolites with a greater vitamin activity such as 25-(OH)-D_3 (Saunders-Blades and Korver, 2006) are necessary to prevent problems in the development and maintenance of bone structure. In bird diets, it is not common to supplement with 1,25-(OH)$_2$-D_3, as this metabolite is neither transferred to the yolk nor participates in embryo development, and it also has possible toxicity problems. Vitamin D requirements are raised when the calcium supply is low and when the calcium-phosphorus ratio is unbalanced.

Authors are unanimous in recommending doses between 2,500 and 3,000 IU/kg of vitamin D in the feed of heavy breeders (Tables II and III). These levels are 10 times higher than those indicated by the NRC (1994) which refer to breeders of light strains.

VITAMIN E

The term vitamin E includes all tocol and tocotrienol derivatives that have α-tocopherol activity. The requirements of an animal and the level in the ration can be found expressed in IU of vitamin E (1 IU is equivalent to 1 mg DL-α-tocopherol acetate) or are expressed in mg of α-tocopherol equivalents (α-TE) which corresponds to the activity of D-α-tocopherol, the most active form (1 mg α-TE = 1 mg D-α-tocopherol = 1.49 mg DL-α-tocopherol acetate). Vitamin E is synthesized in the plant kingdom and tends to be found in free form in nature. Vitamin E in food of animal origin is found principally in the form of α-tocopherol and the quantity depends on the species and the quantity consumed by the animal. Vitamin E is usually incorporated into feeds as DL-α-tocopherol acetate. The ester bond, which increases stability, is hydrolyzed in the small intestine during the digestive process, liberating the active forms which are then absorbed by the enterocytes and transported by the portomicrons and lipoproteins in the plasma to the different tissues.

Vitamin E is essential for the integrity and functioning of the reproductive, circulatory, nervous, immune and muscular systems (**Figure 5**). In fact it is one of the vitamins to which the greatest investigative efforts have been dedicated with a view to finding out its mechanism of action and its requirements (Surai, 2003; Sirri and Barroeta, 2007, among others).

Vitamin E has a crucial role within the cellular defense system in the face of oxidation at both intracellular and extracellular level. α-tocopherol is integrated within the cellular membrane and protects lipids from oxidation, preventing them from being attacked by free radicals. Tocopherols remove the peroxyl radical, donating a hydrogen atom and converting it to peroxide. The majority of symptoms of vitamin E deficiency are related to disorders of the cellular membrane as a result of the oxidative degradation of polyunsaturated fatty acids. This relationship with essential fatty acids and their derivatives with very long chains, precursors of prostaglandins and thromboxanes among others,

means that vitamin E is also involved in the prevention of cardiovascular and carcinogenic diseases. Furthermore, it has been observed that vitamin E promotes the activity of immune system cells (Kolb and Grün, 1995). Vitamin E can alleviate the effects of stress and increase immunocompetence in birds (Cherian and Sim, 1997; Siegel *et al.*, 2001; Yang *et al.*, 2000). It is important to emphasize the need to maintain a balance with other nutrients which exert a complementary action in protecting against free radicals, such as vitamin C, ß-carotene and selenium.

Numerous studies have been aimed at establishing the relationship between vitamin E consumed and the prevention of oxidation. Thus it has been demonstrated how the deposition of α-tocopherol in the animal, as well as in the egg increases in direct proportion to its supply in the diet and is accompanied by a greater oxidative stability (Cortinas *et al.*, 2006, Villaverde *et al.*, 2008, Galobart *et al.*, 2001a). On the other hand, it is known that susceptibility to oxidation increases as the number of double bonds of fatty acids increases. As the profile of fatty acids in the ration is reflected in the fatty acid composition of the different tissues of the animal and of the eggs, increasing the degree of unsaturation in the feed increases susceptibility to oxidation and reduces the quantity of α-tocopherol deposited in the tissues (Galobart *et al.*, 2001b; Cortinas *et al.*, 2003; Villaverde *et al.*, 2004).

The minimum requirements of vitamin E are difficult to establish since different situations can modify the quantity required by the bird. Supplementation of vitamin E should increase in parallel to the quantity of unsaturated fatty acids and the degree of oxidation of the fat added to the feed. Requirements also depend on the presence or absence of other compounds which intervene in the tissue oxidation defense system such as selenium. It should be borne in mind that depending on the feed ingredients and hence the content of tocopherols, carotenoids and other antioxidants, there will be a variation in the oxidative state of the animal and therefore the requirements of antioxidants and

Figure 5. Relationship among the different functions of vitamin E in poultry metabolism

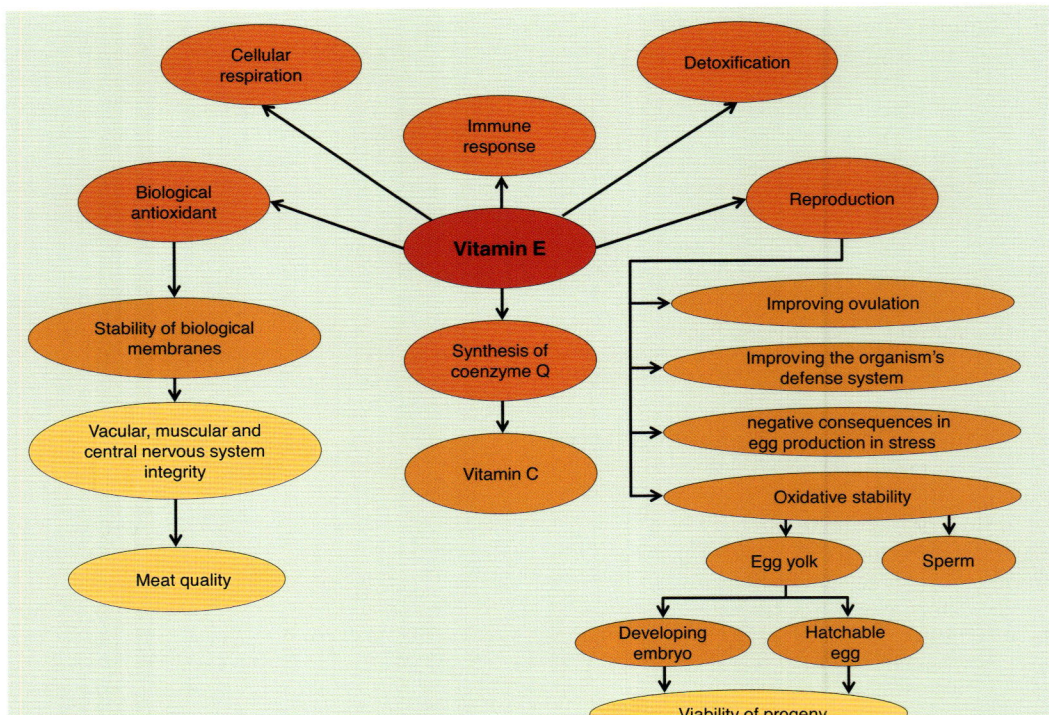

specifically of vitamin E (Surai and Sparks, 2001). It has also been established that there is a negative interaction between vitamin E and vitamin A or β-carotene, as they interfere with each other in their absorption and deposition processes (Haq *et al.*, 1996). This was reported previously by Combs (1976). This author noted that hens fed high vitamin A levels had low plasma levels of vitamin E and therefore low concentrations of the latter in egg yolk. Moreover, Surai *et al.* (1998b) concluded that excessive supplementation with vitamin A in laying hen diets results in an adverse effect on vitamin E in the embryonic/neonatal liver that can compromize the antioxidant status of the progeny.

Vitamin E is also necessary for the normal functioning of the reproductive system. There is evidence that the hormone regulation involved in the reproductive cycle of the birds is also involved in the metabolism of vitamin E (Feingold and Colby, 1992). As it has been mentioned in the section on optimum vitamin nutrition in

laying hens, supplementation of vitamin E above the minimum requirement improves ovulation during the last phase of the laying period, improving the bird's defense system and averting negative consequences on egg production in situations of environmental stress (Siegel *et al.*, 2001). Likewise, it has been observed that an inadequate level of vitamin E in the diets of breeders is detrimental for fertility and hatchability. Vitamin E protects against oxidation in sperm, egg yolk and embryonic tract. (**Figure 5**)

In breeders, the vitamin E supplied in the ration, once absorbed, is transported to the liver, and from there, to the developing oocyte by very low density lipoproteins (VLDL). It has been demonstrated that there is a high efficiency in incorporating α-tocopherol from the maternal feed into the yolk of the chicken egg (Surai, 2003). The quantity of vitamin E in the egg increases linearly with the consumption of vitamin E by the hen. It has been confirmed that the degree of transfer from the feed to the egg and from the egg to the embryo is different for each stereoisomer of vitamin E. Among the different isomers of vitamin E deposited, both in the egg yolk and in the embryonic tissues, α-tocopherol is the most abundant form. However, although α-tocotrienol is in lower concentration, it also has an important role in the antioxidant defense of the developing embryo and a synergistic antioxidant action with α-tocopherol has been described. However, there are still many gaps in the knowledge of the transfer and metabolic action of the different stereoisomers of vitamin E (Cortinas et al., 2004).

The supply of vitamin E in the ration should be continuous, as the hepatic reserve is insufficient to maintain an adequate vitamin concentration in the egg. The quantity of vitamin E deposited in the egg is double that deposited in the liver of the hen and these hepatic reserves diminish rapidly if there is no external supply (Surai et al., 1998a, b and 1999a, b). The vitamin E in the egg yolk is absorbed through the membrane of the yolk sac and subsequently, during the last week of incubation, transferred to the liver, the embryo's principal reserve organ (Surai et al., 1996). Increasing the quantity of vitamin E consumed by the breeder has been shown to increase α-tocopherol, as does the oxidative stability of the hatching egg and the developing embryo (Meydani et al., 1988, Surai et al., 1999b). High levels of oxidation in the membrane of the yolk sac of fertile eggs stored for two weeks correlate with a decrease in their hatchability (Donaldson et al., 1996). It is obvious that a good antioxidant defense system in the fertile egg is important in counteracting situations of stress during embryo development. Vitamin E plays an essential role in this process. Inadequate vitamin E in the diet of breeders gives rise to the production of eggs with low hatchability and high mortality in the last phase of incubation due to failures related to the circulatory system. The existence of a positive correlation between vitamin E in breeder feed and the hatchability and viability of the chicks produced has been demonstrated by Stoianov and Zhekov, 1982 and An et al., 2010. Similar results have been observed by other authors in breeders of laying strains (Leeson et al., 1979a, b),

breeders of heavy strains (Tengerdy and Nockels, 1973; Kristiansen, 1973; Siegel et al., 2001) and in turkey breeders (Atkinson et al., 1955; Jensen and McGinnis, 1957; Jensen, 1968). Hossain et al. (1998), in their research with different levels of vitamin E in breeder feed, observed improvements in the immune development of the chicks with doses of 100 ppm of vitamin E.

Vitamin E supplementation has also been effective in counteracting the negative effects on hatchability provoked by situations of stress such as the presence of toxins (Tobias et al., 1992), of antinutritional factors such as vicine (Muduuli et al., 1982) or by aging (Siegel et al., 2001; Amiri et al., 2006).

Thus an adequate supply of vitamin E in the diets of breeders has a clear effect on their progeny. The physical reserves of newly hatched chicks are very important as their immune, digestive and endocrine systems, among others, are not completely developed until they are 7–10 days old. In particular, vitamin E is important for preventing lipid oxidation and stimulating immune defenses during and after hatching. Hatching and the neonatal period are critical times during which pulmonary respiration starts and changes occur in the metabolism, triggering a rapid tissue growth rate which involves the chick being highly susceptible to oxidation. The presence of antioxidants, in particular α-tocopherol, in the yolk and integrated in the different embryonic tissues has the benefit of protecting against oxidative destruction (Gaal et al., 1995; Speake et al., 1996; Cherian et al., 1996b; Surai et al., 1999b and Surai and Sparks, 2000). A direct relationship has been demonstrated between the level of vitamin E in the liver of a day-old chick and its viability (Yaroshenko et al., 1995, Surai, 2000). In the initial phases of a chicken's life the digestion of lipids, including fat-soluble vitamins, is limited, so the chick's vitamin E reserves depend on their concentration in the egg and on the mother's consumption. Hassan et al. (1990) observed that when the hen's diet contained sufficient vitamin E, the chick's embryonic development was adequate and its reserves were maintained up to two weeks of age. However, chicks coming from breeders which consumed rations deficient in vitamin E presented exudative diathesis at hatching, in other words the deficiency had arisen during incubation.

Supplying vitamin E in the breeders diet is especially critical in turkeys (Surai, 2000) since vitamin E absorption is low, so that not only the level in the egg but also the transfer to the embryo and the reserve in newly hatched turkeys is lower than those described in chickens (Sell et al., 1991; Soto-Salanova et al., 1993; Soto-Salanova and Sell, 1995 and 1996; Surai et al., 1998b). For these reasons, vitamin E supplementation in the rations of female breeder turkeys has important positive repercussions and is able to increase the vitamin E reserve in the progeny during the first 10 days of life.

In recent years research has been carried out on the effect of incorporating different nutrients in the fertile egg during its incubation through the technique of in ovo inoculation. The inclusion of vitamin E in the fertile egg had a positive effect on the physical and immune development of the progeny, although the effects on hatchability remain to be elucidated. Improvements have been observed in weight and feed conversion at 28 and 42 days in meat chickens hatched from eggs inoculated with vitamin E (Hossain et al., 1998, Bhanja et al., 2006).

The relationship between levels of vitamin E and the fertilizing capacity of spermatozoa from breeder males is well established. Vitamin E exerts its antioxidant action on two levels: in the first place on the testicles, where it protects the biological membranes from lipid peroxidation during spermatogenesis. Secondly on the seminal plasma where vitamin E protects against the free radicals which attack the lipids present (Eid et al., 2006). Dietary manipulation can modify the polyunsaturated fatty acid composition of the sperm of broiler and turkey breeder males, improving fertility. The lipid part of the membrane of spermatozoa has a high proportion of polyunsaturated fatty acids, which gives them fluidity and flexibility, facilitating their mobility and the fertilization of the ovum. But these positive effects are only achieved in the presence of antioxidants, in the specific case of vitamin E at a dosage between 120 and 300 ppm

(Surai et al., 1997b, 2000; Zanini et al., 2003; Cerolini et al., 2003, 2005; Biswas et al., 2009). Thus it is important to incorporate antioxidants such as vitamin E to prevent the oxidation of the semen of breeders.

The quantity of α-tocopherol in male sperm is dependent on the availability of vitamin E in the ration (Cerolini et al., 2003, 2005 and 2006). The incorporation of vitamin E in the diet of breeders has been effective in averting loss of fertility (Arscott and Parker, 1967; Yoshida and Hoshi, 1976; Friedrichsen et al., 1980). Thus when breeders are deficient in vitamin E, the males are less fertile due to the lower quantity and quality of sperm produced (Jensen, 1968; Arscott and Kuhns, 1969). Friedrichsen et al. (1980) indicate that a prolonged deficiency of vitamin E in the rations of breeders can give rise to permanent sterility. In a study with turkey breeders, Surai (1992) observed that the best quality of semen was obtained when the feed of males was supplemented with 80 IU/kg of vitamin E and the quantity of vitamin E in the semen was between 3.2 and 6.9 µg/ml which compares to 1.6 µg/ml in unsupplemented birds (Blesbois et al., 1993). Increasing the dose of vitamin E in the feed increases the quantity of α-tocopherol in the sperm. Some studies have included levels of 200–300 mg/kg of vitamin E in the feed, attaining levels of 174 and 188 ng of α-tocopherol/10^9 sperm cells (Surai et al., 1997b; Zaniboni and Cerolini, 2006; Cerolini et al., 2006).

The quantity of vitamin E integrated in the membrane of the spermatozoa may be related to their capacity for fertilization. Supplementation with vitamin E in the final phase of breeding improves the quality and quantity of the semen produced and the antioxidant defenses during their storage in vivo (Surai and Zhedek, 1985; Surai et al., 2000; Brèque et al., 2003; Zaniboni et al., 2006). However in young males this dose-response relationship is not linear (Lin et al., 2005). It has also been demonstrated that vitamin E provides additional protection under conditions in which semen is manipulated in vitro including dilution, storage and freezing (Surai, 2003, Zaniboni and Cerolini, 2009). Some authors point out that breeders need more than 160 IU of vitamin E in the ration to ensure the maintenance of hatchability (Lin *et al.*, 2005). All of the above makes manifest the important role of vitamin E in the structure and functioning of spermatozoa.

The relationship between vitamin E and the immune system has also been an object of great interest. It has been pointed out that supplementation with vitamin E at levels above the minimum requirements indicated by the NRC (1994) either administered in the hen's feed or by means of injection *in ovo* increases the immune response of the progeny (Jackson *et al.*, 1978; Haq *et al.*, 1996; Hossain *et al.*, 1998; Erf *et al.*, 1998; Boa-Amponsem *et al.*, 2001; Amiri *et al.*, 2006). Jackson *et al.* (1978) demonstrated that the production of antibodies was greater in chicks produced by breeders fed 150 mg of vitamin E /kg feed.

As knowledge of the metabolic actions of vitamin E continues to advance, recommendations for incorporating it in feed continue to increase. Different official bodies have increased the recommendations of vitamin E for the breeding stages, above all with a view to combating the free radicals which form as a consequence of situations of physiological and environmental stress, and which make it possible to obtain good reproductive and productive performance in the progeny. The tables published since the year 2000 recommend levels of vitamin E in breeder feed which vary between 30 and 75 mg/kg, and reach 100 mg/kg in the case of turkey breeders. Doses between 100 and 200 mg/kg are necessary to achieve a good immune response.

VITAMIN K

The term vitamin K is used to refer to different compounds of the quinone group with antihemorragic effects. Vitamin K derived from plants is predominantly phylloquinone or vitamin K_1. Vitamin K obtained from bacterial fermentation is mainly menaquinone or vitamin K_2, and vitamin K_3 or menadione is produced by means of chemical synthesis and is the form normally used for feeding animals. The last one is characterized by its water solubility and high stability, being preferentially used in compounds feeds.

The principal function of vitamin K is the control of the blood coagulation period, since it participates in the activation of plasmatic prothrombin. It has also been observed that a large number of proteins with different metabolic functions require vitamin K for their biosynthesis (**Figure 6**). Thus the majority of tissues have relationships depending on vitamin K. Especially noteworthy in the case of breeders is the dependence on vitamin K of osteocalcin, a mineral-binding protein present in the bones of chicken embryos and in the bone matrix. Osteocalcin is essential for the bone mineralization process. However, in the study by Lavelle *et al.* (1994), no functional deficiencies were observed in the bone metabolism of breeders or of their progeny with vitamin K levels below

the minimum requirements. The quantity of vitamin K transferred to the egg is a function of the quantity of vitamin K ingested by the breeder (Almquist, 1971). When the supplementation levels in the breeder rations are inadequate, eggs are produced with low vitamin K content, accompanied by high levels of embryonic mortality due to hemorrhagic processes during the final period of incubation (Nelson and Norris, 1960; Grimminger and Brubacher, 1966). Hatched chicks show a longer coagulation period than normal and any trauma can provoke fatal hemorrhages (Lavelle *et al.*, 1994).

In spite of the fact that menaquinones (vitamin K_2) are produced by microbiota, the birds do not usually have enough vitamin K of microbial origin to meet their requirements, as there may be reduced microbial activity and vitamin K is mainly produced in posterior sections of the digestive tract. The feces of the birds contain relatively high levels of vitamin K, and can be an important source if coprophagy occurs during the production and reproduction process. Vitamin K recommendations should be increased when diseases occur, in the presence of antagonists and in situations which alter the digestion and absorption of vitamin K.

Figure 6. The main function of vitamin K$_3$ is to be a co-factor for the carboxylation of several pre-formed proteins in the liver: prothrombin and other plasma clotting factors and osteocalcin, to develop biological active compounds

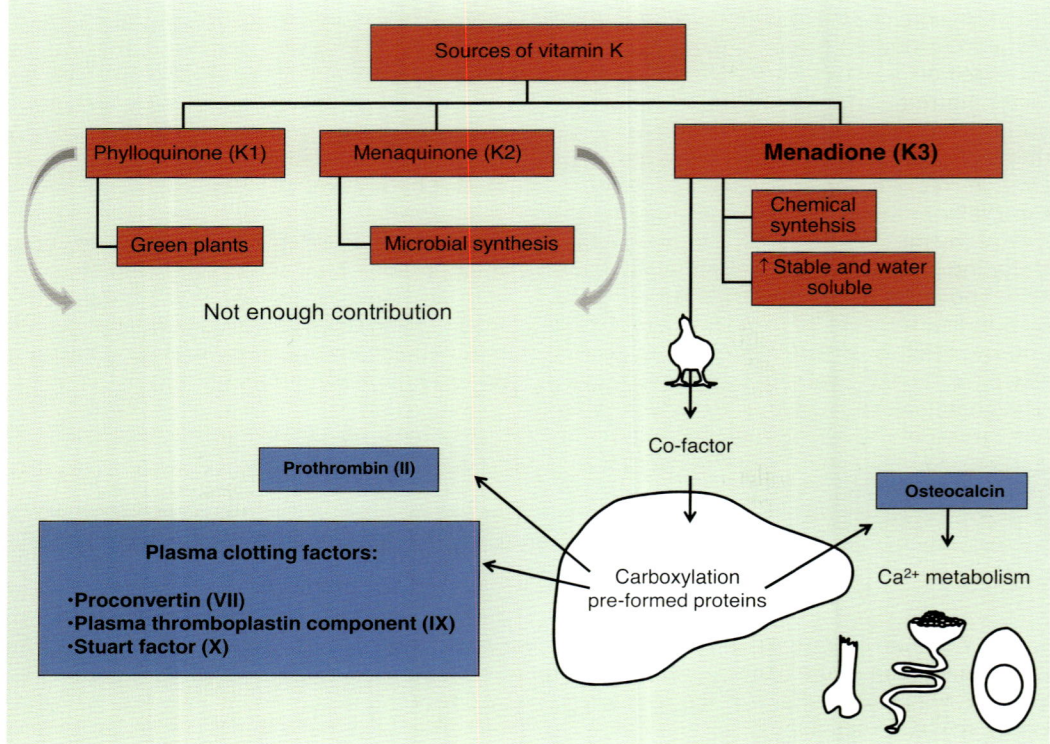

The recommendations indicated in the official tables range between 2 and 4 times the minimum requirements, at 2–4 mg/kg of vitamin K$_3$ for meat bird breeder feeds **(Tables II and III)**.

VITAMIN B COMPLEX WATER-SOLUBLE VITAMINS

Among the water-soluble vitamins are the vitamins of the B complex plus choline and vitamin C.

Most of them cannot be synthesized by the birds or not in sufficient quantities to cover their requirements in different physiological situations. Some can be supplied through the metabolism of the microbiota of the intestinal tract, but since absorption is limited to the posterior sections of the digestive tract, this process is not very efficient and depends on subsequent coprophagy. In general terms they are not stored in significant quantities in the bird (except vitamin B$_{12}$), which prevents toxicity problems but entails the need for a regular supplementation in the ration.

The majority of B group vitamins act as coenzymes on different metabolic pathways and their presence is fundamental for the normal functioning of the organism. An insufficient supply of B group vitamins is usually related to problems in the epithelium and immune system. Studies carried out on B group vitamins show that they affect the production of eggs and the viability of the chicks. Different authors have demonstrated that the content of the majority of water-soluble vitamins depends on the level consumed by the breeder (Souci *et al.*, 1989; Squires and Naber, 1993b). Some vitamins of the B group take between 7 and 10 days to reach the maximum level of deposition in the egg. It is known that the reduced production of hatching eggs by breeders at the start and the end of laying period is related to the composition of the egg, and vitamin composition has been pointed out as a key factor. Nutrition is therefore important not only during the reproduction phase but also during the growth of the breeders, as is covering vitamin requirements with safety margins especially in the pre-laying phase and at the end of laying (Leeson and Summers, 2005). Including levels of biotin, vitamin B6 and folic acid above the requirements in the feeds of breeder turkeys from week 24 of laying improves the rates of embryo survival (Robel, 1983a,b). In this respect, supplementation with vitamins of the B group in drinking water has turned out to be beneficial in batches of chickens coming from young breeders which otherwise have higher mortality early and worse productive performance (Bains, 2001).

In the study described by Leeson and Summers (2005), the rate of incubation responded to the absence or reintroduction of different vitamins in the ration (**Figure 7**). The absence over 3 weeks of the majority of the B group vitamins, individually, caused more than a 10% reduction in hatchability. After 15 weeks of feeding with deficient rations the missing vitamin was reintroduced. After 4 weeks of receiving the proper level of all vitamins, the breeders regained the standard levels of production and hatchability.

The NRC's 1994 publication points out that the vitamin levels needed to produce table eggs may be lower than those needed for hatching eggs (Naber, 1979). It indicates that the water-soluble vitamins and especially riboflavin, pantothenic acid and vitamin B_{12} are critical for good hatchability. It is important to remember that the data supplied by this body refer to breeders of light strains producing hens that lay white table eggs, and only in the case of biotin are minimum requirements specified for breeders of heavy strains producing meat chickens.

Figure 7. Percentage of fertile eggs from breeders fed with deficiencies in B group vitamins, individually. The arrow at 15 weeks indicates the inclusion in the diet of the vitamin being studied which was absent at the start of the experiment.
(adapted from Leeson & Summers, 2005)

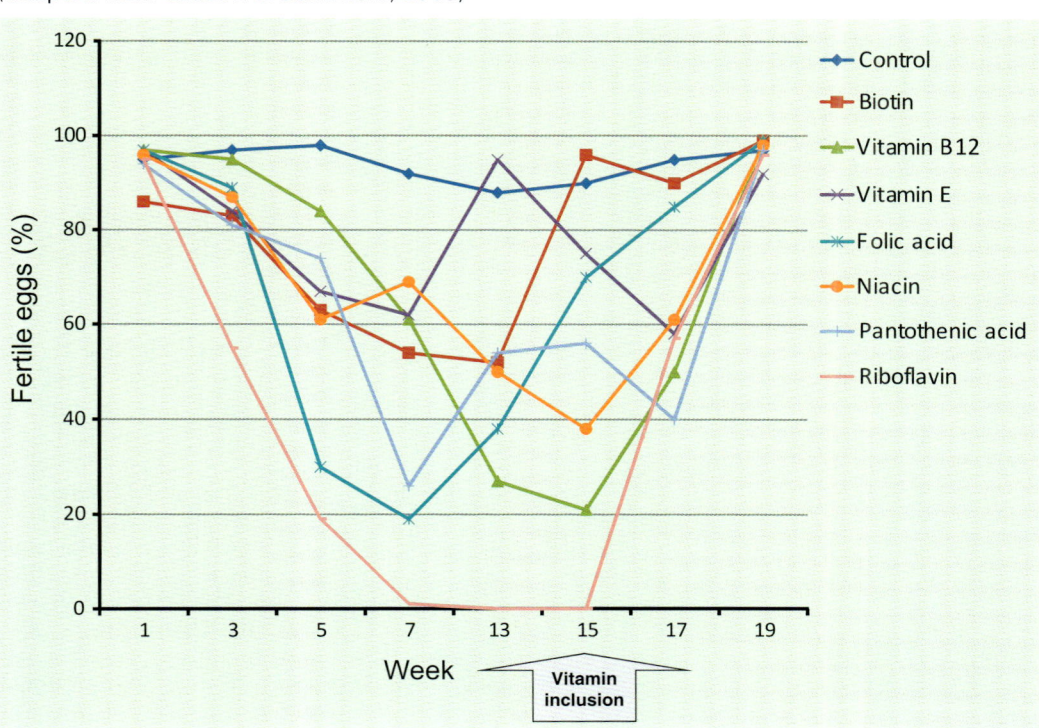

THIAMINE (VITAMIN B$_1$)

Thiamine, vitamin B$_1$, is found in the main raw materials of plant origin used in the typical formulation of poultry feed. However, the frequent presence of antagonists such as mycotoxins and high susceptibility to inactivation by heat must be taken into account.

Thiamine is one of the enzymes critical in the metabolism of branched-chain amino acids, of carbohydrates and in lipogenesis (**Figure 8**). For this reason, thiamine recommendations increase when the main energy source supplied by the feed is carbohydrate.

Thiamine is transported to the egg yolk associated with thiamine binding proteins. The work by Polin *et al.* (1962) and Charles *et al.* (1972) has demonstrated that an inadequate supply of thiamine to breeder hens causes high embryonic mortality and chicks with polyneuritis. Although embryos are capable of synthesizing thiamine from

5–7 days of incubation (Backermann *et al.*, 2008), the quantity of thiamine deposited in the egg is important and allows the newly hatched chick to have a reserve during its first days. Olkowski and Classen (1999) studied the response of broiler chickens to a wide range of thiamine supplementation to the breeder diet (0, 2, 8, 32 mg/kg supplemented to the basal diet) and they observed that the low levels of supplementation increase the thiamine status indices and thiamine metabolism in the offspring. This reserve is important for the initial development of the chick and has repercussions on its subsequent growth. Thus, Bhanja *et al.* (2007) observed that chickens from eggs in which an extra quantity of vitamin B$_1$ had been incorporated, through *in ovo* inoculation, were heavier at 28 days of age.

Heavy breeder strains are less efficient when it comes to incorporating thiamine in the egg, so that their requirements will be

Figure 8. Diagram that represents the pathways in which thiamine is involved.

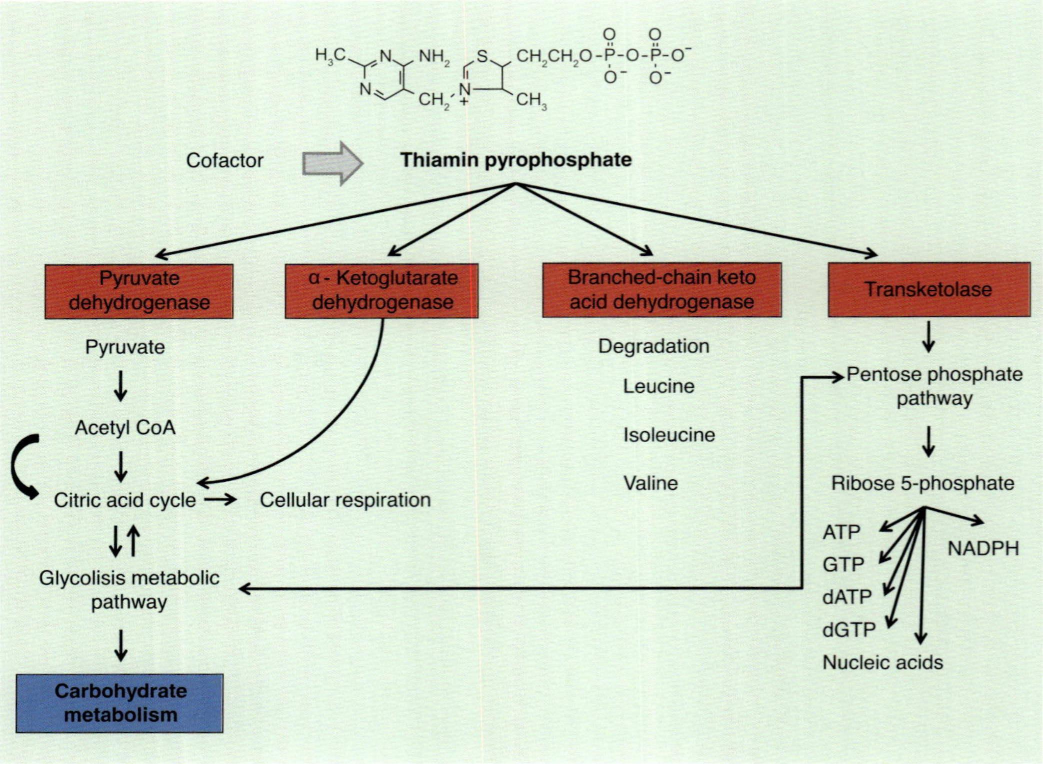

higher than those referenced in light breeder hens such as those indicated by the NRC (1994) set at 0.7 mg/kg. Thus the majority of tables published indicate thiamine recommendations between 1.5 and 2.0 mg/ kg in breeder feed, double that established in the NRC (1994), although little work has been done in relation to thiamine requirements in this type of birds.

RIBOFLAVIN (VITAMIN B$_2$)

Vitamin B$_2$ or riboflavin was first isolated from egg albumin in 1933, and subsequently detected in milk and liver. It is found in appreciable quantities in green plants, although its content is limited in cereals and protein ingredients of plant origin.

Riboflavin recommendations in poultry rise when the quantity of fat or protein in the ration is increased, since vitamin B$_2$, in the forms of flavin mononucleotide (FMN) and flavin adenine dinucleotide (FAD), acts as a cofactor of numerous enzymes involved in the metabolic oxidation processes of these nutrients. More than 100 enzymes are known to bind FAD or FMN. **Figure 9** shows the most important functions of riboflavin.

The riboflavin content in the egg increases in direct proportion to its ingestion by the hen, reaching levels of 5 mg/kg. Not all the quantity of riboflavin contained in the fertile egg is used during embryo development. In fact reserves are generated in the liver and the yolk sac which can cover the chick's requirements for a few days after birth. Squires and Naber (1993b) suggest a supply of riboflavin (4.4 mg/kg) above the minimum requirements to increase production and hatchability and achieve a content of around 2.5 µg of riboflavin per g of egg albumin. When breeders consume levels lower than their requirements, the riboflavin content in the egg is reduced in only 2 days, producing high mortality in the intermediary phase of incubation, accompanied by hatching problems and malformations at birth (Leeson and Summers, 1978, Flores-Garcia, 1992, Flores-Garcia and Stoltyssek, 1992, Squires and Naber, 1993b, Whitehead *et al.*, 1993, Wilson 1997). The lack of riboflavin supply in the feed over 7 weeks caused the hens to practically stop laying eggs, while in contrast reintroducing 7 mg/kg of vitamin B$_2$ over 2–3 weeks restored hatchability up to levels of 95% in the fourth week of reintroducing the vitamin (Leeson and Summers, 2005; **Figure 1**). These data are an endorsement that the quantity of riboflavin in the mother's feed has an obvious influence on the vigour and survival capacity of the chick. (**Figure 9**)

The minimum levels proposed by the NRC in 1994 for light strain breeders stand at 3.6 mg/ kg. Some investigators indicate that the levels for breeders should be triple or quadruple the levels for commercial egg hens (Whitehead and Portsmouth, 1989). In fact, the majority of tables published by recognized bodies recommend levels between 7 and 12 mg/kg of riboflavin for breeder feeds.

Figure 9. Main functions of riboflavin in poultry metabolism

- As a co-enzyme it is involved in the respiratory reaction for obtaining energy from nutrients
- In co-enzyme forms (FAD & FMN) it helps to regulate cellular metabolism as in carbohydrate metabolism
- It is an essential co-facor in the amino acid and fatty acid metabolism
- It is involved in the maintenance of mucus membrane integrity
- It protects myelin sheaths of peripheral nerves
- For maintaining the productive and reproductive demands
- The synthesis of binding proteins in the liver requires riboflavin
- It has functional relationship with several metabolic pathways

Riboflavin

PYRIDOXINE (VITAMIN B$_6$)

The term vitamin B$_6$ refers to a group of three compounds: pyridoxol (pyridoxine), pyridoxal and pyridoxamine. These three compounds have a similar vitamin activity in the different species of birds.

Vitamin B$_6$ is one of the numerous enzymes involved in the metabolism of nutrients, being especially important as a cofactor of enzymes responsible for biosynthesis, catabolism and interconversion of amino acids. The minimum requirements of vitamin B$_6$ have been proposed for rations with moderate levels of protein and a balanced amino acid relationship (Daghir and Shah, 1973). The recommendations for vitamin B$_6$ supply increase feeds with high levels of protein or with an amino acid profile distant from the ideal protein, since a greater quantity of enzymes is needed to metabolize the excess of amino acids and these enzymes are dependent on vitamin B$_6$ (**Figure 10**).

Vitamin B$_6$ is widely distributed in feedstuffs. Furthermore, due to microbial synthesis, coprophagy is a source of vitamin B$_6$ of microbial origin. It is not clearly demonstrated that vitamin B$_6$ from posterior sections of the digestive tract is really absorbed and used in significant quantities by monogastric animals. Only small quantities of vitamin B$_6$ are stored in the organism, and over half, in the case of birds, is found forming part of enzymes in the muscle and liver. Inadequate vitamin B$_6$ will lead to inefficiencies in the utilization of protein in the diet, accompanied by a reduction in the capacity for nitrogen retention and an increase in excretion.

For adult birds, inadequate consumption of vitamin B$_6$ has caused reductions in the production of eggs and in their hatchability. The vitamin B$_6$ content of feed is reflected in the deposition in the egg. The quantity of vitamin B$_6$ needed to obtain maximum fertility is double that for maintaining the number of eggs produced, and furthermore the safety margin is small (Fuller et al., 1961). When, in the study by Robel (2002) increasing levels of pyridoxine (from 12.9 to 24.4 mg/kg) were supplied in the feed of female turkey breeders, no improvement in hatchability

Figure 10. Percentage of hatchability fertile eggs and number of eggs per turkey hen (adapted from Robel, 2002)

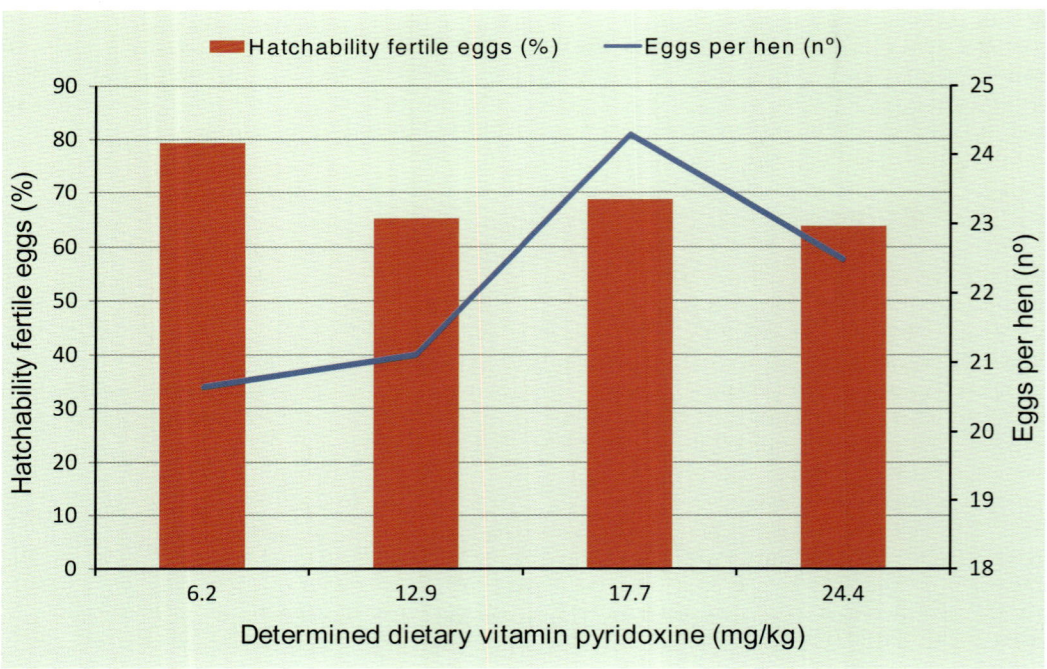

was obtained compared to the basal diet supplemented with 6.2 mg/kg of vitamin B$_6$ (**Figure 10**). In the same study, despite no significant differences obtained in the number of eggs per hen, a slight numerical increase was observed in upper dosages. This lack of effect could be due to the fact that the levels in the basal diet were already much higher than those set by the NRC (3–4 mg/kg of pyridoxine), and a limited efficiency in the transference of vitamin B$_6$ from feed to egg has also been described, especially at high levels of intake (Fuller *et al.*, 1961). It has been demonstrated that inoculating pyridoxine into fertile eggs increases the hatching percentage of chickens (Bhanja *et al.*, 2007) and of turkeys by approximately

4.2% (Robel and Christensen, 1991). On the other hand, severe deficiencies of vitamin B$_6$ cause involution of the genital organs both in females and males (Weiss and Scott, 1979; Scott *et al.*, 1982) and early embryo mortality (Landauer, 1967).

Studies carried out on humans and other animals demonstrate that the depletion of vitamin B$_6$ in the organism affects both humoral and cell-mediated immune response.

The recommendations for dietary supplementation of pyridoxine for heavy breeder hens stand between 3 and 6 mg/kg.

NIACIN

The two forms of niacin or vitamin B$_3$, nicotinic acid and nicotinamide, are functional parts of the coenzymes nicotinamide adenine dinucleotide (NAD) and nicotinamide adenine dinucleotide phosphate (NADP), involved in the cellular respiration processes.

Niacin is not usually found in free form in feedstuffs. In feedstuffs of plant origin, niacin is usually bound to other compounds which, in the case of birds, are difficult to digest resulting in low availability. For example, in cereal grains vitamin B$_3$ is found as a part of more complex structures, bound in covalent form with peptides and carbohydrates, which obstruct its bioavailability. In animal tissue, on the other hand, niacin is found essentially in NAD and NADP, which are hydrolyzed and absorbed efficiently in the intestine.

Tryptophan is a precursor of niacin synthesis in the organism, with a conversion efficiency varying between the different species of birds. Turkeys and ducks are less efficient at converting tryptophan into niacin than chickens and hens. To synthesize 1 mg of niacin, chickens need to consume 50 mg more tryptophan than necessary to cover their protein metabolism related requirements. Therefore a feed which is limiting in niacin would increase tryptophan recommendations by 50%. Furthermore, riboflavin is needed for the synthesis of niacin from tryptophan and for the conversion of vitamin B$_3$ into a

functional coenzyme. A marginal quantity of niacin, accompanied by low levels of niacin, will hinder the production of eggs and their hatchability. On the other hand, during their development and after hatching, chicks obtain niacin through transformation from the tryptophan present in the proteins which are part of the egg yolk. As Cunha (1982) indicates, it is better to supplement niacin in a bird's ration without taking into account the niacin content of cereals since its bioavailability is very low. The same author points out that it is better to ensure that the supply of niacin is adequate to prevent the essential amino acid, tryptophan, from being diverted into the synthesis of niacin.

Some authors indicate that supplementation between 66 and 132 mg/kg of niacin improves the quality of the egg shell (Leeson *et al.*, 1991) and lowers mortality both in the embryo (Briggs, 1946) and in the breeder itself (Jackson, 1992). Harms *et al.* (1988) observed that egg weight increased in parallel with niacin supplementation of breeders, with dosages ranging between 8.4 and 33.4 mg/kg (0.17% of tryptophan in the diet).

The minimum requirements published by the NRC appear to be insufficient and different authors recommend levels between 30 and 55 mg/kg for meat chicken breeders, which would mean tripling or quadrupling the dosage (**Figure 11**).

61

Figure 11. Comparison of recommended niacin levels in broiler breeders' feed. The red line indicates the level recommended by the National Research Council, 1994

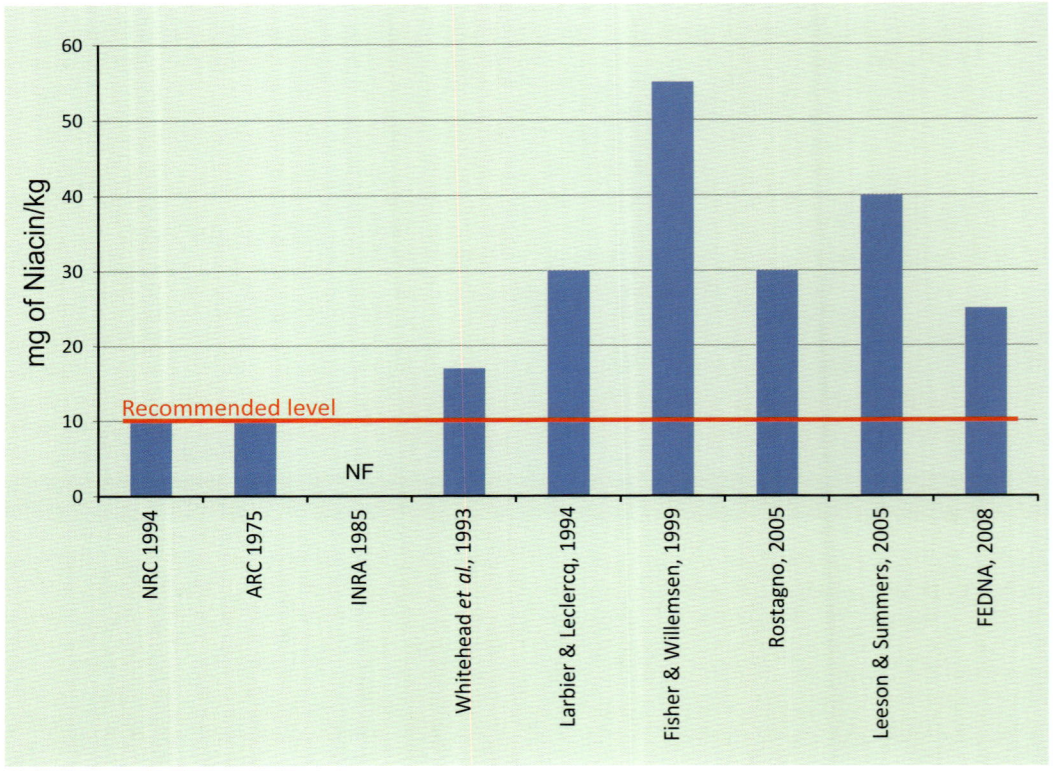

PANTOTHENIC ACID

Pantothenic acid is found forming part of the coenzymes, especially coenzyme A and the carrier protein for acyl groups. It is involved in several metabolic pathways important in endogenous metabolism energy exchange in all tissues (**Figure 12**). Its main functions include the utilization of nutrients, synthesis of fatty acids and participation in the citric acid cycle, as well as in the energy-yielding oxidation of fats, carbohydrates and amino acids. Although this vitamin is found in practically all feedstuffs, complementary supplementation is advisable in the formulation of rations for birds, with the aim of ensuring a high level of production. Cereals have a low or medium pantothenic acid content and, in the case of sorghum, wheat and barley, with a bioavailability of approximately 60%.

Work carried out by Robel (1993b) with female turkey breeders led to the conclusion that in proportion as the pantothenic acid dosage in the hen's feed is increased, the greater the transfer of this vitamin to the egg. A marginal level of this vitamin results in defects in embryo development which reduce the hatchability and viability of the chicks. Embryo death generally occurs in the final days of incubation. There is a direct linear relationship between the pantothenic acid content in the ration of breeders and the proportion of eggs hatched. Supplementation with 4 mg/kg of pantothenic acid prevents losses in reproduction and doses of 8 mg/kg increase hatchable egg production and the viability of offspring (Beer *et al.*, 1963). The requirement for pantothenic acid to ensure viabile offspring may be even greater and Utno and Klieste (1971) set it at 20 mg/kg. Some authors have observed that increasing the pantothenic acid in the ration increases the live weight of the progeny. However this effect is observed in situations of vitamin

Figure 12. Reactions in which coenzyme A (previously synthesised from panthotenic acid, cysteamine and adenosine triphosphate) serves as an acyl transfer agent in a large number of metabolism pathways in the organism (adapted from Hughes, 1952)

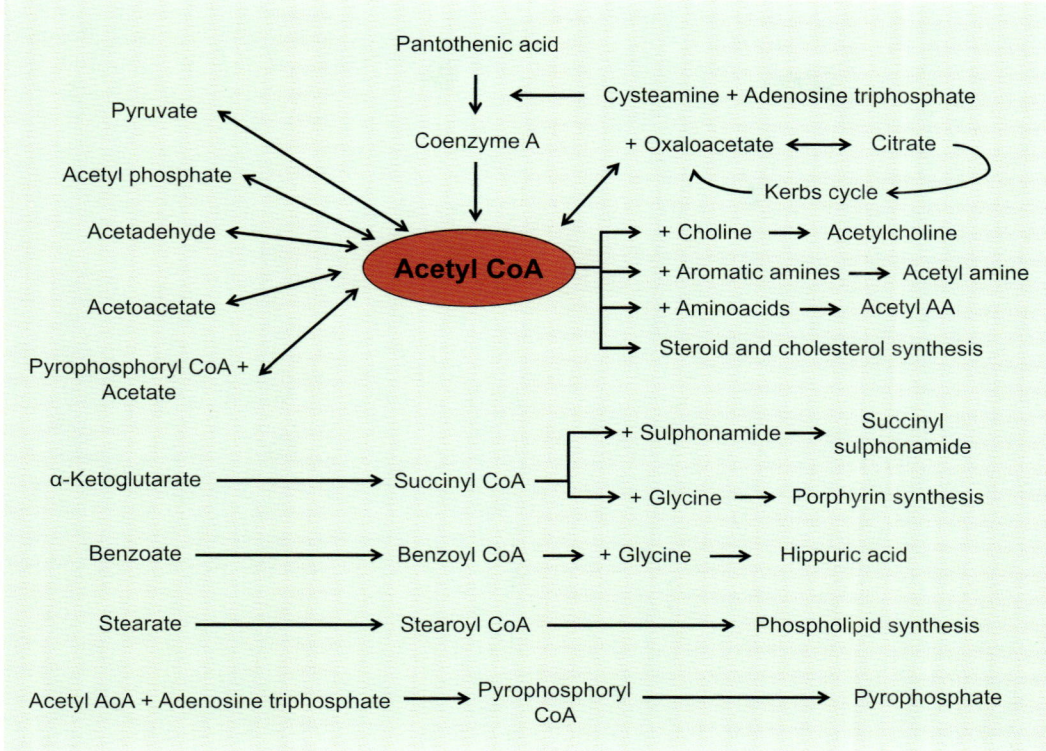

B_{12} deficiency (Balloun and Phillips, 1957).

In a study with breeder males supplemented with 24 mg of pantothenic acid /kg feed, the quantity and quality of the semen increased as well as the weight of the testicles compared with animals fed deficient feeds with 0.38 mg/kg pantothenic acid (Goeger and Arscott, 1984).

When feed intake is restricted, the pantothenic acid content in the ration must be adjusted to ensure the proper level of vitamin ingestion. Furthermore, pantothenic acid requirements may increase when other vitamins are present at marginal levels of bioavailability. The NRC points to pantothenic acid as a critical vitamin for reproduction and sets the minimum requirements for breeders at levels 3.5 times higher than for hens laying table eggs, in both cases referring to light strains. Other authors set recommendations at levels of 12–15 mg/kg for heavy breeder hens and between 16 and 20 mg/kg for female turkey breeders.

BIOTIN

Biotin is a coenzyme essential for gluconeogenesis, lipogenesis and the elongation of essential fatty acids. It is important for the normal functioning of the reproductive and nervous systems and of the thyroid and adrenal glands.

Of all the vitamins present in feed ingredients of plant origin, biotin is the one that presents the most variable content, being affected by numerous environmental factors. Furthermore, the majority of ingredients contain biotin bound to the protein by covalent bonds, which hinders its digestion and availability for the animal. The cecal microbiota of the bird has the ability to synthesize biotin but the quantity is variable and the importance of its utilization on the part of the host is unknown (Scott, 1981).

Biotin is transferred both to the white and to the yolk of the egg through the binding proteins of avidin and biotin, respectively.

The binding proteins of biotin are synthesized in the liver of the hen and provide biotin to the developing follicle, which will constitute the future yolk. The biotin in the yolk is the principal vitamin source for the developing embryo. On the other hand, albumen contains avidin, which is a glycoprotein secreted in the oviduct during the albumen depositing phase and it has important antibacterial properties. Biotin bound to avidin has very low availability during the embryonic phase, however it can be a vitamin source for the newly hatched chick. As with the majority of vitamins, there is a direct relationship between the biotin content in the hen's feed and the egg (Buenrostro and Kratzer, 1984; Whitehead et al., 1985). Biotin dosage levels in breeder feed make it possible to increase the content in the egg (Naber, 1979). Whitehead et al. (1985) have demonstrated a correlation between the quantity of biotin in the egg yolk and the level of biotin in the

Figure 13. Based on the regression curves obtained by Robel (1991), estimations were made for each 5-6 wk production period, for determining approximate dietary biotin level at highest estimated hatchability: in period 1, a straight line without slope was formed, indicating that younger hens did not respond to different dietary biotin levels; in period 2, highest hatchability occured for the diet containing approximately 500 µg biotin/kg; and for hens in period 3, highest hatchability occured for the diet containing approximately 800 µg biotin/kg (adapted from Robel, 2002).

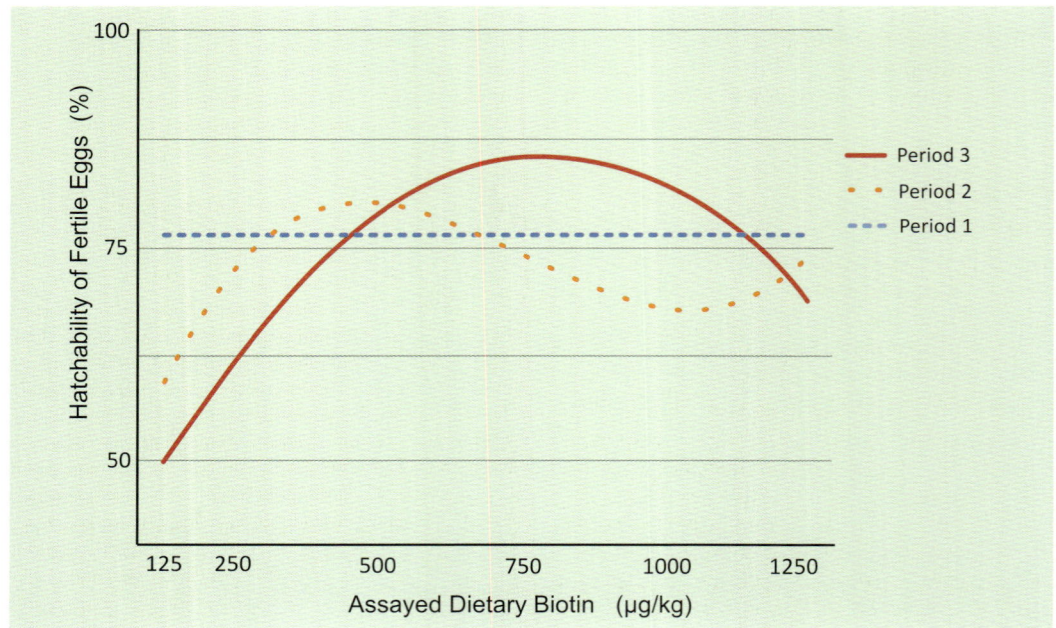

plasma of the progeny, a level inversely related to hatchability, viability and growth after hatching. High levels of biotin in the egg will permit the proper development of the embryo and the chick to achieve its genetic potential.

An inadequate quantity of biotin in a breeder's feed gives rise to a decrease in laying and hatchability with high mortality during the last week of incubation and bone deformaties in the progeny (Ferguson et al., 1961; Cravens et al., 1944; Robel, 1991). Supplementation of 150–252 µg/kg of biotin in the breeder feed ensured an adequate deposition of this vitamin in the egg and hatchability of 80% (Brewer and Edwards, 1972). Furthermore, these authors observed that chicks coming from breeders with higher levels of biotin were heavier at 2 weeks of age. Similarly, Robel (1989) observed that when the breeder feed contained 165 µg/kg of biotin, the fertile eggs had a hatchability of 84%. When the dose of biotin was higher (440 µg/kg), hatchability reached 89%.

In the case of turkey breeders, maximum hatchability was obtained by supplementing the feed with 520 µg/kg of biotin during the initial and intermediary phases of reproduction. This figure increased to 750 µg/kg of biotin in the breeder feed during weeks 50–54 of life, which made it possible to increase hatchable egg production by 22% and chick hatchability by 10% (**Figure 13**) (Robel, 2002). These findings suggested that commercial turkey breeder diets may warrant higher dietary biotin levels in order to optimize hatchability in older turkey hens. Injecting *in ovo*, 87 µg of biotin into each egg it was possible to improve hatchability by 4–5%. These data indicate that metabolic requirements for biotin increase as a breeder gets older.

The results of Harms et al. (1979), demonstrate the relationship between supplementation with biotin in breeders and the repercussion on aspects of welfare and quality of the final product. The incorporation of 200µg/kg of biotin in the hen's feeds made it possible to reduce the incidence of foot pad dermatitis and breast lesions in the progeny.

Biotin is the only vitamin for which the NRC (1994) estimates minimum requirements for meat breeders. That body specifies requirements of 16 µg of biotin per hen per day, which is 60% more than for light breeders (10 µg per hen per day). These data are based on the results of Whitehead et al. (1985), and they consider that this is the minimum level which makes it possible to reach at least a biotin concentration in the egg yolk of 550 ng/g. The level of biotin recommended by genetics companies stands at between 200 and 400 µg/kg for heavy breeder hens and between 300 and 450 µg/kg for female turkey breeders, which is between 2 and 2 ½ times higher than the NRC requirements (1994). There are significant differences in the metabolism and deposition of biotin between breeder hens and turkeys which could be responsible for the different vitamin requirements for the two species (Whitehead, 1988).

FOLACIN

The terms folacin, folate and folic acid can be used interchangeably and refer to a large variety of compounds which possess biological activity of folic acid.

Folacin is essential in the transfer of monocarbonate units in metabolic processes, affecting the synthesis of purines and pyrimidines, which make up the nucleic acids needed for cell division. It is also involved in the interconversion of serine and glycine, in the degradation of histidine and in the addition of methyl groups to compounds such as methionine, choline and thiamine. For this reason, inadequate levels of other methyl group donors (such as vitamin B_{12}, serine, methionine, betaine and choline) increase folic acid requirements. This interaction with other nutrients is especially important in birds, as nitrogen is excreted as uric acid, which entails a high expenditure of methionine and cysteine. Furthermore, methionine tends to be the first limiting amino acid in bird feeding, which entails an increase in requirements of other sources of methyl group donors. Logically,

65

Figure 14. Hatchability of turkey eggs from hens fed a basal diet supplemented with folic acid (0.65, 2.73 and 7.37 mg/kg) over three equal time periods of production (0-5, 6-10 and 11-16 weeks) and vitamin contents of egg yolk (adapted from Robel, 2002)

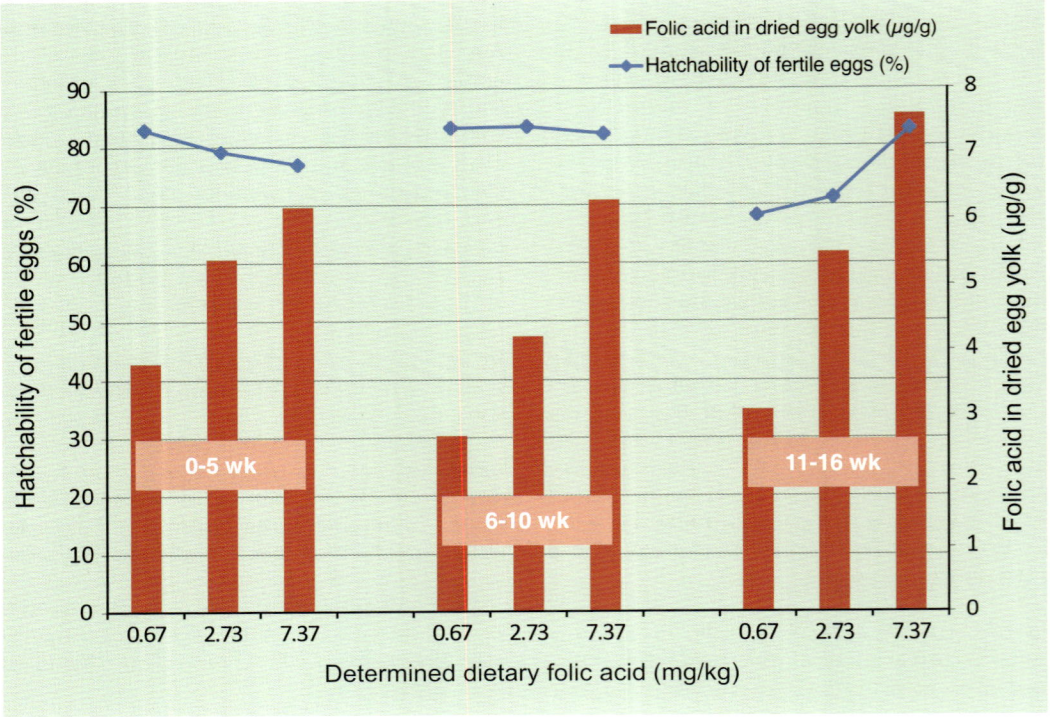

high levels of protein in the diet raise the dietary recommendations for folate. Folacin is present in the majority of feedstuffs used in chicken feeds, but as it tends to present itself in conjugated forms, its absorption efficiency may be reduced.

An inadequate supply of folic acid in hens hinders the normal development and functioning of the oviduct, accompanied by a defective deposition of albumen (Siddons, 1978). Feeds for broiler breeders tend to incorporate 1–1.5 mg/kg of folic acid, while in turkey breeders it ranges between 1 and 2 mg/kg. The transfer of folacin from feed to egg is very high. There are results in the breeding phase of turkeys which indicate that increasing dietary supplementation with folic acid is accompanied by a greater content of this vitamin in the egg (**Figure 14**) and gives rise to increases in the weight of the poult at hatching as well as its subsequent growth rate (Miller and Balloun, 1967; Robel, 1993a, Robel, 2002). Although the incorporation of high levels of folic acid (2.64 and 5.51 mg/kg) in the feed of female turkey breeders did not

increase hatchability, the extra incorporation of folic acid through *in ovo* injection did permit an increase of 8–9% in the weight of the progeny (Robel, 1993a and 2002). In breeder hens, marginal quantities of folacin are accompanied by reduced hatchability, higher mortality and more deformities in the chicks (Leeson *et al.*, 1979b).

It is widely accepted that the folacin requirements for the production of hatching eggs is higher than for the production of table eggs (Taylor, 1947; NRC, 1994; Robel, 1993a). In human nutrition, it is well established that a daily supply of folacin should be administered which amply exceeds the minimum requirements, especially during gestation and lactation.

Some official bodies recommend incorporating folic acid in the feed of heavy breeder hens at levels higher than 1 mg/kg, values which reach 2 mg/kg for female turkey breeders. The recommendations of the genetics companies go so far as to double and triple this figure (**Table II**).

CYANOCOBALAMIN (VITAMIN B₁₂)

Vitamin B_{12} or cyanocobalamin was discovered in 1948 and is an essential part of different enzymatic systems essential for the basic metabolic functions of the organism. The dietary requirements for this vitamin, and consequently its margin of error, are very small. Furthermore, it is characterized by only being synthesized by microorganisms and not being found in feedstuffs of plant origin. Bedding can be a source of vitamin B_{12} for birds housed on solid floors, although there are no data relating to its absorption level.

Vitamin B_{12} requirements increase with the level of production, with the quantity of protein included in the ration, and they depend on the presence of other essential nutrients related to transmethylation and the biosynthesis of methyl groups. The main functions in which vitamin B_{12} is involved are summarized in **Figure 15**.

Despite being a water-soluble vitamin, a certain degree of storage occurs, mainly in the liver. As the vitamin B_{12} content in the hen's feed increases, so does its deposition in the egg, increasing its availability for embryonic development. Chicks from breeders fed levels above the minimum requirements of vitamin B_{12} form an important vitamin reserve for their subsequent development. After 2–5 months of administering a diet with an inadequate quantity of vitamin B_{12} one can already start to observe that the reserves of this vitamin in the newly hatched chick are insufficient and the rate of mortality rises (Patel and McGinnis, 1977; Scott et al., 1982). Inadequate levels of vitamin B_{12} are associated with low hatchability and disorders in the progeny (Olcese et al., 1950; Tuite and Austic, 1974; Patel and McGinnis, 1980; Ward et al., 1985). On the other hand, Squires and Naber (1992) observed that increasing the supplementation of vitamin B_{12} in the feeds of heavy breeders produced an increase in the weight and number of eggs produced and hatched. Panic et al. (1970) observed that supplementing vitamin B_{12} at a level of 20 µg/kg produced an increase in the content of this vitamin in the egg and an increase of 20% in hatchability. The inclusion of 10 µg/kg vitamin B_{12} in the hen's feed improves the live weight and growth of the progeny (Patel and McGinnis, 1977).

It is important to take into account the interaction with other micronutrients such as riboflavin and pantothenic acid (Tuite and Austic, 1974, Balloun and Phillips, 1957).

The majority of tables published recommend a supplementation of vitamin B_{12} in breeder feed which ranges between 10 and 20 µg/kg.

Figure 15. Summary of the main functions of cyanocobalamin in poultry metabolism

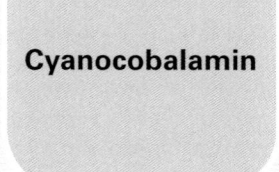

Cyanocobalamin

- It acts as a co-enzyme involved in transmethylation reactions for the synthesis of a number of amino acids and proteins
- It promotes the formation of DNA → essential for the reproduction process
- It participates in the synthesis of tetrahydrofolic acid from folic acid
- It is involved in the metabolism of propionic acid
- It promotes the proper neutral function through maintenance of the myelin sheath on nerve fibers of the spinal cord
- It is essential for the maturation of red blood cells
- It participates in oxidation-reduction system

CHOLINE

Choline is a nutrient essential for birds involved in structural and neurotransmission functions and in the donation of methyl groups.

Choline is considered a vitamin although it does not fulfill some of the prerequisites of this definition. For example, birds require high quantities of choline (less than 1%), levels similar to the amino acids and essential fatty acids. It can be synthesized in the liver of birds from serine and methyl groups, requiring 3 moles of methionine for each mole of choline synthesized. However for the majority of metabolic processes, the quantity and rate of synthesis are insufficient to cover requirements, above all when the supply of precursors such as methionine, vitamin B_{12} or folacin are limited.

Most of the choline in feed ingredients for poultry is integrated in lecithin (phosphatidylcholine) and, to a lesser extent, in free form or as sphingomyelin.

Although choline can be synthesized in the liver from the methylation of ethanolamine, young birds are dependent on the supply of choline in the ration, as they have a less well developed capacity for synthesizing choline from methionine or betaine (Norvell and Nesheim, 1969). It has been described that choline requirements of laying hens are influenced by the vitamin supplies during their growth phase. Furthermore, diets with reduced choline levels during the reproduction phase affect the size of the egg although choline deposition in the egg and embryonic development are not much affected (Klasing, 1998).

As a structural component of lecithin, Chlorine plays an essential role in the formation of the very low density

Figure 16. Abdominal fat deposition was reduced when high levels of choline were fed to broiler breeders (adapted from Rama Rao, 2001).

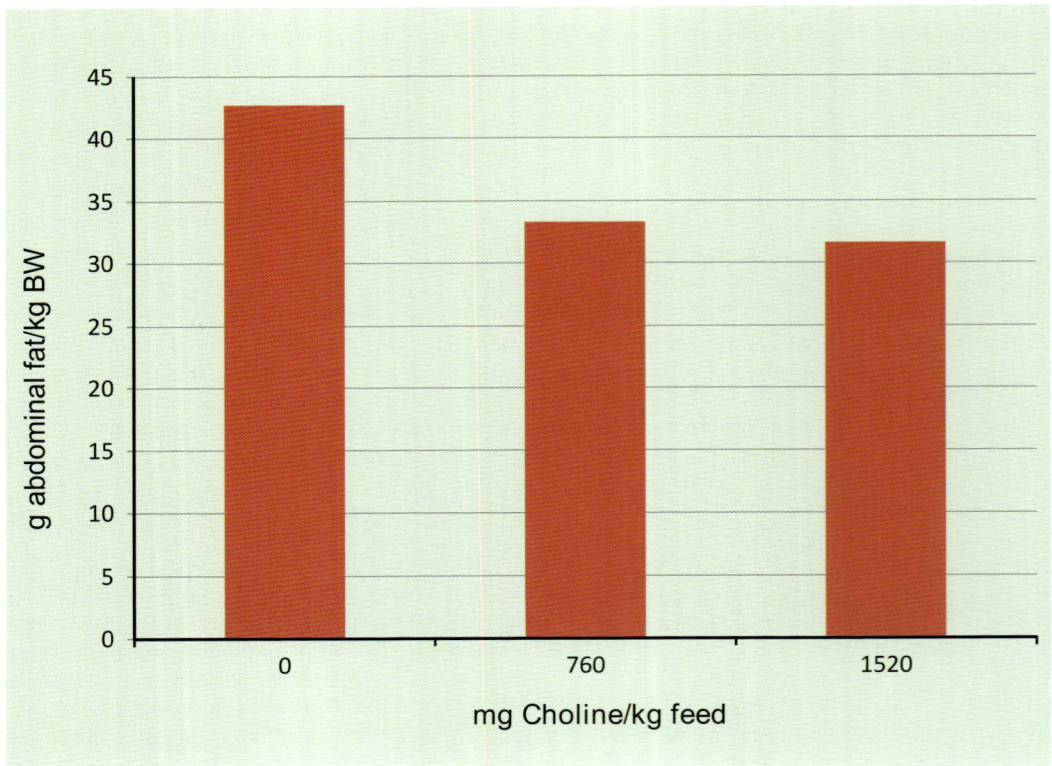

lipoproteins assigned to incorporating and mobilizing the triglycerides present in the liver. Lecithin deficiency is associated with an accumulation of fat in the liver (Rama Rao et al., 2001) and a decrease in the quantity of fat deposited in the egg yolk. In addition, the same authors showed a numerical reduction in the abdominal fat depot when birds were fed increasing amounts of choline (**Figure 16**). In the case of female turkey breeders, results indicate that supplementation with 1,000 mg/kg of choline optimizes the production and hatchability of eggs as well as the normal growth and viability of the progeny (Balloun and Miller, 1964).

The recommendations established for choline are higher for high protein feeds. This is due to the fact that additional methyl groups are needed for the synthesis and excretion of uric acid.

Although the NRC (1994) does not specify minimum requirements for choline, several publications indicate the importance of its supplementation in feed, although the recommendations range widely between 250 and 1,000 mg/kg depending on the safety margin applied, taking into account the variability of the ingredients and the fact that the presence of precursors may be limited.

VITAMIN C

The term vitamin C includes compounds with L-ascorbic acid activity. The functions of ascorbic acid are related to its redox properties, it is a cofactor and protector of different enzymes, it is involved in the reduction of trace minerals and acts as an antioxidant and/or prooxidant. One of the most interesting properties of vitamin C is its ability to act as a reducing agent or electron donor. It reacts rapidly with free radicals and acts synergistically with vitamin E, facilitating its regeneration in biological systems (Rocha et al., 2010).

As knowledge about the role of vitamin C advances, its effect on the maintenance and improvement of the animal's health and well-being is gradually being discovered. Quantities above the minimum requirements are necessary to potentiate its antioxidant role, enabling the deactivation of the free radicals produced by routine cell activity and by the action of stress-inducing agents. Vitamin C participates in the regeneration of vitamin E from its oxidized form (Chan et al., 1991; Chan, 1993). Furthermore, vitamin C is needed for the development of bones and eggshells, being a necessary cofactor for the conversion of vitamin D_3 in its active form, $1,25-(OH)_2-D_3$.

Almost all species of birds can synthesize vitamin C from glucose. However, the endogenous synthesis of ascorbic acid may be insufficient when the animal is subjected to stress, for example from heat or faced with an immune challenge. Increasing the ingestion of vitamin C raises the bird's resistance to infectious diseases. Some investigators have observed birds with the ability to choose feed with higher levels of vitamin C during periods of heat stress (Pardue and Thaxton, 1986; Kutlu and Forbes, 1993; McKee and Harrison, 1995; Kratzer et al., 1996). Furthermore, since ascorbic acid is especially important in the formation of collagen, its presence increases the capacity for the healing of wounds (Rajkhowa et al., 1996).

There is controversy in the literature in relation to the beneficial effects of vitamin C supplementation in poultry feeds. Although some of the work does not show effects on the parameters studied with vitamin C supplementation in breeder feeds, there are others which show improvements at different levels. Most results demonstrate the beneficial effect of vitamin C supplementation in feeds for hens in the laying phase – be it of eggs for consumption or for incubation hatchability – and in stress situations, principally heat-induced. Thus, on supplementing with ascorbic acid, several authors observe improvements in egg production, in strength and thickness of the shell as well as a higher rate of chick survival (Peebles and Brake, 1985; Chung *et al.*, 2005). Furthermore, it is thought that the biosynthesis of ascorbic acid diminishes as the bird ages and therefore in the final phases of reproduction, endogenous synthesis may be insufficient to cover requirements (Bains, 2001).

In breeder males, vitamin C could help to protect spermatozoa from the negative effects of oxidation. The concentration of ascorbic acid in the seminal fluid is higher than in the serum (Luck *et al.*, 1995). It has been demonstrated that supplementation with vitamin C has beneficial effects on fertility. Supplementation of 100 mg/kg of ascorbic acid increased the size of the testicles of growing males (Pardue and Thaxton, 1986). Furthermore, adding doses of ascorbic acid up to 500 ppm to the

feeds of breeder males of heavy strains in high temperature situations produced an increase in the volume of semen, in the number of spermatozoa per ejaculation and in sperm motility (Perek and Snapir, 1963; Monsi and Onitchi, 1991 **Figure 17**).

These benefits have also been described in breeder turkeys: on supplementing with vitamin C levels between 150 and 200 ppm, increases of 16 to 28% were observed in the volume and concentration of spermatozoa of the semen produced (Dobrescu, 1987; Noll, 1993). Other authors, while not observing modifications in sperm parameters on incorporating vitamin C in the diet of breeder turkeys, have indicated that the antioxidant properties of vitamin C can delay the formation of degenerative cells in the testicles (Neuman *et al.*, 2002).

Figure 17. Effect of different ascorbic acid concentrations in broiler breeder males' sperm production and sperm motility. (adapted from Monsi and Onitchi, 1991)

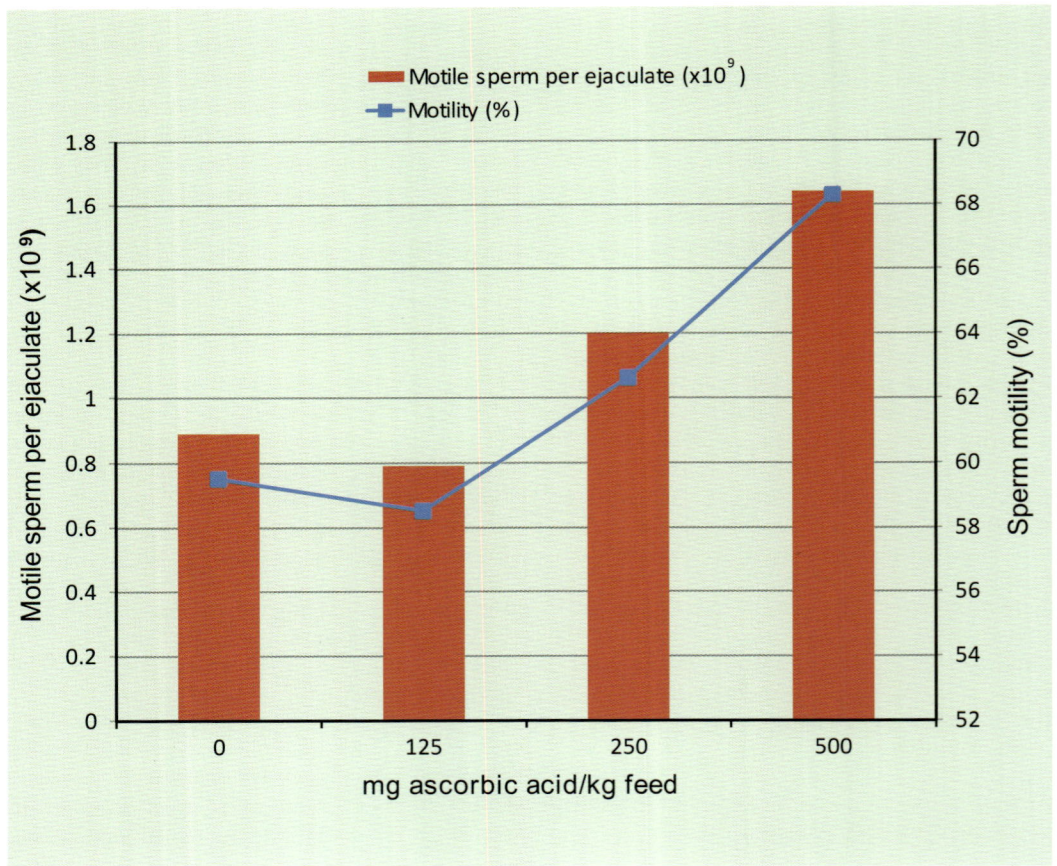

There is practically no storage of vitamin C in the body, which means there is no reservoir for coverage at times of deficiency. Vitamin C is the only vitamin which is not present in the infertile egg, as there is no transfer from the hen. However, vitamin C is found in the developing embryo deriving from endogenous synthesis (Pardue and Thaxton, 1986; Zwaan and Lam, 1992). During the initial phases of embryonic development, ascorbic acid is synthesized in the yolk membrane and liberated to the liver and other peripheral tissues (Surai and Speake, 2000). The antioxidant action of vitamin C is beneficial to the embryo especially if stress situations arise due to excess heat during the incubation process. Inoculation of 3 mg of vitamin C in eggs during the last part of incubation improved the viability and hatch weight of the chicks (Zakaria and Al-Anezi, 1996).

Birds need vitamin C for their metabolism, but due to their capacity for endogenous synthesis, there are no recommendations for supply in the ration from the NRC (1994). However other authors or bodies advise supplying vitamin C in the diet (between 50 and 250 mg/kg) for various reasons. As seen previously, these recommendations are justified because ascorbic acid requirements increase in different circumstances such as exposure to immunological or environmental stress, deficiencies in nutrients such as vitamin A and situations of metabolic alterations. Additionally the consumption of ascorbic acid above the strict physiological requirements has beneficial effects on the immune response of the animal.

Table II. Recommended vitamin levels (IU or mg/kg air-dry feed) for broiler breeders by various sources

	Source / Units	ARC, 1975	INRA, 1984	NRC, 1994	Whitehead et al, 1993*	Larbier and Leclerq, 1994	Fisher and Willemsen, 1999*	Rostagno, 2005	Leeson and Summers, 2005	FEDNA, 2008	DSM OVN (2011)
Vitamin A	IU	2,700	10,000	3,000	11000-12000	10,000	12000-13000	9,000	8,000	11,000	12000-15000
Vitamin D3	IU	600	1,500	300	3,000	2,000	3,000	2,500	3,000	2,800	3000-5000
25-OH-D3 (HyD)**	mg	-	-	-	-	-	-	-	-	-	0.069
Vitamin E	mg	-	15	10	30	25	100	40	75	30	100-150[1][2]
Vitamin K	mg	1.0	4.0	1.0	3.0	2.0	5.0	2.0	3	2.1	5.0-7.0
Vitamin B1	mg	-	-	0.7	-	1.5	3	1.8	2.0	1.1	3.0-3.5
Vitamin B2	mg	4.0	4.0	3.6	12.0	4.0	12.0	7.0	10.0	9	12-16
Vitamin B6	mg	4.0	1.0	4.5	3.0-6.0	3.0	4.0-6.0	2.0	4.0	3.0	4.0-6.0
Vitamin B12	mg	0.002	0.008	0.008	0.015	0.01	0.03	0.02	0.015	0.017	0.03-0.04
Niacin	mg	10	-	10	12-17	30	50-55	30	40	25	50-60
D-Panthothenic acid	mg	6.5	8.0	7.0	12-15	12.0	12-15	13.0	12.0	12	15-25
Folic acid	mg	0.50	0.20	0.35	2.00	0.50	2.00	0.90	0.75	1.1	2.0-4.0
Biotin	mg	0.15	0.1	0.10-0.16	0.15-0.2	0.1	0.25-0.3	0.1	0.15	0.11	0.25-0.4
Vitamin C	mg	-	-	-	200	-	-	-	-	-	100-150[3]
Choline	mg	1,100	500	1,000	-	500	1,000	300	500	250	350-700

* Ranges of vitamins according to predominant cereal in the diet: maize or wheat (higher value)
** Add to HyD 60 mg/kg Carophyll Red (MaxiChick) to improve hatchability. MaxiChick is covered by a DSM International Patent Application WO 2010 057811 nationalized in US and Europe amongst others. MaxiChick is a trademark registered in Europe and the US amongst others.
(1) Add 5 mg/kg for each 1% dietary fat when fat is higher than 3%;
(2) Under heat stress conditions increase level up to 200 mg/kg
(3) Recommended under heat stress conditions; use phosphorylated form in heat treated feeds

Table III. Recommended vitamin levels (IU or mg/kg air-dry feed) by principal broiler meat breeder genetic companies

Grow-out phase	Source / Units	Starter				Grower				Laying				Maximum	Benefits in Scientific Literature
		Cobb*	Ross*	Hubbard	DSM OVN	Cobb*	Ross*	Hubbard	DSM OVN	Cobb*	Ross*	Hubbard	DSM OVN (2011)		
Vitamin A	IU	10000-11000	10000-11000	12,000	10000-12000	10000-11000	10000-11000	15,000	10000-12000	12000-13000	11000-12000	15,000	12000-15000	16000	Increases hatchability and hatching of eggs (Squires and Naber, 1993a).
Vitamin D3	IU	3,000	3,500	3,000	3000-4000	3,000	3,500	3,000	3000-4000	3,000	3,500	3,000	3000-5000	2000-4000	Heavier progeny at hatch, higher bone ash & lower TD incidence (Atencio et al., 2005).
25-OH-D3 (HyD)**	mg	-	-	-	0.069	-	-	-	0.069	-	-	-	0.069	0.069	Improved hatchability
Vitamin E	mg	75-80	60	40	80-100[1][2]	45-50	45	60-150	80-100[1][2]	50-100	100	60-150	100-150[1][4]	300	More eggs produced (Siegel et al., 2001)
Vitamin K	mg	3	3	2	3.0-5.0	3	2	5	3.0-5.0	6	5	5	5.0-7.0	10	Higher prothrombin levels in offsprings (Griminger and Brubacher, 1966)
Vitamin B1	mg	2	3	2	2.0-3.0	2	2	3	2.0-3.0	2.5-3.5	3	3	3.0-3.5	8	Increased thiamine status indices and thiamine metabolism of the offspring (Olkoswki and Classen. 1999)
Vitamin B2	mg	5.0-8.0	6	8	6.0-8.0	5.0-7.0	5	12	6.0-8.0	10-16	12	12	12-16	7	Influence on hatchability, vigor and survival of the chick (Leeson and Summers, 2005)
Vitamin B6	mg	3	3.0-4.0	3	3.0-5.0	3	2.0-3.0	5	3.0-5.0	6	4.0-5.0	5	4.0-6.0	n.a.	See Table V pag. 69
Vitamin B12	mg	0.025	0.02	0.02	0.02-0.03	0.02	0.02	0.03	0.02-0.03	0.03-0.4	0.03	0.03	0.03-0.04	0.02	Hatchability levels are between 88.5 and 92.7 % (panic et al., 1970)
Niacin	mg	20-40	35-30	60	30-60	20-35	30-25	60	30-60	40	55-50	60	50-60	66-132	Improves the quality of the shell (Leeson et al., 1991)
D-Panthothenic acid	mg	8.0-12.0	15-13	10	13-15	8.0-10.0	15-13	15	13-15	25	15-13	15	15-25	24	Increases the quantity and quality of semen (Goeger and Arscott, 1984)
Folic acid	mg	1.5	1.5	1	1.5-2.0	1	1	2	1.5-2.0	4	2	2	2.0-4.0	n.a.	See Table V pag. 69
Biotin	mg	0.25-0.3	0.15-0.2	0.15	0.2-0.4	0.25-0.30	0.15-0.2	0.2	0.2-0.4	0.3-0.38	0.25-0.30	0.2	0.25-0.4	0.44	Better hatchability results (Robel, 1989)
Vitamin C	mg	25	-	-	100-150[3]	25	-	-	100-150[3]	50	-	-	100-150[3]	500	Semen volume, motile sperm per ejaculate and sperm number per ejaculate were increased (Monsi and Onitchi, 1991)
Choline	mg	300-350	1400	750	350-700	200-300	1400	750	350-700	250-450	1000	750	350-700	760-1520	Liver fat content can be reduced in the offspring (Rama Rao et al., 2001)

* Range for some vitamins is referred respectively to maize or wheat diets
** Add 60 mg/kg Carophyll Red (MaxiChick) to improve hatchability. MaxiChick (HyD and Carophyll Red) is covered by a DSM International Patent Application WO 2010 057811 nationalized in US and Europe amongst others. MaxiChick is a trademark registered in Europe and the US amongst others.
(1) Add 5 mg/kg for each 1% dietary fat when fat is higher than 3%;
(2) Higher level for optimum immune function
(3) Recommended under heat stress conditions; use phosphorylated form in heat treated feeds
(4) Under heat stress conditions increase level up to 200 mg/kg

Table IV. Recommended vitamin levels (IU or mg/kg air-dry feed) for turkey breeders (laying phase) by various sources

	Source / Units	ARC, 1975	INRA, 1989	NRC, 1994	Whitehead et al., 1993*	Leeson and Summers, 2005	DSM OVN (2011)
Vitamin A	IU	2,700	10,000	5,000	11000-12000	10000-9000	12000-14000
Vitamin D3	IU	2,000	1,500	1,100	3,000	3,500	4000-5000
25-OH-D3 (HyD)**	mg	-	-	-	-	-	0.092
Vitamin E	mg	60	15	10-25	30	100	100-150[1][2]
Vitamin K	mg	-	4	0.5-1.0	3.0	3.0-4.0	4.0-5.0
Vitamin B1	mg	-	1.0	2.0	2.0	3.0	4.0-5.0
Vitamin B2	mg	3.5	6	2.5-4.0	12.0	8.0-10.0	15-20
Vitamin B6	mg	-	2.0	3.0-4.0	3.0-5.0	5.0-6.0	6.0-7.0
Vitamin B12	mg	-	0.0	0.003	0.002	0.020-0.016	0.040-0.050
Niacin	mg	-	40	40	50-55	60-70	80-120
D-Panthothenic acid	mg	16.0	10	9-16	18-20	18.0	30-35
Folic acid	mg	0.70	1.00	0.7-1.0	2.00	1.0-2.0	4.0-6.0
Biotin	mg	0.2	0.15	0.10-0.20	0.2-0.25	0.25-0.30	0.40-0.60
Vitamin C	mg	-	-	-	-	-	100-200[3]
Choline	mg	1,350	600	800-1000	200-400	800-900	500-1000

* Ranges of vitamins according to predominant cereal in the diet: maize or wheat (higher value)
** Add 60 mg/kg Carophyll Red (MaxiChick) to improve hatchability. MaxiChick (HyD and Carophyll Red) is covered by a DSM International Patent Application WO 2010 057811 nationalized in US and Europe amongst others. MaxiChick is a trademark registered in Europe and the US amongst others.
(1) Add 5 mg/kg for each 1% dietary fat when fat is higher than 3%
(2) Under heat stress conditions increase level up to 200 mg/kg
(3) Recommended under heat stress conditions; use phosphorylated form in heat treated feeds

Table V. Recommended vitamin levels (IU or mg/kg air-dry feed) by principal turkey breeder genetic companies

Grow-out phase	Source / Units	Starter			Grower			Laying			Maximum	Benefits in Scientific Literature
		BUT*	Hybrid	DSM OVN	BUT*	Hybrid	DSM OVN	BUT*	Hybrid	DSM OVN		
Vitamin A	IU	11000-12000	12,000	12000-14000	6000-8000	9,600	8000-10000	11000-12000	12,000	12000-14000	n.a.	See Table III pag. 67
Vitamin D3	IU	5,000	5,000	4000-5000	4,000	4,800	4000-5000	5,000	5,000	4000-5000	2700	Greater live weight and higher ash content in the tibia of the offspring (Stevens et al., 1984)
25-OH-D3 (HyD)**	mg	-	suggested	0.092	-	suggested	0.092	-	suggested	0.092	0.092	Improved hatchability
Vitamin E	mg	100	100	100-250[1] [2]	50	60	60-80	100-120	100	100-150 [4]	120	More spermatozoa concentrations (Zaniboni et al., 2005)
Vitamin K	mg	4.0	4.0	4.0-5.0	2.0	3.0	2.0-4.0	5.0	5.0	4.0-5.0	n.a.	See Table III pag. 67
Vitamin B1	mg	4.0	4.5	4.5-5.0	1.0	2.0	2.0-3.0	4.0	4.5	4.0-5.0	n.a.	See Table III pag. 67
Vitamin B2	mg	10.0	15.0	15-20	5.0	12.0	10-15	20.0	18.0	15-20	n.a.	See Table III pag. 67
Vitamin B6	mg	6.0-7.0	5	6.0-7.0	4.0-5.0	3.5	6.0-7.0	6.0-7.0	5	6.0-7.0	6.2	To assure high hatchability levels (Robel, 1992 and 2002)
Vitamin B12	mg	0.04	0.04	0.04-0.05	0.02	0.02	0.03-0.04	0.04	0.04	0.040-0.050	0.01	Increased the body weight of progeny at 21 days of age (Chen et al., 1993)
Niacin	mg	80-70	110	100-150	55-50	85	60-80	80-70	110	80-120	33.4	Increased the weight of eggs (Harms et al., 1988)
D-Panthothenic acid	mg	28-25	28	30-35	16-15	23	25-30	28-25	30	30-35	37.4-74.8	Vitamin levels are greater in the egg yolk (Robel, 1993)
Folic acid	mg	4.0	3.5	4.0-6.0	2.0	2.5	2.0-3.0	6.0	4.5	4.0-6.0	7.37	Improvements in hatchability, higher body weight and greater vitality in the offsprings (Robel, 2002)
Biotin	mg	0.2-0.3	0.3	0.4-0.6	0.2-0.3	0.17	0.4-0.6	0.35-0.45	0.5	0.40-0.60	0.8	In older turkey hens, better results in hatchability (Robel, 2002)
Vitamin C	mg	-	-	100-200[3]	-	-	100-200[3]	-	-	100-200[3]	300	Reduced formation of multinucleated giant cells in the testes of 65 wk-older breeder toms (Neuman et al., 2002)
Choline	mg	1600	1200	1000-1200	1200	600	1000-12000	1600	1200	500-1000	1000	Increased production and hatchability, normal growth and viability of the progeny (Balloun and Miller, 1964)

** Add 60 mg/kg Carophyll Red (MaxiChick) to improve hatchability. MaxiChick (HyD and Carophyll Red) is covered by a DSM International Patent Application WO 2010 057811 nationalized in US and Europe amongst others. MaxiChick is a trademark registered in Europe and the US amongst others.
* Range for some vitamins is referred respectively to maize or wheat diets
(1) Add 5 mg/kg for each 1% dietary fat when fat is higher than 3%; (2) Higher level for optimum immune function
(3) Recommended under heat stress conditions; use phosphorylated form in heat treated feeds; (4) Under heat stress conditions increase level up to 200 mg/kg

Table VI. Recommended vitamin levels (IU or mg/kg air-dry feed) by the main broiler meat breeder genetic companies for male broiler (mating period)

Grow-out phase	Male breeder (mating period)				
	Source / Units	Cobb*	Ross*	Hubbard	DSM OVN (2011)
Vitamin A	IU	12000-13000	11000-12000	15,000	12000-15000
Vitamin D$_3$	IU	3,000	3,500	3,000	3000-5000
25-OH-D3 (HyD)**	mg	-	-	-	0.069
Vitamin E	mg	50-100	100	60-150	100-150 [1][2]
Vitamin K	mg	6.0	5.0	5.0	5.0-7.0
Vitamin B$_1$	mg	2.5-3.5	3.0	3.0	3.0-3.5
Vitamin B$_2$	mg	10-16	12	12	12-16
Vitamin B$_6$	mg	6.0	4.0-5.0	5.0	4.0-6.0
Vitamin B$_{12}$	mg	0.03-0.4	0.03	0.03	0.03-0.04
Niacin	mg	40	55-50	60	50-60
D-Panthothenic acid	mg	25	15-13	15	15-25
Folic acid	mg	4.0	2.0	2.0	2.0-4.0
Biotin	mg	0.3-0.38	0.25-0.30	0.2	0.25-0.4
Vitamin C	mg	50	-	-	100-150[3]
Choline	mg	250-450	1000	750	350-700
Canthaxanthin (Carophyll Red)**	mg	-	-	-	6

** Add 60 mg/kg Carophyll Red (MaxiChick) to improve hatchability. MaxiChick (HyD and Carophyll Red) is covered by a DSM International Patent Application WO 2010 057811 nationalized in US and Europe amongst others. MaxiChick is a trademark registered in Europe and the US amongst others.
* Range for some vitamins is referred respectively to maize or wheat diets
(1) Add 5 mg/kg for each 1% dietary fat when fat is higher than 3%;
(2) Under heat stress conditions increase level up to 200 mg/kg
(3) Recommended under heat stress conditions; use phosphorylated form in heat treated feeds

Table VII. Recommended vitamin levels (IU or mg/kg air-dry feed) by the main laying hen breeder genetic companies and DSM Optimum Vitamin Nutrition (OVN) levels

Grow-out phase	From day old to end of laying period				
	Source / Units	Lohman Brown (2007)*	ISA (2010)	Hy-Line (2010)	DSM OVN
Vitamin A	IU	12000-15000	15,000	11,000	10000-15000
Vitamin D$_3$	IU	2500-3000	3,200	4,400	3000-4500
25-OH-D3 (HyD)**	mg	-	-	0.055	0.069
Vitamin E	mg	30-50/100	42	66	50-100[1][2]
Vitamin K	mg	3.0-5.0	5.0	2.2	2.0-5.0
Vitamin B$_1$	mg	2.0-4.0	3.5	2.2	2.5-3.5
Vitamin B$_2$	mg	8.0-10.0	10.0	11.0	10.0-12.0
Vitamin B$_6$	mg	4.0-6.0	4.5	5	5.0-6.0
Vitamin B$_{12}$	mg	0.02-0.03	0.035	0.024	0.02-0.04
Niacin	mg	30	55	44	45-60
D-Panthothenic acid	mg	10.0-20.0	17	13	15-20
Folic acid	mg	1.0-2.0	2.8	1.7	2.0-3.0
Biotin	mg	0,1-0,2	0.25	0.022	0,25-0,40
Vitamin C	mg	100-200	suggested	-	150-200[3]
Choline	mg	300-400	1500	220	300-500
Canthaxanthin (Carophyll Red)**	mg	-	-	-	6

** Add 60 mg/kg Carophyll Red (MaxiChick) to improve hatchability. MaxiChick (HyD and Carophyll Red) is covered by a DSM International Patent Application WO 2010 057811 nationalized in US and Europe amongst others. MaxiChick is a trademark registered in Europe and the US amongst others.
* Starter/grower - laying phase
(1) Add 5 mg/kg for each 1% dietary fat when fat is higher than 3%;
(2) Under heat stress conditions increase level up to 200 mg/kg
(3) Recommended under heat stress conditions; use phosphorylated form in heat treated feeds

REFERENCES

Various bibliographical databases have been used in the writing of this review, especially Medline and ISI web of knowledge, as well as other digital resources. The period under review covers the last 30 years. We have also used monographic publications on aviculture and nutrition of high scientific repute.

Abdulrahim, SM, MB Patel, J McGinnis, 1979, Effects of vitamin D_3 and D_3 metabolites on production parameters and hatchability of eggs. Poult. Sci, 58:858-863.

Almquist, HJ, 1971, In The Vitamins: Eds WH Sebrell Jr., and RS Harris, Academic Press, New York, v. 3, 2nd ed, p. 418.

Ameenuddin, S, ML Sunde, HF DeLuca, ME Cook, 1986, Excessive cholecalciferol in a layers diet: Decline in some aspects of reproductive performance and increased bone mineralization of progeny: Br. Poult. Sci, 27:671.

Amiri Andi, M, M Shivazad, SA Pourbakhsh, M Afshar, H Rokni, NE Shiri, A Mohammadi, Z Salahi, 2006, Effects of vitamin E in broiler breeder diet on hatchability, egg quality and breeder and day old chick immunity. Pakistan J. Biological Sci., 9(5): 789-794.

An, SY, YM Guo, SD Ma, JM Yuan, GZ Liu, 2010, Effects of different oil sources and vitamin E in breeder diet on egg quality, hatchability and development of the neonatal offspring. Asian-Australasian J. Anim. Sci., 23(2):234-239.

ARC, 1975, 1984, The nutrient requirements of farm livestock. no. 1. Poultry Agricultural Research Council. London.

Arscott, GH, RV Kuhns, 1969, Packed sperm volume versus optical density as a measure of semen concentration. Poult. Sci, 48:1126-1127.

Arscott, GH, JE Parker, 1967, Effectiveness of vitamin E in reversing sterility of male chickens fed a diet high in linoleic acid. J. Nutr, 91:219-222.

Atencio, A, HM Edwards Jr, G Pesti, 2005a, Effects of vitamin D_3 dietary supplementation of broiler breeder hens on the performance and bone abnormalities of the progeny. Poult. Sci, 84:1058-1068.

Atencio, A, HM Edwards Jr, GM Pesti, 2005b, Effect of the level of cholecalciferol supplementation of broiler breeder hen diets on the performance and bone abnormalities of the progeny fed diets containing various levels of calcium or 25-hydroxycholecalciferol, Poult. Sci, 84:1593-1603.

Atencio, A, GM Pesti, HM Edwards Jr, 2005c, Twenty-five hydroxycholecalciferol as a cholecalciferol substitute in broiler breeder hen diets and its effect on the performance and general health of the progeny: Poult. Sci, 84:1277-1285.

Atencio, A, HM Edwards Jr, GM Pesti, GO Ware, 2006, The vitamin D3 requirement of broiler breeders. Poult. Sci, 85:674-692.

Atkinson, RL, TM Ferguson, JH Quisenberry, JR Couch, 1955, Vitamin E and reproduction in turkeys. J. Nutr, 55:387-397.

Backermann, S, C Poel, W Ternes, 2008, Thiamin phosphates in egg yolk granules and plasma of regular and embryonated eggs of hens and in five- and seven-day-old embryos. Poult. Sci, 87:108-115.

Bains, BS, 2001, Vitamin nutrition for hatchability and chick liveability. World Poultry, Vitamin Special, p. 7-8.

Balloun, SL, DL Miller, 1964, Choline Requirements of Turkey Breeder Hens: Poult. Sci, 43:64-&.

Balloun, SL, RE Phillips, 1957, Interaction effects of vitamin B12 and pantothenic acid in breeder hen diets on hatchability, chick growth and livability. Poult. Sci, 36:929-934.

Beer, A, ML Scott, M Nesheim, 1963, The effects of graded levels of pantothenic acid on the breeding performance of White Leghorn pullets. Br. Poult. Sci, 3:243-253.

Bethke, RM, PR Record, OHM Wilder, CH Kick, 1936, Effect of different sources of vitamin D on the laying bird. Poult. Sci, 15:336-344.

Bhanja, SK, AB Mandal, SK Agarwal and S Majumdar, 2006, Modulation of post-hatch growth and immunocompetence development through in ovo injection of vitamin E and linoleic acid. Proc. XII European Poultry Conf. Verona, Italy.

Bhanja, SK, AB Mandal, SK Agarwal, S Majumdar and A Bhattacharyya, 2007, Effect of in ovo injection of vitamins on the chick weight and post-hatch growth performance in broiler chickens. Proc. 16th European Symp. Poultry Nutrition,

Strasbourg, France.

Biswas, A, J. Mohan, and K. V. Sastry. 2009. Effect of higher dietary vitamin E concentrations on physical and biochemical characteristics of semen in Kadaknath cockerels. Br. Poult. Sci, 50:733-738.

Blesbois, E, I Grasseau, JC Blum, 1993, Effects of vitamin E on fowl semen storage at 4 degrees C. Theriogenology, 39:771-779.

Blesbois, E, M Lessire, I Grasseau, JM Hallouis, D Hermier, 1997, Effect of dietary fat on the fatty acid composition and fertilizing ability of fowl semen. Biology of Rep., 56: 1216.

Boa-Amponsem, K, SE Price, PA Geraert, M Picard, PB Siegel, 2001, Antibody responses of hens fed vitamin E and passively acquired antibodies of their chicks. Avian Dis., 45:122-127.

Bortolotti, GR, JJ Negro, PF Surai, P Prieto, 2003, Carotenoids in eggs and plasma of red-legged partridges: effects of diet and reproductive output. Physiol. Bicohem. Zoology, 76:367-374.

Braeunlich, K, 1974, XV World Poultry Congress, Aug 1974, New Orleans, USA.

Breque, C, P Surai, JP Brillard, 2003, Roles of antioxidants on prolonged storage of avian spermatozoa in vivo and in vitro. Mol. Reprod. Dev, 66:314-323.

Brewer, LE, HM Edwards, 1972, Studies on biotin requirement of broiler breeders. Poult. Sci, 51:619.

Briggs, GM, 1946, Nicotinic acid deficiency in turkey poults and the occurrence of perosis. J. Nutrition, 31:79.

Buenrostro, JL, FH Kratzer, 1984, Use of plasma and egg yolk biotin of White Leghorn hens to assess biotin availability from feedstuffs. Poult. Sci, 63:1563-1570.

Calini F, F Sirri, 2006, Breeder nutrition and offspring performance. XII European Poultry Conference, Sept 2006, Verona.

Cerolini, S, F Pizzi, T Gliozzi, A Maldjiani, L Zaniboni, L Parodi, 2003, Lipid manipulation of chicken semen by dietary means and its relation to fertility: a review. Worlds Poult. Sci. J., 59:65-75.

Cerolini, S, PF Surai, BK Speake, NH Sparks, 2005, Dietary fish and evening primrose oil with vitamin E effects on semen variables in cockerels. Br. Poult. Sci, 46:214-222.

Cerolini, S, L Zaniboni, A Maldjian, T Gliozzi, 2006, Effect of docosahexaenoic acid and alpha-tocopherol enrichment in chicken sperm on semen quality, sperm lipid composition and susceptibility to peroxidation:.Theriogenology, 66:877-886.

Chan, AC, 1993, Partners in defense, vitamin-E and vitamin-C: 71:725-731.

Chan, AC, K Tran, T Raynor, PR Ganz, CK Chow, 1991, Regeneration of vitamin-E in human platelets. J. Biol. Chem, 266:17290-17295.

Charles, OW, DA Roland, HM Edwards Jr, 1972, Thiamine deficiency identification and treatment in commercial turkeys and Coturnix quail. Poult. Sci, 51:419-423.

Chen, F, SL Noll, PE Waibel, DM Hawkins, 1993, Effect of folate, vitamin B_{12} and choline supplementation on turkey breeder performance. Poult. Sci, 72:73, Suppl.1

Cherian, G, ES Sim, 1997, Egg yolk polyunsaturated fatty acids and vitamin E content alters the tocopherol status of hatched chicks. Poult. Sci, 76:1753-1759.

Cherian, G, FH Wolfe, JS Sim, 1996a, Feeding dietary oils with tocopherols: effects on internal qualities of eggs during storage. J of Food Sci, 61:5-18.

Cherian, G, FH Wolfe, JS Sim, 1996b, Dietary oils with added tocopherols: effects on egg or tissue tocopherols, fatty acids, and oxidative stability. Poult.Sci, 75:423-431.

Chung, MK, JH Choi, YK Chung, KM Chee, 2005, Effects of dietary vitamins C and E on egg shell quality of broiler breeder hens exposed to heat stress. Asian-Australasian Journal of Animal Sciences, 18:545-551.

Clark, NB, SK Lee, MJ Murphy, 1990, Vitamin D action on calcium regulation and osmoregulation in embryonic chicks. In: Wada M, Ishii S and Scanes CG: Endocrinology of birds. Springer-Verlag, Berlin, p. 159-170.

Combs, GF, Jr. 1976, Differential effects of high dietary levels of vitamin A on the vitamin e-selenium nutrition of young and adult chickens. J. Nutr, 106: 967-975

Cortinas, L, A Barroeta, J Galobart, SK Jensen, 2004, Distribution of alpha-tocopherol stereoisomers in liver and thigh of chickens. Br. J. Nutr, 92:295-301.

Cortinas, L, MD Baucells, C Villaverde, F Guardiola, SK Jensen, AC Barroeta, 2006, Influence of dietary polyunsaturation level on alpha-tocopherol content in chicken meat. Archiv Fur Geflugelkunde, 70:98-105.

Cortinas, L, C Villaverde, MD Baucells, F Guardiola, AC Barroeta, 2003, Interaction between dietary unsaturation and α-tocopherol levels: Vitamin E content in thigh meat, XVI Eur. Symp. Qual. Poult. Meat. St. Brieuc, France

Cravens, WW, WH McGibbon, EE Sebesta, 1944, Effect of biotin deficiency on embryonic development in the domestic fowl. Anat. Rec, 90:55-64.

Cunha, TJ, 1982, Niacin in animal feeding and nutrition: National Feed Ingredients Association (NFIA) Fairlawn, New Jersey.

Daghir, NJ, MA Shah, 1973, Effect of dietary protein level on vitamin B6 requirement of chicks. Poult. Sci, 52:1247-1252.

Damjanov, I, SW Neilsen, L van der Heide, HD Eaton, 1980, Testicular changes of acute vitamin A deficiency of cockerels: Am. J. Vet. Res, 41:586-590.

Dobrescu, O, 1987, Vitamin C addition to breeder diets increases turkey semen production: Feedstuffs, 59:18.

Donaldson, WE, MJ Wineland, VI Christensen, 1996, The effect of flock age and egg storage on fatty acid composition of yolk membranes from two broiler crosses. Poult. Sci, 75 (Suppl. 1):5. (Abstr.)

Driver, JP, A Atencio, GM Pesti, HJ Edwards, RI Bakalli, 2004, The effect of maternal dietary vitamin D-3 supplementation on the performance and bone quality of broiler chicks. Poult. Sci, 83:1767.

Driver, JP, A Atencio, GM Pesti, HM Edwards Jr, RI Bakalli, 2006, The effect of maternal dietary vitamin D3 supplementation on performance and tibial dyschondroplasia of broiler chicks. Poult. Sci, 85:39-47.

Edwards, HM Jr, 1995, Factors influencing leg disorders in broilers. Proc. Maryland Nutrition Conf. MD Feed Industry Council Inc. Univ Maryland, p. 21-19.

Eid, Y, T Ebeid, H Younis, 2006, Vitamin E supplementation reduces dexamethasone-induced oxidative stress in chicken semen. Br. Poult. Sci, 47:350-356.

Elaroussi, MA, A Uhland-Smith, W Hellwig, HF DeLuca, 1994, The role of vitamin D in chorioallantoic membrane calcium transport. Biochim. Biophys, Acta 1192:1-6.

Erf, GF, WG Bottje, TK Bersi, MD Headrick, CA Fritts, 1998, Effects of dietary vitamin E on the immune system in broilers: altered proportions of CD4 T cells in the thymus and spleen. Poult. Sci, 77:529-537.

FEDNA (Fundación Española para el Desarrollo de la Nutrición Animal), 2008, Necesidades nutricionales para avicultura: pollos de carne y aves de puesta. Lázaro, R. Y Mateos, G.G. Ediciones Peninsular S.L. Madrid

Feingold, IB, HD Colby, 1992, Sex differences in adrenal and hepatic alpha-tocopherol concentrations in rats. Pharmacology, 44:113-116.

Ferguson, TM, CR Creger, CH Whiteside, RL Atkinson, JR Couch, ML Jones, 1961, B-vitamin deficiency in mature turkey hen. Poult. Sci, 40:1151-&.

Fisher, C, C Kemp, 2000, Impact of breeder nutrition on broiler performance: Int. Hatchery Practice, 15:13-15.

Fisher, C and Willemsen, MHA (1999), Nutrition of broiler breeders, in: Garnsworthy PC and Wiseman J (Eds) Recent advantages in Animal Nutrition 1999 pp. 165-168 (Nottingham, Nottingham University Press).

Flores-Garcia, W, 1992, Einfluß verschiedener B-Vitamine, speziell des Riboflavins, auf Reproduktionsmerkmale bei Legehennen. Agricultural dissertation, Hohenheim, Germany.

Flores-Garcia, W, S Scholtyssek, 1992, Effects of levels of riboflavin in the diet on the reproductivity of layer-breeding stocks:. Proc. 19th World's Poult. Congress, Beekbergen, Netherlands, 1:622.

Fraser, DR, JS Emtage, 1976, Vitamin-D in avian egg - its molecular identity and mechanism of incorporation into yolk. Biochem. J, 160:671-682.

Friedrichsen, JV, GH Arscott, DL Willis, 1980, Improvement in fertility of White Leghorn males by vitamin E following a prolonged deficiency. Nutr. Rep. Int, 22:41

Fuller, HL, RC Field, R Roncalli, WS Dunahoo, HM Edwards, 1961, Vitamin B6 Requirements of breeder hens. Poult. Sci, 40:249.

Gaal, T, M Mezes, RC Noble, J Dixon, BK Speake, 1995, Development of antioxidant capacity in tissues of the chick embryo. Comparative Biochemistry and Physiology B-Biochemistry & Molecular Biology, 112:711-716.

Galobart, J, AC Barroeta, MD Baucells, F Guardiola, 2001a, Lipid oxidation in fresh and spray-dried eggs enriched with w3 and w6 polyunsaturated fatty acids during storage as affected by dietary vitamin

E and canthaxanthin supplementation. Poult. Sci, 80:327-337.

Galobart, J, AC Barroeta, MD Baucells, R Codony, W Ternes, 2001b, Effect of dietary supplementation with rosemary extract and alpha-tocopheryl acetate on lipid oxidation in eggs enriched with omega-3 fatty acids. Poult. Sci, 80:460-467.

Galobart, J, AC Barroeta, MD Baucells, L Cortinas, F Guardiola, 2001c, Alpha-tocopherol transfer efficiency and lipid oxidation in fresh and spray-dried eggs enriched with omega-3 polyunsaturated fatty acids. Poult. Sci, 80:1496-1505.

Goeger, MP, GH Arscott, 1984, Effect of pantothenic acid on reproductive performance of adult White Leghorn cockerels. Nutr. Rep. Int. 30:1193.

Gonzales, E, AS Oliveira, CP Cruz, 2003, In ovo supplementation of 25(OH)D3 to broiler embryos. In: European Symposium On Poultry Nutrition, Lillehammer, p.72-74.

Goodwin, TW, 1984, The Biochemistry of Carotenoids. Vol. 2. Animals. Chapman & Hall, London.

Gore, AB, MA Qureshi, 1997, Enhancement of humoral and cellular immunity by vitamin E after embryonic exposure. Poult. Sci. 76:984-991.

Griminger, P, 1966, Influence of maternal vitamin D intake on growth and bone ash of offspring. Poult. Sci. 45:849-851.

Griminger, P, G Brubacher, 1966, The transfer of vitamin K_1 and menadione from the hen to the egg. Poult. Sci, 45:512-519.

Haq, AU, CA Bailey, 1996, Time course evaluation of carotenoid and retinol concentrations in posthatch chick tissue. Poult. Sci, 75:1258-1260.

Haq, AU, CA Bailey, A Chinnah, 1996, Effect of beta-carotene, canthaxanthin, lutein, and vitamin E on neonatal immunity of chicks when supplemented in the broiler breeder diets. Poult. Sci, 75:1092-1097.

Harms, RH, N Ruiz, RE Buresh, HR Wilson, 1988, Effect of niacin supplementation of a corn-soybean meal diet on performance of turkey breeder hens. Poult. Sci, 67:336-338.

Harms, RH, RA Voitle, DM Janky, HR Wilson, 1979, Influence of biotin supplementation on performance of broiler breeder hens and foot pad dermatitis in the progeny. Nutr. Rep. Int, 19:603-606.

Hart, LE, HF DeLuca, 1985, Effect of vitamin D3 metabolites on calcium and phosphorus metabolism in chick embryos. Am. J. Physiol, 248:E281-5.

Hassan, S, J Hakkarainen, L Jonsson, J Tyopponen, 1990, Histopathological and biochemical changes associated with selenium and vitamin E deficiency in chicks. Zentralbl. Veterinarmed A, 37:708-720.

Hill, F, ML Scott, L Norris, G Heuser, 1961, Reinvestigation of the vitamin A requirements of laying and breeding hens and their progeny. Poult. Sci, 40:1245-1254.

Hossain, SM, SL Barreto, AG Bertechini, AM Rios, CG Silva, 1998, Influence of dietary vitamin E level on egg production of broiler breeders, and on the growth and immune response of progeny in comparison with the progeny from eggs injected with vitamin E. Anim. Feed Sci. Technol, 78:307-317.

Hughes, DE, 1952, The metabolism and function of pantothenic acid: Proceedings of the 78th scientific meeting department of biochemistry: The role of vitamins in metabolic processes, Sheffield, United Kingdom.

INRA (Institut scientifique de Recherche Agronomique), 1985, Alimentación de animales monogástrices. Mundi-Prensa. Madrid.

Jackson, M, 1992, Feeding layers: nutritional considerations. Multi-State Poultry Meeting.

Jackson, DW, GR Law, CF Nockels, 1978, Maternal vitamin E alters passively acquired immunity of chicks. Poult. Sci, 57:70-73.

Jensen, LS, 1968, Vitamin E and essential fatty acids in avian reproduction. Fed. Proc, 27:914-919.

Jensen, LS, J McGinnis, 1957, Studies on the vitamin E requirement of turkeys for reproduction. Poult. Sci, 36:212.

Karadas, F, AC Pappas, PF Surai, BK Speake, 2005, Embryonic development within carotenoid-enriched eggs influences the post-hatch carotenoid status of the chicken. Comparative Biochemistry and Physiology, Part B: Biochemistry & Molecular Biology 141: 244-251.

Kidd, MT, 2003, A treatise on chicken dam nutrition that impacts on progeny. World's Poultry Science Journal, 59:475-494.

Klasing, K, 1998, Comparative avian nutrition:.CAB International, p. 277-329.

Kolb, E, E Grün, 1995, Die Bedeutung des Vitamins E und des Selens für das Immunsystem des Rindes, insbesondere für die Eutergesundheit. Prakt. Tierarzt, 76:749-756

Koutsos, EA, AJ Clifford, CC Calvert, KC Klasing, 2003, Maternal carotenoid status modifies the incorporation of dietary carotenoids into immune tissues of growing chickens (Gallus gallus domesticus). J. Nutr. 133: 1132-1138.

Kratzer, FH, HJ Almquist, P Vohra, 1996, Effect of diet on growth and plasma ascorbic acid in chicks. Poult. Sci, 75:82-89.

Kristiansen, F, 1973, Conditions in poultry associated with deficiencies of vitamin E in Norway. Acta Agricultura Scandinavica, 19:51-57.

Kubota, M, E Abe, T Shinki, T Suda, 1981, Vitamin D metabolism and its possible role in the developing chick embryo. Biochem. J, 194:103-109.

Kutlu, HR, JM, Forbes, 1993, Changes in growth and blood parameters in heat-stressed broiler chicks in response to dietary ascorbic-acid. Livest. Prod. Sci, 36:335-350.

Landauer, W, 1967, The hatchability of chicken eggs as influenced by environment and heredity. Storrs Agricultural Experimental Station Monograph 1 (Revised) Storrs Agricultural Experiment Station, Storrs.

Lavelle, PA, QP LLoyd, CV Gay, RM Leach Jr, 1994, Vitamin K deficiency does not functionally impair skeletal metabolism of laying hens and their progeny. J. Nutr, 124:371-377.

Larbier, M, B Leclercq, 1994, Nutrition and Feeding of poultry: Nottingham University Press

Leeson, S, JD Summers, 1978, Effect of vitamin deficiencies on hatchability. Poult. Sci, 57:1152-1152.

Leeson, S, JD Summers, 2001, Nutrition of the chicken. University Books.

Leeson, S, JD Summers, 2005, Commercial poultry nutrition: Nottingham University Press.

Leeson, S, JD Summers, 2008, Commercial poultry nutrition-3. Nottingham University Press.

Leeson, S, LJ Caston, JD Summers, 1991, Response of laying hens to supplemental niacin. Poult. Sci, 70:1231-1235.

Leeson, S, BS Reinhart, JD Summers, 1979a, Response of White Leghorn and Rhode-Island Red breeder hens to dietary deficiencies of synthetic vitamins. 1. Egg-production, hatchability and chick growth: Can. J. Anim. Sci., 59:561-567.

Leeson, S, BS Reinhart, JD Summers, 1979b, Response of White Leghorn and Rhode-Island Red breeder hens to dietary deficiencies of synthetic vitamins. 2. Embryo mortality and abnormalities. Can. J.Anim. Sci., 59:569-575.

Lin, YF, SJ Chang, JR Yang, YP Lee, AL Hsu, 2005, Effects of supplemental vitamin E during the mature period on the reproduction performance of Taiwan Native Chicken cockerels: Br. Poult. Sci, 46:366-373.

Luck, MR, I Jeyaseelan, RA Scholes, 1995, Ascorbic-acid and fertility Biol. Reprod, 52:262-266.

Mattila, P, K Lehikoinen, T Kiiskinen, V Piironen, 1999, Cholecalciferol and 25-hydroxycholecalciferol content of chicken egg yolk as affected by the cholecalciferol content of feed. J Agric Food Chem, 47:4089-4092.

McDowell, L, 1989, Vitamins in animal nutrition, comparative aspects to human nutrition. Cunha, TJ (ed.), Academic Press, Inc.

McDowell, L, 1989, Vitamin supplementation is critical part of good animal nutrition. Feedstuffs, January 16, p. 15-31.

McDowell, L, 2000, Vitamins in animal and human nutrition, 2nd edition: Iowa State University Press.

McDowell, L, 2004, Vitaminas, 1ª edicion. Ediciones S.

McDowell, L, Nelson, 2008, Optimum vitamin nutrition for poultry. International Poultry Production, 16:27-34.

McKee, JS, PC Harrison, 1995, Effects of supplemental ascorbic-acid on the performance of broiler-chickens exposed to multiple concurrent stressors. Poult. Sci, 74:1772-1785.

Meydani, M, JB Macauley, JB Blumberg, 1988, Effect of dietary vitamin E and selenium on susceptibility of brain regions to lipid peroxidation. Lipids, 23:405-409.

Millar, RI, LT Smith, JH Wood, 1977, The study of the dietary vitamin D requirements of ringnecked pheasant chicks. Poult. Sci, 56:1739

Miller, DL, SL Balloun, 1967, Folacin requirements of turkey breeder hens. Poult. Sci, 46:1502-1508.

Monsi, A, DO Onitchi, 1991, Effects of ascorbic-acid (vitamin-C) supplementation on ejaculated semen characteristics of broiler breeder chickens under hot and humid tropical conditions: Anim. Feed Sci. Technol. 34:141-146.

Moriuchi, S, HF Deluca, 1974, Metabolism of vitamin-D3 in chick-embryo. Arch. Biochem. Biophys, 164:165-171.

Muduuli, DS, RR Marquardt, W Guenter, 1982, Effect of dietary vicine and vitamin E supplementation on the productive performance of growing and laying chickens. Br. J. Nutr, 47:53-60.

Murphy, R. R., J. E. Hunter, H. C. Kwandel. 1936. The effects of vitamin D intake of the hen on the bone calcification of the chick. Poult. Sci. 15:284–289.

Naber, EC, 1979, The effect of nutrition on the composition of eggs. Poult. Sci, 58:518-528.

Narbaitz, R, 1987, Role of vitamin D in the development of the chick embryo. J. Exp. Zool. Suppl, 1:15-23.

National Research Council, 1987, Vitamin tolerance of animals.

National Research Council, 1994, Nutrient Requirements for Poultry. [9th edition].

Nelson, TS, LC Norris, 1960, Studies on the vitamin K requirement of the chick. I. Requirements of the chick for vitamin K1, menadione and menadione sodium bisulfite. J. Nutr, 72:137-144.

Neuman, SL, JI Orban, TL Lin, MA Latour, PY Hester, 2002, The effect of dietary ascorbic acid on semen traits and testis histology of male turkey breeders. Poult. Sci, 81:265-268.

Noll, S, 1993, Personal communication to Tillman, P.B, Feed Management, 44(10), p. 31.

Norman, AW, S Hurwitz, 1993, The role of the vitamin-D endocrine system in avian bone biology. J. Nutr, 123:310-316.

Nys, Y, 2000, Dietary carotenoids and egg yolk coloration: a review. Arch Gefluegelk, 64:45-54.

Norvell, MJ, MC Nesheim, 1969, Studies of choline biosynthesis in chicks. Poult. Sci. 48:1852.

Olcese, O, JR Couch, JH Quisenberry, PB Pearson, 1950, Congenital anomalies in the chick due to vitamin B12 deficiency. J. Nutr, 41:423-431.

Olkowski, AA HL Classen, 1999, The effects of maternal thiamine nutrition on thiamine status of the offspring in broiler chickens. Internat. J. Vit. Nutr. Res., 69 (1), 1999, 32:40

Panic, B, D Stosic, V Hristic, M Cuperlovic, M Pesevska-Stoirova, 1970, Potrebl priploduih kokosi za vitamoni B_{12}. Pojoprivredne Nauke, Beograd, 23: 109-114.

Pardue, SL, JP Thaxton, 1986, Ascorbic-acid in poultry - a review. World's Poult. Sci. J. 42:107-123.

Patel, MB, J McGinnis, 1977, The effect of levels of protein and vitamin B12 in hen diets on egg production and hatchability of eggs and on livability and growth of chicks. Poult. Sci, 56:45-53.

Patel, MB, J McGinnis, 1980, The effect of vitamin B12 on the tolerance of chicks for high levels of dietary fat and carbohydrate. Poult. Sci, 59:2279-2286.

Peebles, ED, J Brake, 1985, Relationship of dietary ascorbic-acid to broiler breeder performance. Poult. Sci, 64:2041-2048.

Perek, M, N Snapir, 1963, Seasonal variations in semen production of different breeds of cocks and the effect of vitamin C feed supplementation upon the semen of White Rocks. Br. Poult. Sci, 4:19-26.

Polin, D, ER Wynosky, CC Porter, 1962, Amprolium 10: influence of egg yolk thiamine concentration on chick embryo mortality. Proc. Soc. Exp. Biol. Med, 110:844-846.

Rajkhowa, TK, AK Katiyar, JL Vegad, 1996, Effect of ascorbic acid on the inflammatory-reparative response in the punched wounds of the chicken skin. Indian J. Anim. Sci, 66:120-125.

Rama Rao, S. V., G. S. Sunder, M. R. Reddy, N. K. Praharaj, M. V. Raju, and A. K. Panda. 2001. Effect of supplementary choline on the performance of broiler breeders fed on different energy sources. Br. Poult. Sci, 42:362-7.

Rebel, JM, JT van Dam, B Zekarias, FR Balk, J Post, A Flores Minambres, AA ter Huurne, 2004, Vitamin and trace mineral content in feed of breeders and their progeny: effects of growth, feed conversion and severity of malabsorption syndrome of broilers. Br. Poult. Sci, 45:201-209.

Robel, EJ, 1983, The effect of age of breeder hen on the levels of vitamins and minerals in turkey eggs. Poult. Sci, 62:1751-1756.

Robel, EJ, 1989, Increasing hatchability with biotin. Internat. Hatch. Pract, 4, p. 47-51.

Robel, EJ, 1991, The value of supplemental biotin for increasing hatchability of turkey eggs. Poult. Sci, 70:1716-1722.

Robel, EJ, 1992, Effect of dietary supplemental pyridoxine levels on hatchability of turkey eggs. Poult. Sci, 71:1733-1738.

Robel, EJ, 1993a, Evaluation of egg injection of folic acid and effect of supplemental folic acid on hatchability and poult weight. Poult. Sci, 72:546-553.

Robel, EJ, 1993b, Evaluation of egg injection method of pantothenic acid in turkey eggs and effect of supplemental pantothenic acid on hatchability. Poult. Sci, 72:1740-1745.

Robel, EJ, 2002, Assessment of dietary and egg injected D-biotin, pyridoxine and folic acid on turkey hatchability: folic acid and poult weight. World´s Poult. Sci. J. 58:305-315.

Robel, EJ, VL Christensen, 1991, Increasing hatchability of turkey eggs by injecting eggs with pyridoxine. Br. Poult. Sci, 32:509-513.

Rocha, JSR, LJC Lara, NC Baiao, RJC Vasconcelos, VM Barbosa, MA Pompeu and MNS Fernandes, 2010, Antioxidant properties of vitamins in nutrition of broiler breeders and laying hens. World´s Poult. Sci. J. 66:261-270.

Rostagno, H, 2005, Tablas brasileñas para aves y credos: Horacio Santiago Rostagno.

Saunders-Blades, JL, DR Korver, 2006, Maternal dietary 25-OH-D3 vitamin D-3 improves chick early innate immunity. Poult. Sci, 85:28-28.

Scott, ML, 1981, Importance of biotin for chickens and turkeys. Feedstuffs, 53(8), p. 59-67.

Scott, ML, M Nesheim, R Young, 1982, Nutrition of the chicken, Scott, Ithaca, Nueva York, p.119.

Sell, JL, CR Angel, FJ Piquer, EG Mallarino, HA al-Batshan, 1991, Developmental patterns of selected characteristics of the gastrointestinal tract of young turkeys. Poult. Sci, 70:1200-1205.

Shen, H, JD Summers, S Leeson, 1981, Egg-Production and shell quality of layers fed various levels of vitamin-D3. Poult. Sci, 60:1485-1490.

Siddons, RC, 1978, Nutrient deficiencies in animals - folic acid, In:M. Rechcigl (Ed.) CRC Handbook Series in Nutrition and Food. 11, Nutritional Disorders, CRC Press, West Palm Beach, FL.

Siegel, PB, SE Price, B Meldrum, M Picard, PA Geraert, 2001, Performance of pure-line broiler breeders fed two levels of vitamin E. Poult. Sci, 80:1258-1262.

Sirri, F, AC Barroeta, 2007, Enrichment in vitamin, in bioactive egg compounds, Editores: Houpalahti et al. Springer-Verlag Berlin Heidelberg.

Soto-Salanova, MF, JL Sell, 1995, Influence of supplemental dietary fat on changes in vitamin E concentration in livers of poults. Poult. Sci, 74:201-204.

Soto-Salanova, MF, JL Sell, 1996, Efficacy of dietary and injected vitamin E for poults. Poult. Sci, 75:1393-1403.

Soto-Salanova, MF, JL Sell, EG Mallarino, FJ Piquer, DL Barker, PE Palo, R.C Ewan, 1993, Research note: vitamin E status of turkey poults as influenced by different dietary vitamin E sources, a bile salt, and an antioxidant. Poult. Sci, 72:1184-1188.

Souci, SW, W Fachman, H Kraut, 1989, Food Composition and Nutrition Tables 1989-90 4th Edition.

Souza, RA, PA Souza, RC Souza, ACRS Neves, 2008, Efeito da utilização de Carophyll Red nos índices reprodutivos de matrizes de frangos de corte. Revista Brasileira de Ciência Avícola 10: 32.

Speake, BK, PF Surai, T Gaal, M Mezes, RC Noble, 1996, Tissue-specific development of antioxidant systems during avian embryogenesis. Biochem. Soc. Trans, 24:182S.

Squires, MW, E C Naber, 1992, Vitamin profiles of eggs as indicators of nutritional status in the laying hen: vitamin B_{12} study. Poult. Sci, 71:2075-2082.

Squires, MW, E C Naber, 1993a, Vitamin profiles of eggs as indicators of nutritional status in the laying hen: vitamin A study. Poult. Sci, 72:154-164.

Squires, MW, E C Naber, 1993b, Vitamin profiles of eggs as indicators of nutritional status in the laying hen: riboflavin study. Poult. Sci, 72: 483-494.

Stevens, VI, R Blair, RE Salmon, JP Stevens, 1984, Effect of varying levels of dietary vitamin D3 on turkey hen egg production, fertility and hatchability, embryo mortality and incidence of embryo beak malformations. Poult. Sci, 63:760-764.

Stoianov, P, R Zhekov, 1982, Causes of disorders affecting the hatching and viability of broiler chicks. Vet. Med. Nauki,

19:47-51.

Sunde, ML, CM Turk, HF DeLuca, 1978, The essentiality of vitamin D metabolites for embryonic chick development. Science 200:1067-1069.

Surai, AP, PF Surai, W Steinberg, WG Wakeman, BK Speake, NHC Sparks, 2003, Effect of canthaxanthin content of the maternal diet on the antioxidant system of the developing chick. Br. Poult. Sci. 44: 612-619.

Surai, PF, 1992, Vitamin E feeding of poultry males. World Poultry Congress, Amsterdam, 1:575-577.

Surai, PF, 1999, Tissue-specific changes in the activities of antioxidant enzymes during the development of the chicken embryo. Br. Poult. Sci. 40: 397-405.

Surai, PF, 2000, Effect of selenium and vitamin E content of the maternal diet on the antioxidant system of the yolk and the developing chick Br. Poult. Sci, 41:235-243.

Surai, PF, 2003, Natural antioxidants in avian nutrition and reproduction. Nottingham University Press

Surai, PF, NH Sparks, 2000, Effect of the selenium content of the maternal diet on the antioxidant system of the newly hatched chick. Personal communication.

Surai, PF, NH Sparks, 2001, Comparative evaluation of the effect of two maternal diets on fatty acids, vitamin E and carotenoids in the chick embryo. Br. Poult. Sci, 42:252-259.

Surai, PF, BK Speake, 2000, Antioxidant systems and avian embryonic development. Proc. World Poultry Conf.

Surai, PF, MS Zhedek, 1985, Effect of vitamins A and E on turkey sperm quality. Ptitsevodstvo, Kiev, 37:27-34.

Surai, PF, IA Ionov, N Buzhina, 1995, Vitamin E and egg quality: Egg and egg products quality. Proceedings of the Vi European Symposium on the Quality of Eggs and Egg Products, Zaragoza, Spain, p. 387-394.

Surai, PF, RC Noble, BK Speake, 1996, Tissue-specific differences in antioxidant distribution and susceptibility to lipid peroxidation during development of the chick embryo. Biochim. Biophys. Acta 1304:1-10.

Surai, PF, RC Noble, BK Speake, 1999a, Relationship between vitamin E content and susceptibility to lipid peroxidation in tissues of the newly hatched chick. Br. Poult. Sci, 40:406-410.

Surai, PF, NH Sparks, RC Noble, 1999b, Antioxidant systems of the avian embryo: tissue-specific accumulation and distribution of vitamin E in the turkey embryo during development. Br. Poult. Sci, 40:458-466.

Surai, PF, BK Speake, NHC Sparks, 2001, Carotenoids in avian nutrition and embryonic development. 1. Absorption, availability and levels in plasma and egg yolk. J. Poult. Sci. 38: 1- 27.

Surai, PF, T Gaal, RC Noble, BK Speake, 1997a, The relationship between the alpha-tocopherol content of the yolk and its accumulation in the tissues of the newly hatched chick. J. Sci. Food Agric. 75:212-216.

Surai, PF, IA Ionov, EF Kuchmistova, RC Noble, BK Speake, 1998a, The relationship between the levels of alpha-tocopherol and carotenoids in the maternal feed, yolk and neonatal tissues: comparison between the chicken, turkey, duck and goose. J. Sci. Food Agric., 76:593-598.

Surai, PF, IA Ionov, TV Kuklenko, IA Kostjuk, A MacPherson, BK Speake, RC Noble, NH C. Sparks, 1998b, Effect of supplementing the hen's diet with vitamin A on the accumulation of vitamins A and E, ascorbic acid and carotenoids in the egg yolk and in the embryonic liver. Br. Poult. Sci, 39:257-263.

Surai, PF, E Kutz, GJ Wishart, RC Noble, BK Speake, 1997b, The relationship between the dietary provision of alpha-tocopherol and the concentration of this vitamin in the semen of chicken: effects on lipid composition and susceptibility to peroxidation. J. Reprod. Fertil, 110:47-51.

Surai, PF, RC Noble, NH Sparks, BK Speake, 2000, Effect of long-term supplementation with arachidonic or docosahexaenoic acids on sperm production in the broiler chicken. J. Reprod. Fertil, 120:257-264.

Surai, PF, BK Speake, RC Noble, NHC Sparks, 1999c, Tissue-specific antioxidant profiles and susceptibility to lipid peroxidation of the newly hatched chick. Biol. Trace Element Res. 68: 63-78.

Taylor, LW, 1947, The effect of folic acid on egg production and hatchability: Poult. Sci, 36:372.

Tengerdy, RP, CF Nockels, 1973, Effect of vitamin-E on egg-production, hatchability and humoral immune-response of chickens. Poult. Sci, 52:778-783.

Tobias, S, I Rajic, A Vanyi, 1992, Effect of T-2 toxin on egg production and hatchability in laying hens. Acta Vet. Hung, 40:47-54.

Torres, CA, SL Vieria, RN Reis, AK Ferreira, PX da Silva, FVF Furtado, 2009, Productive performance of broiler breeder hens fed 25-hydroxycholecalciferol. Revista Brasileira de Zootecnia-Brazilian Journal of Animal, 38 (7): 1286-1290.

Tuan, RS, E Suyama, 1996, Developmental expression and vitamin D regulation of calbindin-D-28K in chick embryonic yolk sac endoderm. J. Nutr, 126:S1308-S1316.

Tuite, PJ, RE Austic, 1974, Studies on a possible interaction between riboflavin and vitamin B 12 as it affects hatchability of the hen's egg. Poult. Sci, 53:2125-2136.

Utno, L, E Klieste, 1971, The influence of D- and DL-pantothenate on the hen productivity chick hatching rate and viability. Latvijas PSR Zinat/nu akademijas vestis izdevums, 6:72-79.

Vieira, AV, K Kuchler, WJ Schneider, 1995, Retinol in avian oogenesis: molecular properties of the carrier protein. DNA Cell Biol, 14:403-410.

Villamide, MJ, MJ Fraga, 1999, Composition of vitamin supplements in Spanish poultry diets. Br Poult Sci, 40:644-652.

Villaverde, C, L Cortinas, AC Barroeta, SM Martin-Orue, MD Baucells, 2004, Relationship between dietary unsaturation and vitamin E in poultry. J. Anim. Physiol. Anim. Nutr. (Berl) 88:143-149.

Villaverde, C, MD Baucells, EG Manzanilla, AC Barroeta, 2008, High levels of dietary unsaturated fat decrease alpha-tocopherol content of whole body, liver, and plasma of chickens without variations in intestinal apparent absorption. Poult. Sci. 87:497-505.

Ward, NE, JE Jones, DV Maurice, 1985, Inefficacy of propionic-acid for depleting laying hens and their progeny of vitamin-B12. Nutr. Rep. Int, 32:1325-1332.

Weiss, FG, ML Scott, 1979, Influence of vitamin B-6 upon reproduction and upon plasma and egg cholesterol in chickens. J. Nutr, 109:1010-1017.

Whitehead, CC, 1988, Nutrition of breeding stock (chapter 6): Recent advances in turkey science, 21st Poultry Science Symposium, p. 91-117.

Whitehead, CC, JI Portsmouth, 1989, Vitamin requirements and allowances for poultry. In : Recent Advances in Animal Nutrition (Eds. Haresign, W. & Cole, D.J.A.), p. 35-86.

Whitehead, CC, RA Pearson, KM Herron, 1985, Biotin requirements of broiler breeders fed diets of different protein content and effect of insufficient biotin on the viability of progeny. Br. Poult. Sci. 26:73-82.

Whitehead, CC, JS Rennie, HA McCormack, PM Hocking, 1993, Defective Down syndrome in chicks is not caused by riboflavin deficiency in breeders. Br. Poult. Sci, 34:619-623.

Wilson, HR, 1997, Effects of maternal nutrition on hatchability. Poult. Sci, 76:134-143.

Wilson, JX, EM Lui and RF del Maestro, 1992, Developmental profiles of antioxidant enzymes and trace metals in chick embryo. Mechanisms of Ageing and Development 65: 51-64.

Yang, N, CT Larsen, TE Dunnington, PA Geraert, P M Picard, PB Siegel, 2000, Immune competence of chicks from two lines divergently selected for antibody response to sheep red blood cells as affected by supplemental vitamin E. Poult. Sci, 79:799-803.

Yaroshenko, FA, IA Ionov, PF Surai, 1995, Vitamin E and quality of newly hatched chicks. Proc.Ukranian Conf. Physiol. Biochem. Farm Anim., Lvov, Ukraine, p. 187.

Yoshida, M, H Hoshii, 1976, Effect of dilauryl succinate on reproduction of the cock and hen and preventive effect of vitamin E. J. Nutr, 106:1184-1191.

Zakaria, AH, MA al-Anezi, 1996, Effect of ascorbic acid and cooling during egg incubation on hatchability, culling, mortality, and the body weights of broiler chickens. Poult. Sci, 75:1204-1209.

Zaniboni, L, S Cerolini, 2006, Lipid changes in chicken sperm during ageing and alpha-tocopherol dietary supplementation. World's Poultry Science Journal, 62:415-415.

Zaniboni, L, S Cerolini, 2009, Liquid storage of turkey semen: Changes in quality parameters, lipid composition and susceptibility to induced in vitro peroxidation in control, n-3 fatty acids and alpha-tocopherol rich spermatozoa. Anim. Reprod. Sci. 112:51-65.

Zaniboni, L, R Rizzi, S Cerolini, 2006, Combined effect of DHA and alpha-tocopherol enrichment on sperm quality and fertility in the turkey. Theriogenology 65:1813-1827.

Zanini, SF, CA Torres, N Bragagnolo, JM Turatti, MG Silva, MS Zanini, 2003, Evaluation of the ratio of omega-6, omega-3 fatty acids and vitamin E levels in the diet on the reproductive performance of cockerels. Archiv. fur Tierernahrung, 57:429.

Zwaan, J, KW Lam, 1992, Comparison of ascorbic-acid levels in the eye and remainder of the chicken-embryo during development, Exp. Eye Res, 54:411-413.

OPTIMUM VITAMIN NUTRITION IN LAYING HENS

A. C. Barroeta, R. Davin and M.D. Baucells
Animal Nutrition and Welfare Service,
Department of Animal and Food Science
Universitat Autonoma de Barcelona, 08193 Bellaterra. Spain
ana.barroeta@uab.es

INTRODUCTION

Vitamins were discovered at the beginning of the twentieth century and birds have served as an experimental model for the discovery and characterization of some of them. However, there still remain many gaps in our knowledge of these essential nutrients.

They are organic substances which are not chemically related like other groups of nutrients (carbohydrates, proteins or lipids) and they are active at low levels, which is to say that they are required in very small amounts (mg or µg).

They are vital to the normal working of the body and therefore are required for physiological functions and to maintain an optimum level of health. Not all vitamins can be synthesized by birds in sufficient quantities to meet their requirements in all physiological phases, so dietary supplementation is required. Some vitamins are provided indirectly by gut microflora, and the rest should be included in feed, either in the ingredients or from synthetic vitamin sources, normally integrated in the vitamin-mineral premix.

Sometimes vitamins are present in feedstuffs bound to other structures, so that during the digestive process they must be freed to become available. Other ingredients contain provitamins, compounds which are structurally related to vitamins but which must undergo certain metabolic changes to confer vitamin activity.

Traditional vitamin classification is based on solubility, a property which determines its behavior in the body. Fat-soluble vitamins (A, D, E and K) are associated with food lipids, and are digested and absorbed in the same way as fats. They are stored in fatty tissues, mainly the liver and adipose tissue, which acts as a reserve for the animal. Excess is excreted in bile, through the feces, but can reach toxic levels especially in the case of vitamins A and D.

Water-soluble vitamins (C and B group) are, in general, absorbed passively through the mucosa of the small intestine, and are transported in tissues either freely or bound to protein complexes. Apart from vitamin B_{12} and choline, they do not accumulate in the body in significant quantities so, to avoid deficiencies, a daily amount in feed is necessary, although tissue catabolism may compensate in part for a deficit. They are excreted in urine and therefore it is rare to reach levels of toxicity. These water-soluble vitamins are all involved in the formation of coenzymes and are, therefore, involved in metabolic processes. Although the specific functions are different, symptoms of deficiency are similar. Deficiency affects rapidly growing tissues, such as bone, skin, feathers and blood.

In this review we shall focus on data relating to the beneficial effect of optimum vitamin intake, that is, intake between minimum and maximum recommended levels. More detailed information on vitamins can be found in the reviews by Bains, (1999), Klaising (1998), Leeson (2007), McDowell (1989a and 2000), NRC (1987), World Poultry-Elsevier (2001) and Weber (2009).

Early studies carried out on vitamins were principally directed towards avoiding symptoms of deficiency. However, in recent years there has been an awakening of interest in the important metabolic functions in which this group of nutrients is involved. This brings us to the concept of Optimum Vitamin Nutrition (OVN) and sets the basis for the line of argument on the factors which justify increasing the vitamin supply in the diets of poultry.

Calculations of the requirements of poultry were carried out under experimental conditions. Moreover, in many instances they are estimated or extrapolated from other species and in no case using the current strains. This is particularly evident in the case of laying hens, where the data are scarce and derived from old studies which bear little relation to the type of hens and systems used today.

Current commercial egg-laying strains have changed a great deal in a few years. Birds have changed in size, sexual maturity has advanced, feed consumption has decreased and, above all, egg production has improved in quantity and size. Logically, these changes in themselves should call for increased nutritional requirements in general, and in particular, increased vitamin requirements.

Feed consumption is a key factor to be considered with regard to fulfilling the animals' nutritional requirements. Current egg-laying strains have a better nutrient conversion ratio which results from a lower voluntary intake. It is estimated that the progressive decrease in the feed conversion ratio results in a reduction of vitamin intake in laying hens of 1% per year. Furthermore stress situations, especially the presence of high temperatures, result in a reduction in feed consumption. The majority of nutritionists formulate feeds for commercial laying hens based on feed intake, and logically, as feed intake decreases they balance the energy level and proportionally increase the supply of calcium and essential amino acids. The supply of vitamins should also be adjusted to consumption to ensure an appropriate daily vitamin intake. In these hens with high yields, the vitamins involved in energy and protein metabolism, as well as in the immune system, are doubly important.

Second, in spite of the technical nature of poultry systems today, practical operating conditions are usually poorer than those in experiments, implying the need for greater vitamin allowances to obtain the same results.

Third, possible stress situations and pathological processes should be borne in mind, as these can lead to lower absorption efficiency through the intestinal wall, a higher metabolic rate or reduction in microbial synthesis of vitamins.

Fourth, the vitamin content and its availability in ingredients are not precisely known. Furthermore, the requirements do not take losses in activity through processing or storage conditions into account (McDowell and Nelson, 2008). The amalgamation of poultry companies leads to the formulation of rations for a greater number of birds, and less frequently.

Fifth, requirements have been established on the basis of studies which did not consider the many interactions between vitamins and other compounds which may distort or impede their use. There are no studies such as those conducted on amino acids, to discover whether there is an order of priority or a relationship between the limiting vitamins similar to the concept of the ideal protein. What is certain is that dosage is imprecise.

Sixth, currently, more detailed studies demonstrate that intake of particular vitamins at levels higher than the minimum established requirements may allow birds to achieve their genetic potential. New vitamin requirements must be established taking into account objectives beyond those related solely to production, such as prevention of and defense against certain diseases through an improvement in the immune status. Under commercial production conditions, the great metabolic effort required of birds in production brings about an increase in the nutritional requirements for the immune response, with clear repercussions for vitamin allowances.

Seventh, more importance is being placed on egg quality and its repercussions not only on nutrition but also on consumer health.

All of these points support the idea that optimum vitamin supplementation, over and above the established minimum requirements, and adapted to specific conditions, will bring improvement to the health and well-being of the birds, and maximize their productive potential and quality.

This review is divided into sections on the different vitamins. For each vitamin there is a description of its role in the bird. Then there is a discussion of various studies in which differing vitamin levels are used, and of the effects on production parameters, egg quality, added value and/or well-being of the laying hen. It looks at the vitamin levels used in practice and the recommendations made by the different official agencies, genetics firms and additive companies. Lastly, it shows the average nutritional composition of eggs produced in the United States and in various countries of the European Union, including Spain.

VITAMIN A

Vitamin A is an unsaturated monoalcohol, retinol, which is found naturally only in animal tissues. Plants contain carotene precursors, of which ß-carotene has the greatest biological potency. In the intestinal epithelium of the birds, carotenes are converted into vitamin A. Synthetic vitamin A in pure form is also available and is sold in a stabilized state.

When it is exposed to air, light or high temperatures, it oxidizes rapidly, losing its activity.

In the body of the animal, vitamin A acts at different levels and it carries out many functions. Nevertheless, the main ones may be summarized thus:

- Effect on eyesight, preventing night blindness.
- Skeletal development. Retinoic acid is necessary to maintain increase of tissues during growth.
- Reproductive performance.
- Development and maintenance of epithelial tissue. Vitamin A is necessary for regeneration of the epithelial tissue. The epithelium, apart from its structural function, acts as a line of defense against invasion by pathogenic organisms. Loss of integrity of the cell membrane allows invasion and impairs the bird's immune system, specifically, antibody production and the proliferation of T cells.
- Supplementation with vitamin A has been linked to an anti-stress effect, which may be explained by its involvement in adrenal response. Vitamin A is necessary for the production of corticosteroids in the adrenal gland, essential for the promotion of gluconeogenesis in situations of stress.

One IU of vitamin A activity is equivalent to the activity of 0.3 µg of retinol or 0.6 µg of ß-carotene, in other words 1 mg of ß-carotene is equivalent to 1667 IU of vitamin A. The minimum requirements recommended by the NRC (1994) are 3000 IU/kg and are based on studies from 1961 and 1965. An excess can lead to pigmentation problems and deficiencies of the other fat-soluble vitamins. For this reason, and because of its capacity to be stored, the maximum tolerance level is 20,000 IU/kg.

Vitamin A deficiency causes reduction in egg production, blindness and keratinization of the epithelium. However, as with other fat-soluble vitamins, deficiencies in animals are not often found, due mainly to the fact that animals are able to store these vitamins in fatty tissues, to be released into blood circulation at times of increased demand or when there is little available in feed.

As early as 1961, Hill *et al.* indicated that 2640 IU/kg was the minimum amount necessary to ensure maximum egg production, but that to minimize blood spots in the egg it was necessary to supplement 3520 IU/kg feed. This effect is due to the fact that vitamin A plays an important role in the integrity of epithelial tissue, particularly in the oviduct. Other studies indicate that vitamin A seems to affect the ovary more than the magnum since variations in dosage are reflected in parameters relating to the yolk and ovulation rather than to the formation of albumen which takes place in the magnum and the uterus (Bermudez *et al.*, 1992).

Among the more recent studies on vitamin A levels in laying hen diets, those carried out by Richter's team in Germany stand out. The team carried out various experiments using increasing dosages of vitamin A both in chick starters and chick growers (Richter *et al.*, 1989 and 1996a) and layers (Richter, 1995 and Richter *et al.*, 1990, 1991, 1996b and 1996c). The authors compared different levels of supplementation between 0 and 18,000 IU/kg and focused on the effects on production parameters and vitamin A levels in the liver and, in some studies, immunity parameters. The results indicate that a minimum level of 2500 IU/kg is necessary to prevent a drop in production. The different dosages used did not affect parameters relating to egg quality and feed conversion. Therefore, the authors indicated a linear relationship between dietary dosages used and vitamin A levels in the liver, but did not observe changes in immunity parameters, a fact which agrees with the study by Coskun *et al.* (1998). Following analysis of the different results, the authors noted that optimum allowances to achieve liver stores which permit maximum production are 4000 IU/kg for chick starters, 2000 IU/kg for chick growers and 6000 IU/kg for layers. As for the importance of liver stores, Squires and Naber (1993a) note that in layers who ingest appropriate quantities of vitamin A, liver deposition is higher when they are forming eggs than during an unproductive phase.

Other studies have concentrated on increasing the levels of vitamin A in the egg (for example Naber, 1993 and Mori *et al.*, 2003). In general, the results indicate that as the dietary dose of vitamin A increases, the levels in the egg and the liver also increase. Although it is not the principal objective of these studies, the authors analyze in parallel the effect of supplementation with vitamin A on the production and quality of eggs. Squires and Naber (1993) observed rising improvements in the laying percentage when supplementing vitamin A at levels of 4000, 8000 and 9000 IU/kg. In the study by Mori *et al.* (2003) no changes were observed in the weight and quality of eggs produced with a dose of 30,000 IU/kg, although the conversion ratio deteriorates above 15,000 IU/kg.

These studies also noted that the content of vitamin A in plasma and yolk are not good indicators of nutritional status.

With regard to the effect of vitamin A on immune status, it has been firmly established (Friedman and Sklan, 1989; Friedman *et al.*, 1991) that vitamin A plays a regulatory role in immune response in chicks and that a deficiency or excess of this nutrient leads to a reduction in their resistance to infections (*E. coli*). Similarly, Sklan *et al.* (1994) found that the maximum immune response in broilers was obtained with doses of vitamin A higher than the minimum established by the NRC (1994). However, the study by Coskun *et al.* (1998) conducted on laying hens shows no significant effect on immunity parameters when vitamin A supplementation levels are increased to 24,000 IU/kg. The results from Lin *et al.* (2002) suggest that hens which suffer thermal stress immediately after vaccination need higher levels of vitamin A to achieve the maximum production of antibodies (**Figure 2**). They also demonstrate that supplementation of vitamin A at levels above the NRC recommendations was beneficial for the proportion of peripheral T cells and this effect was maintained with different thermal stress periods and vaccination times. Because of this the

Figure 1. Effect of vitamin A supplementation on egg weight. (adapted from Richter *et al.*, 1990.)

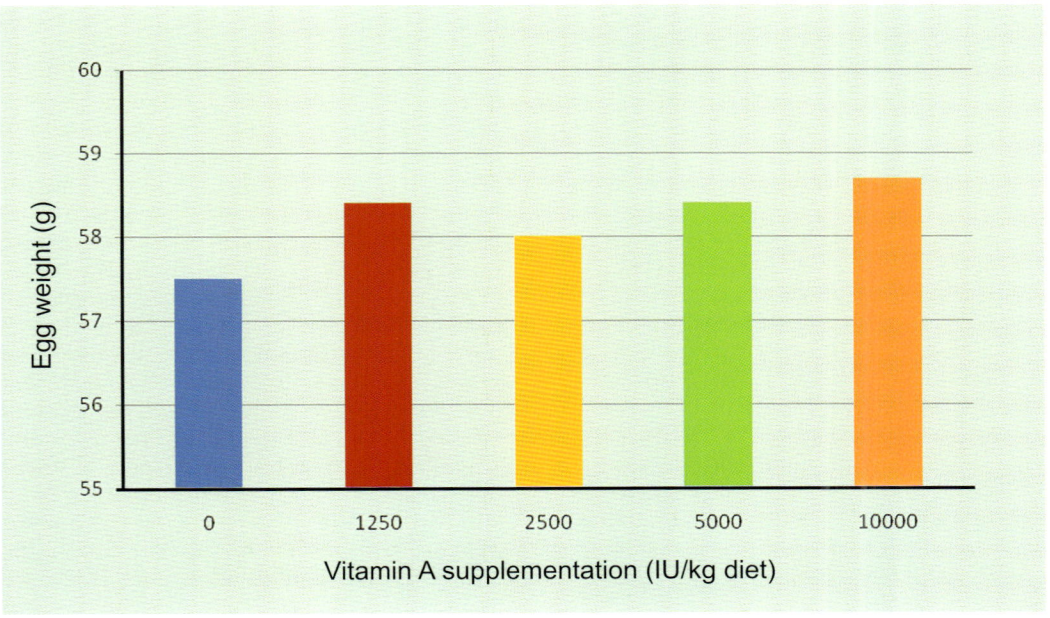

Figure 2. The effects of supplemental vitamin A levels on the immune response under heat stress. (adapted from Lin *et al.* 2002.)

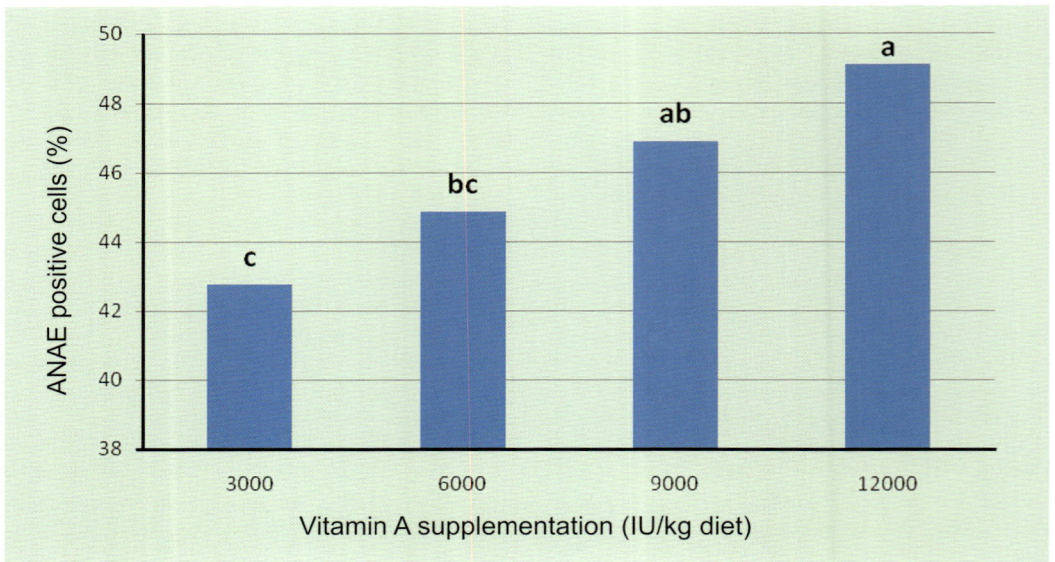

authors indicate that supplementation of high levels of vitamin A (8000 IU/kg) improves production in hens under stress conditions. In this connection, Wang *et al.* (2002) show that the ingestion of vitamin A alleviates the oxidative damage caused by thermal stress and immune challenge.

However, it is important to point out that there is a negative interaction on the level of absorption, between vitamin A and the other fat-soluble vitamins, as well as possible interactions with other nutrients. This is dealt with in the studies by Jiang *et al.* (1994) and Mori *et al.* (2003) which demonstrate a clear interaction between vitamin E and vitamin A in the deposition of both. Another example is the study by Kaya *et al.* (2001) which investigates the interaction between vitamin A supplementation (0 and 10,000 IU) and zinc supplementation (from 0 to 200 ppm), since a connection has been shown between both nutrients with respect to absorption, transport and utilization. No interaction was observed with respect to production in this study, and the authors observed increased blood phosphorus and triglyceride levels related to high levels of vitamin A supplementation and supplies of zinc.

On the one hand, few ingredients contain

high levels of carotene, except for maize and its by-products. On the other, the stability of vitamin A is generally low, especially during heat treatment. This has led to the presence on the market of products based on vitamin A with 70-90% availability for the bird. In practice vitamin A is supplemented with a safety margin of between 2 and 6%. The Spanish feed industry includes on average levels of 2.79 mg retinol (CV = 16) in feed for layers.

A minimum vitamin A requirement of 3000IU for layers (NRC, 1994) was established solely on the grounds of maintaining production parameters, and it is limited by interaction with other fat-soluble vitamins, for example vitamin E, and by the need to stay within the tolerance level. In the light of studies referred to, supplementation at a higher level would increase production. Furthermore, recent studies note that higher levels of vitamin A improve the immune response of the birds in stress situations (including thermal and vaccination stress), contributing to greater comfort for the animals and allowing improvements in the production of commercial eggs. It would be very useful to investigate whether these improvements are accompanied by positive effects on quality of eggs.

VITAMIN D

Vitamin D is a group of ester compounds whose main function is to regulate calcium and phosphorus metabolism, bone mineralization and egg formation. Vitamin D_3 is the form which is most active in birds. The birds can synthesize cholecalciferol or vitamin D_3 from the 7-dehydrocholesterol present in their skin when they receive ultraviolet light through exposure to the sun. In hens, which are housed, endogenous synthesis is insufficient to meet requirements and they must have a supplementary dietary intake.

Cholecalciferol is stored in an inactive form, mainly in the liver and adipose tissue. When the body needs vitamin D it must activate it by hydroxylation to 25-hydroxycholecalciferol. This metabolite is carried to the kidneys where it is converted to 1,25-dihydroxycholecalciferol or calcitriol, which is the active form of vitamin D in animals. The efficiency in hydroxylation reactions that convert 25-hydroxycholecalciferol to 1,25-dihydroxycholecalciferol appears to be affected by the age of the hen (Frost *et al.*, 1990 and Soares *et al.*, 1988).

All metabolic processes involving vitamin D are regulated by two hormones, calcitonin and parathyroid hormone, which are closely connected to the level of calcium in the blood. That is why the main effect of this vitamin is on levels of calcium and phosphorus, and the balance between them.

Main calcitriol functions:

• Stimulating calcium and phosphorus absorption in the intestine.
• Increasing renal reabsorption of calcium and phosphorus.
• Stimulating mobilization and deposition of existing bone calcium and phosphorus with the objective of achieving and maintaining optimum bone mineral content in the hen and the developing egg.

One international unit (IU) of vitamin D_3 is defined as the activity of 0.025 µg vitamin D_3 (cholecalciferol). The minimum requirements established by the NRC (1994) are 300 IU/kg of vitamin D_3.

Figure 3. Effect of vitamin D_3 supplementation on egg integrity. (adapted from Kesharvarz 1996.)

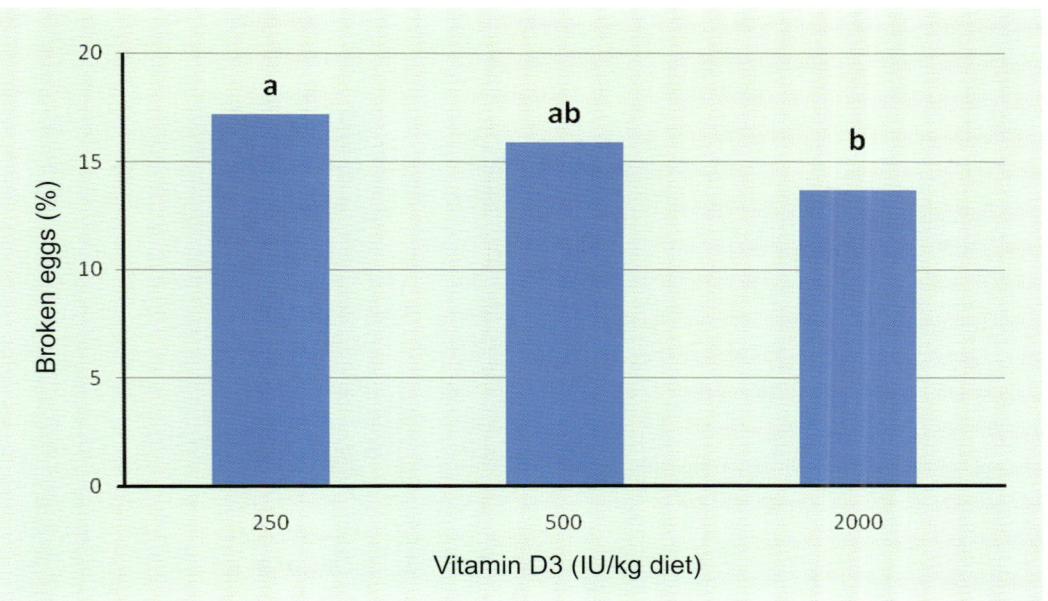

Figure 4. Effect of different sources and levels of vitamin D on tibia bone strength.
(adapted from Mattila 2004.)

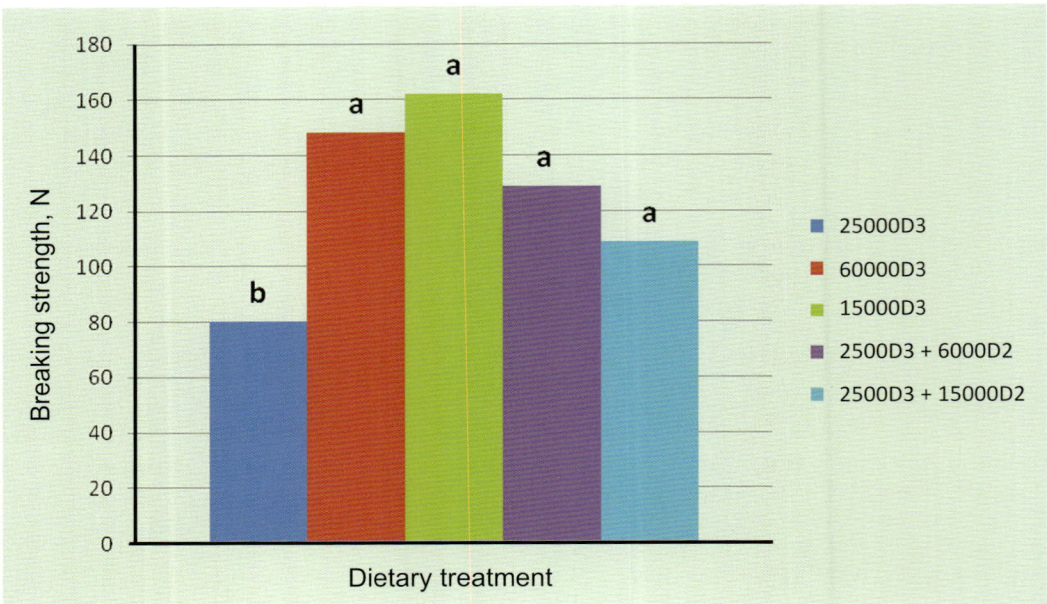

In principle, laying hens have specific calcium needs. In addition to requirements purely for the maintenance and development of bone tissue, they require calcium for shell formation and to ensure medullary bone reserves. Bearing in mind the relationship of vitamin D with calcium, it is logical in practice to use levels above the minimum requirements. However, some studies have not demonstrated under experimental conditions that higher levels of vitamin D improve the quality of the shell.

Kesharvarz (1996) and Kesharvarz and Nakajima (1993) studied the effect of vitamin D_3 supplementation from 250 to 4400 IU/ kg on different production parameters. The percentage of broken eggs (P<0.05) and egg specific gravity (numerically, not statistically) improved with levels of 2000 IU/ kg compared with 250 IU/kg, indicating that this latter level is marginal for metabolism (**Figure 3**). In spite of finding no significant differences in the other factors studied, they point out that the requirements established by the NRC (1994) are marginal and that those set out previously (500 IU; 1984) are more in line with the real needs of the layer. Therefore they suggest the application of a safety margin in the dosage of this vitamin.

These figures agree with the results of Shen *et al.* (1981) which suggest a minimum of 500 IU vitamin D_3 for optimum shell formation.

The supply of vitamin D is essential to maintain the integrity of the skeleton, with clear implications for the birds' state of well-being. The majority of studies demonstrate that doses above the NRC's 1994 recommendations are necessary to promote good bone structure and prevent fractures.

Frost *et al.* (1990) studied vitamin D_3 supplements between 500 and 1,500 IU/ kg, and the results indicate that, as vitamin D_3 levels increase, so do egg production, consumption of feed, egg specific gravity, the percentage and weight of the shell and shell strength, which agree with the results of Faria *et al.* (1999), using from 2,500 to 3,500 IU/kg. Likewise, Mattila *et al.* (2004) observed that supplementation with ergocalciferol (vitamin D_2) and above all cholecalciferol between 6,000 and 15,000 compared with 2,500 IU/kg improves resistance of bones to fracture (**Figure 4**) and does not cause undesirable calcium deposits in vital organs and soft tissues and no changes were observed in the

Figure 5. Effect of vitamin D$_3$ supplementation on egg production, eggshell quality and tibia strength. (adapted from Frost *et al.* 1990.)

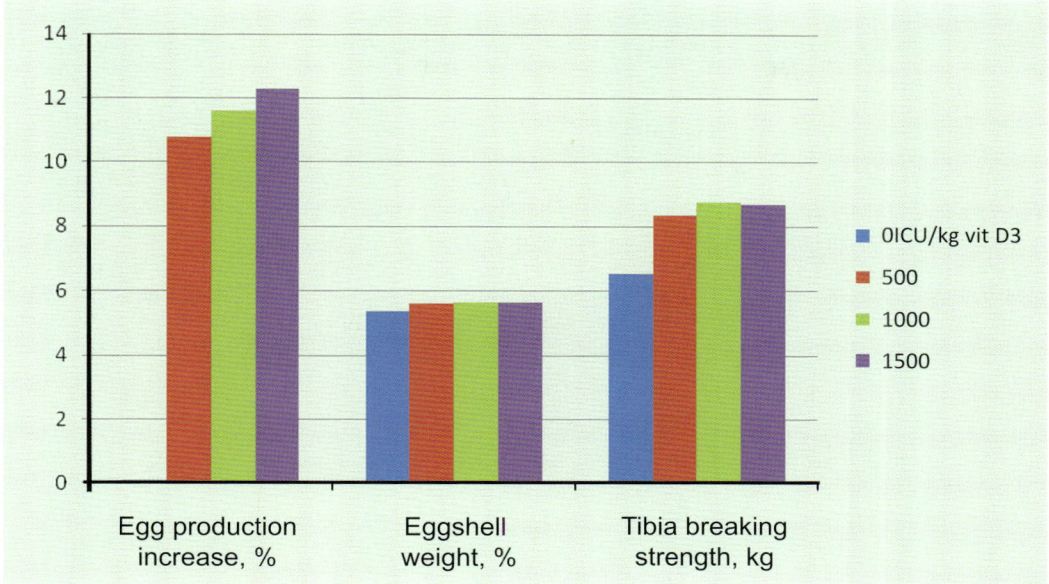

productive parameters of laying hens. Keshawartz (1996) also observed that by increasing the dose of vitamin D$_3$, the weight and breaking stregth of the tibia increased, although no differences in tibia ash content were observed. These authors indicate that the latter observation is not a sensitive method of detecting changes in the level of bone mineralization. The dose quadratically increased serum calcium and phosphorus levels during oviposition. Using more precise methodology, Newbrey *et al.* (1992) demonstrated that supplementing 1,25-dihydroxycholecalciferol [1,25-(OH)$_2$D$_3$] or calcitriol stimulates bone formation and mineral retention in the medullary bone matrix during oviposition.

The improvements in the quality of the shell observed when available phosphorus was reduced from 0.5 to 0.3% appear to be due to a stimulation of the 1,25-(OH)$_2$D$_3$ (Frost *et al.*, 1991). Consequently there is an interest in studying the possibility of supplying preformed metabolites directly and thus not depending on the organism's capacity for conversion to the active compound. Some studies indicate that the addition of vitamin D metabolites together with vitamin D$_3$ (above requirements, >2000 IU/

kg) improves eggshell quality and the levels of calcium and phosphorus in blood to normal phosphorus levels available in the diet (Harms *et al.*, 1990a). Chennaiah *et al.* (2004), Tsang (1992), Tsang *et al.* (1990a) and Tsang and Grunder (1993) demonstrated that layer diets supplemented with calcitriol give rise to fewer egg breakages during classification and washing than diets with normal levels of vitamin D$_3$. These results agree with those of Seeman (1992) and those of Neri (2000) who observed improvements in production and bone mineralization when supplementing with 1,25(OH)$_2$D$_3$.

However, several authors indicate that, when there is an adequate intake of vitamin D$_3$, supplementation of different metabolites has a reduced effect on resistance to bone breakage and on production parameters (Harms *et al.*, 1988 and 1990a; Kesharvarz, 2003a; Newman and Leeson, 1999 and Tsang and Daghir, 1990). Similarly, Frost *et al.* (1990), concluded that the hen can obtain enough 1,25(OH)$_2$D$_3$ from dietary vitamin D$_3$ to maintain production and eggshell quality (**Figure 5**). However, this metabolite is not produced in sufficient levels to maintain the weight and strength of the tibia, particularly in older birds. Koreleski and Swiatkiewicz

(2005) demonstrate that substituting 25% (over 1500 IU/kg) of vitamin D_3 with 25-OH-D_3 improves the density, thickness and resistance to breakage of eggshells produced particularly at the end of laying.

With regard to tolerance levels Tsang et al. (1990b) indicated that 5 µg/kg 1,25(OH)$_2$D$_3$ is the optimum level to improve eggshell quality, and placed the toxic level at 7 µg/kg. The study by Terry et al. (1999) focused on determining the maximum tolerance level for using the 25-OH-D_3 metabolite in layer diets. They studied levels between 41.25 and 825 µg/kg and the effect of these levels on different parameters. The results indicate that using 25-OH-D_3 is safe at a dosage of 82.5 µg/kg, with a safety margin of 5. As we have seen, 1,25(OH)$_2$D$_3$ necessitates supplements at lower levels than with 25-OH-D_3 and logically, as indicated by Soares et al. (1995), maximum tolerance levels in absolute terms are reached sooner.

Problems with pimpling (calcification defects in the egg) have a direct relationship with management and there is an interrelationship with various nutrients.

Goodson-Williams et al. (1986) showed that as age increases, high levels of vitamin D_3 worsen problems of pimpling.

Regarding enrichment of the eggs with vitamin D, Mattila et al. (1999) found a high and positive correlation between the cholecalciferol content of the feed and the cholecalciferol (r = 0.995) and 25-hydroxycholecalciferol (r = 0.941) content of the egg yolk. Eggs enriched with vitamin D can potentially provide the total of the suggested requirement that a person needs, and substantial quantities of 25-OH-D_3 with greater biological activity than that of cholecalciferol (Ward, 2009a).

As Whitehead (1995) points out, vitamin D_3 requirements of layers have not been reevaluated in recent decades. In fact the cholecalciferol level used by the Spanish animal feed industry is 54 µg (2160 IU/kg), i.e. much greater than the minimum recommended level (**Table IV**). In current practice vitamin D_3 metabolites are are now being used and great investigative efforts are being made to observe their usefulness in the nutrition of layers.

VITAMIN E

Vitamin E was discovered in 1922, and it was Bishop and Evans who demonstrated that this fat-soluble factor was essential to rat reproduction. Since then, vitamin E has become of greater interest and our knowledge of its range of activity has broadened.

The term vitamin E includes a range of closely related active components. These components are divided into two groups: tocopherols and tocotrienols. Of the tocopherols the α form exhibits greatest biological activity, has the broadest distribution and is very commonly found in the ingredients used in animal feeds. The natural isomer of α-tocopherol is RRR-α-tocopherol or D-α-tocopherol, and it is the isomer with greatest biological activity, and is usually the reference compound vitamin E.

Most plants can synthesize vitamin E, although animals and human beings do not

have this capacity. This means that meeting vitamin E requirements relies exclusively on food.

The synthetic form of α-tocopherol is a racemic mix of eight stereoisomers, esterified to an acetate group. This form is designated DL-α-tocopherol acetate and is accepted as standard for establishing vitamin E activity. Thus, 1 mg of DL-α-tocopherol acetate is equivalent to one international unit (IU) of vitamin E, while 1 mg of the natural form (D-α-tocopherol) is 1.49 IU. Until α-tocopherol acetate is hydrolyzed in the intestine it is not biologically active in the animal.

Symptoms associated with a deficiency of this vitamin are due to changes in the permeability of cellular membranes. In fact the main function of vitamin E is to act as an antioxidant on a cellular level, specifically protecting the phospholipids in the membranes from lipid oxidation. On a cellular level, vitamin E is integrated in cellular membranes where it neutralizes free radicals, effectively preventing the development of oxidation. The greater the degree of unsaturation of the lipids, the greater their susceptibility to oxidation.

An adequate intake of vitamin E is essential for the following reasons:

- Maintenance of active tissues like muscle, the central nervous system or the vascular system.
- In the particular case of layers, oxidative destruction of ovarian follicles reduces egg production and as a consequence a deterioration in the conversion ratio. Furthermore, there is evidence that vitamin E facilitates the release of vitellogenin, precursor of yolk, from the liver and therefore increases circulation of the compounds necessary for yolk formation.
- Avoiding oxidative destruction or alteration of macrophages, which represent the first line of defense against infections. It also improves the immune response, increasing the production of antibodies.
- Vitamin E also improves immune function by inhibiting the production of immunosuppressive prostaglandins.
- In current systems of table egg production, vaccination is a routine and frequent practice. Vaccination induces immunological stress, which may be aggravated by other environmental situations, such as heat stress.
- Counteraction of the production of peroxides and the toxic effects of mycotoxins (Hoehler and Marquardt, 1996).

The minimum requirement established by the NRC (1994) is 10 mg/kg of feed.

Some authors have studied the effect of supplementation with vitamin E on the production and quality of the shell (Fan et al., 1998). Scheideler and Froning (1996) found that the addition of 50 IU vitamin E slightly improved egg production, 96.1 vs. 94.3 %. However, other researchers (Botsoglou et al., 2005; Florou-Paneri et al., 2006; Richter et al., 1985, 1986 and 1987) found no differences in production parameters with increased dietary content

of vitamin E in layer feeds, but the studies were nearly always carried out under optimum experimental conditions, far from current commercial practice. Only with doses 60 times higher than the minimum requirements (600 mg/kg vitamin E) did Mori et al.(2003) observe a deterioration in production and conversion of feed without repercussions on egg quality.

However, there are numerous conclusive studies which demonstrate the beneficial effect of vitamin E supplementation on alleviating situations of stress, in particular heat stress. Bollengier-Lee et al. (1998) observed that 500 IU vitamin E is successful in reducing the negative effects of chronic heat stress on production (improvements of between 7 and 22%), egg volume and feed conversion ratio of the hens (**Figure 6**). Previous studies had been directed towards determining optimum dosage and time of administration. The same authors (Bollengier-Lee et al., 1999) deduce from a later study that supplementation of 250 IU vitamin E in the layer diets before, during and after heat stress prevented the reduction in laying as a result of exposure to heat. It is important to point out that supplementation must take place not only after but also before and during the period of stress.

These data agree with those of other authors who indicate that vitamin E supplementation before and during heat stress prevents negative effects on production (Bollengier-Lee et al., 1998; Kirunda et al., 2001; Utomo et al., 1994; William 1995; Whitehead, 1998). The team of Scheideler at the University of Nebraska (Puthpongsiriporn et al., 2001 and Scheideler and Froning, 1996) also observed beneficial effects with moderate doses (50-65 IU/kg). Likewise, Bartov et al. (1991) demonstrated that vitamin E supplementation between 125 and 300 mg/kg minimized reduction in egg production, in feed efficiency and in shell density caused by not only of heat stress, but also of some illnesses. The studies by Kucuk et al. (2003) and Panda et al. (2008) detect improvements in the production parameters and antioxidant status of layers subjected to thermal stress (low temperatures 6°C or tropical summer conditions) on the incorporation of vitamin E and vitamin C, with additive effect. All these results indicate that vitamin E

Figure 6. Effect of vitamin E supplementation on egg production under heat stress conditions. (adapted from Bollengier-Lee *et al.* 1998).

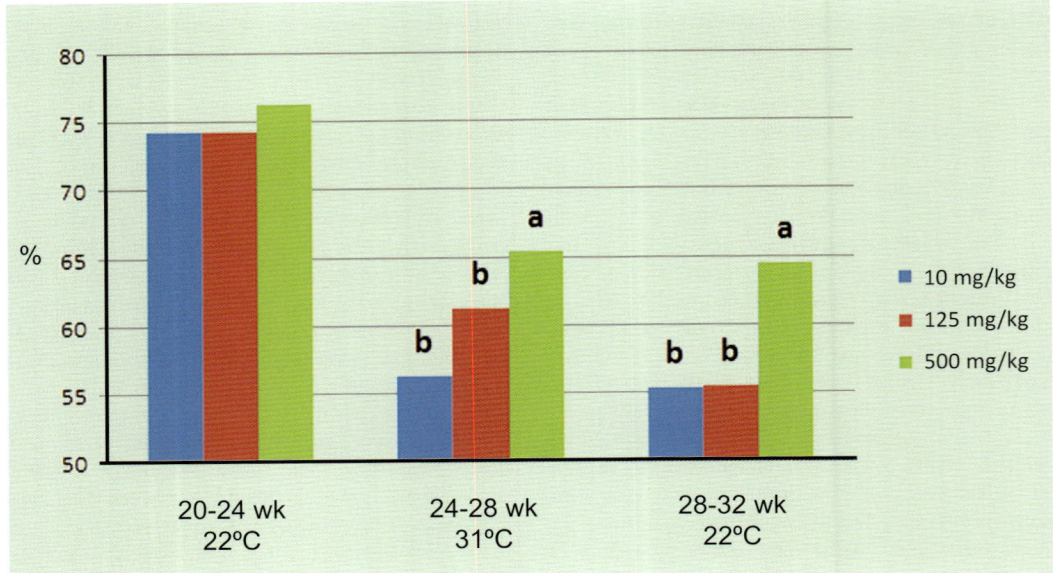

supplementation improves the immune status of the hens, and is potentially beneficial during other stressful situations such as transportation, vaccination, molt and, of course, high temperatures.

Once the basic needs of the animal have been met, the possibility of using higher levels of supplementation can be considered with a view to improving other aspects, in particular those relating to the quality of the food reaching the consumer. Vitamin E can act on two levels: preventing food oxidation and as a way to fortify the food for the consumer.

Interesting observations by Froning (2001) indicate that supplementation with 120 IU/kg vitamin E improves the functional properties of the egg, specifically the percentage of solids. These data agree with the results of other authors who indicate that treatment with vitamin E (250 mg/kg) does not affect egg size, but does affect egg volume by way of its effect on the yolk (Bollengier-Lee *et al.*, 1999). These authors suggest that the antioxidant action of vitamin E counteracts the negative effect of heat stress, and an extra supply results in higher vitellogenin levels in the plasma, which permits greater development of the yolk. Likewise, Kirunda *et al.* (2001) supplemented 60 IU vitamin

E in the diets of hens exposed to high temperatures, and found positive effects on the thickness of the vitelline membrane, yolk and albumen solids and foaming properties, among other parameters.

Vitamin E supplementation could minimize problems of quality and contamination of the egg which occur during summer months, due to high temperatures, and which represent important economic losses for egg processing companies. The effect of vitamin E along with Selenium (Se) supplementation has been studied by Aljamal *et al.*, 2008, who found that including the highest level of vitamin E (100 IU/kg) in the diet of laying hens, the quality of eggs is enhanced significantly. In relation to Se, egg production, feed intake and specific gravity are significantly increased with increasing levels of Se in the hen's diet.

The addition of incremental dosages of vitamin E in hen feed (from 0 to 320 mg α-tocopheryl acetate) does not appear to affect yolk color (Botsoglou *et al.*, 2005; Florou-Paneri *et al.*, 2006; Frigg *et al.*, 1992), although the study by Angela *et al.* (1999) found changes in yolk carotenoid concentrations when 2% vitamin E was added to the basal diet.

100

The oxidative stability of the egg is influenced by its fatty acid composition and the method of processing to which it is subjected. There has been a tendency in recent years to enrich these products with unsaturated fatty acids, specifically from the omega 3 family. However, it has been shown that this greater degree of unsaturation in eggs leads to increased susceptibility to lipid oxidation (Cherian et al., 1996a and b; Galobart et al., 2001a; Grashorn and Steinhilber, 1999; Li et al., 1996). Lipid oxidation reduces the nutritive and organoleptic value of the egg. Furthermore, the consumption of products derived from lipid oxidation has been linked to the development of various pathologies such as cardiovascular disease, ageing, cancer, etc.

Many studies have shown how dietary supplementation with raised levels of vitamin E (different isomers) prevents or reduces the oxidation levels associated with enriching eggs with polyunsaturated fatty acids and subjected to different heat processes (Botsoglou et al., 2005; Cortinas et al., 2001; Cherian et al., 1996a and b; Galobart et al., 2001a, b and c; Li et al., 1996; Qi and Sim, 1998; Wahle et al., 1993) (**Figure 7**). As an example, we will use the results on lipid oxidation obtained by our investigation group, which involved submitting eggs enriched with PUFA omega 3 to an atomization process and subsequent conservation of the egg in powder form (Galobart et al., 2001b). Oxidation levels of fresh egg are very low, but when they are atomized, oxidation values increase by 10-12 times the values of fresh eggs. However, by supplementing the hen's diet with different levels of α-tocopheryl acetate (50, 100 and 200 ppm), oxidation levels decrease considerably (**Figure 8**). Increasing vitamin E levels in the ration reduced TBA values but these differences were only significant between 50 and 200 mg/kg. In other words, the reduction in oxidation values due to vitamin E becomes less as its concentration in the diet increases. This shows us that it would be necessary to adjust dietary supplementation of this compound according to processing and storage conditions of the eggs or of foods of animal origin in general. In this manner the greatest protective effect at lowest economic cost to the producer may be achieved.

The α-tocopherol content of the egg maintains a linear relationship with its level of supplementation in layer feed. Thus, an egg produced by a hen which has

Figure 7. Effect of dietary supplementation with different levels of α-tocopheryl acetate on α-tocopherol concentration in fresh egg, expressed as micrograms per gram of egg. (adapted from Galobart et al. 2001c)

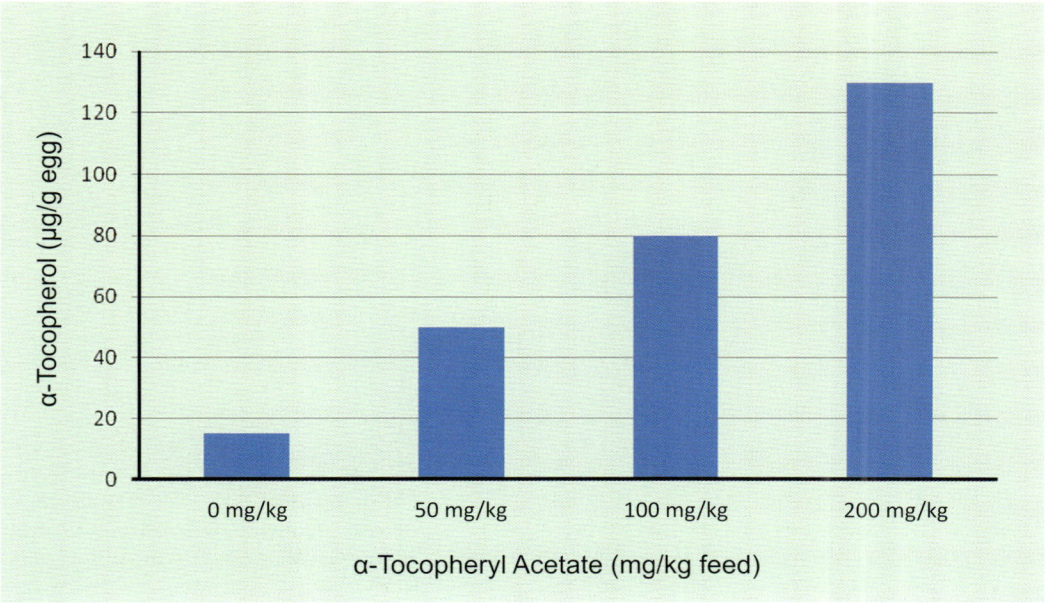

101

Figure 8. Effect of dietary supplementation with different levels of α-tocopheryl acetate on TBA values, expressed as nanograms of malondialdehyde (MDA) per gram of solids, in fresh and spray-dried egg at 0 and 2 months of storage. (adapted from Galobart *et al.* 2001c)

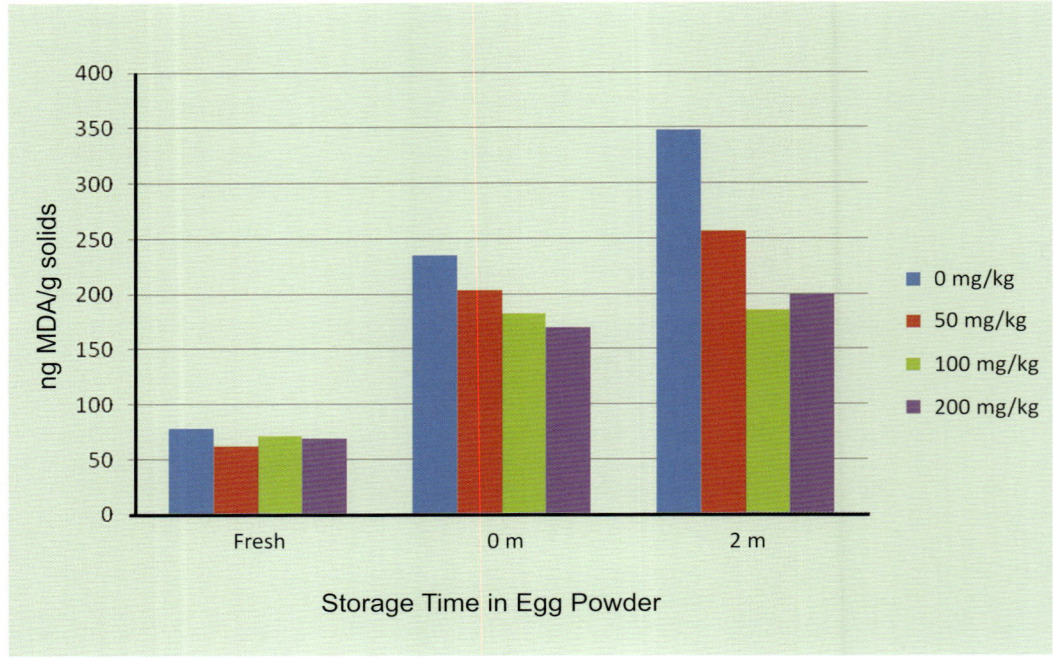

been given 200 mg/kg α-tocopheryl acetate contains around 6-8 mg vitamin E (Galobart *et al.*, 2001c). Recommended consumption of vitamin E (recommended daily amount, RDA) for humans is approximately 10 mg. Therefore, an egg enriched with vitamin E can provide 60-80% of the RDA for this vitamin. Similar observations have been described by a number of authors who have investigated the possibility of increasing the vitamin E content of the egg (Chen *et al.*, 1998; Frigg *et al.*, 1992; Grobas *et al.*, 2002; Jiang *et al.*, 1994; Meluzzi *et al.*, 1999; Mori *et al.*, 2003; Qi and Sim, 1998; Surai *et al.*, 1995). As mentioned before in the section on vitamin A, the interrelation between the two vitamins A and E is very important, as they are involved in its absorption and subsequent deposition in the egg.

Villamide and Fraga (1999) note that, in the Spanish animal feed industry, ingredients provide between 10 and 20 mg vitamin E per kg feed and it is further supplemented by an average of 7.62mg/kg (52% CV). On the basis of all this information, it is logical to conclude that the dosage of vitamin E in layer feeds should be adjusted according to the unsaturated fatty acid content of feed and according to the processing and storage to which the eggs will be subjected. Furthermore, supplementation above the minimum requirements is very beneficial in the face of routine stress situations resulting from vaccinations, beak trimming, heat and transport.

VITAMIN K

Vitamin K includes a range of components called quinones. Vitamin K_1 or phylloquinone is found in green plants and seeds, while K_2 or menaquinone is the result of bacterial synthesis in the large intestine. Vitamin K_3 or menadione is a fat-soluble compound with greater biological activity than the others; it is considered the reference standard for vitamin K activity.

The main function of vitamin K is to regulate the formation of various factors involved in blood clotting. Prothrombin is produced in the liver and used continuously by the body. Continual intake of vitamin K is necessary to activate prothrombin:

- When ovulation takes place, if the follicular sac does not rupture along the stigma line, an area with few blood vessels, blood spots in the yolk may result, which could be avoided with effective blood clotting.
- Layers have a propensity to nervousness, pecking and even cannibalism. If birds are injured, for example following uterine prolapse at oviposition, a longer blood clotting period may trigger cannibalism.
- Beak trimming is a normal practice in management of layers. A delay in the clotting period may delay healing.

The principal bone proteins, such as osteocalcin, are also dependent on vitamin K. Osteocalcin is important in calcium metabolism and is found in bone, in the uterus and in eggshell. Low levels of osteocalcin and bone matrix proteins may impede the mineralization process during skeletal development and eggshell formation (Whitehead, 2004).

In general, layers do not have access to their droppings. Therefore the vitamin K produced by intestinal micro-organisms but not absorbed in the gut does not represent a dietary source. Furthermore, during disease or treatment with antibiotics, this microbial synthesis is reduced or stops.

Requirements for vitamin K by layers have not been established, with the NRC giving a minimum requirement of 0.5 mg/kg in 1994, based on a study from 1964. However, the ARC in 1975 suggests a minimum of 1 mg/kg and recommends levels of 2 mg/kg.

Some studies relating to vitamin K in layers focus on bone metabolism. Lavalle et al. (1994) fed breeding Leghorn hens with a diet deficient in vitamin K, with the object of studying the effect on bone metabolism of layers, embryo development and chick growth. While egg production, shell thickness and other production parameters were not significantly affected, vitamin K deficiency provoked a reduction in concentration of coagulation and osteocalcin factors, which did not affect the initial skeletal development of chicks. Rennie et al. (1997) found no changes in the volume of trabecular bone in the hens on supplementing feed during laying with 20 mg/kg vitamin K. These authors did not consider whether vitamin K stimulated bone development during the whole growth period of the chicks.

With this objective, Fleming et al. (1998) carried out a study which led them to conclude that supplementation of 10 mg/kg menadione in the basal diet (2 mg/kg vitamin K_3) resulted in a greater volume of cancellous bone in the tarsal-metatarsal after 25 weeks of life (**Figure 9**). The authors note that vitamin K could prolong the modeling period of bone formation or inhibit medullary bone loss during the first phases of laying. In a subsequent study (Fleming et al., 2003) they confirmed these results, observing that combined supplementation of extra sources of vitamin K_3, calcium carbonate particles and fluoride improved the quality and resistance of bones at the end of laying, with an improvement of between 12-20% in bone characteristics related to osteoporosis. These authors' results of these authors indicate that these improvements are due mainly to the extra supply of granulated calcium. They also demonstrate that vitamin K_3 supplementation (10 mg/kg added to 2-6 mg/kg in the basal diet) increased the volume of medullary bone in the tarsal-metatarsal both during the starter and grower phase and during laying up to 70 weeks. However, it was not possible to find the explanation for this effect, since the concentration of plasma osteocalcin was not affected by the dietary vitamin K dose during growth.

Figure 9. Effect of additional vitamin K on cancellous bone percentage. (adapted from Fleming 1998.)

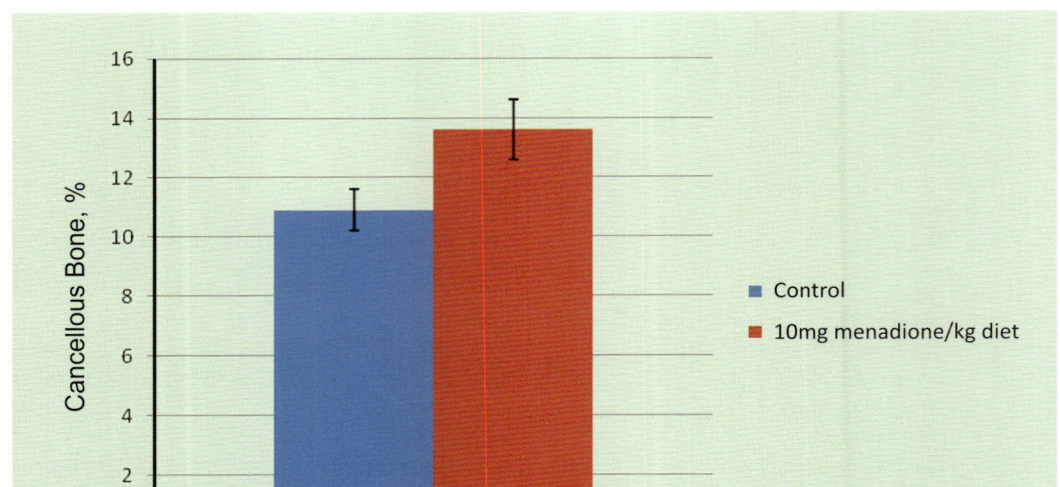

Müller et al (2009) demonstrated that increasing levels of vitamin K (from 0 to 32 mg/kg) to the diet of 67-week-old of age laying hens, improved performance and bone mineralization, but not eggshell quality. (**Figures 10 and 11**)

These data demonstrate that the extra vitamin K_3 supplementation improves the formation of trabecular calcium during the growth period and contributes to preventing osteoporosis in laying hens. However, it would be useful to carry out more studies on the role of vitamin K in the development and maintenance of the skeleton in laying hens to understand the mechanisms involved. Likewise, findings are needed on vitamin K activity in situations of stress, common in practice, in which synthesis or absorption is diminished.

Regarding the possibility of fortifying eggs with vitamin K, the experiment by Suzuki and Okamoto (1997) demonstrates that vitamin K_1 or phylloquinone supplementation between 10 and 100 mg/kg produces eggs with a content of 104-1908 µg vitamin K_1 and 67-192 µg menaquinone per 100 g

yolk. Supplementation with vitamin K_3 or menadione (10-1000 mg/kg) resulted in eggs fortified with menaquinone at a level of 115-240 µg per 100 g yolk, and with menadione at a level of only 1 µg per 100 g yolk. No differences were observed in egg production related to the dosage of vitamin K.

In practice rations are formulated with safety margins of 2. Layer feeds made in Spain include an average menadione level of 1.43 mg/kg (66% CV; Villamide and Fraga, 1999).

These studies are generally inconclusive regarding the interaction between vitamins and between vitamins and other nutrients. The fact that fat-soluble vitamins compete with each other for absorption means that an excess of one may cause deficiency in the others.

Figure 10. Effect of dietary supplementation with different levels of vitamin K on egg weight (g) and egg production (%). (adapted from Müller *et al.* 2009.)

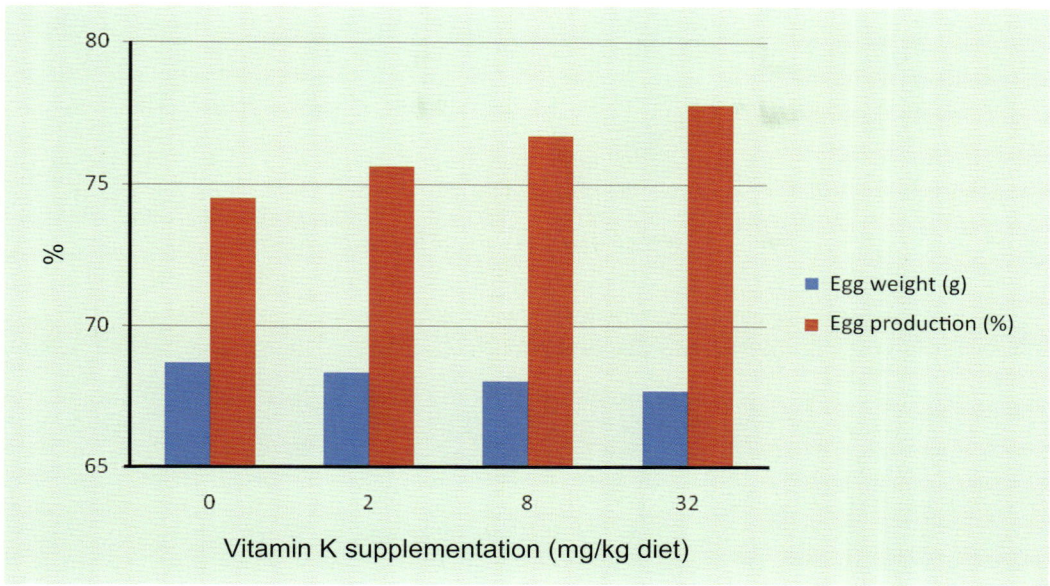

Figure 11. Effect of dietary supplementation with different levels of vitamin K on feed conversion ratio (kg/dozen). (adapted from Müller *et al.* 2009.)

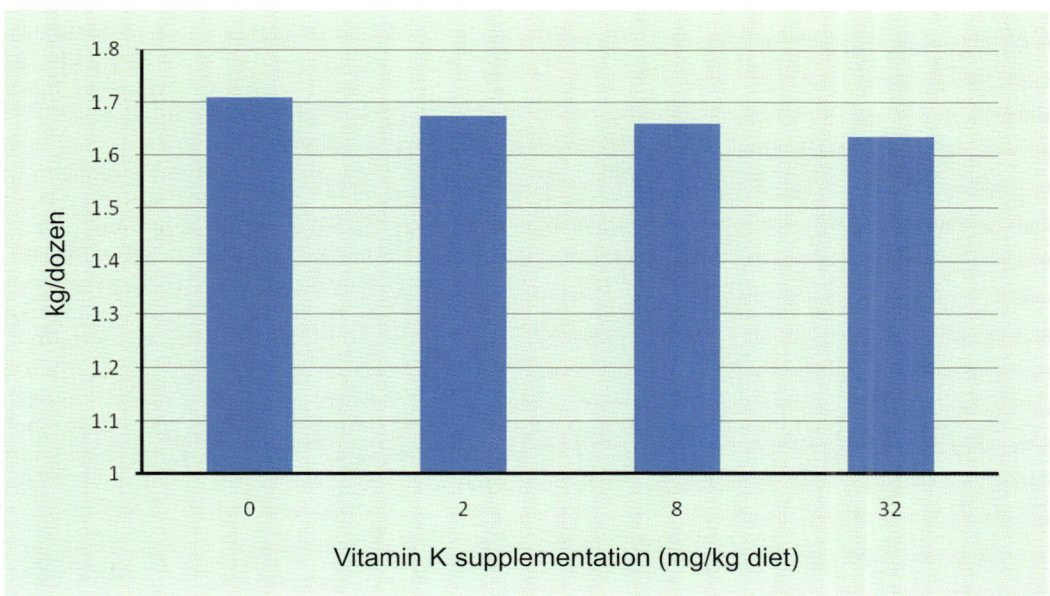

VITAMIN B COMPLEX

The vitamin B complex includes a group of vitamins which, originally, were classified together as one vitamin, since they all have similar metabolic functions.

The vitamins which make up this complex are used by the animal to form coenzymes. Coenzymes are small organic molecules which join to larger enzyme molecules,

assisting these so that chemical reactions may take place with greater efficiency.

The vitamins thiamine, riboflavin, niacin, pyridoxine, pantothenic acid and biotin act principally as coenzymes which are involved in release of energy from feedstuffs. On the other hand, folic acid, cobalamin and choline are required for growth and cell maintenance.

THIAMINE (VITAMIN B$_1$)

Thiamine was the first water-soluble vitamin to be discovered, and for this reason it is also called vitamin B$_1$. It plays a fundamental role in carbohydrate metabolism, as well as in lipid and protein metabolism.

It is found in cereals, soy and its by-products, including oils. In contrast, tapioca and protein products of animal origin contain low levels of thiamine, and it is destroyed by severe heat treatment. It is sold commercially mainly as the hydrochloride and mononitrate salts.

Feed with a high carbohydrate content should be accompanied with additional levels of vitamin B$_1$, since a there is a greater metabolic demand for energy during the tricarboxylic acid cycle. If the quantity of thiamine is insufficient the amount of available energy will be reduced, with negative effects on the production and size of eggs.

In situations of stress, metabolic demands for thiamine for energy release are increased, a problem which is aggravated by the reduced ingestion (lack of appetite) produced by inadequate thiamine intake.

Intestinal dysfunction has a negative effect on thiamine absorption, due to changes in the epithelium and changes in intestinal flora.

The presence of some substances such as mycotoxins, some therapeutic products (amprolium and furazolidone) and, of course, its antagonist thiaminase, may reduce the availability of thiamine in the bird.

There are few studies on thiamine requirements in laying hens. The minimum value recommended by the NRC in 1994 was 0.7 mg/kg. In 1975 the ARC suggested minimum requirements of 1.25 mg/kg, and practical requirements of 1.5 mg/kg. As with other water-soluble vitamins, its low toxicity means only very high levels provoke disorders in animals.

Padhi and Combs (1965) carried out a study using different levels of vitamin B$_1$, from 0 to 1.67 ppm. Best productive yields were obtained with a supplementation level of 1.25 ppm. When dosages lower than or equal to 0.35 ppm were used, egg production ceased after 12 days of feeding and the same occurred after 20 days of the experiment with supplementation levels of up to 0.55 ppm. After 27 days of intake of 0.55 ppm or less, symptoms of polyneuritis appeared, which could be alleviated with parenteral injections of thiamine. Units of activity of RBC transketolase increased proportionally with the level of supplementation.

According to Mills *et al.* (1947), thiamine requirements in chick growers were significantly higher when the ambient temperature was 37° C than 21° C. In this same study no changes were found in the requirements of pyridoxine, nicotinic acid, folic acid or choline.

Levels of supplementation used in practice are above minimum established requirements. González (1987) describes the levels of vitamins used commercially in Spain in feeding laying hens. In the case of thiamine, the levels range from 0 to 1.5 ppm.

In a similar study carried out by Villamide and Fraga in 1999 the average level of thiamine supplementation in layer feed in Spain was 0.91 mg/kg (CV= 72%).

RIBOFLAVIN (VITAMIN B₂)

Riboflavin is named for its yellow color (flavin) and because it contains a simple sugar, D-ribose. It forms an essential part of the enzyme system which carries out the tricarboxylic acid cycle, a group of reactions necessary to obtain energy from nutrients. Riboflavin in the form of a coenzyme is involved in oxidation-reduction reactions, contributing to the maintenance of cellular metabolism and more specifically of carbohydrate, protein and lipid metabolism.

The sources of this vitamin are very varied, and it could be said that all biological material contains riboflavin. Among the main sources are milk, offal, wholegrain cereals and various vegetables. Furthermore, microbial synthesis of riboflavin takes place in the large intestine.

Maintaining the high metabolic demand necessary for optimum egg production depends on the presence of sufficient riboflavin. It provides the energy necessary for the maintenance of various physiological functions, including reproductive functions.

The level of 2.5 mg/kg recommended by the NRC in 1994 is 13.7% higher than the 2.2 mg/kg which they recommended in 1984.

In a study carried out on breeding hens in conditions of a humid tropical environment, supplements from 2.5 to 12.5 mg/kg were administered. Of the various production parameters analyzed, the only one for which a response was obtained was in the production of eggs which improved significantly when the level of riboflavin was increased to 8.5 mg/kg (Arijeniwa *et al.*, 1996). Previously Kirichenko (1991) had found that egg production increased when riboflavin is supplemented at a level 25% higher than that recommended, while in a study carried out by Flores and Scholtyssek (1992), where it was supplemented at levels from 1.7 to 9.7 mg/kg, no significant changes in any production parameter were noted. Squires and Naber (1993b) observed increased production, egg weight and body weight in breeding hens when increasing NRC recommendations from 1984 by 2 and 4 times, but no significant differences between these levels of supplementation were observed.

Squires and Naber (1993b) studied changes produced in the riboflavin content of the egg when supplementing breeding hens with 1.55, 2.20, 4.4 and 8.8 mg/kg for 27 weeks. In the first week of treatment significant differences were observed between the two lower levels of supplementation and the two higher ones. This reduction in egg riboflavin content related to deficient levels of supplementation became even more important as the hens get older. In another study Naber and Squires (1993a) found that when multiplying the requirements by one or two, transfer efficiency of riboflavin from the diet to the egg was 45%, while when four times the requirements was given, transfer efficiency decreased markedly.

In the study by Squires and Naber (1993b), the incidence of blood spots was lower in the eggs of hens which had received supplements of 4.4 and 8.8 mg/kg than those with lower doses. On the other hand these levels of supplementation had a negative effect on shell thickness for several weeks. This deterioration in shell quality is probably linked more to the increase in egg production and weight than to the riboflavin level per se.

Riboflavin deficiency reduces the ability of the hens to deal with heat stress. Onwudike and Adegbola (1984) have documented that in situations of heat stress riboflavin requirements by layers increase. It would also be advisable to increase the dosage of riboflavin in the ration in cases of immunological stress (vaccinations, infections), because of its involvement in antibody synthesis.

These studies indicate that 2.5 mg/kg riboflavin in layer rations may be inadequate. It has been seen that supplementation with 4.4 and 8.8 mg/kg may be beneficial for certain production parameters and egg quality. In this review, no references were found to studies using supplementation levels between 2.2 and 4.4 mg/kg.

Given that the cost of riboflavin supplementation is not high it is usually included in vitamin-mineral premixes at levels higher than minimum requirements, as a safety margin. González (1987) gives a riboflavin range of 2 to 6.5 mg/kg used commercially in layer feed in Spain, and Villamide and Fraga (1999) report an average level of supplementation in Spain of 3.94 mg/kg (CV= 26).

PYRIDOXINE (VITAMIN B$_6$)

Pyridoxine or vitamin B$_6$ is composed of three compounds: pyridoxine, pyridoxal and pyridoxamine, with pyridoxal being the active form. The commercial form of pyridoxine is the hydrochloride salt, which is the most stable form. In the body, vitamin B$_6$ reaches the liver in phosphorylated form, where the conversion which produces pyridoxal phosphate takes place. Niacin and riboflavin are essential to these reactions of conversion and phosphorylation.

Pyridoxine is found in many foods. Ingredients such as offal, fish and wholegrain cereals contain large quantities of this vitamin. Minimum established requirements are of 2.5 ppm (NRC, 1994) based on studies in 1961 and 1946. Normally, this amount is provided in commercial rations for layers (cereals: 3-5 ppm and oil-cakes: 7-14 ppm).

Vitamin B$_6$ acts as a cofactor for a great many enzymes, most of which catalyze reactions involving amino acids. It also takes part in fatty acid and carbohydrate metabolism, and in energy production. Requirements are higher when there is an increase in the protein content of the diet and for feeds formulated to contain high levels of energy from fat.

Given that enzymes, of which pyridoxine is one, take part in many processes, specific symptoms of deficiency are hard to define. Weiss and Scott (1979) studied the effects of administering a diet deficient in pyridoxine. In the short term there was a loss of body weight, anorexia and a marked reduction in body fat reserves, and subsequently reproductive organs altered and egg production ceased. While involution of the

ovaries and oviducts is a result of depletion, regression of the comb and wattles is considered a direct consequence of vitamin B$_6$ deficiency. The authors observed that serum cholesterol reduced while the egg cholesterol content remained similar to that of birds which were fed diets containing appropriate vitamin levels. These effects caused by deficiency were reversed by giving a diet containing the appropriate quantity of pyridoxine. Deficiency has a negative effect on the capacity of the bird to endure situations of stress such as cold or heat. Chronic and acute illnesses may lead to pyridoxine deficiency because of the concomitant reduction in feed intake, and furthermore in these situations pyridoxine requirements are increased to alleviate the additional metabolic demands caused by immunological activity.

The results of Kucuk et al. (2008) suggested that pyridoxine (8 mg/kg) along with zinc (30 mg/kg) supplements improved performance and egg quality, especially eggshell weight, in laying hens. On the other hand, a study carried out on layers of 78 and 72 weeks of age, prior to molt, in which the ration was supplemented with 100 mg/kg pyridoxine, found no changes in egg production, nor in shell formation (Hupfauer, 1993). This may indicate that an excess of pyridoxine in unstressful environmental conditions brings no additional benefits in production.

Pyridoxine does not cause toxicity problems even when given in very large amounts. Abend et al. (1975) observed no significant changes in the chemical composition of the carcass or the egg, or in the pattern of deposition of amino acids in the pectoral muscle on adding gradual increments of vitamin B_6 to the ration. When the ration was deficient in pyridoxine the body protein levels fell. There was a reduction in the glycine-serine quotient.

Weiser *et al.* (1991) indicated, in a study of layers aged 71 and 90 weeks, that a level of 6 mg/kg pyridoxine, mostly provided in the basal diet, is sufficient to prevent bone deformities.

González (1987) mentions that the range of pyridoxine used commercially in layer feed in Spain is between 0 and 2 mg/kg. Villamide and Fraga (1999) record an average supplementation level in Spain of 1.63 mg/kg (CV= 51). Both of these are below the level recommended by the NRC in 1994, but this does not necessarily represent a problem for the health of the bird or for adequate production, if pyridoxine needs are met through the ingredients in the ration. However, factors such as illness or heat stress should be taken into account, since in these conditions a level of pyridoxine which is normally adequate could become marginal.

CYANOCOBALAMIN (VITAMIN B_{12})

Cobalamin, or vitamin B_{12}, was the last vitamin to be discovered, and is the most powerful, so it is needed in very low concentrations to meet the needs of animals. Vitamin B_{12} is the only vitamin to be synthesized in nature solely by microorganisms, so that products of vegetable origin are almost devoid of this vitamin.

Cobalamin contains cobalt in its structure, and it is the only vitamin to have a trace element in its composition.

Unlike the other B group vitamins, cobalamin does not have to be utilized immediately after absorption. It can be accumulated, mainly in the liver, but also, to a lesser degree, in the kidney, muscles, bone and skin. The capacity of the hen to deposit reserves of vitamin B_{12} is not clear. Denton *et al.* (1954) noted that after two unsupplemented weeks deposits were significantly depleted. Scott *et al.* (1982) considered that it takes several months (12 weeks) to exhaust body reserves completely.

The functions of vitamin B_{12} in metabolism include assisting folic acid in the transfer of single carbon atoms for nucleic acid synthesis. It is also involved in cholesterol metabolism and in the biosynthesis of methionine from homocysteine.

It is also necessary for the normal development of erythrocytes and a metabolic deficiency causes macrocytic anemia.

Birds obtain a certain quantity of vitamin B_{12} from bacterial synthesis in the intestine, but it is still considered necessary to provide vitamin B_{12} in the diet of layers, albeit in small amounts, particularly if the main diet is of vegetable origin and coprophagy is not possible. Levels suggested by the NRC in 1994 are of 0.004 mg/kg and are based on studies from the 1950s.

Since vitamin B_{12} is related to choline (via methionine), a reduction in the intake of methionine and choline will increase the requirement for cyanocobalamin.

Deficiency in cyanocobalamin is extremely rare because of the minute quantities required in the daily ration of animals and because of the capacity of the body to store appreciable amounts of this vitamin.

It is generally believed that vitamin B_{12} deficiency does not affect commercial egg production, but early reference was made to a drop in egg weight caused by vitamin B_{12} deficiency (Skinner *et al.*, 1951). Squires and Naber (1992), conducting a study on breeders, observed that best egg production, egg weight, shell thickness, hen weight and optimum hatchability were obtained when the diet contained 8 µg/kg vitamin B_{12} (7.5 µg/kg supplemented). With levels greater than 8 µg/kg slight improvements were obtained, but the differences were not statistically significant. It may be that the nature of the study, carried out over a long period (27 weeks), allowed the detection of differences which had not been observed in shorter-term studies.

These authors suggested that vitamin B_{12} levels above minimum established requirements are necessary for optimum feeding of breeders. Akhmedkhanova and Alisheikhov (1997) and Dzhambulatov *et al.* (1996) estimated that in hot conditions 36 µg is an adequate level to optimize egg production based on different variables (egg production, egg weight, feed conversion ratio, etc.).

As for egg quality, studies by Squires and Naber (1992) and Naber and Squires (1993a) noted that the concentration of vitamin B_{12} in yolk varies rapidly depending on dietary levels, so that the vitamin B_{12} content of the egg could be used as an indicator of the vitamin B_{12} level in the hen and as a

standard of egg quality. This observation confirms the previous results of Denton *et al.* (1954) which suggest that vitamin B_{12} deposits in the body do not sustain the vitamin B_{12} content of the egg over a long period. The same authors noted that the minimum concentration of vitamin B_{12} in the egg for maximum hatchability and egg weight is between 1-3 and 2-6 µg/100g yolk, respectively.

Whitehead (1995) puts vitamin B_{12} requirements for layers at 8 µg/kg, based on the study by Squires and Naber (1992). Villamide and Fraga in 1999 report average levels of vitamin supplementation in feeds for layers in Spain as 12 µg/kg.

NIACIN

Following the isolation of riboflavin from the vitamin B complex, niacin was the third vitamin from this group to be discovered. Niacin, also called nicotinic acid, must convert to nicotinamide to undertake vitamin activity.

Many foods, both of vegetable and animal origin, contain high quantities of niacin. However, a large part of this niacin is bound and not available for absorption. This is the case with some of the niacin contained in cereals and their by-products. The bioavailability of niacin is low in some ingredients, like cereals and oilseeds (10-15%) (Klasing, 1998). The availability of niacin in other feed materials is not well documented. In non-ruminant animals it is considered necessary to supplement niacin with caution if the level calculated in the feedstuffs is below 1.5 times the requirements of the animal (Leclercq *et al.*, 1987).

Niacin is a constituent of two enzymes (NAD and NADP) which transfer hydrogen in fatty acid, carbohydrate and amino acid synthesis and degradation. Furthermore, it assists in the release of energy from feedstuffs and in its delivery to the body's cells.

The conversion of tryptophan to niacin in the body is very inefficient. It has been seen that in breeders 187 mg tryptophan is required to obtain 1 mg niacin (Manoukas *et al.* 1968),

and the presence of vitamins B_1, B_2 and B_6 is also necessary. Sashildar *et al.* (1988) suggested that the presence of mycotoxins in the diet could limit conversion of tryptophan to niacin. According to West *et al.* (1952), an excess of tryptophan did not compensate for a deficiency of niacin in chicks.

Minimum requirements indicated by the NRC in 1994 are 10 mg/kg, based on studies by Ringrose *et al.* (1965).

Several studies have evaluated both production parameters and the metabolism and the cholesterol content in the bird as affected by niacin intake.

Leeson *et al.* (1991) conducted a study with several strains of laying hens to determine the niacin requirements of highly productive birds in terms of production characteristics. The control diet contained 22 ppm niacin and niacin treatment ranged from a supplement level of 44 ppm to 1022 ppm. A slight increase in production was observed when supplementing with 44 ppm compared to the control group. This increase became significant when supplementing with 66 ppm or more. Shell quality (measured as the degree of shell deformity) improved in those hens treated with 44 or 132 ppm. There were no changes in egg weight, feed consumption or weight of the bird. Similar results were obtained by Dikicioglu *et al.*

(2000), feeding rations containing niacin levels varying between 250 and 1500 ppm, observed significant improvements in shell quality and feed conversion efficiency. Body weight was influenced negatively.

The results of Kucukersan (2000) agreed with the conclusions on production parameters. He found that with supplements of 100 ppm niacin, bird weight, egg production and feed conversion efficiency all increased, but his results differ on shell quality, since with this same level of supplementation, shell thickness and weight were reduced. There were no differences between the controls and birds receiving 50 ppm niacin. Jensen et al. (1976) observed no changes in egg production, egg weight, food consumption or body weight with a supplementation of 44 ppm niacin. Similar results were obtained by Ouart et al. (1987) when supplementing with niacin levels from 0 to 22 ppm in diets containing 21.02 ppm (corn-based diet) or 46.11 ppm (wheat-based diet).

Leeson et al. (1991) also investigated whether supplementing niacin in the ration for layers would change the liver content of cholesterol and fat. In other animal species and humans a relationship had been observed between niacin and fat and cholesterol metabolism. In humans it is thought that treatment with niacin helps to reduce blood cholesterol levels. Alderman et al. (1989) suggested that supplementation with 2 g/day was effective in reducing total cholesterol in blood serum and improving the high-density cholesterol-lipoprotein quotient in humans. Witzum (1989) also described reductions of 25-35% in human cholesterol levels when treating with high levels of niacin. Niacin is involved in lipid metabolism, in glycerol synthesis and degradation, in oxidation and synthesis of fatty acids and in steroid synthesis. Leeson et al. (1991) did not observe effects on the cholesterol content of eggs during the 28 days of the experiment and nor did they observe effects on the incidence of fatty liver evaluated according to the accumulation of fat in the liver. This latter point agrees with results previously obtained by Jensen et al. (1976) on adding 44 ppm niacin to the ration and evaluating liver weight and lipid content. Concerning the cholesterol content of the egg, similar results were obtained by Kucukersan (2000) on supplementing 50 and 100 ppm niacin. On the other hand, Dikicioglu et al. (2000) described that adding levels of niacin from 250 to 1500 ppm to the ration increased blood cholesterol levels, while the cholesterol content in yolk was significantly reduced.

It has been suggested that this vitamin controls hysteria or nervousness in birds at a dosage of 200 ppm. At this level mortality rate was reduced when birds were housed at high densities, and the conversion ratio improved. North (1984) agreed that large doses of niacin help to alleviate problems of hysteria in caged birds. However, Ouart et al. (1987) observed no differences between groups which received different levels of supplementation, from 0 to 22 ppm, over supplemented diets containing 21.02 ppm or 46.11 ppm niacin.

Jackson, in a review published in 1992, held that advances in genetics of laying and breeding hens require new thinking on diets. This author believed that there are methods to optimize the genetic potential of the layer, one of which is based on the response to niacin supplementation. He indicated that genetic companies suggest niacin levels of 18-38 ppm.

Economic benefits may be achieved by using higher dosages than those recommended by the NRC (1994). Based on the studies referred to here, 22 ppm niacin is a marginal level if the aim is to maximize egg yield. A level of 66 ppm is sufficient for a good rate of egg production. With a ration supplemented with 100 ppm, feed conversion efficiency probably improves, and with 132-250 ppm positive effects on shell quality would be obtained.

In a review published by Whitehead in 2001 the practical level of supplementation for layers is 50 ppm niacin. In Spain niacin is generally supplemented at levels higher than those indicated by the NRC, but not as high as those quoted here for optimum production. González (1987) reported which place the range of nicotinic acid used commercially in Spain in layer feed at between 2 and 25 mg/kg, and Villamide and Fraga (1999) give an average level of supplementation in Spain of 21.4 mg/kg niacin (CV= 33%).

There appears to be a certain amount of controversy with reference to the effect of niacin on egg cholesterol content. While Dikicioglu *et al.* (2000) state that egg cholesterol is reduced by supplementing with high levels of niacin ranging from 250 to 1500 ppm, Leeson *et al.* (1991) obtained no such results with 1022 ppm niacin.

PANTOTHENIC ACID

As a constituent of coenzyme A and of the carrier protein for acyl groups (ACP), pantothenic acid plays a fundamental role in fatty acid metabolism.

Requirements for this vitamin in laying hens stand at 2 mg/kg (NRC, 1994), with a great variation between individuals of the same breed or strain. Pantothenic acid requirements depends on interactions with other vitamins like vitamin C, biotin and vitamin B_{12}, as well as on the fat content of the ration. Low levels of vitamin B_{12} and high levels of fat increase requirements of pantothenic acid, while the presence of vitamin C could reduce requirements.

Some feed ingredients contain significant amounts of this vitamin, but cereal grains have a relatively low concentration.

The main damage caused by pantothenic acid deficiency involves the nervous system, adrenal insufficiency and the skin, and symptoms are unspecific: dermatosis, changes in feathers, reduction in productive yield. It was initially thought that a deficiency in this vitamin might not affect egg production but might reduce hatchability and embryo survival.

Beer *et al.* (1963), feeding White Leghorn pullets with purified diets concluded that these hens require a minimum of 1.9 ppm to optimize egg production, at least 4.0 ppm to maximize hatchability and 8 ppm to ensure viability of the chicks. Bootwalla and Harms (1991), in their study on minimum pantothenic acid requirements of Single Comb White Leghorn chicks, concluded that a minimum of 4.8 ppm in the diet is necessary to optimize sexual maturity and future performance.

Insufficient information is available to draw conclusions on the pantothenic acid requirements of layers. The requirement has not been re-evaluated for 20 years and, due to its relationship with energy metabolism, it should be adjusted according to the energy content of the diet. Studies on supplementation levels used in practice in Spain report levels ranging from 0 to 15 mg/kg (González, 1987) or average supplementation of 7.45 mg/kg (21% CV; Villamide and Fraga, 1999).

FOLACIN

The term folacin is used to describe a series of compounds derived from folic acid. There are many active biological forms of folates, which makes the amount present in feedstuffs difficult to evaluate. Principal food sources of folacin include leafy green vegetables and offal such as liver or kidneys.

In general terms, absorption of folates is less efficient than other vitamins.

In the body many enzymes use folic acid derivatives for single carbon atom transfer, such as methyl groups, methylene, methenyl, formin and formyl. Folates are necessary for purine and pyrimidine synthesis, glycine and serine interconversion, choline synthesis, histidine degradation and for conversion of homocysteine to methionine. Folate metabolism is entirely related to the metabolism of many other single carbon atom donors, including S-adenosylmethionine, serine, vitamin B_{12} and choline. These nutrients interact in such a way that their respective requirements may be changed. The nutritional importance of these interactions is greater for birds since they have a high rate of uric acid synthesis, a metabolic pathway which uses single carbon atoms from excreted nitrogen. Furthermore, requirements of methionine and cysteine are very high. Methionine is usually the first limiting amino acid, making other sources of methyl groups necessary.

Inadequate levels of other methyl group donors (serine, vitamin B_{12}, choline, etc.) therefore increase requirements, in the same way that high levels of protein in the diet increase requirements to above the recommended levels, due to the need to synthesize high quantities of uric acid for the excretion of nitrogen. Any circumstance affecting intestinal synthesis of folates by microorganisms will also affect requirements. Since they are synthesized by gut microflora, dietary requirements for folates are low (NRC in 1994, 0.25 mg/kg; ARC in 1984, 0.3 mg/kg). The relatively low absorption rate means a good tolerance of high levels of folate.

Sherwood et al. (1993) fed layers with a purified diet deficient in folates (0.07 mg/kg). This had a negative effect on egg production. By increasing the supplementation of folates, folate deposition in yolk and plasma reached saturation point. With 0.72 mg/kg folates in the diet the eggs contained somewhat less than half the maximum possible folate content in the yolk. The study by Keshavarz (2003b) used combinations of reduced supplies of methionine, choline, folic acid and vitamin B_{12} and obtained smaller eggs but improved shell quality the in the final phases of the laying period.

Studies by Hebert et al. (2005) and House et al. (2002) focus on the enrichment of folate in the egg. They used levels between 0 and 128 mg of folic acid per kg of feed and showed how the content in the egg responds to levels above 0.25 mg/kg up to deposit saturation. They observed no changes in production parameters but suggest strains differ in their folate requirements and that a reevaluation of the recommendations is important for highly productive birds.

Husseiny et al. (2008) showed that supplementation up 12 mg/kg diet with folic acid significantly increased egg weight (**Figure 12**). Given the recognized role of folic acid in cellular development, much research into folic acid requirements has been related to hatchability and embryo survival. Some studies even look at the effect of injecting folic acid directly into the egg. Objectives claimed in these studies exceed those of studies specifically on egg production.

The study carried out by Robel (1993) with breeding turkeys using a diet

Figure 12. Effect of dietary supplementation with different levels of folic acid on egg weight. (adapted from Husseiny et al. 2008.)

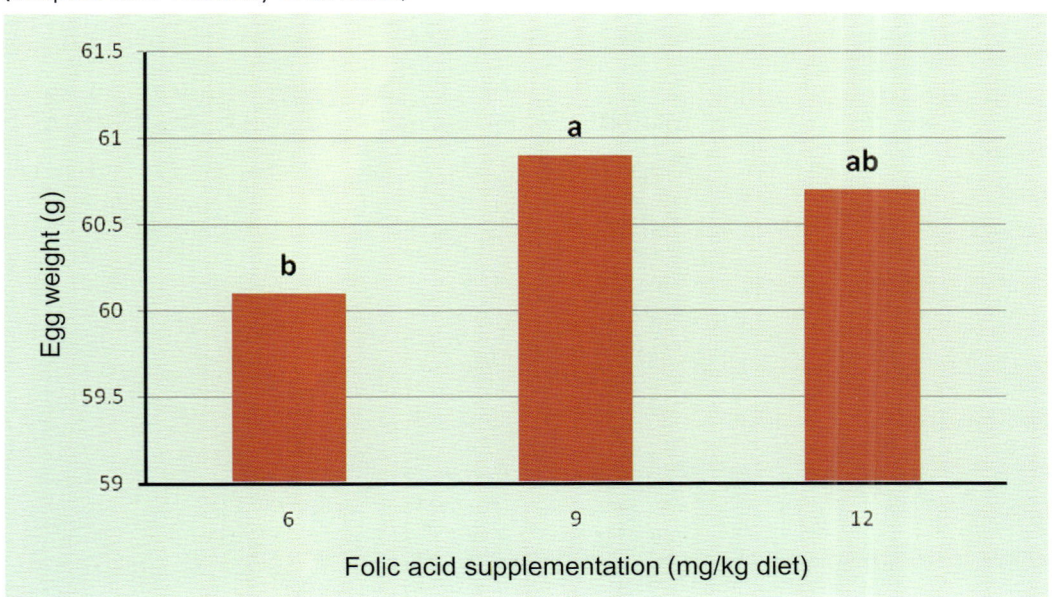

supplemented with 2.64 ppm and 5.51 ppm folic acid suggests that increasing the supplementation dosage above the 1 ppm established by the NRC (1984) as a minimum requirement for this species did not lead to improvements in hatchability of fertile eggs or embryo mortality, although a positive linear response to supplementation was observed in the transfer of folic acid to the egg, specifically the yolk. The production parameters studied did show effects of supplementation with folic acid: higher egg weight and higher bird weight for the 16 days of the experiment with a higher level of supplementation (5.51 vs. 2.64 ppm), the differences in both cases being statistically significant. No differences in the number of eggs produced by the turkey were noted as a result of supplementation.

In relation to egg folate enrichment, hens have the capacity to convert high doses of folic acid added to the feed into natural folates in their eggs (Bunchasak and Kachana, 2009; Hebert *et al.*, 2005; Hoey *et al.*, 2009; and House *et al.*, 2002) (**Figure 13**). It was possible to enhance the folate content of eggs 2-3 fold by feeding hens a folic acid supplemented diet. Folate-enriched eggs could offer consumers a practical means

of increasing folate intake and potentially protecting against disease without the safety concerns relating to folic acid – fortified foods (Ward, 2009b).

Since folic acid is essential to birds, dietry supplementation would probably bring similar benefits to breeding hens and layers, so it would appear prudent to increase dietary recommendations to 2-3 times the minimum established requirements. Liu and Feng (1992) suggested the need to review the minimum requirements established by the NRC in 1984 (0.25 mg/kg), since they observed that levels of 1.5 ppm folic acid increased productive yield in old hens.

González (1987) gives the range of folacin used commercially in Spain in layer feed as 0 to 0.5 mg/kg, and Villamide and Fraga (1999) report an average supplementation level in Spain of 0.32 mg/kg (CV= 80).

The data appears to show that, on a practical level, supplementation is at a somewhat higher level than that indicated by the NRC. Even so, they do not indicate achieving the level of supplementation of 1.5 ppm at which Liu and Feng (1992) observed improvements in production.

Figure 13:.The effect of 12 weeks of dietary treatment with added folic acid (0–32 mg/kg basal feed) on serum folate (µg/L) of laying hens. (adapted from Hoey *et al.* 2009.)

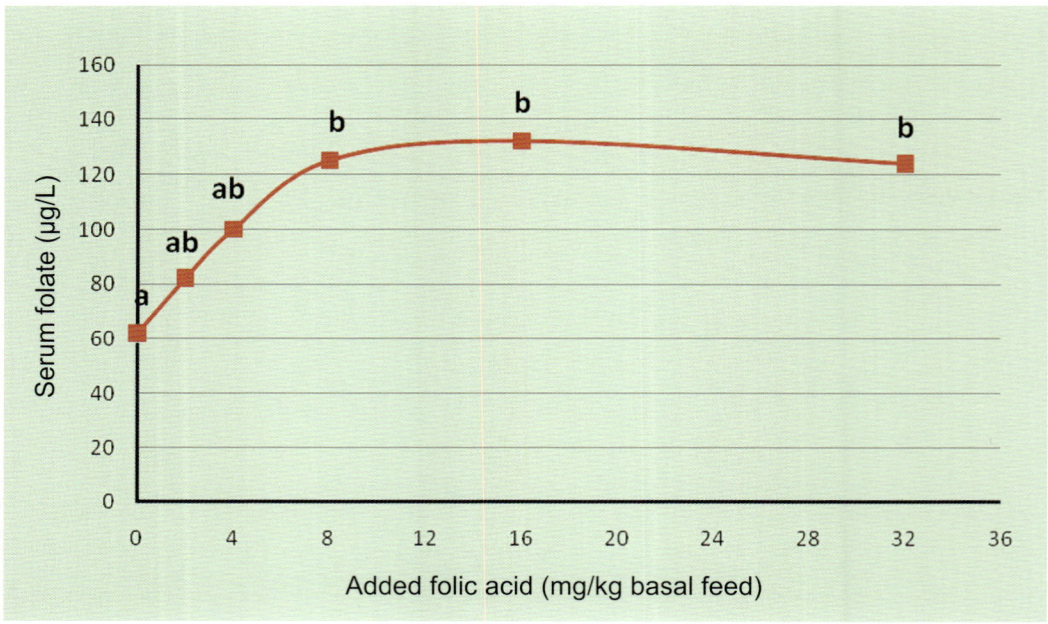

BIOTIN

Natural biotin is widely distributed in vegetable matter, animal tissue, seeds, yeast products and milk products. In sources of natural origin, biotin is bound to lysine or to other amino acids and its bioavailability varies between different feed products (**Table I**), in some of which it is of very limited practical use. In general, biotin from protein sources has greater bioavailability than biotin in most cereals.

The need to supplement biotin depends in part on the type of carbohydrates and fats in the diet and in part on the capacity for synthesis by microorganisms. As this synthesis diminishes, the need for supplementation increases. At the time of supplementation it must be considered whether the animal is able to practice coprophagy and whether there is avidin in the diet. Dietary biotin is absorbed as an intact molecule in the anterior intestine. If this part of the intestine is damaged, for example in cases of coccidiosis, absorption is compromized and therefore also the amount of biotin available to the animal, which is particularly damaging if the ration contains marginal levels of this vitamin. Where there is biotin deficiency, symptoms are non-specific but productive yields are reduced.

In the body, biotin is involved in carboxylation reactions, gluconeogenesis and protein synthesis. For this reason, it is considered essential for life, growth, maintenance of epidermal tissue and reproduction. Carboxylation reactions are important in fatty acid synthesis so biotin is necessary for the synthesis of long-chain fatty acids and for essential fatty acid metabolism.

Marginal levels of biotin may lead to the appearance of fatty liver or kidney syndrome, especially when there is a low level of fat in the diet and lipogenesis is necessary. This scenario may be aggravated by stress, since this drains glycogen reserves. Jensen *et al.* (1976) conducted a study to determine the effects of niacin, biotin or both together on the accumulation of lipids in the liver. They used a diet of maize and soy for 12 weeks, supplemented with 44 mg/kg niacin and/or 110 µg/kg biotin, and saw no changes in the weight of the liver or in lipid content. There were no significant differences in production parameters or body weight. It seems that biotin may prevent fatty liver syndrome but once signs have appeared, it does not seem to have beneficial effects on the accumulation of lipids in the liver. In a study by Whitehead *et al.* (1976), supplements of thiamine, riboflavin, nicotinic acid, pyridoxine, pantothenic acid, biotin, folic acid, vitamin B_{12}, ascorbic acid, choline and inositol were given separately or in combination to chicks. Of all of these, only biotin proved effective in preventing the occurrence of fatty liver or kidney syndrome. The supplementation levels required to prevent this condition were greater than those required to maximize the

Table I. Bioavailability (%) relating to D-biotin from different sources (Baker, 1995)

Source	Bioavailability	Source	Bioavailability
Alfalfa, meal	56	Rice, meal	23
Barley	26	Rye	0
Rapeseed, meal	64	Safflower, meal	32
Maize	100	Sorghum	26
Grass, meal	67	Sunflower, meal	95
Molasses, beet pulp	75	Triticale	6
Oats	37	Wheat, whole	17
Peanut, meal	53	Wheat, germ	55

live weight of the animal, being between 0-5 and 0-15 mg/kg, depending on the diet.

The level of biotin recommended by the NRC in 1994 is 0.1 mg/kg.

No recent literature has been found on studies carried out on layers into the possible repercussions on productive yield of supplementing biotin above requirements. In one study carried out on breeding turkeys (Horrox, 1998) it was found that supplementing with 500 µg/kg biotin increased egg production but it was reduced with 2000 µg/kg. Biotin concentration in the yolk remained stable while that in the albumen depended on the supply of biotin in the diet. Both effects were more marked in older birds, thus confirming that old layers need more biotin in their diet. On the other hand, young hens are less efficient than the older ones in transferring biotin to the yolk and for that reason they need higher supplementation to optimize hatchability (World Poultry, 2001). However, other studies have found a positive relationship between biotin levels in the diet and levels in the yolk (Buenrostro and Kratzer, 1984; Whitehead, 1984). Today's highly productive layers may benefit from biotin supplementation to maximize their productive capacity. González (1987) gives the range of biotin used commercially in Spain in layer feed as 0 to 0.03 mg/kg, and Villamide and Fraga (1999) report an average supplementation level in Spain of 0.016 mg/kg (CV= 96 %). Both of these are below the established requirements.

CHOLINE

Figure 14. Main funcions of Choline

Choline

- It is essential for building and maintaining cell structure
- It plays an important role in liver fat metabolism, preventing abnormal fat accumulation and promoting its transport from the liver as lecithin or by increasing fatty acid catabolism in the liver
- It is necessary for the synthesis of acetylcholine which is required for the transmission of nerve impulses
- It is involved in transmethylation reactions

Although it is an essential nutrient, strictly speaking choline should not be classed as a vitamin, since it is a structural component of fat and nervous tissue. This is why it is required in large amounts, generally more than other vitamins. Choline is also very important in laying hens for the formation of the phospholipid, lecithin, a component of egg yolk.

Choline is widely distributed among feedstuffs of both vegetable and animal origin, and is often found in combined form as a component of phospholipids. Soybean meal, fish meal, egg yolk, offal, vegetables, milk products and wholegrain cereals are all rich sources of choline. Levels shown in the NRC (1994) tables of the natural content of choline in raw foods must be used with caution as the bioavailability varies widely which could give rise to over-estimation of choline levels contained in the feedstuffs (Workel, 1998).

The NRC (1994) indicates a minimum requirement for layers of 1050 ppm choline. Its commercial form is choline chloride.

Birds are able to synthesize choline in the liver from methionine, an amino acid. The ability of animals to synthesize choline is insufficient to meet requirements in conditions of intensive production, however, even in diets with adequate levels of methionine. In diets poor in protein and/or with marginal levels of sulfur amino acids, both choline and methionine may become limiting.

Studies have been carried out to look at the effect of choline in the diet of layers. In most cases the purpose was to observe the response to supplementation of diets with different levels of protein or sulfur amino acids to determine the influence of choline levels on egg production. The results have varied widely.

Pourreza and Smith (1988) suggested that choline supplementation is more or less efficient depending on the dietary methionine content. That is to say, diets with low levels of sulfur amino acids increase the requirements for choline (Workel, 1998). Parsons and Leeper (1984) evaluated the addition of choline and methionine to layer feed containing differing levels of raw protein. They concluded that with crude protein levels of 13-15%, hens respond to supplementation of both nutrients, increasing egg production, feed conversion efficiency and egg weight, with a greater response to supplementation with methionine than with choline. However, with diets containing a crude protein level of 16%, the response to supplementation is not significant.

Likewise, Harms et al. (1990b) and Miles et al. (1986) observed that response to supplementation with respective levels of 660 ppm or 440 ppm choline was evident only in situations where there was a sulfur amino acid deficiency. In these studies, the weight of the egg correlated more to the methionine than to the choline level in the ration.

Tsiagbe et al. (1982) found that layers fed a diet based on maize-soy and meat meal had to be supplemented with choline to maximize production and egg weight. Choline requirements, in the absence of supplementary methionine, appear to be greater than 1000 but not more than 1500 ppm. Sljivovacki et al. (1988) tried different combinations of choline and methionine. When they combined 1100 ppm choline and 200 ppm methionine, egg production and feed intake increased, wheras no changes were observed in feed conversion. Schexnailder and Griffith (1973) found improvements in egg production and weight on supplementing 5 µg vitamin B_{12} and 850 mg choline to a diet containing a low or adequate level of protein and adequate methionine. Furthermore, this increase in production by supplementing choline was in addition to the increase obtained by giving vitamin B_{12} and methionine, thereby indicating that choline cannot be substituted by them. These authors also observed greater feed intake in layers supplemented with choline,

but they attribute this to the increase in production.

Vogt and Harnisch (1991) observed no benefits when supplementing choline levels between 386 and 1222 ppm. These authors concluded that choline content in the basal diet (325-386 ppm) is sufficient to meet requirements. Nesheim (1971) also found no response in production parameters when supplementing practical diets with choline. Only when the diet had been purified to contain very low levels of choline was there, in general, an improvement in production, gain in body weight and reduction in the fat content of the liver following supplementation. Furthermore, Nesheim stated that, based on the choline content of the egg, layers appear to be capable of synthesizing a considerable quantity of choline for egg production when they are fed diets free of choline.

In a study aimed at establishing whether the addition of choline, with or without inositol, could influence production parameters, it was observed that supplementing the basal diet with 660 and 1320 ppm choline chloride did not affect egg production but did improve egg weight and feed conversion efficiency (Couch and Grossie, 1970). Ruiz et al. (1983) concluded that layers of 50 weeks of age require very little choline supplementation when they are fed a diet of maize-soy with adequate levels of methionine.

Tsiagbe et al. (1988) carried out a study to determine the effect of adding choline and methionine to the diet on the egg yolk composition of phospholipids. They used a basal diet containing 976 ppm betaine (equimolar to 1000 ppm choline) and 250 ppm methionine, and this was supplemented with 500 or 1000 ppm choline, with methionine or with both combined. The yolk content of phospholipids and phosphatidylcholine increased significantly when supplementing with choline, while the content of phosphatidylethanolamine diminished during the peak of production (at 36 weeks of age). Furthermore they observed greater egg weight and yolk weight when the hen had been supplemented with 1000 ppm choline compared to the contol birds. The results demonstrate that the increase in egg weight which is seen when supplementing the ration with choline may be linked to changes in the yolk composition of phospholipids. However, Vogt and Harnisch (1991) observed no increase in the phosphatidylcholine content in the egg yolk on supplementing with choline.

Another important parameter when evaluating the addition of choline to the diet of layers is its effect on the reduction of excess fat deposited in the liver. This is due to the role of choline in fat metabolism, both in the utilization and in the transport of fat, thereby preventing abnormal accumulation of fat in the liver. Fatty infiltration of the liver is cited as a clinical sign of choline deficiency, caused by the inability of hepatocytes to export triglycerides and phospholipids, secondary to limited plasma lipoprotein biosynthesis. Phosphatidylcholine is an integral part of the structure of these lipoproteins and of the microsomial membranes which join them (Mookerjea, 1969). Phosphatidylcholine may be synthesized from preexisting choline molecules, via CDP cytidine diphosphocholine (Zeisel, 1981) or via transmethylase allowing de novo synthesis of choline (Blusztajn et al., 1979). March (1981) confirmed a significant reduction in the fat content of the liver when supplementing with 1000 ppm choline. However, March did not confirm that this was directly linked with the prevention of fatty liver, since he did not indicate how much fat in the liver was considered pathological and he did not see differences in the mortality rate between supplemented and unsupplemented hens, nor did he observe changes in production parameters.

The reduction in the fat content of the liver has been confirmed by various authors such as Mendonca et al. (1989) who conducted a study with laying hens of 63-64 days of age, giving them supplements with choline at 500, 1000, 1500 or 2000 ppm. After 4 periods of 28 days it was observed that with supplements of 1500 and 2000 ppm choline, fat deposition in the liver was reduced significantly and that there was a negative correlation between the level of choline in the diet and the total blood concentration of lipids. Similar results were obtained by

Schexnailder and Griffith (1973), who also confirmed that supplementing with choline may be particularly interesting in conditions of heat stress since the deposition of fat in liver increased significantly at higher temperatures.

A study by Armanious et al. (1973) touches on the usefulness of choline in cases of tannic acid toxicity as a result of using sorghum grain with a high tannin content in the diets of laying hens. By adding choline, the authors observed a reduction in the toxic effects of tannic acid such as a reduction in body weight, egg weight, egg production, feed intake and pimpling of the yolk. This beneficial effect of choline, as well as of methionine, confirms the hypothesis that tannic acid and tannins increase the requirements of methyl group donors.

This review leads to the conclusion that choline requirements of layers have not been established. Since choline is not expensive, it is recommended that it be added routinely to the vitamin-mineral premix to ensure that methionine be available for protein synthesis. When formulating metabolic requirements of methyl groups in terms of minimum cost it is better to meet them by way of supplementation with choline (118 mg/hen/day) than methionine (Workel, 1998).

Commercial recommendations for choline content in layer feed are between 1200-1400 mg/kg. Supplementation with choline chloride will depend on the quantity provided in the feed ingredients. Workel (1998) stated that, assuming an approximate dietary content of 1000 mg/kg choline, minimum supplementation should be from 251 to 500 ppm, within the range recommended by INRA (1984). González (1987) gives the range of choline used commercially in Spain in layer feed as 200 to 600 mg/kg, and Villamide and Fraga (1999) report an average supplementation level in Spain of 302 mg/kg (CV= 30).

VITAMIN C

Figure 15. Metabolic functions of Vitamin C.

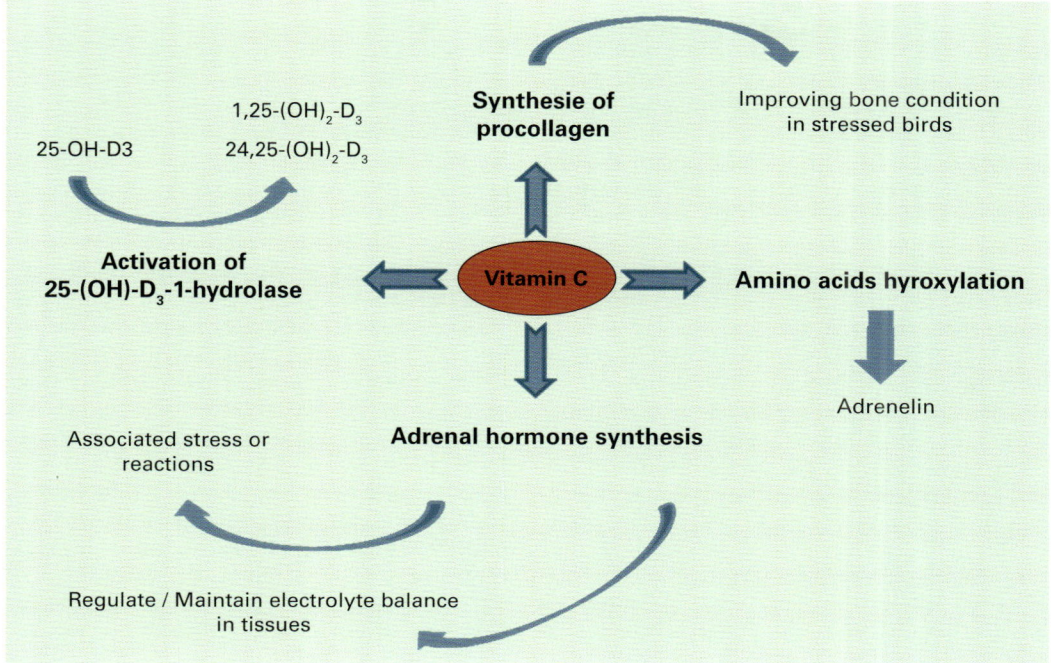

Vitamin C or ascorbic acid is synthesized by birds in the kidney, from glucose, and is not normally considered an essential nutrient. However, in some circumstances, particularly in situations of stress, requirements for this vitamin exceed the bird's capacity for synthesis. Studies have demonstrated beneficial effects of vitamin C supplementation in the diet of birds. The dietary supply of ascorbic acid reduces metabolic and physiological manifestations of stress and prevents negative consequences for production, immunological competence and well-being of birds. Reviews have been carried out by Pardue and Thaxton (1986) and Whitehead and Keller (2003).

Vitamin C is involved in different metabolic reactions which means it has important repercussions on the well-being and production of animals. It is involved in biosynthesis of calcitriol, having the role of regulating calcium homeostasis in the body, collagen and aldosterone. Aldosterone regulates and maintains the electrolytic balance of tissues. It has a preventive rather than reparative function.

Modern layer lines and intensive production lead to an increased demand for vitamin C, especially if there are additional situations of stress. Various results support the use of higher levels in the diets of the birds particularly in specific handling and environmental situations which may cause situations of stress.

Studies examining the influence of supplementation with vitamin C on production parameters have given conflicting results. Some authors (Bell and Marion, 1990; Cheng et al., 1990; Peebles et al., 1992) did not observe differences in egg production with feed supplementation levels from 0 to 400 ppm vitamin C, nor even with levels of 1000 ppm in feed or water (Keshavarz, 1996; Puthpongsiriporn et al., 2001).

However, other studies did find an improvement in production after supplementation with vitamin C. In a study carried out by Zapata and Gernat (1995), an increase in production of approximately 5% was observed on supplying 250 or 500 ppm vitamin C in feed compared to the unsupplemented control group. Where there was heat stress, the increase in egg production in supplemented hens was 20% higher than the unsupplemented hens, and this result appeared more quickly the greater the dosage. This is corroborated by other studies (Sahota and Gillani, 1995; Seven 2008; Sushil *et al.*, 1998a and 1998b) and in a review carried out by Kolb and Seehawer (2001). The authors concluded that at high ambient temperatures, supplementation with 100-300 ppm vitamin C improved production. Njoku and Nwazota (1989) found that at high temperatures, the inclusion of ascorbic acid improved egg production and the feed conversion index, and 400 ppm proved the most effective level of supplementation. A positive effect has been observed from the combined ingestion of vitamin C and vitamin E by hens subjected to low temperatures (6°C), improving production parameters and egg quality (Kucuk *et al.*, 2003).

With respect to egg weight, studies carried out by Balnave *et al.* (1991), Cheng *et al.* (1990), Keshavarz (1996), Khalafalla and Bessei (1996), Puthpongsiriporn *et al.* (2001) and Zapata and Gernat (1995) revealed no significant differences as a result of supplementing with ascorbic acid. On the other hand, Bell and Marion (1990) reported that supplementing with 400 ppm/kg feed slightly increased egg weight in comparison with the eggs of the unsupplemented hens. Abd-Ellah (1995) carried out a study on layers during summer months and observed that hens receiving feed supplemented with 250 or 500 ppm laid eggs significantly heavier than those receiving unsupplemented feed or feed supplemented at a level below 125 ppm. Orban *et al.* (1993) devised a study on layers of 76 or 96 weeks of age which received a diet supplemented with 0, 1000, 2000 or 3000 ppm for 4 weeks. Egg weight increased between 1 and 5% in the birds receiving 2000 or 3000 ppm vitamin C. These authors linked improvement in egg weight and density with the influence of vitamin C on calcium homeostasis. Other authors who also observed greater egg density when supplementing with ascorbic acid were Bell and Marion (1990) and Zapata and Gernat (1995). This improvement appears to be linked to an increase in

shell thickness. Thus, giving high levels of vitamin C would give rise to an increase in calcium deposition in the shell (Orban *et al.*, 1993).

Ascorbic acid at high dosages of 2000-3000 ppm (Orban *et al.*, 1993) may favor both intestinal absorption of calcium and bone reabsorption, which would result in an increase in the blood concentration of calcium, thereby improving bone mass of the bird and shell quality. Zapata and Gernat (1995) observed an improvement in shell quality when supplementing with 250-500 ppm vitamin C in feed, and this was corroborated by other studies (Ahmed *et al.*, 2008; Kassim and Norziha, 1995; Lin *et al.*, 1997; Oruwari *et al.*, 1995) (**Figure 16**). Sahin and Sahin (2002) showed that a combined supplementation with chromium (400 µg/kg) and vitamin C (250 mg/kg) may be a strategy for improving production in laying hens subjected to low temperatures (6.2°C). They demonstrate better mineral retention and a reduction in the excretion of nitrogen, calcium, zinc, iron and chromium. On the other hand, Keshavarz (1996) observed no effect on shell quality or on bone calcium content when supplementing hens exposed to temperatures within the thermoneutral range with 0, 250, 500 or 1000 ppm vitamin C. With respect to bone growth, supplementation with ascorbic acid (250-300 mg/kg) during the growth of layer pullets did not affect the formation and structure of the bones at 15 weeks of age (Fleming *et al.*, 1998) nor alter the volume of the medullary or trabecular bone at the end of laying (Rennie *et al.*, (1997).

Several studies (Abd-Ellah, 1995; Andrews *et al.*, 1987; Bell and Marion, 1990; Cheng *et al.*, 1988; Cheng *et al.*, 1990; Dzhambulatov *et al.*, 1996; Pardue *et al.*, 1984 and 1985) have confirmed that supplementing ascorbic acid during periods of heat stress, during molt or in old birds results in a significant reduction in mortality. Some studies indicate that vitamin C prevents increases in body temperature and it is suggested that it might increase heat loss in animals and their capacity for tolerating high temperatures. It is known that in layers over 40-45 weeks of age, biosynthesis of ascorbic acid is reduced. This is reflected in the low rate of calcitriol biosynthesis.

Figure 16. Effect of dietary supplementation with different levels of vitamin C on hen-housed egg production and egg weight. (adapted from Ahmed *et al.* 2008.)

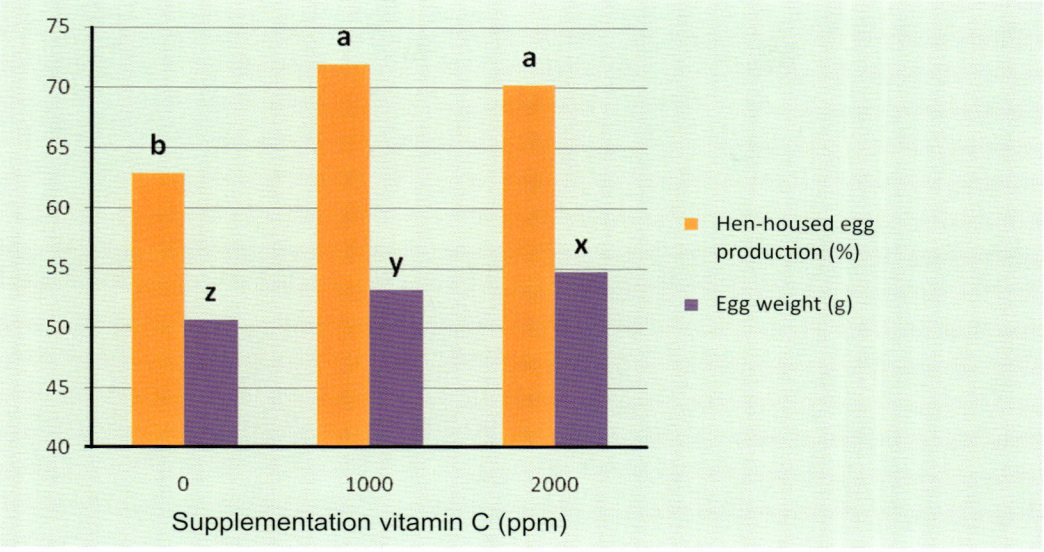

The hens were kept at high ambient environmental temperature (average of 34.5°C; range 28–42°C) throughout the experimental period of 12 weeks.

Ascorbic acid has a protective effect on macrophages during phagocytosis, thereby contributing to an improvement in cellular immune response. This vitamin is also necessary for regulation of corticosterone production during periods of environmental or immunological stress (Sahin and Önderci, 2002). In a recent review by Kolb and Seehawer (2001), supplementing 300 ppm vitamin C in the feed or 5000 ppm vitamin C in water 5 days before and after vaccination contributed to the stimulation of antibody formation, and supplementing 500 ppm vitamin C in feed increased immune response capacity in cases of infection or coccidiosis. On adding 1000 ppm to water administered 24 hours before transportation, vitamin C has an antistress effect. Layers that suffered high temperatures improved their egg weight and immune response thanks to supplementation with ascorbic acid (Lin *et al.*, 2003), and a greater response has also been observed in lymphocyte proliferation as a result of immune challenges on combining a supplementation of vitamin C with 65 mg/kg vitamin E (Puthpongsiriporn *et al.* (2001).

Some studies have looked at the capacity of ascorbic acid to mitigate the effects of ingesting toxic elements such as vanadium (Toussant and Latshaw, 1994). Balnave *et al.* (1991) carried out a study in which saline water was combined with supplementation of ascorbic acid (from 0.25 to 1 g/l) and concluded that vitamin C helps to reduce the damaging effect of saline water on shell quality, and that in these situations vitamin C is better as a preventive measure (Balnave and Zhang, 1992), since its therapeutic effect is more limited. Odabasi *et al.* (2006) show that supplementation with 100 ppm vitamin C is effective not only in preventing but also reversing pigment loss caused by an excess of vanadium in the diet of hens laying brown eggs.

In conclusion, laying hens under stress conditions, and specifically heat stress, respond positively to supplementation with ascorbic acid. Concentrations of vitamin C between 250 and 400 mg/kg result in an improvement in survival, feed consumption, production and egg quality. Doses between 1-2g of ascorbic acid per kg of feed or liter of drinking water is adequate to counteract the adverse effects on shell quality of consuming water with high salt concentrations.

NUTRITIONAL COMPOSITION OF EGGS

There is a great variation in data provided from different countries. (**Table III**) These differences are due in part to the methods of analysis but also to aspects of genetics, management and particularly feeding of the birds. The range of variation is especially evident in foods of a lipid nature and specifically in the fat-soluble vitamins which are clearly affected by their level of inclusion in diet. It has been demonstrated that for certain vitamins there is a direct relationship between the level of inclusion in rations and deposition in the egg.

FORTIFICATION

The purpose of the use of vitamins in animal feeds has moved from being exclusively to avoid deficiency symptoms toward playing an important role in the improvement of the quality of food of animal origin. Using high dosages of some vitamins leads to the fortification of these vitamins in eggs. This fortification allows diversification of the egg market and enables the production of products with added nutritional and commercial value.

Vitamins as a source of fortification are not the objective of this review. Data on this subject have been referred to in the different chapters. More detailed information on the subject can be found in the reviews by Naber (1993), Leeson (2007), Leeson and Caston (2003), Schiavone and Barroeta (2011), Sirri and Barroeta (2007), and Squires and Naber (1993b) which indicate the efficiency of transfer to the egg of different vitamins (**Table II**).

Table II. Classification of vitamins according to efficiency of relative transfer of food to egg. (Leeson, 2007; adapted from Naber, 1993b)

Efficiency of transfer	Vitamin
Low (5 to 10%)	Vitamin K Thiamine Folacin
Medium (15 to 25%)	Vitamin D_3 Vitamin E
High (40-50%)	Riboflavin Pantothenic Acid Biotin Vitamin B_{12}
Very high (60-80%)	Vitamin A

Table III. Nutritional composition of whole eggs in the US and different countries of the European Union (adapted from Seuss-Baum, 2011)

Composition per 100 g of edible portion	Spain 2008[1]	USDA 2009[2]	France 2008[3]	Germany 2009[4]	Italy 1997[5]	UK 2002[6]
Water (g)	76.9	75.84	75.6	74.09	77.1	75.2
Energy (kcal)	141	143	142	154	128	147
Proteins (g)	12.7	12.57	12.6	12.9	12.4	12.6
Carbohydrates (g)	0.68	0.78	0.8	0.7	-*	-
Lipids (g)	9.7	9.94	9.86	11.2	8.7	10.9
SFA (g)	2.8	3.1	2.64	3.33	3.17	3.1
MFA (g)	3.6	3.81	3.66	4.46	2.58	4.7
PUFA (g)	1.6	1.36	1.65	1.51	1.26	1.2
Cholesterol (mg)	410	423	378	396	371	-
Vitamin A (Retinol Eq.; µg)	227	140	179	278	225	190
Carotenoids (ß-carotene Eq.; µg)	10	-	-	-	-	-
Vitamin D (µg)	1.8	1.2	1.62	2.9	1.79	1.7
Vitamin E (α- tocopherol Eq.; mg)	1.9	1.51	1.42	2	1.11	1.1
Vitamin K (µg)	8.9	0.3	-	48	-	-
Thiamine B_1 (mg)	0.11	0.07	0.08	0.1	0.09	0.1
Riboflavin B_2 (mg)	0.37	0.48	0.46	0.3	0.3	-
Vitamin B_6 (mg)	0.12	0.14	0.13	0.12	0.12	0.12
Folate Eq. (µg)	51.2	47	45	65	50	50.4
Vitamin B_{12} (µg)	2.1	1.29	1.36	2	2.5	2.5
Niacin (mg)	3.3[a]	0.07	0.08	3.10[a]	0.1	3.80
Pantothenic acid (mg)	1.8	1.44	1.58	1.6	1.77	1.8
Biotin (µg)	20	-	-	25	20	19.4
Vitamin C (mg)	0	0	0	0	0	0
Calcium (mg)	56.2	53	72.4	56	48	56
Phosphorus (mg)	216	191	181	216	210	200
Iron (mg)	2.2	1.83	1.7	2.1	1.5	1.9
Iodine (µg)	12.7	-	38.3	10	53	52.3
Zinc (mg)	2	1.11	1.01	1.35	1.2	1.4
Magnesium (mg)	12.1	12	11.1	12	13	12
Sodium (mg)	144	140	125	144	137	140
Potassium (mg)	147	134	104	147	133	130
Copper (mg)	0.014	0.10	0.06	0.14	0.06	0.1
Selenium (µg)	10	31.7	13	-	5.8	11.6
Fluoride (µg)	0.11	1.1	-	0.11	-	-

SFA = saturated fatty acids, MFA = monounsaturated fatty acids, PUFA = polyunsaturated fatty acids
* Some databases or tables do not include all nutrients or values are not indicated.
(a) Niacin equivalents (niacin + tryptophan)
(1) Aparicio *et al.* 2008 Tabla de composición del huevo de gallina. In: 'Etiquetado Nutricional', Guía de etiquetado del huevo. Ed.: Instituto de Estudios del Huevo. Madrid, Spain. www.institutohuevo.com/
(2) USDA-National Nutrient Database for Standard Reference-Release 22 (2009), Nutrient Data Laboratory Home Page, http://www.ars.usda.gov/ba/bhnrc/ndl
(3) Composition nutritionnelle des aliments (2008), CIQUAL, AFSSA France
(4) BLS [Bundeslebensmittelschlüssel – Federal foodstuffs database (Germany)] – Version II.3 (2009)
(5) Tabelle di composizione degli alimenti – Istituto Nazionale della Nutrizione, Edra, Milan (1997)
(6) The Composition of Foods, Sixth summary edition Food Standards Agency (2002) McCance and Widdowson's. Cambridge:Royal Society of Chemistry

VITAMIN REQUIREMENTS AND RECOMMENDATIONS FOR LAYERS

Vitamin requirement values for layers established by the National Research Council and other official bodies are shown in **Table V**. The NRC points out that these figures do not allow for a safety margin and their purpose is clearly to avoid deficiency symptoms.

Unlike the previous edition of 1984, the more recent one (NRC, 1994) refers to hens producing brown eggs. Experimental findings are limited, but their requirements have been estimated to be 10% higher than those of layers producing white eggs, on the basis of greater body weight, higher feed intake and greater egg volume.

This new edition also indicates that there have been no published works on vitamin requirements to support a significant change as compared with the previous edition, with the exception of choline. In fact, minimum requirements of vitamins A, D_3, B_1, B_6 and pantothenic acid have been reduced, while those of vitamin B_2 and choline have been increased.

The scientific literature used to establish or estimate requirements is shown. As pointed out by Whitehead (1995, **Table IV**), studies on minimum requirements are old and have not been reviewed in the meantime, although, in some cases, new functions of the vitamins have been described. That is to say that, in many cases, previous values have been retained and it has not been possible to update them. The author concluded that in the case of pantothenic acid, thiamine and folic acid experimental evidence is of doubtful validity.

A study of recommendations by various official bodies, genetic companies and manufacturers of vitamins, and even the dosages used in commercial diets in Spain shows that levels are above requirements to include a safety margin (**Table V**). The recommendations for vitamin supplies are based on the premise of allowing the animal to express its maximum genetic potential, without limitations under practical conditions. The values recommended in practice are between 2 and 10 times higher than those recommended by the NRC (1994) which have remained practically unchanged for more than 30 years.

Multivitamin fortification has resulted in improvements in productive parameters, welfare and the quality of the eggs (Hatta, 2009; Zang et al. 2010a; Zang et al. 2010b).

Increased supplementation of vitamins is based on the specific reasons already outlined in the introduction to this study, of which the following are key factors:

- Vitamin requirements suggested by the NRC were established on the basis of criteria far removed from the current situation. They have not been reevaluated for more than 30 years, and have not been adapted for current strains, methods of production or qualitative demands of the market.

- Production conditions are not homogeneous and vitamin supplies in feed should be adapted to the different management conditions, keeping a safety

Table IV. Vitamin requirements of layers and degree of confidence in validity of the value (Whitehead, 1995)

A	D	E	K	B1	B2	B6	B12	Pantothenic Acid	Niacin	Biotin	Folic Acid	Choline
IU	IU	mg	mg	mg	mg	mg	µg	mg	mg	µg	mg	mg
3600	400	10	0.7	0.7	2.5	2	8	7	8	30	0.3	800
B2	B2	-	B3	C3	A1	B2	A1	C3	B3	A2	C3	B2

Confidence value: A: High,   B: Medium,   C: Low.

Relevance of data: 1: Based on research carried out within the last 10 years
                               2: Based on research carried out between 10 and 20 years ago.
                               3: Based upon research carried out more than 20 years ago,
                               4: Satisfactory research information not available, estimate only.

Table V. Vitamin requirements for laying hens (unit per kg of diet, 90% dry matter) established by different official bodies

	A	D_3	E	K3	B_1	B_2	B_6	B_{12}	Niacin	Pantothenic Acid	Folic Acid	Biotin	C	Choline
	IU	IU	mg	mg	mg	mg	mg	mg	mg	mg	mg	mg	mg	mg
NRC 1994 White/Brown-egg	3000	300	5	0.5	0.7	2.5	2.5	0.004	10	2	0.25	0.1	-	1050
NRC 1984 White/Brown-egg	4000	500	5	0.5	0.8	2.2	3.0	0.004	10	2.2	0.25	0.1	-	-
INRA 1984 (minimum requirements)	4000	500	-	-	0.8	3.8	4.5	0.003	10	10	0.35	0.15	-	-
ARC 1975 (minimum requirements)	2700	600	-	10	1.25	2.5	2.0	-	8.0	1.5	0.3	-	-	600
INRA 1984 (practical recommendations)	8000	1000	5	2	1.5	4.0	3.0	0.004		4	0	0	-	250
ARC 1975 (practical recommendations)	19000	3000	-	2.0	3.0	3.0	0	-	10.0	2.3	0.6	-	-	600

margin which ensures their availability to the animal. A number of factors may alter the animal's vitamin requirements and the supply of vitamins from feed.

- Strains of laying hens are evolving through genetic selection, and rates of growth, conformation, voluntary intake and production are all changing. This has repercussions on metabolic activity and on the bird's immune response. Vitamin requirements should be updated.

- Environmental situations such as high temperatures, the presence of infectious agents and other stress situations may make it difficult to achieve adequate vitamin intake as the requirements increase and the birds eat less.

- Information on the vitamin content of ingredients is limited and inexact, and moreover depends on availability. The processes to which feed is currently subjected, such as pelleting and extrusion, destroy vitamins to a greater or lesser degree. The loss in vitamin activity during the extrusion process is greatest for vitamins A, E, B_1 and C but it may also be significant for other vitamins (Schulde, 1986).

- Finally, the minimum requirements do not take into account objectives such as the well-being of birds, preventing the occurrence and development of pathological disorders, or improving the quality of eggs.

For breeding hens and broilers there are sufficient studies to indicate that increasing the vitamin level has beneficial effects, and this warrants consideration of an increase in vitamin requirements. However, for commercial egg layers, there is a lack of recent data and a need for work on this issue, especially towards reevaluating the vitamin requirements in today's highly productive strains.

Table VI. Recommended vitamin levels (IU or mg kg air-dry feed) for laying hens by principal genetic companies and other sources

	Source / Units	ISA Brown (2010)	Hy-Line (2010)	Lohman (2009)	Villamide and Fraga (1999)[1]	FEDNA (2008)	Leeson and Summers (2005)	DSM OVN (2011)	Maximum level in literature	Reference
Vitamin A	IU	10000	8800	10000	9300	8000-10000	8000	8000-12000	12000	Lin et al., 2002: better immune response in heat stress
Vitamin D3	IU	2500	3300	2500	2160	2000-3000	3500	3000-4000	3500; 6000; 15000	Faria et al. 1999; Mattila 2004: improved bone strenght in laying hens
25-OH-D3 (HyD)	mg	-	0.055	-	-	-	-	0.069	0.069	Terry et al., 1999: improved egg production
Vitamin E	IU	20	16.5	10-30	7.6	8-20	50	20-30[2]	500	Bollingier et al., 1998: reduced effect of chronic heat stress
Vitamin K	mg	3.0	2.2	3.0	1.4	1.4-2.1	3	2.5-3	10	Fleming et al., 1998 and 2003: improved bone strength in layers and pullets
Vitamin B1	mg	2.0	1.7	1.0	0.9	0.4-1.5	2	2-2.5	1.25	Padhi and Combs 1965: better productive performance
Vitamin B2	mg	5.0	5.5	4.0	3.9	4-6	5	5-7	8.8	Squires and Naber, 1993b: improved production and reduced blood spots in breeders
Vitamin B6	mg	5.0	3.3	3.0	1.6	1.5-3	3	3.5-5	6	Weiser et al., 1991: prevention of bone deformities
Vitamin B12	mg	0.015	0.022	0.015	0.012	0.009-0.015	0.01	0.015-0.025	0.036	Akhmeddkanove et al., 1997: optimal production in heat stress
Niacin	mg	40	28	30	21.4	18-35	40	30-50	250-1550	Dikicioglu et al., 2000: better shell quality and feed conversion; lower cholesterol in yolk
D-Panthothenic acid	mg	12	6.5	8	7.45	7-10	10	8-12	-	-
Folic acid	mg	0.75	0.6	0.5	0.31	0.2-0.6	1	1-1.5	1.5	Liu and feng, 1992: improved performance in old hens
Biotin	mg	0.05	0.055	0.025	0.02	0.035-0.08	0.1	0.1-0.15	-	-
Vitamin C	mg	100	-	-	-	-	-	100-200[3]	2000	Orban et al.,1993: improved bone and shell mineralization
Choline	mg	1400	110	400	247	150-250	400	300-500	1500-2000	Mendoca et al., 1989: reduced fat deposition in liver

(1) Average vitamin supplementation in laying hens by Spanish industry
(2) Under heat stress conditions increase level up to 200 mg/kg
(3) Recommended under heat stress conditions; use phosphorylated form in heat treated feeds

REFERENCES

Abas, I., R. Kahraman, H. Eseceli and N. Toker. 2008. The effect of high levels of folic acid on performance and egg quality of laying hens fed on diets with and without ascorbic acid from 28-36 weeks of age. *Journal of Animal and Veterinary Advances.* 7, 389-395.

Abd-Ellah, A. M. 1995. Effect of ascorbic acid supplementation on performance of laying hens during hot summer months. *Assiut Veterinary Medical Journal.* 34, 83–95.

Abend, R., H. Jeroch & A. Hennig. 1975. Studies on the influence of various vitamin B_6 uptake in the hen on the nutrient content of liver, pectoral muscle, total body and egg. *Arch Tierernahr.* 25, 565–573.

Ahmed, W., S. Ahmad, Ahsan-ul-haq and Z. Kamran. 2008. Response of laying hens to vitamin C supplementation through drinking water under sub-tropical conditions. *Avian Biology Research.* v.1, 59-63.

Akhmedkhanova, R. R. & A. M. Alisheikhov. 1997. Use of vitamins C and B_{12} under laying hens heat stress. *11th European Symposium on poultry nutrition.*

Alderman, J., R. Pasternak, F. Sachs, H. Smith, E. Monrad & W. Grossmann. 1989. Effect of a modified, well-tolerated niacin regimen on serum total cholesterol, high density lipoprotein cholesterol and the cholesterol to high density lipoprotein ratio. *Am J Cardiol.* 64, 725–729.

Aljamal, A. A., M. K. Masa'deh and S. E. Scheideler. 2008. Vitamin E and selenium supplementation in laying hens. *Poultry Sci.* 87 (Suppl. 1).

Andrews, D., W. Berry and J. Brake. 1987. Effect of lighting program and nutrition on reproductive performance of molted single comb white leghorn hens. *Poultry Sci.* 66, 1298–1305.

Angela,S, G. Flachowsky G. and Schubert R, 1999, Effects of high vitamin E dosage on the concentration of various lipid soluble substances in the organism of laying hens. 7th Symposium Jena-Thuringen, 403–406.

Aparicio, A., A. C. Barroeta, A. M. López-Sobaler and R. M. Ortega. 2008. Tabla de composición del huevo de gallina. In: 'Etiquetado Nutricional', *Guía de etiquetado del huevo.* Ed.: Instituto de Estudios del Huevo. Madrid, Spain. www.institutohuevo.com/

ARC, 1975, 1984, *The nutrient requirements of farm livestock* no. 1. Poultry. Agricultural Research Council. London.

Arijeniwa, A., I. Ikhimioya, O. K. Bamidele & B. K. Ogunmodede. 1996. Riboflavin requirement of breeding hens in a humid tropical environment. *J Appl Animal Research.* 10, 163–166.

Armanious, M., W. Britton & H. Fuller. 1973. Effect of methionine and choline and tannic acid and tannin toxicity in the laying hen. *Poultry Sci.* 52, 2160–2168.

Bains, B. 1999. *A guide to the application of vitamins in commercial poultry feed.* Rath Design Communications, Australia.

Baker, D. 1995. *Bioavailability of nutrients for animals: Vitamin bioavailability.* Ammerman, C. B., Baker, D. H., Lewis, A. J. (eds). Academic Press, San Diego, 399–431.

Balnave, D., D. Zhang and R. Moreng, 1991, Use of ascorbic acid to prevent the decline in eggshell quality observed with saline drinking water. *Poultry Sci.* 70, 848–852.

Balnave, D. and D. Zhang. 1992. Responses in eggshell quality from dietary ascorbic acid supplementation of hens receiving saline drinking water. *Australian Journal of Agricultural Research.* v.43, p.1259–1264.

Bartov, I.,Y. Weisman and E. Wax. 1991. Effects of high concentrations of dietary vitamin E and ethoxyquin on the performance of laying hens. *British Poultry Sci.* 32, 525–534.

Beer, A., M. L. Scott and M. Nesheim. 1963. The effects of graded levels of pantothenic acid on the breeding performance of White Leghorn pullets. *British Poultry Sci.* 3, 243–253.

Bell, D.E. and J. E. Marion. 1990. Vitamin C in laying hen diets. *Poultry Sci.* 69, 1900–1904.

Bermudez, A., M. Swayne, M. W. Squires and M. Radin. 1992. Effect of vitamin A deficiency on the reproductive system of mature White Leghorn hens. *Avian Diss.* 37, 274–283.

Blair, R., N. Daghir, H. Morimoti, V. Peter and T. Taylor. 1983. *Nutr Abs Rev.* 53, 669.

BLS (Bundeslebensmittelschlüssel – Federal foodstuffs database). 2009. version II.3, Germany.

Blusztajn, J., S. Zeisel and R. Wurtman. 1979. Synthesis of lecithin (phosphatidylcholine) from phosphatidylethanolamine in bovine brain. *Brain Res.* 179, 319–327.

Bollengier-Lee S., M. A. Mitchell, D. B. Utomo, P. E. V Williams and C. C. Whitehead. 1998. Influence of high dietary vitamin E supplementation on egg production and plasma characteristics in hens subjected to heat stress. *Br Poult Sci.* 39, 106–112.

Bollengier-Lee S., P. E. Williams and C. C. Whitehead. 1999. Optimal dietary concentration of vitamin E for alleviating the effect of heat stress on egg production in laying hens. *Br Poult Sci.* 40, 102–107.

Botsoglou, N., P. Florou-Paneri, E. Botsoglou, V. Dotas, I. Giannenas, A. Koidis and P. Mitrakos. 2005. The effect of feeding rosemary, oregano, saffron and alpha-tocopheryl acetate on hen performance and oxidative stability of eggs. *South African Journal of Animal Sci.* 35, 143–151.

Bootwalla, S. and R. Harms. 1991. Reassessment of pantothenic acid requirement for Single Comb White Leghorn pullets from 0 to 6 weeks of age and its subsequent effect on sexual maturity. *Poultry Sci.* 70, 80–84.

Buentrostro, J. and F. Kratzer. 1984. Use of plasma and egg yolk biotin of white Leghorn hens to asses biotin availability from feedstuffs. *Poultry Sci.* 63, 1563–1570.

Bunchasak, C. and S. Kachana. 2009. Dietary folate and vitamin B_{12} supplementation and consequent vitamin deposition in chicken eggs. *Trop Animal Health Prod.* v.41, 1583-1589.

Chen, J. Y., J. D. Latshaw, H. O. Lee and D. B. Min. 1998. α-tocopherol content and oxidative stability of egg yolk as related to dietary α-tocopherol. *J of Food Sci.* 63, 919–922.

Cheng, T., C. Coon and M. Hamre. 1988. Effect of vitamin C and environmental stress on layer performance. *Poultry Sci.* 67, 67.

Cheng, T., C. Coon and M. Hamre. 1990. Effect of environmental stress on the ascorbic acid requirement of laying hens. *Poultry Sci.* 69, 774–780.

Chennaiah, S., S. S. Y. H. Qadri, S. V. R. Rao, G. Shyamsunder and N. Raghuramulu. 2004. Cestrum diurnum leaf as a source of 1,25(OH)(2) vitamin D-3 improves egg shell thickness. *Journal of Steroid Biochemistry and Molecular Biology.* 89–90, 589–594.

Cherian, G., F. H. Wolfe and J. S. Sim. 1996a. Feeding dietary oils with tocopherols: effects on internal qualities of eggs during storage. *J of Food Sci.* 61, 15–18.

Cherian, G., F. W. Wolfe and J. S. Sim. 1996b. Dietary oils with added tocopherols: effects on egg or tissue tocopherols, fatty acids, and oxidative stability. *Poultry Sci.* 75, 423–431.

CIQUAL (Center informatique sur la Qualité des aliments). 2008. *Composition nutritionnelle des aliments.* Table Ciqual, AFSSA

Cortinas, L., J. Galobart, A. C. Barroeta, M. D. Baucells and M. A. Grashorn. 2001. Alpha-tocopherol content and lipid oxidation in fresh, cooked and scrambled eggs enriched with omega-3 fatty acids. 13th European Symposium of Poultry nutrition, Oct 2001, Blankenberge Belgium. 68–69.

Coskun, B., F. Inal, I. Celik, O. Erganis, A. M. Tiftik, F. Kurtoglu, Y. Kuyucuoglu and U. Ok. 1998. Effects of dietary levels of vitamin A on the egg yield and immune responses of laying hens. *Poultry Sci.* 77, 542–546.

Couch, J. and B. Grossie. 1970. Choline and inositol in laying hen nutrition. *Poultry Sci.* 49, 1731–1733.

Denton, C., W. Kellogg, J. Sizemore and R. Lillie. 1954. Effect of injecting and feeding vitamin B_{12} to hens on content of the vitamin in the egg and blood. *J of Nutrition.* 54, 517–577.

Dikicioglu, T., A. A. Yigit and E. Ozdemir. 2000. The effects of niacin on egg production and egg quality. *Lalahan Hayvancilik Arastirma Enstitusu Dergisi.* 40, 65–74.

Dzhambulatov, M. M., P. I. Viktorov, A. M. Alisheikhov and R. R. Akhmedkhanova. 1996. Setting norms for vitamins C and B_{12} in feeds for laying hens and broiler chickens subjected to heat stress. *Russian Agricultural Sciences.* 10, 14–16.

Fan, S., Y. Han, R. Li, S. J. Fan, Y. W. Han and R. W. Li. 1998. Effect of adding anti-oxidative micronutrients to the diets on the performance of layers exposed to high ambient temperature. *Chinese Journal of Veterinary Science.* 18, 606–610.

Faria, D. E., O. M. Junqueira, P. A. Souza, M. R. Mazalli and D. Salvador. 1999. Influence of different levels of vitamins D and C and age of laying hens on performance and egg quality. 1 – summer. *Revista Brasileira de Ciencia Avicola.* 1, 193–201.

FEDNA (Fundación Española para el Desarrollo de la Nutrición Animal). 2008. Necesidades nutricionales para avicultura: pollos de carne y aves de puesta. Lázaro, R. Y. y Mateos, G. G. Ediciones Peninsular S.L. Madrid

Fleming, R. H., H. A. McCormack and C. C. Whitehead. 1998. Bone structure and strength at different ages in laying hens and effects of dietary particulate limestone, vitamin K and ascorbic acid. *Br Poultry Sci.* 39, 434–440.

Fleming, R. H., H. A. McCornmack, L. Mc Teir and C. C. Whitehead. 2003. Effects of dietary particulate limestone, vitamin K_3 and fluoride and photostimulation on skeletal morphology and osteoporosis in laying hens. *Br Poultry Sci.* 44, 683–689.

Flores, G. W. and S. Scholtyssek. 2001. Effect of levels of riboflavin in the diet on the reproductivity of layer breeding stocks: Proceedings, 19th World's Poultry Congress, Amsterdam, Netherlands, 19 24 September 1992, 622.

Florou-Paneri, P., D. Dotas, I. Mitsopoulos, V. Dotas E. Botsoglou, I. Nikolakakis and N. Botsoglou. 2006. Effect of feeding rosemary and alpha-tocopheryl acetate on hen performance and egg quality. *Journal of Poultry Sci.* 43, 143–149.

Fraga, M. J., C. de Blas and G. G. Mateos. 1991. Alimentación mineral y vitamínica de la gallina ponedora: Nutrición y alimentación de gallinas ponedoras: Ed. Mundi-Prensa, Madrid, 174–185.

Friedman, A., A. Meidovsky, G. Leitner and D. Sklan. 1991. Decreased resistance and immune response to Escherichia coli infection in chicks with low or high intakes of vitamin A. *J of Nutrition.* 121, 395–400.

Friedman A. and D. Sklan 1989. Impaired T lymphocyte immune response in vitamin A depleted rats and chicks. *Br J Nutr.* 62, 439–449.

Frigg, M., C. C. Whitehead and S. Weber. 1992. Absence of effects of dietary alpha-tocopherol on egg yolk pigmentation. *Br Poultry Sci.* 33, 347–353.

Froning, G. 2001. Vitamin E dietary supplementation improves egg quality of eggs from heat stressed hens. *Egg industry.* November 2001, 20.

Frost, T. J., D. A. S. Roland and G. G. Untawale. 1990. Influence of vitamin D3, 1alpha-hydroxyvitamin D3, and 1,25-dihydroxyvitamin D3 on eggshell quality, tibia strength, and various production parameters in commercial laying hens: *Poultry Sci.* 69, 2008–2016.

Frost, T. J., S. Roland and D. Marple. 1991. Effects of various dietary phosphorus levels on plasma 1,25-(OH)2D3, ionized and total calcium, and phosphorusin commercial leghorns: *Poultry Sci.* 70, 1570.

Galobart, J., A. C. Barroeta, M. D. Baucells and F. Guardiola. 2001a. Lipid oxidation in fresh and spray-dried eggs enriched with omega-3 and omega-6-polyunsaturated fatty acids during storage as affected by dietary vitamin E and canthaxanthin supplementation. *Poultry Sci.* 80, 327–337.

Galobart, J., A. C. Barroeta, M. D. Baucells, R. Codony and W. Ternes. 2001b. Effect on dietary supplementation with rosemary extract and α-tocopheryl acetate on lipid oxidation in eggs enriched with omega-3-fatty acids. *Poultry Sci.* 80, 460–467.

Galobart, J., A. C. Barroeta, M. D. Baucells, L. Cortinas and F. Guardiola. 2001c. α-Tocopherol transfer efficiency and lipid oxidation in fresh and spray-dried eggs enriched with omega-3-polyunsaturated fatty acids during storage. *Poultry Sci.* 80, 1496–1505.

Gonzalez Mateos, G. 1987. Nutrición y alimentación del ganado: Ed. Mundi-Prensa. Madrid.

Goodson-Williams, R., D. Roland and J. McGuire. 1986. Effects of feeding graded levels of vitamin D3 on egg shell pimpling in aged hens. *Poultry Sci.* 65, 1556–1560.

Grashorn, M. A. and S. Steinhilber. 1999. Effect of dietary fat with different relations between omega-6 and omega-3 fatty acids on egg quality: Proceedings of the VIII European Symposium on the Quality of Eggs and Egg Products. Bologna, Italy. 95-100.

Grobas, S., J. Mendez, C. Lopez Bote, C. De Blas and G. G. Mateos. 2002. Effect of vitamin E and A supplementation on egg yolk α-tocopherol concentration. *Poultry Sci.* 81, 376–381.

Harms, R. H., H. R. Wilson and R. D. Miles. 1988. influence of 1,25-Dihydroxyvitamin D3 on the performance of commercial laying hens. *Poultry Sci.* 67, 1233–1235.

Harms, R. H., S. M. Bootwalla, S. A. Woodward, H. R. Wilson and G. A. Untawale. 1990a. Some observations on the influence of vitamin D metabolites when added to the diet of commercial laying hens. *Poultry Sci.* 69, 426–432.

Harms, R. H., N. Ruiz and R. D. Miles. 1990b. Research note: Conditions necessary for a response by the commercial laying hen to supplemental choline and sulfate. *Poultry Sci.* 69, 1226–1229.

Hatta, H., N. Hamada, M. Nishii, T. Hayakawa and J.M. Hernández. 2009. Effects of enriched multi-vitamin & canthaxanthin combination on performance of laying hens & egg quality. *European Symposium on Poultry Nutrition, Scotland.*

Hebert, K., J. D. House and W. Guenter. 2005. Effect of dietary folic acid supplementation on egg folate content and the performance and folate status of two strains of laying hens. *Poultry Sci.* 84 1533–1538.

Hill, F., M. L. Scott, L. Norris and G. Heuser. 1961. Reinvestigation of the vitamin A requirements of laying and breeding hens and their progeny. *Poultry Sci.* 40, 1245–1254.

Hoehler, D. and R. R. Marquardt. 1996. Influence of vitamins E and C on the toxic effects of ochratoxin A and T-2 toxin in chicks. *Poultry Sci.* 75, 1508–1515.

Hoey, L., H. McNulty, E. M. E. McCann, K. J. McCracken, J. M. Scott, B. B. Marc, A. M. Molloy, C. Graham and K. Pentieva. 2009. Laying hens can convert high doses of folic acid added to the feed into natural folates in eggs providing a novel source of food folate. *Br J Nutr.* 101, 206–212.

Horrox, N. 1998. Biotin - the breeder booster. *International Hatchery Practice.* 12, 7–8.

House, J. D., K. Braun, D. M. Ballance, C. P. O'Connor and W. Guenter. 2002. The enrichment of eggs with folic acid through supplementation of the laying hen diet. *Poultry Sci.* 81, 1332–1337.

Hupfauer, M. 1993. Effect of vitamins C and B_6 and various vitamin D_2 and D_3 metabolites on laying performance and egg shell quality in old layers. Ludwig Maximilians Universität München , Germany, 117 pp.

Husseiny El O.M., A. Z. Soliman, I. I. Omara, H. M. R. El-Sherif. 2008. Evaluation of dietary methionine, folic acid and cyanocobalamin (B12) and their interactions in laying hen performance: *International J. of Poultry Sci.* 7, 461-469.

INRA (Institut scientifique de Recherche Agronomique). 1985. Alimentación de animales monogástricos. Mundi-Prensa. Madrid.

Istituto Nazionale della Nutrizione. 1997. Tabelle di composizione degli alimenti, Edra Milan, Italy

Jackson, M. 1992. Feeding layers: nutritional considerations: Multi-State Poultry Meeting.

Jensen, L. S., C. Chang and D. Maurice. 1976. Effect of biotin and niacin on lipid content of livers in the laying hen. *Poultry Sci.* 55, 1771–1773.

Jiang, Y., R. McGeachin and C. Bailey. 1994. Alpha-tcopherol, beta-carotene, and retinol enrichment of chicken eggs. *Poultry Sci.* 73, 1137–1143.

Kassim, H. and I. Norziha. 1995. Effects of ascorbic acid (vitamin C) supplementation in layer and broiler diets in the tropics. *Asian-Australasian Journal of Animal Science* 8, 607–610.

Kaya, S., H. Umucalilar, S. Haliloglu and H. Ipek. 2001. Dietary vitamin A and Zinc on egg yield and some blood parameters of laying hens. Proc. Symposium on Egg and egg products quality, Kusadasi-Turkey.

Keshavarz, K. 1996. The effect of different levels of vitamin C and cholecalciferol with adequate or marginal levels of dietary calcium on performance and eggshell quality of laying hens. *Poultry Sci.* 75, 1227–1235.

Keshavarz, K. 2003a. A comparison between cholecalciferol and 25-OH-cholecalciferol on performance and eggshell quality of hens fed different levels of calcium and phosphorus. *Poultry Sci.* 82, 1415–1422.

Keshavarz, K., 2003b. Effects of Reducing Dietary Protein, Methionine, Choline, Folic Acid, and Vitamin B12 During the Late Stages of the Egg Production Cycle on Performance and Eggshell Quality. *Poultry Sci.* 82, 1407–1414.

Keshavarz, K. and S. Nakajima. 1993. Re-evaluation of calcium and phosphorous requirements of laying hens for optimum performance and eggshell quality. *Poultry Sci.* 72, 144–153.

Khalafalla, M. K. and W. Bessei. 1997. Effect of ascorbic acid supplementation on egg shell quality of laying hens receiving saline drinking water. *Archiv fur Geflugelkunde.* 61, 172–175.

Kirichenko, A. 1991. Proportion of group

B vitamins in diets for table hens. *Ptitsevodstvo.* 5, 13–14.

Kirunda, D., S. E. Scheideler and R. Mckee. 2001. The efficacy of vitamin E (DL-alpha-tocopheryl acetate) supplementation in hen diets to alleviate egg quality deterioration associated with temperature exposure. *Poultry Sci.* 80, 1378–1383.

Klaising, K. 1998. Comparative avian nutrition: CAB International, 277–229.

Kolb, E. and J. Seehawer. 2001. Significance and application of ascorbic acid in poultry. *Archiv fur Geflugelkunde.* 65, 106–113.

Koreleski, J. and S. Swiatkiewicz. 2005. Efficacy of different levels of a cholecalciferol 25-OH-derivative in diets with two limestone forms in laying hen nutrition. *Journal of Animal and Feed Sciences.* 14, 305–315.

Kucuk, O., N. Sahin, K. Sahin, M. F. Gursu, F. Gulcu, M. Ozcelik and M. Issi. 2003. Egg production, egg quality, and lipid peroxidation status in laying hens maintained at a low ambient temperature (6 degrees C) and fed a vitamin C and vitamin E-supplemented diet. *Veterinarni Medicina.* 48, 33–40.

Kucuk, O., A. Kahraman, I. Kart, N. Yildiz and A. C. Onmaz. 2008. A combination of zinc and pyridoxine supplementation to the diet of laying hens improves performance and egg quality. *Biol Trace Elem Res.* 126, 165–175.

Kucukersan, S. 2000. The effect of niacin added to the laying hen rations on egg production and egg quality with some blood metabolites. Ankara *Universitesi Veteriner Fakultesi Dergisi.* 47, 201–212.

Lavelle, P. A., Q. P. Lloyd, C. V. Gay and R. M. Leach. 1994. Vitamin K deficiency does not functionally impair skeletal metabolism of laying hens and their progeny. *J of Nutrition.* 124, 371–377.

Leclercq, B., J. C. Blum, B. Sauveur and P. Stevens. 1987. Nutrition of laying hens: Feeding of non-ruminant livestock, Wiseman, J (ed.), Butterworths, 78–85.

Leeson, S. 2007. Vitamin requirements: is there basis for re-evaluating dietary specifications. *World's Poultry Science Journal.* 63, 255–266.

Leeson, S., L. J. Caston and J. D. Summers. 1991. Response of laying hens to supplemental niacin. *Poultry Sci.* 70, 1231–1235.

Leeson, S. and L. J. Caston. 2003. Vitamin enrichment of eggs. *Journal of Applied Poultry Research.* 12, 24–26.

Leeson, S. and J. D. Summers. 2005. Commercial poultry nutrition. Nottingham University Press.

Leeson, S. and J. D. Summers. 2008. Commercial poultry nutrition-3. Nottingham University Press.

Li, S. X., G. Cherian and J. S. Sim. 1996. Cholesterol oxidation in egg yolk powder during storage and heating as affected by dietary oils and tocopherol. *J of Food Sci.* 61, 721–725.

Lin, P., J. Lu, P. H. Lin and J. J. Lu. 1997. The effects of different dietary nutrients levels and ascorbic acid supplementations on performances, egg shell quality and blood parameter of laying hens in a hot season in Taiwan. *Journal of the Chinese Society of Animal Sci.* 26, 395–408.

Lin, H., L. F. Wang, J. L. Song, Y. M. Xie, Q. M. Yang. 2002. Effect of dietary supplemental levels of vitamin A on the egg production and immune responses of heat-stressed laying hens. *Poultry Sci.* 81, 458–465.

Lin, H., J. Buyse, Q. K. Sheng, Y. M. Xie and J. L. Song. 2003. Effects of ascorbic acid supplementation on the immune function and laying hen performance of heat-stressed laying hens. *Journal of Feed, Agriculture and Environment.* 1, 103–107.

Liu, A. and L. Feng. 1992. Effect of supplementation of folic acid, ascorbic acid and cyanocobalamin on the performance of layers. *Ningxia Journal of Agro-Forestry Science and Technology.* 6, 40–42.

Lohmann, 2007. Lohmann brown-classic. Layer management guide. http://www.lohmanngb.co.uk/lohmann-brown.pdf

Lohmann, 2009. Lohmann brown-classic. Layer management guide. http://www.hastavuk.com.tr/en/kitapciklar_en/0/brown.pdf

Manoukas, A., R. Ringrose and A. Terri. 1968. The availability of niacin in corn, soybean meal and wheat middlings for the hen. *Poultry Sci.* 47, 1836–1842.

March, B. 1981. Choline supplementation of layer diets containing soybean meal or rapeseed meal as protein supplement. *Poultry Sci.* 60, 823.

Mattila, P., K. Lehikoinen, T. Kiiskinen and V. Piironen. 1999. Cholecalciferol and 25-hydroxycholecalciferol content of chicken egg yolk as affected by the cholecalciferol content of feed. *J Agric*

Food Chem. 47, 4089–4092.

Mattila, P., J. Valaja, L. Rossow, E. Venalainen and T. Tupasela. 2004. Effect of vitamin D-2- and D-3-enriched diets on egg vitamin D content, production, and bird condition during an entire production period. *Poultry Sci.* 83, 433–440,

McDowell, L. 1989a. Vitamins in animal nutrition, comparative aspects to human nutrition. Cunha, TJ (ed.), Academic Press, Inc.

McDowell, L. 1989b. Vitamin supplementation is critical part of good animal nutrition. *Feedstuffs* 16, 15–31.

McDowell, L. 2000. Vitamins in animal and human nutrition, 2nd edition: Iowa State University Press.

McDowell, L. & Nelson. 2008. Optimum vitamin nutrition for poultry. *International Poultry Production.* 16, 27–34.

Meluzzi, A., F. Sirri, N. Tallarico and L. Vandi. 1999. Dietary vitamin E in producing eggs enriched with n-3 fatty acids. 2: Egg and egg products quality, VIII European symposium on the quality of egg and egg products, Bologna, Italy.

Mendonca, C. X. J., E. M. Guerra and C. A. Oliveria. 1989. Choline supplementation in Hisex Brown and Hisex White laying hens. 2. Deposition of lipids in liver and lipids in plasma: *Revista da Faculdade de Medicina Veterinaria e Zootecnia da Universidade de Sao Paulo.* 26, 93–103.

Miles, R. D., N. Ruiz and R. H. Harms. 1986. Response of laying hens to choline when fed practical diets of supplemental sulfur amino acids. *Poultry Sci.* 65, 1760–1764.

Mills, C., E. Cottingham and E. Taylor. 1947. The influence of environmental temperature on dietary requirement for thiamine, pyridoxine, nicotinic acid, folic acid and choline in chicks. *American Journal of Physiology.* 149, 376–379.

McCance & Widdowson's. 2002. The composition of foods, 6th summary edition. Food Standards Agency. Royal Society of Chemistry, Cambridge, UK.

Mookerjea, S. 1969. Studies on the plasma glycoprotein synthesis by isolated perfused liver: Effect of early choline deficiency. *Can.J. Biochemistry.* 47, 125–133.

Mori, A. V., C. X. Mendonca, C. R. M. Almeida and M. C. G. Pita. 2003. Supplementing hen diets with vitamins A and E affects egg yolk retinol and alpha-tocopherol levels.

Journal of Applied Poultry Research. 12, 106–114.

Müller, J. I., A. E. Murakami, C. Scapinello, I. Moreira and E. Varela. 2009. Effect of vitamin K on bone integrity and eggshell quality of white hen at the final phase of the laying cycle. *Revista Brasileira de Zootecnia.* 38, 488-492.

Naber, E. 1993. Modifying vitamin composition of eggs: a review. *J of Appl Poultry Research.* 2, 385–93.

Naber, E. C. and M. W. Squires. 1993a. Vitamin profiles of eggs as indicators of nutritional status in the laying hen: diet to egg transfer and commercial flock survey. *Poultry Sci.* 72, 1046–1053.

Naber, E. C. and M. W. Squires. 1993b. Research note: early detection of the absence of a vitamin premix in layer diets by egg albumen riboflavin analysis. *Poultry Sci.* 72 1989–1993.

National Research Council. 1987. Vitamin tolerance of animals.

National Research Council. 1994. Nutrient Requirements for Poultry. [9th edition].

Neri, M. 2000. Use of 25-0H-D3 in fowl diets. *Rivista di Avicoltura.* 69, 16–19.

Nesheim, M., M. Norvell, E. Ceballos and R. Leach. 1971. The effect of choline supplementation of diets for growing pullets and laying hens. *Poultry Sci.* 50, 820–831.

Newbrey, J. W., S. T. Truitt, D. A. Roland, T. J. Frost and G. G. Untawale. 1992. Bone histomorphometry in 1,25(OH)2D3- and vitamin D3-treated aged laying hens. *Avian Diss.* 36, 700–706.

Newman, S. and S. Leeson. 1999. The effect of dietary supplementation with 1,25-dihydroxycholecalciferol or vitamin C on the characteristics of the tibia of older laying hens. *Poultry Sci.* 78, 85–90.

Njoku, P. and O. Nwazota. 1989. Effects of dietary inclusion of ascorbic acid on the performance of laying hens in a tropical enviroment. *Br Poultry Sci.* 30, 831–845.

North, M. 1984. Commercial chicken production manual. AVI Publ.Co., Inc. Westport, CT.

Odabasi, A. Z., R. D. Miles, M. O. Balaban, K. M. Portier and V. Sampath. 2006. Vitamin C overcomes the detrimental effect of vanadium on brown eggshell pigmentation. *J Appl. Poult Res.* 15, 425–432.

Onwudike, O. and A. Adegbola. 1984.

Riboflavin requirement of laying hens for egg production and reproduction in the humid tropics. *Trop Agric.* 61, 205–207.

Orban, J., D. A. Roland, K. Cummins and R. Lovell. 1993. Influence of large doses of ascorbic acid on performance, plasma calcium, bone characteristics, and eggshell quality in broilers and Leghorn hens. *Poultry Sci.* 72, 691–700.

Oruwari, B. M., O. O. Mbere and B. T. Sese. 1995. Ascorbic acid as a supplement for Babcock hen in a tropical condition. *Journal of Applied Animal Research.* 8, 121–128.

Ouart, M., R. H. Harms and H. R. Wilson. 1987. Effect of graded levels of niacin in corn-soy and wheat-soy diets on laying hens. *Poultry Sci.* 66, 467–470.

Padhi, P. and G. Combs. 1965. Effect of dietary thiamine intake on red blood cell transkelotase activity in laying hens. *Poultry Sci.* 44, 1405.

Panda, A. K., S. V. Ramarao, M. V. L. N. Raju and R. N. Chatterjee. 2008. Effect of dietary supplementation with vitamins E and C on production performance, immune responses and antioxidant status of White Leghorn layers under tropical summer conditions. *Br Poultry Sci.* 49, p.592-599.

Pardue, S. L., J. P. Thaxton, J. Brake. 1984. Plasma ascorbid acid concentration following ascorbic acid loading in chicks. *Poultry Sci.* 63, 2496.

Pardue, S. L., J. P. Thaxton and J. Brake. 1985. Influence of supplemental ascorbic acid on broiler performance following exposure to high temperature. *Poultry Sci.* 64, 1338.

Pardue, S. L. and J. P. Thaxton. 1986. Ascorbic acid in poultry. *World's Poultry Science j.* 42, 107–123.

Parsons, C. and R. Leeper. 1984. Choline and methionine supplementation of layer diets varying in protein content. *Poultry Sci.* 63, 1604–1609.

Peebles, E. D., E. H. Miller, J. D. Brake and C. D. Schultz. 1992. Effects of ascorbic-acid on plasma thyroxine concentrations and eggshell quality of Leghorn chickens treated with dietary thiouracile. *Poultry Sci.* 71 553–559.

Pourreza, J. and W. Smith. 1988. Performance of laying hens fed on low sulfur amino acids diets supplemented with choline and methionine. *Br Poultry Sci.* 29, 605–611.

Puthpongsiriporn, U., S. E. Scheideler, J. Sell,

M. Beck. 2001. Effects of vitamin E and C supplementation on performance, in vitro lymphocyte proliferation, and antioxidant status of laying hens during heat stress. *Poultry Sci.* 80, 1190–1200.

Qi, G. H. and J. S. Sim. 1998. Natural tocopherol enrichment and its effect in n-3 fatty acid modified chicken eggs. *J of Agricultural and Food Chemistry.* 46, 1920–1926.

Rennie, J. S., R. H. Fleming, H. A. McCormack, C. C. McCorquodale and C. C. Whitehead. 1997. Studies of nutritional factors on bone structure and osteoporosis in laying hens. *Br Poultry Sci.* 38, 417–424.

Richter, G., I. Rodel, E. Wunderlich, E. Marckwardt. 1985. Evaluation of laying-hen feed with varied vitamin E and antioxidant supplementation. *Arch Tierernahr.* 35, 707–714.

Richter, G., E. Marckwardt, A. Hennig, G. Steinbach. 1986. Vitamin E requirements of laying hens. *Arch Tierernahr.* 36, 1133–1143.

Richter, G., A. Lemser, G. Jahreis, G. Steinbach. 1987. Vitamin E requirement of chicks and young hens. *Arch Tierernahr.* 37, 1029–1039.

Richter, G., A. Hennig and H. Jeroch. 1989. The vitamin A supply of laying hens including during rearing. 1. Testing of mixed feed with a varied vitamin A supplementation in chicks and young hens. *Arch Tierernahr.* 39, 1053–1064.

Richter, G., E. Sitte and M. Petzold. 1990. The vitamin A supply of laying hens including during rearing. 2. Effect of varied vitamin A supplementation of mixed feed in rearing on production in the laying period. *Arch Tierernahr.* 40, 221–227.

Richter, G., A. Lemser, E. Sitte, C. Ludke, G. ed Flachowsky, F. ed Schone and A. Hennig. 1991. Vitamin A requirements of chicks, young and laying hens: RefType: Personal Comunication.

Richter, G. 1995. Incorporation and mobilization of vitamin A in laying hens. *Arch Tierernahr.* 48, 337–345.

Richter, G., A. Lemser, C. Ludke, G. Steinbach and P. Mockel. 1996a. Studies on the vitamin A requirements and recommendations for laying hens. *Archiv fur Geflugelkunde.* 60, 174–180.

Richter, G., A. Lemser, G. Jahreis, U. Wanka, M. Matthey, K. Schubert and G. Steinbach. 1996b. Studies in vitamin A requirement and recommendations for chicken and pullets. *Archiv fur Geflugelkunde.* 60, 193–202.

Richter, G., A. Lemser and J. Bargholz. 1996c. Is vitamin A supply of laying hens sufficient?: *Muhle + Mischfuttertechnik.* 133, 49–50.

Ringrose, R., A. Manoukas, R. Hinkson and A. Terri. 1965. The niacin requirement of the hen. *Poultry Sci.* 44, 1053–1065.

Robel, E. 1993. Evaluation of egg injection of folic acid and effect of supplemental folic acid on hatchability and poult weight. *Poultry Sci.* 546–553.

Ruiz, N., R. D. Miles, H. R. Wilson and R. H. Harms. 1983. Choline supplementation in the diets of aged White Leghorn hens grouped according to body weight. *Poultry Sci.* 62, 1028–1032.

Sahin, K. and N. Sahin. 2002. Effects of chromium picolinate and ascorbic acid dietary supplementation on nitrogen and mineral excretion of laying hens reared in a low ambient temperature (7 degrees C). *Acta Veterinaria Brno.* 71, 183–189.

Sahin, K. and M. Önderci. 2002. Optimal dietary concentrations of vitamin C and chromium for alleviating the effect of low ambient temperature on serum insulin, corticosterone, and some blood metabolites in laying hens. *Journal of Trace Elements in Experimental Medicine.* 15, 153–161.

Sahota, A. W. and A. H. Gillani. 1995. Effect of ascorbic acid supplementation on performance and cost of production in layers maintained under high ambient temperatures. *Pakistan Veterinary Journal.* 15, 155-158.

Sashidhar, F., K. Jaya Rao and B. Narasinga Rao. 1988. Effect of dietary aflatoxins on tryptophan-niacin metabolism. *Nutr Rep Int.* 37, 515–521.

Scheideler S. E. and G. W. Froning. 1996. The combined influence of dietary flaxseed variety, level, form and storage conditions on egg production and composition among vitamin E-supplemented hens. *Poultry Sci.* 75, 1221–1226.

Schexnailder, R. and M. Griffith. 1973. Liver fat and egg production of laying hens as influenced by choline and other nutrients. *Poultry Sci.* 52, 1188–1194.

Schiavone, A. and A. C. Barroeta. 2011. Egg enrichment in vitamins and minerals. In: Improving egg and egg product safety

and quality, Chapter 15 volume 2. Eds: Y. Nys, M. Bain, F. Van Immerseel. Woodhead Publishing Ltd., UK.

Schulde, M. 1986. Extrusion technology for the food industry: The stability of vitamin in extrusion cooking, in: O'Connor, C. (ed.), Elsevier Applied Science, London, 22–23.

Scott, M. L., M. Nesheim and R. Young. 1982. Nutrition of the chicken. Scott, M. L. and Associates, Ithaca, NY.

Seemann, S. 1992. Effect on laying performance and egg shell quality of vitamin C and 1, 25-dihydroxivitamin D3 in old layers. Ludwing Maximilians Universität München, Germany.

Seven, P. T. 2008. The effects of dietary Turkish propolis and vitamin C on performance, digestibility, egg production and egg quality in laying hens under different environmental temperatures. *Asian-Australasian Journal of Animal Sciences.* 21, 1164-1170.

Shen, H., J. Summers and S. Leeson. 1981. Egg production and shell quality of layers fed various levels of vitamin D3. *Poultry Sci.* 60, 1485–1490.

Sherwood, T., R. Alphin, W. Saylor and H. White. 1993. Folate metabolism and deposition in eggs by laying hens. *Arch Biochem Biophys.* 15, 66–72.

Sirri, F. and A. Barroeta. 2007. Enrichment in Vitamin, in Bioactive Egg Compounds, Editores: Houpalahti *et al.* Springer-Verlag Berlin Heidelberg.

Skinner, J., J. Quisenberry and J. Couch. 1951. High efficiency and APF concentrates in the ration of the laying fowl. *Poultry Sci.* 30, 319–324.

Sklan, D., D. Melamed and A. Friedman. 1994. The effect of varying levels of dietary vitamin A on immune response in the chick. *Poultry Sci.* 73, 843–847.

Sljivovacki, K., Z. Jokic and D. Popov. 1988. Effect of the concentration of methionine and choline in the diet on productive performance of laying hens. *Veterinarski Glasnik.* 42, 315–321.

Soares, J. H., M. Ottinger and E. Buss. 1988. Potential role of 1,25 dihydroxicholecalciferol in egg shell calcification. *Poultry Sci.* 67, 1322–1328.

Soares, J. H., J. Kerr and R. Gray. 1995. 25-hydroxycholecalciferol in poultry nutrition. *Poultry Sci.* 74, 1919–1934.

Squires, M. W. and E. C. Naber. 1992. Vitamin

profiles of eggs as indicators of nutritional status in the laying hen: vitamin B$_{12}$ study. *Poultry Sci.* 71, 2075–2082.

Squires, M. W. and E. C. Naber. 1993a. Vitamin profiles of eggs as indicators of nutritional status in the laying hen: vitamin A study. *Poultry Sci.* 72, 154–164.

Squires, M. W. and E. C. Naber. 1993b. Vitamin profiles of eggs as indicators of nutritional status in the laying hen: riboflavin study. *Poultry Sci.* 72, 483–494.

Suess-Baum, I., H. Fulda, F. Nau and C. Guérin-Dubiard. 2011. The nutritional quality of eggs, chapter 11 volume 2. Eds: Y. Nys, M. Bain, F. Van Immerseel. Woodhead Publishing Ltd., UK.

Surai, P. F., I. A. Ionov and N. Buzhina. 1995. Vitamin E and egg quality: Egg and egg products quality, proceedings of the VI European symposium on the quality of eggs and egg products, Zaragoza, Spain, 387–394.

Sushil, P., C. K. Aggarwal and S. K. Chopra. 1998a. Effect of feeding anti-stress agents on the performance of egg type pullets housed in cages during summer. *Indian Journal of Poultry Sci.* 33, 1–7.

Sushil, P., C. K. Aggarwal and S. K. Chopra. 1998b. Effect of supplementation of anti-stress agents in the ration on egg quality of pullets during summer. *Indian Journal of Animal Sci.* 68, 667–668.

Suzuki, Y. and M. Okamoto. 1997. Production of hen's eggs rich in vitamin K. *Nutrition Research.* 17, 1607–1615.

Terry, M., M. Lanenga, J. L. McNaughton and L. E. Stark. 1999. Safety of 25-hydroxyvitamin D3 as a source of vitamin D3 in layer poultry feed. *Veterinary and Human Toxicology.* 41, 312–316.

Toussant, M. and J. Latshaw. 1994. Evidence of multiple metabolic routes in vanadium's effects on layers. Ascorbic acid differential effects on prepeak egg production parameters following prolonged vanadium feeding. *Poultry Sci.* 73, 1572–1580.

Tsang, C. 1992. Calcitriol reduces egg breakage. *Poultry Sci.* 71, 215–217

Tsang, C., A. Grunder, J. H. Soares and R. Narbaitz. 1990a. Effect of 1-alpha,25-dihydroxycholecalciferol on egg shell quality and egg production. *Br Poultry Sci.* 31, 241–247.

Tsang, C., A. Grunder and R. Narbaitz. 1990b. Optimal dietary level of 1-alpha, 25-dihydroxycholecalciferol for eggshell quality in laying hens. *Poultry Sci.* 69, 1702–1712.

Tsang, C. and N. Daghir. 1990c. Research note: The effect of 1-alpha ,25-dihydroxyvitamin D3 added to a layer diet containing adequate amounts of vitamin D3 on the performance of layers. *Poultry Sci.* 69, 1822–1825.

Tsang, C. and A. Grunder. 1993. Effect of dietary contents of cholecalciferol, 1 alpha,25-dihydroxycholecalciferol and 24,25-dihydroxycholecalciferol on blood concentrations of 25-dihydroxycholecalciferol, 1a,25-dihydroxycholecalciferol, total calcium and eggshell quality. *Br Poultry Sci.* 34, 1021–1027.

Tsiagbe, V., C. Kang and M. Sunde. 1982. The effect of choline supplementation in growing pullet and laying hen diets. *Poultry Sci.* 61, 2064.

Tsiagbe, V., M. Cook, A. Harper and M. Sunde. 1988. Alterations in phospholipid of egg yolks from laying hens fed choline and methionine-supplemented diets. *Poultry Sci.* 67, 1717–1724.

U.S. Department of Agriculture, Agricultural Research Service. 2009. National Nutrient Database for Standard Reference. Release 22.

Utomo, D. B., M. A. Mitchell and C. C. Whitehead. 1994. Effects of α-tocopherol supplementation on plasma egg yolk precursor concentrations in laying hens exposed to heat stress. *Br Poultry Sci.* 35, 828.

Villamide, M. J. and M. J. Fraga. 1999. Composition of vitamin supplements in Spanish poultry diets. *Br Poult Sci.* 40, 644–652.

Vogt, H. and S. Harnisch. 1991. Choline in layer diets. *Archiv fur Geflugelkunde.* 55, 236–240.

Wahle, K. W. J., P. P. Hoppe and G. McIntosh. 1993. Effects of storage and various intrinsic vitamin E concentrations on lipid oxidation in dried egg powders. *J Science of Food and Agriculture.* 61, 463–469.

Wang, L. F., H. Lin and Q. M. Yang. 2002. The effect of inoculated and heat-stressed laying hens. *Acta Veterinaria et Zootechnica Sinica.* 33, 443–447.

Ward N. E. 2009a. Potential vitamin D role in eggs explored. *Feedstuffs* 81, 1-2.

Ward, N. E. 2009b. Folate-fortified eggs have niche. *Feedstuffs*. 81, 1-3.

Weber, G. M. 2009. Improvement of flock productivity through supply of vitamins for higher laying performance and better egg quality. *World's Poultry Science Journal*. 65, 443-458.

Weiser, H., M. Schlachter, H. P. Probst, G. Flachowsky and F. Schone. 1991. Importance of vitamins D_3, C and B_6 for bone metabolism. Friedrich Schiller Universität Jena Germany. Vitamine und weitere Zusatzstoffe bei Mensch und Tier. 3. Symposium, Jena, 26–27.

Weiss, F. and M. Scott. 1979. Influence of vitamin B_6 upon reproduction and upon plasma and egg cholesterol in chickens. *J Nutrition*. 109, 1010–1017.

West, J., C. Carrick, S. Hauge and E. Mertz. 1952. The tryptophan requirement of young chickens as influenced by niacin. *Poultry Sci*. 31, 479–487.

Whitehead C. C. *et al*. 1976. The involvement of biotin in preventing the Fatty Liver and Kidney Syndrome in chicks. *Research in Veterinary Sci*. 20, 180–184.

Whitehead, C. C. 1984. Biotin intake and transfer to the egg and chick in broiler breeder hens on litter cages. *Br Poultry Sci*. 25, 287–292.

Whitehead, C.C. 1995. Current knowledge on vitamin requirements of poultry: World's Poultry Science Association Proceedings, 10th European Symposium on poultry nutrition.

Whitehead, C. C. 1998. The influence of vitamins on the performance and health status of laying hens and turkeys. Multi-State Poultry meeting.

Whitehead, C. C. 2001. Nicotinic acid in poultry nutrition. *Feed Mix*. 9.

Whitehead, C. C. 2004. Overview of bone biology in the egg-laying hen. *Poultry Sci*. 83, 193–199.

Whitehead, C. C. and T. Keller. 2003. An update on ascorbic acid in poultry. *Worlds Poultry Science Journal*. 59, 161–184.

Witzum, J. 1989. Current approaches to drug therapy for the hyper-cholesterolemic patient. *Circulation*. 80, 1101–1114.

Workel, H.,T. Keller, A. Reeve and A. Lauwaerts. 1998. Choline - the rediscovered vitamin: *World poultry magazine on production processing and marketing*. 14, 22–25.

World Poultry-Elsevier. 2001. Vitamins. World poultry, magazine on production processing and marketing special 2001.

Zang H., K. Zhang, X. Ding, J.M. Hernández and D. Yao. 2010a. Effects of dietary vitamin level on the laying performance of laying hens. *International Scientific Poultry Forum. Atlanta*.

Zang H., K. Zhang, X. Ding, J.M. Hernández and D. Yao. 2010b. Effects of dietary vitamin level on the egg quality and vitamin contents in egg of laying hens. *International Poultry Forum. Atlanta*.

Zapata, L. and A. Gernat. 1995. The effect of four levels of ascorbic acid and two levels of calcium on eggshell quality. *Poultry Sci*. 74, 1049–1052.

Zeisel, S. 1981. Dietary choline: Biochemistry, physiology and pharmacology. *Annu Rev Nutr*. 1, 95–121.

OPTIMUM VITAMIN NUTRITION IN BROILERS AND TURKEYS

R. Cepero Briz and A. Blanco Pérez
Department of Animal Production and Food Science
Faculty of Veterinary Science. University of Zaragoza, Spain

139

INTRODUCTION

Vitamins were once regarded as "unknown growth factors," and were mostly discovered in the course of the 20th century. The quantities of vitamins required are very small, but they are essential for tissue integrity, normal development of organic functions, and the maintenance of health. Their physiological and metabolic roles are very varied and of great importance, as they are involved in many biochemical reactions and they take part in the metabolism of the nutrients derived from the digestion of carbohydrates, lipids and proteins. A single vitamin may have several different functions, and many interactions between them are known.

Broiler and turkey feed should be supplemented with vitamins as the primary materials do not contain them in sufficient quantities, and (apart from vitamin C) the birds are either unable to synthesize them, or do so in very limited quantities (B group, K_2), most of which are excreted in any case. An animal's body is able to store some vitamins, principally in the liver (A, D_3, B_{12}, and to a lesser extent E and K_3). Vitamin deficiencies produce non-specific signs of illness (loss of appetite, retarded growth, defective plumage, rise in mortality) as well as specific signs, amply described in the basic literature on poultry pathology and nutrition (Scott et al., 1982; Klasing, 1998; Austic and Scott, 2000; Leeson and Summers, 2001), among which neurological disorders are prominent (Burgos et al., 2006). **Table I** summarizes the active forms and most important functions of vitamins, as well as the symptoms of vitamin deficiency.

VITAMIN REQUIREMENTS: CONCEPT AND DEFINITION

Vitamins can almost never be regarded as nutrients in isolation because they display a wide variety of interactions with each other and also with other nutrients (Bains, 1999). The fat-soluble vitamins compete for intestinal absorption, with the result that an excess of one may cause deficiencies of the others: this has frequently been observed when employing very high levels of vitamin A. The vitamins of the B group are regulators of intermediary metabolism, and some of the metabolic processes are independent: For example choline, B_{12} and folic acid interact in the metabolism of the methyl groups, so that a lack of one of them increases the requirement for the others, and the same thing happens between B_{12} and pantothenic acid. It may also happen that an excess of one vitamin induces a deficiency of others; thus, biotin status deteriorates if the diet is supplemented with choline and other vitamins of the B group. High choline levels may have a similar effect on other vitamins during the storage of feed.

Vitamins are also known to interact in various ways with other nutrients, such as amino acids. For example, there is a notable genetic variability in birds' capacity to synthesize nicotinic acid from tryptophan, so that their requirements differ between strains. Both methionine and choline can be a source of methyl groups, which are needed to synthesize both of them, and this relationship is of commercial importance because supplementation incurs an economic cost. Other vitamins (biotin, folic acid and B_6) play a part in metabolic interconversions of amino acids, so that the requirement for them increases if protein levels are high. The same applies to those vitamins which play a role in the metabolism of carbohydrates (biotin, B_1), the requirements for which are higher with low-fat diets. Finally, there are also interactions between minerals and vitamins, the best documented being that between selenium and vitamin E.

All this makes it somewhat difficult to estimate precisely the requirements for each vitamin separately, and it is probably more appropriate to focus on the problem generally.

Whitehead (1987) gives a clear explanation of the situation. The classic evaluation of the dose-response curve, so widely used to estimate the requirements of other nutrients, is not an appropriate technique in the case of vitamins, as their cost is generally low in

Table I. Vitamins: active forms, summary of functions and signs of deficiency

	Natural forms	Commercial forms	Function	Deficiency symptoms
Vitamin A	A_1 = Retinol or Retinal	Vitamin A_1 acetate and palmitate	Vision Steroid synthesis Epithelialization	Severely retarded growth Blindness Skin problems Higher susceptibility to infections
	A_2 = 3-Dehydroretinal	Retinal on protective/hydrodispersible support		
Vitamin D	D_2 = Ergocalciferol	Vitamin D_2	Absorption and fixing of calcium. D_2 shows no activity in birds	Rickets Osteomalacia
	D_3 = Cholecalciferol	Vitamin D_3 free or fixed on protective/hydrodispersible support		
Vitamin E	α-Tocopherol	DL-α-Tocopherol	Antioxidant Stimulates defenses at 20 times its minimum requirements	Muscular dystrophy Exudative diathesis Encephalomalacia
	α-Tocopherol	dl-α-tocopherol acetate		
Vitamin K	K_1 = Phylloquinone	K_1	Anticoagulant	Hemorrhages Anemia
	K_2 = Menaquinone	K_3 = menadione		
Vitamin B_1	Thiamine (aneurine)	Thiamine hydrochloride	Sugar degradation	Chick polyneuritis
		Thiamine mononitrate		
Vitamin B_2	Riboflavin	Riboflavin	Hydrogen transport Respiratory chain	Retarded growth Leg problems and paralysis
		Riboflavin-5-sodium phosphate		
Vitamin B_6	Pyridoxine	Pyridoxine hydrochloride	In enzymes which control amino acid metabolism	Low appetite Slow growth Skin disorders
	Pyridoxal			
	Pyridoxamine			
Vitamin B_{12}	Cyanocobalamin	Cyanocobalamin	Co-factor in the synthesis of nucleic acids	Slow growth
	Methylcobalamin	Hydroxycobalamin		
Pantothenic acid	Co-enzyme A	Ca and Na pantothenate	Interconversions between fatty acids, carbohydrates and amino acids	Loss of weight Skin disorders Nervous system disorders
		Pantothenol		
Niacin (PP)	Nicotinic acid	Nicotinic acid	Group active in enzymes of the respiratory chain	Slow growth Dermatitis Leg problems
	Nicotinamide	Nicotinamide		
Folic acid	Pteroylmonoglutamate	Folic acid (pteroylmonoglutamic)	Nucleic acid biosynthesis	Slow growth Anemia Leg problems
	Pteroylpolyglutamate			
Biotin	Free and combined D-Biotin	D-Biotin	Coenzyme in synthesis of fatty acids, amino acids and purines	Skin lesions Retarded growth Foot problems
Choline	Choline (ester)	Choline chloride	Transmethylations Phospholipid component	Slow growth Perosis Fatty liver
Vitamin C	Ascorbic acid	Ascorbic acid	Corticosteroid hormone genesis	Lower resistance to stress
	Dehydroascorbic acid	Ca or Na ascorbate		

relation to the value of the response value and the potential consequences of inadequate levels. For these reasons, the usual practice is to define vitamin requirements by taking into account the maximum response obtained with the chosen evaluation criteria, which are traditionally of the production type (growth rates and conversion index). However, growth is not a specific response; it may be affected by other factors associated with the feed (palatability, particle size, levels of other nutrients, etc.). This may explain the great variability in response levels between studies on a particular vitamin, even if they are almost concurrent. For Whitehead (1987) it will be not possible to establish precise mathematical relationships regarding vitamin requirements until all their interactions are known in detail. Moreover, it is very difficult to account in the equations for various diet types, changes in physical composition, etc.

Another consideration is the ever changing productive responses over time, resulting from the rapid and continuous genetic improvement in broilers and turkeys. After only a few years the experimental data tend to underestimate actual requirements. This also occurs in those studies where the maximum expression of genetic potential has not been achieved. In some cases it has been demonstrated mathematically and using biochemical criteria that animals which grow more rapidly have greater requirements (Whitehead and Bannister, 1980). Using experimental data from 1976 these authors estimated a biotin requirement in the starter phase of 170 μg/kg of feed, but when using the same model to recalculate it in line with 1984 production results, they estimated it had increased by 5% in only 8 years (Whitehead, 1987).

Another important aspect is that the requirements defined in scientific publications are normally based on data obtained under experimental conditions, where the birds are maintained in ideal environmental and operational conditions, and so do not take into account these aspects or pathological challenges that may lead to an increase in vitamin requirements in practical situations (Cooke and Raine, 1987). In this type of study the differences in mortality are not usually statistically significant; however in practice

they are of great economic importance, above all if losses occur in the final phases of fattening.

The problem is further complicated if other criteria as well as the purely productive are considered, such as improvement in meat quality (Morrissey et al., 1998; Sheehy et al., 1995; Jensen et al., 1998; Weber, 2001; Surai et al., 1993; Chung, 2006; Fellenberg and Speisky, 2006) This is closely related to fat oxidation processes, which can be reduced by using larger doses of some vitamins, especially vitamin E. Another very important criterion today is the well-being of the animals, which involves the prevention of stress and disease.

The interrelationships between nutrition, stress and pathology have received growing attention. This is demonstrated by the many reviews published in the last 20 years, whether on general aspects (Jensen, 1986; Whitehead and Portsmouth, 1989; Leeson et al., 1995; Whitehead, 1999, 2000, 2001, 2002b; Broz and Ward, 2007), or on their effects on immunity (Franchini and Bertuzzi, 1991; Latshaw, 1991; Chew, 1995; Ferket and Qureshi, 1999; Humphrey and Klasing, 2003; Kidd, 2004; Klasing, 2007), or on specific pathologies such as coccidiosis (Crevieu-Gabriel and Naciri, 2001; Dalloul and Lillehoj, 2005), ascites (Dale and Villacres, 1986; Malan et al., 2001; Baghbanzadeh and Decuypere, 2008), thermal stress (Puchal, 1989; Daghir, 1995a, b, 1996; Balnave, 2004; Gous and Morris, 2005; Lin et al., 2006) and foot problems (Sauveur, 1984, 1988; Cook, 1988; Whitehead, 1991, 1995, 2000, 2002a, 2005; Watkins, 1993; Thorp, 1994; Bains et al., 1996; Edwards, 1992, 2000; Rath et al., 2000; Nixey, 2005; Waldenstedt, 2006). All of them devote a large amount of space to discussing investigations on vitamins.

The process of adapting to a stress situation implies among other mechanisms an increase in basal metabolism and in body temperature, which require additional energy that must be obtained from the diet and/or physical reserves. But consumption of feed drops rapidly under stress conditions, and reserves only exist if the nutrient intake was previously above the animal's normal daily requirements (Dunn, 1996; Bains, 1997). This means the requirements for adaptation to stress are achieved at the cost of other functions less important for survival.

Stress reduces growth rate and the carcass and breast yield, and impairs feed conversion. It has frequently been demonstrated both experimentally and in practice that a higher than normal level of supplementation has a beneficial effect on these parameters (Ferket and Qureshi, 1992; Deyhim and Teeter, 1993, 1996; Deyhim *et al.*, 1994, 1995, 1996). The conversion of nutrients into energy takes place through metabolic processes (including lipolysis and gluconeogenesis) which depend on cofactors, principally vitamins of the B group and ascorbic acid. An essential requirement in coping with stress is the hormone corticosterone, without which energy production through gluconeogenesis stops, and the synthesis of which requires vitamin C.

Immunological stress is produced when the tissues are invaded by a pathogenic agent, whether by natural infection or vaccination. The primary defensive barrier depends on the integrity of the epithelia and mucous membranes, in which vitamin A plays a fundamental role (Chew and Park, 2004). The physiological response is initiation of the phagocytic activity of macrophages and the production of specific antibodies. Protecting the macrophages from self-destruction by the same mechanism by which they combat the pathogens requires the antioxidant activity of vitamins E and C (Chew, 1995). Vitamins A, D and E modify the leukocyte response (Klasing, 2007). Moreover, the synthesis of antibodies, which are proteins, requires an adequate and continuous supply of vitamins of the B group (Bains, 2001). Under field conditions it is well known that vitamin treatments help sick animals recover better, but investigation has focused on studying the contribution of vitamins to improving immunity and to the prevention of specific pathologies only recently.

For these reasons the concept of *Optimum Vitamin Nutrition* was introduced (Svendsen and Weber, 2001; McDowell and Ward, 2008). The concept attempts to cover all these objectives rather than simply deal with the prevention of clinical deficiencies.

VITAMIN SUPPLEMENTATION: GENERAL ASPECTS

The key reference work on the vitamin requirements of chickens and turkeys continues to be the latest edition of the US National Research Council publication on the nutritional needs of birds (NRC, 1994). The levels established guarantee the absence of serious deficiencies, the classic signs of which are infrequently detected today, unless due to occasional mixing errors in the factory (especially in starter feed). Many of the studies were conducted with purified diets that were difficult to granulate and therefore consumed in meal form, and under laboratory conditions (Leeson, 2007). The NRC's vitamin recommendations do not ensure the expression of the genetic potential of today's birds. In fact, other than in the cases of niacin and pyridoxine, these levels have not been altered in more than 30 years, and are based on outdated experimental data (**Table II**). There is greater doubt about requirements in the finishing phase, and even more so for turkeys, which are based on studies from the 1950s and 1960s. With some exceptions, such as vitamins C, D$_3$ and E, little research on vitamin requirements has been carried out in the last 40 years.

In practice, the poultry industry has tended over time to increase vitamin levels considerably, above all for vitamin D, niacin and folic acid and, to a lesser extent, for riboflavin, biotin and pantothenic acid. In the majority of cases levels are 50–100% higher than the NRC's, and in some cases 5–10 times more (Villamide and Fraga, 1999; Coelho, 2000; Maiorka *et al.*, 2002). In many cases what was a high level in the 1990s is now considered to be moderate or even low. Broiler and turkey genetic selection companies also recommend levels considerably higher than the NRC (**Tables X** and **XIV**), and may differ depending on whether the basal cereal in the diet is wheat or corn, and the climate hot or temperate.

Table II. Vitamin requirements for chickens (NRC, 1994) and degree of confidence for values proposed at the same date (Whitehead, 1996)

FATTENING PHASE	STARTER			GROWTH		
	VALUE	CONFIDENCE LEVEL	DATA ORIGIN (YEARS)	VALUE	CONFIDENCE LEVEL	DATA ORIGIN (YEARS)
Vitamin A (IU/kg)	1,500	*medium*	> 20	1,500		E
Vitamin D (IU/kg)	200	*medium*	< 10	200		E
Vitamin E (mg/kg)	10	-----	-----	10		E
Vitamin K (mg/kg)	0.5	*medium*	> 20	0.5		E
Thiamine B$_1$ (mg/kg)	1.8	*low*	> 20	1.8		E
Riboflavin B$_2$ (mg/kg)	3.6	*high*	< 10	3.6		E
Pyridoxine B$_6$ (mg/kg)	3.5	*medium*	> 20	3.5		E
Vitamin B$_{12}$ (µg/kg)	10	*low*	> 20	10		E
Niacin (mg/kg)	35	*medium*	< 10	30	*medium*	< 10
Pantothenic acid (mg/kg)	10	*medium*	10-20	10		E
Folic acid (mg/kg)	0.55	*low*	< 10	0.55		E
Biotin (µg/kg)	150	*medium*	10–20	150		E
Choline (mg/kg)	1,300	*high*	< 10	1,000	*high*	10–20

E: estimates

There are many reasons in the poultry industry to strengthen vitamin supplementation, working with high safety margins:

1. Changes in the genetic makeup of broilers and turkeys

In the past decade broilers have reached commercial weight 0.8 days earlier each year (**Figure 1**), and the starter phase, in which complex physiological processes are initiated, has become a greater proportion of their short lives. In turkeys the situation is even more marked, with the birds increasing their weight by a factor of 20 in 4 weeks, and 300 in males aged 20 weeks. Moreover, the continuous improvement in the conversion index means modern birds consume less and less feed per kg of weight (**Figure 2**), so that their vitamin intake is proportionally smaller. Leeson (2007) calculates that the average ingestion of vitamin E per kg of weight by a 2-kg chicken has decreased by 0.8% per year in the last 20 years, and by 0.6% in a 14-kg turkey, leading to the suggestion that vitamin levels should be increased by 0.6 and 1% per year simply to maintain the same intake level.

Moreover, selection to achieve more rapid growth has directly or indirectly produced profound modifications in different aspects of the birds' physiology. Dunnington and Siegel (1996) summed up the results of studies carried out over 38 generations of selection to increase daily gain: modifications in appetite control and thermoregulatory mechanisms, in oxygen consumption, body temperature and heat production, in the capacity to absorb nutrients and in the activity of digestive enzymes, in hormone and serum levels in general, in physical composition (**Tables III and IV**), in the immune response and in resistance to stress. Some vitamins are involved in all these processes.

It would seem logical to raise vitamin levels in accordance with the increase in meat yield. The higher growth rate means the energy levels in the diet must be raised, and it should not be forgotten that the vitamins of the B group play an important role in energy metabolism. The use of higher protein levels and of lysine and methionine to maximize breast yield increase requirements for vitamin B$_{12}$, biotin and pyridoxine.

144

Figure 1. Reduction in the time needed for a broiler to achieve 1.5 kg of live weight

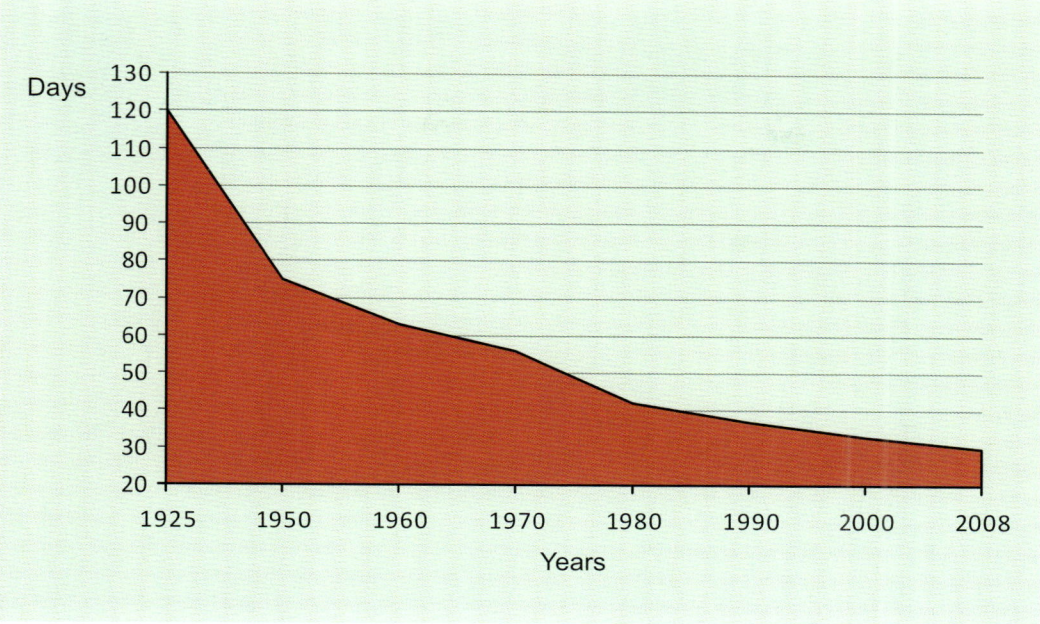

Figure 2. Development of consumption/bird and feed conversion in broilers
(Source: Broiler management guides)

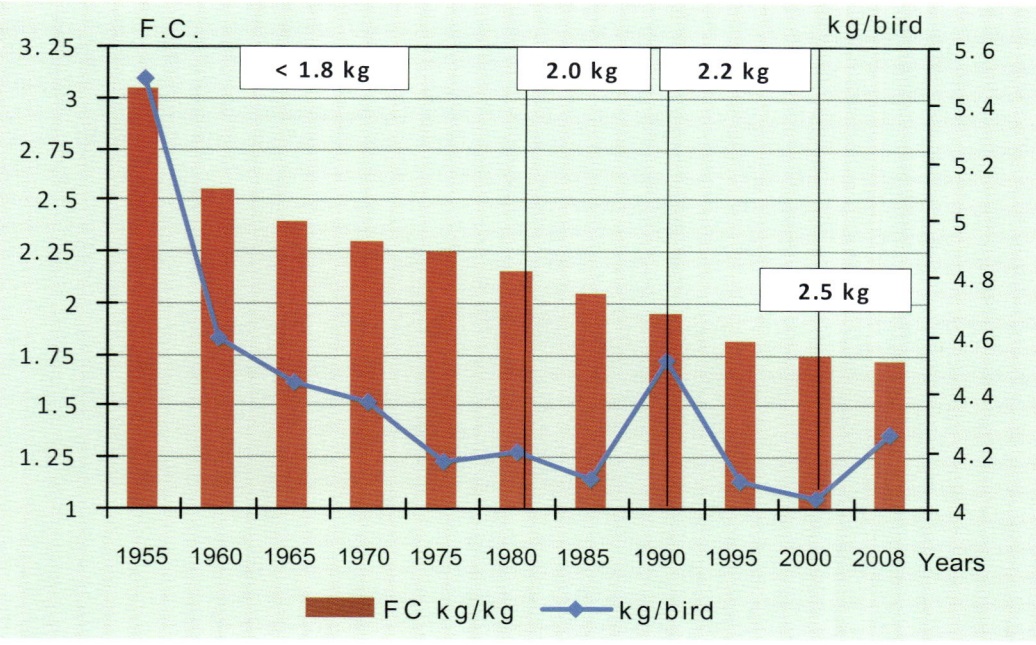

Table III. Improvements in chicken carcass yield and composition (Havenstein *et al.*, 1994, 2003)

Characteristic	1957	1991	2003
Age, days	84	42	42
Live weight, kg	1.41	2.13	2.67
Carcass weight, kg	0.91	1.39	1.93
Carcass yield, %	65.1	67.7	72.3
% breast	13.0	15.0	20.0
% carcass fat	12.3	14.2	13.7
% abdominal fat	1.1	1.5	1.4

2. Animal health and well-being

Intensive rearing means considerable pressure on the birds, which are exposed to many stress factors, whether environmental (high density, high temperatures, damp bedding), immunological (vaccinations, infections) or nutritional (fat rancidity, fungus contamination, etc.). Modern broilers and turkeys have a high productive potential but are more susceptible to infections (Bayyari *et al.*, 1997; Yunis *et al.*, 2000). Clear positive effects of general vitamin fortification for stress conditions arising from one of these factors, or a combination of several of them, have been demonstrated in both species (Ferket and Qureshi, 1992; Coelho and McNaughton, 1995; McKnight *et al.*, 1995b; Taranu *et al.*, 1995; Deyhim and Teeter, 1996; Dunn, 1996). Already well established in particular are the roles of vitamin C in alleviating heat stress and the improvement in the immune response due to vitamin E. Other vitamins (D_3, E and most of the B group) have also shown positive effects in preventing or reducing metabolic problems (ascites, foot problems) caused by rapid growth (Leeson *et al.*, 2005; Malan *et al.*, 2001; Whitehead, 2000).

3. Product quality

Today it is more necessary than ever to take into account this important aspect which was also neglected in the requirements established by the NRC. In recent years numerous studies have demonstrated that a higher supplementation with some vitamins, especially vitamin E, can reduce skin problems and improve not only carcass and breast yield but also the stability of meat against oxidation (Sheehy, 1995; Jensen *et al.*, 1998; Weber, 2001). Furthermore, the enrichment of vitamin content in poultry meat achieved by using higher doses in feed (Hernández *et al.*, 2002; Pérez-Vendrell *et al.*, 2003; Castaign *et al.* 2003) could be attractive to many consumers.

4. Variations in the content and bioavailability of vitamins in feed ingredients

These may be caused by many factors, such as interactions with other vitamins

Table IV. Improvements in turkey carcass yield and composition (Herendy *et al.*, 2004)

Characteristic	Males 1967 rate	Males 1999 rate	Females 1967 rate	Females 1999 rate
Live weight, kg				
6 weeks	0.91	2.59	0.74	1.60
10 weeks	2.42	6.72	1.71	5.24
16 weeks	4.64	13.90	3.17	10.19
20 weeks	6.12	19.14	3.89	12.62
% carcass yield, 20 weeks	62.5	77.3	65.0	83.4
% breast/live weight 20 weeks	13.6	24.9	13.8	26.2
% abdominal fat/l.w., 20 weeks	0.9	0.9	1.8	2.5

and nutrients, mycotoxins, etc. In Europe, diets are more varied than in the US and the predominance of wheat rather than corn makes it more necessary to supplement with niacin and biotin, as well as pantothenic acid and vitamins A and B_6 (Whitehead, 1993). There have been recent changes in feed formulation which may affect vitamin requirements, such as the ban on meat meal (an important source of cyanocobalamin and pantothenic acid) and the greater use of completely vegetarian diets, rich in unsaturated fats, which may involve higher requirements of vitamin E for its antioxidant effect. The ban on growth-promoting antibiotics in the EU may make vitamins with immunomodulatory functions

Table V. Vitamin loss (%) in granulated broiler feed stored under different conditions.
Taken from Ross management guide (data originating from BASF Co.).

	Form	Premix type	Ideal conditions	Stored premix	Stored premix and feed
Vitamin A	AD₃ pellets	V	8	9	16
		VM	9	13	19
		VMC	10	17	23
Vitamin D₃	AD₃ pellets	V	8	9	17
		VM	9	11	18
		VMC	9	15	22
Vitamin E	Acetate	V	7	7	10
		VM	7	10	13
		VMC	7	13	16
Vitamin K	Menadione bisulfite complex (MBSC)	V	35	36	49
		VM	39	46	56
		VMC	39	53	62
Vitamin B₁	Thiamine HCl	V	17	18	27
		VM	21	35	42
		VMC	39	40	47
Vitamin B₂	Riboflavin	V	10	10	16
		VM	10	14	19
		VMC	12	17	22
Vitamin B₆	Pyridoxine	V	13	13	19
		VM	14	18	23
		VMC	16	22	27
Pantothenic acid	Ca pantothenate	V	10	10	15
		VM	10	10	15
		VMC	11	21	25
Folic acid		V	11	11	13
		VM	12	16	16
		VMC	13	25	26
Niacin	Nicotinic acid	V	13	13	20
		VM	15	18	25
		VMC	15	21	28
Biotin		V	13	13	20
		VM	14	17	23
		VMC	16	22	28
Vitamin C	Ascorbic acid	V	56	57	70
		VM	58	69	78
		VMC	58	69	78
Vitamin C	Protected	V	27	29	42
		VM	30	37	49
		VMC	30	44	55
Storage conditions and time	Vitamins tel quel		0 days	0 days	0 days
	Premixes, 15°C, 60% RH		14 days	56 days	56 days
	Feeds, 20°C, 60% RH		7 days	7 days	28 days

V= vitamins; VM = vitamins and minerals; VMC = choline

more beneficial.

Pelleting, heat treatments, extrusion and expansion are manufacturing processes that are becoming more aggressive and may cause vitamin losses between 15 and 40%, which will increase if feed is kept for any length of time or in unsuitable conditions (**Table V**).

These and other technological aspects such as how well vitamin sources are protected, composition of premixes, when these are added to the feed, etc. may cause the concentrations which reach the animal to be considerably different from those expected (Putnam, 1983; Cooke and Raine, 1987; Putnam and Taylor, 1997; Whitehead, 2002c; Lauzon et al. 2008).

5. Cost-benefit relationship

Greater vitamin fortification today makes up around 1–1.5% of the cost of feed is small in relation to the possible improvement it may bring and the prevention of risks that may be very economically damaging. Studies carried out under practical field conditions by Coelho and McNaughton (1995) on broilers and by McKnight et al. (1995a) on turkeys demonstrated that the group of companies which used higher supplementation levels achieved improved growth, feed conversion and viability of birds, especially in conditions of moderate stress (Figures 3, 4 and 5), and improved yield at the slaughterhouse, which amply compensated for the additional cost.

This was confirmed specifically in similar investigations for vitamin E (Kennedy et al., 1992; Bird and Boren, 1999) with levels of 180–240 ppm, and for some vitamins of the B group (Coelho et al., 2001) supplemented levels four times higher than the levels normal in the North American poultry industry and 16 times more than the NRC level. There is no reason why these increases in vitamin content should be harmful, since the toxic levels are 100–1,000 times higher than the minimum requirements (NRC, 1987; Leeson et al., 1997), except for vitamins A and D_3 for which toxicity occurs at approximately 10 times higher than the given requirement.

Figure 3. **Effect of vitamin supplementation levels on broiler mortality at 42 days** (Coelho and McNaughton, 1995)

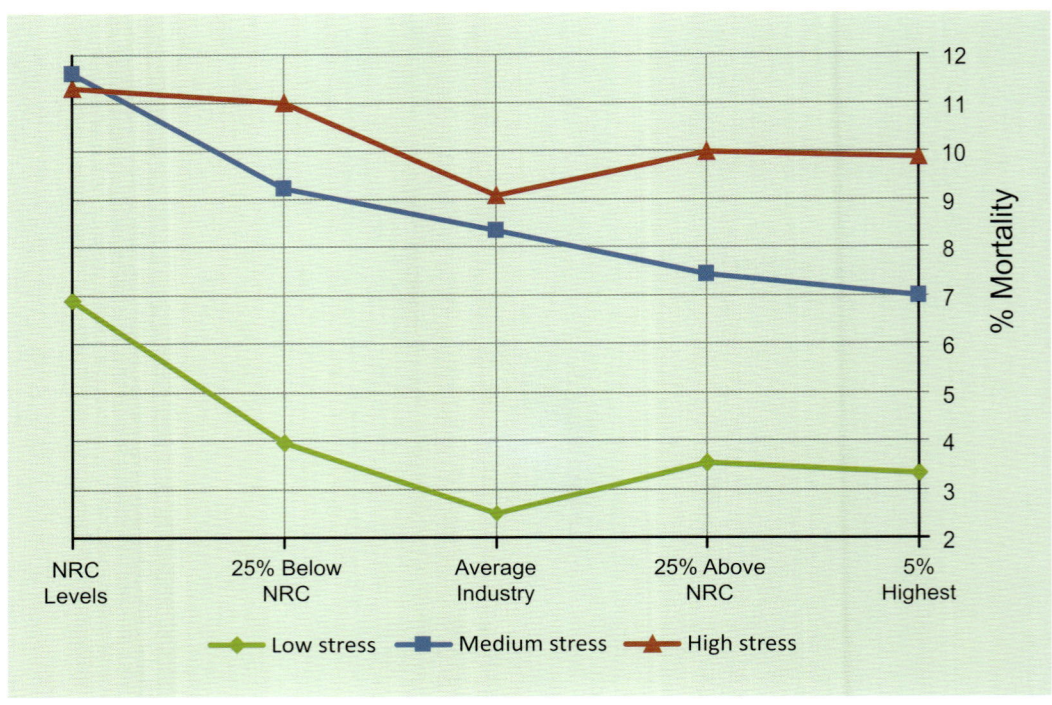

Figure 4. Effects of vitamin level on broiler performance to 51 days under various stress conditions (Coelho and McNaughton, 1995)

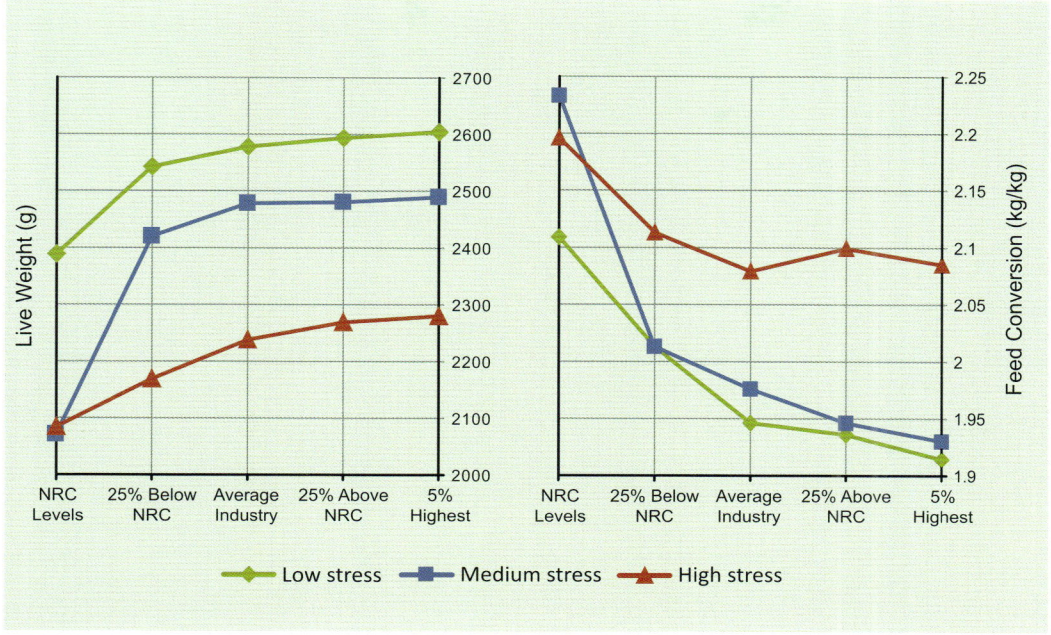

Figure 5. Effects of vitamin supplementation levels on broiler carcass yield (Coelho and McNaughton, 1995)

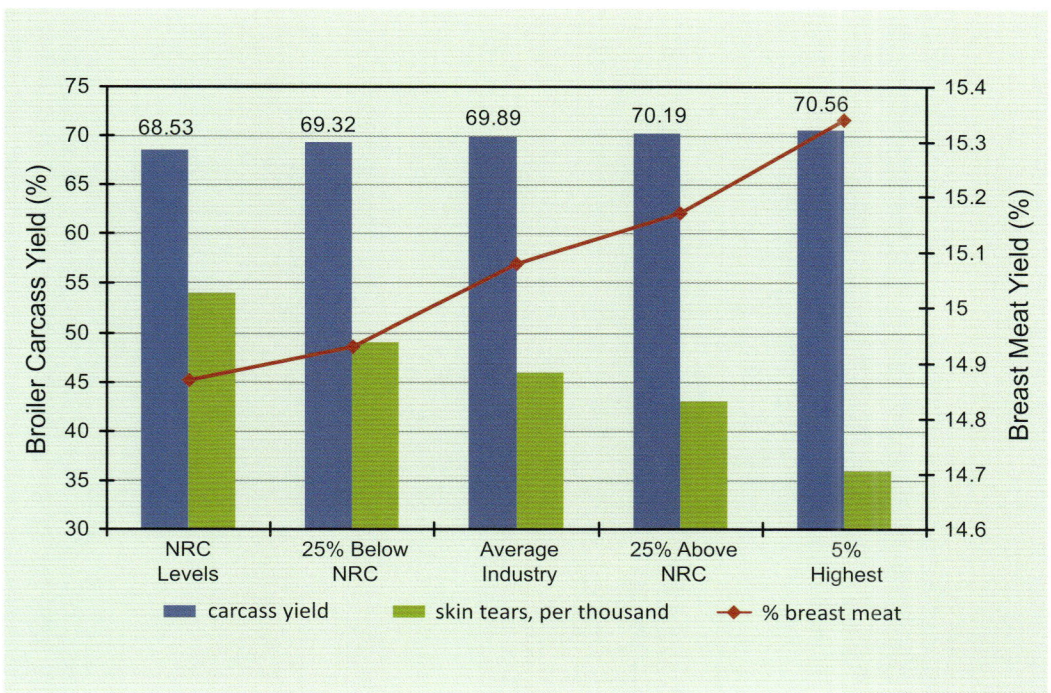

CURRENT RECOMMENDATIONS

As previously indicated, higher levels of vitamin supplementation are used in practice than those recommended by the NRC, and they have been increasing over the past 10–15 years (Ward, 1993; Troescher and Coelho, 1996; Whitehead, 1996; Coelho and McNaughton , 1995; Coelho, 2000). This applies above all to D_3, niacin and folic acid, and to a lesser extent to riboflavin, biotin and pantothenic acid. In Spain, vitamin C is only included in 10% of premixes, principally during hot periods, and at least 40% of producers add choline separately, due to its adverse effects on the stability of other vitamins.

Table VI shows the levels used in the diets of broilers by the poultry industry in Spain and the United States (Villamide and Fraga, 1999; Coelho, 2000), with data that represent 85–90% of production. In general, the levels used in Spain are somewhat higher than in the US, except for vitamin D_3. In both countries there is considerable variability, above all in the finishing feeds, in which values 20–35% lower than those for starter feeds are normally used. The divergence

between companies is greatest for biotin, thiamine and vitamin E, while the range is narrower for A, D, riboflavin and pantothenic acid, probably because of cost. The safety margins are greater for the fat-soluble vitamins (3–6 times the NRC values) than for those of the B group. Maiorka et al. (2010) have described a similar situation in the Brazilian poultry industry.

Table VI also shows that some companies withdraw some vitamins (or even all of them) in finisher feed. Pressure to reduce feeding costs in the 1990s introduced the concept of withdrawing vitamin supplements in feed for the last 5–7 days (or even 14 days); but in the US this strategy has declined distinctly since 1993 (Coelho, 2000). Several studies aimed at evaluating the consequences of this withdrawal found no statistically significant effects on productivity, foot problems, or carcass quality from withdrawing the vitamin-mineral premix (Christmas et al. 1995; Vo et al., 1997; Khajali et al., 2006). However, others observed an increase in locomotor problems and tibial dyschondroplasia, as well as loss of

Table VI. Average composition and range (mg/kg*) of vitamin supplements used in Spain and the United States (Villamide and Fraga, 1999; and Coelho, 2000)

Period	Starter		Growth/Finishing		Finishing/Withdrawal	
	SP 0–28 days	USA 0–21 days	SP > 28 days	USA > 21 days	SP last 5 days	USA > 42 days
Vitamin A	11.6 (7.7–15.0)	7.67 (6.0–9.2)	9.9 (6.0–13.3)	7.17 (6.1–8.2)	3.90 (0–6.7)	5.78 (3.4–8.2)
Vitamin D_3	2.8 (1.5–4)	2,70 (2.1–3.1)	2.29 (1.2–3.6)	2.51 (2.0–3.0)	0.89 (0–2.1)	2.01 (1.3–2.9)
Vitamin E	27.9 (7.5–50)	23.21 (14.3–41.6)	23.2 (6–45)	17.93 (12.7–24.1)	17.5 (3.6–50)	14.21 (7.3–20.2)
Vitamin K	2.54 (0.75–5.4)	1.37 (0.7–2.0)	2.57 (0.5–5)	1.27 (0.8–1.7)	2.83 (0.3–10)	1.01 (0.6–1.7)
Vitamin B_1	1.64 (0–3)	1.67 (1.17–2.2)	1.49 (0–3)	1.53 (1.02–2.04)	0.46 (0–1.1)	1.19 (0.7–1.8)
Vitamin B_2	6.50 (5.4–8)	6.68 (5.3–8.5)	5.30 (3.9–8)	6.24 (5.4–7.1)	2.25 (0–4)	5.03 (2.9–6.9)
Vitamin B_6	3.35 (1.8–5)	2.48 (1.7–3.4)	2.62 (1–5)	2.28 (1.7–2.9)	0.58 (0–1.5)	1.83 (1.0–2.7)
Vitamin B_{12}	16.6 (12–30)	12.66 (9.8–16.2)	15.0 (9–30)	11.76 (10.1–13.4)	5.88 (0–12.5)	9.46 (5.6–13.3)
Niacin	46.4 (25–86)	39.3 (30.8–48.1)	34.0 (20–66)	37.0 (30.4–41.3)	12.9 (0–30)	29.8 (17.9–41.3)
Pantothenic	13.1 (8–19)	10.74 (8.9–12.8)	11.0 (6.4–15)	10.07 (8.8–11.2)	5.59 (0–10)	8.11 (4.7–10.5)
Folic acid	1.08 (0.5–1.5)	0.80 (0.6–1.1)	0.85 (0.4–1.5)	0.74 (0.6–0.9)	0.31 (0–0.95)	0.59 (0.4–0.8)
Biotin	0.13 (0–0.25)	0.074 (0.05–0.1)	0.09 (0–0.2)	0.068 (0.04–0.09)	0.023 (0–0.1)	0.055 (0.03–0.08)
Choline	352 (200–540)	----	285 (200–420)	----	212 (100–420)	-----

* Vitamins A and D_3, thousands IU/kg; B_{12}, µg/kg

uniformity in chicken carcasses (Skinner *et al.*, 1992). These researchers suggested that supplementation should continue if stress conditions prevail (heat, mycotoxins, high density). For Whitehead (2002), eliminating the vitamin premix from the withdrawal feed is inadvisable from the viewpoint of animal well-being, since the birds would shortly have to deal with the stress of loading and transport to the slaughterhouse, and vitamins E and C are particularly important in counteracting this stress.

Dehyim and Teeter (1993) attributed the absence of statistical significance observed in these experiments to the small number of birds used, the scant replication of treatments, and the use of diets with animal byproduct meal, which contains double the amount of B vitamins of soy. In their own study they found differences very close to significance for growth (- 6%) and feed conversion index (- 8%), carcass yield (+ 0.2 points) and breast meat percentage (+ 0.8 points) with respect to the unsupplemented control group, and they emphasized that these numerical differences are significant economically. Similar results were found in a subsequent experiment (Dehyim *et al.,* 1995). Patel *et al.* (1997) confirmed the negative effects of the

withdrawal of vitamins in 3 different strains, in particular withdrawal of riboflavin, which caused a linear reduction in growth. Maiorka *et al.* (2002) withdrew supplementation during the last 4 and 7 days and obtained a worse feed conversion index and a tendency towards reduction of slaughtering weight. Ferket and Qureshi (1992) removed the vitamin premix from 21 days of age, which resulted in a weight loss of 68 g at 43 days and a feed conversion index 7% higher than the broilers with vitamin supplementation. Furthermore, when heat stress was induced the supplemented birds had lower mortality and exhibited a higher level of IgG immunoglobulins. Dehyim *et al.* (1994) also found a better immune status in broilers which received vitamin supplements until the end of the cycle under hot environmental conditions. Furthermore, Dehyim and Teeter (1996) and Patel *et al.* (1997) observed a 30–50% reduction in vitamin B_1 and B_2 breast content in unsupplemented birds, especially in thermal stress situations.

For turkeys, there is only data from North America (Ward, 1993; McKnight *et al.*, 1995a; Coelho, 2000). Although in practice between 6 and 8 feeding phases are employed, in **Table VII** these are grouped into 3. In general,

Table VII. Average composition and range (mg/kg*) of vitamin supplements used in turkey production in the United States (Coelho, 2000)

Period	Starter 0–6 weeks	Growth 7–12 weeks	Finishing > 13 weeks
Vitamin A, IU/kg	**9.61** (7.1–12.2)	**7.58** (5.8–9.4)	**5.57** (4.1–7.5)
Vitamin D_3, IU/kg	**4.42** (3.0–6.6)	**3.11** (1.7–4.7)	**2.30** (1.4–3.4)
Vitamin E	**44.52** (17.0–81.5)	**26.9** (12.2–43.3)	**18.41** (6.8–32.5)
Vitamin K	**1.85** (1.1–5.2.8)	**1.49** (0.7–2.6)	**1.14** (0.6–2.0)
Vitamin B_1	**2.19** (1.1–3.0)	**1.25** (0.7–1.7)	**0.91** (0.2–1.5)
Vitamin B_2	**7.81** (6.3–9.7)	**5.88** (4.7–7.0)	**3.99** (2.8–5.2)
Vitamin B_6	**3.19** (0.8–4.9)	**2.10** (0.6–3.1)	**1.71** (0.7–2.6)
Vitamin B_{12}	**16.0** (11.0–22.0)	**12.0** (8.0–17.0)	**7.0** (5.0–10.0)
Niacin	**72.87** (45.9–98.6)	**56.49** (43.2–65.5)	**40.59** (28.1–51.9)
Pantothenic	**16.45** (12.5–21.1)	**13.38** (10.2–17.9)	**8.83** (7.1–10.9)
Folic acid	**2.01** (1.0–3.3)	**0.87** (0.2–1.5)	**0.68** (0.3–1.0)
Biotin	**0.15** (0.07–0.23)	**0.10** (0.04–0.14)	**0.09** (0.04–0.15)

* B_{12}, µg/kg

the levels used for starters are twice those for the finishing phase, with a smaller drop in vitamin A, riboflavin, niacin, biotin and pantothenic acid, and a greater decrease in D, E, K, thiamine and cyanocobalamin. Variability is particularly high in finisher feed, reflecting the uncertainty arising from insufficient scientific information, above all for vitamins of the B group. In starter feeds, the divergence between different companies are smaller for vitamins A, B_2, niacin and pantothenic acid. The majority of levels used at present exceed those published by Ward in 1993.

It is also of interest to compare the vitamin recommendations of the principal scientific sources which constitute habitual reference points for poultry nutrition specialists. It should be pointed out that the NRC expresses them as total requirements, while in the other cases they are recommendations for feed supplementation. In practice the vitamin content of the basal feed ingredients is ignored(Whitehead, 1993). **Tables VIII** and **IX** reflect the recommendations for broiler nutrition which have steadily risen over time.

It is evident that the NRC values fall well below those of the other sources. In starter and grower feeds they are 4–6 times lower for vitamins A, E, K, and B_{12}, and 10–20 times lower for D_3. There is less difference with regard to vitamins B_1, B_6, niacin and biotin. For choline the NRC figures are 2–5 times higher than the other sources but this is because they refer to total requirements and not supplementation levels.

The highest supplementation levels are those proposed by the company DSM, in accordance with its concept of Optimum Vitamin Nutrition (OVN), but they are now more in line with the figures indicated by the best-known nutrition specialists. The recommendations for vitamin supplementation by Larbier and Leclerq of the INRA agree largely with DSM's specifications (except for vitamin E), and in the majority of cases raise the INRA's old recommendations, especially for pantothenic acid, folic acid, vitamin K, and the B group in general. Leeson and Summers (1997) also far exceeded the levels indicated by the NRC, and a few years later (Leeson and Summers, 2005) they again

increased their recommendations, which are now fairly close to DSM's. When making comparisons it should be kept in mind that the authors are referring exclusively to corn-soy diets as used in the US. The Spanish nutritional association, FEDNA, proposes feeding programs of different duration, and in general adopts somewhat more conservative recommendations than DSM's, with the greatest differences relating to supplies of biotin and vitamin E. The current vitamin supplementation recommendations by DSM are largely in agreement, except for vitamins E and C, with the specifications of management guides for the principal commercial broiler strains, which can be seen in **Table X**.

In finishing feeds, the NRC levels are still well below those of other sources, except for vitamins of the B group when compared with the INRA. Moreover, in the majority of cases it specifies the same values as in the preceding phase. This may be due to the relative scarcity of studies on requirements in this period of fattening (Whitehead, 1987, 2000). Larbier and Leclerq generally reduce their recommendations for the first phase by 25–50%, and also agree largely with those proposed by DSM (except, again, for vitamin E), in most cases raising the figures published 8 years previously by INRA, especially for the same aforementioned vitamins. DSM maintains the levels of A, D, K, B_1, niacin and folic acid. As in the starter phase, only this firm currently proposes supplementing vitamin C under certain circumstances.

The recommendations for turkey nutrition are shown in **Tables XI–XIII**, and **Table XIV** shows those of the most important genetics companies. The situation is similar to that already described for broilers, although there are differences in the vitamin recommendations for different commercial turkey strains. From the 17th week onwards DSM proposes lower levels (20–50%) in most cases (data not shown).

Finally, it is worthwhile commenting on some studies that have specifically evaluated the OVN concept from the firm of DSM, which for the majority of vitamins includes supplementation between 30 and 50% higher than the levels currently used commercially (except for vitamin E, which is some 10 times

Table VIII. Recommended vitamin levels (IU or mg/kg air-dry feed) for broilers starter and grower (0-21 days) by various sources

Source / Units		NRC, 1994	INRA, 1984	Larbier and Leclerq, 1992	Leeson and Summers, 1997	Whitehead, 2002	Leeson and Summers, 2005	FEDNA, 2008 (0-18days)	DSM OVN (2011) Starter	Grower
Vitamin A	IU	1,500	10,000	12,000	6,500	10000-15000	8,000	9000-15000	11000-15000	10000-12500
Vitamin D3	IU	200	1,500	2,000	3,000	4000-5000	3,500	3000-3800	3000-5000	3000-5000
25-OH-D3 (HyD)	mg	-	-	-	-	-	-	-	0.069	0.069
Vitamin E	IU	10	15	30	30	30-180	50	20-45	150-300 [1][2]	50-100 [3]
Vitamin K	mg	0.5	5.0	2.5	2.0	2-3	3.0	2-3.1	3-4	3-4
Vitamin B1	mg	1.8	0.50	2.0	4.00	1.5-2.5	4.00	1-2.5	3-4	2-3
Vitamin B2	mg	3.6	4.0	6.0	5.50	6-8	5.00	5-7.5	8-10	7-9
Vitamin B6	mg	3.5	-	-	4.00	4.00	4.00	2.5-4	4-6	4-6
Vitamin B12	mg	0.01	0.01	0.02	0.013	0.01-0.016	0.012	0.016-0.022	0.02-0.04	0.02-0.03
Niacin	mg	35	25	30	40	35-60	40	40-65	60-80	60-80
D-Panthothenic acid	mg	10	5.0	15	14	12-18	14	10-16	15-20	12-18
Folic acid	mg	0.55	0.20	1.0	1.0	1.5-2.5	1.0	1-1.5	2.0-2.5	2.0-2.5
Biotin	mg	0.15	-	0.10	0.20	0.18-0.25	0.10	0.09-0.18	0.2-0.4	0.2-0.3
Vitamin C	mg	-	-	-	-	-	-	-	100-200 [5]	100-200 [5]
Choline	mg	1300	500	600	800	250-350	400	300-500	400-700	400-700

(1) Add 5 mg/kg for each 1% dietary fat when fat is higher than 3%;
(2) Higher level for optimum immune function
(3) Under heat stress conditions increase level up to 200 mg/kg
(5) Recommended under heat stress conditions; use phosphorylated form in heat treated feeds

Table IX. Recommended vitamin levels (IU or mg/kg air-dry feed) for broilers finisher by various sources

	Source / Units	NRC, 1994	INRA, 1984	Larbier and Leclerq, 1992	Leeson and Summers, 1997	Whitehead, 2002	Leeson and Summers, 2005	FEDNA, 2008	DSM OVN (2011)
Vitamin A	IU	1,500	10,000	10,000	5,850	10000-15000	8,000	7000-9000	1000012500
Vitamin D3	IU	200	1,500	1,500	2,700	4000-5000	3,500	2000-2800	3000-5000
25-OH-D3 (HyD)	mg	-	-	-	-	-	-	-	0.069
Vitamin E	IU	10	10	20	27	30-180	50	20-25	50-100 [4]
Vitamin K	mg	0.5	4.0	2.0	1.8	2-3	3.0	1.7-2.2	3-4
Vitamin B1	mg	1.8	-	2.0	3.6	1.5-2.5	4.0	0.3-1.3	2-3
Vitamin B2	mg	3.6	4.0	4.0	5.0	6-8	5.0	3-5.5	6-8
Vitamin B6	mg	3.5	-	2.5	3.6	4.0	4.0	0.6-2.4	4-6
Vitamin B12	mg	0.01	0.01	0.01	0.012	0.01-0.016	0.012	0.008-0.015	0.02-0.03
Niacin	mg	30	15	20	36	35-60	40	20-35	50-80
D-Panthothenic acid	mg	10	5.0	10	12.6	12-18	14	8-10	10-15
Folic acid	mg	0.55	-	0.2	0.9	1.5-2.5	1.0	0.3-0.7	2.0-2.5
Biotin	mg	0.15	-	0.05	0.18	0.18-0.25	0.10	0.02-0.095	0.2-0.3
Vitamin C	mg	-	-	-	-	-	-	-	100-200 [5]
Choline	mg	1000	500	500	720	250-350	400	175-250	400-600

(4) For optimum meat quality additional 150 mg/kg
(5) Recommended under heat stress conditions; use phosphorylated form in heat treated feeds

Table X. Recommended vitamin levels (IU or mg/kg air-dry feed) by principal broiler genetic companies and DSM Optimum Vitamin Nutrition (OVN) levels

Grow-out phase	Source / Units	Starter				Grower				Finisher			
		Cobb (2008)*	Ross (2007)*	Hubbard (2006)	DSM OVN (2011)	Cobb (2008)*	Ross (2007)*	Hubbard (2006)	DSM OVN (2011)	Cobb (2008)*	Ross (2007)*	Hubbard (2006)	DSM OVN (2011)
Vitamin A	IU	13000-14000	11000-12000	15000	11000-15000	11000-12000	9000-10000	12500	10000-12500	11000	9000-10000	10000	10000-12500
Vitamin D3	IU	5000	5000	3000	3000-5000	5000	5000	3000	3000-5000	5000	4000	2000	3000-5000
25-OH-D3 (HyD)	mg	-	-	0.0625	0.069	-	-	-	0.069	-	-	-	0.069
Vitamin E	IU	80	75	50-100	150-300 [1][2]	60	50	30-100	50-100 [3]	50	50	30-100	50-100 [4]
Vitamin K	mg	4	3	3	3-4	4	3	3	3-4	3	2	2	3-4
Vitamin B1	mg	4	3	3	3-4	4	3	3	2-3	2	2	2	2-3
Vitamin B2	mg	9	8	8	8-10	9	8	9	7-9	8	5	6	6-8
Vitamin B6	mg	4	4-5	4	4-6	4	4-5	3	4-6	3	2-3	3	4-6
Vitamin B12	mg	0.02	0.016	0.03	0.02-0.04	0.015	0.016	0.016	0.02-0.03	0.015	0.01	0.01	0.02-0.03
Niacin	mg	60	60-55	60	60-80	50	60-55	50	60-80	50	40-35	50	50-80
D-Panthothenic acid	mg	15	15-13	15	15-20	12	15-13	10	12-18	12	15-13	10	10-15
Folic acid	mg	2	2	1.5	2.0-2.5	2	2	1.5	2.0-2.5	1.5	1.5	1	2.0-2.5
Biotin	mg	0.15-0.2	0.15-0.2	0.2	0.2-0.4	0.15-0.2	0.15-0.2	0.2	0.2-0.3	0.12-0.18	0.1	0.1	0.2-0.3
Vitamin C	mg	-	-	200	100-200 [5]	-	-	200	100-200 [5]	-	-	200	100-200 [5]
Choline	mg	400	1600	700	400-700	400	1500	600	400-700	350	1400	600	400-600

* Range for some vitamins is referred to maize (lower) or wheta (higher) diets
(1) Add 5 mg/kg for each 1% dietary fat when fat is higher than 3%;
(2) Higher level for optimum immune function
(3) Under heat stress conditions increase level up to 200 mg/kg
(4) For optimum meat quality increase level up to 200 mg/kg
(5) Recommended under heat stress conditions; use phosphorylated form in heat treated feeds

higher). In general, positive and significant responses in productivity were obtained (Hernández et al., 2002; Pérez-Vendrell et al., 2003; Castaign et al., 2003; Moslehi et al., 2004; Castaign et al., 2007), especially under stress conditions, and it is notable that an increase in feed intake is usually observed.

Carcass and breast yield has also improved, with a reduction in abdominal fat (Hernández et al., 2002; Castaign et al., 2003), as has oxidative stability of the meat (Pérez-Vendrell et al., 2003; Pérez-Vendrell and Weber, 2005) and its vitamin content, especially of thiamine, pantothenic acid and vitamin E (Pérez-Vendrell et al., 2003; Castaign et al., 2003). When the OVN vitamin-mineral premix also included the metabolite of vitamin D_3 25-OH-D3 hydroxycholecalciferol (Hy-D), locomotor problems were reduced, and resistance and bone ash were increased, in both chickens and turkeys (Pérez-Vendrell and Weber, 2007; Philippe et al., 2005). Moslehi et al. (2004) compared 7 different levels of supplementation, and found that the OVN levels reduced mortality and the feed conversion index in broilers, and yet did not increase production costs any more than the majority of the other treatments In fact the highest cost per kg of weight came from applying the NRC recommendations.

Table XI. Recommended vitamin levels (IU or mg/kg air-dry feed) for turkey starter and grower (0-8 weeks) by various sources

	Source / Units	NRC, 1994 (0-8 wks)	INRA, 1984	Larbier and Leclerq, 1992	Leeson and Summers, 1997	Leeson and Summers, 2005	DSM OVN (2011) Starter (0-6 wks)	DSM OVN (2011) Grower (7-12 wks)
Vitamin A	IU	5,000	10,000	15,000	9,500	10,000	12000-15000	10000-12000
Vitamin D3	IU	1,100	1,500	3,000	2,700	3,500	4000-5000	3000-5000
25OHD3 (HyD)	mg	-	-	-	-	-	0.092	0.092
Vitamin E	IU	12	20	25	40	100	100-250 [1][2]	60-80 [1]
Vitamin K	mg	1.75/1.5	4.0	3.0	2.0	3.0	4.0-5.0	3.0-4.0
Vitamin B1	mg	2.0	2.00	2.0	3.0	3.0	4.5-5.0	3.0-5.0
Vitamin B2	mg	4/3.6	6.0	8.0	6.0	10.0	15-20	10-15
Vitamin B6	mg	4.5	2.0	4.0	6.0	6.0	6.0-7.0	5.0-7.0
Vitamin B12	mg	0.003	0.015	0.02	0.014	0.020	0.040-0.050	0.030-0.040
Niacin	mg	60	60	65	80	60	100-150	80-100
D-Panthothenic acid	mg	10.0/9.0	10	20	17	18	30-35	20-25
Folic acid	mg	1.0	1.2	1.0	1.0	2.0	4.0-6.0	2.0-3.0
Biotin	mg	0.25/0.20	0.3	0.20	0.25	0.25	0.25-0.40	0.25-0.30
Vitamin C	mg	-	-	-	-	-	100-200	100-200 [3]
Choline	mg	1600/1400	800	800	1900	800	1000-1200	500-1000

(1) Add 5 mg/kg for each 1% dietary fat when fat is higher than 3%;
(2) Higher level for optimum immune function
(3) Recommended under heat stress conditions; use phosphorylated form in heat treated feeds

Table XII. Recommended vitamin levels (IU or mg/kg air-dry feed) or turkey grower (phase 2) and finisher (9-16 weeks) by various sources

	Source / Units	NRC, 1994 (9-12 & 13-16 wks)	INRA, 1984 (9-16 wks)	Larbier and Leclerq, 1992 (9-16 wks)	Leeson and Summers, 1997 (9-16 wks)	Leeson and Summers, 2005 (9-16 wks)	DSM OVN (2011) Grower (7-12 wks)	DSM OVN (2011) Finisher 1 (13-18 wks)
Vitamin A	IU	5,000	8,000	10,000	8,500	10,000	10000-12000	8000-10000
Vitamin D3	IU	1,100	1,200	2,000	2,400	3,500	3000-5000	3000-4000
25-OH-D3 (HyD)	mg	-	-	-	-	-	0.092	0.092
Vitamin E	IU	10	15	20	30	100	60-80 [1][2]	30-50 [1][2]
Vitamin K	mg	1.0/0.75	3.0	2.0	2.0	3.0	3.0-4.0	3.0-4.0
Vitamin B1	mg	2.0	1.00	1.0	3.0	3.0	3.0-5.0	3.0-4.0
Vitamin B2	mg	3.0	4.0	4.0	5.0	10.0	10-15	8.0-10
Vitamin B6	mg	3.5	-	3.0	5.0	6.0	5.0-7.0	3.0-6.0
Vitamin B12	mg	0.03	0.01	0.01	0.014	0.02	0.030-0.040	0.020-0.030
Niacin	mg	50	50	50	70	60	80-100	60-80
D-Panthothenic acid	mg	9.0	12	12	15	18	20-25	15-20
Folic acid	mg	0.8/0.7	1.0	1.0	0.75	2.0	2.0-3.0	2.0-2.5
Biotin	mg	0.125	0.05	0.10	0.20	0.25	0.25-0.30	0.20-0.25
Vitamin C	mg	-	-	-	-	-	100-200 [3]	100-200 [3]
Choline	mg	1,100	800	600	1700	800	500-1000	400-600

(1) Add 5 mg/kg for each 1% dietary fat when fat is higher than 3%;
(2) For optimum meat quality increase level up to 200 mg/kg
(3) Recommended under heat stress conditions; use phosphorylated form in heat treated feeds

Table XIII. Recommended vitamin levels (IU or mg/kg air-dry feed) for turkey finisher (>16 weeks) by various sources

	Source / Units	NRC, 1994 (>16 wks)	INRA, 1984	Larbier and Leclerq, 1992	Leeson and Summers, 1997	Leeson and Summers, 2005	DSM OVN (2011) Finisher 2 (>18 wks)
Vitamin A	IU	5,000	8,000	10,000	7,000	10,000	6000-9000
Vitamin D3	IU	1,100	1,200	2,000	2,200	3,500	2000-3000
25-OH-D3 (HyD)	mg	-	-	-	-	-	0.092
Vitamin E	IU	10	10	20	20	100	30-50 [1][2]
Vitamin K	mg	0.75/0.5	2.0	2.0	1.5	3.0	3.0-4.0
Vitamin B1	mg	2.0	-	1.0	2.5	3.0	2.0-3.0
Vitamin B2	mg	2.5	4.0	4.0	5.0	10.0	8.0-10
Vitamin B6	mg	2.0/4.0	-	3.0	3.0	6.0	3.0-6.0
Vitamin B12	mg	0.003	0.01	0.01	0.012	0.02	0.015-0.025
Niacin	mg	40	40	50	60	60	50-60
D-Panthothenic acid	mg	9.0	5	12	15	18	15-20
Folic acid	mg	0.7	0.5	1.0	0.50	2.0	2.0-2.5
Biotin	mg	0.1		0.10	0.15	0.25	0.20-0.25
Vitamin C	mg	-	-	-	-	-	100-200[3]
Choline	mg	950/800	500	600	1500	800	400-600

(1) Add 5 mg/kg for each 1% dietary fat when fat is higher than 3%;
(2) For optimum meat quality increase level up to 200 mg/kg
(3) Recommended under heat stress conditions; use phosphorylated form in heat treated feeds

Table XIV. Recommended vitamin levels (IU or mg/kg air-dry feed) by principal turkey genetic companies and DSM Optimum Vitamin Nutrition (OVN) levels

Grow-out phase	Source / Units	Starter			Grower			Finisher			
		BUT & Nicholas 0-4 wks	Hybrid 0-6 wks	DSM OVN 0-6 wks	BUT & Nicholas 5-12 wks	Hybrid 7-14 wks	DSM OVN 7-12 wks	BUT & Nicholas >13	Hybrid >15	DSM OVN 13-18 wks	DSM OVN (2011) >18 wks
Vitamin A	IU	15,000	12,000	12000-15000	10,000	9,600	10000-12000	8,000	8,000	8000-10000	6000-9000
Vitamin D3	IU	5,000	5,000	4000-5000	3,000	4,800	3000-5000	2,000	4,000	3000-4000	2000-3000
25-OH-D3 (HyD)	mg	-	suggested	0.092	-	suggested	0.092	-	suggested	0.092	0.092
Vitamin E	IU	100	100	100-250 [1][2]	80	60	60-80	50	30	30-50 [4]	30-50 [4]
Vitamin K	mg	5	4	4.0-5.0	3	3	3.0-4.0	3	2.5	3.0-4.0	3.0-4.0
Vitamin B1	mg	5	4.5	4.5-5.0	1	2	3.0-5.0	1	2	3.0-4.0	2.0-3.0
Vitamin B2	mg	8	15	15-20	6	12	10-15	6	10	8.0-10.0	8.0-10.0
Vitamin B6	mg	7	5	6.0-7.0	5	3.5	5.0-7.0	3	2.5	3.0-6.0	3.0-6.0
Vitamin B12	mg	0.02	0.04	0.040-0.050	0.02	0.02	0.03-0.04	0.02	0.015	0.020-0.030	0.015-0.025
Niacin	mg	75	110	100-150	50	85	80-100	40	55	60-80	50-60
D-Panthothenic acid	mg	25	28	30-35	15	23	20-25	15	17	15-20	15-20
Folic acid	mg	3	3.5	4.0-6.0	2	2.5	2.0-3.0	2	2	2.0-2.5	2.0-2.5
Biotin	mg	0.3	0.3	0.25-0.40	0.3	0.17	0.25-0.30	0.2	0.16	0.20-0.25	0.20-0.25
Vitamin C	mg	-	-	100-200 [3]	-	-	100-200	-	-	100-200 [3]	100-200 [3]
Choline	mg	400	1200	1000-1200	300	900	500-1000	200	600	400-600	400-600

(1) Add 5 mg/kg for each 1% dietary fat when fat is higher than 3%;
(2) Higher level for optimum immune function
(3) Recommended under heat stress conditions; use phosphorylated form in heat treated feeds
(4) For optimum meat quality increase level up to 200 mg/kg

159

LATEST INVESTIGATIONS IN VITAMIN NUTRITION

The best specialists agree on the need to reevaluate the vitamin requirements of broilers and turkeys (Portsmouth, 1996; Bains, 1999; Whitehead, 2001, 2002; Leeson, 2007). In the past 10–15 years there have been investigations on vitamins E and D_3, principally focusing first on discovering their functions and applications in immunity and the oxidative stability of meat, and second on preventing foot problems; as well as to a lesser extent on the effects of vitamin C under heat stress conditions. For the remainder of vitamins there are few recent studies.

WATER-SOLUBLE VITAMINS

The deficiencies shown in vitamins of the B group are rare nowadays (Whitehead, 2002). However, an inadequate supply of these vitamins with important roles in the regulatory processes of bone growth, usually manifests itself in disorders of the epiphyseal growth plate, with reduction in the proliferation of chondrocytes, which results in shortened and twisted bones and in deformity of the condyles of the tibiotarsal articulation, which rotates 90–180°, causing displacement of the gastrocnemius tendon (slipped tendon), an abnormal condition known as chondrodystrophy or perosis (Rama-Rao et al., 2003; Waldenstedt, 2006). This problem can also be caused indirectly by microplasmas, since they reduce the supply of nutrients the growth plate receives (Whitehead, 2005). Of particular importance in preventing the condition are pyridoxine and folic acid (especially if the diet is high in protein), riboflavin, niacin, biotin and choline, and in the initial phases birds respond well to extra supplementation with vitamins of the B group (Klein-Hessling, 2006).

The principal functions of the B-group vitamins are connected with energy metabolism from carbohydrates, fatty acids and proteins. Except in organs with high metabolic requirements such as heart, liver and kidneys, birds lack reserves of these vitamins, while even in these organs the reserve is very small after hatching, which

means a continuous supply is needed. The presence of aflatoxins in feed reduces the level of most of these vitamins in plasma and liver by 50 and 20%, respectively, if their concentration reaches 5 mg/kg of feed (Bains, 2001). Furthermore, a greater supply of these vitamins reduces the adverse effects of mycotoxins by favoring their break-down and detoxification in the liver.

Stress conditions increase energy requirements and reduce feed consumption, and a higher supplement of these vitamins, even over short periods, helps birds to overcome the consequences of stress prejudicial to their productivity and immune status. Thus Ferket and Qureshi (1992), who administered a combination of water-soluble vitamins and electrolytes in the drinking water of broilers, which they intermittently subjected to heat stress for 4–5 days, for 24 hours prior to and during the entire period of stress, obtained better growth rates and feed conversion and a higher level of IgG immunoglobulins, which were in fact comparable to those obtained with a complete vitamin shock also including vitamins A, D_3 and E.

In an experiment under practical conditions, Coelho et al. (2001) compared, under different degrees and conditions of stress (population density, new or permanent bedding, E. coli and coccidia infection, etc.), the effects of multiplying by various factors (1x, 2x, 4x, 8x and 16x) the levels indicated by the NRC for riboflavin, niacin, folic acid, pantothenic acid and vitamin B_{12}. These vitamins were chosen specifically for their role in protein deposition, which has increased in modern strains with high breast yields. Under intense stress conditions the increased levels were unable to compensate fully for the reduction in performance, but the most favorable results came with dosages higher than fourfold. In the groups subjected to a low or moderate stress level, the live weight, viability and feed conversion index improved in proportion to the supplementation level. The sixteen-fold level produced the maximum benefits (+16.4% live weight and –6.6% in feed conversion compared to the NRC level).

Carcass and breast yield and the percentage of abdominal fat also improved significantly. At fourfold inclusion, the profits per bird were $0.17, and at 16 times the dose $0.30, and returns on investment were calculated as 4.2% and 1.5%, respectively.

Other researchers have looked at the effects on product quality. Swierczewska *et al.* (2005) evaluated the chemical and sensory composition of the breast and leg of chickens fed with quantities of vitamins B_2, B_6, B_{12} and folic acid twice as high as those recommended by the NRC. Analysis of the muscle composition revealed more protein and less fat than the birds in the control group. The cholesterol level, very much depending on the type of muscle considered, was higher in the legs of the birds which received a supplement and any level of vitamins, probably because of the fat contained in the supplement. The smallest quantity of collagen was found in the diets which included a standard level of vitamins. There were no negative effects on the sensory quality of the meat.

THIAMINE (VITAMIN B_1)

Functions

Thiamine has an important role in carbohydrate metabolism and therefore in energy metabolism, especially in the heart and nervous system. It is also necessary for the synthesis of nucleic acids and of acetylcholine, essential in the transmission of nervous impulses. Requirements differ for different organs; the content of B_1 in the heart is higher than in the liver and brain, and it responds in greater measure to changes in the level of B_1 in the diet (Olkowski and Classen, 1996).

Sources

Cereals and soy have a high thiamine content and are thus unlikely to lead to a deficiency, although on occasion deficiencies have been confirmed in the field, with symptoms such as anorexia, polyneuritis and foot problems. Vitamin B_1 requirements increase if the diet is high in carbohydrates, so if there is a thiamine deficiency the body's reserves are rapidly exhausted. Including fish meal (which contains thiaminases) or amprolium (an antagonist of B_1) increases the requirement for this vitamin in the diet. In premixes that include choline and trace minerals its stability is relatively low; at ambient temperature vitamin B_1 content may be reduced by up to 50%. This occurs to a greater extent in feed contaminated by mycotoxin-producing fungi such as *Aspergillus* and *Fusarium*, where the B_1 concentration can drop by a factor of up to 10 (Nagaraj and Wu, 1993).

Requirements and recommendations for supplementation

The NRC (1994) recommends a supplementation in broiler feed of 1.8 ppm, based on studies carried out in the 1960s. Thiamine requirements have been investigated very little in the last 30 years but they appear to be higher than those indicated by the NRC (Portsmouth, 1996). With higher supplementation levels, some reports show improvements in weight gain and conversion index in broilers (Wagstaff, 1978) and a reduction of mortality in young turkeys (Cook, 1992). Olkowski and Classen (1996) found that with 2–4 ppm the plasma content of B_1 decreased with age, but it was higher and more constant at 8 ppm, and increased continuously with 16 and 32 ppm. Leeson and Summers (1997) and all the genetics companies suggest levels 2–3 times higher than the NRC's, especially in hot climates since it is known that at 32°C the requirements for preventing polyneuritis are triple those appropriate at 21°C (Whitehead and Portsmouth, 1989). In turkeys the difference is 50%.

Other factors which affect optimum thiamine levels are the hen's nutrition, which influences the reserves and metabolism of her progeny (Olkowski and Classen, 1999), and the existence of pathological processes. In feeds containing *Fusarium proliferatum*, vitamin B_1 supplementation at levels higher than those recommended by the NRC (22 and 89 ppm) improved weight gain in the starter phase, and were effective in preventing

161

immunosuppression (Nagaraj and Wu, 1993; Yang and Wu, 1997). It is also known that coccidia compete with the birds for this vitamin, the plasma level of which correlates to the severity of the disease. On the other hand, Deyhim et al. (1996) found a 23% reduction in thiamine content of the breast when the vitamin premix was withdrawn during the finishing period.

RIBOFLAVIN (VITAMIN B$_2$)

Functions

This vitamin, in its phosphorylated form or as constituent of the flavoproteins, is a coenzyme and cofactor of more than 50 enzymes involved in redox reactions, in the metabolism of carbohydrates and amino acids, and in the synthesis and oxidation of fatty acids and transporting proteins. It plays an important role in maintaining the integrity of mucous membranes and the nervous system. It interacts with other vitamins: pyridoxine, niacin and pantothenic acid. Squires and Naber (1993) demonstrated that the concentration of riboflavin in the egg diminishes as the laying hen gets older.

Riboflavin is more likely than other vitamins to become deficient under practical conditions, especially under stressful conditions (Ruiz and Harms, 1988b, 1989; Whitehead, 2000) and when aflatoxins are present (Leeson et al., 1995), for which reason an ample safety margin should be applied in poultry nutrition (Ibrahim, 1998). Deficiency is characterized by poor plumage, deterioration in growth rates and feed conversion, paralysis and claw curvature, a lowering of resistance to heat stress, enteritis and diarrhea, and an increase in mortality in the first week (Summers et al., 1984; Leeson et al., 1995; Klasing, 1998). Portsmouth (1996) indicates that riboflavin deficiency can periodically be observed in newly hatched chicks, manifested as clubbed down, although Whitehead (2004) points out that according to recent research the cause of this problem may be not nutrition but infection.

According to Yang and Wang (1996a, b), the maximum deposition of riboflavin in the liver is achieved with 17 ppm in the first week, and with 6 and 4 ppm in the second and third weeks, respectively; the absorption of methionine also increased if the maximum concentration was used.

The withdrawal of vitamin B$_2$ from the diet during the last weeks reduces its content in breast tissue by 37% (Deyhim et al., 1996), which is of interest from the consumer's point of view, since normally 100 g of breast meat contributes 9% of the recommended daily intake of this vitamin.

Sources

Riboflavin is fairly abundant in by-products of animal origin and in dehydrated alfalfa, but scarce in cereals and protein-rich feed ingredients. Corn-soy diets usually contain 2–2.6 mg/kg riboflavin, 60% of which is bioavailable (Chung and Baker, 1990). But the increase in pelleting temperatures and the use of expanders to control contamination by Salmonella has increased its degradation (Ibrahim, 1998).

Requirements and recommendations for supplementation

The levels recommended by the NRC are based on studies carried out over 20 years ago. Ruiz and Harms (1988d), with broiler starter diets containing vitamin B$_2$ at 2.6 ppm, found that reduced growth rates, severe paralysis and high mortality were confirmed at 2.6 ppm. They found 3.6 mg/kg was needed to achieve maximum productivity, and 4.6 ppm to prevent foot problems. Rutz et al. (1989) obtained optimum performance by supplementing 2 mg/kg riboflavin, with higher levels not bringing further improvements. Subsequent studies, carried out with a higher number of replicates, raised the optimum dosage to 5.0–7.2 (Deyhim et al., 1990, 1991; Olkowski and Classen, 1998).

Whitehead (1999) pointed out that riboflavin requirements for growth, expressed as a percentage of the diet, had not changed in spite of the considerable genetic progress in broiler productivity; but that if the well-being of the birds was adopted as an additional criterion they could be doubled under stress conditions. The recommendations of the principal genetic selection companies tend in this direction.

Deyhim *et al.* (1991) used a vitamin B_2 concentration 2 times higher than that recommended by the NRC, and achieved an increase of 6% in live weight; when broilers were subjected to cyclical heat stress (24–35–24°C) the improvement was maintained at 5%, while the feed conversion index and mortality fell by 2% and 6%, respectively compared to the control. Whitehead (1999) induced chronic heat stress in chickens of 7 to 21 days of age, supplemented with 2.8, 3.3, 7 and 15 ppm. Heat stress reduced growth rate by an average of 10%. No significant effects on the riboflavin level were detected, but curved claws were observed even at 7 mg/kg (**Table XV**). At normal temperatures 3.3 mg/kg was sufficient. Under tropical conditions

positive responses were found at 5.1–10 ppm (Ogunmodede, 1977; Ibrahim, 1998).

In turkeys, the most recent studies on riboflavin requirements were conducted by Lee (1982), who proposed 4 mg/kg as the most suitable level, and by Ruiz and Harms (1988a, 1989), on whose results the current NRC recommendations are based. In young turkeys of 0–21 days it was estimated that a total provision of 3.5 mg/kg was enough to achieve maximum production, although to prevent paralysis and curved claws it was necessary to increase to 4.4 ppm. The same investigators determined that to maximize the live weight of males of 4–8 and 9–11 weeks the optimum dietary levels were 3.6 and 2.5 mg/kg, respectively. However, Leeson and Summers (1997) and the majority of North American companies (Coelho, 2000) were using appreciably higher supplementation levels.

Table XV. Live weight and incidence of paralysis and curved claws in broilers fed on diets with different riboflavin concentrations, under normal temperature conditions or chronic heat stress conditions. (Whitehead, 1999)

	Temperature	Riboflavin mg/kg			
		2.8	3.3	7	15
Live weight 21 days, g	Normal	526	661	625	598
	Heat stress	507	567	539	558
% paralysis, curved claws	Normal	22	0	0	0
	Heat stress	20	4	2	0

PYRIDOXINE (VITAMIN B_6)

Functions and sources

Vitamin B_6 includes 3 compounds with similar actions: pyridoxal, pyridoxamine and pyridoxine. Pyridoxine is the most active and commonly found in feed ingredients. The majority of the ingredients are good sources of this vitamin, but its bioavailability is relatively low (40–60%), particularly in soy.

Like the rest of the vitamins in the B group, B_6 has numerous metabolic functions, principally in the metabolism and transport of amino acids, especially methionine and tryptophan. This means the use of high

levels of these amino acids increases the requirement for pyridoxine, and a deficiency of which reduces the nitrogen retention. Vitamin B_6 is stored principally in muscular tissue. It participates in the incorporation of iron into hemoglobin and in the synthesis of immunoglobulins, so that a marginal deficiency will cause normochromic microcytic polycythemia (the increase of small red cells), and a fall in IgM and IgG (Blalock and Thaxton, 1984; Blalock *et al.*, 1984).

Requirements and recommendations for supplementation

Few recent investigations into vitamin B_6 requirements have been carried out because it is generally considered that practical diets provide sufficient vitamin B_6. However, it should be kept in mind that modern birds consume less feed per kg of live weight, so that vitamin intake falls proportionately. Moreover, the optimum requirements of pyridoxine are related to the levels of protein and amino acids in the diet (Daghir and Shah, 1973), for which reason it has been suggested that when using high protein diets, as is normal nowadays for broilers and turkeys, its requirement would increase by 25% (Portsmouth, 1996). The NRC position is based on studies from the early 1970s, and it proposes 3.5 mg/kg for broilers and turkeys from 8 weeks onwards and 4.5 mg/kg for turkeys of 0–2 months. According to Villamide and Fraga (1999), the majority of vitamin premixes in Spain provide lower levels. A dosage of 4 mg/kg is sufficient to counteract the toxic effects of the inclusion of high proportions of some legumes in feeds (Walters et al., 1991). Other authors consider that the supplement should be up to 6 mg/kg (Leeson and Summers, 1997; Bains, 1999). A previous study on turkeys estimated requirements of 6 mg/kg (Waldroup et al., 1976). The content of B_6 in eggs decreases as the age of the laying hen increases (Robel, 1983).

Vitamin B_6 also seems to be important from the point of view of animal well-being. It has been shown that high levels of pyridoxine (500–1,000 mg/kg) can reduce fear reactions in broilers, as assessed by the duration of the tonic immobility reaction (Schwean and Classen, 1995). These high doses reduced growth, but they improved the conversion index. Supplementing with 3 ppm pyridoxine was found beneficial, either on its own or in combination with 60 ppm L-carnitine under conditions of thermal stress (Celik et al., 2006). This combination improved weight gain and feed intake, as well as carcass weight, something which was not observed when pyridoxine alone was used. This synergy may be attributable to the potential in both substances to regulate energy metabolism and modulate oxidative stress.

Attention has also been given to vitamin B_6 in relation to foot problems (**Table XVI**), because supplementation reduces the incidence (Cope et al., 1979, Beirne and Jensen, 1981). According to Sauveur (1984), pyridoxine is involved in the formation of picolinic acid (derived from tryptophan), in turn linked to the intestinal absorption of zinc, and all of them would act synergically in preventing foot problems. Masse et al. (1994, 1996) demonstrated that a marginal deficiency of vitamin B_6 leads to incomplete development of the collagen and an anarchic invasion of the bone growth plate by irregular blood vessels, together with long bone deviation, problems which could be reduced with higher supplementation. They considered this vitamin essential for the integrity of the conjunctive tissue matrix and the development of the skeleton.

Table XVI. Effect of pyridoxine supplementation on foot problems in broilers
Cope et al., 1979, cit. by Sauveur, 1988

	Basal diet 4.7 ppm	+ 10 ppm	+ 30 ppm	+ 110 ppm
Normal claws and feet	31 %	66 %	82 %	79 %
Twisted claws, or slightly affected feet	50 %	20 %	16 %	11 %
Severe deformity of claws and feet	19 %	13 %	2 %	11 %

VITAMIN B$_{12}$

Functions and sources

Cyanocobalamin is involved in the metabolism of fatty acids and the synthesis of proteins, and also in reactions which involve the transfer of methyl and hydrogenated/hydrogen groups. It interacts with methionine and with folic and pantothenic acids. It is present only at low levels in poultry diets, especially if they do not include meal of animal origin, although it is the most stable vitamin during feed pelleting and storage processes. It is estimated that 100 g of breast meat provides 8.5% of daily requirements in humans.

Requirements and recommendations for supplementation

Vitamin B$_{12}$ requirements are very small – they are measured in micrograms – and it is moreover the vitamin stored in the greatest quantities, principally in the liver. Requirements were estimated as 12 µg/kg in the 1970s (Whitehead and Portsmouth, 1989). Portsmouth (1996) considered that its level should be increased by about 20% in diets without animal byproduct meal. No recent papers have been published, either for broilers or turkeys, except for a study by Alisheilkhov *et al.* (2000) where the combination of 35 µg/kg vitamin B$_{12}$ and of 103 mg/kg vitamin C increased live weight by 7.5% and energy use by 6.7% compared to the control group.

NIACIN$_2$

Functions

Niacin includes two active compounds, nicotinic acid and niacinamide, both available commercially; the biopotency of the second is 24% greater (Maurice and Lightsey, 1996; Ruiz and Harms, 1988e). There are 14 known metabolic reactions in which it participates, forming part of the NAD and NADP coenzymes. It is therefore essential in the metabolism of carbohydrates, amino acids and fatty acids, and in obtaining energy through the Krebs cycle.

Niacin interacts with other nutrients, principally with tryptophan, from which it may be obtained given sufficient quantities of riboflavin and pyridoxine; the reaction is irreversible. Tryptophan is converted into niacin at a ratio of 45–50:1 in chickens (Whitehead and Portsmouth, 1989) or 102–119:1 in turkeys (Ruiz and Harms, 1988c). This difference is due to the higher level of picolinic acid and lower amount of the picolinic acid carboxylase enzyme present in the later species, making its requirements much higher than those of broilers. In practice the production of niacin from tryptophan is minimal, since this amino acid is not normally found in excess in diets. Moreover, high levels of fat in feed, especially saturated fat, will inhibit this reaction (Whitehead, 2001).

Sources

Niacin is abundant in by-products of animal origin and distilling, as well as in cereals, but its bioavailability is low, especially in wheat and sorghum (10–15%), as it is found in combination with a peptide or a carbohydrate (niacytin) which cannot be assimilated by birds. In oilseeds, bioavailability is 40%. It is fairly stable under normal conditions. Chicken meat is an excellent source of niacin, providing some 14 mg/100 g (78% of recommended daily intake).

Requirements and recommendations for supplementation

The requirements for niacin are uncertain since its availability varies depending on cereal type and the influence of tryptophan levels. It is assumed that requirements have increased in correlation to the improvement in growth rate, but very little research has in fact been carried out in the last 25 years. In broilers, Whitehead and Porstmouth (1989) proposed a level two times higher than the NRC's (35 ppm), and later Whitehead (1993) estimated requirements at 50–60 mg/kg. Waldenstedt (2006) points out that that the proportion of birds with foot defects is higher in birds whose diet is low in this vitamin.

165

North American studies, based on corn-soy diets, are somewhat contradictory. Waldroup *et al.* (1985), in a series of 4 experiments with broilers fattened to 42 days, used supplements of 33–66 ppm to a basal diet with 33 mg/kg, and observed significant improvements in live weight (with a greater response in males) and in some cases in the feed conversion index. However, Ruiz and Harms (1990) found no significant differences above the same basal level. In turkeys, Ruiz and Harms (1988a) and Ruiz and Harms (1989), who worked with 30% higher tryptophan levels, concluded that daily niacin requirements were 32 and 27 mg/kg of feed from 0 to 3 and 3 to 7 weeks, respectively, which would make supplementation in corn-soy diets unnecessary.

Whitehead (2001) considers that these levels are totally inadequate for diets based on wheat and for current growth rates, and conducted and published two experiments, in which the best results for live weight and conversion at 3 and 6 weeks were achieved with 80–100 mg/kg. Under heat stress conditions the niacin requirement for maximum growth dropped to 50 mg/kg, due to the lower weight gain caused by the high temperatures (**Table XVII**).

The data for turkeys are also inconsistant. Ruiz and Harms (1988a) tried supplementation levels up to 88 ppm in young turkeys of 0–21 days old, and concluded that a minimum of 44 ppm was sufficient to maximize productive results and reduce the incidence and severity of foot problems. In contrast, Maurice *et al.* (1990), obtained significant improvements in live weight at 8 weeks with diets containing 140 mg/kg, twice as much as proposed by the NRC, an improvement maintained to a lesser extent under stress conditions from damp bedding. In a subsequent investigation, Maurice (1996) found that in turkeys older than 8–12 weeks the high dose of niacin counteracted the reduction in growth caused by high population density, and also improved the composition of the carcass. In respiratory infections from *Bordetella* on the other hand, positive effects were obtained from the addition of niacin to drinking water (Yersin *et al.*, 1989). Whitehead (2001) proposed adding 70 mg/kg niacin to feeds up to 12 weeks.

Table XVII. Responses to niacin supplementation at normal temperature or under chronic heat stress. Whitehead (2001)

Niacin, mg/kg	0	20	40	50	60	80
Experiment 1						
Live weight 42 days, kg	2.50 a	2.54 a	2.49 a	---	2.50 a	2.59 b
Feed efficiency (gain/feed)	0.56	0.57	0.56	---	0.57	0.58
Experiment 2						
Wt. 21 d., g Normal temp.	660 a	629 a	---	636 a	---	713 b
Wt. 21 d., g, Heat Stress	573 a	584 a	---	655 b	---	618b

Different letters indicate significant differences at P<0,05

PANTOTHENIC ACID

Functions and sources

This vitamin is a constituent of the acetyl-coenzyme A, which is essential in the utilization of nutrients for obtaining energy in the Krebs cycle, and of other enzymes and coenzymes. It takes part in the synthesis of fatty acids, cholesterol and steroid hormones. It is also involved in the production of antibodies, in the activity of the adrenal glands, and in the acetylation of choline for nervous impulse transmission. It has a relationship with vitamin B_{12}; if the latter is deficient it accentuates the lack of pantothenic acid. It also interacts with folic acid, biotin and copper. Pantothenic acid is present at low levels in basic feed ingredients such as corn, barley and soy, and more abundant in green plants and by-products of animal origin. It is fairly stable under normal conditions.

Requirements and recommendations for supplementation

The established requirements for chickens and turkeys (10 mg/kg feed) are based on studies from the late 1970s. There are very few more recent experimental data although, contrary to the situation with other vitamins, they tend to confirm earlier findings. Dehyim *et al.* (1992) tried concentrations 2 and 4 times higher than normal in broilers without obtaining improvements in their growth rate or energy balance. Harms and Nelson (1992) tried supplementation levels of up to 14.4

mg/kg in chicks (0–21 days) without finding significant differences in growth rate or feed conversion index compared to the levels currently established by the NRC. Studies in turkeys have produced similar results, both in the starter period (Ruiz and Harms, 1989) and between 4 and 12 weeks, where the use of levels lower than those of the NRC (4–8 mg/kg) in corn-soy diets did not entail significant changes in these parameters (Harms and Bootwalla, 1992).

However, the current recommended levels for commercial strains are 2–3 times higher, probably because of the role attributed to pantothenic acid in general resistance to stress and in the prevention of skin lesions (Bains, 1999). The study by Dehyim *et al.* (1992) offers another interesting aspect; the possibility of enriching pantothenic acid content in poultry meat. At the dosage used pantothenic acid in breast meat increased by 35–74%.

FOLIC ACID

Functions and sources

Folic acid is structurally one of the most complex vitamins. Its principal functions are related to the synthesis of protein and nucleic acids and the interconversions of various amino acids. It is also necessary for the maturation process of red corpuscles and the functioning of the immune system.

It is present in the majority of the ingredients of poultry diets, especially in those of animal origin, but in insufficient quantity (Bains, 1999). Chicken meat contains some 12 mg/100, providing 6% of the recommended daily intake in humans.

Requirements and recommendations for supplementation

The NRC recommendations (0.55 mg/kg) have not changed in 25 years, and few recent studies have been published, but in general these have found responses at higher dosages. Ryu *et al.* (1995) consider that the requirements are not well established due to inadequacies of the analytical methods, to the widespread belief that soy-based diets do not require supplementation, and to the fact that many nutritional factors

may modify their requirements. Pesti *et al.* (1991) demonstrated that corn-soy diets with a theoretical content of 1.5 ppm produced clear signs of folic acid deficiency, because its actual concentration was 3 times lower.

Folic acid requirements vary according to the composition of the diet. They increase if the protein level is high, since it is required for the synthesis of uric acid (Creek and Vasaitis, 1963). They are also influenced by the levels of certain amino acids (methionine, glycine, serine) and of other vitamins – they increase if B_{12} and especially choline are deficient. With choline and methionine levels close to those recommended by the NRC, supplements of 1.2 mg/kg have been suggested (Pesti *et al.*, 1991; Ryu *et al.*, 1995). Others have found positive responses in growth and feed conversion even with 1.8–2 mg/kg (Pesti and Rowland, 1989; Ryu and Pesti, 1993; Ryu *et al.*, 1994). Based on these production criteria, Ryu *et al.* (1995) estimated the total requirements at 1.45 mg/kg, and recommended adding 1.2–1.3 mg/kg depending on the levels of choline in the diet.

However, Whitehead *et al.* (1995) did not observe this supposed dependence on choline levels, and they suggest that methionine deficiency may be more significant for folic acid requirements. In their experiments maximum growth and conversion results were obtained with a total content in the starter diet (meal) of 1.7–2.0 mg/kg, thus requiring supplementation with an estimated 1.5 mg/kg. For granular feeds the authors recommend a supplement of 2.5 to 3 mg/kg. Along the same lines El Husseiny et al. (2007) presented a study which evaluated the efficacy of folic acid and betaine in situations where methionine was adequate or limiting. In both cases improvements were obtained in production parameters, digestibility of nutrients and carcass yield with levels of both folic acid and betaine of 0.5–0.75 or 1 ppm. No information is available for turkeys.

Folic acid appears to be effective in preventing certain pathological disorders. In the case of reovirus infection, lesions decreased if the concentration of folic acid in diets was two times higher than that proposed by the NRC (Cook et al., 1983, 1984b). A trial using thiram (tetramethylthiuram disulfide) to induce tibial dyschondroplasia in chickens (Rath et al. 2006) evaluated the protective capacity of various vitamins (A, D, B$_6$ and folic acid) against this condition, and concluded that folic acid levels five times higher than those recommended by the NRC were the most effective for this purpose. The low levels of folic acid in high-protein diets increase the incidence of foot problems (Ryu et al., 1995; Waldenstedt, 2006).

BIOTIN

Functions

Biotin acts as cofactor for many enzymes that take part in gluconeogenesis, in protein synthesis, and in carboxylation reactions produced in the metabolism of carbohydrates, lipids and proteins, which are important for the synthesis of long chain fatty acids. Thus in cases of biotin deficiency specific alterations have been described in the lipid profile of bird tissues, consisting of a proportional reduction in the concentrations of fatty acids with a greater number of carbon atoms (Watkins and Kratzer, 1987 abc; Watkins, 1989; Chee and Chang, 1995). Hypoglycemia is also typical (Balnave et al., 1977), since biotin helps to maintain glucose levels when carbohydrate intake is low. The classic symptoms of biotin deficiency are dermatitis, growth reduction and foot deformities, with alterations in bone formation (Bain and Newbrey, 1988). The biotin content of the hatchable egg increases with the age of the hen (Whitehead et al., 1985).

Sources

The majority of ingredients show great variability in content and bioavailability of biotin (Whitehead et al., 1982; Frigg, 1984, 1987; Misir and Blair, 1988). The best known case is wheat (bioavailability 0–5%); in

barley it is 11%, and in corn and soy 75–100% (Whitehead et al., 1982). Diets based on these cereals without biotin supplementation lead to higher mortality and slower growth rates. Other influences are some nutrients, such as fiber, which interfere with its intestinal absorption (Misir and Blair, 1984; Oloyo, 1991); the protein level with greater requirements at 18% than at 22% crude protein (Whitehead and Blair, 1974); the level of choline and the other water-soluble vitamins, which at high levels reduce the bioavailability of biotin (Whitehead et al., 1976; Whitehead and Randall, 1982); the proportion of added fat (Whitehead et al., 1976), and even the composition of the fat. Various studies carried out in the 1970s, cited by Whitehead and Portsmouth (1989) indicated an increase of biotin requirements in diets high in PUFA and the addition of tallow reduced mortality from FLKS (Balnave et al., 1977). Biotin requirements thus depend in great measure on the composition of the diet.

Steam pelleting does not affect the stability of biotin (Whitehead and Bannister, 1980), and there has even been an increase of 10% measured in its bioavailability (Buenrostro and Kratzer, 1984). As with the majority of the vitamins of the B group, there is a certain amount of recycling through the ingestion of shavings with feces; but at 3 weeks this is negligible, and at 7 weeks, it only amounts to 0.01 mg/kg (Whitehead and Bannister, 1980).

Requirements and recommendations for supplementation

The study of this vitamin received a great boost as a result of the appearance in the 1970s of a serious metabolic problem in broilers known as fatty liver and kidney syndrome, FLKS, described in detail by Whitehead (1988) and Bryden (1991). The syndrome's biochemical manifestations correspond to those described above. The imbalance between two enzymes dependent on biotin prevented hepatic gluconeogenesis from re-establishing levels of glycemia in cases of greater demand due to fasting or heat stress. The mobilization of lipid reserves to obtain glucose failed and led to fatty infiltration of the organs and death by acidosis. Whitehead et al. (1976) demonstrated clearly that FLKS is due to insufficient biotin in the diet. This pathology was seen in particular when broiler diets were relatively low in fat and protein. Whitehead (2000) indicated that the problem was again being found in the United Kingdom.

Studies carried out more than 25 years ago (Whitehead and Bannister, 1980) established a level of 170 µg/kg as the biotin requirement for growth in broilers, although the NRC maintained its recommendation at 150 µg/kg, based on older data. Other authors (Misir and Blair, 1984; Watkins and Kratzer, 1987; Oloyo, 1991, 1994; Chee and Chang, 1995) found linear responses up to 200 µg/kg. Whitehead (1988) indicated that the biotin requirement

could increase under conditions of nutritional or environmental stress, and that with diets slightly low in fat or protein, 250–300 µg/kg might be necessary to minimize mortality. Oloyo (1991, 1994) specified 200 µg/kg to prevent FLKS, pododermatitis, and foot deformities completely, a level rather higher than that required to achieve optimum live weight and feed conversion. Some diets with unshelled sunflower seeds required up to 240 µg/kg biotin to achieve the same results.

In sunsequent investigations responses have been obtained to even higher values. Balios and Poupulis (1992) obtained significant improvements in live weight and feed conversion with 550 µg/kg when the proportion of fat added to the feed was 1.5% instead of 6.5%. Brufau et al. (1995) significantly increased the growth rate and feed conversion efficiency by adding 200 µg/kg to diets with 50% wheat, and Jian et al. (1996), also with wheat-based diets, increased live weight at 21 days by using up to 300 µg/kg. With feeds based on wheat and 6 supplementation levels (between 0 and 250 µg/kg of biotin available), Whitehead (2000) obtained 100 g more live weight at 40 days with the maximum level (300 µg/kg of total content) than with the base level (**Table XVIII**). No statistical significance was found for the feed conversion index, but it showed numerical improvement.

Biotin is also related to other aspects of animal health and well-being. It has been observed that sudden death syndrome tends to decrease when higher levels of biotin are used (Hulan et al., 1980; Whitehead and

Table XVIII. Responses to biotin supplementation of a diet with wheat and 50 µg/kg available biotin (Whitehead, 2000)

Total biotin	50	120	170	200	250	300
Live weight 21 days, g	720 a	739	726	742	740	763 b
Feed efficiency (gain/feed) 0–21 days	0.587	0.608	0.600	0.600	0.605	0.633
Live wt. 40 days, kg	2.18 a	2.22	2.24	2.24	2.23	2.29 b
Feed efficiency (gain/feed) 0–42 days	0.502	0.514	0.499	0.511	0.482	0.520

Different letters indicate significant differences at P<0.01

169

Randall, 1982), although the etiology of this condition remains unclear. A significant reduction in lesions from reovirus infection (tenosynovitis and twisted feet) has also been found when the biotin concentration in the diet is 200% higher than that indicated by the NRC (Cook et al., 1984a, b).

Another disorder related to biotin is plantar pododermatitis. Various now outdated studies have established a clear relationship between biotin deficiency and digital and plantar lesions (Harms and Simpson, 1975; Harms et al., 1977; McIlroy et al., 1987). The incidence of these conditions has increased over recent years (Ekstrand et al., 1997; Martrenchar et al., 2002; Folegatti et al., 2006; Pagazaurtundúa and Warris, 2006) and there is pressure in the EU to reduce it for reasons of animal welfare. The causes are known to be multifactorial and there is now known to be a genetic link.

The primary cause of pododermatitis stems from breeding poultry on excessively damp bedding (Haslam et al., 2007; Mayne et al., 2007 b), be it due to insufficient ventilation flow (Folegatti et al., 2006) and/or excessive population density (Ekstrand et al., 1997), certain types of bedding and their depth (Martrenchar et al., 2002; Haslam et al., 2007), or through the influence of certain ingredients or of nutritional imbalances, which lead to wet droppings (Oloyo, 1991, 1994; Bilgili et al., 2005; Eichner et al., 2007). As yet, there are no studies on the possible benefits of biotin to combat the factors which lead to the appearance of plantar pododermatitis.

FLKS appears rarely in turkeys, although it has been induced experimentally with low biotin diets and an 18-hour fast (Whitehead and Siller, 1983). However, under commercial conditions the characteristic signs of biotin deficiency (dermatitis, perosis) have been observed much more than in chickens (Whitehead, 1988; Waldenstedt, 2006), and turkeys, especially the males, are more prone than females to plantar pododermatitis, which causes pain and impaired mobility.

Biotin requirements are especially high in this species of poultry (Whitehead, 1977; Mayne, 2005). In early studies, levels of 300 mg/t feed were needed to reverse plantar lesions (Dobson, 1970, Whitehead, 1977). Around 1970 the biotin requirement of fattening turkeys were estimated at some 250 µg/kg feed, and the subsequent literature recommended levels of 200 to 325 µg/kg in the starter phase (Misir and Blair, 1988; Whitehead and Portsmouth, 1989), although male turkeys needed 50 µg/kg more than females. According to Mayne (2005) pododermatitis was still be observed with these levels.

The recommended biotin dosage today might be higher, considering the genetic improvement achieved in the last 30 years (Clark et al. 2002). Biotin requirements fall with age, but they increase if there is a high proportion of soy in the ration and/or the bedding is damp. Mayne et al. (2007a), in an experiment in which they evaluated supplements of 200, 800 and 1,600 µg/kg in turkeys from 2 to 14 weeks, found no significant effects from the higher biotin doses with regard to preventing plantar pododermatitis, although they used bedding that was poor in terms of humidity and hygiene, which could have affected their results. Whitehead (2002) and Mayne et al. (2007b) consider that in such a case it is highly advisable to increase biotin levels. According to Buda (2000), a level of 300 µg/kg was ineffective in preventing pododermatitis in turkeys of 9 to 20 weeks of age, but this objective was completely achieved using 2,000 µg/kg.

There is little information about possible effects of biotin on meat quality. Oloyo (1991) indicated that 200 µg/kg was necessary to maximize muscle percentage and the meat to bone relationship, while 160 µg/kg was sufficient to achieve maximum weight and carcass yield. Balios and Poupulis (1992) compared diets with 1.5% and 6.5% fat, and 120–150 vs. 550 µg/kg of biotin. With the higher dosage they observed a tendency towards a reduction in abdominal fat and a significant increase in its degree of saturation.

CHOLINE

Functions

Birds are able to synthesize choline, and this capacity increases with age. However, the amounts and the speed at which they are synthesized may sometimes be inadequate. Choline is a lipotropic factor for the liver, so that its requirements are higher for high-fat diets. It is essential for the formation of the neurotransmitter acetylcholine and of the lecithins, which form part of the cell membranes, and choline is involved in the formation of the cartilaginous matrix which facilitates the growth of the bones. In some trials an increase in choline and folic acid has led to a decrease in foot problems (Ryu *et al.*, 1995). It does not appear to affect immunity (Wang *et al.*, 1987).

Choline also acts as methyl group donor for transmethylation reactions important in the formation of many substances. This is a role it shares with methionine and betaine, which means that all these substances are able partially to substitute for each other, although their interrelations, recently reviewed by Simon (1999), are complex and still under discussion (Pillai *et al.*, 2006 a, b). Folic acid and cyanocobalamin also take part in these reactions. Thus their requirements increase if the choline supply is insufficient (Ryu *et al.*, 1995).

Sources

The extent to which choline is absorbed from raw materials is doubtful. (Anonymous, 1997; Workel *et al.*, 1999). Choline is more abundant in fish meal and oilseeds, although in this last case its bioavailability varies greatly; in soy it is estimated at between 75 and 100% (Menten *et al.*, 1997; Simon, 1999), while rapeseed, which contains 3 times more, it is only 25–40% (Emmert and Baker, 1997). Corn contains half the amount of choline of wheat and barley, so that a higher amount needs to be provided in diets where corn predominates. These situations, together with the interrelationship of choline with methionine and betaine, may explain the discrepancies on choline requirements found in the literature, although the majority of the published studies which form the

basis for the current NRC recommendations are 20–40 years old. When interpreting the effects of adding choline one needs to be aware of the methionine and betaine levels of the different treatments and the choline content in the basal diets.

Requirements and recommendations for supplementation

Choline requirements are very high in the starter phase, the one most studied, and they diminish as the synthesizing capacity of the birds increases with age; they are also lower in slower growing genotypes. Quilin *et al.* (1961) determined that 1 g of choline could substitute 2.3–2.4 g of methionine as methyl group donor, a ratio that falls to 2:1 in the work of Wang *et al.* (1987). Whitehead *et al.* (1992) calculated that using a total level of 1,250 mg of choline between 0 and 3 weeks of age could substitute for 0.13 g/kg methionine.

This relationship depends on the concentrations of the two nutrients. Choline requirements increase if the diet is relatively low in sulphur amino acids, and at these levels productive responses to the supplementation of choline were observed (Pillai *et al.*, 2006). The growth reduction caused by lack of methionine is aggravated if there is also a choline deficiency (Whitehead and Portsmouth, 1989). When methionine is very deficient it becomes the major limiting factor, and extra supplies of choline have no effect (Whitehead *et al.*, 1992), as also happens if there is excessive methionine (Miles *et al.*, 1987).

Several experiments have verified that the addition of choline produces significant improvements in growth, feed consumption and feed conversion index, and that the dose-response relationship was linear (Tillman and Pesti, 1985; García *et al.*, 1999), although in some cases this was only found in the starter phase (Bond *et al.*, 1985). The estimated optimum supplementation levels in corn-soy diets (whose theoretical content is some 1,350 mg/kg) vary widely, between 120 and 1,000 ppm, which may be due to differences in the composition of the feeds used. Emmert and Baker (1997) ascertained an almost linear growth response from 10–22 days up to supplementation levels of 1,115 mg/kg, and observed further improvements up to 2,000. A supplement of 800 ppm (total dietary content: 1,900 ppm) was sufficient to optimize feed conversion. These values are much higher than those proposed by the NRC. Based on this work and other INRA trials, Workel et al. (1999), recommend a feed supplement of 500–800 mg/kg for older broilers, depending on the phase of fattening.

However, Whitehead et al. (1992) found no positive effect in broilers 3 to 6 weeks old when supplementing choline at 500 mg/kg (total dietary content: 1,120 mg/kg) with 6 different levels of methionine. In more recent experiments, conducted under controlled conditions, choline only had positive effects on growth and hepatic remethylation of homocysteine in diets unsupplemented by methionine. If methionine levels were adequate or slightly deficient these improvements were no longer significant (Pillai et al., 2006a, b).

That there is no advantage in working with diets deficient in choline, since in such cases its requirements will be covered in part through methionine, which is one of the most limiting nutrients in poultry diets from the economic viewpoint.

Another aspect that has been investigated is whether it might be possible to substitute betaine for choline as a methyl group donor in broilers diets, since it is known that 55–62% of choline converts to betaine in the liver after oxidization (Kettunen et al., 1999). This is possible only to a limited extent. Lowry et al. (1987) showed that 75% of choline requirements must be provided by choline itself. In experiments by Emmert and Baker (1997) the addition of 500 ppm betaine to diets with a total of 600 mg choline produced no effect, while performance improved linearly with the addition of choline. In studies by Pillai et al. (2006a) an increase in the choline level improved the liver's capacity for homocysteine remethylation in methionine-deficient diets. This was also achieved with betaine, but to a lesser extent and less consistently. On the other hand, Waldroup et al. (2006) found that the addition of 1,000

mg/kg betaine or choline from the first day of life, or a combination of each of them at 500 mg/kg, improved the feed conversion index and breast yield at 35 and 42 days, and this independently of methionine levels.

In contrast, Waldroup et al. (2005) studied the effects of betaine or choline, alone or in combination in situations of threat from coccidiosis and found few or no benefits in terms of weight gain, feed conversion or mortality. The increases in carcass yield resulted from betaine supplementation, and the improvement in breast yield at 42 days of age to choline supplementation, although this was no longer the case at 49 days. Nassiri Moghaddam et al. (2007) also studied the efficacy of substituting betaine with choline. The results were unclear, since live weight and conversion index improved from 0 to 21 days and from 22 to 42 days, but not between 42 and 49 days. There was also an increase in breast yield and decrease in percentage of abdominal fat. The results of both investigations suggest that the age of the broilers may be an important factor in the efficacy of the combination of these two substances.

In slower growing chickens a significant drop in the proportion of abdominal fat has also been observed with the use of betaine and choline supplements (Hassan et al., 2005). The different combinations used improved weight gain, feed conversion index and levels of serum proteins. The addition of 0.072% and 0.144% betaine to feed led to improvements similar to those obtained with the use of 1,170 and 1,470 ppm choline (**Table XIX**). Choline at 1,170 mg/kg produced a reduction of 8.7% in abdominal fat, regardless of the betaine level. Surprisingly at 1,470 ppm choline the results for this parameter were no different from those obtained with the basal diet. On the other hand increasing the betaine level linearly reduced the levels of abdominal fat, regardless of choline level. The conclusion was that a choline level of 1,170 mg/kg is adequate for the growth of this type of chickens, but it can be reduced to 870 mg/kg if 0.072% betaine is added to the diet.

The majority of estimates for choline requirements of turkeys are based on research published decades ago. Christmas and Harms (1988, 1989) observed that the addition of choline improved growth between 8 and 12 weeks, especially if methionine levels were relatively low, but this was not the case between 4 and 8 weeks. On the other hand Ferket *et al.* (1993) obtained maximum growth at 16 days with supplements of

750 ppm, and at 9 days with 1,000 ppm, and they indicate that at this age betaine can replace choline by up to 50%. According to Whitehead and Portsmouth (1989), the diet of young turkeys must provide a total of 1,600 mg/kg from 0 to 4 weeks.

Table XIX. Effects of choline and betaine levels on growth and feed conversion of slow-growing chickens. (Hassan *et al.*, 2005)

Treatments		Growth			Feed conversion index		
		1–28 days	29–56 days	1–56 days	1–28 days	29–56 days	1–56 days
Interaction of effects between choline and betaine							
Choline	**Betaine**						
0.0	0.00	257.9	430.1	688.0	2.57	3.49	3.15
0.0	0.07	276.1	439.0	715.1	2.41	3.41	3.02
0.0	0.14	283.6	438.9	722.5	2.36	3.40	3.00
300	0.00	275.2	435.0	710.2	2.42	3.42	3.04
300	0.07	287.0	452.2	739.2	2.33	3.31	2.93
300	0.14	290.3	454.6	744.9	2.31	3.29	2.91
600	0.00	260.1	424.8	648.9	2.56	3.51	3.15
600	0.07	276.9	430.0	719.9	2.42	3.37	3.00
600	0.14	280.2	435.1	715.3	2.39	3.42	3.02
Effects of choline supplementation							
0.0		272.5 b	436.0 b	708.5 b	2.45 a	3.43 a	3.06 a
300		284.2 a	447.3 a	731.5 a	2.35 b	3.34 b	2.96 a
600		272.4 b	434.3 a	706.7 b	2.46 a	3.43 a	3.06 a
Effects of betaine supplementation							
0.00		264.4 b	430.0 b	694.4 b	2.52 a	3.47 a	3.11 a
0.07		280.0 a	444.7 a	724.7 a	2.35 b	3.36 b	2.98 b
0.14		284.8 a	442.9 a	727.7 a	2.39 b	3.37 b	2.98 b

Different letters indicate significant differences at P<0.01

VITAMIN C

Functions

Ascorbic acid is involved in fundamental biological and metabolic processes: conversion of vitamin D_3 to its active form, biosynthesis of collagen, absorption of minerals (iron), control of glucocorticoid synthesis, stimulation of phagocytic activity and as an antioxidant on a cellular level. Thus its action is important in calcification processes, in immune response, adaptation to stress and in the maintenance of electrolytic balance. These functions, along with a great number of investigations on the effects of vitamin C, were reviewed in detail by Pardue and Thaxton (1986), and more recently by Whitehead and Keller (2003).

Sources

Birds can synthesize this vitamin in the kidney, so that it is usually assumed they need no supplementation. It should however be borne in mind that the ability to do this is reduced in the first week of life, especially in males, as manifested by the decline in its concentration in plasma; thereafter it progressively increases (Bains et al., 1998). Pardue and Thaxton (1982) estimated that day-old chicks can only synthesize 16% and 33% of what they are able to at 20 and 30 days, respectively. It also falls at time of stress (Pardue and Thaxton, 1986; Pardue, 1989; Hooper et al., 1989; Seemann, 1991; Jones, 1996). For these reasons, and based on experiences in the field, Bains et al. (1998) recommend supplementing feed with vitamin C at 150 ppm during the first 2–3 weeks, especially to prevent later foot problems.

In stress situations, so common in commercial production, supplementation with ascorbic acid at 150–300 ppm has shown various physiological effects: reduction in the corticosterone and potassium concentration in plasma, and increase in the plasma concentration of sodium, triglycerides and vitamin C itself; reduction in the heterophil/lymphocyte ratio and fear reactions (Pardue and Thaxton, 1984; Aguilera-Quintana et al., 1989; Kutlu and Forbes, 1993; Jones and Satterlee, 1997; Andreasen and Frank, 1999;

Zulkifli et al., 2001); improvement in cellular and humoral immune response (Gross, 1988, 1992); and increase in feed consumption and digestibility of nutrients (Pardue et al., 1985; Murray et al., 1987a, b; Kutlu and Forbes, 1994, 1995; McKee et al., 1995; McKee and Harrison, 1995, 1996; Dzhambulatov et al., 1996).

However, a wide variation has been observed in the level of these responses and therefore in the zootechnical results obtained, which may be due to diverse factors: low stability of vitamin C in feed, which improves in encapsulated forms (Whitehead and Keller, 2003), and also in drinking water, especially if alkaline and/or unchlorinated (Pardue, 1989; Krautmann, 1989); level and duration of dosage; the age of the birds (van Niekerk et al., 1989); and intensity and combination of stress factors (McKee and Harrison, 1995; Teeter and Belay, 1996; Balnave, 2004).

Requirements and recommendations for supplementation

Resistance to stress
In experiments carried out under excellent operating conditions, the response to adding ascorbic acid to feed tended to be statistically insignificant (Kafri et al., 1988; Kutlu and Forbes, 1994; Marron et al., 2001), although other researchers have found positive responses in weight gain, digestibility of nutrients and carcass yield with diets supplemented with 200 ppm (Lohakare et al., 2005b). The situation changes when stress is induced (Pardue and Thaxton, 1982; Pardue et al., 1984; McKee and Harrison, 1995; Mahmoud et al., 2004), or if trials are conducted under commercial conditions, although in these cases too the responses vary depending on the degree of stress (Balnave, 2004). It has been established that vitamin C supplementation in feed or drinking water reduces the plasma levels of ACTH and corticosterone (Sahin et al., 2002), of T_3 and T_4 (Sahin et al., 2003), and the respiratory quotient of birds (McKee et al., 1997). All this helps to limit metabolic stress symptoms and alleviate their consequences, which allows the productivity and the immunocompetence of the birds to improve (Whitehead and Keller, 2003).

174

High temperature is among the stress factors which in practice most frequently affect finishing birds, inducing oxidative stress which ascorbic acid, being one of the most important organic antioxidants, can help to counteract. The scientific literature is inconsistent with respect to the effect of vitamin C. Plenty of studies have found no significant effects on production parameters when using concentrations between 125 and 1,000 ppm (Stilborn et al., 1988; Orban et al., 1993; Puron et al., 1994; Teeter and Belay, 1996; Rose and Peter, 2000); but in many others, significantly better results have been found, with increased feed consumption and live weight and reduced mortality and feed conversion index. It is notable that these include nearly all the trials carried out in hot countries, where supplementation with this vitamin is normal commercial practice (Ogbuinya, 1991; Daghir, 1996). Qureshi et al. (2000) obtained positive responses by adding vitamin C to the feed if at the same time electrolytes were added to the drinking water, suggesting that this could be a factor explaining the discrepancies observed.

In general, the dosages considered optimum are from 200–250 mg/kg, although in extreme conditions further improvements have been confirmed at 500 and 1,000 ppm (Kafri and Cherry, 1984; Njoku, 1984, 1986; Pardue et al., 1985; Kovar et al., 1990; Cier et al., 1992; Rajmane and Ranade, 1992; Hussein, 1995; Daghir, 1996; Dzhambulatov et al., 1996; Díaz-Cruz et al., 2001). In a recent study, Curça et al. (2006) concluded that 2,000 ppm improved the weight of broilers kept at high temperatures by 12% at 4 weeks. Benefits are more evident when other stress factors, such as coccidiosis, or beak trimming in turkeys, are present as well as heat (McKee and Harrison, 1995; Seokand and Singh, 1996). Satterlee et al. (1989) observed a reduced duration of the tonic immobility reaction in birds supplemented with vitamin C, indicating a situation of less fear.

In feed selection experiments, when temperatures rose broilers chose to eat the feed supplemented with 200 ppm vitamin C, increasing their intake in 3–5 days (Kutlu and Forbes, 1995). Moreover, levels of ascorbic acid in feed show a negative correlation with those of HSP 70, or heat shock protein (Mahmoud et al., 1999).

Bottje et al. (1998) observed a reduction of vitamin C concentration in the pulmonary fluid under low temperature conditions; this is possibly why similar dosages of vitamin C have also had positive results in the face of cold stress (Gross, 1988). The addition of 1,000 ppm to the drinking water of day-old chicks that had suffered prolonged transportation significantly reduced mortality (Vo et al., 1996). At normal temperatures supplementation with ascorbic acid appears to offer few advantages, however (Gous and Morris, 2005).

Immunity

There is more agreement on the capacity of vitamin C to improve immune response of chickens and turkeys in the face of particular diseases and so reduce mortality and the consequent drop in production. There are many papers, reviewed by Pardue (1989), Lattshaw (1991), Chew (1996), Klasing (1998), Ferket and Qureshi (1999), and Whitehead and Keller (2003). To this end it has been recommended that before and during a threat from pathogens vitamin C levels of 300–330 mg/kg be used – in severe cases up to 1,000 ppm have been used – although some researchers report that efficacy was lower with dosages above 400 ppm (Gross et al., 1988; Davelaar and van der Bos, 1992; Wen et al., 1997). The effects most commonly observed consist of significant reduction in mortality and lesions, and improvement in cellular immunity and the amounts of specific antibodies (Gross, 1992). Also important is its antioxidant effect, which allows the stability of cellular membranes to be maintained (Dimanov et al., 1994; van Dyck and Adams, 2003) and important organs such as the liver to be protected from oxidation (Hayashi et al., 2004).

Favorable immune responses, frequently accompanied by decreases in morbidity and mortality, have been observed in various pathologies: coccidiosis (McKee and Harrison, 1995; Crevieu-Gabriel and Naciri, 2001), Newcastle disease (Edrise et al., 1986; Franchini et al., 1994; Gross et al., 1988; Lohakare et al., 2005b), infectious bronchitis (Davelaar and van der Bos, 1992; Okoye et al., 2000), Gumboro disease (Wu et al., 2000, Amakye-Anim et al., 2000; Hayashi et al., 2004, Lohakare et al., 2005), colibacillosis (Gross et al., 1988; van Niekerk et al.,

1989), Marek's disease (Yotova et al., 1990), aflatoxicosis and other intoxications (Pardue et al., 1987; Maynard et al., 1989; Tudor and Bunaciu, 2001), and ascites (Decuypere et al., 1994; Bottje and Wideman, 1995, 1998; Ladmakhi et al., 1997; Díaz-Cruz et al., 2001; Walton et al., 2001; Xiang et al., 2002). Nevertheless vitamin C supplementation alone is not enough to prevent or cure all these diseases.

Bone quality

Other investigations have been directed at discovering the possible role of vitamin C in preventing foot problems. Ascorbic acid stimulates renal synthesis of the active form of vitamin D_3 (calcitriol, or 1,25-di hydroxycholecalciferol), acting as cofactor of the enzyme 25-(OH)-D_3-1 hydroxylase. Ascorbic acid at a level of 250 ppm, combined with calcitriol in the feed, can reduce rickets under certain conditions (Roberson and Edwards, 1994; Rennie, 1995). At 2,000 ppm femur bone strength improved by 16% (Orban et al., 1993), although the combination of 200 ppm vitamin C and 200 IU vitamin D was enough to improve bone strength (Lohakare et al., 2005a). Weiser et al. (1990) also demonstrated greater bone strength with levels of 100 ppm and variable levels of vitamin D in the diet. According to Whitehead (2002, 2005) these benefits are greater in hot environments.

Vitamin C has also been used to prevent tibial dyschondroplasia. Initial studies in which very high levels were tried (500–1,000 mg/kg) did not succeed in showing positive effects, or rather they were inconclusive, since improvements were found in some experiments but not repeated in others (Edwards, 1989; Roberson and Edwards, 1994). The only consistent finding was a reduction of bone ash (Leach and Burdette, 1985; Edwards, 1989), which by contrast increased when lower dosages were applied, both when vitamin C alone was used (Whitehead, 1995) and when it was combined with higher calcium levels (Doan, 2000). Rennie (1995) indicated that dosages of 250–500 ppm were only effective with normal levels of calcium.

According to Whitehead (2000) the combined addition of 250 ppm vitamin C and 10 μg/kg calcitriol to feed completely

prevents tibial dyschondroplasia, and counteracts the reduction in the rate of growth usually provoked by calcitriol. This synergy, considered dubious by Edwards (2000), would be due not only to the stimulation of 1,25-dihydroxycholecalciferol production, but also to the fact that vitamin C promotes an increase in receptors for vitamin D and collagen biosynthesis, and therefore stimulates bone matrix production (Farquharson et al., 1998). This is why Whitehead and Keller (2003) conclude in their review that the combination of ascorbic acid and calcitriol is potentially useful for preventing tibial dyschondroplasia. Petek et al. (2005) published positive results with the addition of 150 mg/l to drinking water.

Meat quality

The relationship between vitamin C and the quality of meat has also been widely studied. The addition of 0.1% ascorbic acid to the drinking water of chickens and turkeys 24–36 hours before their collection and transport to the slaughterhouse significantly increased the carcass yield (on average by 1%) in practically all of the conducted tests (**Figure 6**), and frequently also the breast percentage (Farr et al., 1988; Quarles and Adrian, 1989; Krautmann et al., 1991; Fletcher and Cason, 1991; Völker and Fenster, 1991; Grashorn and Völker, 1993). Although some variation can be seen in the responses, these effects are more pronounced the more stressful the conditions of these operations, and that this treatment reduces the levels of stress indicators (Satterlee et al., 1991). Kutlu (2001) found that supplementing with 250 ppm reduced the lipid content in the carcass and increased carcass yield in broilers exposed to 35–37°C for 8 hours a day. The improvement in yield is based on the reduction of shrinkage during transport and on increased water retention (Grashorn and Völker, 1993; McKnight et al., 1996). The latter may be due to the fact that in treated birds less change has been found in the plasma concentration of aldosterone and in the sodium/potassium ratio (Pardue et al., 1985; Satterlee et al., 1991).

Leeson et al. (1995) cited sources from the turkey industry which indicated positive effects of vitamin C on the prevention of pale, soft exudative meat (PSE), which are known to be linked to the stress situations suffered before the slaughter of the birds. Yin et al.

(1993) demonstrated *in vitro* its antioxidant activity on myoglobin, which could improve color stability of the meat. Lohakare *et al.,* 2005a found an improvement in color stability at levels of 200 ppm.

Vitamin C has an antioxidant effect *in vivo* by reducing the radical tocopheroxyl and thus restoring the antioxidant activity of vitamin E. It was therefore supposed that supplementing with it might favor the oxidative stability of meat fat. However, Morrisey *et al.* (1998) concluded in their review that this effect was small or non-existent. Neither the addition of 1,000 ppm to drinking water 24 hours before slaughtering (King *et al.*, 1993, 1995) nor supplementation of feed with 110 mg/kg ascorbic acid (Grau *et al.*, 2001a, b; Bou *et al.*, 2001) proved to have a protective effect against fat oxidation (measured by TBARS values), and they did not improve the organoleptic quality of the meat (Bou *et al.*, 2001).

In contrast McKnight *et al.* (1996) found that in stress situations the TBARS concentrations in the breast were reduced if a level of 200–300 ppm was used during the 3 weeks prior to slaughtering. Young *et al.* (2003) obtained similar results when supplementing 1,000 ppm vitamin C for 6 weeks together with 200 ppm vitamin E. These effects of protecting against oxidation and the synergic action of the two vitamins were also confirmed in the experiment by Gheisari *et al.* (2004).

Interactions

The interactions of vitamin C with other substances have been studied in recent years. Vitamin C in combination with citric acid and phytase improved live weight and conversion index; there have also been reports of 27% increases in AMEn digestibility in diets low in calcium and phosphorus compared to values obtained when using phytase alone (Afsharmanesh *et al.*, 2004). In a later study, Afsharmanesh *et al.* (2005) also added vitamin D_3 to this type of diet, increasing live weight and protein digestibility by 18 and 60%, respectively. Feed consumption and conversion also improved compared to low phosphorus diets.

Under heat stress conditions vitamin C used at 250 ppm in combination with chromium supplemented at 400 ppm improved live weight, feed intake and feed conversion index, which demonstrated the synergic action of the two substances (Sahin *et al.*, 2003). The serum concentrations of insulin, T_3, T_4, vitamin E and vitamin C itself also increased while plasma levels

Figure 6. Effect of adding vitamin C to drinking water (0.1%, 24 h) on carcass yield
(1. Krautmann, 1989 2. Volker and Fenster, 1991 3. Grashorn and Volker, 1993)

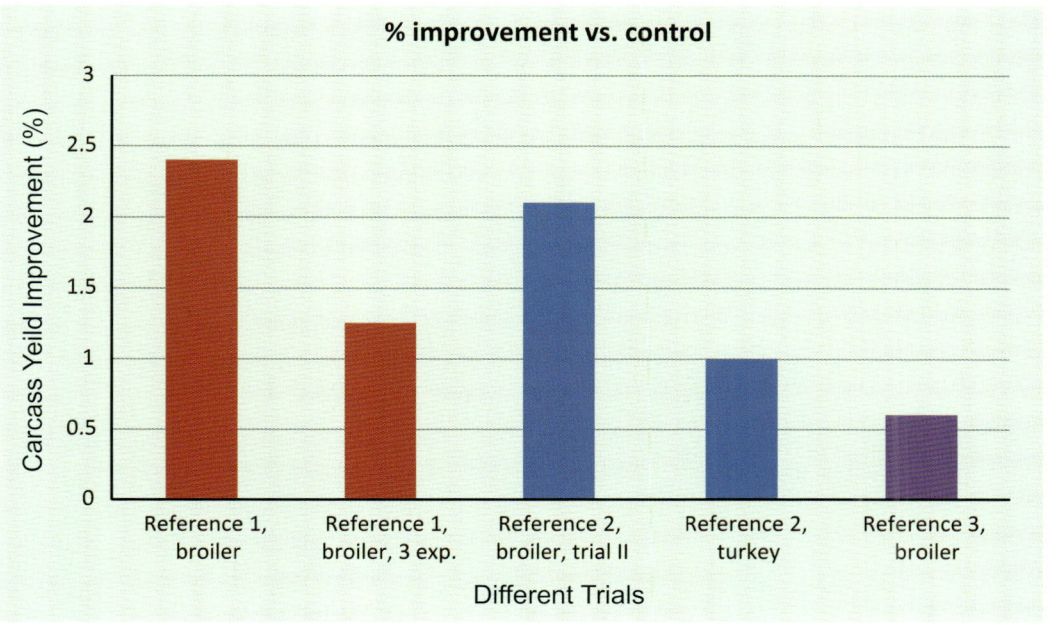

of corticosterone, glucose, cholesterol and MDA fell. These researchers indicate that the synergism between the two nutrients might be due to the increase in insulin synthesis induced by the chromium, since the hormone contributes to the transport of vitamin C to the red cells. Vitamin C used in conjunction with acetyl salicylic acid (ASA) boosted the immune response, increasing the weight of

the bursa of Fabricius, thymus and spleen, and the serum levels of antibodies, even if the birds were subjected to high temperatures (Naseem *et al.,* 2005). The combined use of ASA, sodium bicarbonate and potassium chloride in drinking water produced improvements in production parameters in heat stress situations (Roussan *et al.,* 2008).

FAT-SOLUBLE VITAMINS

VITAMIN A

Sources

In its active form vitamin A is scarce in nature, as it is found only in fish oil, meat meal, and oilseeds. Green plants contain ß-carotene, a precursor of vitamin A, although the content varies greatly according to the species, state of maturity, preservation, etc. The efficacy of its conversion to vitamin A is greater in birds (2:1) than in other species, but it falls to 5:1 with increased ingestion of carotene. Jensen and Edberg (1999) estimated that, in broilers, 1 mg ß-carotene is equivalent to 393 IU vitamin A, approximately 25% of the normally accepted ratio. Maize and its derivatives contain significant quantities of pigmenting carotenoids, but their provitamin activity is much lower. Provision of vitamin A in the diet of broilers and turkeys is therefore achieved mainly through synthetic forms, retinyl acetate or palmitate. Nowadays its stability is much improved, but losses through pelleting (5–40%), storage or fungal contamination may be significant.

Intestinal absorption of vitamin A is calculated as between 40 and 80%. It may be modified by many factors, either in a positive way, such as the inclusion of fats in the diet, the addition of antioxidants, and the use of moderate levels of vitamin E (Abawi *et al.,* 1985; Noel and Brinkhaus, 1998), or in a negative way, such as high levels of vitamin E, the presence of aflatoxins, or enteric infections (West *et al.,* 1992). Thus coccidiosis reduces its levels in plasma and hepatic

reserves, which increases requirements of vitamin A because of poor absorption and oxidation induced by the cellular immune response (Augustine and Ruff, 1983; Allen, 1988, 1997; Allen *et al.,* 1996). Vitamin A deficiencies reduce resistance to coccidiosis (Chew, 1995; Dalloul *et al.,* 2002; Dalloul and Lillehoj, 2005).

Functions

Vitamin A deficiency is unlikely in practice (Kidd, 2004). However, the efficiency of conversion of ß-carotene to vitamin A is reduced in situations of stress and illness, or due to mycotoxins. Marginal deficiencies may therefore result when working with minimum levels in feed (Bains, 1997), characterized by changes in skeletal development (Whitehead and Portsmouth, 1989), a fall in the numbers of antibodies and reduction in cellular immunity (Friedman *et al.,* 1991; Sklan *et al.,* 1994, 1995; Dalloul *et al.,* 2002), rapid depletion of hepatic reserves (Aye *et al.,* 2002a), and a drop in muscle glycogen reserves (Sundeen *et al.,* 1980). With more pronounced deficiencies severe disruptions occur in respiratory and intestinal epithelia (Uni *et al.,* 1998; Aye *et al.,* 2000a; Chew and Park, 2004), and in extreme cases, blindness and death.

Since the 1930s vitamin A has been known to be important in protecting the epithelial tissues and mucous membranes, which are natural barriers against pathogens, and therefore in preventing infections (Latshaw, 1991, Dalloul and Lillehoj, 2005). Vitamin A also has desirable effects related to immunity, which require a greater supply than that recommended by the NRC, and estimated as between 3 and 10 times more for chickens (Xu et al., 1989; Friedman and Sklan, 1989, 1997; Halevy et al., 1994; Lessard et al., 1997). Vitamin A is needed for the proper functioning of such important lymphoid organs as the thymus and bursa of Fabricius, and modifies leukocyte response, in particular of the CD_4+T cells (Halevy et al., 1994), which is impaired in cases of deficiency (Sklan et al., 1994, 1995; Chew, 1995; Dalloul et al., 2002; Chew and Park, 2004; Klasing, 2007). This has been confirmed by studies with chickens and turkeys, using various pathogenic agents (Davis and Sell, 1989; Sijtsma et al., 1990, 1991; Friedman et al., 1991; Rombout et al., 1992; Chew, 1995; Aye et al., 2000b; Dalloul et al., 2000).

Requirements and recommendations for supplementation

Minimum requirements for growth have been estimated at between 1,500 (chickens) and 2,000 IU/kg (turkeys). For broilers, the NRC (1994) recommended 1,500 IU/kg feed, although in practice levels 5–10 times greater than these are used. For turkeys NRC recommends 5,000 IU, where the industry uses twice that amount. Using 15,000 IU/kg improves growth and feed conversion index in broilers compared to lower dosages (Kucuk et al., 2003). Higher levels produce no further improvements in these parameters (Ballard and Edwards, 1988; Wyatt, 1991); in fact, in trials using extreme dosages (of the order of 50,000 IU/kg), these parameters have worsened in both chickens and turkeys (Jensen et al., 1983; Veltmann et al., 1986; Jiakui et al., 2008). A level of 65,000 IU/kg increases the incidence of tibial dyschondroplasia in chickens (Jiakui et al., 2008).

Immunity
The optimum dosage of vitamin A most appropriate to preventing or reducing certain pathologies is apparently not the same for all diseases. Faced with the Newcastle virus and other antigens, Seeman and Hazijah (1985) and Sklan et al. (1994, 1995) observed an increase in chickens and turkeys in the proliferation of lymphocytes and macrophages and in the numbers of specific antibodies up to a dosage of 18,999 IU. Faced with E. coli the immune response improved until 60,000 IU/kg vitamin A was reached (Tengerdy and Nockels, 1975; Tengerdy and Brown, 1977). Using 20,000 IU/kg Sklan et al. (1995) observed a greater increase in specific antibodies in the face of the chiken pox and Newcastle disease viruses after vaccination against these diseases than if they used 6,700 IU/kg. However, in other studies an excess of vitamin A led to a depression of the humoral immune response (Friedman and Sklan, 1989; Friedman et al., 1991, Lessard et al., 1997).

A balance needs to be maintained between the fat-soluble vitamins, since they compete to be absorbed. An excess of one will alter the plasma concentrations of the others, and this may have critical concequences(Abawi and Sullivan, 1989; Aburto and Britton, 1998a, b). An excess of vitamin A reduces the absorption of vitamin E and its concentration in the plasma and liver (Aburto and Britton, 1998a, b), and can even affect the proper functioning of the lymphoid organs (She et al., 1997). In turkeys, adding vitamin E (30–40 mg), vitamin A (12,000–15,000 IU) and a high level of oxidants (100–150 meq O_2/kg) to the diet did not adversely affect health, but the turkeys' vitamin E reserves diminished, as did hepatic lactate-dehydrogenase activity. A certain predisposition to infection by the virus causing hemorrhagic enteritis was also observed (Zduncyk et al., 2002). These risks, and the existence of legal upper limits on the inclusion of vitamin A in feed, have induced subsequent research directed at improving immunity by nutritional means to concentrate principally on vitamin E (Whitehead, 2002).

Nevertheless, a synergy between the two vitamins in birds suffering stress situations has been demonstrated using normal dosages of vitamin A. The use of 15,000 IU vitamin A in conjunction with 250 mg/kg vitamin E reduced serum and hepatic levels of MDA (a lipid oxidation indicator) in broilers subjected to thermal stress (Sahin et al., 2002).

179

Bone quality

Other investigations have studied the role of vitamin A in preventing skeletal development anomalies such as rickets and tibial dyschondroplasia, but the responses obtained have been contradictory or not statistically significant (Waldenstedt, 2006). This appears to be related to the interactions between vitamins A and D_3 (Jensen et al., 1983; Ballard and Edwards 1988; Luo and Huang, 1991; Aburto et al., 1998). An excess of vitamin A (more than 20,000 IU/kg) impairs the metabolism of vitamin D_3, reducing its availability, and the inverse also occurs (Aburto and Britton, 1998a, b). In this situation reductions in growth and in bone ash content have been observed, as well as the appearance of osteodystrophies such as rickets, especially in turkeys (Veltmann et al., 1983; Britton, 1994; Aburto and Britton, 1998a, b), and swelling of the growth cartilage (Veltmann et al., 1983; Tang et al., 1984; Ruksomboonde and Sullivan, 1985). At normal dosages of 8,000–15,000 IU/kg there appears to be no interaction (Whitehead et al., 2004a), but if the vitamin D_3 level is marginal by 500 IU/kg, even normal vitamin A supplementation levels can have negative effects which disappear on the inclusion of at least 100 IU vitamin D (Luo and Huang, 1991).

Meat quality

Excessive levels of vitamin A can have adverse effects on carcass pigmentation (Jensen et al., 1981; Wyatt, 1991; Jiakui et al., 2008). Moreover some studies have been conducted on the possible benefits of a higher dietary supplementation of vitamin A or ß-carotene to improve meat stability against oxidation, but they have proved to be much less effective than vitamin E (King et al., 1995; Ruiz et al., 1998). However, there appear to be no adverse interactions in this area such as those described above, as the use of 30,000 IU/kg vitamin A did not impair the antioxidant action of vitamin E at 150 ppm, although it had no protective effect against fat oxidation either (Bartov et al., 1997).

VITAMIN K

Functions and sources

This term covers a series of compounds based on the structure of menadione (2-methyl-1.4-napthoquinone). Natural forms are phylloquinone (vitamin K_1) and the menaquinones (vitamin K_2), which are found only in green plants such as alfalfa and in fish and meat meal, but they are unstable. In practice, intake is provided by a synthetic product, vitamin K_3, in the form of various bisulfite complexes with nicotinamide or pyrimidine (MNB, MSB-gelatin, MPB, MSB), which are more stable and potent (Huyghebaert, 1991).

Birds can synthesize vitamin K in the intestine, but to only a very limited degree. Furthermore, its anticoagulant action is impaired by aflatoxins (Daghir, 1996) and by prolonged treatment with antimicrobials, which eliminate the intestinal flora that synthesize it (Bains, 1999). The most damaging of these is sulfaquinoxaline. According to Esmail (2002), in the case of coccidiosis vitamin K requirements rise to 8 mg/kg – between 2 and 4 times higher than the current recommended supplementation, and 20 times higher than that indicated by the NRC.

Requirements and recommendations for supplementation

Portsmouth (1996) indicated that the values recommended by the NRC, based on work carried out more than 50 years ago, may be too low for current conditions and the stress produced by illness, but there is no confirmation of this because no studies have been published recently. Vitamin K requirements in turkeys between 7 and 14 days of age were estimated in accordance with the concentration of prothrombin in the plasma and the coagulation time. The estimated requirements range between 0.079 and 0.13 mg/kg. The biopotency of various compounds was also evaluated, and it was found that while vitamin K_1 itself is the most potent and MBP is twice as effective as MBSC (Jin et al., 2001).

Trials conducted with dicumarol (a vitamin K antagonist) found higher shrinkage from bleeding, and therefore a lower carcass yield (Marion et al., 1985), which led the authors to suggest that under field conditions the same could happen where there is a vitamin K deficiency. Scott et al. (1982) attributed the capillary fragility and the presence of muscular hematomas and petechiae to marginal deficiencies in vitamin K, but there is no clear evidence that this is the cause of such defects, which are now quite common in carcasses.

There is somewhat more information on the interaction of vitamin K with other fat-soluble vitamins. Vitamin K activity is impaired by excessive levels of vitamins A and E, which has repercussions on coagulation time (which maybe three times longer) and on broiler mortality (Abawi and Sullivan, 1989; Frank et al., 1997). An excess of vitamin K,

on the other hand, causes focal necrosis and hemorrhages in the lymphoid organs (She et al., 1997). An imbalance between vitamins D and K adversely affects the feed conversion index (Abawi and Sullivan, 1989). In turkeys, the addition of 2 ppm vitamin K contributed to improved recovery from a case of rickets, and it was verified that in diets low in vitamin D, supplementation with up to 2.9 ppm vitamin K improved feed consumption and growth. This did not happen if the vitamin D level was adequate (Jin and Sell., 2001). Zhang et al. (2003) evaluated the effects of increasing vitamin K on bone development, and they obtained the best results with 8 ppm in the starter phase and 2 ppm subsequently. However, the possible importance of vitamin K for skeletal development under practical conditions is not well established (Whitehead, 2002a; Waldenstedt, 2006).

VITAMIN D_3

Functions and sources

The term vitamin D covers many compounds, such as provitamin D (ergosterol) from green plants, which undergoes a photochemical reaction caused by ultraviolet radiation from sunlight to form previtamin D (ergosterol), and this then becomes vitamin D_2 (ergocalciferol). Much more important in birds is vitamin D_3 or cholecalciferol. Except in some fish oil and meal, vitamin D_3 is scarce in feed ingredients, so supplementation is required.

Birds can obtain vitamin D_3 in quantities equivalent to 20–40 µg/kg through the action of sunlight on 7-dehydrocholesterol, a lipid secreted by the uropygial gland and which is present in feathers (Edwards, 2000). Where animals are kept indoors, this mechanism is of little significance, so vitamin D_3 must be provided in the feed. Following its absorption in the intestine, cholecalciferol converts in the liver to 25-hydroxycholecalciferol (25-OH-D_3), and in the kidney to the physiologically more active (but with a shorter average life) form of 1,25 dihydroxycholecalciferol or calcitriol (1,25 $(OH)_2 D_3$). Vitamin C is involved in this stage. There are further renal metabolites, such as 24,25 $(OH)_2 D_3$ or 1,24,25 $(OH)_3 D_3$, but they are of less practical interest.

Calcitriol (1,25-DH) acts in a similar way to steroid hormones: together with the parathyroid hormone it regulates the absorption, transport, deposition and mobilization of calcium. Increasing the dosage of vitamin D_3 increases the plasma concentration of ionized and total calcium, and reduces the concentration of phosphorus and sodium (Shafey et al., 1990). It also improves the absorption and retention of phosphorus and the utilization of phytic phosphorus (Shafey et al., 1990; Mohammed et al., 1991), and intervenes in the differentiation and maturation of chondrocytes (Whitehead et al., 1994a). Thus vitamin D_3 plays an essential role in the metabolism and development of the skeleton in chickens and turkeys, maintaining complex balances with calcium and phosphorus, although other vitamins (B_6, folic acid, C and K) and mineral trace elements (Cu, B, F, Al) are also involved in the ossification process. 1,25-DH is 10 times more efficient than cholecalciferol in the prevention and cure of rickets (Ameenudin et al., 1985). It has also been credited with functions regulating the cells of the immune system (Mireles, 1997; Aslam et al., 1998).

Its precursor, 25-OH-D3, is also more potent than vitamin D_3 (2.5–4 times more), and a greater proportion of it is absorbed.

However, it is 5–10 times more toxic; at 1 mg/kg it induces calcification of the renal tubules. Of less importance is 24,25 $(OH)_2$ D_3. Its physiological role is less clear, but it is excreted and eliminated very rapidly. To become active it has to be hydroxylated again to position 1, but it is 2.5 times less potent than calcitriol (Ameenudin et al., 1985), and in practice it appears to be non-existent (Mitchell et al., 1997a). A recent study evaluated 1-α-OH-D_3 (Edwards et al., 2002). It appears to have similar activity to 1,25-DH, inducing much faster absorption and mobilization of calcium than vitamin D_3, and it is 8 times more effective in increasing bone ash content.

Requirements and recommendations

Vitamin D_3 deficiency is manifested at the biochemical level by hypocalcaemia and hypophosphatemia. Cases of rickets due to lack of this vitamin show an enlargement in the proliferative zone of the growth plate, while if they are due to lack of phosphorus it is the hypertrophic zone which is enlarged. There are other skeletal anomalies associated with vitamin D, such tibial dyschondroplasia (TD). Up to 12 different types of skeletal disorder have been identified in broilers and turkeys, entailing great losses to the poultry industry due to resulting mortality and seizures, which are valued in the United States at more than $120 million per year (Cook, 2000). Furthermore, the continuous improvement in growth rate imposes a great strain on the skeleton, and for some time now foot problems have been a significant concern in breeding broilers and turkeys (Thorp, 1994; Bains, 1994; Whitehead, 2004, 2005).

Although it has been recognized for 40 years now, the incidence of tibial dyschondroplasia (TD) has increased in the last 15 years. This problem consists of the formation in the bone growth matrix of a non-vascularized cartilage mass which does not mineralize and causes fragility and deviation of the tibia. TD produces clinical lameness in chickens from 3 weeks of age, and also appears in turkeys aged between 11 and 14 weeks, although with less severity (Hocking et al., 2002; Whitehead, 2005). This disorder and its genetic implications have been described, among others, by Whitehead (2004) and

Leach and Monsonego-Ornan (2007) and it seems clear that it results from an interaction between genetics and nutrition (Broz and Ward, 2007), certainly involving the metabolism of calcium and vitamin D. Diets low in Ca and/or high in P and chlorine may induce TD, although increasing calcium or establishing an adequate Ca/P ratio does not prevent it completely (Edwards, 1992).

Nutritional factors are therefore the most important in increasing bone quality, both through greater mineralization and better organization of the collagen matrix (Rath et al. 2000), and among them vitamin D and its metabolites are of paramount importance. This is why the tendency has been to supplement with ever higher levels of vitamin D.

The NRC indicates requirements of 200 IU/kg for broilers of any age, which corresponds to 5 µg/kg (1 µg/kg = 40 IU/kg), based on studies from the 1960s, and aimed at the prevention of rickets. Whitehead (2000) considers these figures very low, especially in the absence of ultraviolet light (in windowless sheds), and that at times they do not even fulfill their original objective.

In practice the normal supplement is between 3,000 and 5,000 IU/kg (75–125 µg/kg) depending on the age of the broilers, due to uncertainty as to whether the birds are receiving an adequate quantity given the possible presence of stress, mycotoxins and poor absorption processes, which hamper the absorption and hydroxylation of vitamin D (Cook, 1988; Whitehead, 2002a; Leeson and Summers, 2005; Rama Rao et al., 2007). Allowances must also be made for the possible presence in feed of antinutritional factors that interfere with vitamin D absorption and/or metabolism, as happens with raw soy and rice (Pierson and Hester, 1982), and of high levels of fat in feed, which lower calcium retention and bone calcification due to soap formation. Additional allowances must be made for the adverse effects on renal calcitrol synthesis of pathogens that affect the kidney, such as certain infectious bronchitis viruses or the Gumboro disease virus, even if they come from vaccines (Bains, 1999). Furthermore, it has been found on occasion that the various sources of vitamin D_3 show variable biopotency (40–134% in turkeys) (Yang *et al.*, 1973), although this variability currently appears to be lower (86–118% in broilers) (Kasim and Edwards, 2000).

Scientific research has also investigated vitamin D levels far higher than those recommended by the NRC. The earliest work was reviewed by Pierson and Hester (1982) and Ameenudin *et al.* (1985). Soares and Lofton (1986), after testing levels up to 8,000 IU/kg, considered 400 IU/kg to be the most appropriate concentration to achieve optimum growth and calcification at any age. Subsequently, minimum requirements for growth have been estimated at 275 IU/kg (6.9 µg/kg), at 550 (13.8 µg/kg) to achieve the maximum concentration of vitamin D in blood plasma, and at 900 (22.6 µg/kg) to prevent rickets in 800–1,000 IU/kg (Edwards *et al.*, 1994; Edwards, 1999).

Whitehead (1995b) compared the effects of using 400 or 800 IU/kg, and with the higher level increased growth and the plasma concentration of 25 (OH)$_2$. More recently, the same author indicated that 1,000–1,250 IU/kg will still not achieve total prevention of rickets nor maximum bone ash content (Whitehead, 2002a, 2003). Kasim and Edwards (2000) obtained a maximum bone ash level within this range, with 1,100 IU/kg vitamin D. In the absence of ultraviolet light these requirements would increase to 1,600 IU/kg (Edwards *et al.*, 1992a, Mitchell *et al.*, 1997a), based on bone ash content and growth. Mireles (1997) compared the use of 2,100 IU/kg in the starter phase and 1,300 IU/kg during growth with levels 3 times higher, with no effects on production indices or on the incidence of tibial dyschondroplasia.

The estimation of vitamin D$_3$ requirements can be affected not only by the evaluation criterion used but also by genetics, chick quality and vitamin nutrition of breeders, and the levels of calcium and phosphorus in the diet. These last factors present the most obvious interactions with vitamin D requirements (Huyghebaert *et al.*, 2005), and will be dealt with in the section devoted to bone quality.

The vitamin status of chicks after hatching appears to be of importance to their subsequent vitamin D requirements (Hocking, 2007), which is explained by the fact that at an early age the 25-hydroxylase enzyme shows little activity (Rama Rao *et al.*, 2007). Driver *et al.* (2006) used 250 and 2,000 IU/kg in the nutrition of breeder hens and found that the higher level reduced the incidence of tibial dyschondroplasia in their offspring, although only in the hatchings of the middle and final laying phases, possibly because when egg production fell, more vitamin D$_3$ was deposited in the eggs. Atencio *et al.* (2005a) supplied breeders with vitamin D supplementation between 125 and 4,000 IU/kg, and their offspring between 200 and 3,200 IU/kg. The broilers that received the higher level and that came from hens supplemented with 2,000–4,000 IU/kg were the ones that showed the best growth and highest bone ash. These results were repeated in other experiments (Atencio *et al.*, 2005b), and these chickens also responded better to low calcium diets, exhibiting a lower degree of rickets and tibial dyschondroplasia. Rama Rao *et al.* (2007) state that if the hens' diet contains insufficient vitamin D, the progeny will have leg problems whatever their own supplementation level.

Various studies have revealed the action of ultraviolet light emitted by fluorescent lighting but not by incandescent lamps. If broiler diets contain 200–2,000 IU/kg vitamin D$_3$, or are supplemented with 1,25-DH, there is limited incidence of TD if the calcium level is correct. In the absence of UV light, however, TD is observed even with 2,000 IU/kg. Where there is UV light, TD starts to decrease with 1,100 IU/kg except in genetic strains with a high incidence of the problem, which require much higher supplementation (Edwards *et al.*, 1992a, 1994; Elliot and Edwards, 1997; Mitchell and Edwards, 1997a). TD is more prevalent with infections and vaccinations with the bronchitis virus (Mireles, 1997; Bains *et al.* 1998).

As indicated, clear differences in vitamin D metabolism have been found between genetic strains with high or low predisposition to tibial dyschondroplasia (TD). Those prone to TD respond better to higher levels of vitamin D (Shafey *et al.*, 1990; Whitehead, 1995b; Mitchell *et al.*, 1997b; Shirley *et al.*, 2003). Growth rate during the first 2 weeks has a strong effect on the incidence of TD and on requirements for vitamin D and/or its metabolites; both are reduced if birds gain weight more slowly in this period (Thorp 1994; Elliot and Edwards, 1994).

The vitamin D requirements of turkeys are higher than chickens although, as with the other vitamins, few studies have been published. The situation is somewhat different, since in commercial production turkeys may suffer from rickets as a result of vitamin D_3 deficiency. The NRC recommended 1,100 IU/kg for all ages, but the North American industry has been using 4 times more on average in the starter phase, and 2–3 times more thereafter (Coelho, 2000).

Even at these levels, rickets sometimes appears in the field, whether due to interference with vitamin D_3 absorption caused by mycotoxins, to which this species is particularly sensitive, or to poor absorption processes, or to imbalances of Ca and P, or to unknown factors (Riddell, 2000). Bar et al. (1987) reported 22 cases of rickets which occurred in Israel, in which there were clear signs of vitamin D_3 deficiency (low plasma concentrations of Ca, 25-OH-D3, and of the calcium carrier protein). The diet included 111 µg/kg, i.e. 4 times the level indicated by the NRC. They were unable to identify the cause, but it is significant that the process was not repeated on an experimental farm, even using the same feed that had caused the problems in the field.

Rickets develops more readily in turkeys than in chickens, and is more persistent (Perry et al., 1991). For this reason, vitamin D_3 supplementation needs to be raised above the level recommended by the NRC. A minimum level of 1,200 IU/kg was already being recommended in 1980 (Whitehead and Portsmouth, 1989), and in 1991 Sanders and Edwards showed that at 21 days no less than 2,700 IU/kg were required to prevent rickets induced by low-calcium diets, and that continuing supplementation at this level improved growth up to 14 weeks of age.

Bone quality

As previously indicated, the effects of vitamin D and its metabolites are dependent on the levels of Ca and P in the diet. If concentrations of these minerals are adequate, 35–50 µg/kg (1 µg = 40 IU; 1 IU = 0.025 µg) is enough to achieve good cortical bone quality (Waldenstedt, 2006), and 40–45 µg/kg to prevent rickets completely (Ledwaba and Robeson, 2003), although other researchers have assessed this requirement to be as high as 77.5 µg/kg (Elliot and Edwards, 1997). 25–75 µg/kg have generally been used to prevent TD, with poor results. Whitehead et al. (2004a) consider these levels ineffective, and according to their own results, 125–250 µg/kg are needed for this purpose.

By increasing the calcium/phosphorus ratio in the diet, growth and feed consumption improved with levels of 660 µg/kg vitamin D_3, and bone ash improved with 6,600 µg/kg (Quian et al., 1997). The addition of incremental dosages of vitamin D_3 was most effective where there was an excess of calcium, and utilization of phytate phosphorus improved, thus confirming the previous results of Edwards (1993). Baker et al. (1998) investigated the effects of various mineral combinations: adequate levels of Ca and P, marginal deficiency in calcium, and deficiency in both minerals. In the latter two cases they found the most effective level to be 8 times higher than that of the NRC; but where diets were deficient in phosphorus, supplementation at 250 times higher than the NRC resulted in an increase in bone ash, with no negative effect on growth or feed conversion index as in the other treatments. From this they deduced that chickens have a high tolerance to an excess of vitamin D if their diets are deficient in phosphorus.

Subsequently Rama Rao et al. (2006) found that to improve ash content and feed conversion index with diets low in Ca and P, a minimum of 3,600 IU/kg vitamin D_3 was needed in the starter phase. In another experiment using up to 9,600 IU/kg with diets both low and adequate in Ca and P, they observed improvements similar to those published by Whitehead et al. (2004a), although the improvement in growth was not as great as that which can be achieved with the correct levels of Ca and P (Rama Rao et al., 2008). In another publication (Rama Rao et al., 2003) the same authors indicate that at available levels of 1% Ca and 0.5% P, vitamin D_3 requirements for maximum growth do not exceed 200 IU/kg, but that 800 to 7,900 IU/kg are needed as Ca and P increase.

There are discrepancies in the literature on the efficacy of vitamin D in preventing TD. Almost all the studies induced the condition with diets unbalanced in Ca and P, and most used between 1,000 and 3,000 IU/kg vitamin D_3. Sometimes no positive responses were achieved under these conditions (Edwards, 1989; Rennie et al., 1993; Mitchell et al., 1997a; Whitehead, 2000), but in other papers significant reductions were obtained with 2,000–4,000 IU/kg vitamin D_3 (Edwards et al., 1992a; Xu et al., 1997; Fritts and Waldroup, 2003). In some experiments TD even increased with the same dosages (Edwards et al., 1992a). Edwards et al. (2002) suggest that when studying this vitamin there are inevitably factors, nutritional or otherwise, which vary between experiments (and even more so in the field), which may give rise to results which are hard to explain as a group, but which appear clear within one experiment.

Whitehead (1995b) stated that at available levels of 1.2% and 0.6% Ca and P, respectively, 25 µg/kg vitamin D_3 is enough to prevent TD, but that the same dose is not effective if the diet has an unbalanced Ca/P ratio. Rama Rao et al. (2007) indicate that under these conditions there is a fall of 1–2% in the incidence of TD for every additional 400 IU vitamin D_3 up to 2,800 IU/kg. Saxena (1996) considered that under practical conditions and with normal mineral levels (Ca, 1%; available P, 0.45%), broilers needed 4,000 IU/kg (20 times NRC), and demonstrated that the NRC levels increased the incidence of TD.

It has since been confirmed that much higher vitamin D_3 levels are needed to eliminate TD or reduce it to minimum levels. McCormack et al. (2002) and Whitehead et al. (2004a) compared levels of 200 to 10,000 IU/kg in starter feeds, and found a linear increase in ash content and tibia strength as well as better growth and a total absence of TD. These improvements were achieved with 5,000 IU/kg in diets balanced in Ca and P and to a greater extent, but with 10,000 IU/kg, if they were unbalanced (**Table XX**). Whitehead et al. (2004b) concluded that current broiler

Table XX. Live weight, incidence of tibial dyschondroplasia (TD) and fracture resistance of the tibia in 14-day-old broilers fed on diets with different calcium, available phosphorus and vitamin D_3 content. (Whitehead et al., 2004b)

	Mineral levels		Vitamin D (µg/kg)			
	% Ca	% av. P	5	20	125	250
Exp. 1 Live weight, g	1.0	0.45	302 a	298 a	307 a	327 b
	0.8	0.35	315 a	311 a	316 a	336 b
TD incidence, %	1.0	0.45	78 a	39 b	4 c	4 c
	0.8	0.35	88 a	51 b	6 c	8 c
Tibia fracture resistance (N)	1.0	0.45	59.5 a	80.4 b	92.1 c	101.3 c
	0.8	0.35	61.0 a	78.1 b	90.9 c	93.5 c
Exp. 2 Live weight, g	0.8	0.35	295 a	297 a	303 a	351 b
	0.8	0.50	308 a	307 a	339 b	349 b
	1.3	0.35	257 a	258 a	303 b	261 a
	1.3	0.50	301 a	306 a	343 b	333 b
TD incidence, %	0.8	0.35	78 a	84 a	22 b	0 c
	0.8	0.50	79 a	78 a	52 b	20 b
	1.3	0.35	4	0	4	0
	1.3	0.50	40 a	39 a	8 b	0 b
Tibia fracture resistance (N)	0.8	0.35	36.4 a	44.5 a	61.4 b	76.1 c
	0.8	0.50	47.9 a	59.6 a	94.7 c	83.0 d
	1.3	0.35	26.8 a	30.2 a	44.6 b	43.3 b
	1.3	0.50	54.2 a	65.4 b	89.0 c	88.9 c

Different letters indicate significant differences at P<0.01

vitamin D requirements to prevent TD may be above the maximum limit permitted in the EU (5,000 IU/kg/125 µg/kg).

This limit does not appear to be currently justified. The tolerance of birds to high doses of vitamin D$_3$ appears to be very high, especially if the levels of Ca and P in the diet are not the most appropriate. In early studies, Lofton and Soares (1986) observed a higher incidence of TD using 500 µg/kg vitamin D$_3$, and Cruishank and Sim (1987) an increase in valgus-varus bone deformities with 100 µg/kg. Subsequently Yarger et al. (1995a) observed no renal calcification until they supplemented the diet with 3,450 µg/kg (148,000 IU/kg), and Qian et al. (1997), with 6,600 µg/kg, also indicated no negative consequences. Baker et al. (1998), who used 1,250 µg/kg (50,000 IU/kg, 250 times the NRC level) found no signs of toxicity or reduced growth; in fact this dose produced good results in phosphorus-deficient diets. Papesova and Fucikova (2000), with diets supplemented with 2,500–125,000 IU/kg found toxicity from 25,000 IU/kg, i.e. 10–15 times the normal supplementation, but only after administering it for 3 months.

The review by Waldenstedt (2006) indicates that it is not known what concentration of vitamin D$_3$ is excessive for current genotypes, although a recent experiment provides some indication (Nain et al., 2007). When the researchers used 80,000 IU/kg instead of 5,000 IU/kg in broilers, the higher dosage produced a 2.5 times higher mortality from sudden death syndrome, and they observed twice the number of birds with moderate arrhythmia and tachycardia after a stress event. Intense and prolonged hypercalcemia caused by the high dose of vitamin D proved harmful, since an adequate level of calcium is important for the proper functioning of the cardiac muscle.

The justification for higher vitamin D$_3$ levels would be in the increase in calcium requirements of modern, faster growing strains that need to form their skeletons more rapidly, which leads to more porous bones. The Ca/P ratio in bones is now 2.6:1 and not the traditional 2:1 (Williams et al., 2000a, b), with the effect that today's broilers would require starter diets with 1.2% Ca and 0.45% available P, which raises requirements for vitamin D$_3$ (Whitehead, 2005).

EU legislation imposes a maximum limit of 5,000 IU/kg vitamin D$_3$ in feed (Directive 85/429), although some countries have stricter standards. Research and commercial practice have focused on increasing supplies of vitamin D$_3$ by including some of its metabolites in feed, in particular 25-OH-D3, given that they are more active than vitamin D itself.

Interactions with other nutrients

High levels of vitamins A and E may reduce the status of vitamin D (Aburto and Britton, 1998a, b). Vitamin A at very high dosages of 45,000 IU/kg proved deleterious, increasing tibial dyschondroplasia. This negative effect was already apparent at practical levels, from 1,500 to 15,000 IU/kg, if the concentration of vitamin D was low (500 IU/kg), since growth and bone ash were reduced, and the requirement of vitamin D to overcome these negative effects was 3 times greater. The adverse effect of vitamin D, in contrast, took place at levels of 10,000 IU, which are impossible in practice. Luo and Huang (1991) also observed that an excess of vitamin A reduced growth and increased the incidence of tibial dyschondroplasia unless the feed was supplemented with vitamin E levels 5 times higher than those recommended by the NRC.

The possible synergy between ascorbic acid and vitamin D$_3$, and with its metabolite 1,25-DH, based on the role of the first in the biosynthesis of the second, is dealt with in more detail in the section on vitamin C. In some trials the combination of vitamins C and D has succeeded in reducing rickets (Roberson and Edwards, 1994) and increasing bone strength (Weiser et al., 1990; Lohakare et al., 2005). Whitehead and Keller (2003) indicate that combined supplementation of 1,25-DH and vitamin C has a potential application in reducing TD. However, Edwards (2000) and Waldenstedt (2006) consider that the experiments conducted to date offer no conclusive results.

The metabolism of vitamin D$_3$ may also be related to electrolyte balance. In cases of acidosis, generally induced by an excess of chlorine and low levels of sodium and potassium, calcitriol biosynthesis falls by 50% (Leeson and Summers, 2005).

186

Immunity

There are many studies on humans and laboratory animals that link vitamin D_3 with immune status (De Luca and Zierold, 1998; Lal *et al.*, 1999; Huff *et al.*, 2000; Praslickova *et al.*, 2008). While there is still little information on birds, the results point to a relationship with cell-meditated immunity, since it is needed for the maturation and functioning of macrophages, especially in the first two weeks of a chicken's life (Garlich *et al.*, 1992; Rama Rao *et al.*, 2007; Saunders-Blades and Korver, 2008).

Aslam *et al.* (1998) found a reduced immune response at cellular level and a reduction in thymus weight if there was a vitamin D_3 deficiency, which did not appear with a supplementation of 800 IU/kg; but Fritts *et al.* (2004) found no improvement with levels between 2,000 and 4,000 IU/kg. Praslickova *et al.* (2008) demonstrated that resistance to Marek's disease is connected to a marker in the vitamin D receptor gene, with the vitamin inducing a change in T lymphocyte response favorable to combating this virus. These actions seem to be more effective if the metabolite 25-dihydroxycholecalciferol is used. Saunders-Blades and Korver (2008) infected chicks of 1 and 4 days from hens that had received 2760 UI vitamin D or 60 µg/kg 25-OH-D3 in their diet with *E. coli* and with *Salmonella typhimurium*. They observed that the latter treatment improved maturation of the macrophages and increased the proportion of bacteria destroyed by the phagocytes.

VITAMIN D_3 METABOLITES

The discovery that vitamin D metabolites may reduce TD (Edwards, 1989; Rennie *et al.*, 1993) opened up a new field of research on their role in broiler nutrition and in foot problems. The most effective are the 1-hydroxylated, 1α-OH, and calcitriol or 1,25 DH (Rennie *et al.*, 1995; Elliot and Edwards, 1997; Rennie *et al.*, 1995), the metabolite which was the subject of most of the research carried out in the 1990s.

Bone quality

Initially all the studies focused on evaluating the efficacy of the metabolite 1,25-dihydroxycholecalciferol (1,25-DH), since there is a low concentration of this metabolite in the blood plasma of birds with tibial dyschondroplasia (Vaiano *et al.*, 1994), and it has often been confirmed that supplementing it in feed increases bone ash content (Edwards, 2000). Using 5 µg/kg calcitriol reduces TD significantly (Rennie and Whitehead, 1996a; Roberson and Edwards, 1996; Mitchell *et al.*, 1997b), and at 10 µg/kg it disappears completely (Edwards *et al.*,. 1992a). It was originally suggested that this supplementation be limited to the first weeks of life, given the fact that at this age chicks have a lower capacity for producing it (Vaiano *et al.*, 1994), but this strategy was ineffective in reducing TD (Rennie *et al.*, 1993). This metabolite has proven much more effective than levels of vitamin D even 10 times higher (2,000 IU/kg) than those recommended in 1994 by the NRC (Rennie, 1994; Elliot and Edwards, 1997).

The use of 1,25-DH is constrainedby its high cost and limited availability, and especially because of its toxic effects, which are most evident in high calcium diets (> 0.9–1% Ca). Hypercalcemia and reduced growth have been observed at 5 µg/kg, and are marked at 10 µg/kg (Rennie *et al.*, 1995; Elliot *et al.*, 1995; Roberson and Edwards, 1996; Mitchell *et al.*, 1997a; Elliot and Edwards, 1997). If calcium levels are low, however, or the Ca/P ratio is unbalanced, the birds' tolerance is higher and their growth is not impaired (Edwards *et al.*, 1992a; Rennie *et al.*, 1993, 1995; Whitehead, 1995a; Roberson and Edwards, 1996). The use of 1,25-DH reduces TD with a dosage-dependent response (Edwards, 1989, 1990; Rennie *et al.*, 1993), but its efficacy, as with other metabolites, depends on the incidence of this disorder (Rennie and Whitehead, 1996): in genetic strains with a higher predisposition to TD, higher supplementation is needed, from 10–15 µg/kg, and in this case weight gain is not reduced (Thorp *et al.*, 1993; Whitehead, 1995a; Xu *et al.*, 1997; Mitchell *et al.*, 1997b).

The safe limit appears to be 3.5 µg/kg at

normal calcium concentrations, but even under these conditions the safety margin between effective and toxic dosages is narrow, so that care would have to be taken with a possible commercial application (Whitehead, 2000). A practical strategy could be to combine it with ascorbic acid, since there appears to be synergy between the two substances (Völker and Fenster, 1991; Rennie, 1995).This aspect is discussed in more detail in the section on vitamin C.

The metabolite 1α-hydroxycalciferol (1α-OH) has also been assessed as 8–10 times more active than vitamin D_3. It promotes the absorption and mobilization of calcium in only 2 hours instead of 24 (Edwards et al., 2002), and appears to be about as effective as 1,25-DH, but at a much lower cost. In experiments with vitamin D_3 levels between 0 and 40 μg/kg, and dosages of 1α-OH from 0.635 to 10 μg/kg, the bioavailability of the metabolite was 1.9 to 21.2 times higher than that of vitamin D_3 (Kasim and Edwards, 2000). The percentage of bone ash proved to be the most appropriate assessment criterion, and it increased by 35% with the maximum level of vitamin D_3, and by 40% with 10 μg/kg 1α-OH.

Using this metabolite, Rennie and Whitehead (1996b) were able to reduce TD at 21 days to minimal figures (5%). Biehl and Baker (1997) observed no negative effects when using up to 40 μg/kg in a low-calcium diet. Edwards et al. (2004) used 5–10 μg/kg 1α-OH and obtained good results for weight at 16 days, bone ash and plasma calcium concentration, both in high – and low – calcium diets, but they still observed rickets where the calcium level was low. On the other hand, with a normal calcium level 20 μg/kg 1α-OH produced hypercalcemia and reduction in growth, so that the authors recommended reducing the calcium level if this metabolite is used.

Driver et al. (2005) evaluated the efficacy of 5 μg/kg 1α-OH and 1,000 units phytase in diets very low in calcium and phosphorus during the starter and growth phases. The birds which had not been given the supplements presented many cases of twisted legs (valgus-varus), and those which had been had growth rates and foot conditions similar to those from diets with normal calcium and phosphorus. There were however differences between the two experiments for unknown reasons, which the authors attributed to a different quality of the day-old chicks. This influence has been demonstrated by Shim et al. (2008), who found that the age of breeders had a significant effect on the presence of rickets when feeding their offspring with low-phosphorus diets. Using 5 μg/kg 1α-OH increased the live weight of broilers, but this increase was lower in those originating from young hens. In general, the use of this metabolite reduced both mortality and rickets caused by low phosphorus, and increased phosphorus retention and bone ash content.

In common with 1,25 DH, 1α-OH improves phosphorus retention synergistically or additively with phytases (Edwards, 1993; Mitchell and Edwards, 1996; Biehl and Baker, 1997). This allows calcium and phosphorus to be saved in diets (Roberson and Edwards, 1994; Biehl et al., 1995). In more recent experiments, Snow et al. (2004) assessed the use of phytases (300 units), 1α-OH (5–15 μg/kg) and citric acid 3–4%. The three products increased the utilization of phytic phosphorus, thereby providing from 0.02–0.04% of the available phosphorus. The use of 5 μg/kg 1α-OH reduced the requirement for available phosphorus by 0.04% to 5 μg. These effects were additive, so that the combination of the three substances liberated 0.13% of the available phosphorus.

The metabolite 25-OH-hydroxycholecalciferol (25-OH-D3), although less effective than calcitriol (Edwards, 1989), is in practice more useful for reducing TD, since the toxic dose is some 10 times higher than the effective one (Yarger et al., 1995b; Rennie and Whitehead, 1996a, b), so that it has been used commercially for some time now. 25-OH-D3 is seen as possessing an activity 2–2.5 times greater than vitamin D itself (Edwards et al., 1994; Ledwaba and Roberson, 2003), and higher intestinal absorption (90% vs. 70–75%).

In general, much higher concentrations are required (40–75 μg/kg) than if 1,25-DH is used (Rennie and Whitehead, 1996a, Yarger et al., 1995b; Ledwaba and Robeson,

2003; Parkinson and Cransberg, 2004), but it is more effective in preventing TD than vitamin D_3 itself (Fritts and Waldroup, 2003). Although these supplements do not eliminate TD, they do reduce clinical lameness and improve production results in proportion to dosage (Yarger et al., 1995a; Ward, 1995; Rennie and Whitehead 1996b) and time of administration (Mireles et al., 1996; Mireles, 1997, **Table XXI**).

Early tests showed some variability (Edwards, 2000), and in stress-free situations supplementation was often ineffective (Roberson, 1999). In more practical situations, marked and progressive improvements have generally been achieved reducing the incidence and severity of TD at 25-OH dosages between 70 and 250 µg/kg (Rennie and Whitehead, 1996a; Mitchell et al., 1997a; Zhang et al., 1997).

The effect is clearer if diets are low in calcium or their Ca/P ratio is unbalanced (Rennie and Whitehead, 1996a; Ledwaba and Robeson, 2003). Results also vary according to the birds' predisposition to TD (Mireles et al., 1999); if this is low, the improvement is slight (Roberson et al., 2005), but if it is very high then low doses will not work (Mitchell et al., 1997). Ledwaba and Roberson (2003) published a series of five experiments conceived to try and elucidate the question. In the diets designed to induce TD, supplementation with 40 or 70 µg/kg 25-OH-D3 reduced the incidence and severity of this disorder, especially if calcium was low and/or no vitamin D_3 was supplemented. However, the TD was reduced even more when 1,100 IU vitamin D_3 was added together with 10 µg/kg 25-OH-D3. If the feed had a higher vitamin D_3

content (2,200 IU/kg), the addition of 25-OH-D3 no longer improved the weight of the birds or their feed conversion index.

Productivity and quality of the product
Recent experiments have confirmed the benefits of 25-OH-D3 on production indices and product quality. Saunders-Blades and Korver (2006), using a commercial product (Hy D®) increased the rate of growth at all ages, as well as carcass yield and the weight and proportion of legs and breast. The plasma concentration of 25-OH-D3 did not fall between 0 and 10 days of age, something which is observed with vitamin D, and consequently the mineral density and strength of the femur increased. Santos and Soto-Salanova (2005) conducted a commercial trial in 4 sheds of 20,000 broilers to compare the effects of using 3,000 IU/kg vitamin D_3 and additionally including 300 mg/kg Hy D. This last treatment improved live weight by 53 g (1.7%), reduced the feed conversion index by 56 g (-2.6%), increased bone strength by 9%, and reduced drip shrinkage in the carcass (20–40%) and breast (25–50%). With these improvements they calculated a benefit of €60,000 for every million broilers reared under these conditions.

More research is needed to determine to what degree Hy D may substitute vitamin D_3 intake, although in some studies the latter has been eliminated completely with no adverse effects (Rennie and Whitehead, 1996b). Mireles (1997) used 69 µg/kg without vitamin D supplementation from either the first or seventh day of the chickens' life. In both cases a greater reduction in TD was achieved than with the control diet, with adequate vitamin D supplements. In the

Table XXI. Effect of the metabolite 25-OH-D$_3$ (68.9 µg/kg) on productivity at 49 days and the incidence and gravity of tibial dyschondroplasia (TD) in 52 day old males. (Mireles, 1997.)

Days administered	Weight, kg	Consumption, kg	Conversion index	% losses	% severe TD	Lesion rate
0	2.31 a	4.49 a	1.94 ab	3.56	16.0	0.8
21	2.33 ab	4.55 ab	1.95 b	2.19	12.0	0.4
33	2.34 b	4.51 ab	1.93 ab	2.53	12.0	0.5
42	2.38 b	4.57 ab	1.92 a	3.35	8.0	0.4
49	2.42	4.60b	1.90 b	4.48	4.0	0.2

first case growth increased compared to the control diet, but the result was reversed in the second, which suggests that the first week of life is a critical period for response to this metabolite.

More recently, Parkinson and Cransberg (2004) reduced TD and increased body weight up to 14 days with the same dosage of 25-OH-D3 and without vitamin D supplements. In other experiments they showed that 25-OH-D3 was more effective than vitamin D_3 in increasing bone ash content, and that the advantages of using this metabolite are greater when working with low dosages of vitamin D_3 (500 IU/kg), but that the benefits diminish at higher levels (2,000–4,000 IU/kg). Philips et al. (2005) presented data obtained with dosages between 35 and 560 µg/kg in diets without vitamin D supplementation. The weight of the broilers increased linearly up to 280 µg/kg, the feed conversion index fell by 5% from 140 µg/kg and the plasma concentration of 25-OH-D3 increased with the inclusion level. Koreleski and Swiatkiewicz (2005) tried substituting 50–60% vitamin D_3 with equivalent quantities of 25-OH-D3 and were able to improve bone strength and production indices, while Papesova et al. (2008) report a synergy between vitamin D and its metabolite, as they obtained better results with 62.5 and 50 µg/kg, respectively, than with only 50 µg 25-OH-D3 or 125 µg/kg vitamin D_3. It therefore seems possible, as Huyghebaert et al. (2005) indicated, that the two substances perform specific and complementary actions.

Other papers indicate the existence of a relationship between the vitamin nutrition of breeders and the efficacy of 25-OH-D3 in their offspring (Atencio et al., 2005 b, c). The initial work combined levels of vitamin D_3 up to 2,000 IU/kg and 12.5 µg/kg 25-OH-D3 in the feed of breeder hens and subsequently the chicks received 27.5 µg/kg 25-OH-D3. Live weight and tibia ash content increased by over 20% if the hens had received supplementation very low in vitamin D (125 IU/kg), but with 500 IU/kg there was already little difference from the controls. The best results in all evaluated parameters were achieved if the breeders received 2,000 IU/kg vitamin D in feed. Rickets and TD increased in broilers whose mothers received only 3.1 or 12.5 µg/kg 25-OH-D3, which clearly indicates that these quantities are severely deficient (Atencio et al., 2005b). Another series of experiments with higher levels of 25-OH-D3 and vitamin D (Atencio et al., 2005c) revealed that chickens which received unbalanced calcium and phosphorus diets supplemented with 40 µg/kg 25-OH-D3 had a lower incidence of TD and rickets, gained more weight and had a higher level of calcium in bones and serum. These advantages were also achieved by including 4,000 IU/kg in the breeders feed, but the best results came from broilers whose mothers received this high level of vitamin D and an adequate calcium level as well as including 40 µg/kg 25-OH-D3.

The metabolite 25-hydroxycholecalciferol also seems to be useful in preventing another bone problem in broilers known as black bone syndrome (BBS), which is characterised by the blackening of the leg bones, more usually in the tibia but sometimes also in the femur of the broiler, and with the discoloration extending to the adjacent meat, especially after cooking (Lyon and Lyon, 2002; Saunders-Blades and Korver, 2006). This problem now appears more widespread than previously appreciated. It appears to be linked with diffusion of blood from the medulla through the bone structure, particularly when deboned cuts are frozen. Cooking can exacerbate the defect, as well as blackening the blood. The problem is already showing an impact on the market (Kam et al., 2007).

The cause of BBS appears to be a disruption of intramembranous ossification, due to the fact that the structure of the cortical bone is more porous in modern broilers (Rath et al., 2000; Whitehead, 2005). Saunders-Blades and Korver (2006) demonstrated that improving bone mineral density and including 25-OH-D3 in the feed can reduce blood diffusion and discoloration, and improve acceptance of poultry meat by consumers.

To prevent rickets in turkeys, better results have been obtained by adding the metabolite $1,25\,(OH)_2$ D3 at a dosage of 5–10 µg/kg than with higher levels of vitamin D supplementation (Sanders and Edwards, 1991; Perry et al., 1991; Atia et al., 1994) and 25-OH-D3, at 40–100 µg/kg (Owens and

Ledoux, 2000; Owens and Ledoux, 2001). These supplements increased weight as well as, with the higher concentrations, bone strength and bone ash content, even without supplementing vitamin D_3. At 90 µg/kg, 25-OH-D3 produced effects similar to the inclusion of 3,650 IU vitamin D_3 in combination with phytases (Owens and Ledoux, 2001). However, the response depends on the strain of turkey and the type of diet (Mireles et al., 1999), and these effects were small or non-existent when feed was very deficient in calcium and phosphorus (Owens and Ledoux, 2000).

However, no appreciable effect of vitamin D_3 metabolites on tibial dyschondroplasia in turkeys has been observed (Sanders and Edwards, 1991; Nixey, 2005). Although the characteristics of the lesion are similar to those in broilers, it is less severe and does not cause deformities or poor gait and it tends to heal with age (Whitehead, 2005). Unlike in broilers, TD in turkeys appears to have no relation to calcium or phosphorus levels (Hocking et al., 2002), and Nixey (2005) proposed that the etiology of this disorder may be different in chickens and turkeys. In the latter it may be due to the lack of some trace element at an early age, possibly copper, given that TD may be induced by the fusarium fungus and some fungicides responds well to treatments with copper. Pines et al. (2005) indicate that the two species show differences in the regulation of angiogenesis in the growth plate, which means that TD prevention would have to be accomplished by different strategies.

Immunity

Positive effects of the use of the metabolite 25-OH-D3 on humoral immunity in the face of certain pathologies have also been published. Mireles (1997) reported a better immune response after vaccinating against Newcastle disease with the inclusion of 69 µg/kg of this metabolite in feed and other experiments established an increase in the titer of infectious bronchitis antibodies, and a general increase in the titers of antibodies in the presence of coccidiosis (Mireles et al. 1999).

Gill (2002) published the results of a trial in which broilers were infected with the virus causing malabsorption syndrome. Adding 37.5 µg/kg 25-OH-D3 to feed, as well as greatly increasing the concentration of this metabolite in blood plasma, also reduced mortality and resulted in better growth and feed conversion than 1,500 or 2,200 IU/kg vitamin D_3/kg. In turkeys, Huff et al. (2000, 2002) investigated the effects of 25-OH-D3 on the prevention of turkey osteomyelitis complex, a disease involving E. coli and S. aureus. Using turkeys immunodepleted with dexamethasone and inoculated with E. coli, and administering 25-OH-D3 at 2,100–4,100 IU/kg of bodyweight in drinking water, they found a reduction in losses, in airsaculitis and the lesions typical of this complex, and a lower heterophil/lymphocyte ratio. In a trial with the inclusion in feed of 99 µg/kg 25-OH-D3 or 10 µg/kg 1,25-OH-D3 they were able to suppress colibacillosis lesions, although 1,25-OH-D3 resulted in higher mortality and lower live weight in the turkeys than 25-OH-D3.

Utilization of phytic phosphorus

Interest in the metabolites of vitamin D_3 has also increased in the US due to strict regulations on the use of bedding as fertilizer according to its concentration of phosphorus. In the European Union the limit continues to be that of nitrogen. The vitamin D metabolites liberate phytic phosphorus used separately or in combination with phytases (McNaughton and Murray, 1990; Soares et al., 1995), which allow reductions in the inorganic phosphorus supply in the diet and its excretion. According to Applegate et al. (2003), the likely mechanism is not a direct influence on the activity of intestinal phytases, but rather an intestinal calcium absorption, reducing its chelation with the phytin molecule and its solubility, which would make it more accessible to phytase action.

In the 1990s a number of trials were conducted with the aim of assessing the possibilities of reducing the available phosphorus in the diet by using different vitamin D metabolites in feed. Using 1,25-OH-D3 at 5 µg/kg allowed the available phosphorus to be reduced by 0.030–0.059% (Edwards, 1993, 1995, 1999); with 1α (OH)D3, at 5 µg/kg, between 0.025–0.03%, and 0.06% at 20 µg/kg (Biehl and Baker, 1997); and with 25-OH-D3 there were no significant effects at 5 µg/kg (Edwards, 1995, 1999), but with

191

35–70 µg/kg a reduction of 0.03–0.035% was demonstrated (Angel et al. 2001a).

Angel et al. (2001a) conducted two experiments directed at improving phosphorus utilization by broilers housed in cages and receiving a diet with low levels of calcium and phosphorus, comparing the efficacy of 200–500 units of phytase, 35–70 µg/kg 25-OH-D3, 3% citric acid, and all combinations there of. The percentage of bone ash improved in all cases. The combination of the three additives saved 0.116–0.126% of available phosphorus in the formulation, 25-OH-D3, 0.037%, and 500 units of phytase 0.065%. The two last treatments combined reduced requirements for available phosphorus by between 0.067% and 0.092%.

Subsequently, in another trial with 3 flocks of broilers reared on bedding and with feed lower in phosphorus than the NRC recommendations, Angel et al. (2005, 2006) demonstrated that it was possible to reduce the cumulative available phosphorus consumption per bird from 18.2 to 8.65–11 g, at the same time as reducing the total content of phosphorus in the bedding by 60% with the use of these additives, and the quantity of soluble phosphorus by another 60%. Neither growth nor bone fractures at slaughter were influenced by these treatments, in spite of using diets low in phosphorus.

More clarification is needed on the specific conditions under which available phosphorus can be reduced and by how much in the context of supplementation with 25-OH-D3 and/or phytases, since there are some contradictory data. Ledwaba and Robeson (2003) found a linear increase in the retention of phytic phosphorus in low-calcium diets when adding 27.5 µg/kg 25-OH-D3 and incremental dosages of vitamin D_3 (up to 2,800 IU/kg). This retention also increased with higher 25-OH-D3 supplementation levels (40 and 70 µg/kg) in diets lower in vitamin D, but the difference dimished when higher concentrations of vitamin D were used. With caged broilers that received no vitamin D supplementation, Philips et al. (2005) tried levels of 25-OH-D3 between 35 and 560 µg/kg. They found improvements in phosphorus utilization of 49% and 51% at the highest dosages of

25-OH-D3. Calcium utilization improved by around 40% with all levels of 25-OH supplementation.

Subsequently, Philips et al. (2008) assessed the effects of 69 µg/kg 25-OH-D3 and 750 units of phytase in diets with three levels of vitamin D (200, 500 and 2,000 IU/kg). With the lower vitamin D concentrations the combination of phytase and 25-OH-D3 improved production results, tibia bone strength and ash content, as well as the utilization of calcium and phosphorus. Phosphorous utilization improved even further if the feed included 2,000 IU vitamin D, in contrast to the experiments of Ledwaba and Robeson (2003).

Angel et al. (2001b) reported 3 experiments in cages with turkeys with the same objectives as with broilers. The results, statistically and economically significant, are shown in **Table XXII**.

In another trial with 2 flocks of turkeys reared in floor pens, the same researchers compared the efficacy of 600 units of phytase and/or 50 µg/kg 25-OH-D3 in diets with phosphate levels in accordance with the NRC or the higher levels used by the North American industry. They estimated a saving of 0.03% available phosphorus, practically the same as with the battery trials. Phytase and 25-OH-D3 reduced the concentration of phosphorus in bedding when used both in combination and separately. Growth was not affected by these treatments. Bar et al. (2003) however conducted a series of experiments with different levels of 25-OH-D3, concluding that the benefits were more evident in diets low in calcium or phosphorus, but only up to 20–30 µg/kg, and that at 75 µg/kg there was a decline in growth. It should nevertheless be pointed out that the results from different trials are not comparable and that in the majority of them the vitamin D_3 supplements were below 3,000 IU/kg in the starter phase, when the current recommendation is 4,000–5,000 IU/kg.

Some recent studies on broilers and turkeys have revealed that supplementation with 69 µg/kg 25-OH-D3 was linked to the use of a higher level of all the vitamins in general. With this treatment, which included 90 µg/

Table XXII. Effect of using 25-OH-D$_3$ and other additives on the requirements of available phosphorus in turkeys. (Angel *et al.*, 2001b)

	Treatment	Available P saving (g/kg)
Experiment 1	25-OH-D3, 35–105 µg/kg	0.033–0.046
	Phytase, 600 units	0.092
	25-OH-D3, 70 µg/kg + phytase, 300 units	0.074
	25-OH-D3, 70 µg/kg + phytase, 600 units	0.124
Experiment 2	25-OH-D3, 35–70 µg/kg	0.032–0.049
	Phytase, 600 units	0.087
	25-OH-D3, 35 µg/kg + phytase, 600 units	0.106
	25-OH-D3, 35 µg/kg + phytase, 600 units + citric acid, 2%	0.112
Experiment 3	25-OH-D3, 70 µg/kg + phytase, 500 units	NS
	Phytase, 500 units	0.063
	Citric acid, 3%	0.0.031
	Phytase, 500 units + citric acid, 2%	0.130

kg 25-OH-D3-D3 up to the 6th week and 50 µg/kg subsequently, Philippe *et al.* (2005) were able to delay locomotor problems in turkeys until 15 weeks of age and improve productivity and breast yield compared to the standard vitamin levels in France, with or without addition of 25-OH-D3. Pérez Vendrell and Weber (2007) conducted a similar trial with broilers using 62.5 µg/kg 25-OH-D3 throughout the cycle, compared to the vitamin levels typically used in Spain, and without supplementing 25-OH-D3. The level of vitamin D$_3$ (2,500 IU/kg) was used throughout in both treatments. The higher vitamin levels, combined with the 25-OH-D3 supplementation, resulted in better growth and feed conversion index in the starter phase as well as better meat quality, higher breast proportion and improved lipid oxidative stability.

VITAMIN E

Sources

Vitamin E is a generic term referring to a group of compounds called tocopherols present in natural form in the lipid fraction of feed ingredients, mainly in oilseeds and by-products of animal origin, although with very low stability. In oilseed meal the content is minimal, since it is eliminated on extraction of the oil. In practice, supplements are added in the more stable form of α-tocopherol acetate. Intestinal absorption of vitamin E depends on a number of factors but averages at 42% (Barroeta, 2007).

Functions

Vitamin E is the main antioxidant in blood and on a cellular level, it maintains the integrity of the cellular and vascular membranes. It also acts as a detoxifier and takes part in many other biochemical reactions. Vitamin E is essential for the fertility of adult birds. It has been found only relatively recently that this vitamin is involved in immune response, on a cellular as well as humoral level.

Requirements and recommendations

Requirements established by the NRC in 1994 for the prevention of the typical signs of vitamin E deficiency, namely encephalomalacia and exudative diathesis, are based on studies from the 1950s and 1960s and are relatively low. However, it was already common practice then to fortify the diets of broilers and turkeys with supplements at a level of 20–30 mg/kg (Ward, 1993). It has been calculated that broilers selected for increased lean tissue have requirements 50% higher using the vitamin E plasma concentration as a criterion (Whitehead, 1991). In general, the use of much higher levels (150–400 ppm) has not led to improvements in production indicators on an experimental level, either in chickens (Blum et al., 1990; Bartov and Frigg, 1992; Macklin et al., 2000; Coetzee et al., 2001) or in turkeys (Applegate and Sell, 1996; Sell et al., 1995, 1997; Kalbfleisch et al., 2000). However, these very high levels are associated with benefits in other criteria, such as immunity and resistance to stress, and meat quality. These aspects have been studied extensively over the last 20 years.

The long recognized relationship between vitamin E and selenium has been further reinforced by experiments conducted recently. Thus improvements have been found in production parameters (Okolelova et al., 2006), the immune status of birds (Singh et al., 2006), and the oxidative stability of the product (Özkan et al., 2007; Ryu et al., 2005).

Vitamin E metabolism is different in chickens and turkeys. In young turkeys, 7–10 days after hatching there is a marked drop in its levels in the liver, from 144 to only 0.5 µg/g, and in plasma between 7 and 21 days, and these remain low until 21 days of age (Soto-Salanova et al., 1991; Waibel et al., 1994; Soto-Salanova and Sell, 1995, 1996; Surai et al., 1997). This phenomenon occurs, albeit to a lesser degree, even when the vitamin E level in starter feed is raised to 150 ppm (Applegate and Sell, 1996) or when the diet of breeding turkeys is fortified. However, Surai et al. (1999) found that using 365 ppm in breeder feed raised the concentration of vitamin E in the liver, brain and lungs of the chick between 3 and 5 times, which reduced the susceptibility of these organs to oxidation.

Following a series of experiments focusing on the starter phase, Sell (1996) concludes that vitamin E requirements in young turkeys

depend on the chosen evaluation criterion: growth (a maximum of 20 ppm), increased resistance of red blood cells to hemolysis (85 ppm), increased tissue concentration of vitamin E (more than 115 ppm), or achieving sufficient plasma levels of over 2 µg/l (minimum 150 ppm).

Resistance to stress

There are signs that vitamin E requirements increase under conditions of stress. In chickens subjected to excessive temperatures, positive physiological responses have been shown, such as a smaller rise in body temperature, reduced mortality, and a large increase of the hormone triiodothyronine in plasma (Kan et al., 1993; Qureshi et al., 2000), and Sahin et al. (2002) using a combination of vitamins E and A, which caused a reduction of 50% in the concentration of malonaldehyde in the liver and serum of broilers subjected to heat stress. Erf et al. (2000) demonstrated that the use of 150 IU/kg vitamin E in turkeys reduced immunological stress caused by vaccinations against Newcastle disease and hemorrhagic enteritis, given that the lymphocyte count increased while that of heterophils decreased. This reduced the relationship between the two, which is usually interpreted as a lower degree of stress.

More recent experiments have gone deeper into the physiological effects of vitamin E in stress situations. Maini et al. (2007) found that supplementing starter feed with 200 ppm vitamin E reduced peroxidation of erythrocytes and in various tissues at 3 and 5 weeks of age in chickens subjected to heat stress. With turkeys, Siegel et al. (2006) found that in cases of cold stress the mortality of day-old turkeys was significantly reduced when the hens had been supplemented with 300 ppm vitamin E instead of only 10, and observed that the α-tocopherol concentration in the plasma of the offspring wa 7-fold higher.

A field trial with 1.5 million chickens, using 33 or 240 mg/kg vitamin E, obtained the following improvements: feed conversion index, -2.3%; live weight, +0.7%; viability, +0.1%; downgrading, -34%; septicaemia-toxaemia, -25%; inflammatory processes, -61% (Boren and Bond, 1996). Subsequently other studies (Bird and Boren, 1999; Siegel et al., 2000) with this same level achieved improvements in all production parameters. The large-scale trial run by Bird and Boren (1999) also confirmed an increase in breast yield, and a reduction in downgrading and the proportion of defects in the carcass and its cuts (**Figure 7**). In turkeys, McKnight et al. (1996) found that starter supplementation with 100–200 mg/kg vitamin E improved growth and feed conversion in different stress situations typical of commercial conditions. Sowinska et al. (1997) reported that transportation shrinkage was reduced from 2.3% to 1.5% after administering 30 mg/l in drinking water to turkeys.

Results of this type have led some researchers to state that "the only valid scientific method to study optimum vitamin requirements is by evaluation in field tests using a large number of birds, provided that these be controlled in a precise and uniform manner" (Rice and McIllroy, 1988, quoted by Kennedy et al., 1992).

Immunity
The role of vitamin E in the functioning of the immune system has been studied in depth over the last few years by several research groups, although there remains much to be learned (Klasing, 2007). It is believed that this action is based on the function of vitamin E as a lipophilic antioxidant, capable of preventing lipid peroxidation in membranes caused by free radicals. Disease is an important factor in the production of free radicals, either during prostanoid synthesis, or as a consequence of macrophage function.

The relationship between vitamin E and immunity first came to light in 1975, when researchers improved immune response using 300 ppm and reduced mortality in birds facing an E. coli challenge (Tengerdy and Nockels, 1975; Tengerdy and Brown, 1997). Subsequent studies have found similar effects, with dosages between 100 and 300 mg/kg, in cases of colibacillosis (Siegel et al., 2000), coccidiosis (Colnago et al., 1984), and listeriosis in turkeys (Zhu et al., 2003); and also in the immune response to vaccinations against Newcastle disease (Franchini et al., 1986, Hesabi, 2007) and bronchitis (Klasing, 1998, **Figure 8**; Hesabi, 2007). Erf et al. (2000) recorded an increase in vitamin E concentration in the principal immune organs when using 150 IU/kg, which they related to the greater immune response

Figure 7. Improvement in carcass quality of broilers supplemented with vitamin E (240 vs. 50 ppm) in starter feed
(Field study, China, 1.1 million broilers. Bird and Boren, 1999)

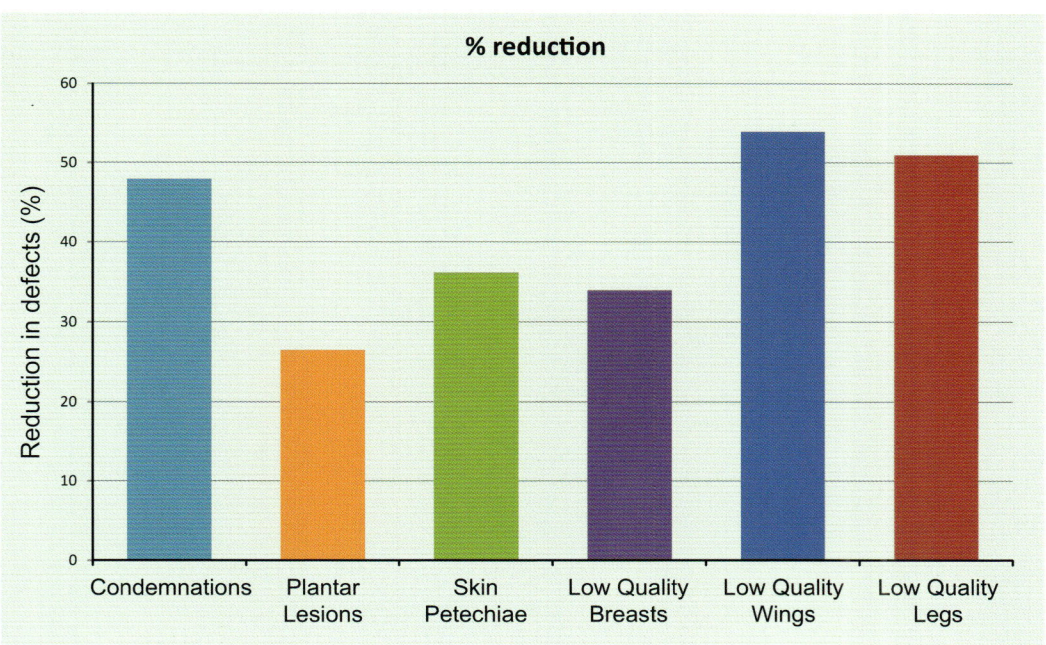

Figure 8. Effect of vitamin E supplementation level on titers of infectious bronchitis antibodies (Klasing *et al.*, 1997)

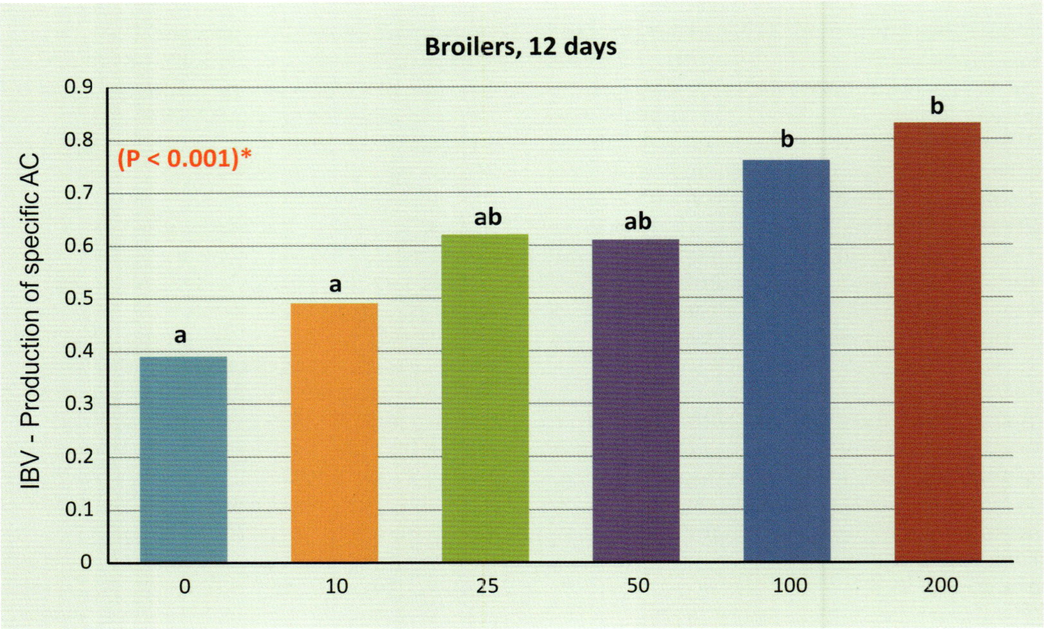

elicited following vaccinations for Newcastle disease and hemorrhagic enteritis.

It has been shown that vitamin E is promotes the phagocytic activity of macrophages, especially at thymus level (Konjufca *et al.*, 2004) and in other immune mechanisms mediated by cells (Chang *et al.*, 1990; Erf *et al.*, 1998; Konjufca *et al.*, 2004; Leshchinsky and Klasing, 2003).

Abdukalikoba *et al.* (2006, 2008) assessed the improvement in the cell response to challenges from vaccination against infectious bronchitis and in the humoral response to SRBC inoculation. Levels of 200 and 400 IU/kg did not improve on results obtained with 80 IU/kg. The authors suggest that average supplementation levels are adequate if combined with arginine. Further research is required to clarify the question.

In general, the dosages of vitamin E proposed for improving immune status are much greater (100–300 ppm) than those for growth, which means that they represent an important extra cost. This raises the subject of their cost/benefit relationship, which has been assessed in some studies. Kennedy *et al.* (1992) monitored 168 flocks

with a total of 3 million broilers and found significant improvements in growth and feed conversion indexes as a result of the continued use of 160 mg/kg vitamin E. The economic evaluation produced a benefit of 8.4%, and, after deducting the cost of vitamin E (certainly high as this high level was maintained throughout the cycle) of 2.7% on average. This improvement was considerably higher for those producers who usually had poorer results. McIlroy *et al.* (1993) supervised 79 flocks in Northern Ireland, during a Gumboro epidemic, using either 48 or 178 mg/kg vitamin E. Clinical symptoms were not detected because all the birds were vaccinated, but in 43 flocks subclinincal IBD was diagnosed by bursal lesions. With 48 ppm vitamin E there was a reduction of 28% in the net income, but with 128 mg/kg it improved by 10%. In healthy chickens a much lower improvement of 2% was obtained. Whitehead (2002) considers that more virulent strains of Gumboro virus vaccine, which are currently used in many countries and which entail greater immunological stress, may increase the benefits of using a higher vitamin E supplementation in feed.

However, contradictory results abound in scientific literature. Allen and Fetterer (2002)

196

considered that the results of Colnago were inconsistent, and in their own experiments they did not find improvements in live weight or in the prevalence of lesions after an infection of *Eimeria maxima*. Friedman *et al.* (1998) found the humoral immune response impared with 30 ppm rather than with 10 ppm following colibacillosis infection and vaccination against Newcastle disease, while for Leschinsky and Klasing (2001) levels of 25–50 ppm vitamin E are immunomodulatory in broilers, and they concluded that supplements of 100 and 200 mg/kg were less effective in increasing the production of antibodies following bronchitis vaccination.

Various hypotheses have been proposed to explain these discrepancies. First, the effect of vitamin E on humoral response appears to differ according to the antigen under consideration. Hesabi (2007) indicates that 50 IU/kg were needed to improve the number of antibodies in the face of Newcastle disease, 75 IU/kg for better protection against bronchitis, and up to 100 IU/kg to increase defenses against mycotoxins. On the other hand, in certain pathological processes the humoral immune response is the most relevant and in others, such as bronchitis, it is immunity mediated by cells which has special importance. An anti-inflammatory role has also been indicated for this vitamin, since it inhibits the production of certain cytokines in a dose-dependent manner (Leshchinsky *et al.*, 2003).

Other authors report that the magnitude of the response differs according to the degree of the pathogen challenge, which appears to vary between the different experiments. It is thought that the relationship between vitamin E and immunity can be altered by various factors such as genetic selection (Boa-Amponsem *et al.*, 2006; Siegel *et al.*, 2006) and the strain of bird used, since some studies have found different responses depending on the strain under consideration (Maurice *et al.*, 1993; Siegel *et al.*, 2000; Boa-Amponsem *et al.*, 2001). However, Yang *et al.* (2000) found no clear relationship between vitamin E supplementation and the production of antibodies in the face of the SRBC antigen or of a challenge from *E. coli* in chickens from strains selected for a low or high production of antibodies against SRBC.

Maternal immunity still active at the time of the outbreak may also have an influence (Leshchinsky and Klasing, 2001), as may the vitamin status of the day-old chick, which is related to the vitamin E supplementation level of breeders. These factors determine the efficiency of the chick's antioxidant systems in the embryonic and early postnatal periods (Surai *et al.*, 1997, 1999; Surai, 2000). The concentration of vitamin E in the chick's tissues depends on the hen's diet and its consequent accumulation in the egg yolk. Thus if breeders receive 365 ppm vitamin E instead of 150, the vitamin E content in the lung, liver and brain of the chick will be 6, 4 and 2 times higher, respectively (Surai *et al.*, 1999). After hatching Vitamin E concentration falls rapidly in the yolk sac in only 9 days from 566 µg/kg to 26.7 in broilers and from 156 to only 0.1 µg/kg in turkeys (Surai *et al.*, 1997; Surai, 2000). If the breeder and starter feed of broilers contain high levels of unsaturated fats, the high levels of PUFA adversely affect the vitamin status of chickens and turkeys after hatching (Cherian and Sim, 1997, 2003).

Haq *et al.* (1996) showed that chicks from hens that received supplementation of 300 ppm vitamin E presented better humoral immunity and more active lymphocytes, which has recently been confirmed by Rebel *et al.* (2004). Hossain *et al.* (1998) found that increasing vitamin E to 75 ppm in the diet of breeders increased its concentration in the egg yolk and improved the antibody titers of their offspring after vaccination against Newcastle disease. Rebel *et al.* (2004) showed that broilers infected with the virus causing malabsorption syndrome suffered less damage and recovered sooner if the breeders had received a higher vitamin E supplementation.

Research with turkeys, as with broilers, has centered on the effects of vitamin E on immunity, and the picture here is unclear . With 150 ppm vitamin E, Ferket *et al.* (1995) obtained lower mortality from colibacillosis and better feed conversion in coccidiosis challenge situations. Huff *et al.* (2004), using 30 IU/kg per day in drinking water together with sodium salicylate 5 days before and during an *E. coli* challenge, were able to reduce mortality and colibacillary lesions and maintain growth rate. In contrast, Friedman *et al.* (1998) obtained worse results with 150

197

ppm vitamin E than with 50ppm, and Sell *et al.* (1997) used 300 ppm in an *E. coli* challenge without detecting significant improvements.

Qureshi *et al.* (1993) state that it takes 250 ppm to induce an increase in IgG (which was confirmed by Ferket and Qureshi, 1999), and to stimulate proliferation of T-lymphocytes with these levels. Heffels-Redman *et al.* (2000, 2001) also observed this phenomenon, although 400–800 ppm vitamin E did not improve the rate of hemagglutination-inhibiting antibodies following vaccination against Newcastle disease. The same was found in the experiment by Kalbfleisch *et al.* (2000), who did however confirm an improved humoral response to vaccination against hemorrhagic enteritis. It appears that vitamin E may act on immunity by several mechanisms, and it would be worth conducting similar studies to those previously indicated for broilers.

In conclusion, it is difficult to indicate with precision the optimum levels and period of vitamin E supplementation needed to improve the immunity of broilers and turkeys, since the degree of protection necessary will depend on the type and degree of immunological pressure induced by different vaccination programs, nutritional and environmental conditions, as well as by potential exposure to different pathogens. With regard to vitamin E the focus should be the improvement of its metabolic status, rather than merely preventing its deficiency.

One example of this approach is the study by Gore and Qureshi (1997), who injected 10, 20, or 30 IU vitamin E into the amniotic fluid of turkey embryos 3 days before hatching. Levels above 10 IU led to a drop in hatchability, but at this dosage they observed more antibodies than in the control groups, and a greater proportion of macrophages in a post-hatch challenge with sheep red blood cells. The same occurred with chicken embryos. In broilers, Hossain *et al.*, (1998) obtained similar results, improving titers against Newcastle disease, as well as significant improvements in weight at 42 days, in viability, and in the feed conversion index. This may offer a promising way of improving the immune status of birds.

Prevention of disease

The antioxidant action of vitamin E has led to a number of studies on its relationship with hypoxic syndrome or ascites, a metabolic disease which continues to cause important economic losses, although less now than in previous years. In 1986, Dale and Villacres analyzed the first studies to note a possible relationship, and more recently, Malan *et al.* (2001) and Baghbanzadeh and Decuypère (2008) have reviewed the published evidence. Ascitic chickens exhibit a high production of reactive oxygen and a reduction in levels of ascorbic acid and vitamin E in liver and lungs and consequently indications of lipid peroxidation in these organs (Iqbal *et al.*, 2001; Envetchakul *et al.*, 1993). Bottje *et al.* (1995) demonstrated that mortality from ascites was reduced when vitamin E implants were used, which liberated some 15 mg per day.

However, tests using higher feed levels of vitamin E, mainly in starter feeds (100–500 ppm), with or without the addition of selenium (whose synergies with this vitamin are well known), have only been partially successful or have not reduced the incidence of ascites (Bottje *et al.*, 1997, 1998; Stanley *et al.*, 1997; Roch *et al.*, 2000b; Villar-Patino *et al.*, 2002), while another study (Walton *et al.*, 2001) even linked the use of 50 ppm vitamin E to an increase in ascites, although it was combined with megadosages of vitamin C, which could have had a pro-oxidant effect. Belay *et al.* (1996) observed no reduction in mortality with a supplement of antioxidant vitamins 25% higher than the levels used commercially at the time, although the birds were significantly heavier without this entailing a higher incidence of ascites. More recently, supplementation with vitamin E, on its own or in combination with arginine, did not improve pulmonary relaxation following epinephrine challenge or bioavailability of the nitric oxide synthetase enzyme, although vitamin E levels of the order of 400 IU were associated with long periods of recovery from arteriopulmonary pressure (Lorenzoni and Ruiz-Feria, 2006).

Whitehead (2002) indicates that nutrition is not the root cause of hypoxic syndrome, so it is doubtful whether it can really be prevented by changes in composition of the diet. Broz and Ward (2007) consider that since ascites is a condition of multifactorial origin it is necessary to conduct more research under practical conditions to confirm whether either vitamin E or vitamin C can have a protective effect against this pathology.

Another line of research relates to "cellulitis" – a subcutaneous infection, generally by *E. coli* – a problem which is becoming the primary cause of downgrading in broiler slaughterhouses. Until now the results have been inconsistent, although in some experiments certain improvements have been noticed, particularly if the vitamin E supplement (50–100 ppm) is linked with zinc complexes (Downs *et al.*, 1999; 2000; Macklin *et al.*, 2000). In broilers intoxicated with ochratoxins the combination of 500 IU/kg vitamin E and 0.1 ppm selenium improved growth and allowed the birds to recover better (Kurkure *et al.*, 2004).

The scientific literature makes mention of a possible role of vitamin E in the reduction of skeletal problems, given that its deficiency increases the incidence of twisted feet, with deviations of the distal portion of the tibia or the tarsus at proximal level (Summers *et al.*, 1984). However, vitamin E at levels 5–10 times higher than normal can affect the utilization of vitamin D_3 if this is at marginal levels (500 IU/kg), and thus adversely affect ossification (Aburto and Britton, 1998a, b).

In turkeys particular attention has been paid to the efficacy of vitamin E in improving health, and it is usually added to the diet at levels 3–4 times higher than those recommended by the NRC to prevent deficiencies (Ward, 1993), although Sell *et al.* (1997a) considered that the NRC levels might be adequate in the absence of diseases. However, cases of encephalomalacia at 3–4 weeks have been reported (Klein *et al.*, 1994) as does so-called "fatigue syndrome", in which a significant reduction in the plasma concentration of vitamin E has been found in affected turkeys (Meldrum *et al.*, 2000), which respond well to vitamin E supplementation in drinking water (Sell, 1996). Problems have also been observed with the inclusion of some fat sources in feeds, probably due to their state of rancidity, since an increase in oxidation products was found in plasma together with a corresponding reduction in vitamin E concentration (Csallany, 1988; Soto-

Salanova and Sell, 1995). This problem, and the protective effect of supplementing these diets with selenium and vitamins A and E has been described by Zdunczyk *et al.* (2002).

Meat quality

The beneficial effects of including high dosages of α-tocopherol acetate in feed on the oxidative stability and sensory quality of meat have been extensively researched. Oxidation processes are responsible for the occurrence of unpleasant smells and flavors, for changes in the nutritive value (reduction in the meat's polyunsaturated fatty acid and fat-soluble vitamin content) and even for the appearance of components which are potentially harmful to health, such as cholesterol oxides.

The risk of oxidation is increased if meat undergoes prolonged defrosting, and when restructured and pre-cooked meat products are manufactured, since salt and cooking accelerate oxidation processes. The problem is greater if the fat in the meat contains a high level of polyunsaturated fatty acids, which are highly valued nowadays from a nutritional point of view, but which are also very susceptible to oxidation (Barroeta, 2007). The amount of published material on all of these aspects is vast, and important aspects now seem clear, such as optimum levels of supplementation, the required period of supplementation, and effects on composition, oxidative stability and sensory quality of the meat. Much information can be found on the subject, which may be found in reviews such as those by Morrissey *et al.* (1998), Sheehy *et al.* (1995), Jensen *et al.* (1998), Weber (2001), Fellenberg and Speisky (2006), and Barroeta (2007).

Vitamin E content of meat

The most immediate effect of supplementing vitamin E above the levels recommended by the NRC is the enrichment of poultry meat with this vitamin (Marusich *et al.*, 1974; Koreleski *et al.*, 2006; Hsiesh *et al.*, 2002; Villaverde *et al.*, 2008), which improves the nutritional content of the meat, although transfer efficiency is lower than in the egg (Flachowsky *et al.*, 2001). The increase is more rapid in liver and kidney tissue than in muscle and fat (Sheehy *et al.*, 1991; Surai *et al.*, 1993; Flachowsky *et al.*, 2001), and greater in the darker muscles of the thigh and leg, which have a higher fat content and are rich in type I and IIa oxidative metabolism fibers, than in glycolytic metabolism fibers such as pectorals (Brandon *et al.*, 1993; Jensen *et al.*, 1998; Malczyk *et al.*, 1999), in which the vitamin E concentration also diminishes more rapidly (Sheldon *et al.*, 1997). Vitamin E is deposited in cellular membranes, where the process of oxidation begins (Asghar *et al.*, 1990), and in subcellular organelles such as mitochondria and microsomes (Lauridsen *et al.*, 1997; Mercier *et al.*, 1998).

The enrichment of meat with vitamin E is directly proportional to its levels in the diet and the length of the supplementation period (Sheehy *et al.*, 1991; Bartov and Frigg, 1992), although a plateau is reached above 500 ppm (Jakobsen *et al.*, 1995; Flachowsky *et al.*, 2001). Sheehy *et al.* (1995) calculated that every additional 100 ppm vitamin E in the diet increased the vitamin E content of meat by 7% of the recommended daily human intake. Thus, just 10 ppm would achieve 1–2%, while 300 ppm could provide 21%.

It has however been demonstrated that the lipid composition of feed modifies the deposition of vitamin E, which in diets with a high degree of unsaturation is reduced by between 25 and 100%, in proportion to the degree of unsaturation (Maurice and Lightsey, 1995; Ahn *et al.*, 1995). However, this level is 25 times higher than meat from unsupplemented chickens (Cortinas *et al.*, 2001). Cortinas *et al.* (2003, 2005) and Villaverde *et al.* (2004b) demonstrated that the extent of enrichment varies in inverse proportion to the PUFA content in the diet, and that with an increase of 32 g/kg PUFA, the α-tocopherol content of meat was reduced by 52% when 100 ppm vitamin E was added to feed. If feed has a high PUFA content (45–61 g/kg) the vitamin E in the thigh rises by 0.6 mg/kg for every 10 ppm increase of its dose in feed, while with a lower concentration (15–34 g/kg PUFA) this increase rises to 1.14 g/kg. The vitamin E required to maintain its thigh content at a constant level rises between 2.5 and 3.7 ppm for every gram of PUFA in the diet, and this makes supplementation of 200 ppm necessary for broiler diets containing 30 g/kg PUFA or more (Barroeta, 2007).

In feed with a normal composition, and using 200 ppm vitamin E over 4–5 weeks, it has been possible to increase the vitamin E content in chicken meat by 4–6 times, from 3.5 to 14–20 mg/kg (Brandon *et al.*, 1993; De Wynne and Dirinck, 1996; Maraschiello *et al.*, 1999). This means that a portion of chicken would provide up to 10–15% of the recommended daily intake in human nutrition (10 mg/day). Bou *et al.* (2004) found that in diets with high levels of fish oil this percentage can vary between 14 and 19% if levels of 70–140 ppm vitamin E are used. Barroeta (2007) indicates that vitamin E requirements increase between 2.5 and 3.7 mg for every gram of PUFA in the diet to achieve the same α-tocopherol concentrations in tissue.

Supplementing feed with organic selenium can also increase vitamin E content in the liver and muscles. Skrivan *et al.* (2008) found that, in diets with 50 mg/kg vitamin E, the vitamin E content of breast and thighs increased by about 25% when 0.3 mg/kg organic selenium was included in the diet.

The capacity of turkeys for depositing vitamin E in their tissue is 4–5 times lower than that of broilers, even where the lipid composition of their meat is similar (Marusich *et al.*, 1974, Sheldon, 1984; Surai *et al.*, 1993). This has been explained by reduced intestinal absorption and greater tocopherol catabolism in this species of poultry (Sklan *et al.*, 1982; Viau *et al.*, 1998). The concentrations of vitamin E achieved fall with some rapidity in frozen meat, although if turkeys have received extra supplementation, the speed of the process is slowed to half (Wen *et al.*, 1996; Higgins *et al.*, 1998a). The concentration also depends on the muscle under consideration (Viau *et al.*, 1998; Higgins *et al.*, 1998b). Including oxidized fats in the diet considerably reduced hepatic reserves of vitamin E in turkeys (Zdunczyk *et al.*, (2002).

Using supplementation levels twice as high as the NRC's, the vitamin E content of muscle falls rapidly in the first three weeks and remained low subsequently. Even with 600 ppm vitamin E in feed, its deposition is slow, equivalent to 0.3 μg per week (Wen *et al.*, 1997). Turkeys therefore require a higher and continuous vitamin E supply than broilers to achieve the same effects (Sklan *et al.*, 1982; Morrissey *et al.*, 1997). It takes 13 weeks to reach the accumulation plateau in the thigh muscle (Wen *et al.*, 1997). The vitamin E content in turkey meat rose with an increase in its level in feed to 275 ppm only between 16 and 18 weeks of age, but the improvement is minimal, from 0.1 to 0.5 mg/kg (Sheldon, 1984). Using 200 ppm over 6 weeks is also insufficient, especially if soy oil is used in the feed, and using 400 mg/kg between 11 and 16 weeks of age the vitamin E content in meat is less than that in chickens that received 200 ppm over 5 weeks (Genot et al., 1998; Viau et al., 1998). It took a minimum of 300 ppm for 13 weeks or 200 ppm for 16 weeks to increase the vitamin E content of turkey meat by 6 times (Wen et al., 1997; Mercier et al., 1998).

A relationship has also been demonstrated between vitamin E content in feed and meat, and treatments with the antimicrobial, enrofloxacin. Both substances are fat-soluble and compete for penetration of the cellular membranes, which has an influence on the pharmacokinetic characteristics of enrofloxacin and the incorporation of vitamin E. Carreras et al. (2004) confirmed in chickens that the administration of 50 mg/l enrofloxacin, applying a withdrawal period of 12 days, caused no excess residues of the drug in the breast, with a feed supplementation of both 20 and 100 IU/kg α-tocopherol acetate. However, treatments with the higher dosage of vitamin E without a withdrawal period produced a significant fall in the enrofloxacin content in the thigh and liver. The accumulation of vitamin E was significantly higher in the thigh than in the breast. This fact was confirmed in turkeys by Sárraga et al. (2006).

However, in the same study the interaction between the two substances presented itself differently from the previous experiment. The turkeys were supplemented with 30 or 200 IU/kg vitamin E, and were given the same pharmacological treatment. This time the use of more vitamin E did not affect the concentration of the drug in the thigh and liver if an enrofloxacin withdrawal period was applied, but otherwise a higher level of residues of the medication was determined in the liver and thigh of the birds which received a higher vitamin E supplementation. There was no obvious explanation for this discrepancy with the results previously obtained in broilers.

Oxidative stability
Most of the published studies on vitamin

E and meat quality have been aimed at studying its effects on oxidative stability, which in poultry meat is lower than for beef or pork due to its higher polyunsaturated fatty acid content (Rhee et al., 1996). The determination of thiobarbituric acid reactive substances (TBARS), the most important of which is malonaldehyde, has mainly been used to assess these effects. Although the TBARS method has often been criticized for not being sufficiently specific, it is the one that has been used in the great majority of studies conducted on chickens and turkeys.

A significant negative correlation has been found between the TBARS values obtained and vitamin E ingestion (Bartov and Frigg, 1992; Sheehy et al., 1993, 1997; Sheldon et al., 1997; Guo et al., 2003; Pesut et al., 2005; Cortinas et al., 2005; Sárraga et al., 2006, 2008; Koreleski and Swiatkiewicz, 2006), as well as its content in meat (Gatellier et al., 1998; Ruiz et al., 1999; Hsieh et al., 2002; Bou et al., 2004; Yan et al., 2006) and liver, and plasma concentration in vivo (Guo et al., 2001). Using more sophisticated methods, such as the determination of volatile substances profiles, it has been established that higher levels of vitamin E in feed reduces the concentration of secondary oxidation products (aldehydes and ketones) by around 50%, especially hexanal (De Wynne and Dirinck, 1996; Wen et al., 1996; García Regueiro et al., 1998). Vitamin E supplementation in feed is much more effective in maintaining oxidative stability than adding it to meat post-mortem, since it is not then incorporated in cellular membranes (Vara-Ubol and Bowers, 2001).

Reduction of TBARS in fresh chicken meat normally ranges from 40% to 90%, and from 39% to 66% in processed and/or pre-cooked products (Jensen et al., 1998). This wide range of variation suggests there are many factors which affect the levels, such as composition of the feed (principally, its lipid fraction), conditions of storage and packaging of the meat, type of product derived and, of course, dosage and administration time of α-tocopherol acetate. According to Barroeta (2007), the use of 200 ppm vitamin E prevents 84–88% of TBARS. In addition to the reduction in TBARS, other favorable effects of vitamin E have been shown, such as the reduction in protein oxidation in turkey meat

201

(Mercier *et al.,* 2001; Batifoulier *et al.*, 2002; Gatellier *et al.*, 2003), and the reduction in the content of oxidized cholesterol compounds in chicken meat – an aspect of great nutritional interest, since these are substances which have been linked to the risk of cardiovascular disease. In general the compounds are found in meat after 6–12 days, and increase with time, showing a positive correlation with the TBARS index. Supplementation with 200 ppm vitamin E reduces oxidized cholesterol compounds in chicken meat by 50%, and with 800 ppm a reduction of 70-75% is possible (Galvin *et al.*, 1998; Grau *et al.*, 2001b).

The interrelationships between vitamin E and other vitamins also impact the oxidative stability of meat. Carreras *et al.* (2004) confirmed that α-tocopherol acetate increased the levels of vitamin E in raw breast, but the presence of 1.5 ppm ß-carotene reduced its deposition, and resulted in TBARS values no different from those of the control. Both vitamin E and ß-carotene reduced rancidity in meat; the combination of both of them modified its texture in terms of pastiness and firmness. Similar results were obtained by Sárraga *et al.* (2006).

It is necessary to include high levels of fat in the diets of broilers and turkeys to satisfy their high energy requirements and achieve maximum growth with the lowest possible feed conversion indices. This makes it necessary to include vegetable oils in the formulation of feed, mainly soy and sunflower oil, whose proportions in the diet are increasing given the tendency to aviod fats of animal origin. This may increase the likelyhood of meat becoming rancid, since the lipid composition of fat in birds is in a great measure a reflection of that in the diet, and these oils are abundant in polyunsaturated fatty acids. It is now well known that the optimum level of vitamin E supplementation to protect meat from fat oxidation depends on the lipid composition of the diet (Ahn *et al.*, 1995; Cortinas *et al.*, 2001; Barroeta, 2007).

Comparisons abound in the literature between different sources of fat (tallow, olive, rape, soy, sunflower, palm, etc.), and the consensus is that if the most unsaturated ones are used, vitamin E at 200 ppm needs to be added for several weeks to maintain the oxidative stability of chicken meat (Sárraga

and García-Regueiro, 1999; Malczyk *et al.*, 1999; Grau *et al.*, 2000, 2001b; Cortinas *et al.*, 2001; Villaverde *et al.*, 2004b; Rebole *et al.*, 2006). Less vitamin E is necessary if tallow or olive oil is used – not economically viable today – but improvements can be observed nevertheless (Lauridsen *et al.*, 1997; O'Neill *et al.*, 1998a).

In turkeys, if the feed contains soy oil, 200 ppm is insufficient to maintain the oxidative stability of the meat (although the improvements are proportionally more than with rape or tallow), and it is no different from that in meat from turkeys which have not received extra supplementation. Using 400 ppm vitamin E provides much better results if the fat in the feed has a high level of unsaturation (Genot *et al.*, 1998; Viau *et al.*, 1998; Mercier *et al.*, 1998a, b).

Supplementation with high levels of vitamin E is even more important if the fat incorporated in the feed is altered by oxidation or by heat, which is more likely if soy, sunflower or linseed oil is used (Sweeney *et al.*, 1992; Sheehy *et al.*, 1993; Engberg *et al.*, 1996; Galvin *et al.*, 1997; Jensen *et al.*, 1997). In this case, levels of 30–50 mg/kg are ineffective. **Table XXIII** demonstrates the high degree of rancidity in frozen breast meat from chickens consuming oxidized fats, and the preventive effect of high dosages of vitamin E in the diet.

An increase in the dosage of vitamin E is required if the aim is to raise the concentration of omega-3 polyunsaturated fatty acids in meat, which are of great nutritional interest, but also the most easily oxidized, the strategy thus entails a potential risk of abnormal flavors occurring (rancidity, fish). Incorporating fish and linseed oil in feed has been tried to achieve this objective. To prevent rancidity and its undesirable effects, a minimum of 100 ppm α-tocopherol acetate is required if the degree of enrichment is moderate (Lin *et al.*, 1989a, b; Huang and Miller, 1994; Zanini *et al.*, 2003a, b), but this dosage should be raised to 250–300 mg/kg if these oils are included at a level of 2% or more (Gualtieri *et al.*, 1993; Khattak *et al.*, 1995; Nam *et al.*, 1997), especially if the meat is to be stored for long periods (Miller and Huang, 1993). On the other hand, supplementation with vitamin E or with mixtures of tocopherols permits a greater degree of enrichment with omega-3

Table XXIII. Effect of diets with oxidized (OX) or normal (N) sunflower oil and different levels of α-tocopherol acetate (0, 30, 200 ppm) on the oxidative stability of chicken breast cooked after freezing. TBARS values (mg malonaldehyde/kg meat) (Galvin et al., 1993)

Months / Diet	0	1	2	3
OX 0	6.79	8.02	18.89	25.27
OX 30	2.20	4.19	4.39	4.80
OX 200	0.46	1.00	1.11	1.41
N 30	0.46	1.60	1.87	1.57
N 200	0.46	1.07	1.27	1.21

PUFAs, especially in thighs (Ahn et al., 1995; Ajuyah et al., 1993; Surai and Sparks, 2001).

In a similar way to that indicated above for the muscle content of vitamin E, the protective effect is lower in fresh meat or in meat refrigerated for a very short time than in meat stored for 7–12 days and frozen meat, in which dosages around 200 mg/kg have been successful in preventing signs of rancidity in chicken carcasses (abnormal smell, discoloration), even after 9 months of freezing (Brandon et al., 1993; Coetzee and Hoffman, 2001; Fellenberg et al., 2006; Bou et al., 2004, 2006). In turkeys, supplementation with 150 ppm throughout the fattening period maintains frozen meat in good condition for up to 108 days (Bartov and Kahner, 2006), and with 300 ppm for up to 12 months (Higgins et al., 1998b).

The risk of oxidation is also increased by the manufacturing processes of meat products, such as mincing (Pikul et al., 1997), adding salt (O'Neill et al., 1999) or cooking (Grau et al., 2000). In these studies the dosages of vitamin E were effective in preventing the occurrence of bad flavor in pre-cooked products (warmed-over flavor), already detectable after being refrigerated for 48 hours (Mielche and Bertelsen, 1994; Weber, 2001). These positive effects were confirmed in raw and cooked turkey burgers, either refrigerated or frozen (Wen et al., 1996; Nam et al., 2003), and also in minced and frozen chicken meat (Pikul et al., 1997). Reduction in TBARS normally ranges between 39 and 66% in processed and/or precooked chicken products, and between 50 and 77% in turkey products (Jensen et al., 1998; Higgins et al., 1999). The effect is more evident in products packaged normally than in vacuum-packed products, a procedure which has its own protective effect against oxidation (Ahn et al., 1995; Higgins et al., 1998a; Ruiz et al., 1999). On the other hand, supplementation with 600 ppm in turkey feed for 147 days removed the need to use nitrites as meat preservers, maintaining oxidation indexes and color stability (Walsh et al., 1998).

Meat irradiation, a decontaminating process now legal in the US, reduces its vitamin E content and accelerates oxidation, which is already intense in just 3 days (Lakritz and Thayer, 1992, 1994), particularly in turkey meat (Lakritz et al., 1995; Ahn et al., 1997). Fortification with 200 ppm vitamin E in the last 2 weeks did not succeed in counteracting this effect (Eslick et al., 1997), which is better overcome with continuous supplementation of 100 ppm, followed by 400–600 ppm in the last 14 days of fattening, provided that the meat is vacuum-packed (Ahn et al., 1998; Nam and Ahn, 2003). Similar conclusions were reached by Yan et al. (2006) following an experiment in which they also included conjugated linoleic acid to stabilize the final product.

All these results demonstrate the difficulty of establishing recommendations for vitamin E supplementation which are applicable to all situations, since there are many factors which may affect optimum dosages, starting with the desired outcomes; and, as has been pointed out, the polyunsaturated fatty acid content of the feed is decisive (**Figure 9**). However, it is clear that the efficacy of vitamin E supplementation increases in line with the dosage and the period of administration. Barton and Frigg had already demonstrated in 1992 that increased supplementation to broilers two weeks before slaughter gave meat moderate protection against oxidation, although this protection was improved if the higher level was applied throughout the fattening cycle, and Brandon *et al.* (1993) advised supplementing broiler diets with 150–200 mg/kg α-tocopherol acetate for 4–5 weeks. These findings were confirmed by subsequent research (Morrissey *et al.*, 1997; Grau *et al.*, 2000). The latter authors believe that using 225 ppm for 3 weeks before slaughter is equivalent to using 150 ppm in the last 32 days, which may be more economical (**Figure 10**). For turkeys, Morrissey *et al.* (1998) calculate the minimum supplementation needed as 300 ppm for 13 weeks, based on the results of Wen *et al.* (1997) and Sheldon *et al.* (1997).

Finally, it is worth discussing the work aimed at finding alternatives to the use of vitamin E. It seems evident that the protective effect of α-tocopherol acetate is superior to that of other vitamins or provitamins with antioxidant action, such as vitamin A (Bartov *et al.*, 1997; Sallman *et al.*, 1998), ß-carotene (Barroeta and King, 1991; King *et al.*, 1993; Ruiz *et al.*, 1999) or vitamin C (Grau *et al.*, 2001a, b; Bou *et al.*, 2001). King *et al.*(1995) found an improvement in TBA values and in the sensory quality of the meat with a dosage of 150 IU α-tocopherol acetate throughout the fattening period, while ß-carotene, at 25 ppm, or administering 0.15% vitamin C in drinking water did not have positive effects. Nevertheless, in situations of heat stress the combination of 250 ppm ascorbic acid and 280 ppm vitamin E significantly increased the oxidative stability of meat during storage (Gheisari *et al.*, 2004).

Some studies have also compared the effectiveness of vitamin E with that of essential oils of aromatic plant seeds, such as rosemary and sage (López Bote *et al.*, 1998b), oregano (Botsoglou *et al.*, 2002; Young *et al.*, 2003; Basmacioglu *et al.*, 2004; Messikommer *et al.*, 2005: Smet *et al.*, 2005), grape skins and seeds (Mielnik and Skrede, 2003; Goñi *et al.*,

2007; Brenes *et al.*, 2008), mustard (Khattak *et al.*, 1996), sesame (Yoshida and Takagi, 1999; Du *et al.*, 2002), mint (Maini *et al.*, 2007) and tea catechins (Tang *et al.*, 2001; Gheisari *et al.*, 2006). Although all these ingredients succeeded in reducing TBARS values and cholesterol oxide, vitamin E activity at a dosage of 200 ppm was superior by between 30 and 50% (**Table XXIV**).

Other trials assessed the results of using feed with high levels of oats but, while there was an important reduction in TBARS values and cholesterol oxide (López Bote *et al.*, 1998a), the effect of vitamin E again proved to be much higher, and furthermore weight gain and feed intake of broilers reduces linearly in response to the increase in the oat content of the diet (Valaja *et al.*, 2001). The incorporation of 1.5% carnosine (a natural muscular dipeptide) in feed has also been investigated; in this case a more comparable antioxidant effect was found, which was additive to that of vitamin E (O'Neill *et al.*, 1998b, 1999). However, it may have potential as more than just a feed additive, as it may be added to meat during processing, together with vitamin E (Morrissey *et al.*, 1998).

Organoleptic quality

Some studies have more directly evaluated the effects of high levels of vitamin E on the sensory quality of meat, using objective methods and/or panels of trained tasters. Olivo *et al.* (1998) found a lower drop in post-mortem pH, which indicates a potential use in the prevention of pale, soft and exudative meat syndrome (PSE). Drip losses diminish (O'Neill *et al.*, 1998a; Olivo *et al.*, 1998), even when supplements are given only in the last 2–3 weeks of fattening (McKnight *et al.*, 1996; Malczyk *et al.*, 1999).

Sheehy *et al.* (1995) found an improvement in meat taste using 160 mg/kg vitamin E compared to the usual level of 20 ppm. An improvement in flavor was detected with just 80 ppm (Ristic and Lidner, 1992) and this continued up to 160 ppm (Blum *et al.*, 1990). De Wynne and Dirinck (1996) and Janssens *et al.* (1999) found that continuous use of 200 ppm vitamin E instead of 50 ppm significantly improved perceptions of texture, succulence, flavor, abnormal flavors and general acceptability, and that evaluation of flavor corresponded with the lowest concentration

Figure 9. Effects of vitamin E dosage and degree of dietary unsaturation on oxidative stability of chicken meat (Cortinas *et al.*, 2001)

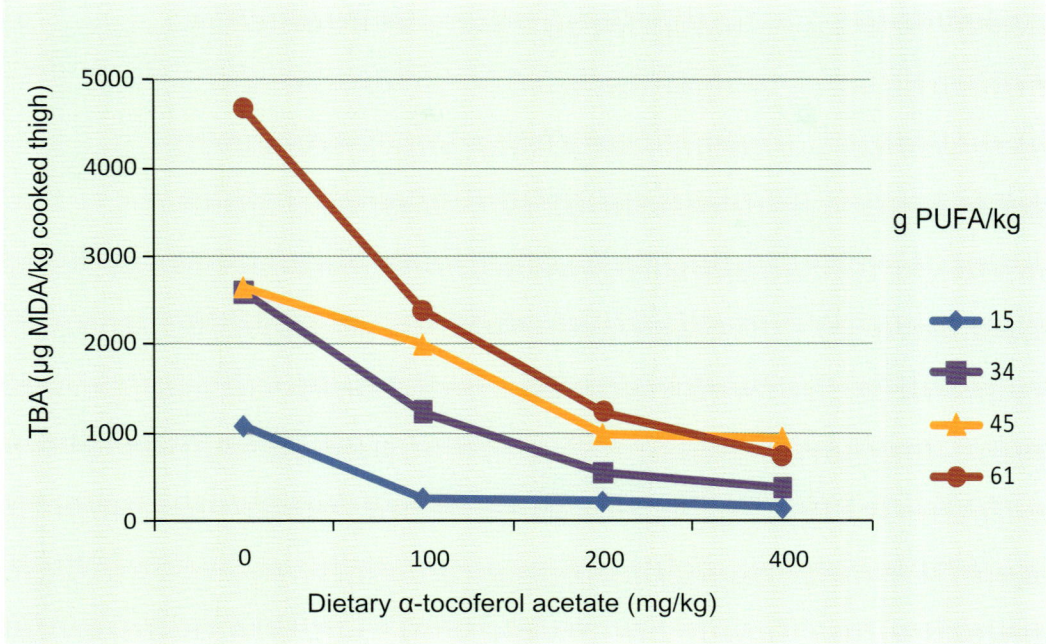

Figure 10. Effects of vitamin E dosage and administration time on oxidative stability of chicken meat (Grau *et al.*, 2000)

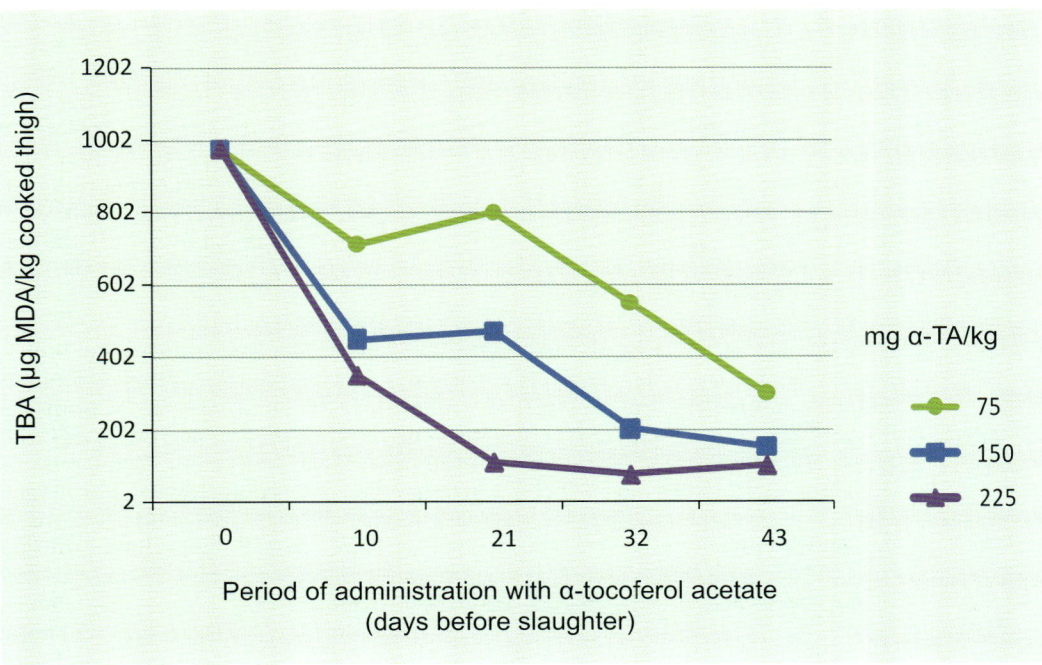

205

Table XXIV. Comparative effects of vitamin E and other antioxidants on the oxidative stability of chicken thighs

Reference	Antioxidant and dosage	Type of sample	TBARS mg/kg
King *et al.*, 1995	Vit. E, 150 ppm	Cooked meat	0.29
	ß-carotene, 30 ppm		1.85
Khattak *et al.*, 1996	Mustard oil, 4%	Fresh meat	0.67
López-Bote *et al.* 1998a	Vit. E, 10 ppm	Refrigerated meat, 9 days	0.51
	Vit. E, 200 ppm		0.19
	Oat, 20%		0.37
López-Bote *et al.* 1998b	Vit. E, 200 ppm	Cooked meat, 4 days	2.71
	Rosemary oil, 500 ppm		4.58
	Sage oil, 500 ppm		6.28
Tang *et al.*, 2001	Vit. E 200 ppm	Frozen meat, 1 month	0.15
	Tea catechins, 100 ppm		1.10
Botsoglou *et al.*, 2002	Vit. E, 200 ppm	Fresh meat	0.42
	Oregano oil, 50 ppm		0.25
	Oregano oil, 100 ppm		0.10
Goñi *et al.*, 2007	Vit. E, 200 ppm	Refrigerated meat, 7 days	0.28
	Grape residues, 3%		0.35
Grau *et al.*, 2001b	Vit. E 225 ppm	Cooked meat	2.91
	Vit. C 110 ppm		4.08

of aldehydes, especially hexanal. These effects are less pronounced in very fresh meat after 1–4 days (Ruiz *et al.*, 2001), but clearly evident with longer storage times of 7–12 days (Blum *et al.*, 1990; Janssens *et al.*. 1999). The effects are undetectable if the diet is fortified only in the last week of fattening (Thomas *et al.*, 1988). An improvement in the color stability of meat may also be expected, by way of preventing the oxidation of myoglobin to metamyoglobin. This has been clearly demonstrated in other species, although the meat of birds, especially breast meat, has a lower pigment content (Jensen *et al.*, 1998).

More data on the subject are available for turkey meat, but using higher levels of supplementation, between 250 and 600 ppm. *In vitro* studies have shown that myoglobin oxidation is reduced (Yin and Cheng, 1997; Lynch *et al.*, 1998), which has also been confirmed on a practical level (Santé *et al.*, 1992), together with an improvement in the red (a*) value by spectrophotometry (Santé and Lacourt, 1994; Higgins *et al.*, 1998b) and subjective color evaluation (Sheldon *et al.*, 1997; Janssens *et al.*, 1999). A reduction has been observed in the frequency of pale, PSE-type meat (Ferket and Allen, 1994), a problem which is now more prevalent in turkeys than in chickens. Significant differences have also been demonstrated in tasting tests: the frequency of "typical flavor" assessments increase, those of "abnormal flavors" decrease (Sheldon *et al.*, 1997), and assessments of texture, succulence, flavor and general appreciation improve (Janssens *et al.*, 1999).

CONCLUSIONS

This review shows that much is known today about vitamin nutrition, but also that there are important gaps in our knowledge. In the last 15–20 years great advances have been made in research in some fields, such as the role of vitamin D metabolites in the prevention of foot and leg problems, or the effects of vitamin E on meat quality. But for other vitamins few studies are available and many of these are out of date. There is a lack of clarity over requirements in the final phases of broiler fattening, and the information on turkeys is deficient in many aspects. The relationship between vitamins and immunity is one of the areas which merits new research. Although considerable information is now available on this subject, our understanding is still incomplete. Its applications may turn out to be of great importance in the current situation in the European Union, in which the preventive and therapeutic pharmacological options are becoming ever more limited by regulation.

It is clear that the current recommendations by the National Research Council, directed toward the prevention of serious vitamin deficiency, are excessively conservative and are based on studies which are outdated; in some cases they are not even adequate to achieve their primary objective. In most cases they no longer correspond with either the requirements of birds whose genetic potential has progressed spectacularly in the last few years, or with the practical conditions in which production takes place, which often entails some degree of stress for the animals. But above all, they are not in line with the achievement of objectives which exceed the simple attainment of maximum productivity and which are ever more decisive, such as the well-being of broilers and turkeys and the quality and safety of their meat. Optimum vitamin nutrition should take all of these aspects into account.

Vitamins constitute a relatively small part of the cost of feed, yet they have a considerable potential impact on the health and production of birds, given the diversity and importance of the functions they carry out in many areas of animal physiology. The complexity of their interactions in many processes, the need to maintain delicate balances, and data arising from the most recent research, especially that carried out in field conditions, suggest that a general increase in vitamin fortification in broiler and turkey feed could be the most appropriate strategy in many cases.

REFERENCES

Abawi, F.G. and Sullivan, T.W. (1989). Interactions of vitamins A, D3, E, and K in the diet of broiler chicks. Poultry Sci., 68:1490-1498.

Abawi, F.G., Sullivan, T.W., and Schedeiler, S.E. (1985). Interaction of dietary fat with levels of vitamins A and E in broiler chicks. Poultry Sci., 64:1192-1198.

Abawi, F.G.and Sullivan, T.W. (1989). Interactions of vitamins A, D3, E, and K in the diet of broiler chicks. Poultry Sci., 68:1490-1498.

Abdukalykova, S. and Ruiz-Feria, C.A. (2006). Arginine and vitamin E improve the cellular and humoral inmune response of broiler chickens. Int. J. of Poultry Sci., 5(2): 121-127.

Abdukalykova, S.T., Zhao, X., and Ruiz-Feria, A. (2008). Arginine and vitamin E modulate the subpopulations of T lymphocytes in broiler chickens. Poultry Sci., 87:50-55.

Aburto, A. and Britton, W.M. (1998a). Effects of different levels of vitamins A and E on the utilization of cholecalciferol by broiler chickens. Poultry Sci. 77: 570-577.

Aburto, A. and Britton, W.M. (1998b). Effects and interactions of dietary levels of vitamins A and E and cholecalciferol in broiler chickens. Poultry Sci. 77: 666-673.

Aburto, A., Edwards, H.M., and Britton, W.M. (1998). The influence of vitamin A on the utilization and amelioration of toxicity of cholecalciferol, 25-hydroxy cholecalciferol and 1,25 dihydroxy cholecalciferol in young broiler chickens. Poultry Sci. 77: 585-593.

Afsarmaneh, M., Pourreza, J., and Samie, A.H. (2004). Influences of citric and ascorbic acids as mineral chelators, and vitamin D3 on efficacy of microbial phytase in broilers fed wheat-based diets. Proc. XXII World's Poultry Congress, Istanbul, CD-rom.

Afsharmanesh, M, Edriss, M.A., Pourreza, J., and Rahmani, H. (2004). Influences of citric and ascorbic acids as mineral chelators, and vitamin D3 with microbial phytase on AME digestibility. Proc. XXIII World's Poultry Congress, Istanbul, CD-rom.

Afsharmanesh, M. and Pourreza, J. (2005). Effects of calcium, citric acid, ascorbic acid, vitamin D, on the efficacy of microbial phytase in broilers starters fed wheat-based diets I. Performance, bone mineralization and ileal digestibility. Int. J. Poultry Sci., 4 (6): 418-424.

Aguilera-Quintana, I., Munn, B.J., and Krautmann, B.A. (1989). The influence of ascorbic acid on broiler pre-slaughter levels and heterophyl/lymphocite ratios. Poultry Sci., 68 (suppl. 1): 166 (abstract).

Ahn, D.U., Sell, J.L., Jeffery, M., Jo, C., Chen, X., Wu, C., and Lee, J.I. (1997). Dietary vitamin E affects lipid oxidation and total volatiles of irradiated raw turkey meat. J. Food Sci. 62 (5):954-958

Ahn, D.U., Sell, J.L., Jo, C., Chen, X., Wu, C., and Lee, J.I. (1998). Effects of dietary vitamin E supplementation on lipid oxidation and volatiles content of irradiated, cooked turkey meat patties with different packaging. Poultry Sci. 77: 912-920.

Ahn, D.U., Wolfe, F.H., and Sim, J.S. (1995). Dietary α-linolenic acid and mixed tocopherols and packaging influences on lipid stability in broiler chicken breast and leg muscle. J. Food Sci. 60, (5): 1013-1018.

Ajuyah, A.O., Ahn, D.U., Hardin, R.T., and Sim, J.S. (1993). Dietary antioxidants and storage affect chemical characteristics of omega-3 fatty acid enriched broiler chicken meats. J. Food Sci. 58, (1): 43-46.

Alisheilkhov, A.M., Akhmedkhanova, R.R., and Jamboulatov, M.M. (2000). The problem of inter-reaction of vitamins C and B12 and fermentation preparations in broiler feeding. Proc. XXII World's Poultry Congress, Istanbul, CD-rom.

Allen, P.C. (1988). Physiological basis for carotenoid malabsorption during coccidiosis. Proc. Maryland Nutr. Conf., 18.

Allen, P.C. (1997). Production of free radicals species during Eimeria maxima infections in chickens. Poultry Sci., 76: 814.

Allen, P.C. and Fetterer, R.H. (2002). Interaction of dietary vitamin E with Eimeria maxima infections in chickens. Poultry Sci. 79: 41-48.

Allen, P.C., Danforth, H.D., Morris, V.C., and Levander, O.A. (1996). Association of lowered plasma carotenoids with protection against cecal coccidiosis by diets higher in n-3 fatty acids. Poultry Sci., 75:966.

Amakye-Anim, J., Lin, T.L., Hester, P.Y.,

Thiagarajan, D., Watkins, B.A., and Wu, C.C. (2000). Ascorbic acid supplementation improved antibody response to infectious bursal disease vaccination in chickens. Poultry Sci., 79:680-688.

Ameenudin, S., Sunde, M.L., and Cook, M.E. (1985). Essentiality of vitamin D3 and its metabolites in poultry nutrition: A review. WPSJ., 41 (1):52-62.

Andreasen, C.B. and Frank, D.E. (1999). The effects of ascorbic acid on in vitro heterophyl function. Avian Dis. 43: 656-663.

Angel, R., Dhandu, A.S., Applegate, T.J., and Christman, M. (2001a). Phosphorus sparing effect of phytase, 25-hydroxycholecalciferol, and citric acid when fed to broiler chicks. Poultry Sci., 80 (suppl. 1):133-134 (abstract).

Angel, R., Dhandu, A.S., Applegate, T.J., and Christman, M. (2001b). Non-phytate phosphorus sparing effect of phytase and citric acid when fed to poults. Poultry Sci., 80 (suppl. 1):134 (abstract).

Angel, R., Saylor, W.W, Dhandu, A.S., Powers, P., and Applegate, T.J. (2005). Effects of dietary phosphorus, phytase, and 25-hydroxycholecalciferol on performance of broiler chickens growing in floor pens. Poultry Sci., 84:1031-1044.

Angel, R., Saylor, W.W. Mitchell, A.D., Powers, P., and Applegate, T.J. (2006). Effects of dietary phosphorus, phytase, and 25-hydroxycholecalciferol on broiler chicken bone mineralization, litter phosphorus, and processing yields. Poultry Sci., 85:1200-1211.

Anonymous (1997). Choline – An essential nutrient. Int. Poultry Prod., 5(2):11-15.

Applegate, T.J. and Sell, J. L. (1996). Effect of dietary linoleic to linolenic acid ratio and vitamin E supplementation on vitamin E status of poults. Poultry Sci. 75: 881-890.

Applegate, T.J., Angel, R., and Classen, H.L. (2003). Effects of dietary calcium, 25-hydroxycholecalciferol, or bird strain on small intestinal phytase activity in broiler chickens. Poultry Sci., 82:1140-1148.

Asghar, A., Lin, C.F., Gray, J.I., Buckley, D.J., and Booren, A.M. (1990). Effects of dietary oils and a α-tocopherol supplementation on membrane lipid oxidation in broiler meat. J. Food Sci., 55:46-50.

Aslam, S.M., Garlich, J.D., and Qureshi, M.A. (1998). Vitamin D deficiency alters the immune responses of broiler chicks. Poultry Sci., 77:842-849.

Atencio, A., Edwards, H.M., and Pesti, G. (2005a). Effects of vitamin D3 dietary supplementation of broiler breeder hens on the performance and bone abnormalities of the progeny. Poultry Sci., 84:1058-1068.

Atencio, A., Edwards, H.M., and Pesti, G. (2005b). Effects of the level of cholecalciferol supplementation of broiler breeder hens on the performance and bone abnormalities of the progeny fed diets containing various levels of calcium or 25- hydroxycholecalciferol. Poultry Sci., 84:1593-1603.

Atencio, A., Pesti, G., and Edwards, H.M. (2005c). Twenty-five hydroxycholecalciferol as a choleclaciferol substitute in broiler breeder hen diets and its effect on the performance and general health of the progeny. Poultry Sci., 84:1277-1285.

Atia, F.A., Waibel, P.E., Hermes, I., and Carlson, C.W. (1994). Effect of dietary cholecalciferol and 1,25-dihydroxycholecalciferol on turkey poults in the absence and presence of ascorbic acid. Poultry Sci., 73 (suppl.1):91 (abstract).

Augustine, D.C. and Ruff, M.D. (1983). Changes in carotenoid and vitamin A levels in young turkeys infected with Eimeria meleagrimitis or Eimeria adenoides. Avian Dis., 27:963.

Austic, R.E and Scott, M.L. (2000). Nutritional diseases. In: Diseases of poultry (10th ed.). Edited by Calnek, B.W. Iowa State University Press, 48-64.

Aye, P., Morishita, T.Y., Saif, Y.M., and Onas, M. (2000b). The effect of hypovitaminosis A on the pathogenesis of Pasteurella multocida in turkeys. Avian Dis. 44: 818-826.

Aye, P., Morishita, T.Y., Saif, Y.M., Latshaw, J.D., Harr, B.S., and Cihla, F.B. (2000a). Induction of vitamin A deficiency in turkeys. Avian Dis. 44: 809-817.

Baghbanzadeh, A. and Decuypere, E. (2008). Ascites syndrome in broilers: physiological and nutritional perspectives. Avian Pathol, 37 (2):117-126.

Bain, S.D. and Newbrey, J.W. (1998). Biotin deficiency may alter tibiotarsal bone growth and modeling in broiler chicks. Poultry Sci., 67: 590-595.

Bains, B. (1997). Important role for vitamins

during stress. World Poultry, 13(2): 30-35.

Bains, B. (1999). A guide to the application of vitamins in commercial poultry feed. Pub. by Rath Design Communications, Australia, 200 pp.

Bains, B. (2001). Impaired health reduces impact of vitamins. World Poultry vitamin special 2001, 9-11

Bains, B. (2001). Impaired health reduces impact of vitamins. World Poultry, Vitamin special, 9-11.

Bains, B., Brake, J.T., and Pardue, S.L. (1996). Reducing leg weakness in commercial broilers. World Poultry. 14 (1): 24-27.

Bains, B.S. (1994). Broilers suffer from dyschondroplasia and femoral necrosis. World Poultry, 10 (10):109-111.

Bains, B.S., Brake, J.T., and Pardue, S.L. (1998). Reducing leg weakness in commercial broilers. World Poultry, 14 (1):24-27.

Baker, D.H., Biehl, R.R., and Emmert, J.L. (1998). Vitamin D3 requirement of young chicks receiving diets varying in calcium and available phosphorus. Brit. Poultry Sci., 39:413-417.

Balios, J. and Poupulis, C. (1992). Effect of biotin on the fatty acid composition of abdominal fat, liver fat and blood serum fat of broilers fed high fat diets. Proc. XIX World´s Poultry Congress, Amsterdam.

Ballard, R. and Edwards, H.M. (1988). Dietary zeolite and vitamin A on tibial dyschondroplasia in chickens. Poultry Sci., 67:113-119.

Balnave, D. (2004). Challenges of accurately defining the nutrient requirements of heat-stressed poultry. Poultry Sci. 83:5-14.

Balnave, D., Berry, M.N., and Cumming, R.B (1977). Clinical signs of fatty liver and kidney syndrome in broilers and their alleviation by the short-term use of biotin or animal tallow. Brit. Poultry Sci. 18: 749-753.

Bar, A., Razaphkovsky, V., Vax, E., and Plavnik, I. (2003). Performance and bone development in broiler chickens given 5-hydroxycholecalciferol. Brit. Poultry Sci., 44:224-233.

Bar, A., Rosenberg, J., Perlman, R., and Hurwitz, S. (1987). Field rickets in turkeys: Relationship to vitamin D. Poultry Sci., 66:68-72.

Barroeta, A. and King, A.J. (1991). Effects of carotenoids on lipid oxidation in stored poultry muscle. Poultry Sci., 70 (suppl. 1, p. 11).

Barroeta, A.C. (2007). Nutritive value of poultry meat:relationship between vitamin E and PUFA. WPSJ, 63:277-284.

Bartov, I. and Frigg, M. (1992). Effect of high concentrations of dietary vitamin E during various age periods on performance, plasma vitamin E and meat stability of broiler chicks at 7 weeks of age. Brit. Poultry Sci. 33: 393-402.

Bartov, I. and Kanner, J. (1996). Effect of high levels of dietary iron, iron injection, and dietary vitamin E on the oxidative stability of turkey meat during storage. Poultry Sci. 75: 1039-1046.

Bartov, I., Sklan, D., and Friedman, A. (1997). Effect of vitamin A on the oxidative stability of broiler meat during storage: lack of interactions with vitamin E. Brit. Poultry Sci. 38: 255-257.

Basmacioğlu, H, Toku ğlu, Ö., and Ergül, M. (2004). Effect of dietary natural antioxidants on lipid oxidation in stored broiler meat enriched with N-3 PUFAs. Proc. XXII World's Poultry Congress, Istanbul, CD-rom.

Batifoulier, F, Mercier, Y, Gatellier, P., and Renerre, M. (2002). Influence of vitamin E on lipid and protein oxidation induced by H2O2-activated MetMb in microsomal membranes from turkey muscle. Meat Sci., 61:389-395.

Bayyari, G.R., Huff, W.E., Rath, N.C., Balog, J.M., Newberry, L.A., Villines, J.D., Skeeles, J.K., Anthony, N.B., and Nestor, K.E, (1997). Effect of genetic selection of turkeys for increasing body weight and egg production on immune and physiological responses. Poultry Sci., 76:289-296.

Beirne, M. J. and Jensen, L.S. (1981). Influence of high levels of pyridoxine on twisted legs in broilers. Poultry Sci., 60:1026-1029.

Belay, T., Vanhooser, S.L., Mcknight, F.M., and Teeter, R.G. (1996). An evaluation of short term low atmospheric oxygen exposure and antioxidant supplementation effects on subsequent broiler growth rate and ascites incidence. Poultry Sci. 72 (suppl. 1): 13 (abstract).

Biehl, R.R. and Baker, D.H. (1997). Utilization of phytate and non-phytate phosphorus in chicks as affected by source and amount of vitamin D. J. Anim. Sci., 75:2986-2993.

Bilgili, S.F., M.A. Alley, M.A., J.B. Hess, J.B., and Moran, E.T. (2005) Influence of strain-cross, sex, and feeding programs on broiler chicken paw (feet) yield and quality. Proc. XVII th European Symposium on the Quality of Poultry Meat Doorwerth, The Netherlands,342-349

Bird, N. and Boren, B. (1999). Vitamin E and immunity in commercial broiler production. World Poultry 15(7):20-21.

Blalock, T.L. and Thaxton, J.P. (1984). Hematology of chicks experiencing marginal vitamin B6 deficiency. Poultry Sci., 63:1243.

Blalock, T.L., Thaxton, J.P., and Garlich, J.D. (1984). Humoral immunity in chicks experiencing marginal vitamin B6 deficiency. J. Nutr. 114:312.

Blum, J.C., Touraille, C., Salichon, Y., and Ricard, F. H. (1990). Influence des apports eleves de vitamin E sur les performances de croissance du "broiler" et la conservation des carcasses refrigerees. VIII Eur. Poultry Conf., Barcelona, 228-231.

Boa-Amponsem, K., Orice, S.E., Geraert, P.A., Picard, and Siegel, P.B. (2001). Antibody responses of hens fed vitamin E and passively acquired antibodies of their chicks. Avian Dis., 45:122-127.

Boa-Amponsem, K., Picard, M, Blair, M.E, Meldrum, B., and Siegel, P.B. (2006) Memory antibody responses of broiler and leghorn chickens as influenced by dietary vitamin E and route of sheep red blood cell administration. Poultry Sci., 85:173-177.

Bond, P.L. and Boren, B. (1997). Factors affecting vitamin E in turkeys investigated. Feedstuffs, 69(49):12-13, 18.

Bond, P.L., Meinecke, C.F., Miller, M.A., and Stephenson, E.L. (1985). Choline-methionine interrelationships in broiler diets when measuring at different growth stages. Poultry Sci., 64 (suppl. 1):6 (abstract).

Boren, B. and Bond, P. (1996). Vitamin E and immunocompetence. Broiler Ind., November, 26-33.

Botsoglou, N.A., Florou-Paneri, P., Christaki, E., Fletouris, D.J., and Spais, A.B. (2002). Effect of dietary oregano essential oil on performance of chickens and on iron-induced lipid oxidation of breast, thigh and abdominal fat tissues. Brit. Poultry Sci., 43:223-230.

Bottje, W., Envetchakul, B., Moore, R., and Mcnew, R. (1995). Effect of α-tocopherol on antioxidants, lipid peroxidation, and the incidence of pulmonary hypertension syndrome (ascites) in broilers. Poultry Sci., 74:1356-1369.

Bottje, W., Erf, G., Bersi, T., Wang, S., Barnes, D., and Berrs, K. (1997). Effect of dietary DL-α-tocopherol on tissue α- and γ-tocopherol and pulmonary hypertension syndrome (ascitis) in broilers. Poultry Sci., 75:1507-1512.

Bottje,W.,Wang, S, Beers, K.W., and Cawthon, D. (1998). Lung lining fluid antioxidants in male broilers: age-related changes under thermoneutral and cold temperature conditions. Poultry Sci., 77:1905-1912.

Bottje, W.G. and Wideman, R.F. (1995). Potential role of free radicals in the pathogenesis of pulmonary hypertension syndrome. Poultry and Avian Biol. Reviews, 6:221-231

Bottje, W.G. and Wideman, R.F. (1998). Lung lining fluid antioxidants in male broilers: age-related changes under thermoneutral and cold temperature conditions. Poultry Sci., 77: 1905-1912.

Bou, R, Guardiola, F, Tres, A, Barroeta, A.C., and Codony, R. (2004). Effect of dietary fish oil, α-tocopheryl acetate, and zinc supplementation on the composition and consumer acceptability of chicken meat. Poultry Sci., 83:282-292.

Bou, R., Guardiola, F., Grau, A., Grimpa, S., Manich, A., Barroeta, A., and Codony, R. (2001). Influence of dietary fat source, α-tocopherol and ascorbic acid supplementation on sensory quality of dark chicken meat. Poultry Sci. 80: 800-807.

Brandon, S., Morrissey, P.A., Buckley, D.J., and Frigg, M. (1993) Influence of dietary α-tocopheryl acetate on the oxidative stability of chicken tissues. 11th European Symposium on the Quality of Poultry Meat, 397-403.

Brenes, A, Viveros, A, Goñi, I, Centeno, C, Sáyago-Ayerdy, S.G, Arija, I., and Saura-Calixto, F. (2008). Effect of grape pomace concentrate and vitamin E on digestibility of polyphenols and antioxidant activity in chickens. Poultry Sci., 87:307-316.

Britton,W.M. (1994). Effects of dietary vitamin A at marginal levels of cholecalciferol. Poultry Sci. 73 (suppl 1): 52 (abstract).

Broz, J. and Ward, N.E. (2007). The role of vitamins and feed enzymes in combating metabolic challenges and disorders. J. Appl. Poult. Res. 16:150-159.

Brufau, J., Llauradó, Ll, Pérez-Vendrell, A.,

and Esteve-García, E. (1995). Effect of biotin supplementation on broiler diets based on wheat or corn. Poultry Sci., 74 (suppl.1): abstract 398.

Bryden, W.L. (1991). Tissue depletion of biotin in chickens and the development of deficiency lesions and the fatty liver and kidney syndrome. Avian Pathol. 20: 259-269.

Buda, S. (2000). Effects of biotin on the skin of turkey foot pads. World Poultry, 16 (12):47-48.

Buenrostro, J.L. and Kratzer, F.H. (1984). Use of plasma and egg yolk biotin of white leghorn hens to assess biotin availability from feedstuffs. Poultry Sci., 63:1563-1569

Burgos, S., Bohorquez, D.V., and Burgos, S.A. (2006). Vitamin deficiency-induced neurological disease in poultry. Int. J. Poult. Sci., 5 (9):804-807.

Carreras, I., Castellari, M., Garcia Regueiro, J.A., Guerrero, L, Esteve-Garcia, E., and Sárraga, C. (2004). Influence of enrofloxacin administration and α-tocopheryl acetate supplemented diets on oxidative stability of broiler tissues. Poultry Sci., 83:796-802.

Castaing, J., Larroudé, P, Pcyhorgue, A., Hamelin, C., and Manroufi, C. (2003). Incidence de deux niveaux d'apports en vitamines sur les performances du poulet de chair. V Journées Rech. Avicoles, Tours, 261-264.

Castaing, J., Larroudé, P., Hamelin, C., and Ball, A. (2007). Effect de deux niveaux d'apports en vitamines sur les performances zootechniques de poulets type labels. VII Journées Recherches Avicoles, Tours, 288-292.

Celik, L, Tekeli, A., Kutlu, H. R., and Gorgulu, M. (2006) Effects of dietary vitamin B6 and L-carnitine on growth performance and carcass characteristics of broilers reared under high temperature regime. Proc. XII Eur. Poultry Conf., Verona 2006, CD rom.

Chang, W.P., Marsh, J.A., Dietert, R.R., and Combs, G.F. (1990). The effect of dietary vitamin E and selenium deficiencies on chicken lymphocyte surface marker expression and proliferation. Poultry Sci., 69 (suppl. 1):32 (abstract).

Chee, K.W. and Chang, M.I. (1995). Biotin deficiency and plasma fatty acids patterns in broilers. Poultry Sci., 74 (suppl.1):abstract 398.

Cherian, G. and Sim, J.S. (1997). Egg yolk polyunsaturated fatty acids and vitamin E content alters the tissue tocopherol status of hatched chicks. Poultry Sci., 76:1753-1759.

Cherian, G. and Sim, J.S. (2003). Maternal and posthatch dietary polyunsaturated fatty acids alter tissue tocopherol status of chicks. Poultry Sci., 82:681-686.

Chew, B.P. (1995). Antioxidant vitamins affect food animal immunity and health. J. Nutr. 125:1804S-1808S.

Chew, B.P. (1996). Importance of antioxidant vitamins in immunity and health in animals. Anim. Feed Sci. Technol. 9: 103-114.

Chew, B.P. and Park, J.S. (2004). Carotenoid action on the immune response. J. Nutr. 134:257S-261S.

Christmas, R.B, Harms, R.H., and Sloan D.R. (1995). The absence of vitamins and trace minerals and broiler perfomance. J. Appl. Poultry Res. 4: 407-410.

Christmas, R.B. and Harms, R.H. (1988). The choline requirement of the four to twelve week old turkey poult as affected by dietary methionine. Poultry Sci., 67 (suppl. 1):9 (abstract).

Christmas, R.B. and Harms, R.H. (1989). Further evaluation on the methionine effect on the supplemental choline needs of the four to twelve week old male turkey poult. Poultry Sci., 68 (suppl. 1):30 (abstract).

Chung, T.K. (2006). Vitamins and poultry products quality. Int. Poultry Prod. 14 (5):11-15.

Chung, T.K. and Baker, D.H. (1990). Riboflavin requirement of chicks fed purified amino acid and conventional corn-soybean meal diets. Poultry Sci. 69: 1357-1363.

Cier, D., Rimsky, Y., Rand, N., Polishuk, O., Gur, N., Ben Shoshan, A., Frish, Y., and Ben Moshe, A. (1992). The effects of supplementing ascorbic acid on broilers performance under summer conditions. Proc. XIX World's Poultry Congress, Amsterdam, 586-589.

Clark, S., Hansen, G., Mclean, P., Bond, P., Wakeman, W., Meadows, R., and Buda, S. (2002). Pododermatitis in turkeys. Avian Dis. 46:1038–1044.

Coelho, M. (2000). Update on commercial poultry, swine and dairy vitamin supplement. Feed Info.com.

Coelho, M., Mcknight, W., and Cousins, B. (2001). Impact of a targeted B-vitamin regimen on rate and efficiency of fast growing broilers from 0 to 49 days. Proc. PSA Symp., 201

Coelho, M.B. and Mcnaughton, J.L. (1995) Effect of composite vitamin supplementation on broilers. J. Appl. Poultry Res. 4:219-229.

Coetzee, G.J.M. and Hoffman, L.C. (2001). Effect of dietary vitamin E on the performance of broilers and quality of broiler meat during refrigerated storage. South African J. of Anim. Sci., 31(3):161-176.

Colnago, G.L., Jensen, L.S., and Long, P.L. (1984). Effects of selenium and vitamin E on the development of immunity to coccidiosis in chickens. Poultry Sci., 63:1136-1143.

Cook, M.E, Springer, W.R, Kerr, K.M., and Herbert, J.A. (1983). Severity of tenosynovitis reovirus-infected chickens fed various dietary levels of choline, folic acid, manganese, biotin and niacine. Avian Dis. 18:502.

Cook, M.E, Springer, W.T, Kerr, K.M., and Herbert, J.A. (1984b). Severity of tenosynovitis in reovirus-infected chickens fed various dietary levels of choline, folic acid, manganese, biotin or niacin. Avian Dis. 28 (3): 562-573.

Cook, M.E, Springer, W.T., and Herbert, J.A. (1984a). Enhanced incidence of leg abnormalities in reovirus wvu 2937-infected chickens fed various dietary levels of selected vitamins. Avian Dis. 28 (3): 548-561.

Cook, M.E. (1988). Factors enhancing the incidence of skeletal deformities. Proc. Maryland Nutr. Conf., 24-29.

Cook, M.E. (2000). Skeletal deformities and their causes: Introduction. Poultry Sci., 79:982-984.

Cook, M.E., (1992). Performances Of Turkeys Fed Thiamine, Riboflavin and Vitamin E In Excess Of NRC Requirements. Basf Seminars, Fresno, California.(

Cooke, B.C. and Raine, H.D. (1987). The application of nutritional principles by the commercial nutritionist. In: Nutrient requirements of poultry and nutritional research, 191-200. Ed. by Fisher, C. and Boorman, K.N. Ed. Butterworths.

Cope, F.O., Stuart, M., and Stake, P.E. (1979). Reducing the incidence and severity of curled toes and perosis-like leg abnormalities in cage-reared broilers by high dietary levels of pyridoxine or choline. Poultry Sci., 58:1046.

Cortinas, L., Barroeta, A.C., Villaverde, C., Galobart, J., Guardiola, F., and Baucells, M.D. (2005). Influence of the dietary polyunsaturation level on chicken meat quality: Lipid oxidation. Poultry Sci., 84:48-55.

Cortinas, L., Galobart, J., Barroeta, A.C., Castillo, M.S., and Jensen, S.K. (2001). Influencia del nivel de insaturación dietética sobre el depósito y efecto antioxidante del α-tocopherol en muslo de pollo (crudo, cocido y cocido-refrigerado). XXXVIII Symp. Sec. Esp. WPSA, Córdoba, 141-148.

Cortinas, L., Villaverde, C., Baucells, M.D., Guardiola, F., and Barroeta, A.C. (2003). Interaction between dietary unsaturation and α-tocopherol levels: vitamin E content in thigh meat. Proc. XVI Eur. Symp. on the Quality of Poultry Meat, St. Brieuc, France, 192-198.

Creek, R.D. and Vasaitis, V. (1963). The effect of excess dietary protein on the need of folic acid by the chick. Poultry Sci., 42:1136-1140.

Crevieu-Gabriel, I. and Naciri, M. (2001). Effect de l'alimentation sur les coccidiosis chez le poulet. INRA Prod. Anim., 14 (4):231-246.

Cruishank, J.J. and Sim, J.S. (1987). Effects of excess vitamin D3 and cage density on the incidence of leg abnormalities in broiler chickens. Avian Dis., 31.332-338.

Csallany, A.S., Menken, B.Z., and Waibel, P. (1988). Research note: Hepatic tocopherol concentration in turkeys as influenced by dietary vitamin and fat. Poultry Sci., 67:1814-1816.

Curça, D., Andonie, V., Andronie, I.C., and Pop, A. (2006). The influence of feed supplementation with ascorbic acid and sodium ascorbate on broilers, under thermal stress. Proc. XII Eur. Poultry Conf., Verona, CD rom.

Daghir, N.J. (1995a). Broiler feeding and management in hot climates. In: Poultry Production in Hot Climates, 185-218. CAB International.

Daghir, N.J. (1995b). Nutrient requirements of poultry at high temperatures. In Poultry Production in Hot Climates, 106-122. CAB International.

Daghir, N.J. (1996). Nutrition and climatic stress. Proc. XX World's Poultry Congress,

Delhi, 141-150

Daghir, N.J. and Shah, M.A. (1973). Effect of dietary protein level on vitamin B6 requirements of chicks. Poultry Sci., 52:1247.

Dale, N.M. and Villacres, A. (1986). Dietary factors affecting the incidence of ascites in broilers. Proc. Georgia Nutr. Conf., 79-85.

Dale, N.M. and Villacres, A. (1986). Dietary factors affecting the incidence of ascites. Proc. Georgia Nutr. Conf., 79-85.

Dalloul, R.A. and Lillehoj, H.S. (2005). Recent advances in immunomodulation and vaccination against coccidiosis. Avian Dis. 49:1-8.

Dalloul, R.A., Lillehoj, H.S., and Doerr, J.A. (2000). Effect of vitamin A deficiency on local and systemic immune responses of broiler chickens. Poultry Sci. 79 (suppl 1): 98-99 (abstract).

Dalloul, R.A., Lillehoj, H.S., Shellem, T.A., and Doerr, J.A. (2002). Effect of vitamin A deficiency on host intestinal immune response to *Eimeria acervulina* in broiler chickens. Poultry Sci. 81:1509–1515.

Davelaar, F.G. and Van Den Bos, J. (1992). Ascorbic acid and infectious bronchitis infections in broilers. Avian Pathol., 21: 581-589.

Davis, C.Y. and Sell, J.L. (1989). Immunoglobulin concentrations in serum and tissues of vitamin A-deficient broiler chicks after Newcastle disease virus vaccination. Poultry Sci., 68:136-144.

De Luca, H.F. and Zierold, C., (1998). Mechanisms and functions of vitamin D. Nutr. Rev., 37:161-193.

De Wynne, A. and Dirinck, P. (1996). Studies on vitamin E and meat quality: Effect of feeding high vitamin E levels on chicken meat quality. J. Agric. Food Chem., 44:1691-1696.

Decuypere, E., Vega, C., Barthat, A.A., Buyse, J., Zoons, J., and Albers, J.G. (1994). Increased sensitivity to triiodothyronine (T3) of broiler lines with a high susceptibility for ascites. Brit. Poultry Sci., 35:287-297.

Dehyim, F., Belay, T., and Teeter, R.G. (1992). An elevation of dietary pantothenic acid needs of broilers through eight weeks post-hatching. Nutr. Res., 12:1549.

Dehyim, F., Wiernusz, C.J., Belay, T., Teeter, R.G., Coelho, M.B., and Halley, J.T. (1990). Riboflavin and pantothenic acid requirement of broilers through eight weeks posthatching. Poultry Sci., 69 (suppl. 1):43 (abstract)

Dehyim, F., Wiernusz, C.J., Belay, T., Teeter, R.G., Coelho, M.B., and Halley, J.T. (1991). A re-evaluation of the male broilers riboflavin and pantothenic acid dietary requirement in thermoneutral and heat distress environment. Poultry Sci., 70 (suppl. 1):157 (abstract).

Deyhim, F. and Teeter, R.G. (1993). Dietary vitamin and/or trace mineral premix effects on performance, humoral mediated immunity and carcass composition of broilers during thermoneutral and high ambient temperature distress. J. Appl. Poultry Res. 2: 347-355.

Deyhim, F. and Teeter, R.G. (1996). Vitamin withdrawal effects on performance, carcass composition, and tissue vitamin concentration of broilers exposed to various stress types. Poultry Sci., 75 (suppl. 1):113 (abstract).

Deyhim, F., Stoecker, B.J., Adeleye, P.G., and Teeter, R.G. (1994). The effects of heat distress environment, and vitamin or trace mineral supplementation on growth and cell mediated immunity in broiler chickens. Nutr. Res., 14 (4):587-592.

Deyhim, F., Stoecker, B.J., Adeleye, P.G., and Teeter, R.G. (1995). The effects of heat distress environment, vitamin, and trace mineral supplementation on performance, blood constituents, and tissue mineral concentration in broiler chickens. Nutr. Res., 15 (4):521-526.

Deyhim, F., Stoecker, B.J., and Teeter, R.G. (1996). Vitamin and trace mineral withdrawal effects on broiler breast tissue riboflavin and thiamin content. Poultry Sci. 75: 201-202.

Diaz-Cruz, A., Avila, G.E., Guinzberg, P.R., and Iña, E.P. (2001). Effects of vitamins E and C and lipoic acid on productive perfomance and oxidative stress in broiler chicks. 13th Eur. Symp. on Poultry Nutrition. Blankenberge, Belgium, 335.

Dimanov, D.J., Petkov, G.S., Georgiev, S.G., and Mitev, J.E. (1994). Influence of selenium and ascorbic acid on the activity of plasma glutathione peroxidase and peroxidase resistance of erithrocite lipids in chickens. Proc. 9th European Poultry Conference, Glasgow, 183-185.

Doan, B.H. (2000). Effects of different levels of dietary calcium and supplemental vitamin C on growth, survivability, leg abnormalities, total ash in the tibia, serum calcium and phosphorus in 0-4 week old chicks under tropical conditions. Livestock Res. for Rural Develop. 12:14.

Dobson, D. C. (1970). Biotin requirement of turkey poults. Poultry Sci. 49:546–553.

Downs, K.M., Macklin, K.S, Norton, P.A., and Hess, J.B. (1999). The effectiveness of dietary vitamin E and organic zinc complexes for reducing the incidence of cellulitis. Poultry Sci., 78 (suppl. 1):129 (abstract).

Downs, K.M., Norton, P.A., Macklin, K.S., and Hess, J.B. (2000). The influence of supplemental vitamin E and Zinc-amino acid complex on avian cellulitis. Poultry Sci., 79 (suppl. 1):108 (abstract).

Driver, J.P., Atencio, A., Pesti, G.M., Edwards, H.M., and Bakalli, R.I. (2006). The effect of maternal dietary vitamin D3 supplementation on performance and tibial dyschondroplasia of broiler chicks. Poultry Sci., 85:39-47.

Driver, J.P., Pesti, G.M., Bakalli, R.I., and Edwards, H.M. (2005) Phytase and 1-α-hydroxycholecalciferol supplementation of broiler chickens during the starting and growing/finishing phases. Poultry Sci., 84:1616-1628.

DSM (2008). Óptima nutrición vitamínica de los animales para la producción de alimentos de calidad.

Du, M. and Ahn, D.U. (2002). Effect of antioxidants on the quality of irradiated sausages prepared with turkey thigh meat. Poultry Sci. 81:1251-1256.

Dunn, N. (1996). The vital vitamin boost for broilers under stress. World Poultry vol.12, no.6: 45-47.

Dunnington, E.A. and Siegel, P.B. (1996). Long-term divergent selection for eight-week body weight in White Plymouth Rock chickens. Poultry Sci., 75:1168-1179.

Dzhambulatov, M.M., Viktorov, P.I., Alisheikhov, A.M., and Akhemedkhanova, R.R. (1996). Setting norms for vitamins C and B12 in feeds for laying hens and broiler chickens subjected to heat stress. Rus. Agric. Sci., 10:14-16.

Edrise, B.M., Khair El-Din, A.W., and Soliman, R. (1986). The immunopotentiating effect of ascorbic acid against Newcastle disease in chickens. Vet. Med. J., 34:251-264.

Edwards, H. M. (1989). The effect of dietary cholecalciferol, 25-hydroxycholecalciferol and 1,25-dihydroxy-cholecalciferol on the development of tibial dyschondroplasia in broiler chickens in the absence and presence of disulfuram. J. Nutr, 119:647-652.

Edwards, H. M. (1992). Nutritional factors and leg disorders. In: Bone Biology and Skeletal Disorders in Poultry. Ed. by C.C. Whitehead. Carfax Pub., Oxfordshire, England., Chapter 10, 167-193

Edwards, H.M. (1989). Effects of vitamin C, environmental temperature, chlortetracycline, and vitamin D3 on the development of tibial dyschondroplasia in chickens. Poultry Sci., 68:1527-1534.

Edwards, H.M. (1990). Efficacy of several vitamin D compounds in the prevention of tibial dyschondroplasia in broiler chickens. J. Nutr., 120:1054-1061.

Edwards, H.M. (1993). Dietary 1,25-dihydroxycholecalciferol increases natural phytate phosphorus utilization in chickens. J. Nutr., 123:567-577.

Edwards, H.M. (1995). Efficacy of several vitamin D compounds in increasing phytate phosphorus utlization in chickens. Poultry Sci., 74 (supp. 1):107 (abstract).

Edwards, H.M. (1999). Responses to vitamin D3 metabolites tend to vary. Feedstuffs, July 5:14-15.

Edwards, H.M. (2000). Nutrition and skeletal problems in poultry. Poultry Sci., 79:1018-1023.

Edwards, H.M. (2002). Studies on the efficacy of cholecalciferol and derivatives for stimulating phytate utilization in broilers. Poultry Sci., 81:1026-1031.

Edwards, H.M., Elliot, M.A., and Sooncharernying, S. (1992a). Effect of dietary calcium on tibial dyschondroplasia. Interaction with light, cholecalciferol, 1,25-dihydroxycholecalciferol, protein and synthetic zeolite. Poultry Sci., 71:2041-2055.

Edwards, H.M., Elliot, M.A., and Sooncharernying, S. (1992b). Quantitative substitution of 1,25-dihydroxy-cholecalciferol and 1-hydroxy-cholecalciferol for cholecalciferol in broiler diets. XIX World´s Poultry Congress, Amsterdam, 567-571.

Edwards, H.M., Elliot, M.A., and Sooncharernying, S., Britton, W.M. (1994). Quantitative requirement for cholecalciferol in the absence of ultraviolet light. Poultry Sci., 73:288-294.

Edwards, H.M., Shirley, R.B., Escoe, W.B. and Pesti, G.M. (2002). Quantitative evaluation of 1-α-hydroxycholecalciferol as a cholecalciferol substitute for broilers. Poultry Sci., 81:664-669.

Edwards, H.M., Shirley, R.B: Atencio, A., and Pesti, G.M. (2004). Effect of dietary Ca levels on the efficacy of 1-α-hydroxycholecalciferol in the diets of young broilers. Proc. XXII World's Poultry Congress, Istanbul, CD-rom.

Eichner, G., Vieira, S.L., Torres, C.A., Coneglian, J.L.B., Freitas, D.M., and Oyarzabal, O.A. (2007). Litter moisture and footpad dermatitis as affected by diets formulated on an all-vegetable basis or having the inclusion of poultry by-product. J. Appl. Poultry Res. 16:344-350.

Ekstrand, C., Algers, B., and Svedberg, J. (1997) Rearing conditions and foot-pad dermatitis in Swedish broiler chickens. Prev. Vet. Med., 31: 167–174.

El-Husseiny, O.M., Abo-El-Ella, M.A., Abd-Elsamee, M.O., Magda, M., and Abd-Elfattah. (2007). Response of broilers performance to dietary betaine and folic acid at different methionine levels. Int. J. Poultry Sci. 6 (7): 515-523.

Elliot, M.A. and Edwards, H. M. (1994). Effect of genetic strain, calcium and feed withdrawal on growth, tibial dyschondroplasia, plasma 1,25-dihydroxycholecalciferol, and plasma 25-hydroxycholecalciferol in sixteen-day-old chickens. Poultry Sci., 73:509-519.

Elliot, M.A. and Edwards, H.M. (1997). Effect of 1,25-dihydroxycholecalciferol, cholecalciferol, and fluorescent lights on the development of tibial dyschondroplasia and rickets in broiler chickens. Poultry Sci., 76:570-580.

Elliot, M.A., Roberson, K.D., Rowland, G.N., and Edwards, H.M. (1995). Effects of dietary calcium and 1,25-dihydroxycholecalciferol on the development of tibial dyschondroplasia in broilers during the starter and grower periods. Poultry Sci., 74:1495-1505.

Emmert, J.L. and Baker, D.H. (1997). A chick bioassay approach for determining the bioavailable choline concentration in normal and overheated soybean meal, canola meal and peanut meal. J. Nutr., 127:745-752.

Engberg, R.M., Lauridsen, C., Jensen, S.K., and Jakobsen, K. (1996). Inclusion of oxidized vegetable oil in broiler diets. Its influence on nutrient balance and on antioxidative status of broilers. Poultry Sci. 75: 1003-1011.

Enkvetchakul, B., Bottje, W., Anthony, N., and Moore, R. (1993). Compromized antioxidant status associated with ascites in broilers. Poultry Sci. 72:2272-2280.

Erf, G.F., Bottje, W.G., Bersi, T.K., Headrick, M.D., and Fritts, C.A. (1998). Effects of dietary vitamin E on the immune system in broilers: altered proportions of CD4 T cells in the thymus and spleen. Poultry Sci. 77: 529-537.

Erf, G.F., Noll, S., Bersi, T.K., Wang, X., Kalbfleisch, J., Bottje, W.G., and Erf, G.F. (2000). Effects of dietary vitamin E supplementation in young male turkey poults. II. Tissue levels of vitamin E, proportions and concentrations of immune cells. Poultry Sci. 79 (suppl. 1):47-48 (abstract).

Eslick, N.L., Ahn, D., and Sell, J. (1997). Effect of vitamin E and irradiation on tocopherol content and lipid oxidation of turkey breast and thigh meat. Poultry Sci., 75 (suppl. 1):abstract 352.

Esmail, S.H.M. (2002). Nutrition is a major player in disease prevention. World Poultry, 18(6):16-17.

Farqhuarson, C., Berny, E.B., Mawer, E., Seawright, E., and Whitehead, C.C. (1998). Ascorbic acid-induced chondrocyte differentiation: The role of the extracellular matrix and 1,25 dihydroxycholecalciferol. Eur. J. Cell Biol., 76:110-118.

Farr, A.J., Salman, H.K., Krautmann, B.A., Gonzales, L., and Mcdonald, A. (1988). Effect of high level of vitamin C dosage 32 hours prior to slaughter on processing parameters of broiler chickens. Poultry Sci., 67 (suppl. 1): 85 (abstract).

Fedna (2008). Necesidades nutricionales para avicultura: Pollos de carne y gallinas de puesta. Ed. Fundación Española para el Desarrollo de la Nutrición Animal, 73 pp.

Fellenberg, M.A. and Speisky, H. (2006). Antioxidants: their effects on broiler oxidative stress and its meat oxidative stability. WPSJ., 62:53-70.

Fellenberg, M.A., Peña, C., and Speisky, H. (2006). Effect of dietary supplementation of vitamin E on the antioxidant status of broilers and the oxidative stability of its cooled meat. Proc. XII Eur. Poultry Conf., Verona, CD rom.

Ferket, P.R. and Allen, E. (1994). How nutrition and management influence PSE in poultry meat. Broiler Ind., 57(9).

Ferket, P.R. and Qureshi, M.A. (1992). Performance and immunity of heat-stressed broilers fed vitamin- and electrolyte supplemented drinking water. Poultry Sci., 71:88-97.

Ferket, P.R. and Qureshi, M.A. (1999). The turkey immune system and nutritional immunomodulators. Proc. 12th Eur. Symp. on Poultry Nutrition, Veldhoven, The Netherlands, 17-29.

Ferket, P.R., Garlich, J.D., and Thomas, L.N. (1993). Dietary choline and labile methyl donor requirement of turkey poults. Poultry Sci., 72 (suppl. 1):13 (abstract).

Ferket, P.R., Qureshi, M.A., Garlich, J.D., Rives, D.V., and Kidd, M.T. (1995). Vitamin E affects performance, immunity and meat quality. World Poultry, 11 (2): 10-11.

Fisher, H.H. (1974). Niacine requirements. Proc. Roche Symposium, 11-29.

Flachowsky, G., Engelman, D., Sünder, A., Halle, I., and Sallman, H.P. (2001). Eggs and poultry meat as tocopherol sources in dependence on tocopherol supplementation of poultry diets. Food Res. Int., 35:239-243.

Fletcher, D.L. and Cason, J.A. (1991). Influence of ascorbic acid on broiler shrink and processing yields. Poultry Sci., 70:2191-2196.

Folegatti, E, Sirri, F., Meluzzi, A., and Toscani, Tt (2006). Prevalence of foot pad lesions and carcass injuries as indicators of broiler welfare conditions in Italy. Proc. XII Eur. poultry Conf., Verona, CD-rom.

Franchini, A. and Bertuzzi, S. (1991). Micronutrients and immune functions. 8th Eur. Symp. on Poultry Nutrition, Venezia-Mestre, 63-80.

Franchini, A., Bertuzzi, S., and Meluzzi, A. (1986). The influence of high doses of vitamin E on immune response of chicks to inactivated oil adjuvant vaccine. La Clinica Veterinaria, 109:117-127.

Franchini, A., Bertuzzi, S., Tosarelli, C., Ianelli, S., Nanni Costa, A., and Stefoni, S. (1994). Chronobiological influence of vitamin C on chicken immune functions. Archiv fur Geflugelk., 58:165-175.

Frank, J., Weiser, H., and Biesalski, H.K. (1997). Interaction of vitamins E and K: Effects of dietary vitamin E on phylloquinone activity in chickens. Int. J. Vit. Res., 67:242.

Friedman, A. and Sklan, D. (1989). Antigen–specific immune response impairment in the chicken as influenced by dietary vitamin Am. J. Nutr., 119:790.

Friedman, A. and Sklan, D. (1997). Effects of retinoids on immune response impairment in birds. WPSJ., 53.185.

Friedman, A., Bartov, I., and Sklan, D. (1998). Humoral immune response impairment following excess vitamin E nutrition in the chick and turkey. Poultry Sci. 77: 956-962.

Friedman, A., Meidovsky, J., Leitner, G., and Sklan, D. (1991). Decreased resistance and immune response to *E. coli* infection in chickens with low and high intakes of vitamin A. J. Nutr., 121:395-400.

Frigg, M. (1984). Available biotin content of various feed ingredients. Poultry Sci., 63:750-753.

Frigg, M. (1987). Biotin in poultry and swine rations and its significance for optimum performance. Proc. Maryland Nutr. Conf., 101-108.

Fritts, C.A. and Waldroup, P.W. (2003). Effect of source and level of vitamin D3 on live performance and bone development in growing broilers. J. Appl. Poultry Res., 12:45-52.

Fritts, C.A. and Waldroup, P.W. (2004). Effect of source and level of vitamin D3 on immune function in growing broilers. J. Appl. Poultry Res., 13:263-273.

Fritts, C.A. and Waldroup, P.W. (2005). Comparison of cholecalciferol and 25-hydroxycholcalciferol in broiler diets designed to minimize phosphorus excretion. J. Appl. Poultry Res., 14:156-166.

Galvin, K., Morrissey, P.A., and Buckley, D.J. (1997). Influence of dietary vitamin E and oxidised sunflower oil on the storage stability of cooked chicken muscle. Brit. Poultry Sci. 38: 499-504.

Galvin, K., Morrissey, P.A., and Buckley, D.J. (1998). Cholesterol oxides in processed chicken muscle as influenced by dietary α -tocopherol supplementation. Meat Sci. 48: 1-9.

Galvin, K., Morrissey, P.A., Buckley, D.J., and Rigg, M. (1993). Influence of oil quality and α-tocopheryl acetate supplementation on α-tocopherol and lipid oxidation in chicken tissues. 11th Eur. Symp. on the Quality of Poultry Meat, Tours, pp: 423-429.

Garcia Regueiro, J.A., Diaz, I., and Hortós, M. (1998). Volatile compounds of meta from broilers fed with different dietary oils and antioxidants. Proc. 44th ICoMST, 644-645.

Garcia, M.N., Pesti, G.M., and Bakalli, R.J. (1999). The effects of three methyl sources (methionine, betaine and choline) on the performance of growing chicks. Poultry Sci., 78 (suppl. 1):137

Garlich, J.D., Qureshi, M.A., Ferket, P.R., and Aslam, S.M. (1992). Immune system modulation by dietary calcium. Proc. XIX World's Poultry Congress, Amsterdam, 618-619.

Gatellier, P., Lessire, M., Hermier, D., Maaroufi, C., and Renerre, M. (2003). Influence of nitrite and vitamin E percentage on myoglobin and lipid oxidation in packaged cooked cured-hams. 2003 Spring Meeting of the WPSA French Branch meeting abstracts.

Gatellier, P., Mercier, Y., Remignon, H., and Renerre, M. (1998). Effects of dietary fat and vitamin E content on lipid and protein oxidation in turkey meat homogenates after a chemical induction. Proc. 44th ICoMST, 636-637.

Genot, C., Meynier, A., Viau, M., Métro, B., and Gandemer, G. (1998). Dietary fat and vitamin E supplementation affect lipid oxidation in cooked turkey meat. Proc. 48 ICoMST, 632-633.

Gheisari, A.A., Samie, A., Pourreza, J., Khoddami, A., and Gheisari, M.M. (2004). Effect of dietary fat, α-tocopherol, and ascorbic acid supplementation on the performance and meat oxidative stability of heat stressed broiler chicks. Proc. XXII World's Poultry Congress, Istanbul, CD-rom.

Gheisari, A.A., Taheri, R., Rahmani, H.R., Toghyani, M., Bahadoran, R., and Khoddami, A. (2006). Effects of dietary vitamin E and green tea powder on performance of broiler chicks and meat lipid peroxidation during different storage times. Proc. XII European Poultry Conference, Verona, Italy, CD-rom.

Gill, C. (2002). Vitamin D3 metabolite versus MAS in broilers. Feed Int., Feb. 2002, 16-17.

Goñi, I., Brenes, A., Centeno, C., Viveros, A., Saura-Calixto, F., Rebolé, A., Arija, I., and Estevez, R. (2007). Effect of dietary grape pomace and vitamin E on growth performance, nutrient digestibility, and susceptibility to meat lipid oxidation in chickens. Poultry Sci., 86:508-516.

Gore, A.B. and Qureshi, M.A. (1997). Enhancement of humoral and cellular immunity by vitamin E after embryonic exposure. Poultry Sci., 76:984-991.

Gous, R.M. and Morris, T.R. (2005). Nutritional interventions in alleviating the effects of high temperatures in broiler production. WPSJ., 61:463-475.

Grashorn, M.A. and Völker, L. (1993). Effects of an application of Vitamin C before transportation on carcass yield of broiler chickens. Proc. 11th Eur. Symp. on the Quality of Poultry Meat, Tours, 191-195.

Grau, A., Codony, R.L, Grimpa, S., Baucells, M.D., and Guardiola, F. (2001a). Cholesterol oxidation in frozen dark chicken meat: influence of dietary fat source, and α-tocopherol and ascorbic acid supplementation. Meat Sci. 57: 197-208.

Grau, A., Guardiola, F., Bou, R., and Codony, R. (2000). Influencia de la dosis y el tiempo de suplementación del pienso con acetato de α-tocoferol en la calidad de la carne de pollo. Alimentación, nutrición y salud, 7 (4):pp. 91-98.

Grau, A., Guardiola, F., Grimpa, S., Barroeta, A.C., and Codony, R. (2001b). Oxidative stability of dark chicken meat through frozen storage: Influence of dietary fat and α-tocopherol and ascorbic acid supplementation. Poultry Sci., 80:1630-1642.

Gross, W.B, Jones, D. and Cherry, J. (1988). Effect of ascorbic acid on the disease caused by Escherichia coli challenge infection. Avian Dis., 32: 407-409.

Gross, W.B. (1988). Effect of ascorbic acid on antibody response of stressed and unstressed chickens. Avian Dis., 32: 483-485.

Gross, W.B. (1992). Effects of ascorbic acid on stress and disease in chickens. Avian Dis. 36: 688-692.

Gualtieri, M., Poli, B.M., and Rapaccini, S. (1993). Fatty acid composition of broiler meat as influenced by diet supplementation with fish oil. Proc. XI Eur. Symp on the Quality of Poultry Meat, Tours, 136-143.

Guo, Y, Zhang, G, Yuan, J., and Hie, W. (2003). Effects of source and level of magnesium and vitamin E on prevention of hepatic peroxidation and oxidative deterioration of broiler meat. Anim. Feed Sci. Technol. 107: 143-150.

Guo, Y., Tang, Q., Yuan, J., and Jiang, Z. (2001). Effects of supplementation with vitamin E on the performance and the tissue peroxidation of broiler chicks and the stability of thigh meat against oxidative deterioration. Anim. Feed Sci. Technol. 89: 165-173.

Halevy, O., Arazi, Y., Melamed, D., Friedman, A., and Sklan, D. (1994). Retinoic acid receptor-alpha gene expression is modulated by dietary vitamin A and by retinoic acid in chicken T lymphocytes. J. Nutr., 124:2139-2146.

Haq, A.U., Bailey, C.A., and Chinnah, A. (1996). Effect of beta-carotene, canthaxantin, lutein, and vitamin E on neonatal immunity of chicks when supplemented in the broiler breeder diets. Poultry Sci., 75:1092-1097.

Harms, R.H. and Nelson. (1992). Research note: A lack of response to pantothenic acid supplementation of corn-soybean meal diet on performance of turkey breeder hens. Poultry Sci., 71:1952.

Harms, R.H. and Simpson, C.F. (1975) Biotin deficiency as a possible cause of swelling and ulceration of foot pads. Poultry Sci. 54:1711-1713.

Harms, R.H., Damron, B.L., and Simpson, C.F. (1977). Effect of wet litter and supplemental biotin and/or whey on the production of foot pad dermatitis in broilers. Poultry Sci. 56:291-296.

Harms, R.H. and Bootwalla, S.M. (1992). Do turkey starter diets need pantothenic acid supplementation? J. Appl. Poultry Res., 1:19-21.

Haslam, S.M., Knowles, T.G., Brown, S.N., Wilkins, L.J., Kestin, S.C., Warriss, P.D., and Nicol, C.J. (2007). Factors affecting the prevalence of foot pad dermatitis, hock burn and breast burn in broiler chicken, Brit. Poultry Sci., 48:264-275.

Hassan, R. A., Attia, Y.A., and El-Ganzory, E.H. (2005). Growth, carcass quality and serum constituents of slow growing chicks as affected by betaine addition to diets containing different levels of choline. Int. J. Poultry Sci. 4 (11): 840-850.

Havenstein, G.B., Ferket, P.R., and Qureshi, M.A. (2003). Carcass composition and yield of 1957 vs 2001 broilers when fed representative 1957 and 2001 broiler diets. Poultry Sci., 82:1509-1518.

Havenstein, G.B., Ferket, P.R., Scheideler, S., and Larson, B.T. (1994). Carcass composition and yield of 1957 vs 1991 broilers when fed "typical" 1957 and 1991 broiler diets. Poultry Sci., 73:1785-1804.

Hayashi, K, Yoshizaki, R, Ohtsuka, A, Torada, T., and Tuduki, T. (2004). Effects of ascorbic acid on performance and antibody production in broilers vaccinated against infectious bursal disease under a hot environment. Proc. XXII World's Poultry Congress, Istanbul, CD-rom.

Heffels-Redmann, U., Redmann, Th., and Weber, G. (2001) Vitamin E supplementation in turkeys influences immune reactions and performance. World Poultry Special issue on Vitamins.

Heffels-Redmann, U., Redmann, Th., Lange, K., Schröder-Gravendyck, S.E., and Sallmenn, H. P. (2000). Influence of vitamin E on immune reactions of turkeys. Arch. Geflügelk 65 (2): 68-75.

Herendy, V., Süto, Z., and Horn, P. (2004). Comparison of turkey strains and feeding management of the 1967´s and the 1999's regarding growth and slaughter characteristics. Proc. XXII World's Poultry Congress, Istanbul 2004, CD-rom.

Hernández, J.M., Pérez-Vendrell, A.M., and Brufau, J. (2002). Effect of vitamin level in broiler diets in productive parameters and meat deposition Proc. 11th Eur. Poultry Conf., Bremen, Germany. CD rom.

Hesabi, H. (2007). Effect of vitamin E on performance and immune response of broiler chicks. Proc. 16th Eur. Symp. on Poultry Nutrition, Strasbourg, p. 321.

Higgins, F.M., Kerry, J.P., Buckley, D.J., and Morrissey, P.A. (1998a). Assessment of α-tocopheryl acetate supplementation, addition of salt and packaging on the oxidative stability of raw turkey meat. Brit. Poultry Sci. 39: 596-600.

Higgins, F.M., Kerry, J.P., Buckley, D.J., and Morrissey, P.A. (1998b). Effect of dietary α-tocopheryl acetate supplementation on α-tocopherol distribution in raw turkey muscles and its effect on the storage stability of cooked turkey meat. Meat Sci. 50 (3): 373-383.

Higgins, F.M., Kerry, J.P., Buckley, D.J., and Morrissey, P.A. (1999). Effects of dietary α-tocopheryl acetate supplementation and salt addition on the oxidative stability (TBARS) and warmed-over flavor (WOF) of cooked turkey meat. Brit. Poultry Sci. 40: 59-64.

Hocking, P.M (2007). Optimum feed

composition of broiler breeder diets to maximize progeny performance. Proc. 16th Eur. Symp. on Poultry Nutrition, Strasbourg, 101-108.

Hocking, P.M., Wilson, S., Dick, L.N., Robertson, G.W., and Nixey, C. (2002). Role of dietary calcium and available phosphorus in the aetiology of tibial dyschondroplasia in growing turkeys. Brit. Poultry Sci., 43:432-441.

Hooper, C.L., Lightsey, S.F, Toler, J.E., and Maurice, D.U. (1989). Effect of age, sex, and food deprivation on the biosynthesis of ascorbic acid in meat-type chickens. Poultry Sci., 68 (suppl. 1): 116 (abstract).

Hossain, S.M., Barreto, S.L, Bertechini, A.G., Ríos, A.M., and Silva, C.G. (1998). Influence of dietary vitamin E level on egg production of broiler breeders, and on the growth and immune response of progeny in comparison with the progeny from eggs injected with vitamin E. Anim. Feed Sci. Technol., 73:307-317.

Hsieh, H.F, Chiang, S.H., and Lu, M.Y. (2002). Effect of dietary monounsaturated/ saturated fatty acid ratio on fatty acid composition and oxidative stability of tissues in broilers. Anim. Feed Sci. and Technol., 95:189-204.

Huang, X.X. and Miller, E.L. (1994). Stability of meat from broilers fed vitamin E in conjuction with lipids from fish oil and fish meal. Proc. 9th Eur. Poultry Conf., Glasgow, 217-218.

Huff, G.R., Huff, W.E., Balog, J.M., and Rath, N.C. (2000). The effect of vitamin D3 on resistance to stress-related infection in an experimental model of turkey osteomyelitis complex. Poultry Sci., 79:672-679.

Huff, G.R., Huff, W.E., Balog, J.M., Rath, N.C., and Izard, R.S. (2004). The effects of water supplementation with vitamin E and sodium salicytate (UNI-SOL®) on the resistance of turkeys to Escherichia coli respiratory infection. Avian Dis. 48:324-331.

Huff, G.R., Huff, W.E., Balog, J.M., Rath, N.C., Xie, H., and Horst, R.L. (2002). Effect of dietary supplementation with vitamin D metabolites in an experimental model of turkey osteomyelitis complex. Poultry Sci., 81:958-965.

Hulan, H.W., Proudfoot, F.G., and Mcrae, K.N. (1980). Effect of vitamins on the incidence of mortality and acute death syndrome ("flip-over") in broiler chickens. Poultry Sci., 59:927-931.

Humphrey, B.D. and Klasing, K.C. (2003). Modulation of nutrient metabolism and homeostasis by the immune system. Proc. 14th Eur. Symp. on Poultry Nutrition, Lillehammer, 137-142.

Hussein, A.S. (1995). Effects of dietary energy and vitamin C on growth performance of broiler chicks raised in hot climates. Poultry Sci., 74 (suppl. 1):151 (abstract).

Hussein, A.S., Cantor, A.H., Pescatore, A.J., and Johnson, T.H. (1993). Effect of dietary aluminum and vitamin D interaction on growth and calcium and phosphorus metabolism of broiler chicks. Poultry Sci., 72:306-309.

Huyghebaert, A. (1991). Stability of vitamin K in a mineral premix. World Poultry, 7:71.

Huyghebaert, G., Lippens, M., Lescoat, P., and Nys, Y. (2005). The interaction between the macrominerals calcium and phosphorus, vitamin D and phytase in broilers. Proc. 15th Eur. Symp. on Poultry Nutrition, Balatonfured, Hungary, 151-165.

Ibrahim, M. (1998). Riboflavin deficiency in chicken. World Poultry, 20-21.

Inra (1984). Alimentación de los animales monogástricos. Ed. MundiPrensa, Madrid 1985, 279 pp.

Iqbal, M., Cawthon, D., Beers, K., Wideman, R.F., and Bottje, W.G. (2002). Antioxidant enzyme activities and mitochondrial fatty acids in pulmonary hypertension syndrome (PHS) in broilers. Poultry Sci., 81:252-260.

Iqbal, M., Cawthon, D., Wideman, R.F., and Bottje, W.G. (2001). Lung mitochondrial dysfunction in pulmonary hypertension syndrome. II. Oxidative stress and inability to improve function with repeated additions of adenosine diphosphate. Poultry Sci., 80:656-665.

Jakobsen, K., Enberg, R.M., Andersen, J.O., Jensen, S.K., and Lauridsen, C. (1995). Supplementation of broiler diets with all-rac- α-tocopheryl acetate or a mixture of RRR-α-γ- tocopheryl acetate. 1. Effect on the vitamin status of broilers in vivo and at slaughter. Poultry Sci., 74:1984-1994.

Janssens, G., Cheetham, V., Fitt, T., and Taylor, A. (1999). Effect of dietary vitamin E on consumer acceptance of fresh poultry meat. XIV Eur. Symp. of Poultry Meat Quality, Bologna, pp: 173-179.

Jensen, C., Engberg, R., Jakobsen, K.,

Skibsted, L.H., and Bertelsen, G. (1997). Influence of the oxidative quality of dietary oil on broiler meat storage stability. Meat Sci. 47: 211-222.

Jensen, C., Lauridsen, C., and Bertelsen, G. (1998). Dietary vitamin E: Quality and storage stability of pork and poultry. Trends in Food Sci. and Technol. 9: 62-72.

Jensen, L.S. (1986). Interaction of nutrition with stress and disease. Proc. Georgia Nutr. Conf., 27-37.

Jensen, L.S., Fletcher, D.L., Lilburn, M.S., and Akiba, Y. (1981). Relationship of level of dietary vitamin A supplementation to broiler performance. Poultry Sci., 59 (suppl 1):1603 (abstract).

Jensen, L.S., Fletcher, D.L., Lilburn, M.S., and Akiba, Y. (1983). Growth depression in broiler chicks fed high vitamin A levels. Nutr. Rep. Int., 28:171-179.

Jensen, S.K. and Edberg, R.M. (1999). Bioavailability of various α-tocopherol esters in relation to age and feed formulation and vitamin A activity of ß-carotene in broilers. Proc. 12th Eur. Symp. on Poultry Nutrition, Veldhoven, 132-133.

Jiakui, L., Bi Dingren, P.S., Yanhong, Z., and Donghai, Z. (2008). Effects of high dietary vitamin A supplementation on tibial dyschondroplasia, skin pigmentation and growth performance in avian broilers. Res. in Vet. Sci., 84: 409–412

Jian, L., Shuisheng, H., and Hunchun, H. (1996). Studies of the biotin deficiency and its requirement for broiler chicks. Proc. XX World´s Poultry Congress, Delhi, India, IV, 179.

Jin, S. and Sell, J.L. (2001). Dietary vitamin K1 requirement and comparison of biopotency of different vitamin K sources for young turkeys. Poultry Sci,. 80:615–620.

Jin, S., Sell, J.L., and Haynes, J.S. (2001). Effect of dietary vitamin K1 on selected plasma characteristics and bone ash in young turkeys fed diets adequate or deficient in vitamin D3. Poultry Sci., 80:607–614.

Jones, R.B. and Satterlee, D.G. (1997). Vitamin C and fear in poultry: An overview. Poultry Sci., 76 (suppl. 1): 104 (abstract).

Jones, R.D. (1996). Fear and adaptabilty in poultry: Insights, implications and imperatives. WPSJ., 52:131.

Julian, R.J. (1998). Rapid growth problems: Ascites and skeletal deformities. Poultry Sci., 77:1773-1780.

Kafri, I. and Cherry, J.A. (1984). Supplemental ascorbic acid and heat stress in broiler chicks. Poultry Sci., 63 (suppl. 1): 125 (abstract).

Kafri, I., Rosebrough, R.W., Mcmurtry, J.P., and Steele, N.C. (1988). Corticosterone implants and supplementary ascorbic acid effects on lipid metabolism in broiler chicks. Poultry Sci., 67:1356-1359.

Kalbfleisch, J., Erf, G.F., Brannon, J., and Noll, S. (2000). Effects of dietary vitamin E supplementation in young male poults. I. Growth performance and lymphoid organ characteristics. Poultry Sci. 79 (suppl. 1):116 (abstract).

Kam, M., Saunders-Blades, J., Wisher, W.V., and Korver, D.R. (2007). Sensory acceptability of thighs from chickens fed vitamin D3 or 25-hydroxycholecalciferol.

Kan, P., Mitchell, M.A., and Carlisle, A.J. (1993). Effect of vitamin E on thyroid hormone production in heat stressed broiler chickens. Proc. 4th Eur. Symp. on Poultry Welfare, Edinburgh,295-297.

Kasim, A.B. and Edwards, H.M. (2000). Evaluation of cholecalciferol sources using broiler chicks assays. Poultry Sci., 79:1617–1622.

Kennedy, D.G., Rice, D.A., Bruce, D.W., Goodall, E.A., and Mcilroy, S.G. (1992). Economic effects of increase vitamin E supplementation of broiler diets on commercial broiler production. Brit. Poultry Sci., 36: 848-849.

Kettunen, H., Peuranen, S., Remus, J.C., Tiihonen, K., and Virtanen, E. (1999). The bioefficacy of dietary betaine and choline in broiler chicks. Poultry Sci., 78 (suppl. 1):140 (abstract).

Khajali, F., Asadi Khoshoei, E. and Zamani Moghaddam, A.K. (2006). Effect of vitamin and trace mineral withdrawal from finisher diets on growth performance and immunocompetence of broiler chickens. Brit. Poult. Sci., 47(2):159-162.

Khattak, F.M., Scaife, J.R. ,and Acamovic, T. (1996). Influence of whole mustard seed and supplemental vitamin E on lipid oxidation in broiler meat. Brit. Poultry Sci., 37:S58-S59 (abstract).

Khattak, F.M., Scaife, J.R., and Acamovic, T. (1995). Influence of dietary alpha-tocopherol supplementation on lipid oxidation in poultry meat obtained from broilers fed marine oil or rapeseed based diets. Brit. Poultry Sci. 36:848-849.

Kidd, M.T. (2004). Nutritional modulation of immune function in broilers. Poultry Sci., 83:650-657.

King, A.J., Uijttenboogaart, T.G., and De Vries, A.W. (1993). A comparative study: alpha-tocopherol, beta-carotene and ascorbic acid as antioxidants in stored poultry muscle. Proc. XI Eur. Symp on the Quality of Poultry Meat, Tours (France), 435-441.

King, A.J., Uijttenboogaart, T.G., and De Vries, A.W. (1995). α-tocopherol, ß-carotene and ascorbic acid as antioxidants in stored poultry muscle. J. Food Sci., 60 (5):1009-1012.

King, A.J., Uijttenboogaart, T.G., and De Vries, A.W. (1995). α-tocopherol, ß-carotene and ascorbic acid as antioxidants in stored poultry muscle. J. Food Sci.: 60 (5): 1009-1012.

Kjaer, J.B., Su, G, Nielsen, B.L., and Sørensen, P. (2006) Foot pad dermatitis and hock burn in broiler chickens and degree of inheritance. Poultry Sci, . 85:1342–1348.

Klasing, K.C. (1998). Vitamins. In: Comparative avian nutrition. CAB International, chapter 11, 227-329

Klasing, K.C. (2007). Nutrition and the immune system. Brit. Poultry Sci., 48 (5);525-537.

Klein, D.R., Novilla, M.N., and Watkins, K.L. (1994). Nutritional encephalomalacia in turkeys: diagnosis and growth performance. Avian Dis. 38: 653-659.

Klein-Hessling, H. (2006). Chondrodystrophy in turkeys and broilers. World Poultry, 22 (9):35-36.

Konjufca, V.K., Bottje, W.G., Bersi, T.K., and Erf, G.F. (2004). Influence of dietary vitamin E on phagocytic functions of macrophages in broilers. Poultry Sci., 83:1530-1534.

Koreleski, J. and Swiatkiewicz, S. (2006). Fatty acids and TBA-RS in frozen stored breast meat of chickens fed diets with rapeseed oil supplemented with fish oil and vitamin E. Proc. XII European Poultry Conference, Verona, Italy, CD-rom.

Koreleski, J. and Swiatkiewicz, S. (2005). Performance and tibia bones quality in broilers fed diet supplemented with particular limestone and 25-hydroxycholecalciferol. Proc. 15th Eur. Symp. on Poultry Nutrition, Balatonfured, 215-218.

Kovar, S.J., Ingram, D.R., Hagedorn, T.K.,

Klemperer, M.D., Barnes, D.G., and Laurent, S.M. (1990). Broiler performance as influenced by dietary sodium zeolite-A and ascorbic acid. Poultry Sci., 69 (suppl. 1): 75 (abstract).

Krautmann, B.A. (1989). Practical application of ascorbic acid in combating stress. In The role of vitamin C in poultry stress management. Animal health and nutrition. Hoffmann- La Roche Inc., 37-48.

Krautmann, B.A., Gwyther, M.J., Lentz, E.L., and Peterson, L.A. (1991). Effect of ascorbic acid on carcass yield in broiler chickens. Poultry Sci., 70 (suppl. 1):67 (abstract).

Kucuk, O., Sahin, N., and Sahin, K. (2003). Supplemental zinc and vitamin A can alleviate negative effects of heat stress in broiler chickens. Biol. Trace Elem. Res., 94:225-235.

Kurkure, N.V., Kalorey, D.R., and Bhandarkar, A.G. (2004) The effect of vitamin E and selenium on reversal of ochratoxicosis in broilers: Growth, haematological and immunological study. Proc. XXII World's Poultry Congress, Istanbul, CD-rom.

Kutlu, H.R. (2001). Influence of wet-feeding and supplementation with ascorbic acid on performance and carcass composition of broiler chicks exposed to high ambient temperature. Archiv fur Geflugelk., 61:172-175.

Kutlu, H.R. and Forbes, J.M. (1993). Changes in growth and blood parameters in heat-stressed broiler chicks in response to dietary ascorbic acid. Livest. Prod. Sci., 36:375-350.

Kutlu, H.R. and Forbes, J.M. (1994). Responses of broiler chicks to dietary ascorbic acid and corticosterone. Brit. Poultry Sci, 35:184-185.

Kutlu, H.R. and Forbes, J.M. (1995). Self-selection for ascorbic acid by broiler chicks in response to changing environmental temperature. Brit. Poultry Sci, 36: 820-821.

Ladmakhi, H.M., Buys, N., Dewil, E., Rahimi, G., and Decuypere, E. (1997). The prophylactic effect of vitamin C supplementation on broiler ascites incidence and plasma thyroid hormone concentration. Avian Pathol. 26: 33-34.

Lakritz, L. and Thayer, D.W. (1992). Effect of ionizing radiation on unesterified tocopherols in fresh chicken breast muscle. Meat Sci. 32: 257-265.

Lakritz, L. and Thayer, D.W. (1994). Effect of

gamma radiation on total tocopherols in fresh chicken breast muscle. Meat Sci. 37: 439-448.

Lakritz, L., Fox, J.B., Hampson, J., Richardson, R., Kohout, K., and Thayer, D.W. (1995). Effect of gamma radiation on levels of α-tocopherol in red meats and turkey. Meat Sci., 41 (3): 261-271.

Lal, H., Pandey, R., and Agarwal, S.K. (1999). Vitamin D: Non-skeletal actions and effects on growth. Nutr. Res., 19:1683-1718.

Larbier, M. and Leclercq, B. (1992). Nutrition et alimentation des volailles. Institut National de la Recherche Agronomique (INRA), 7: 139-170.

Larroudé. P., Castaing, J., Hamelin, C., and Ball, A. (2005). Effet d'une supplementation en Hy-D® pour deux niveaux d'apports en vitamins sur les performances, le developpement osseux et les troubles locomoteurs des dindons. 6th Journées de la Recherche Avicole, St. Malo, 244-248.

Latshaw, J.D. (1991). Nutrition-mechanisms of immunosuppression. Vet. Immunol. and Immunopathol., 30 (1):111-120.

Lauridsen, C., Buckley, D.J., and Morrissey, P.A. (1997). Influence of dietary fat and vitamin E supplementation on α-tocopherol levels and fatty acid profiles in chicken muscle membranal fractions and on susceptibility to lipid peroxidation. Meat Sci. 46: 9-22.

Lauzon, D.A, Johnston, S.L, Southern, L.L., and Xu, Z. (2008). The effect of carrier for vitamin E on liver concentrations of vitamin E and vitamin E excretion in broilers. Poultry Sci., 87:934-939.

Leach, R.M. and Burdette, J.H. (1985). The influence of ascorbic acid on the occurrence of tibial dyschondroplasia in young broiler chickens. Poultry Sci., 64:1188-1191.

Leach, R.M. and Monsonego-Ornan, E. (2007). Tibial dyschondroplasia 40 years later. Poult. Sci., 86:2053-2058.

Ledwaba, M.F. and Roberson, K.D. (2003). Efectiveness of twenty-five hydroxycholecalciferol in the prevention of tibial dyschondroplasia in Ross cockerels depends on calcium level. Poultry Sci., 82:1769-1777.

Lee, D.J.W. (1982). Growth, erythrocyte gluthatione reductase and liver flavine as indicators of riboflavin status in turkey poults. Brit. Poultry Sci., 23:263.

Leeson, S. and Summers, J.D. (1997). Commercial Poultry Nutrition, 2nd edition. Ed.University books. Ontario, Canada, 350 pp.

Leeson, S. and Summers, J.D. (2001). Vitamins. In: Scott's Nutrition of the Chicken Ed. University books. Ontario, Canada, 176-330.

Leeson, S. and Summers, J.D. (2005). Feeding programs for broiler chickens. In: Commercial Poultry Nutrition 3rd ed.University Books, Ontario, Canada, 229-295.

Leeson, S. Summers, J.D. 2005). Feeding Programs For Turkeys. In: Commercial Poultry Nutrition 3Rd Ed.University Books, Ontario, Canada, 345-358.(

Leeson, S., Díaz, G,. and Summers, J.D. (1995). Poultry metabolic disorders and mycotoxins. Ed. University Books, Ontario, Canada, 351 pp.

Leeson. S. (2007). Vitamin requirements: is there basis for re-evaluating dietary specifications? WPSJ., 63:255-266.

Leshchinsky, T.V. and Klasing, K.C. (2003). Profile of chicken cytokines induced by lipopolysaccharide is modulated by dietary α-tocopheryl acetate. Poultry Sci., 82:1266-1273.

Leshchinsky, T.V. and Klasing, K. C. (2001). Relationship between the level of dietary vitamin E and the immune response of broiler chickens. Poultry Sci. 80: 1590-1599.

Lessard, M. Hutchings, D., and Cave, N.A. (1997). Cell-mediated and humoral immune responses in broiler chickens maintained on diets containing different levels of vitamin A. Poultry Sci., 76:1368–1378.

Lin, C.F, Asghar, A., Gray, J.I., Buckley, D.J., Boren, A.M., Crackel, A.M., and Flegal, C.J. (1989a). Effects of oxidised dietary oil and antioxidant supplementation on broiler growth and meat stability. Brit. Poultry Sci., 30:855-864.

Lin, C.F, Gray, J.I., Asghar, A., Buckley, D.J., Boren, A.M., and Flegal, C.J. (1989b). Effects of dietary oils and alpha-tocopherol supplementation on lipid composition and stability of broiler meat. J. Food Sci., 54:1457-1460.

Lin, H., Du, R. and Zhang, Z.Y. (2000). The peroxidation in tissues of heat-stressed broilers. Aust. J. Anim. Sci., 13:1373-1376.

Lin, H., Jiao, H.C., Buyse, J., and Decuypere,

E. (2006). Strategies for preventing heat stress in poultry. WPSJ., 62:71-95.

Lofton, J.T. and Soares, J.H. (1986). The effects of vitamin D3 on leg abnormalities in broilers. Poultry Sci., 65:749-756.

Lohakare, J.D., Kim, J.K, Ryu, M.H., Hahn, T.W., and Chae, B.J. (2005a). Effects of vitamin C and vitamin D interaction on the performance, immunity, and bone characteristics of commercial broilers. J. Appl. Poult. Res. 14:670-678.

Lohakare, J.K., Ryu, M.H, Hahn, T.W., Lee, J.K., and Chae, B.J. (2005b). Effects of supplemental ascorbic acid on the performance and immunity of commercial broilers. J. Appl. Poult. Res. 14:10-19.

López-Bote, C.J., Gray, J.I., Gomaa, E.A., and Flegal, C.J. (1998a). Effect of dietary oat administration on lipid stability in broiler meat. Brit. Poultry Sci. 39: 57-61.

López-Bote, C.J., Gray, J.I., Gomaa, E.A., and Flegal, C.J. (1998b). Effect of dietary administration of oil extracts from rosemary and sage on lipid oxidation in broiler meat. Brit. Poultry Sci. 39: 235-340.

Lorenzoni, A.G. and Ruiz-Feria, C.A. (2006). Effects of vitamin E and L-arginine on cardiopulmonary function and ascites parameters in broiler chickens reared under subnormal temperatures. Poultry Sci., 85:2241-2250.

Lowry, K.R., Izquierdo, O.A., and Baker, D.H. (1987). Efficacy of betaine relative to choline as a dietary methyl donor. Poultry Sci., 66 (suppl. 1):135 (abstract).

Luo, L. and Huang, J. (1991). Effects of vitamin A and D supplementation on tibial dyschondroplasia in broilers. Anim. Feed Sci. Technol., 34:21-27.

Lynch, M.P., Faustman, C., Chan, W.K.M., Kerry, J.P., and Buckley, D. J. (1998). A potential mechanism by which α-tocopherol maintains oxymyoglobin pigment through cytochrome b5 mediated reduction. Meat Sci., 50: 333-342.

Lyon, B.G. and Lyon, C.E. (2002). Color of uncooked and cooked broiler leg quarters associated with chilling temperature and holding time. Poultry Sci., 81: 1916-1920.

Macklin, K.S., Norton, R.A., Hess, J.B., and Bilgili, S.F. (2000). The effect of vitamin E on cellulites in broiler chickens experiencing scratches in a challenge model. Avian Dis., 44:701-705.

Mahmoud, K.Z., Edens, F.W., and Eisen, E.J. (1999). Vitamin C reduces HSP70 and plasma corticosterone response in broilers subjected to cyclic heat stress. Poultry Sci., 78 (suppl. 1):106 (abstract).

Mahmoud, K.Z., Edens, F.W., Eisen, E., and Havenstein, G.B. (2004). Ascorbic acid decreases heat-shock protein 70 and plasma corticosterone response in broilers (Gallus gallus domesticus) subjected to cyclic heat stress. Comp. Biochem. Physiol., B 137:35-42.

Maini, S., Rastogi, S.K., Korde, J.P, Madan, A.K., and Shukla, S.K. (2007). Evaluation of oxidative stress and its amelioration through certain antioxidants in broilers during summer. J. Poultry Sci., 44:339-347.

Maiorka, A., Laurentiz, A.C., Santin, E., Araújo, L.F., and Macari, M. (2002). Dietary vitamin or mineral mix removal during the finisher period on broiler chicken performance. J. Appl. Poult. Res. 11:121-126.

Maiorka, A., Portella Félix, A., Sorbara, J.O.B., and Lecznieski, J., 2010 Niveles vitamínicos para una producción moderna y eficiente de carne de pollo. Selecciones Avícolas, Mayo, 2010.

Malan, D.D., Buyse, J., and Decuypere, E. (2001). Nutrition: An exogenous factor in broiler ascites. Proc. 13th Eur. Symp. on Poultry Nutrition, Blankenberge, Belgium, 319-326.

Malczyk, E., Kopec, W., and Smolinska, T. (1999). Influence of oil and vitamin E (alpha-tocopherol) supplementation on lipid oxidation and flavor of poultry meat. XIV Eur. Symp. of Poultry Meat Quality, Bologna, 167-173.

Maraschiello, C., Sárraga, C., and García-Regueiro, J.A. (1999). Gluthatione peroxidase activity, TBARS and α-tocopherol in meat from chickens fed different diets. J. Agric. Food Chem., 47:367-382.

Marion, J.E., Harms, R.H., and Arafa, A.S. (1985). Effect of dicumarol and vitamin K source on blood loss and processed yields of broilers. Poultry Sci., 64:1306-1309.

Marron, L., Bedford, M.R., and Mccracken, K.J. (2001). The effects of adding xylanase, vitamin C and copper sulphate to meat-based diets on broiler performance. Brit. Poultry Sci. 42: 493-500.

Martrenchar, A., Boilletot, E., Huonnic, D., and Pol, F. (2002). Risk factors for foot-pad dermatitis in chicken and turkey broilers in France. Prev. Vet. Med., 52: 213–226.

Marusich, W.L., Ogrinz, E.F., Brand, M. and Mitrovic M. (1970). Induction, prevention and therapy of biotin deficiency in turkey poults. Poultry Sci., 49:412-421.

Marusich, W.L., Ritter, E., Ogrinz, E.F., Keating, J., and Mitrovic, M. (1974). Effect of supplemental vitamin E in control of rancidity in poultry meat. Poultry Sci., 54:331-344.

Masse, P.G, Pritzker, K.P-H., Mendes, M.G., Boskey, A.L., and Weiser, H. (1994). Vitamin B6 deficiency experimentally induced bone and joint disorder. Brit. J. Nutr. 71:919-932.

Masse, P.G., Rimnac, C.M., Yamauchi, M., Coburn, S.P., Rucker, R.B., Howell, D.S., and Boskey, A.L. (1996). Pyridoxine deficiency affects biomechanical properties of chick tibial bone. Bone, 18:567-574.

Maurice, D.V. (1996). Anabolic agents, vitamins, and fermentation co-products as growth promoters in poultry. Proc. XX World's Poultry Congress, Delhi, p.255.

Maurice, D.V. and Lightsey, S.F (1996). Toxicity of coproducts of niacinamide synthesis and bioefficacy of niacin sources. Poultry Sci., 75 (suppl.1):11 (abstract)

Maurice, D.V. and Lightsey, S.F. (1995). Effect of three grade fats on performance and tissue vitamin E content of broiler chickens. Poultry Sci., 74 (suppl. 1):204 (abstract).

Maurice, D.V., Jones, J.E., Lightsey, S.F., and Rhoades, J.F. (1990). Response of male poults to high levels of dietary niacinamide. Poultry Sci., 69:661-668.

Maurice, D.V., Jones, J.E., Lightsey, S.F., Rhoades, J.F., and Ulaiman, S. (1988). Response of tom poults to high dietary niacinamide. Poultry Sci., 67: (suppl.1):24 (abstract).

Maurice, D.V., Lightsey, S.F., and Gaylord, T.C. (1993). Immunoenhancement in chickens fed excess dietary vitamin E is dependent on genotype and concentration. Poultry Sci., 72 (suppl. 1):55 (abstract).

Maynard, M., Johnstone, B.J., and Klasing, K.C. (1989). Influence of source and valence on vanadium toxicity in broiler chicks. Poultry Sci., 68 (suppl.1):91 (abstract).

Mayne, R. K., Else, R. W., and Hocking, P. M. (2007b). High litter moisture alone is sufficient to cause footpad dermatitis in growing turkeys. Brit.Poultry Sci., 48: 538 -545.

Mayne, R.K., Else, R.W., and Hocking, P.M. (2007a). High dietary concentrations of biotin did not prevent foot pad dermatitis in growing turkeys and external scores were poor indicators of histopathological lesions. Brit. Poultry Sci., 48 (3): 291-298.

Mbajiorgu, C.A, Ng´Ambi, J.W., and Norris, D. (2007). Effect of time of initiation of feeding after hatching and influence of dietary ascorbic acid supplementation on productivity, mortality and carcass characteristics of Ross 308 broiler chickens in South Africa. Int. J.of Poultry Sci. 6 (8): 583-591.

McCormack, H.A, McTeir, L., Fleming, R.H., and Whitehead, C.C. (2002). Vitamin D requirements of broilers at different dietary concentrations of calcium, phosphorus, and vitamin A.Proc. 11th Eur. Poultry Conf., Bremen, CD-rom.

McDowell, L. and Ward, N.E. (2008). Optimum vitamin nutrition for poultry: Int. Poultry Prod., 16:27-34.

Mcilroy, S.G., Goodall, E.A., and Mcmurray, C.H. (1987). A contact dermatitis in broilers: Epidemiological findings. Avian Pathol., 16:93-105.

Mcilroy, S.G., Goodall, E.A., Rice, D.A., Mcnulty, M.S., and Kennedy, D.G. (1993). Improved performance in commercial broiler flocks with subclinical infectious bursal disease when fed diets containing increased concentrations of vitamin E. Avian Pathol. 22: 81-92.

Mckee. J.S. and Harrison, P.C. (1995). Effects of supplemental ascorbic acid on the performance of broiler chickens exposed to multiple concurrent stressors. Poultry Sci., 74:1722-1785.

Mckee. J.S. and Harrison, P.C. (1996). Ascorbic acid-induced reductions in the respiratory quotient of heat-stressed chicks may result from increased availability of fatty acids for energy purposes. Poultry Sci., 75 (suppl.1): 1 (abstract).

Mckee. J.S., Harrison, P.C., and Riskowski, G.L. (1997). Effects of supplemental ascorbic acid on the energy conversion of broiler chicks during heat stress and feed withdrawal. Poultry Sci., 76:1278-1286

Mcknight, W.F, Coelho, M., and Mcnaughton, J.L. (1996). Effect of antioxidant vitamins on broiler meat quality. Poultry Sci., 75: (suppl. 1):129 (abstract)

Mcknight, W.F., Coelho, M.B., and Mcnaughton, J.L. (1995a). Turkey vitamin fortification. I. Commercial U.S. turkey vitamin survey. Poultry Sci., 74 (suppl. 1):185 (abstract).

Mcknight, W.F., Coelho, M.B., and Mcnaughton, J.L. (1995b). Turkey vitamin fortification. II. Performance of turkeys fed industry levels of vitamins. Poultry Sci., 74 (suppl. 1):205 (abstract).

Mcnaughton, J.L. and Murray, R. (1990). Effect of 25- hydroxycholecalciferol (25-0H-D3) and vitamin D3 on phosphorus requirement of broilers. Poultry Sci., 69 (suppl. 1):178

Meldrum, J.B., Evans, R.D., Robertson, J.L., Watkins, K.L., and Novilla, M.N. (2000). Alterations in levels of various host antioxidant factors in turkey knockdown syndrome. Avian Dis., 44:891-895.

Menten, J.F.M., Pesti, G.M., and Bakalli, R.J. (1997). The availability of choline in soybean meal. Poultry Sci., 76 (suppl. 1):81 (abstract).

Mercier, Y., Gatellier, P., Viau, M., Remignon, H., and Renerre, M. (1998a). Effect of dietary fat and vitamin E on color stability and on lipid and protein oxidation in turkey meat during storage. Meat Sci. 48: 301-308.

Mercier, Y., Gatellier, P., Viau, M., Remignon, H., and Renerre, M. (1998b). Protein and lipid oxidation in turkey Sartorius muscle during frozen storage as influenced by dietary fat sources and vitamin E supplementation. Proc. 41st ICoMST, 638-639.

Mercier, Y., Gatellier, P., Vincent, A., and Renerre, M. (2001). Lipid and protein oxidation in microsomal fraction from turkeys: influence of dietary fat and vitamin E supplementation. Meat Sci. 58: 125-134.

Messikommer, R., Balzer, S., and Wenk, C. (2005). Impact of oregano essential oil on production data and lipid oxidation parameters in broiler chickens. Proc. 15th Eur. Symp. on Poultry Nutrition, Balatonfured, Hungary, 298-303.

Mielche, M. M. and Bertelsen, G. (1994). Approaches to the prevention of warmed-over flavor. Trends in Food Sci. and Technol. 5: 322-327.

Mielnik, M.B. and Skrede, G. (2003). Antioxidative properties of grape seed extract in cooked turkey meat. Proc. XVI Eur. Symp. On the Quality of Poultry Meat, St. Brieuc, France, 298-303.

Miles, R.D., Ruiz, N., and Harms, R.H. (1987). Dietary conditions necessary for a methyl donor response in broilers and laying hens fed a corn-soybean meal diet. Poultry Sci., 66 (suppl. 1):29-30 (abstract).

Miller, E.L. and Huang, Y.X. (1993). Improving the nutritional value of broiler meat through increased n-3 fatty acid and vitamin E content. 11th Eur. Symp. on the Quality of Poultry Meat, Tours, 404-411.

Mireles, A. (1997). The impact of using 25-hydroxyvitamin D3 on performance and the immune system of broilers. Memoria Jornada Internacional Avicultura de Carne, Trouw Nutrition, Madrid, 30-38.

Mireles, A., Kim, S., Douglas, J., and Ghazikhanian, G.Y. (1999). Effect of 25-hydroxycholecalciferol (25-0H-D3), breed, and low nutrient starter feeds on heavy turkey tom performance, meat yield, tibial dyschondroplasia (TD), and incidence of leg problems. Poultry Sci., 78

Mireles, A., Kim, S., Krautmann, B., Yarger, J., and Stark, L. (1996). Effect of 25-hydroxycholecalciferol (25-0H-D) on broiler field performance and incidence of tibial dyschondroplasia (TD): minimum D3 metabolite consumption period. Poultry Sci., 75

Mireles, A., Klasing, K.C., and Kim, S. (1999). Evidence that dietary 25-hydroxycholecalciferol (25-0H-D3) supplementation affects commercial broiler performance by modification of their immune response. Poultry Sci., 78 (suppl. 1):50

Misir, R. and Blair, R. (1984) Bioavailable biotin from cereal grains for broiler chicks as affected by added dietary fiber. Poultry Sci. 63, Suppl.1: 152 (abstract).

Misir, R. and Blair, R. (1988). Biotin bioavailability of protein supplements and cereal grains for starting turkey poults. Poultry Sci. 67: 1274-1280.

Mitchell, R.D., Edwards, H.M. (1996). Effects of phytase and 1,25-dihydroxy-cholecalciferol on phytate utilization and the quantitative requirement for calcium and phosphorus in young broiler chickens. Poultry Sci., 75:95-110.

Mitchell, R.D., Edwards, H.M., and Mcdaniel, G.R. (1997a). The effects of ultraviolet light and cholecalciferol and its metabolites in the development of leg abnormalities in chickens genetically selected for a high and low incidence of tibial dyschondroplasia. Poultry Sci., 76:346-354.

Mitchell, R.D., Edwards, H.M., Mcdaniel, G.R., and Rowland, G.N. (1997b). Dietary 1,25-dihydroxy-cholecalciferol has variable effects on the incidence of leg abnormalities, plasma vitamin D metabolites, and vitamin D receptors in chickens divergently selected for tibial dyschondroplasia. Poultry Sci., 76:338-345.

Mohammed, A., Gibney, M.J., and Taylor, T.G. (1991). The effects of dietary levels of inorganic phosphorus, calcium and cholecalciferol on the digestibility of phytate-P by the chick. Brit. J. Nutr., 66:251-259.

Morrissey, P.A., Brandon, S., Buckley, D.J., Sheehy, P.J.A., and Frigg, M. (1997). Tissue content of α-tocopherol and oxidative stability of broiler receiving dietary α-tocopheryl acetate supplement for various periods pre-slaughter. Brit. Poultry Sci. 38: 84-88.

Morrissey, P.A., Sheehy, P.J.A., Galvin, K., Kerry, J.P., and Buckley, D.J. (1998). Lipid stability in meat and meat products. Meat Sci., 49, Suppl. 1:S73-S86.

Moslehi, H., Irani., M., and Shivazad, M. (2004). Investigation in the optimum level of vitamin premix in broiler performance. Proc. XXII World's Poultry Congress, Istanbul, CD-rom.

Muir, W.J., Husband, A.J., and Bryden. W.L. (2002). Dietary supplementation with vitamin E modulates avian intestinal immunity. Brit. J. Nutr., 87:579-595.

Murray, D.L., Brake, J., and Thaxton, J.P. (1987a). Effects of adrenocorticotropin and dietary ascorbic acid on cutaneous basophil hipersensitivity to phytohemagglutinin in chickens. Poultry Sci., 66:1846-1852.

Murray, D.L., Brake, J., Thaxton, J.P., and Gildersleeve, R.P. (1987b). Effects of adrenocorticotropin and dietary ascorbic acid on delayed hypersensitivity to human gamma globulin in chickens. Poultry Sci., 66:1859-1869.

Nagaraj, R.Y. and Wu, W. (1993). Toxicity of F. proliferatum and nutritional intervention in chickens. Poultry Sci., 74 (suppl. 1): 58. (abstract).

Nain, S., Laarveld, B., Wojnarowicz, C., and Olkowski, A.A. (2007). Excessive dietary vitamin D3 supplementation as a risk factor for sudden death syndrome in fast growing commercial broilers. Comp. Biochem. and Physiol., A1 48:828-833.

Nam, K.C, Min, B.R, Yan, H, Lee, E.J, Mendoça, A, Wesley, I., and Ahn, D.U. (2003). Effect of dietary vitamin E and irradiation on lipid oxidation, color, and volatiles of fresh and previously frozen turkey breast patties. Meat Sci., 65:523-521.

Nam, K.C. and Ahn, D.U. (2003). Use of double packaging and antioxidant combinations to improve color, lipid oxidation, and volatiles of irradiated raw and cooked turkey breast patties. Poultry Sci., 82: 850-857.

Nam. K.T., Lee, H.A., Min, B.S., and Kang, C.W. (1997). Influence of dietary supplementation with linseed and vitamin E on fatty acids, α-tocopherol and lipid peroxidation in muscles of broiler chicks. Anim. Feed Sci. Technol., 66:149-158

Naseem, S, Younus, M, Anwar, B, Ghafoor, A, Aslam, A., and Akhter, S. (2005). Effect of ascorbic acid and acetylsalicylic acid supplementation on performance of broiler chicks exposed to heat stress. Int. J. Poultry Sci., 4: 900-904.

Nassiri Moghaddam, H., Maghoul, M. A., Hahanian Najafabadi, R., Danesh Mesgaran, M., and Kermanshahi, H. (2007). The effect or different levels of choline and betaine on broiler performance and carcass characteristics. Proc. 16th Eur. Symp. on Poultry Nutrition, Strasbourg, 687-690.

National Research Council (1987). Vitamin tolerance of animals. National Academy Press, Washington D.C., 96 pp.

National Research Council (1994). Nutrient requirements of poultry. National Academy Press, Washington D.C., 155 pp.

Nixey, C. (2005). The role of nutrition in tibial dyschondroplasia occurrence in turkeys. Proc. 15th Eur. Symp. on Poultry Nutrition, Balatonfured, 166-178.

Njoku, P.C. (1984). The effect of ascorbic acid supplementation on broiler performance in a tropical environment. Poultry Sci. 63 (suppl. 1):156.

Njoku, P.C. (1986). Effect of dietary ascorbic acid (vitamin C) supplementation on the performance of broiler chickens in a tropical environment. Anim. Feed Sci. and Technol. 16: 17-24.

Noel, K. and Brinkhaus, F. (1998). Vitamin A retention of a high pigment broiler

227

growing feed treated with endox or ethoxyquin. Poultry Sci. 77 (suppl 1): 144 (abstract).

O´Neill, L.M., Galvin, K., Morrissey, P.A., and Buckley, D.J. (1998a). Comparison of effects of dietary olive oil, tallow and vitamin E on the quality of broiler meat and meat products. Brit. Poultry Sci. 39: 365-371.

O´Neill, L.M., Galvin, K., Morrissey, P.A., and Buckley, D.J. (1998b). Inhibition of lipid oxidation in chicken by carnosine and dietary α-tocopherol supplementation and its determination by derivative spectrophotometry. Meat Sci., 50:479-488.

O´Neill, L.M., Galvin, K., Morrissey, P.A., and Buckley, D.J. (1999). Effect of carnosine, salt and dietary vitamin E on the oxidative stability of chicken meat. Meat Sci. 52: 89-94.

Ogbuinya, P. (1991). Vitamin C increased broiler bodyweight. Poultry Int. March´91: 24.

Ogunmodede, B.K. (1977). Riboflavin requirement of starting chickens in a tropical environment. Poultry Sci., 56:231.

Okolelova, T.M, Grigorieva, E.N, Posviryakobao.A, Papzyan,T.T., and Nollet, L. (2006). The vitamin E improvement of broiler performance depends also on the form of Se administration. Proc. XII European Poultry Conference, Verona, Italy, CD-rom.

Okoye, J.O.A., Okwor, L.J.E., Ezema, W.S., Okosi, L.I., Chiwuba, A.R.S., Adeyeye, O.V., and Amadi, C.H. (2000). Effect of ascorbic acid supplementation on body weight gain, antibody response and resistance to infectious bursal disease. Proc. XXI World Poultry Conf., Montreal (CD-rom).

Olivo, R., Ida, E.I., Franco, F.O., Carneiro, A.L., and Shimokomaki, M. (1998). The effect od supplemented vitamin E on poultry PSE. Proc. 44th ICoMST, 644-645.

Olkowski, A.A. and Classen, H.L. (1996). The study of thiamine requirement in broiler chickens. Int. J. Vit. Nutr. Res. 66:332

Olkowski, A.A. and Classen, H.L. (1998). The study of riboflavin requirements in broiler chickens. Int. J. Vit. Nutr. Res., 68:316.

Olkowski, A.A. and Classen, H.L. (1999). The effect of maternal thiamine nutrition on thiamine status of the offspring in broiler chickens. Int. J. Vit. Nutr. Res., 66:32.

Oloyo, R.A. (1991). Responses of broilers fed guineacorn/palm kernel meal based ration to supplemental biotin. J. Sci. Food Agric., 55: 539-550.

Oloyo, R.A. (1994). Studies on the biotin requirement of broilers fed sunflower seed meal based diets. Arch. Anim. Nutr., 45: 345-353.

Orban, J.I., Roland, D.A., Cummings, K., and Lovell, R.T. (1993). Influence of large doses of ascorbic acid on performance, plasma calcium, bone characteristics, and eggshell quality in broilers and leghorn hens. Poultry Sci., 72: 691-700.

Owens, G.M. and Ledoux, D.R. (2000). Effects of 25-hydroxycholecalciferol and vitamin D on phosphorus utilization by turkey poults fed a typical corn-soybean meal diet. Poultry Sci. 79 (suppl. 1):113 (abstract).

Owens, G.M. and Ledoux, D.R. (2001). Effects of 25-hydroxyvitamin D3, vitamin D3, low phytic acid corn, and phytase on phosphorus utilization by turkey poults fed dietary treatments from hatch to six weeks of age. Poultry Sci., 80 (suppl. 1), abstract 1981.

Özkan, S., Basmacioğlu Malayoğlu, H., Yalcin, S., Karadas, F., Koçtürk, S., Çabuk, M., Oktay, G., Özdemir, S., and Ergül, M. (2007). Dietary vitamin E (α-tocopherol acetate) and selenium supplementation from different sources: performance, ascites-related variables and antioxidant status in broilers reared at low and optimun temperatures. Brit. Poultry Sci., 48 (5):580-593.

Pagazaurtundua, A., and Warriss, P.D. (2006). Levels of foot pad dermatitis in broiler chickens reared in 5 different systems. Brit. Poultry Sci., 47: 529-532.

Papesova, L. and Fucikova, A. (2000). Acute and long-term toxicity of coated vitamin D3. Proc. XXII World's Poultry Congress, Istanbul, CD rom.

Papesova, L., Fucikova, A., Pipalova, M., and Tupy, P. (2008). The synergic effect of vitamin D3 and 25-hydroxycholcalciferol in broiler fattening. Proc. XXIII World's Poultry Congress, Brisbane, CD-rom.

Pardue, S.L. (1989). Ascorbic acid: adrenal functions, stress and supplementation. In The role of vitamin C in poultry stress management. Animal health and nutrition. Hoffmann- La Roche Inc: 1-15.

Pardue, S.L. and Thaxton, J.P. (1982). Enhanced livability and improved immunological responsiveness in ascorbic acid supplemented cockerels during acute heat stress. Poultry Sci., 61 (suppl. 1):1522 (abstract).

Pardue, S.L. and Thaxton, J.P. (1984). Evidence for amelioration of steroid-mediated immunosuppression by ascorbic acid. Poultry Sci., 63:1262.

Pardue, S.L. and Thaxton, J.P. (1986). Ascorbic acid in poultry: a review. WPSJ. 42 (2): 107-123.

Pardue, S.L., Thaxton, P., and Brake, J. (1984). Plasma ascorbic acid concentration following ascorbic acid loading in chicks. Poultry Sci. 63: 2492-2496.

Pardue, S.L., Thaxton, P., and Brake, J. (1985). Influence of supplemental ascorbic acid on broiler performance following exposure to high environmental temperature. Poultry Sci. 64: 1334-1338.

Pardue, S.L., Uhf, W.E., Kubena, L.F., and Harvey, R.B. (1987). Influence of ascorbic acid on aflatoxicosis in broiler cockerels. Poultry Sci., 66 (suppl. 1):156 (abstract).

Parkinson, G.B. and Cransberg, P.H. (2004). Effect of casein phosphopeptide and 25-hydroxycholecalciferol on tibial dyschondroplasia in growing broiler chickens. Brit. Poultry Sci., 45:802-806.

Patel, K., Hardy, H, Edwards, M., and Baker D.H. (1997). Removal of vitamin and trace mineral supplements from broiler finisher diets. J. Appl. Poultry Res. 6: 191-198.

Pérez-Vendrell, A.M. and Weber, G.M. (2007). The effects of elevated dietary vitamins (OVN) combined with Hy D(25-hydroxycholecalciferol) on performance, health and processing yield of broilers. Proc. 16th Eur. Symp. on Poultry Nutrition, Strasbourg, France. 213-216.

Pérez-Vendrell, A.M., Hernández, J.M., Llauradó, L., and Brufau, J. (2003). Improving the nutritive value of broiler meat by feeding optimum vitamin nutrition (OVNTM). Proc. XVI Eur. Symp. on the Quality of Poultry Meat, Saint-Brieuc, France. 185-189.

Perry, R.W., Rowland, G.N., and Britton, W.M. (1991). Pathology of experimental vitamin D deficiency in turkeys and the effects of various vitamin D supplements. Avian Dis., 35:542-553.

Pesti, G.M. and Rowland, G.N. (1989). The influence of folic acid supplementation to corn and soybean meal based diets in broiler growth. Poultry Sci., 68 (suppl. 1):198.

Pesti, G.M., Rowland, G.N., and Ryu, K.S (1991). Folate deficiency in chicks fed diets containing practical ingredients. Poultry Sci., 70:600-604.

Pesut, O., Jovanivic, I., Noller, L., and Tucker, L. (2005). Effect of Se (Sel-Plex®) in combination with α-tocopherol on GSH- Px activity and TBARS in plasma of broilers. Proc. 15th Eur. Symp. on Poultry Nutrition, Balatonfured, Hungary, 502-504.

Petek, M, Sönmez, S, Yildiz, H., and Baspinar, H. (2005). Effects of different management factors on broilers performance and incidence of tibial dyschondroplasia. Brit. Poultry Sci.,46 (1): 16-21.

Philippe, L, Castaing, J., Larroudé, P., Hamelin, C., and Ball, A. (2005). Effect et supplémentation de Hy-D pour deux niveaux d'apports en vitamines sur les performances, le développment osseux et les troubles locomotives des dindons. VI Journées Recherches Avicoles, St. Malo.

Philips, P., Aureli, R., Fru, F. and Weber, G. (2008). Effects of 25-hydroxycholecalciferol and a peniphora lycii phytase on the growth performance and the apparent utilization of Ca and P in broiler chickens fed basal diets low in phosphorus and with different levels of vitamin D3. Proc. 16th Eur. Symp. on Poultry Nutrition, Strasbourg, 609-612.

Philips, P., Aureli, R., Weber, G., and Klünter, A.M. (2005). Effects of 25-hydroxycholecalciferol (Hy-D) at doses from 35 to 560 µg per kg feed on the performance of broiler chickens fed a diet based on maize, wheat and soybean meal. Proc. 15th Eur. Symp. on Poultry Nutrition, Balatonfured, 189-191.

Pierson, F.W. and Hester, P.Y. (1982). Factors influencing leg abnormalities in poultry: A review. WPSJ., 38(1):5-17.

Pikul, J., Holownia, K., and Plewinsky, A. (1997). Influence of dietary alpha-tocopheryl acetate on lipid oxidation in chicken meat. XIII Eur. Symp. of Poultry Meat Quality, Poznan , 223-229.

Pillai, P.B., Fanatico, A. C., Blair, M.E., and Emmert, J. L.(2006b). Homocysteine remethylation in broilers fed surfeit choline or betaine and varying levels and sources of methionine from eight to twenty-two days of age. Poultry Sci. 85:1729–1736.

Pillai, P.B., Fanatico, A.C., Beers, K.W., Blair, M.E., and Emmert, J.L. (2006a)

Homocysteine remethylation in young broilers fed varying levels of methionine, choline, and betaine. Poultry Sci. 85:90–95.

Pines, M., Hasdai, A.M., and Monsonego-Ornan, E. (2005). Tibial dyschondroplasia – tools, new insights and future prospects. WPSJ., 61: 285-297.

Porstmouth, J. (1996). Requerimientos vitamínicos de los broilers y las reproductoras pesadas. Proc. XXXIII Symp. WPSA's Spanish Branch, Toledo, 115-137.

Praslickova, D., Sharif, S., Sarson, A., Abdul-Careem, M.F., Zadworny, D., Kulenkamp. A., Ansah, G., and Kuhnlein, U. (2008). Association of a marker in the vitamin D receptor gene with Marek's disease resistance in poultry. Poultry Sci., 87:1112-111.

Puchal, F. (1989). Broiler nutrition and heat stress. Proc. 7th Eur. Symp. on Poultry Nutrition, Lloret de Mar, Spain, 65-81.

Puron, D., Santamaria, R., and Segura, J.C. (1994). Effects of sodium bicarbonate, acetylsalicylic, and ascorbic acid on broiler performance in a tropical environment. J. Appl. Poultry Res. , 3 (2): 141-145.

Putnam, M. (1983). Composición de los alimentos y estabilidad vitamínica. Reunión de la Sociedad de Técnicos en Alimentación, York, Inglaterra. Reimpresión Roche Information Service, Animal Nutrition Dept., 14 pp.

Putnam, M. and Taylor, A. (1997). Vitaminas en alimentos animales: Los factores críticos. Avicultura Profesional, 15 (5/6) pp. 24-28.

Quarles, C.L. and Adrian, W,J. (1989). Evaluation of ascorbic acid for increasing carcass yield in broiler chickens. InThe role of vitamin C in poultry stress management. Animal health and nutrition. Hoffmann- La Roche Inc: 16-36.

Quian, H., Kornegay, E.T., and Denbow, D.M. (1997). Utilization of phytate phosphorus and calcium as influenced by microbial phytase, cholecalciferol, and the calcium:total phosphorus ratio in broiler diets. Poultry Sci., 76:37-46.

Quillin, E.C., Combs, G.F., Creek, R.D., and Romoser, G.L. (1961). Effect of choline on the methionine requirements of broiler chickens. Poultry Sci. 40 (3): 639-645.

Qureshi, M.A., Ferket, P.R., and Garlich, J.D. (1993). Effect of dietary supplementation of vitamin E on the immune function of turkey poults. Poultry Sci., 72 (suppl. 1): 89 (abstract).

Qureshi, M.A., Vanhooser, S.L., and Teeter, R.G. (2000). Dietary vitamin E, vitamin C and drinking water electrolyte effects on broiler performance and immunity during exposure to high cycling ambient temperature. Poultry Sci., 79 (suppl. 1): 89 (abstract).

Rajmane, B.V. and Ranade, A.S. (1992). Remedial measures to control high mortality during summer season in tropical countries. Proc. XIX World's Poultry Congress, Amsterdam, 1, 343-345.

Rama Rao, S.V., Raju, M.V.L.N., Panda, A.K., and Reddy, M.R. (2007). Vitamin supplementation could lower feed costs, reduce environmental risks. Feed Int., May/June 2007, 8-11.

Rama Rao, S.V., Raju, M.V.L.N., Panda, A.K., Shaharai, P.N., Reddy, M.R., Sunder, G.S., and Sharma, R.P. (2008). Effect of surfeit concentrations of vitamin D3 on performance, bone mineralization, and mineral retention in commercial broiler chicks. J. Poultry Sci., 45: 25-30.

Rama Rao, S.V., Raju, M.V.L.N., Panda, A.K., Sunder, G.S., and Sharma, R.P. (2006). Effect of high concentration of cholecalciferol on growth, bone mineralization, and mineral retention in broiler chicks fed suboptimal concentrations of calcium and non-phytate phosphorus. J. Appl. Poultry Res., 15: 493-501.

Rama Rao, S.V., Raju, M.V.L.N., Sharma, R.P., Nagalakshmi, D., and Reddy, M.R. (2003). Lameness in chickens: alleviation by dietary manipulation. Poultry Int., Sept.2003, 53-61.

Rath, N. C., Huff, G.R., and Huff, W.E. (2006). Thiram-induced tibial dyschondroplasia: a model to study its pathogenesis and prevention. Proc. XII Eur. Poultry Conf., Verona, CD rom.

Rath, N. C., Huff, G.R., Huff, W. E., and Balog, J.M.(2000). Factors regulating bone maturity and strength in poultry. Poultry Sci.,79:1024-1032.

Rath, N.C., Huff, G.R., Huff, W.E., and Balog, J.M. (2000). Factors regulating bone maturity and strength. Poultry Sci., 79:1024-1032.

Rebel, J.M.J., Van Dam, J.T.P., Zekarias, B., Balk, F.R.M., Post, J., Flores Miñambres,

A., and Ter Huurne, A.A.H.M. (2004). Vitamin and trace mineral content in feed of breeders and their progeny: Effects on growth, feed conversion and severity of malabsorption syndrome of broilers. Brit. Poultry Sci., 45:201-209.

Rebole, A., Rodriguez, M.L., Ortiz, L.T., Alzueta, C., Centeno, C., Viveros., A, Brenes, A., and Arija, I. (2006). Effect of dietary high-oleic acid sunflower seed, palm oil and vitamin E supplementation on broiler performance, fatty acid composition and oxidation susceptibility of meat. Brit. Poultry Sci., 47 (5):581-591.

Rennie, J. S. (1994). Vitamin D metabolites and the prevention of tibial dyschondroplasia. Proc. 9th Eur. Poultry Conf., Glasgow, 207-210.

Rennie, J.S. (1995). Vitamin D, ascorbic acid and tibial dyschondroplasia. Poultry Int., April 1995: 50-52.

Rennie, J.S. and Whitehead, C.C. (1996a). Dietary 25-hydroxycholecalciferol and tibial dyschondroplasia. Brit. Poultry Sci., 37:S74-S76.

Rennie, J.S. and Whitehead, C.C. (1996b). Effectiveness of dietary 25- and 1-hydroxycholecalciferol in combating tibial dyschondroplasia in broiler chickens. Brit. Poultry Sci., 37:213-221.

Rennie, J.S., Mccormack, H.A., Farquhatson, C., Berry, J.L., Mawer E.B., and Whitehead, C.C. (1995). Interaction between dietary 1,25-dihydroxycholecalciferol and calcium and effects of management on the occurrence of tibial dyschondroplasia, leg abnormalities and performance in broiler chickens. Brit. Poultry Sci., 36:465-477.

Rennie, J.S., Whitehead, C.C., and Thorp, B.H. (1993). The effect of dietary 1,25-dihydroxy-cholecalciferol in preventing tibial dyschondroplasia in broilers fed on diets imbalanced in calcium and phosphorus. Brit. J. Nutr., 69:809-816.

Rennie, S. (1995). Vitamin D, ascorbic acid and tibial dyschondroplasia. Poultry Int., April '95: 50-52.

Rhee, K.S., Anderson, L.M., and Sams, A.R. (1996). Lipid oxidation potential of beef, chicken, and pork. J. Food Sci., 61(1):8-12.

Riddell, C. (2000). Management of skeletal disease. Proc. XXI World's Poultry Congress, Montreal, CD rom.

Ristic, M. and Lidner, H. (1992). Influence of vitamin E supplementation on the meat quality and storage capability of broilers. XIX World's Poultry Congress, Amsterdam, p. 146.

Robel, E.J. (1983). The effect of age of breeder hen on the levels of vitamins and minerals in turkey eggs. Poultry Sci., 62:1751-1756.

Roberson, K.D. (1999). 25-hydroxycholecalciferol fails to prevent tibial dyschondroplasia in broiler chicks raised in battery brooders. 1999 J. Appl. Poultry Res., 8:54-61.

Roberson, K.D. and Edwards, H.M. (1994). Effects of ascorbic acid and 1,25-dihydroxycalciferol on alkaline phosphatase and tibial dyschondroplasia in broiler chickens. Brit. Poultry Sci., 35:763-773.

Roberson, K.D. and Edwards, H.M. (1996). Effect of dietary 1,25-dihydroxycholecalciferol level on broiler performance. Poultry Sci., 75:90-94.

Roberson, K.D., Ledwaba, M.F., and Charbeneau, R.A. (2005). Studies on the efficacy of twenty-five-hydroxycholecalciferol to prevent tibial dyschondroplasia in Ross broilers fed marginal calcium diet. Int. J. Poultry Sci., 4 (2) 85-90.

Roch, G., Boulianne, M., and De Roth, L. (2000a). Dietary antioxidants reduce ascites in broilers. World Poultry, 16 (11): 18-22.

Roch, G., Boulianne, M., and De Roth, L. (2000b). Effects of dietary vitamin E and selenium on incidence of ascites, growth performances and blood parameters in cold stressed broilers. Poultry Sci. 79 (suppl. 1):41 (abstract).

Rombout, J.H.W.M., Van Rens, B.T.T.M., Sijtsma, S.R., Van Der Weide, M.C., and West, C.E. (1992). Effects of vitamin A deficiency and Newcastle disease virus infection on lymphocyte subpopulations in chicken blood. Vet. Immunol. and Immunopathol., 31: 155-166.

Rose, S.P. and Peter, J.S. (2000). Dietary ascorbic acid and tocopherol acetate supplements for broiler chickens kept at high temperatures. Proc. XXI World's Poultry Congress, Montreal, CD-rom.

Roussan, D.A, Khwaldeh, G.Y, Haddad, R.R., Shaheen, I.A, Salameh, G., and Al Rifai, R. (2008). Effect of ascorbic acid, acetylsalicylic acid, sodium bicarbonate, and potassium chloride supplementation in water on the performance of broiler chickens exposed to heat stress. J. Appl.

Poult. Res., 17.141-144.

Ruiz, J.A., Guerrero, L., Arnau, J., Guardia, M.D., and Esteve-Garcia, E. (2001). Descriptive sensory analisis of meat from broilers fed diets containing vitamin E or ß-carotene as antioxidants and different supplemental fats. Poultry Sci., 80:976-982.

Ruiz, J.A., Perez-Vendrell, A.M., and Esteve-Garcia, E. (1998). Antioxidant properties of ß-carotene in poultry meat as affected by its concentration in feed during storage. Proc. 44 ICoMST:642-643.

Ruiz, J.A., Pérez-Vendrell, A.M., and Esteve-Garcia, E. (1999). Effect of beta-carotene and vitamin E on oxidative stability in leg meat of broilers fed different supplemental fats. J. Agric. Food Chem., 47:448-454.

Ruiz, N, Harms, R.H., and Linda, S.B. (1990). Niacin requirement of broilers fed a corn-soybean meal diet from 1 to 21 days of age. Poultry Sci., 69: 433-439.

Ruiz, N. and Harms, R.H. (1987). The niacin requirement of broiler chickens fed a corn-soybean meal diet from three to seven weeks of age. Poultry Sci., 66 (suppl.1):37 (abstract)

Ruiz, N. and Harms, R.H. (1988a). Niacin requirement of turkey poults fed a corn-soybean meal diet from 1 to 21 days of age. Poultry Sci., 67:760-765.

Ruiz, N. and Harms, R.H. (1988b). Riboflavin requirement of turkeys from 4 to 11 weeks of age. Poultry Sci. 67 (suppl. 1): 32 (abstract).

Ruiz, N. and Harms, R.H. (1988c). Determination of tryptophan to niacin conversion ratio in turkey poults. Poultry Sci., 67 (suppl.1):148 (abstract) .

Ruiz, N. and Harms, R.H. (1988d). Riboflavin requirement of broiler chicks fed a corn-soybean meal diet. Poultry Sci. 67: 794-799.

Ruiz, N. and Harms, R.H. (1988e). Comparison of the biopotencies of nicotinic acid and nicotinamide for broiler chicks. Brit. Poultry Sci., 29:491-498.

Ruiz, N.and Harms, R.H. (1989). Riboflavin requirement of turkey poults fed a corn-soybean meal diet from 1 to 21 days of age. Poultry Sci. 68: 715-718.

Ruksomboonde, A. and Sullivan, T.W. (1985). Vitamins A, D3, and K interactions in broiler chicks and turkey poults. Poultry Sci. 64 (suppl 1):175 (abstract).

Rutz, F., Cantor, A.H., Pescatore, A.J.,

Johnsson, T.H., and Pfaff, W.K. (1989). Effect of dietary riboflavin and selenium on metabolism and performance of young broiler chicks. Poultry Sci. 68 (suppl.1): 202 (abstract)

Ryu, K.S and Pesti, G.M (1993). Effects of supplemental folic acid on the performance of starting broiler chicks. . Poultry Sci., 72 (suppl.1):118 (abstract)

Ryu, K.S, Pesti, G.M., and Edwards, H.M. (1994). Folic acid and methionine requirements of broiler chicks. Poultry Sci., 73 (suppl.1):73 (abstract).

Ryu, K.S., Roberson, K. D., Pesti, G. M., and Eitenmiller, R.R. (1995). The folic acid requirements of starting broiler chicks fed diets based on practical ingredients. Interrelationships with dietary choline. Poultry Sci. 74: 1447-1455,

Ryu, Y.C., Rhee, M.S, Lee, K.M., and Kim, B.C. (2005). Effects of different levels of dietary supplemental selenium on performance, lipid oxidation, and color stability of broiler chicks. Poultry Sci., 84:809-815.

Sahin, K, Sahin, N., and Kucuk, O. (2003). Effects of chromium, and ascorbic acid supplementation on growth, carcass traits, serum metabolites, and antioxidant status of broiler chickens reared at a high ambient temperature (32°C). Nutr. Res., 23:225-238.

Sahin, K., Sahin, N., Onderci, M., Gursu, F., and Cikim, G. (2002). Optimal dietary concentrations of chromium for alleviating the effect of heat stress on growth, carcass qualities, and some serum metabolites of broiler chickens. Biol. Trace Elem. Res., 89:53-64.

Sahin, K., Sahin, N., Sari, M., And.Gursu, M.F. (2002). Effects of vitamins E and A supplementation on lipid peroxidation and concentration of some mineral in broilers reared under heat stress (32°C). Nutr. Res., 22:723–731.

Sallmann, H.P., Furhrmann, H., and Götzke, S. (1998). The effect of the vitamins A and E and dietary fat on the oxidative stability of turkey muscle in vivo. J. Anim. Physiol. and Anim. Nutr., 80:226-231.

Sanders, A.M. and Edwards, H.M. (1991). The effects of 1,25-dihydroxycholecalciferol on the performance and development in the turkey poult. Poultry Sci., 70:853-866.

Santé, V. and Lacourt, A. (1994). The effect of dietary α-tocopherol supplementation and antioxidant spraying on color stability and lipid oxidation of turkey meat. J. Sci. Food Agric. 65: 503-507.

Santé, V., Renerre, M., and Lacourt, A. (1992). Effect of dietary vitamin E supplementation on color stability and lipid oxidation in turkey meat. Proc. 38th ICoMST,591-594.

Santos, Y. and Soto-Salanova, M.F. (2005). Effect of Hy-D addition on performance and slaughter results of broilers. Proc. 15th Eur. Symp. on Poultry Nutrition, Balatonfured, 219-221.

Sárraga, C. and Garcia Regueiro, J.A. (1999). Membrane lipid oxidation an proteolytic activity in thigh muscles from broilers fed different diets. Meat Sci. 52: 213-219.

Sárraga, C., Carreras, I., Garcia Regueiro, J.A., and Castellari, M. (2006). The combined effects of α-tocopheryl acetate supplementation and enrofloxacin administration on oxidative stability of turkey meat. Brit. Poultry Sci., 47 (6):708-713.

Sárraga, C., Guàrdia, M.D., Díaz, I, Guerrero, L., and Arnau, J. (2008). Nutritional and sensory qualites of raw meat and cooked brine-injected turkey breast as affected by dietary enrichment with docosahexaenoic acid (DHA) and vitamin E. J. Sci. Food and Agricult., 88:1448-1454.

Satterlee, D.G , Ryder, F.H., and Godber, J.S. (1991). Effect of ascorbic acid on plasma aldosterone and electrolyte levels in broiler chickens being prepared for slaughter. Poultry Sci., 70 (suppl. 1):181 (abstract)

Satterlee, D.G, Aguilera-Quintana, I., and Munn, B.J. (1989). Vitamin C reduces stress responses associated with pre-slaughter management practices in broiler chickens. In The role of vitamin C in poultry stress management. Animal health and nutrition. Hoffmann- La Roche Inc: 16-36.

Saunders-Blades and Korver, D.R. (2006). Hy-D and poultry: bones and beyond. Proc. DSM meeting, XII Eur. Poultry Conf., Verona, 1-11.

Saunders-Blades and Korver, D.R. (2008). Effect of maternal and dietary 25-OH on broiler production and immunity. Proc. XXIII World's Poultry Congress, Brisbane, CD-rom.

Sauveur, B. (1984). Dietary factors as causes of leg abnormalities in poultry: a review. WPSJ., 40:195-206.

Sauveur, B. (1988). Lésions osseuses et articulaires des pattes des volailles: roles de l´alimentation. INRA Prod. Anim., 1 (1): 35-45.

Saxena, H. C. (1996). Need for reappraisal: Practical aspects of calcium, phosphorus and vitamin D3 nutrition for broilers World Poultry 12 (10):52.

Schwean, K. and Classen, H.L. (1995). The effects of high dietary pyridoxine on broiler productivity and tonic immobility. Poultry Sci., 74 (suppl. 1):94 (abstract).

Scott, M.L., Young, R.J., and Nesheim, M.C. (1982). Alimentación de las aves. Ed. GEA, 1984.

Seeman, V. and Hazija, H. (1985). Effects of nutrition on the strength of acquired immunity against Newcastle disease. Veterinarski Archiv, 55(1):1.

Seemann, M. (1991). Is Vitamin C essential in poultry nutrition? World Poultry: 17.

Sell, J.L. (1996). Recent developments in vitamin E nutrition of turkeys. Anim. Feed Sci. Technol. 60: 229-240.

Sell, J.L., Soto-Salanova, M., Jeffrey, M, Ahn, D., and Palo, P.E., (1995). Further evaluation of the dietary vitamin E requirement of growing turkeys. Poultry Sci. 74 (suppl. 1):149 (abstract).

Sell, J.L., Soto-Salanova, M., Palo, P.E., and Jeffrey, M. (1997a). Influence of supplementing corn-soybean meal diets with vitamin E on performance and selected physiological traits of male turkeys. Poultry Sci. 76:1405-1417.

Sell, J.L., Trampel, D.W., and Griffith, R.W. (1997b). Adverse effects of Escherichia coli infection of turkeys were not alleviated by supplemental dietary vitamin E. Poultry Sci. 76: 1682-1687.

Seokand, B.S. and Singh, R.A. (1996) Effect of ascorbic acid supplementation during summer and winter months on performance of broilers. Proc. XX World´s Poultry Congress, Delhi, p. 258.

Shafey, T.M., Mcdonald, M.W., and Pym, R.A.E. (1990). Effects of dietary calcium, available phosphorus and vitamin D on growth rate, food utilization, plasma and bone constituents and calcium and phosphorus retention of commercial broiler strains. Brit. Poultry Sci., 31:587-602.

She, R.P., Xia, Z.F., Zhang, J.L., Meng, Y., Ma, X., and Liu, F. (1997). Toxic effects of excessive vitamin A and K on the immune system of chickens. Poultry Sci. 76 (suppl 1):78 (abstract).

Sheehy, P.J.A., Morrissey, P.A., and Buckley, D.J. (1995). Advances in research and application of vitamin E as an antioxidant for poultry meat. Proc. XII Eur. Symp. on the Quality of Poultry Meat, Zaragoza, 425-436.

Sheehy, P.J.A., Morrissey, P.A., and Buckley, D.J. (1997). Influence of vegetable oils and alpha-tocopheryl acetate supplementation in lipid peroxidation in chick muscle. Proc. 47th ICoMST,1285-1289.

Sheehy, P.J.A., Morrissey, P.A., and Flynn, A. (1991). Influence of dietary α-tocopherol on tocopherol concentrations in chick tissues. Brit. Poultry Sci. 32: 391-397.

Sheehy, P.J.A., Morrissey, P.A., and Flynn, A. (1993). Influence of heated vegetable oils and α-tocopheryl acetate supplementation on α-tocopherol, fatty acids and lipid peroxidation in chicken muscle. Brit. Poultry Sci. 34: 367-381.

Sheehy, P.J.A.; Morrissey, P.A., and Buckley, D.J. (1995). Advances in research and application of vitamin E. Proc. XII Eur. Symp. on the Quality of Poultry Meat, Zaragoza, Spain, 425-436.

Sheldon, B.W. (1984). Effect of dietary tocopherol on the oxidative stability of turkey meat. Poultry Sci. 63: 673-681.

Sheldon, B.W., Curtis, P.A., Dawson, P.L., and Ferket, P.R. (1997). Effect of dietary vitamin E on the oxidative stability, flavor, color, and volatile profiles of refrigerated and frozen turkey breast meat. Poultry Sci. 76: 634-641.

Shim, M.Y., Pesti, G.M., Bakalli, R.I., and Edwards, H.M. (2008). The effect of breeder age and egg storage time on phosphorus utilization by broiler progeny fed a phosphorus deficiency diet with 1α-OH vitamin D3. Poultry Sci., 87:1138-1145.

Shirley, R.B., Davis, A.J., Compton. M.M., and Berry, W.D. (2003). The expression of calbindin in chicks that are divergently selected for high or low incidence of tibial dyschondroplasia. Poultry Sci., 82:1965-1973.

Siegel, P.B., Blair, M., Gross, W.B., Meldrum, B., Larsen, S.C., Boa-Amponsem, K., and Emmerson, D.A. (2006). Poult performance as influenced by age of dam, genetic line, and dietary vitamin E. Poultry Sci., 85:939-942.

Siegel, P.B., Larsen, S.T., Emmerson, D.A., Geraert, P.A., and Picard, M. (2000). Feeding regimen, dietary vitamin E and genotype influences on immunological and production traits of broilers. J. Appl. Poultry Res., 9:269-278.

Sijtsma, S.R., Rombout, J.H.W.M., Dohmen, M.J.W, West, C.E., and Van Der Zijpp, A.J. (1991). Effect of vitamin A deficiency on the activity of macrophages in Newcastle diseased virus-infected chickens. Vet. Immunol. and Immunopathol., 27:17-27.

Sijtsma, S.R., Rombout, J.H.W.M., West, C.E., and Van Der Zijpp, A.J. (1990). Vitamin A deficiency impairs cytotoxic T lymphocyte activity in Newcastle disease virus-infected chickens. Vet. Immunol. and Immunopathol., 26: 191-201.

Simon, J. (1999). Choline, betaine and methionine interactions in chickens, pigs and fish (including crustaceans) WPSJ., 55:353-374.

Singh, H., Sodhi, S., and Kaur, R. (2006). Effects of dietary supplements of selenium, vitamin E or combinations of the two on antibody responses of broilers. Brit. Poultry Sci., 47 (6):714-719.

Skinner, J.T, Waldroup, A.L., and Waldroup, P.W. (1992). Effects of removal of vitamin and trace mineral supplements from grower and finisher diets on live performance and carcass composition of broilers. J. Appl. Poultry Res. 1:280-286.

Sklan, D., Bartov, I., and Hurwitz, S. (1982). Tocopherol absorption and metabolism in the chick and the turkey. J. Nutr., 112:1394-1400.

Sklan, D., Melamed, D., and Friedman, A. (1994). The effect of varying levels of dietary vitamin A on immune response in the chick. Poultry Sci., 73: 843-847.

Sklan, D., Melamed, D., and Friedman, A. (1995). The effect of varying dietary concentrations of vitamin A on immune response in the turkey. Brit. Poultry Sci., 36: 385-392.

Skrivan, M., Marounek, M., Dlohuá, G., and Sevcíkova, S. (2008). Dietary selenium increases vitamin E content of egg yolk and chicken meat. Brit. Poultry Sci., 49:482-486.

Smet, K., Raes, K., Huyghebaert, G., and Haak, L. (2005). Influence of feed enriched with natural antioxidants and the oxidative stability of broiler meat. Proc. XVII Eur. Symp. On the Quality of Poultry Meat, Doorwerth, The Netherlands, 99-106.

Snow, J.L., Baker, D.H., and Parsons, C.M. (2004). Phytase, citric acid and

1-α-hydroxycholecalciferol improve phytate phosphorus utilization in chicks fed a corn-soybean meal diet. Poultry Sci., 83:1187-1192.

Soares, J.H. and Lofton, J.T. (1986). Recent studies on vitamin D and skeletal problems in broilers. Proc. Maryland Nutr. Conf., 1-6.

Soares, J.H., Kerr, J.M., and Gray, R.W. (1995). 25-hydroxycholecalciferol in poultry nutrition. Poultry Sci., 74:1919-1934.

Soto-Salanova, M.F. and Sell, J.L. (1995). Influence of supplemental dietary fat on changes in vitamin E concentration in livers of poults. Poultry Sci., 74:201-205.

Soto-Salanova, M.F. and Sell, J.L. (1996). Efficacy of dietary and injected vitamin E for poults. Poultry Sci., 75:1393-1403.

Soto-Salanova, M.F., Sell, J. L., Mallarino, E.G., Piquer, J., Barker, D., Palo, P., and Ewan, R.C. (1991). Unalleviated depletion of vitamin E in poults. Poultry Sci., 70 (suppl. 1):116 (abstract).

Sowinska, J., Filus, K., Wójcil, A., and Gierczynski, S. (1997). Quality of turkey meat from birds that were treated with vitamin E and selenium before preslaughter handling. XIII Eur. Symp. of Meat Quality, Poznan, Poland, 120-123.

Squires, M.W. and Naber, E.C. (1993). Vitamin profiles of eggs as indicators of nutritional status in the laying hen: Riboflavin study. Poultry Sci., 72:483-494.

Stanley, V.G., Chukwu, H., Thompson, D., Jones, G., and Gray, C. (1997). Singly and combined effects of organic selenium (Se-yeast) and vitamin E on ascites reduction in broilers. Poultry Sci. 76 (suppl. 1):28

Stilborn, H.L., Harris, G.C., Botje, W.G., and Waldroup, P.W. (1988). Ascorbic acid and acetylsalicylic acid (aspirin) in the diet of broilers maintained under heat stress conditions. Poultry Sci., 67:1183-1187.

Sullivan, T.W., Heil, H.M. and Armintrout, M.E. (1967). Dietary thiamine and pyridoxine requirements of young turkeys. Poultry Sci., 46:1560-64.

Summers, J.D., Shen, H., Leeson, S., and Julian, R.J. (1984). Influence of vitamin deficiency and level of dietary protein on the incidence of leg problems in broiler chickens. Poultry Sci., 63:115-1121.

Sundeen, G., Richards, J.F., and Bragg, D.B. (1980). The effect of vitamin A deficiency on some postmortem parameters in avian muscle. Poultry Sci., 59: 2225-2236.

Surai, P.F. (2000). Effect of selenium and vitamin E content of the maternal diet on the antioxidant system of the yolk and the developing chick. Brit. Poultry Sci., 41:235-243.

Surai, P.F. (2003). Natural antioxidants in avian nutrition and reproduction. Nottingham University Press.

Surai, P.F. and Sparks, N.H.C. (2001). Tissue specific fatty acid and α-tocopherol profiles in male chickens depending on dietary tuna oil and vitamin E provision. Poultry Sci., 79:1132-1142.

Surai, P.F., Gaal, T., Noble, R.C., and Speake, B.K. (1997). The relationship between the α-tocopherol content of the yolk and its accumulation in the tissues of the newly hatched chick. J. Sci. Food Agric., 75:212-216.

Surai, P.F., Ionov, I.A., Kuchmistova, E.F., Noble, R.C., and Speake, B.K. (1998). SAKHATSY, N.I., and KUKLENKO, T.V. (1998). The relationship between the levels of α-tocopherol and carotenoids in the maternal feed, yolk, and neonatal tissues: Comparisons between the chicken, turkey, duck, and goose. J. Sci. Food Agric., 76:593-598.

Surai, P.F., Ionov, I.A., Sakhatsy, N.I., and Kuklenko, T.V. (1993). Vitamins A and E content in poultry meat and its quality. 11th Eur. Symp. on the Quality of Poultry Meat, Tours, 455-460.

Surai, P.F., Noble, R.C., and Speake, B.K. (1999). Relationship between vitamin E content and susceptibility to lipid peroxidation in tissues of the newly hatched chick. Brit. Poultry Sci. 40: 406-410.

Svendsen, O.L. and Weber, G.M. (2001). Optimum vitamin nutrition (OVN) for poultry. Hoffmann- La Roche Ltd.

Sweeney, G., Morrissey, P.A., and Buckley, D.J. (1992). Effect of dietary α-tocopheryl acetate supplementation on α-tocopherol levels in broiler tissues and on lipid oxidation. XIX World's Poultry Congress, Amsterdam, 582-585.

Swierczewska, E., J,. Skomial, T., Smolinska, J., and Kopowski. (2005). The quality of meat of broiler chickens fed with doubled amount of vitamins B group and fat-mineral preparation. Proc. XVII Eur.Symp. on the Quality of Poultry Meat, Doorwerth, 185-189.

Tang, K-N, Rowland, G.N., and Veltmann, J.R. (1984). Vitamin A toxicity: comparative

235

changes in bone of the broiler and leghorn chicks. Avian Dis., 29 (2):416-428.

Tang, S.Z., Kerry, J.P., Sheehan, D., Buckley, D.J., and Morrissey, P.A. (2001). Antioxidative effect of dietary tea catechins on lipid oxidation of long-term frozen stored chicken meat. Meat Sci., 57:331-336.

Taranu, I.(1999) Optimizing vitamin supplementation in broilers. Poultry Int., Sept.´99: 104-105.

Taranu, I., Criste, R.D., Burlacu, R., Olteanu, M., and Burlacu, G. (1995). Influence of vitamin and mineral nutrition and of low ambiental temperature on broiler performance and quality of body composition. Proc. XII Eur. Symp. on Poultry Meat Quality, Zaragoza, 83-90.

Teeter, R.G. and Belay, .T (1996). Broiler management during acute heat stress. Anim. Feed Sci. Technol., 58: 127-142.

Teeter, R.G. and García, R. (1993). Optimización de la producción durante el stress por calor. Selecciones avícolas, abril 1993: 230-240.

Tengerdy, R.P. and Brown, J. (1977). Effect of vitamin E and A on hummoral immunity and phagocytosis on E. coli affected chickens. Poultry Sci., 56:957-963.

Tengerdy, R.P. and Nockels, C. (1975). Vitamin E or Vitamin A protects chickens against E. coli infection. Poultry Sci., 54:1292-1296.

Thomas, R.A., Izat, A.L., and Waldroup, P.W. (1988). Effects of high levels of vitamin E on finisher diets on quality of broiler meat. Poultry Sci. (suppl. 1) (abstract).

Thorp, B.H., (1994). Skeletal disorders in the fowl: A review. Avian Pathol., 23:203-236.

Thorp, B.H., Ducro, B., Whitehead, C.C., Farquharson, C., and Sorensen, P. (1993). Avian tibial dyschondroplasia: the interaction of genetic selection and dietary 1,25-dihydroxycholecalciferol. Avian Pathol., 22:311-324.

Thorp, P. (1994). Skeletal disorders in the fowl: A review. Avian Pathol., 23:203-236.

Tillman, B. and Pesti, G.M. (1985). Response from male broilers to L-methionine and choline supplementation in a corn-soybean meal diet. Poultry Sci., 64 (suppl. 1):44 (abstract).

Troescher, A.H.A. and Coelho, M.B. (1996). Vitamins levels in the US feeds and effect of graded vitamin levels on stress challenged broiler. XX World´s Poultry Congress, Delhi, 130.

Tsiagbe, V.K., Cook, M.E., Harper, A.E., and Sunde, M.L. (1987). Enhanced immune responses in broiler chicks fed methionine-supplemented diets. Poultry Sci., 66:1147-1154.

Tudor, D. and Bunaciu, P. (2001). Can vitamin C help fight aflatoxicosis. Poultry Int. April 2001:10-14.

Uni, Z., Zaiger, G., and Reifen, R. (1998). Vitamin A deficiency induces morphometric changes and decreased functionality in chicken small intestine. Brit. J. Nutr., 80:401-407.

Vaiano, S.A., Azuolas, J.K., and Parkinson, G.B. (1994). Serum total calcium, phosphorus, 1,25-dihydroxycholecalciferol, and endochondral ossification defects in commercial broiler chickens. Poultry Sci., 73:1296-1305.

Valaja, J., Pertilla, S., Tupasela, T., and Helander, E. (2001). Effect of high-oil oats and vitamin E supplementation on broiler production. 13th Eur. Symp. of Poultry Nutrition, Blankenberge, Belgium,: 33-34.

Van Dyck, S.M.O. and Adams, C.A. (2003). Dietary antioxidants-antiradical active nutricines. Int. Poultry Prod., 11 (6):15-19.

Van Niekerk, T., Garber, T.K., Dunnington, E.A., Gross, W.B., and Siegel, P.B. (1989). Response of White Leghorn chicks fed ascorbic acid and challenged with Escherichia coli or corticosterone. Poultry Sci., 68: 1631-1636.

Vara-Ubol, S. and Bowers, J.A. (2001). Effect of α-tocopherol, β-carotene, and sodium tipolyphosphate on lipid oxidation of refrigerated cooked ground turkey and ground pork. J. Food Sci., 66 (5): 662-667.

Veltmann, J.R. and Jensen, L.S. (1983). Vitamin A toxicosis in turkey poults: detrimental effects induced by excess vitamin A ameliorated by extra dietary vitamin D3. Poultry Sci., 62: 1518.

Veltmann, J.R., Jensen, L.S., and Rowland, G.N (1986). Excess dietary vitamin A in the growing chick: effects of fat source and vitamin D. Poultry Sci., 65:153-163.

Viau, M., Métro, B., Genot, C., Rémignon, E., and Gandemer, G. (1998). Vitamin E status of muscle as related to vitamin E supply and dietary fat in the turkey. Proc. 44th ICoMST, 640-641.

Villamide, M.J. and Fraga, M.J. (1999). Composition of vitamin supplements in Spanish poultry diets. Brit. Poultry Sci. 40: 644-652.

Villar-Patino, G., Díaz-Cruz, A., Ávila-González, E., Guinzberg, R., Pablos, J.L., and Pina, E. (2002). Effects of dietary supplementation with vitamin C or vitamin E on cardiac lipid peroxidation and growth performance in broilers at risk of developing ascites syndrome. Am. J. Vet. Res., 63(5):673-676.

Villaverde, C., Baucells, M.D., Bou, R., and Barroeta, A.C. (2004a). Use of oxidized sunflower oil: Effect on vitamin E deposition in different tissues in poultry. Proc. XXII World's Poultry Congress, Istanbul, CD-rom.

Villaverde, C., Baucells, M.D., Manzanilla, E.G., and Barroeta, A.C. (2008). High levels of dietary unsaturated fat decrease α-tocopherol content of whole body, liver, and plasma of chickens without variations in intestinal apparent absorption. Poultry Sci., 87:497-505.

Villaverde, C., Cortinas, L., Barroeta, A.C., Martin-Orue, S.M., and Baucells, M.D. (2004b). Relationship between dietary unsaturation and vitamin E in poultry. J. Anim. Physiol. and Anim. Nutr., 88:143-149.

Vo, K.V-, Adefope, N.A., Fenderson, C.L., and Kolison, S.H. (1999). Effect of vitamin and trace mineral withdrawal on performance of broilers reared under high density stress. Poultry Sci., 78 (suppl. 1):58 (abstract).

Vo, K.V., Bashaw, A.J., Adefope, N.A., Catlin, C., and Wakefield, T. (1996). Effect of ascorbic acid and sucrose supplementation to broiler chicks subjected to delayed placement on early mortality, hemo-stress response, and growth performance. Poultry Sci., 75 (suppl. 1): 150 (abstract).

Völker, L. and Fenster, R. (1991) Supplementation with ascorbic acid for increasing carcass yield in broiler chickens and turkeys prior to slaughter. Proc. 8th Eur. Symp. on Poultry Nutrition, Venice, 274-276.

Wagstaff, R.K. (1978). Two hidden vitamins worth 0.137 lb 0.024 FC. Broiler Ind., 41 (8):93.

Waibel, P.E., Felice, L.J., Brannon, J.A., Chen, F., and Chen, M. (1994). Vitamin E forms for turkeys. 1994. J. Appl. Poultry Res. 3: 261-267.

Waldenstedt, L. (2006). Nutritional factors of importance for optimal leg health: a review. Anim. Feed. Sci. and Technol., 126:291-207.

Waldroup, P.W. and Fritts, C.A. (2005). Evaluation of separate and combined effects of choline and betaine in diets for male broilers. Int. J. Poultry Sci. 4 (7): 442-448, 2005

Waldroup, P.W., Hellwig, H.M., Spencer, G.K., Smith, N.K., Fancher, B.I., Jackson, M.E., Johnson, Z.N., and Goodwin, T.L. (1985). The effects of increased levels of niacin supplementation on growth rate and carcass composition of broiler chickens. Poultry Sci., 64:1777-1784.

Waldroup, P.W., Maxey, J.F., Latter, L.W., Jones, B.D., and Meshew, M.L. (1976). Bull. 805 Exp. Arkansas Univ, (cit. by Whitehead C.C. and Portsmouth P.I., 1989 see reference).

Waldroup, P.W., Motl, M.A., Yan, F., and Fritts, C.A. (2006). Effects of betaine and choline on response to methionine supplementaction to broiler diets formulated to industry standards. J. Appl. Poult. Res. 15:58-71.

Walsh, M.M., Kerry, J.F., Buckley, D.J., Arendt, E.K., and Morrissey, P.A. (1998). Effect of dietary supplementation with α-tocopheryl acetate on the stability of reformed and restructured low nitrite cured turkey products. Meat Sci., 50:191-201.

Walters, B.S., Wu, W., and Maurer, A.J. (1991). Effect of flat peas (Lathyrus silvestris) on broiler chicks. Poultry Sci., 70 (suppl. 1):127

Walton, J.P., Julian, R.J., and Squires, E.J. (2001). The effects of dietary flax oil and antioxidants on ascites and pulmonary hypertension in broilers using a low temperature model. Brit. Poultry Sci., 42: 123-129.

Wang, J-H, Rogers, S.R., and Pesti, G.M. (1987). Influence of choline and sulfate on copper and toxicity and substitution of and antagonism between methionine and copper supplements to chick diets. Poultry Sci., 66:1500-1507.

Ward, N.E. (1993) Vitamin supplementation rates for U.S. comercial broilers, turkeys and layers. J. Appl. Poultry Res. 2: 286-296.

Ward, N.E. (1995). Research examine use of 25-0H vitamin D3 in broiler chicks. Feedstuffs, 67:12-15.

Watkins, B.A. (1989). Levels of dihomo-γ-linoleate are depressed in heart phosphatydilcholine and phosphatydilethanolamine in the biotin-deficient chick. Poultry Sci., 68:698-705.

Watkins, B.A. (1993). Diet and leg weakness in poultry. In: Recent Advances in Animal Nutrition. P.C. Garnsworthy and D.J.A. Cole (eds.). Nottingham University Press, 131-141.

Watkins, B.A. and Kratzer, F.H. (1987a). Tissue lipid fatty acid composition of biotin-adequate and biotin-deficient chicks. Poultry Sci., 66:306-313.

Watkins, B.A. and Kratzer, F.H. (1987b). Dietary biotin effects on polyunsaturated fatty acids in chick tissue lipids and prostaglandin E2 levels in freeze-clamped hearts. Poultry Sci., 66:1818-1828.

Watkins, B.A. and Kratzer, F.H. (1987c). Effects of dietary biotin and linoleate on polyunsaturated fatty acids in tissue phospholipids. Poultry Sci., 66:2024-2031.

Weber, G. (2001). Nutritional effects on poultry meat quality, stability and flavor. Proc. 13th Eur. Symp. on Poultry Nutrition, Blankenberghe, Belgium, 9-16.

Weiser, H., Schlachter, M., Probst, H.P., and Kormann, Aw. (1990). The relevance of ascorbic acid for bone metabolism. Proc. 2nd Symposium Ascorbic Acid in Domestic Animals, Kartause Ittingen, Switzerland, ETH, Zurich, 73-95.

Wen, J., Lin, J., and Wang, H.M. (1997). Effect of dietay vitamin E and ascorbic acid on the growth and immune function of chicks. Chinese Agric. Sci. 145-149.

Wen, J., Mccarthy, S.N., Higgins, F.M.J., Morrissey, P.A., Buckley, D.J., and Sheehy, P.J.A. (1997). Effect of dietary α-tocopheryl acetate on the uptake and distribution of α-tocopherol in turkey tissue and lipid stability. Irish J. Agric. Food Res., 36:65-74.

Wen, J., Morrissey, P.A., Buckley, D.J., and Sheehy, P.J.A. (1996). Oxidative stability and α-tocopherol retention in turkey burger during refrigerated and frozen storage as influenced by dietary α-tocopheryl acetate. Brit. Poultry Sci. 37: 787-795.

West, C.E., Sijstma, S.R., Kouwenhoven, B., Rombout, J.H.W.M., and Van Der Zijpp, A.J. (1992). Epithelia-damaging virus infections affect vitamin A status in broiler chickens. J. Nutr., 122:333-339.

Whitehead, C. (1995). Nutrition and skeletal disorders in broilers and layers. Poultry Int. Dec.'95: 40-48.

Whitehead, C. C. (1977). The use of biotin in animal nutrition. WPSJ., 33:140-154

Whitehead, C. C. (1988). Biotin in animal nutrition. Roche Animal Nutrition and Health, 58 pp.

Whitehead, C. C. (1991). Relationships between tissue and dietary levels of vitamins A and E in lines of genetically lean and fat broilers. Proc. 8th Eur. Symp. on Poultry Nutrition, Venice, 295-297.

Whitehead, C. C. (2001). Nicotinic acid in poultry nutrition. Feed Mix, g(1): 32-34.

Whitehead, C.C, Armstrong, J.A., and Waddington, D. (1982). The determination of the availability to chicks of biotin in feed ingredients by a bioassay based on the response of blood pyruvate carboxylase (EC 6. 4. 1.1) activity. Brit. J. Nutr., 48: 81-88.

Whitehead, C.C, Bannister, D.W, Evans, A.J, Siller, W.G., and Wight, P.A.L. (1976). Biotin deficiency and fatty liver and kidney syndrome in chicks given purified diets containing different fat and protein levels. Brit. J. Nutr. 35: 115-125.

Whitehead, C.C, Blair, R, Bannister, D.W, Evans, A.J., and Morley Jones, R (1976). The involvement of biotin in preventing the fatty liver and kidney syndrome in chicks. Res. Vet. Sci. 20: 180-184.

Whitehead, C.C, Pearson, R.A., and Herron, K.M. (1985). Biotin requirement of broiler breeders fed diets of different protein content and effect of insufficient biotin on the viability of progeny. Brit. Poultry Sci., 26:73-82.

Whitehead, C.C, Rennie, J.S., Farquharson, C., and Fleming, R.H. (1994b), Recent findings on tibial dyschondroplasia in broilers and osteoporosis in caged layers. Brit. Poultry Sci., 35:168-170.

Whitehead, C.C. (1987). Requirements for vitamins. In: Nutrient requirements of poultry and nutritional research, Ed. by Fisher, C. and Boorman, K.N. Ed. Butterworths. 173-190.

Whitehead, C.C. (1991). Effects of vitamins on leg weakness in poultry. Proc. 7th Eur. Symp. on Poultry Nutrition, Venezia-Mestre, 157-166.

Whitehead, C.C. (1993). Vitamin supplementation of cereal poultry. Animal Feed Sci. and Technol., 45: 81-95.

Whitehead, C.C. (1995a). Nutrition and skeletal disorders in broilers and layers. Poultry Int., Dec. 1995, 40-48.

Whitehead, C.C. (1995b). The role of vitamin

D metabolites in the prevention of tibial dyschondroplasia. Anim. Feed Sci. and Technol., 53:205-210.

Whitehead, C.C. (1996). Nutrition Issues: Changing standard requirements. Poultry Int., Sept. 1996. 24-26.

Whitehead, C.C. (1999). The impact of vitamins on health and performance in fowls. Proc. 12th Eur. Symp. on Poultry Nutrition, Veldhoven, 73-82.

Whitehead, C.C. (1999). The impact of vitamins on health and performance in fowls. Proc. 12th Eur. Symp. on Poultry Nutrition, Veldhoven, The Netherlands, 73-82.

Whitehead, C.C. (2000). Recent developments on the effects of nutrition on skeletal disease. Proc. XXI World`s Poultry Congress, Ontario, Canada, CD-rom.

Whitehead, C.C. (2000). Recent developments on the effects of nutrition on skeletal disease. Proc. XXI World's Poultry Congress, Montreal, CD-rom.

Whitehead, C.C. (2000). Update on vitamin and trace mineral requirements for poultry. Proc. Maryland Nutr. Conf.

Whitehead, C.C. (2001). Nutrition and poultry welfare. Proc. 6th Eur. Symp. on Poultry Welfare, Zollikofen, Switzerland. 159-167.

Whitehead, C.C. (2002). Nutrition and poultry welfare. WPSA. J., 58:349-356.

Whitehead, C.C. (2002a). Influence of vitamins and minerals on bone formation and quality. Proc. 11th Eur. Poultry Conf., Bremen, Germany (CD-rom).

Whitehead, C.C. (2002b). Nutrition and poultry welfare. WPSA. J., 58:349-356.

Whitehead, C.C. (2002b). Nutrition and poultry welfare. WPSA. J., 58:349-356.

Whitehead, C.C. (2002c). Vitamins in feedstuffs. In: Poultry Feedstuffs, supply, composition and nutritive value. Ed. by J.M. McNab and K.N. Boorman. CABI Pub, 181-190.

Whitehead, C.C. (2003). Papel de la nutrición para mejorar el bienestar y la calidad de vida de las aves. Proc. 40th Symp. WPSA's Spanish Branch, Girona.

Whitehead, C.C. (2004). Nutritional and metabolic disorders in meat poultry. Proc. XXI World Poultry Congress, Istanbul, CD-rom.

Whitehead, C.C. (2005). Mechanisms and nutritional influences in skeletal development: Influence of macro- and microelements on bone formation. Proc.

15th Eur. Symp. on Poultry Nutrition, Balatonfured, 142-150.

Whitehead, C.C. and Bannister, D.W. (1980). Biotin status, blood pyruvate carboxylase (EC 6.4.1.1) activity and performance in broilers under different conditions of bird husbandry and diet processing. Brit. J. Nutr., 43: 541-549.

Whitehead, C.C. and Blair, R.B. (1974). The involvement of biotin in the fatty liver and kidney syndrome in broiler chickens. WPSJ., 30:231.

Whitehead, C.C. and Keller, T. (2003). An update on ascorbic acid in poultry. WPSJ., 59:161-184.

Whitehead, C.C. and Porstmouth, J.I. (1989). Vitamin requirements and allowances for poultry. In: Recent advances in animal nutrition. Haresign, W. and Cole, D.G.A. (Eds). Ed. Butterworth.

Whitehead, C.C. and Randall, C.J. (1982). Interrelationships between biotin, choline and other B-vitamins and the occurrence of fatty liver and kidney syndrome and sudden death syndrome in broiler chickens. Brit. J. Nutr. 48: 177-184.

Whitehead, C.C. and Siller, W.G. (1983). Experimentally induced fatty liver and kidney syndrome in the young turkey. Res. Vet. Sci. 34: 73-76.

Whitehead, C.C., Farquharson, C., Rennie, J.S., and Mccormack, H.A. (1994a). Nutrition and cellular factors affecting tibial dyschondroplasia in broilers. Proc. Aust. Poultry Sci. Symp., Sydney, 13-19.

Whitehead, C.C., Mccormack, H.A., and Webster, C. (1992). A quantitative estimate of the replaceability of methionine by choline in broiler diets. Proc. XIX World's Poultry Congress, Amsterdam, 639-640.

Whitehead, C.C., Mccormack, H.A., Mcteir, L., and Fleming, R.H. (2004a). High vitamin D3 requirements in broilers for bone quality and prevention of tibial dyschondroplasia and interactions with dietary calcium, available phosphorus and vitamin A. Brit. Poultry Sci., 45:425-436.

Whitehead, C.C., Mccormack, H.A., Mctier, L., and Fleming, R.H. (2004b). The maximum legal limit for vitamin D3 in broiler diets need to be increased. Brit. Poultry Sci., 45 (suppl. 1):S24-S26.

Whitehead, C.C., Mccormack, H.A., Rennie, J.S., and Frigg, M. (1995). Folic acid requirements of broilers. Brit. Poultry Sci. 36: 113-121.

Williams, B., Solomon, S., Waddington, D., Thorp, D., and Farquharson, C. (2000a). Skeletal development in the meat-type chicken. Brit. Poultry Sci., 41:141-149.

Williams, B., Waddington, D., Solomon, S., and Farquharson, C. (2000b). Dietary effects on bone quality and turnover, and Ca and P metabolism in chickens. Res. Vet. Sci., 69:81-87.

Workel, H. A., Keller, Th., Reeve, A., and Lauwaerts, A. (1999). Choline - The rediscovered vitamin. Poultry Int., April ´99: 44-47.

Wu, C.C., Dorairajan, T. and Lin, T.L. (2000). Effect of ascorbic acid supplementation on the immune response of chickens vaccinated and challenged with infectious bursal disease virus. Vet. Immunol. and Immunopathol. 74: 145-152.

Wyatt, C.L. (1991). Effect of high levels of vitamin A supplementation on skin pigmentation and growth performance in broiler chicks. Poultry Sci., 68 (suppl. 1):161 (abstract).

Xiang, R.P, Sun, W.D, Wang, J.Y, and Wang, X.L. (2002). Efect of vitamin C on pulmonary hypertension and muscularisation of pulmonary arterioles in broilers. Brit. Poultry Sci., 43: 705- 712

Xu, T., Cook, M.E., and Blake, J.P. (1989). Vitamin supplementation for performance and immune response of young turkeys. Poultry Sci., 68 (suppl. 1):161 (abstract).

Xu, T., Cook, M.E., and Blake, J.P. (1989). Vitamin supplementation for performance and immune response of young turkeys. Poultry Sci., 70 (suppl. 1):134 (abstract).

Xu, T., Leach, R.M., Hollis, B., and Soares, J.H. (1997). Evidence of increased cholecalciferol requirement in chicks with tibial dyschondroplasia and interactions with dietary calcium, available phosphorus and vitamin A. Brit. Poultry Sci., 76:47-53.

Yan, H.J., Lee, J., Nam, K.C., Min, B.R., and Ahn, D.U. (2006). Dietary functional ingredients: performance of animals and quality and storage stability of irradiated raw turkey breast. Poultry Sci., 85:1829-1837.

Yang, H.S., Waibel, P.E., and Brenes, J. (1973). Evaluation of vitamin D3 supplements by biological assay using the turkey. J. Nutr., 103:1187-1194.

Yang, L. and Wang, H. (1996b). Effect of riboflavin on the utilization of methionine and metabolism of protein of liver. XX World´s Poultry Congress, Delhi, India, IV: 212.

Yang, L. and Wang, H. (1996a). Effect of dietary riboflavin level on performance and nutritional status of broilers. XX World´s Poultry Congress, Delhi, India, IV: 148.

Yang, M. and Wu, W. (1997). Dietary supplementation of thiamine in excess of NRC recommendation can prevent immunosupression caused by toxic Fusarium proliferatum. Poulty Sci., 78 (suppl. 1): 125. (abstract).

Yang, N., Larsen, C.T., Dunnington, E.A., Geraert, P.A., Picard, M., and Siegel, P.B. (2000). Immune competence of chicks from two lines divergently selected for antibody response to sheep red blood cells as affected by supplemental vitamin E. Poultry Sci., 79:799-803.

Yarger, J.G., Saunders, C.A., Mcnaughton, J.L, Quarles, C.L., Hollis, B.W., and Gray, R. W. (1995a). Comparison of dietary 25-hydroxycholecalciferol and cholecalciferol in broiler chickens. Poultry Sci., 74:1159-1167.

Yarger, J.G., Saunders, C.A., Quarles, C.L., Hollis, B.W., and Gray, R. W. (1995b). Safety of 25-hydroxycholecalciferol as a source of cholecalciferol in poultry rations. Poultry Sci., 74:1437-1446.

Yegani, M.D, Miles, R, H,.Nilipour, A.D., and Butcher,G. (2001). Vitamin C - practical applications in modern poultry production. World Poultry, (17)10.

Yersin, A.G., Edens, F.W., and Simmons, D.G. (1989). The effects of Bordetella avium on tracheal cilia of turkey poults receiving exogenous niacine. Poultry Sci., 70 (suppl. 1):162 (abstract):

Yin, M.C, Faustman, C., Riesen, J.W., and Williams, S.N. (1993). α- Tocopherol and ascorbate delay oxymyoglobin and phospholipid oxidation in vitro. J. Food Sci., 58 (6): 1273-1276.

Yin, M.C. and Cheng, W.S. (1997). Oxymyoglobin and lipid oxidation in phosphatidylcholine liposomes retarded by α-tocopherol and ß-carotene. J. Food Sci., 62 (6): 1095-1097.

Yoshida, H. and Takagi, S. (1999). Antioxidative effects of sesamol and tocopherols at various concentrations in oils during microwave heating. J. Sci. Food Agric. 79: 220-226.

Yotova, I., Yotsov, S., Pashov, D., Afanasov,

K., Sotirov, L., and Stoyanccev, E. (1990). Effect of vitamin C on some factors of immune reactivity of broiler chicks infected with Marek's disease virus. Vet. Bull., 12:1200.

Young, J.F., Stagsted, J., Jensen, S.K., Karlsson, A.H., and Henckel, P. (2003). Ascorbic acid, α-tocopherol, and oregano supplements reduce stress-induced deterioration of chicken meat quality. Poultry Sci., 83:1343-1351.

Yunis, R., Ben-David, A., Heller, E,D., and Cahaner, A. (2000). Immunocompetence and viability under commercial conditions of broiler groups differing in growth rate and in antibody response to *Escherichia coli* vaccine. Poultry Sci., 79:810-816.

Zanini, S.F, Torres, C.A.A, Bragagnolo, N, Turatti, J.M, Silva, M.G., and Zanini, M.S. (2003a). Oil sources and vitamin E levels in the diet on the composition of fatty acid in roosters meat. Proc. XVI Eur. Symp. On the Quality of Poultry Meat, St. Brieuc, France, 199-210.

Zanini, S.F, Torres, C.A.A, Bragagnolo, N, Turatti, J.M., Silva, M.G., and Zanini, M.S. (2003b). Effect of oil sources and vitamin E levels in the diet on the concentration of total lipids, cholesterol, vitamin E in thigh and chest meat of cockerels. Proc. XVI Eur. Symp. on the Quality of Poultry Meat, St. Brieuc, France, 278-284.

Zaviezo, D., Mac Auliffe, T. and Mcginnis, J. (1977). The choline requirement of turkey poults. Poultry Sci., 56:82-87.

Zdunczyk, Z., Jankowski, J., and Koncicki, A. (2002). Growth performance and physiological state of turkeys fed diets with higher content of lipid oxidation products, selenium, vitamin E and vitamin A. WPSJ., 58 (3):357-364.

Zhang, C., Li, D., Wang, F., and Dong, T. (2003). Effects of dietrary vitamin K levels on bone quality in broilers Archiv Anim. Nutr., 57 (3):197-206.

Zhang, X., Liu, G., Mcdaniel, G.R., and Roland, D.A. (1997). Response of broiler lines selected for tibial dyschondrplasia incidence to supplementary 25-hydroxycholecalciferol. J. Appl. Poultry Res., 6:410-416.

Zhu, M., Wesley, I.V., Nannapaneni, R., Cox, M., Mendoca, A., Johnson, M.G., and Ahn, D.U., (2003). The role of dietary vitamin E in experimental listeria monocytogenes infections in turkeys. Poultry Sci., 82:1559-1564.

Zulkifli, I., Norma, M.T.C., Chong, C.H., and Loh, T.C. (2001). The effects of crating and road transportation on stress and fear responses of broiler chickens treated with ascorbic acid. Archiv für Geflugelk., 65: 33-37.

OPTIMUM VITAMIN NUTRITION IN PIGS

B. Isabel, A. I. Rey and C. López Bote
Department of Animal Production
Faculty of Veterinary Science
Complutense University 28040 Madrid, Spain
clemente@vet.ucm.es

INTRODUCTION

Minimum and optimum vitamin recommendations

Vitamins are defined as organic compounds necessary in small quantities to maintain animal life and production. The discovery of the existence and physiological functions of vitamins during the first half of the 20th century has been one of the most exciting chapters in the history of scientific discovery. It proved a milestone in the development of quantitative and applied animal nutrition, leading to an adjustment in nutrient supply corresponding to the needs of animals in each productive situation. However, it is much more difficult to establish with precision the requirements and recommendations for the different types of vitamin than for energy, protein, essential amino acids and macrominerals. In the first place, even small, not easily quantifiable variations may provoke marked effects when dealing with micronutrients. In this respect, small variations in the analytical methodology used for each vitamin from laboratory to laboratory and over the course of time (during which more precise instruments have been developed) are undoubtedly responsible

for the great diversity in published results. Secondly, in most cases there are important concentrations of vitamins in ingredients used in ration formulation, although their values and availability to animals vary considerably and can also vary depending on storage time or the technological treatment applied. This makes it exceedingly difficult to establish precisely the quantity actually ingested by animals. All this means that, in practice, it is not possible to invoke the factorial method to calculate requirements and it is necessary to resort to empirical tests of feed to which different levels of vitamins are added and the response measured.

In most cases, this type of test is done by including vitamins in conventional feeds (which contain a more or less constant concentration of naturally-occurring vitamins), and obtaining a dose-response curve which shows the optimum vitamin concentration which should be included to supplement that provided by the ingredients. The dose-response curve obtained in this type of trial is similar to those obtained for any other nutrients (**Figure 1**). The lack of an essential nutrient for a sufficiently

Figure 1. Relation between quantity of vitamin intake and theoretical productive response.

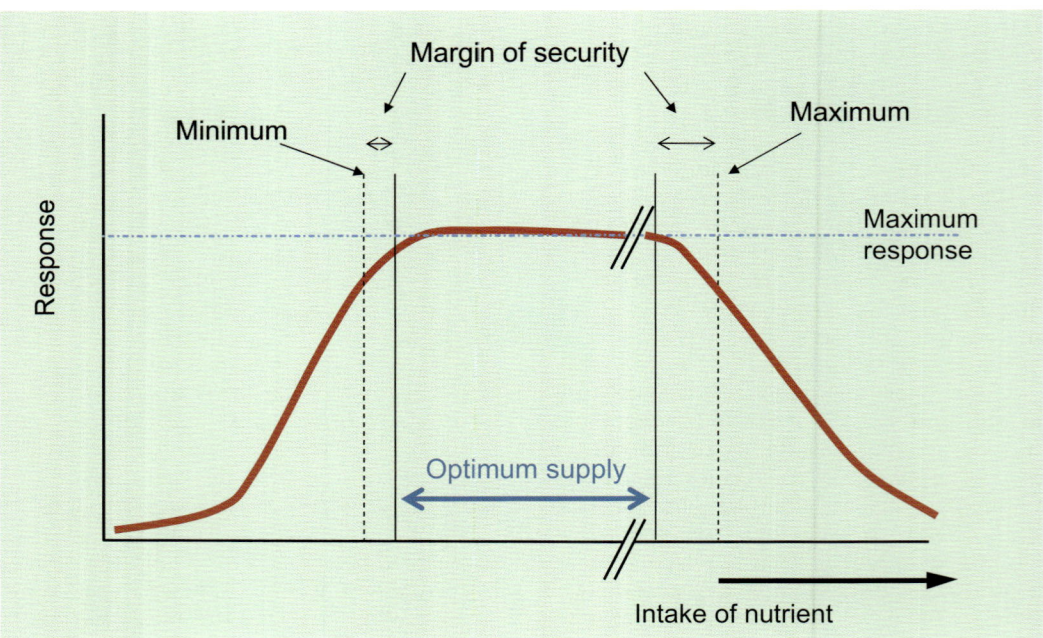

prolonged period is not compatible with production levels and with health. Thus, any increment in supply allows a substantial improvement in productive response, which may be adjusted according to an exponential equation which from a certain point follows the law of diminishing returns. That is to say that the benefit obtained by increasing the concentration of the nutrient in food is proportionally smaller every time until what may be called a plateau phase is reached where the maximum productive response is located. This curve enables the need for a particular nutrient to be determined, that is to say the minimum quantity which a healthy animal should receive daily to meet requirements for maintenance and a given production level. As these are "minimum" quantities, the values are usually increased within so-called "safety margins" whose objective is to correct deviations resulting from the biological variability of both animals and feed. The values obtained are referred to as optimum nutrient provision, and have a relatively wide range (**Figure 1**).

In some cases this optimum supply may be exceeded, leading to surplus and even toxicity. In the case of vitamins toxic effects have only been observed with vitamins A and D (and only when administering quantities far greater than the ones used in practice). Since supplying a given nutrient in high concentrations increases the cost of a ration, in practice a quantity is chosen which represents the minimum supply that provides the maximum productive response within a safety margin (**Figure 1**).

The introduction of the economic factor, essential in ration formulation and in the establishment of nutrient restrictions, represents an additional area of difficulty. As maximum productive response is approached, returns become smaller and therefore increments in the concentration of nutrients may become economically unviable. For this reason, ultimately, the establishment of each recommendation has an economic base, hence the concept of "economic optimum" which may be the minimum concentration of a nutrient which produces the maximum response, or even a slightly lower concentration which does not produce the maximum response but does produce the greatest economic benefit of the process. The need to introduce the economic factor in animal nutrition is linked to the fact that each productive situation is unique and therefore production strategy is also unique and the definition of formulation needs and criteria should also be specific to each case.

Calculation of the most appropriate level of supplementation in conventional feed may be confusing because feeds which are considered normal in some geographical areas or production conditions may not be used in other parts of the world. For example, a good deal of North American scientific production is obtained using feeds based on corn and soy, in which the content and availability of vitamins is very different from that in manioc, barley or sunflower.

Is it necessary to revise vitamin recommendations for swine nutrition?

Most recommendations for vitamins in swine nutrition are based on studies carried out several decades ago. The question of revising these values is often discussed, although this is a topic that raises some controversy due to the fact that in some cases the information available is unclear and that commercial interests may at times make the actual need to update recommendations seem less than credible. Nevertheless, from our point of view, there are several reasons to suggest the need to review recommendations for vitamins (and other nutrients) for swine periodically. These include the following:

- The majority of vitamin recommendations derived from different trials is expressed in concentration per kilogram feed. In pigs, changes brought about by genetic improvement geared to reducing the feed conversion index have had the marked indirect effect of reducing voluntary ingestion over the last few decades. These changes do not affect pigs during all productive phases with the same intensity, nor is the effect on both sexes the same.
- There has simultaneously been a marked increase in the productive capacity of the animals, ever approaching the physiological limit. It is likely that as the productive limit

is approached, more attention should be paid to the supply of the different nutrients to avoid imbalances. However, genetics continue to evolve. We are probably on the threshold of a revolution thanks to the massive application of techniques based on molecular biology. It will therefore be necessary to take the conditions for the optimization of feed formulation to the limit in order to maintain that rate of improvement in production.

- With the increase in knowledge of the science behind the phenomena which regulate animal physiology and productive processes, studies must consider other factors besides those strictly related to a lack of deficiency or to the mere optimization of response. Aspects like immune response capacity, breeder longevity, viability of neonatal pigs, adaptation to stress, response to vaccinations, susceptibility to pathological problems (edema, etc.), the capacity to overcome disease, the variability (and not only average values) in any production parameter calculated, etc., deserve ever increasing attention in modern swine production and have not until now been evaluated in sufficient depth. In **Figure 2**, different response curves for the same vitamin according to the parameter measured (growth, resistance to disease, meat quality, immune response, etc.) are represented schematically.

- In the last few years consumers have been playing a more active role in the production process, and are becoming far more selective in their choices. For this reason, attention must be paid to their opinions and specific demands. Thus aspects like diversification of production, animal well-being, the content of potentially toxic compounds or residues, fortification of food with natural compounds etc. acquire particular relevance. Optimum vitamin nutrition in swine offers some interesting alternatives which must be studied and applied appropriately.

- During the past few years conditions in production have been modernized significantly, with improved genetics, facilities etc. The consequences of the technical revolution that this implies call for the optimization of nutrition.

- The costs of the different ingredients (including vitamins) which are used in pig feed are variable and so too, therefore, are the vitamin levels which permit the optimum economic return in each case. In general, scientific and technical processes and large scale industrial production mean that production of synthetic vitamins is more efficient, and so the price of the vitamin supply is becoming proportionally lower in comparison with the other ingredients used in ration formulation. For that reason, the vitamin concentration in feed which corresponds to the economic optimum is tending to become higher, ever approaching the recommended concentration for optimum production. This fact demands special attention, since not all commercial vitamin preparations are of the same quality, nor are they of equal benefit to the animals.

- Some changes to feed guidelines (e.g. ban on meal of animal origin, ban on antibiotics) and other changes which will undoubtedly take place, mean that the entire production strategy (housing, vaccination regime, handling, etc.) should be reviewed, entailing re-evaluation in economic terms of the supply of different micronutrients in different phases of the productive cycle.

Figure 2. Schematic representation showing different response curves for the same vitamin according to the parameter measured (growth, resistance to disease, meat quality, immune response, etc.).

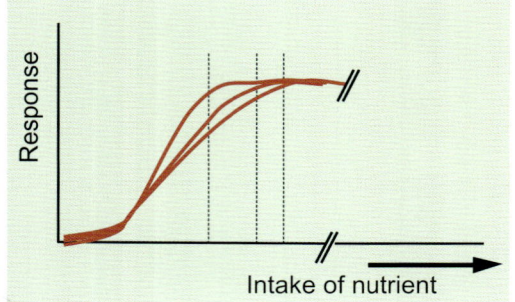

Taking all these considerations into account, this review looks at the study of vitamin requirements in swine nutrition and feed in the light of the latest discoveries.

FAT-SOLUBLE VITAMINS

VITAMIN A

Chemical structure and units

Vitamin A is an unsaturated alcohol of 20 carbon atoms (retinol), (**Figure 3**), although it also exists in esterified form (usually with acetic, palmitic or propionic acid). It is a yellow substance, insoluble in water, but soluble in fats and organic solvents. The molecule is very susceptible to oxidation, especially in its alcohol form. One international unit of vitamin A is equal to 0.3 µg retinol (1 mg retinol = 3333 IU vitamin A), 0.344 µg in acetate form, 0.359 µg propionate or 0.55 µg palmitate. Other forms included in the generic denomination of vitamin A are the aldehyde or retinal form, which plays an important role in the development of vision and in reproduction, and the acid form (retinoic acid) essential in cellular growth and differentiation.

Metabolism

Being a fat-soluble compound, vitamin A is insoluble in the aqueous media mainly found in the intestine. For this reason, attention must be paid to the fat-soluble fraction when formulating rations, in order to achieve good capacity for emulsion and micelle formation in the duodenum, the target site of vitamin A absorption. Interactions between different fat-soluble compounds competing for the same absorption mechanism have been described. This interaction has for instance been described for vitamin E in chickens (Pudelkiewicz *et al.*, 1964) and in rats (Bieri *et al.*, 1981) and in pigs there is evidence of the inhibition of retinyl acetate over tocopherol acetate in vitro (Lauridsen *et al.*, 2001).

Esterified forms must undergo hydrolysis to free the alcohol, which is actually absorbed. The alcohol is esterified in enterocytes, and

Figure 3. Schematic representation of vitamin A (retinol) and its provitamin form (ß-carotene).

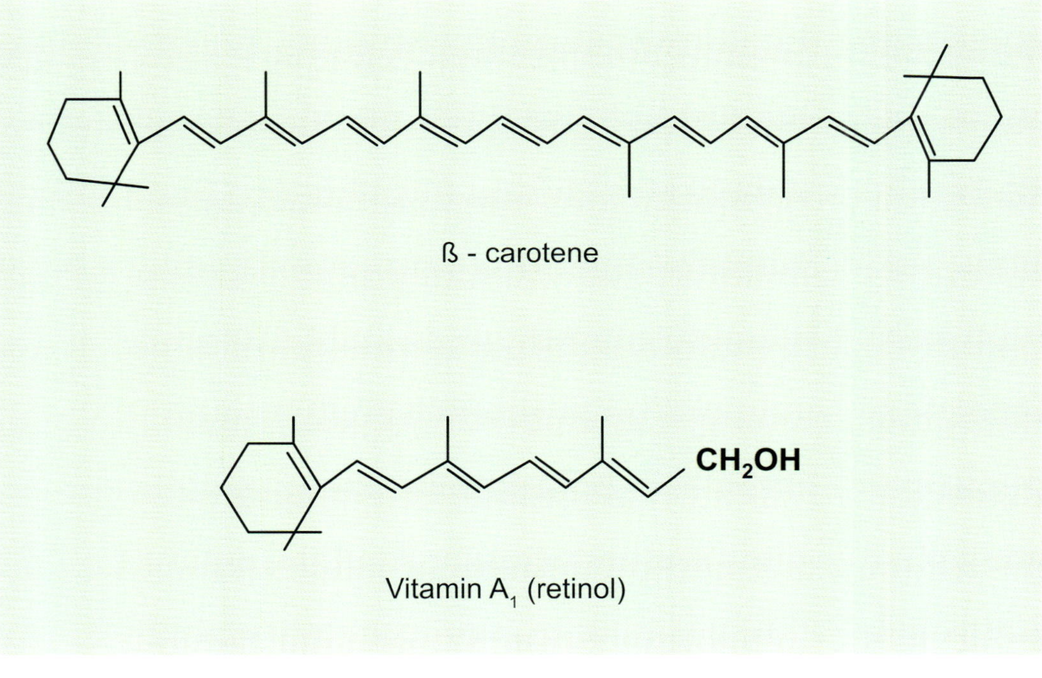

ß - carotene

CH$_2$OH

Vitamin A$_1$ (retinol)

is delivered by chylomicrons to the liver, where it accumulates. The liver is estimated to contain around 90% of vitamin A deposits. When retinol is released from hepatocytes it binds, with great affinity, to a protein (retinol binding protein, RBP) which transports it to different target cells. The cytoplasm of these cells contains another protein, which also strongly binds retinol.

Vitamin A is not found as such in vegetables, but is present in provitamin form, such as certain carotenoids which animals convert easily to vitamin A. About 100 molecules with provitamin A activity are known. Of these, ß-carotene is the most abundant and active. Green foods contain a large amount of ß-carotene, which is very sensitive to oxidation.

In pigs, conversion of carotene to vitamin A takes place essentially in the small intestine. Although, in theory, the cleavage of the ß-carotene molecule may yield two molecules of retinol, in practice this conversion is not very efficient, especially in swine. Theoretically, 1 mg retinol is equivalent to 3333 IU vitamin A, but in the National Research Council (NRC) (1998) publication it is calculated that in practice 1 mg retinol is only equivalent to 267 IU, that is to say, 12.5 times less.

Vitamin A performs a number of functions. Probably the most studied and well-known is the function related to the physiology of vision. In this process, retinol is oxidized until an aldehyde is formed, which is also isomerized from the trans form to the cis form (**Figure 4**). From this, it can combine with a

Figure 4. Representation of vitamin A participation in the physiology of vision.

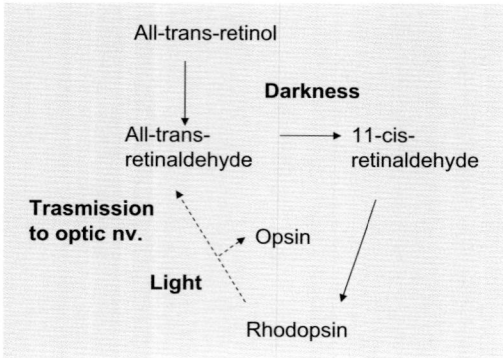

protein to form rhodopsin. On exposure to light, rhodopsin cleaves and releases the aldehyde in cis form which converts back to the trans form, producing a nerve stimulation responsible for vision.

Vitamin A is also implicated in the formation, protection and secretory activity of skin and mucosa. It has also been linked to corticosteroid production in the adrenal glands. For these reasons vitamin A is attributed with an important function in resistance to diseases, especially those related to the respiratory tract. Although the implication of vitamin A in resistance to disease has scarcely been defined, there are data to indicate a negative effect of insufficient vitamin A supply (even at levels which do not give rise to other manifestations of deficiency) on antibody production and on the number of lymphocytes (Kelly and Easter, 1987; Bebravicious et al., 1987).

Vitamin A is essential for maintenance of reproductive physiology and fetal development. Deficiency in this vitamin gives rise to an increase in mortality in sows and weakness in newborn piglets. Previous studies of the effects of injections of vitamin A or supplementation of the ration have demonstrated positive effects on reproductive yield in primiparous sows with deficiencies (Brief and Chew, 1985) or in the number of piglets born alive when it was administered in concentrations of 11,000 IU (Coffey and Britt, 1993). Vitamin A has been linked to the capacity of the ovary to produce steroid hormones, particularly progesterone (Talavera and Chew, 1988). Furthermore, it is likely that vitamin A is involved in the preparation of uterine mucosa. One protein has been identified which has a great affinity for retinol in the endometrium, the ovary, the testicle and the embryo. In the case of the uterus, progesterone is involved in regulation of the synthesis of this protein. Its participation has not been sufficiently clarified, although it could be linked to intracellular transport of vitamin A and its passage to the embryo, where it is probably needed to regulate cellular differentiation and proliferation, steroid production (Talavera and Chew, 1988), immune response (Hoskinson et al., 1992), transcription of specific genes, etc. In this respect it has also been demonstrated in pigs that mutations in the gene of the RBP4 (retinol binding protein 4) are directly related to the number of piglets born and weaned (Terman *et al.*, 2007).

Vitamin A has also been associated with certain characteristics related to meat quality such as intramuscular fat content or the percentage of certain fatty acids, thanks to the possible action of the vitamin in controlling the differentiation of adipocytes (Gregoire *et al.*, 1998) and in the activity of certain desaturating enzymes (Miller *et al.*, 1997; Olivares *et al.*, 2008). There are almost no data on the effects of vitamin A on the content of intramuscular fat in fattening pigs (D´Souza *et al.*, 2003). However, experiments developed in cattle (Siebert *et al.*, 2006), have demonstrated a negative relationship between vitamin A content in feed and percentage of intramuscular fat. The same authors (Siebert *et al.*, 2006) observed that restricting the vitamin A content in the ration increased the proportion of saturated fatty acids in subcutaneous fat in cattle. However, the data are not consistent in this respect since other authors (Gonocica-Buefil *et al.*, 2007) found no alterations in the fatty acid profile.

In most if not all cases the mechanism of vitamin A action is similar to that of steroid hormones and is carried out by binding to specific receptors located in the cellular cytoplasm of target tissues. When the active form (retinoic acid) is bound to the receptor, the receptor translocates to the nucleus where it binds to chromatin acceptors and causes production of a messenger RNA and, as a consequence, of a specific cytoplasmic protein (Shin and McGrane, 1997).

Some research carried out in the 1980s indicates that the role of ß-carotene in reproduction could be quite different to that of retinol. It probably raises uterine protein concentration. Brief and Chew (1985) periodically administered 228 mg of ß-carotene parenterally to gestating sows from conception to weaning and they observed reduced embryo mortality and an increase in the number of weaned pigs and in weaning weight. Coffey *et al.* (1983) observed a similar effect, although they indicated that it was impossible to determine whether in fact embryo mortality dropped or the production of ova increased. The same authors observed

no effects in primiparous sows. However, Stender *et al.* (1999) observed no beneficial effects when administering ß-carotene to high performance sows, indicating that the effect is probably limited to sows maintained in operations of low reproductive efficiency. It has not been possible to reproduce this effect in experiments adding raised levels of ß-carotene to feed for sows, probably due to the low absorption of carotenes in this species. In bovine livestock, where absorption is greater, the possible specific effect of ß-carotene in female breeders has been studied, and a high corpus luteum content and a specific location in microsomes described. This suggests a possible antioxidant function similar to that described for vitamin E. The identification of possibly different roles for vitamin A and ß-carotene opens up an interesting field of research and requires the establishment of appropriate administration strategies in the pig industry. One interesting aspect which needs to be clarified is the interaction between vitamin A and ß-carotene, as well as the importance of reserve levels of these compounds in the liver and their capacity for mobilization. Furthermore, recent research has shown that pigs can absorb ß-carotene, albeit in small quantities (Schweigert *et al.*, 1995), and that as soon as it is absorbed they convert it to vitamin A (in contrast to other species).

Although an antioxidant effect of ß-carotene has been shown in other species, this is unlikely to prove useful in pigs due to its poor absorption and limited accumulation in muscular tissue.

Deficiency symptoms

One of the first symptoms of vitamin A deficiency is night blindness, also known as hemeralopia. In breeding animals, deficiency can give rise to infertility, and in gestating animals to abortion or birth of dead, weak or blind young. In less serious cases, reduced appetite and delayed growth are observed.

Sources

Vitamin A is present in food of animal origin. It is found abundantly for example in milk, egg yolk and liver, associated with the fatty part. Foods of vegetable origin (basically green plants) contain the form of provitamin (carotenoids) which are converted to vitamin A in animals. There is a synthetic form (retinyl acetate) which can be synthesized in the laboratory.

Recommendations

As has been pointed out, both vitamin A and carotenoids are very susceptible to oxidation reactions, so significant losses may result from feed being stored, ground, exposed to air or heated. For this reason it is difficult to determine the actual supply from ingredients used in pig feed, and stable vitamin A is often added in sufficient quantity to meet all requirements, regardless of the contribution from other ingredients.

Vitamin A participates in a great variety of vital processes, some of which have not been studied sufficiently, and depends on many factors which are difficult to control. These include genetics, productive status, level of reserves in the liver, vitamin or provitamin content of ingredients, storage and technological treatments of feed, capacity for absorption of retinol or of different provitamin forms, capacity for conversion from provitamins to vitamin A, oxidative status of the animals, consumption, etc. For these reasons, establishing precise recommendations is complicated.

The NRC (1998) recommends 2200 IU/kg feed for piglets up to 10 kg and 1750 for piglets up to 20 kg (**Table I**). During fattening and finishing, the recommendation is 1300 IU/kg (**Table II**). In feeds for gestation and for boars the recommendation increases to 4000 IU, while for lactation it is set at 2000 IU/kg (**Table III**). These recommendations should be understood as minimum values. A more realistic view could probably be obtained from studies of the actual situation.

In a recent review of the vitamin content of feeds used in Spain, Fraga and Villamide (2000) found an average value of 13800 IU/kg of feed for piglets, 7800 UI/kg for fatteners and 11765 UI/kg for breeders (Tables 1-3). Thus the actual quantities are 5.5, 5.2 and 2.6 times those recommended. Variations between different companies are very high. In a similar study carried out in the USA, Coelho (2000) obtained similar values, which supports the view that levels suggested by the NRC are widely exceeded in practice. In any case, the high variability described indicates the lack of information available and the prevailing confusion.

The only available work on the evolution of vitamin A content in commercial feeds in recent years indicates that in the last 10 years its average value in feeds for gestating sows has increased in the US by around 12%, probably due to the discovery and confirmation of its implication in reproductive processes described earlier. In this respect, a recent study carried out by Lindemann et al. (2008), in which intramuscular injections of high concentrations of vitamin A (250,000 IU and 500,000 IU) were given to sows of different ages from weaning to breeding, demonstrated positive effects in the number of piglets born and weaned for younger sows (1st and 2nd litters), while in older sows (3rd to 6th litters) the effects were not so marked. This work once again demonstrates that the vitamin A requirements for maximum reproductive yield may vary according to age, and again raises the need for a revision of the recommendations currently in use.

Another aspect of interest which should be considered when establishing dosage in the formulation of compound feeds is possible interaction with other nutrients with similar characteristics, as in the case of vitamin E. There is evidence that the use of high doses of vitamin A in feed causes a depletion of vitamin E in the tissue of young pigs. However, the available data for fattening pigs are scarce and sometimes not very conclusive. Thus while Anderson et al. (1995) found no interference in growing-fattening pigs when using concentrations of 20,000 IU of vitamin A, Hoppe et al. (1992) found interaction in the hepatic tissue when using doses of 20,000-40,000 IU of vitamin A upwards, while no effects were found with lower concentrations (10,000 IU). Young pigs are more sensitive to the use of high doses of vitamin A, with a clear interaction being observed on the vitamin E content of tissues when concentrations of 13,000 IU of vitamin A were used in the feed (Hoskinson et al., 1992).

Table I. Recommended vitamin levels (IU or mg/kg air-dry feed) for piglets by principal genetic companies and other sources

	Source / Units	NRC (1998)			Average industry levels in Spain (2000)* Piglets		Average industry levels in USA (2000)** Grower		PIC		DanBred		DSM OVN (2011)	
		<5 kg	5-10 kg	10-20 kg	Average	CV%	Average	CV%	<5 kg	5-25 kg	<9 kg	9-30 kg	<5 kg	5-30 kg
Vitamin A	IU	2,200	2,200	1,750	13,800	51	11,300	26	11,000	10,000	8,000	5,000	10000-20000	10000-15000
Vitamin D3	IU	220	220	200	2,120	22	1,528	45	1,750	1,650	800	500	1800-2000	1800-2000
25-OH-D3 (HyD)	mg	-	-	-	-	-	-	-	-	-	-	-	0.05	0.05
Vitamin E	IU	16.0	16.0	11.0	31.4	77	52.0	26	85.0	80.0	130.0	130.0	100-150 [1][2]	100-150 [1]
Vitamin K	mg	0.5	0.5	0.5	1.85	69	3.58	49	5.5	4.5	2.0	2.0	8.0-10.0	5.0-6.0
Vitamin B1	mg	1.5	1.0	1.0	1.53	56	0.77	138	3.500	3.500	2.0	2.0	3.5-5.5	3.0-5.0
Vitamin B2	mg	4.0	3.5	3.0	5.88	43	8.4	38	13.0	10.0	4.0	4.0	10.0-15.0	10.0-15.0
Vitamin B6	mg	2.0	1.5	1.5	2.43	54	1.24	96	7.0	4.500	3.0	3.0	6.0-8.0	6.0-8.0
Vitamin B12	mg	0.02	0.0175	0.015	0.03	30	0.037	41	0.06	0.04	0.02	0.02	0.05-0.07	0.04-0.06
Niacin	mg	20.0	15.0	12.5	33.0	52	46	37	70.0	45.0	20.0	20.0	60-80	35-55
D-Panthothenic acid	mg	12.0	10.0	9.0	15.6	34	27.0	33	40.0	35.0	10.0	10.0	30-50	25-45
Folic acid	mg	0.3	0.3	0.3	0.44	111	1.0	89	1.0	0.800	-	-	1.5-3.0	1.5-2.5
Biotin	mg	0.08	0.05	0.05	0.090	76	0.261	175	0.300	0.150	0.02	0.02	0.20-0.40	0.2-0.4
Vitamin C	mg	-	-	-	-	-	-	-	130	-	-	-	100-200 [3]	100-200 [3]
Choline	mg	-	-	-	-	-	-	-	440	330	-	-	500-800	250-400

* Villamide and Fraga, 2000; ** Coelho, 2000
(1) Add 5 mg/kg for each 1% dietary fat when fat is higher than 3%;
(2) For optimum immune health additional 100 mg/kg feed
(3) Recommended under heat stress conditions; use phosphorylated form in heat treated feeds

Table II. Recommended vitamin levels (IU or mg/kg air-dry feed) for growing-finishing pigs by principal genetic companies and other sources

Source /Units		NRC (1998)			Average industry levels in Spain (2000)*		Average industry levels in USA (2000)**				PIC		DanBred	DSM OVN (2011)	
		20-50 kg	50-80 kg	80-120 kg	Grower/ Finisher		Grower		Finisher		25-70 kg	>70 kg	30-100 kg	30-70 kg	> 70 kg
					Average	CV%	Average	CV%	Average	CV%					
Vitamin A	IU	13000	13000	13000	7800	18	7500	27	5700	40	6500	5000	4000	7000-10000	5000-8000
Vitamin D3	IU	150	150	150	1650	22	1110	48	841	47	1200	1000	400	1500-2000	1000-1500
25-OH-D3 (HyD)	mg	-	-	-	-	-	-	-	-	-	-	-	-	0.05	0.05
Vitamin E	IU	11.0	11.0	11.0	9.5	50	27.7	35	20.0	37	35.0	20.0	36.0	60-100 [1]	60-100 [1,2]
Vitamin K	mg	0.5	0.5	0.5	0.7	130	2.3	48	1.7	59	3.5	2.0	2.0	2-4	2-4
Vitamin B1	mg	1.0	1.0	1.0	0.8	94	0.4	163	0.6	169	-	-	2.0	2-3	1-2
Vitamin B2	mg	2.5	2.0	2.0	3.35	39	5.4	26	3.8	37	6.0	4.0	2.0	7-10	6-10
Vitamin B6	mg	1.0	1.0	1.0	1.0	82	0.4	179	0.9	171	-	-	3.0	2.5-4.5	2-3.5
Vitamin B12	mg	0.010	0.005	0.005	0.02	18	0.024	32	0.019	48	0.03	0.02	0.02	0.03-0.05	0.03-0.05
Niacin	mg	10.0	7.0	7.0	15.5	30	29	28	22.0	41	25.0	20.0	20.0	20-40	20-40
D-Panthothenic acid	mg	8.0	7.0	7.0	9.00	27	18.0	31	15.0	45	20.0	15.0	10.0	25-45	25-45
Folic acid	mg	0.3	0.3	0.3	0.04	317	0.19	182	0.3	186	-	-	-	1.0-1.5	0.5-1
Biotin	mg	0.05	0.05	0.05	0.007	257	0.046	149	0.06	153	-	-	0.1	0.15-0.30	0.10-0.20
Choline	mg	-	-	-	-	-	-	-	-	-	-	-	-	150-300	100-200

* Villamide and Fraga, 2000; ** Coelho, 2000
(1) Add 5 mg/kg for each 1% dietary fat when fat is higher than 3%;
(2) For optimum meat quality additional 150 mg/kg

Table III. Recommended vitamin levels (IU or mg/kg air dry feed) for breeder pigs by principal genetic companies and other sources

	Source / Units	NRC (1998)			Average industry levels in Spain (2000)* Breeders		Average industry levels in USA (2000)** Gestation		PIC		DanBred		DSM OVN (2011)		
		Gestation	Lactation	Boars	Average	CV%	Average	CV%	Gest./Lact.	Boars	Gestation	Lactation	Gilts	Sows	Boars
Vitamin A	IU	4,000	2,000	4,000	11,765	29	11,377	24	10,000	11,000	8,000	8,000	10000-12500	10000-15000	10000-15000
Vitamin D3	IU	200	200	200	1,720	15	1,602	56	1,750	1,750	800	800	1800-2000	1500-2000	1500-2000
25-OH-D3 (HyD)	mg	-	-	-	-	-	-	-	-	-	-	-	0.05	0.05	0.05
Vitamin E	IU	44	44	44	24	49	54	26	65	110	36	150	80-100 [1]	100-150 [1][2]	100-150
Vitamin K	mg	0.5	0.5	0.5	1.54	105	3.50	57	4.4	4.4	2.0	2.0	1.5-3.0	4.5-5.0	4.5-5.0
Vitamin B1	mg	1.0	1.0	1.0	0.67	81	0.90	114	2.2	2.2	2.0	2.0	1.0-2.0	2.0-2.5	1.0-2.0
Vitamin B2	mg	3.75	3.75	3.75	4.25	32	7.8	42	10.0	10.0	5.0	5.0	6.0-10.0	6.0-10.0	6.0-10.0
Vitamin B6	mg	1.0	1.0	1.0	1.66	68	1.15	102	3.3	3.3	3.0	3.0	3.5-5.5	3.5-5.5	3.5-5.5
Vitamin B12	mg	0.015	0.015	0.015	0.02	20	0.034	41	0.04	0.04	0.02	0.02	0.03-0.05	0.03-0.05	0.03-0.05
Niacin	mg	10.0	10.0	10.0	21.0	21	42	30	45.0	45.0	20.0	20.0	20-30	25-45	25-45
D-Panthothenic acid	mg	12.0	12.0	12.0	11.9	26	25.0	38	35.0	35.0	15.0	15.0	15-30	30-35	20-30
Folic acid	mg	1.3	1.3	1.3	1.34	101	1.7	62	1.3	1.7	1.1	1.1	3.5-5.5	3.5-5.5	3.5-5.5
Biotin	mg	0.20	0.20	0.20	0.150	61	0.330	137	0.220	0.550	0.02	0.02	0.30-0.50	0.50-0.80	0.50-0.80
Vitamin C	mg	-	-	-	-	-	-	-	-	-	-	-	200-300	200-300 [3]	200-500 [3]
Choline	mg	-	-	-	-	-	-	-	650	650	-	-	250-500	500-800	500-800
ß-carotene***	mg	-	-	-	-	-	-	-	-	-	-	-	-	300 [4]	-

* Villamide and Fraga, 2000; ** Coelho, 2000; *** mg/head day
(1) Add 5 mg/kg for each 1% dietary fat when fat is higher than 3%;
(2) For optimum piglet health: during late pregnancy and lactation total 250 mg/kg feed
(3) Recommended under heat stress conditions; use phosphorylated form in heat treated feeds
(4) Per animal per day from after weaning up to confirmed conception

VITAMIN D

Chemical structure and units

The two most important forms of vitamin D are ergocalciferol (D_2) and cholecalciferol (D_3). One IU of vitamin D is defined as the activity of 0.025 µg of cholecalciferol (1 mg of cholecalciferol = 40,000 IU of vitamin D).

Metabolism

Cholecalciferol can be formed from 7-dehydrocholesterol, a derivative of cholesterol which can be synthesized by pigs. Thus in certain circumstances it is not considered an essential nutrient (**Figure 5**). Vitamin D_3 can also be formed from ergosterol of vegetable origin. Both precursors or provitamins can convert to the corresponding vitamins by the action of ultraviolet rays (especially between 290 and 315 nm), usually from sunlight. In animals produced in confinement this activation is not possible (even when there are windows), so in practice it is necessary to include vitamin D forms in feed. Due to their fat-soluble properties the two forms

Figure 5. Schematic representation of vitamin D metabolism.

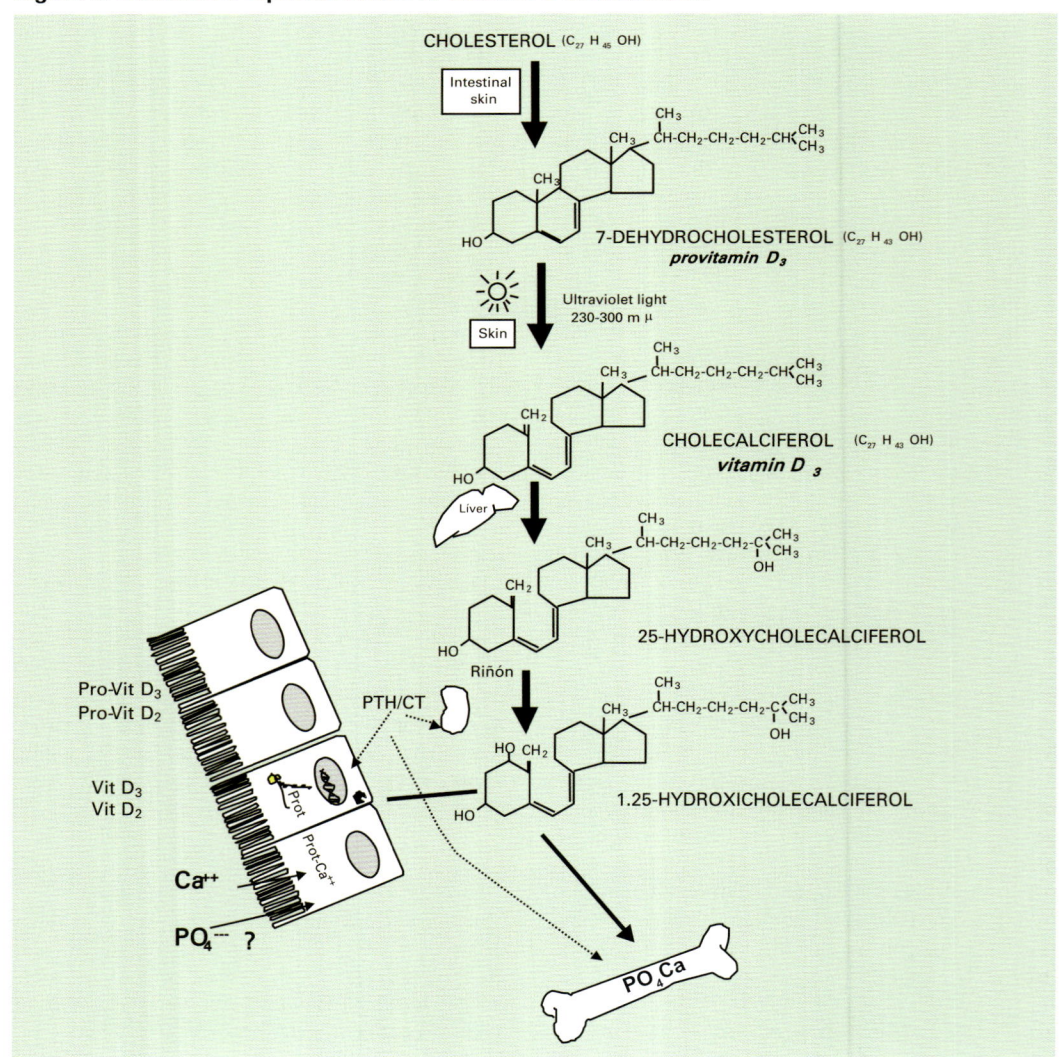

of vitamin D can be absorbed in the small intestine from micelles. Regardless of their origin (conversion in the skin or absorption), the vitamins are carried by blood to the liver, where they convert to 25-hydroxycalciferol. This compound enters the bloodstream and migrates to the kidney, where it converts to 1,25-dihydroxycholecalciferol, the biologically active form (**Figure 5**). This compound is carried in the bloodstream to the target tissues, intestine and bone.

The 1.25-dihydroxy derivatives of the two vitamin forms enter intestinal mucosal cells, interacting with chromatin and producing a specific messenger RNA to form a calcium-binding protein and other proteins with less well-known activity, which together stimulate calcium and phosphorous absorption. It is probable that they also modulate magnesium absorption. The mechanism of action of the 1,25-hydroxy derivatives is identical to hormone action as they are formed in a gland, enter the bloodstream and perform their function of modulating chromosome expression. A calcium carrier protein has also been found in the kidney where it probably regulates calcium reabsorption although it is probably of little quantitative importance.

Because of their link with calcium and phosphorous metabolism, there is a strong relationship between vitamin D derivatives and the hormones calcitonin and parathyroid hormone (PTH). PTH regulates synthesis of 1,25-hydroxy derivatives in the kidney. When the Ca concentration in blood is low, production of PTH increases, stimulating the formation of 1,25-hydroxy derivatives in the kidney and as a consequence increases intestinal absorption of calcium and probably reabsorption in the kidney, thereby increasing circulating calcium.

It has been observed that vitamin D deficiency causes insufficient bone mineralization, causing rickets in young pigs and osteomalacia in adults. The presence of 1,25-hydroxy derivatives corrects this problem. It has also been observed that other hydroxylated derivatives of vitamin D may regulate physiological bone development (Bar *et al.*, 1982).

In certain circumstances vitamin D can participate in the mobilization of bone calcium, which requires the participation of PTH. Moreover, it is possible that vitamin D may participate in the formation of organic bone matrix (Gonnerman *et al.*, 1976).

In the last few years a series of effects of vitamin D on meat quality have been described. These effects are due to its relationship with calcium and the fact that several proteolytic enzymes are calcium-dependent. Some studies carried out in the 1980s and early 1990s have shown that injection of calcium before slaughter leads to an increase in the concentration of intracellular calcium (McFarlane *et al.*, 1996). Also the inclusion of raised levels of vitamin D in the days before slaughter may lead to an increase in the concentration of cytoplasmic calcium (Sparks *et al.*, 1999). In cattle, it has been possible to verify that this procedure causes activation of calcium-dependent proteases and therefore an improvement in meat tenderness. Swanek *et al.* (1997) have shown that the inclusion of greater quantities of vitamin D (between 5 and 7 million IU/day) in cattle feed during a period ranging from 7 to 10 days before slaughter reduces the strength needed to cut meat by between 7% and 18%, and the proportion of chops which can be classified as firm by around 22%. In the case of swine, however, this treatment is less effective, and could even have a negative effect on problems from an abrupt drop in pH (closely related to a massive input of calcium to muscle after slaughter), and therefore on so-called pale, soft and exudative (PSE) meat. Problems of lack of tenderness in meat from pigs are not necessarily comparable with those in beef.

However, Enright *et al.* (1998) have pointed out a positive effect of vitamin D supplementation in feed on the water holding capacity and color stability during storage. Lack of verification in other publications means that these results must be viewed with caution for the time being.

Deficiency symptoms

Vitamin D deficiency gives rise to a slower growth rate. Problems of ossification have already been mentioned (rickets, osteomalacia) may also be due to a lack of calcium or phosphorous.

Sources

Vitamin D is not abundant in feedstuffs used in pig feed. It is not usually found in food of vegetable origin, except in sun-dried forage. In the animal kingdom, vitamin D_3 is found only in small quantities in some tissues such as liver and in fish oils.

Recommendations

Although in some circumstances vitamin D requirements may be obtained entirely by endogenous synthesis, in practice it is useful to include a sufficient quantity in feed to obtain all requirements.

The National Research Council (NRC) recommends 220 IU/kg feed for piglets, 200 IU/kg for pigs between 10 and 20 kg and 150 IU/kg during the remainder of the fattening period. The quantity for breeders is identical in all cases and the recommendation is 200 IU/kg (**Tables I – III**).

In their review of vitamin content of commercial feeds in Spain, Fraga and Villamide (2000) found average values of 2120, 1112 and 1720 IU/kg feed for piglets, fatteners and breeders respectively, that is, approximately 10 times more than the figures indicated by the NRC. The coefficient of variation in this case is smaller than that given for vitamin A and is between 15% and 22%. The review by Coelho (2000), carried out using data obtained from commercial feeds in the US, found slightly smaller values (1528, 8418 and 1602 IU/kg for piglets, fatteners and gestating sows, respectively). Surprisingly in this case the coefficient of variation is higher and is between 45% and 56%, which indicates a very wide range of variation. The results provided by Coelho (2000) indicate that in the US there are probably two well-defined positions: while some companies use relatively high concentrations of vitamin D (similar to those described in Spain), others use a much lower level. Also, when studying evolution over time, from 1992 to 1999, a surprising drop of 16.7% is observed in the level of inclusion of vitamin D in feeds for gestating sows.

VITAMIN E

Chemical structure units

Vitamin E has a hydroquinol nucleus or chromanol ring with an isoprenoid chain (four carbon atoms in a straight chain and a side chain of a single carbon) which is repeated three times in succession (**Figure 6**). If the side chain is completely saturated, the product is given the name of tocopherol, but if it has an unsaturate for each isoprenoid group (that is to say a total of three unsaturates) it is called tocotrienol. In nature there are four natural tocopherols (α, β, δ and γ) and four tocotrienols (α, β, δ and γ) which demonstrate vitamin E activity. The differences between the different forms are due to the position and number of methyl groups in the chromanol ring. The different position of the methyl groups gives rise to the different racemic forms of tocopherols and tocotrienols. If the methyl groups are located on the same plane, they are called R forms, but if they are located on different planes, they are called S forms. The natural isomer of α-tocopherol possesses three methyl groups in positions 2, 4 and 8 of the isoprenoid chain on the same plane and for that reason is called 2R, 4R, 8R or RRR α-tocopherol, or sometimes D-α-tocopherol. The synthetic form, known as DL-α-tocopherol or all-rac-α-tocopherol, is a mixture in the same proportion of the R and S isomers. The differences between the distinct racemic forms and their comparison with the natural form are becoming a subject of active investigation. In a recent study Lauridsen and Jensen (2005) find that of the 8 possible isomers, approximately 99% of what is found in tissues consists of R isomers in position 2, probably because of differences in the affinity of the α-tocopherol transporting hepatic protein. Of the total tocopherol retained in the tissues, the RRR form predominates (more than 30%),

Figure 6. Schematic representation of vitamin E.

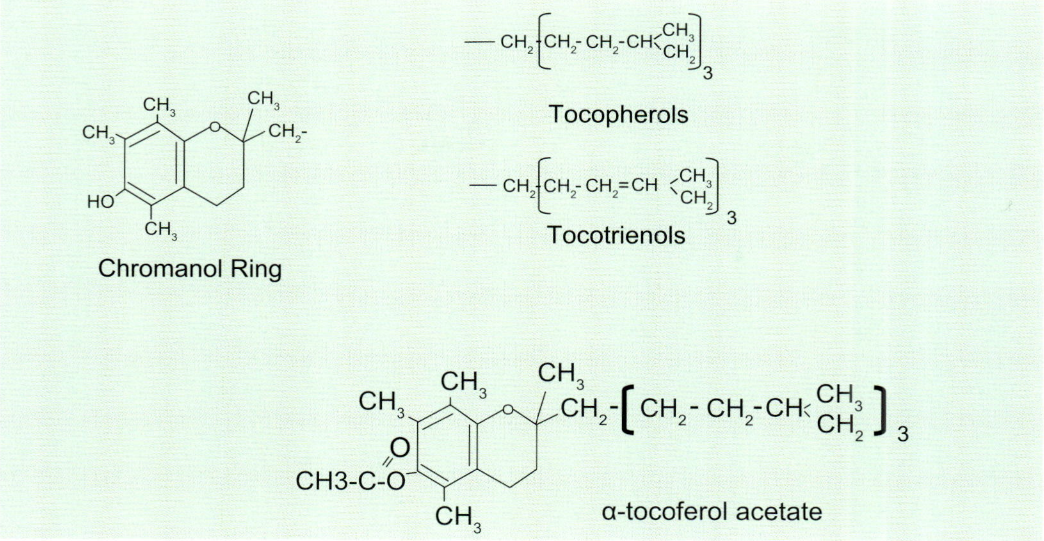

Tocopherols

Tocotrienols

Chromanol Ring

α-tocoferol acetate

followed by the RRS and RSR (around 27%) and the RSS (around 17%). The four isomers SSS, SRR, SSR and SRS together make up a quantity of less than 1%, even if the animals have a high supplementation of all-rac-α-tocopherol (Lauridsen and Jensen, 2005). Mahan et al. (2000) have observed a greater absorption of the natural forms in breeding sows and Wilburn et al. (2007) observed the same effect.

In all cases, position 6 of the chromanol ring has a hydroxyl (alcohol) group which oxidizes very easily, producing a structural change in the molecule and giving rise to α-tocopherol quinone (with two ketone groups). Since it prevents other compounds being oxidized vitamin E acts as an antioxidant, and is therefore very susceptible to oxidation. To prevent it oxidizing so readily, the hydroxyl group from position 6 can be esterified in the laboratory with a fatty acid (usually acetic acid, although it may also be palmitic, propionic, etc.), giving rise to forms which are completely resistant to oxidation, although they also have no vitamin activity. In order for these esters to be active in vivo they must be hydrolyzed in the intestine, releasing the hydroxyl group.

Many tests have been carried out to establish the vitamin activity of the different tocopherols and tocotrienols and it has been observed that the relative activity differs according to the function under consideration (capacity to prevent fetal reabsorption, hemolysis, and muscular dystrophy). Nevertheless, in all cases, the greatest activity is found in the α-tocopherol isomer, followed by β-tocopherol (between 12% and 40% of activity depending on the function studied). The other compounds are much less active – γ-tocopherol between 3% and 20%, δ-tocopherol between 0.3% and 1%, α-tocotrienol between 17% and 29%, β-tocotrienol between 1% and 5%. The other tocotrienols can be considered to lack vitamin activity (Machlin, 1984). Of all the possible compounds (including esters) with vitamin E activity, the one which is most widely used in animal nutrition is DL-α-tocopherol acetate. Indeed, this is the compound used as the reference in establishing international units (1 IU = 1 mg DL-α-tocopherol acetate).

Metabolism

Vitamin E is absorbed in the intestine, so tocopherol ester forms have to have been hydrolyzed previously by action of esterases (Mathias et al., 1981), which represents the point at which it becomes functionally active. It is absorbed in the form of bile salt micelles together with lipids from the ration, mainly where the upper and middle

257

Figure 7. Effect of supplying all-rac-α-tocopherol (70 vs. 250 IU) in the feed of breeder sows on the profile of α-tocopherol stereoisomers in alveolar macrophages of piglets one week after weaning (adapted from Lauridsen and Jensen, 2005).

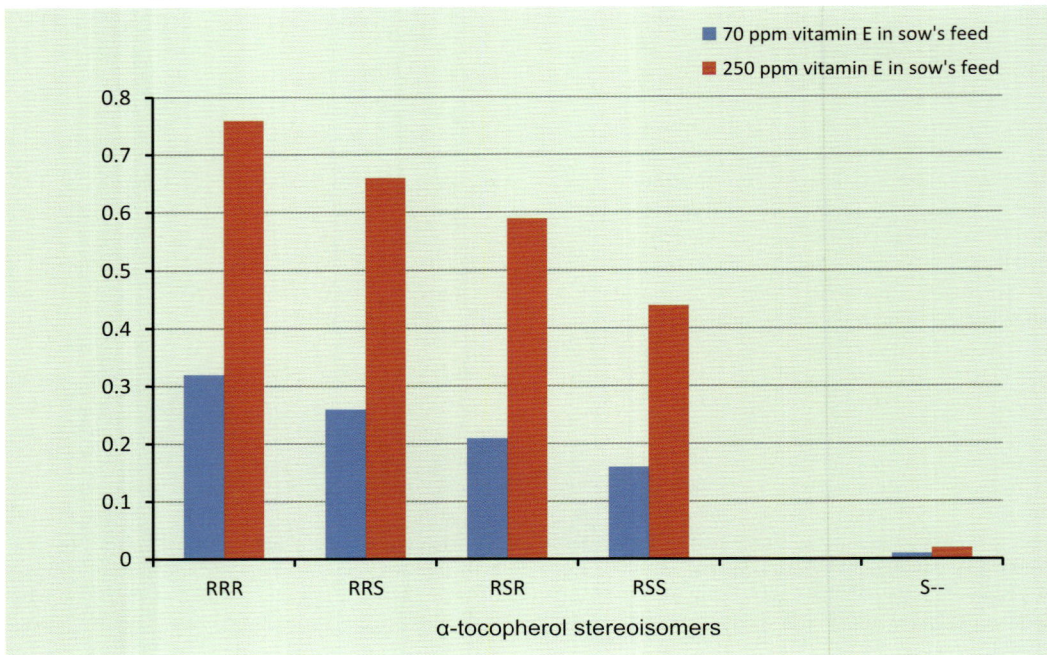

third of the small intestine meet (Gallo-Torres, 1980). The molecule is incorporated into chylomicrons and is transported in the lymphatic system, carried by lipoproteins (McCormick *et al.*, 1960). Tissue distribution is explained by the presence of specific receptors in tissues for lipoprotein carriers, by passive diffusion from membrane lipoproteins to tissues or by action of the lipoprotein lipase which acts as a carrier protein (Parker, 1989; Traber *et al.*, 1985). In studies carried out on humans using raised concentrations of the synthetic form it has been shown that consumption of more than 900 mg DL-α-tocopherol acetate per day limits hydrolysis of the ester bond (Baker *et al.*, 1986). It has also been shown that there is competition between fat-soluble vitamins for absorption, probably due to lipase-mediated hydrolysis or due to competition for entry into micelles.

The efficiency of absorption of α-tocopherol and of the different forms of vitamin E is, however, relatively low (Machlin, 1984). It depends on the effectiveness of the digestive system (Hollander, 1981), on the presence of vitamin A, which could reduce absorption

(Morrissey, 1994), or of the ferric ion which could destroy vitamin E. Absorption increases with the addition of fat to the ration, in particular medium chain triglycerides, since the presence of polyunsaturated fatty acids reduces absorption efficiency (Gallo-Torres and Miller, 1971). Other authors, however, have found more recently that the polyunsaturated fatty acid content of the ration does not change the apparent absorption of vitamin E (Lilian *et al.*, 1997). In studies carried out with rats, Gallo-Torres (1980) found that absorption of α-tocopherol and/or its esters when ingested orally was 20-40%. Similar data have been described in swine. In some cases, such as that of piglets, digestibility may be even less.

When comparing feeds with or without added fat, a higher concentration of α-tocopherol (between 10% and 15%) is generally observed in pigs given fatty feeds. This may be due partially to the high content of tocopherols in vegetable oils, although not exclusively so, because the same phenomenon is observed (to a lesser extent) when they are given animal fats (with very low vitamin E content), so it is likely that tocopherol absorption is helped by the inclusion of fat in the feed.

Once absorbed, α-tocopherol is distributed by all cellular membranes (including intracellular structures such as the endoplasmic reticulum or the nuclear membrane) (**Figure 8**). Nevertheless, this distribution is not homogeneous in all animal cells. Marked differences have been observed in α-tocopherol deposition depending on the oxidative capacity of muscle fiber. Oxidative muscles present a greater concentration of vitamin E associated with a greater phospholipid content, increased vascular development and greater activity of mitochondrial enzymes (Jensen *et al.*, 1988a).

Vitamin E is the main antioxidant in vivo, acting in a coordinated way with a whole series of biological protection mechanisms against oxidation, which includes other vitamins (vitamin A, ß-carotene, vitamin C), a whole series of enzymes, such as catalase, the superoxide dismutase (dependent on Zn and Cu), the glutathione peroxidase (dependent on Se), etc., and even small

quantities of some natural or synthetic antioxidants (Wenk *et al.*, 2000, López Bote, 2000). The crutial feature of vitamin E is that it is located mainly within cellular membranes and specifically prevents the oxidation of polyunsaturated fatty acids which constitute phospholipids (**Figure 8**). Vitamin E neutralizes free radicals and gives way (as has been shown) to an oxidized form (α-tocopheryl quinone). The coordinated performance of fat-soluble antioxidants, principally ascorbic acid, enables regeneration of α-tocopherol and therefore allows it to continue to exercise its antioxidant function.

By protecting phospholipid polyunsaturated fatty acids from oxidation, vitamin E carries out two clearly established functions. First, it allows maintenance of the structural integrity of membranes, even in the presence of free radicals. Second, vitamin E carries out an important function in the maintenance of cellular physiology, and is necessary for a multitude of functions, some of which are difficult to establish accurately. Thus, the role of vitamin E is linked to that of essential polyunsaturated fatty acids which

Figure 8. Schematic representation of the location of the α-tocopherol molecule in the interior of the membrane and of the regenerative mechanism of free radicals formed thanks to the intervention of vitamin C (From Morrissey *et al.*, 2000).

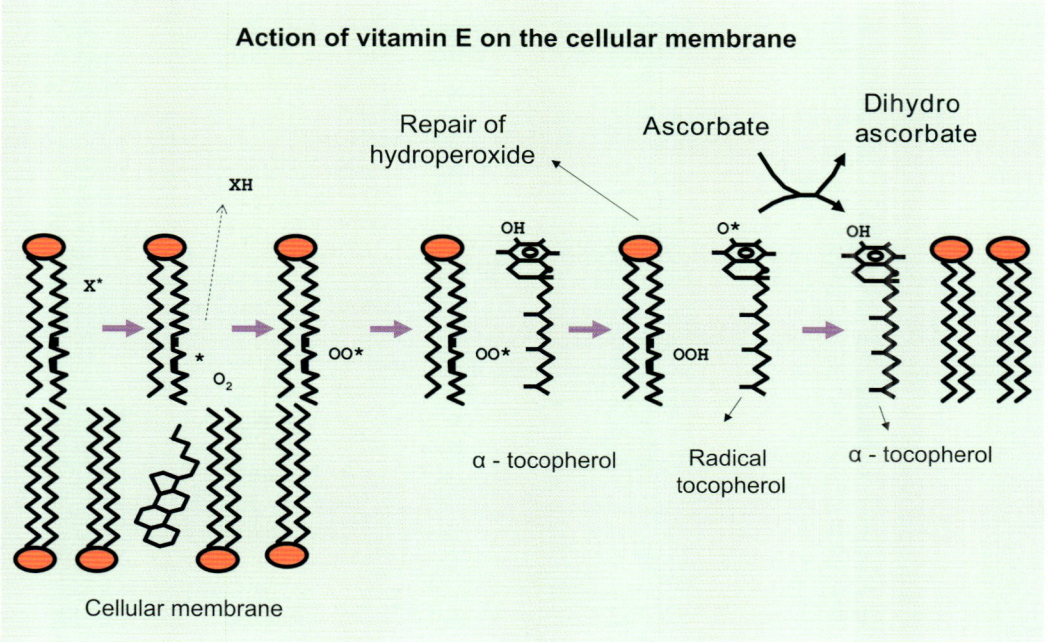

constitute cellular membranes and generate highly metabolically active compounds, such as prostaglandins, prostacyclins, thromboxanes and leukotrienes. Vitamin E concentration has been directly linked to the functioning of the reproductive, muscular, circulatory and nervous systems, and even to immune response and resistance to various pathological conditions.

As with most fat-soluble compounds, once absorbed by the animal's body any surplus not required to carry out short-term biological functions can be stored, remaining dissolved in animal lipids. Thus there is a direct relationship between ingestion and tissue concentration. For this reason, unlike with water-soluble vitamins, in some circumstances it might be useful to administer higher quantities than the minimum levels established to obtain an additional benefit.

Deficiency symptoms

The first tests on the existence of vitamin E were related to the reproductive function, hence it was first classed as an anti-sterility vitamin. Other deficiency symptoms are muscular weakness, muscular degeneration (myopathy), hepatosis, discoloration of adipose tissue (waxy pigmentation), edema and even sudden death.

Sources

Vitamin E is abundant in food of vegetable origin. In most cases, the available analytical data refer to α-tocopherol which, as has been pointed out, is the main active compound. Content is especially high in green forage (especially in leaves and buds). Tender grass contains around 200 mg/kg (Rey et al., 1997). Cereals are also a good source of vitamin E, with an approximate range of concentration between 10 and 40 mg/kg. Barley (around 35-40 mg/kg) and oats (20-25 mg/kg) are the cereals which contain the largest quantity. In cereals, vitamin E is concentrated particularly in the germ, so cereal by-products (rice bran, wheat germ, some by-products of corn) usually have much larger quantities (50-70 mg/kg), although these are very variable depending on the technological treatment applied. In general, legumes have a moderate α-tocopherol content (around 10 mg/kg). Oleaginous

foods have very variable values depending on whether or not the oil has been extracted and on the extraction procedure itself. For example, the α-tocopherol content of whole soy seed is around 50 mg/kg. Cake obtained by mechanical extraction, however, contains around 7-10 mg/kg and cake obtained from solvent extraction has a value of around 3 mg/kg. In general, products of animal origin have very low quantities, because in live animals the concentration rarely exceeds 2-4 mg/kg of tissue, and the processing methods are usually very aggressive to tocopherols.

As has already been pointed out, vitamin E is highly susceptible to oxidation, therefore storage or some technological treatments (milling, dehydration, etc.) cause marked losses in a few days or weeks (up to 90%). For this reason, the vitamin E content of products like dried alfalfa can vary considerably depending on the production process (from 30 mg/kg or even less, up to a value of around 180 mg/kg).

Recommendations

Owing to the many processes in which it is involved and the possibility of using larger quantities to boost some aspects related to health or the quality of products, vitamin E recommendations can be established by different methods, so the figures recommended in the bibliography also vary considerably. This review will first study the established recommendations aiming at obtaining optimum productive efficiency, pointing out when necessary the existence of data to indicate the possible usefulness of modifying the supply according to the situation or to production objectives desired in certain circumstances. In the second part, we will look at the possible usefulness of providing higher quantities with the objective of improving meat characteristics.

Vitamin E and productive efficiency

Some studies carried out in the last few years on breeder sows have demonstrated a positive relationship between vitamin E administration and the number of piglets born. Mahan (1991) included four concentrations of vitamin E (0, 16, 33 and 66 mg/kg) in feed for breeder sows during three consecutive reproductive cycles and observed a characteristic exponential response (**Figure 9**). This information has led the NRC (1998) to increase its previous recommendations for breeder sows to a level of 44 mg/kg. However, there is some information to indicate that use of vitamin E in the breeder sow goes much beyond improving number of piglets born or survival to 7 days. First, in cattle there is a relationship between vitamin E intake and some problems characteristic of the breeder female, such as retained placentas and the incidence of some pathologies. Also in bovine livestock, an apparent relationship has been shown between vitamin E intake and the number of somatic cells found in milk (Batra *et al.*, 1992). Some of these functions could be affected by deficient production of prostaglandins whose concentration depends to quite an extent on the oxidative status of animals. The situation is not as clear for the sow, but an increase in the duration of parturition has been shown when vitamin E intake is reduced, which could be due to inadequate contraction of the smooth musculature. A relationship between vitamin E intake and the incidence of mastitis, metritis and agalactia (Mahan, 1991) has also been shown.

It is worth pointing out that vitamin E transfer through the placenta is very limited so piglets are born with very low levels of α-tocopherol. This is supremely important because it has been demonstrated experimentally that vitamin E increases immune response capacity (Wuryastuti *et al.*, 1993). What is more, the administration of iron in the neonatal period means an overloading of the piglet's limited antioxidant capacity (Hill *et al.*, 1999). Thus, the importance has been recognized of establishing strategies which allow the concentration of α-tocopherol in the piglet to be increased, foremost among them the diet of the dam during the final stages of gestation and during the lactation period (Mahan *et al.*, 2000). Given good physiological condition in sows fed with conventional feed, colostrums provides a very high concentration of α-tocopherol (more than 20 μg/ml), which permits a considerable increase in tissue concentration of α-tocopherol in piglets during the first few days of their life (**Figure 10**). This is achieved by the sow drawing on her physical reserves of α-tocopherol, which in the days following parturition causes a sharp drop in the concentration of α-tocopherol in her serum (which goes from a value close to 2 μg/ml to a value less than 1 μg/ml). The concentration of α-tocopherol in the milk falls during lactation until it reaches a figure close to 2 μg/ml and in consequence the concentration in the serum of the piglet also does so, until it

Figure 9. **Effect of administering vitamin E in breeder sows** (From Mahan *et al.*, 1991).

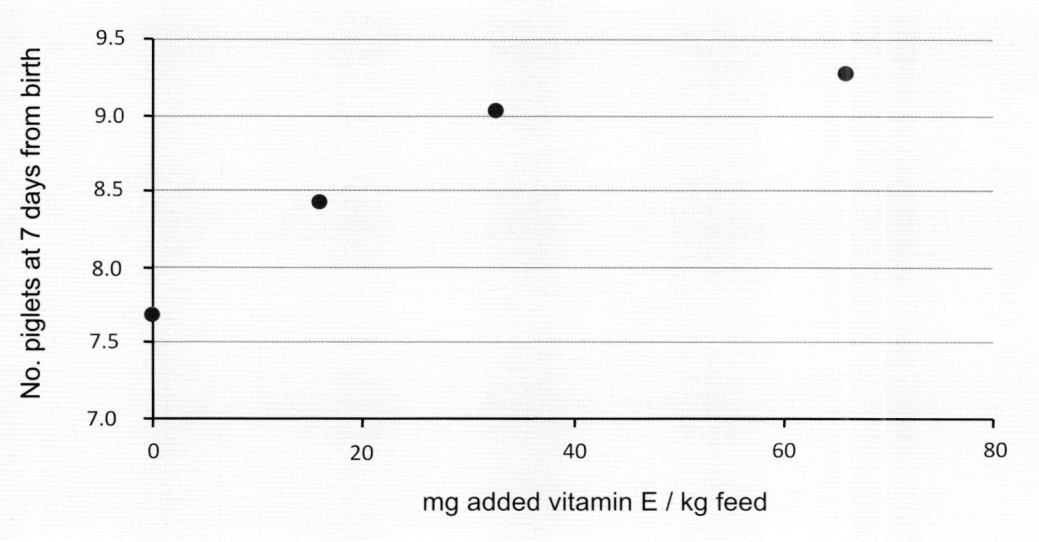

Figure 10. Estimate of the approximate evolution of the concentration of α-tocopherol in blood serum of a breeder sow (▬▬), in the colostrum and milk (▬ ▬) and in the blood serum of the piglet (▪ ▪ ▪) from birth until weaning in pigs fed with feed with a vitamin E concentration within the range of commercial feed use.
(From Lauridsen and Jensen 2005, Moreira and Mahan, 2002, Mahan *et al.*, 2000).

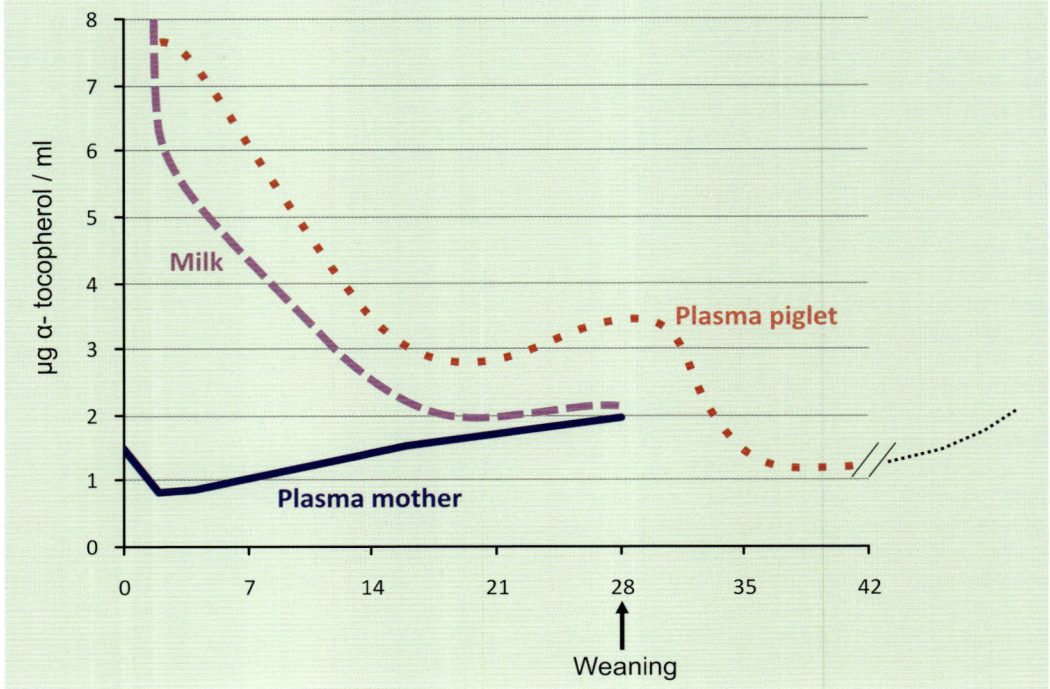

Figure 11. Effect of the concentration of vitamin E in the feed of breeder sows on the concentration of α-tocopherol in the liver of weaned piglets
(From Lauridsen and Jensen, 2005).

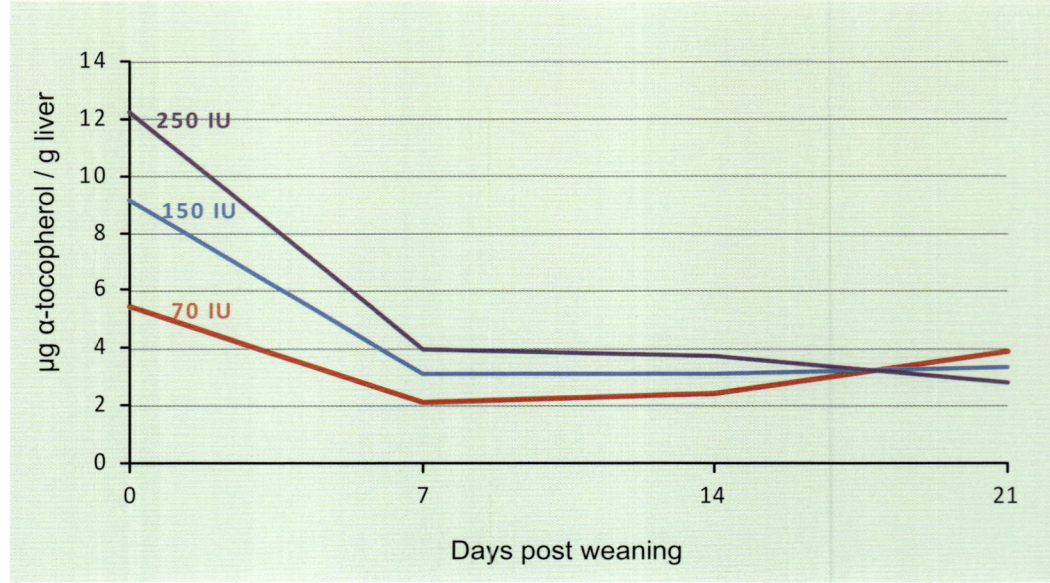

reaches a figure close to 3-4 µg/ml. This behavior seems to indicate that it might be useful to increase the supply of vitamin E to the breeder sow in gestation and/or lactation so that there is a greater possibility of transfer to the piglet. Hidiroglou *et al.* (1993) observed a linear response in the α-tocopherol content of milk when including between 22 and 88 mg vitamin E/kg in feed. More recently, Lauridsen and Jensen (2005) have observed that the content in the sow's plasma and in the milk rises linearly when the concentration of vitamin E in the feed is increased from 70 to 250 IU and this response is maintained throughout lactation. **Figure 11** shows the concentration of α-tocopherol in the hepatic tissue of piglets according to the concentration of vitamin E in the dam's feed during the lactation period. At the time of weaning (at 28 days) the concentration of α-tocopherol in the liver of piglets whose mothers received 250 IU is more than double that of piglets whose mothers received 70 IU. Babinsky (1992) observed that inclusion of up to 136 mg vitamin E/kg in feed for sows during the pre-weaning period improved immune response in weaned piglets.

Another key moment in the life of the pig is when it is weaned, since while vitamin E continues to play a very important role as the pig's limited digestive capacity at this stage leads to the concentration in the tissues diminishing markedly (**Figure 10**). In the case of blood serum the concentration can fall to less than half in just one week after weaning. This implies a high susceptibility to suffering oxidation processes during this critical moment in the life of the piglet (Soares, 1999). Teige *et al.* (1982) have found an inverse relationship between the presentation of clinical symptoms after experimental infections and the intake of vitamin E, and have consequently found an improvement in productive indices when the sanitary situation was poor.

Different strategies have been established to minimize this dramatic fall in the concentration of α-tocopherol. Moreira and Mahan (2002) have demonstrated that the inclusion of vitamin E in high concentrations (up to 200 IU/kg of feed) results in an increase in the serum concentration of α-tocopherol (**Figure 12**). Nevertheless, effectiveness is limited due to digestive inefficiency and antagonism

Figure 12. Concentration of α-tocopherol in the blood serum of weaned piglets as affected by the concentration of vitamin E in the feed (between 0 and 200 IU/kg) (From Moreira and Mahan, 2002).

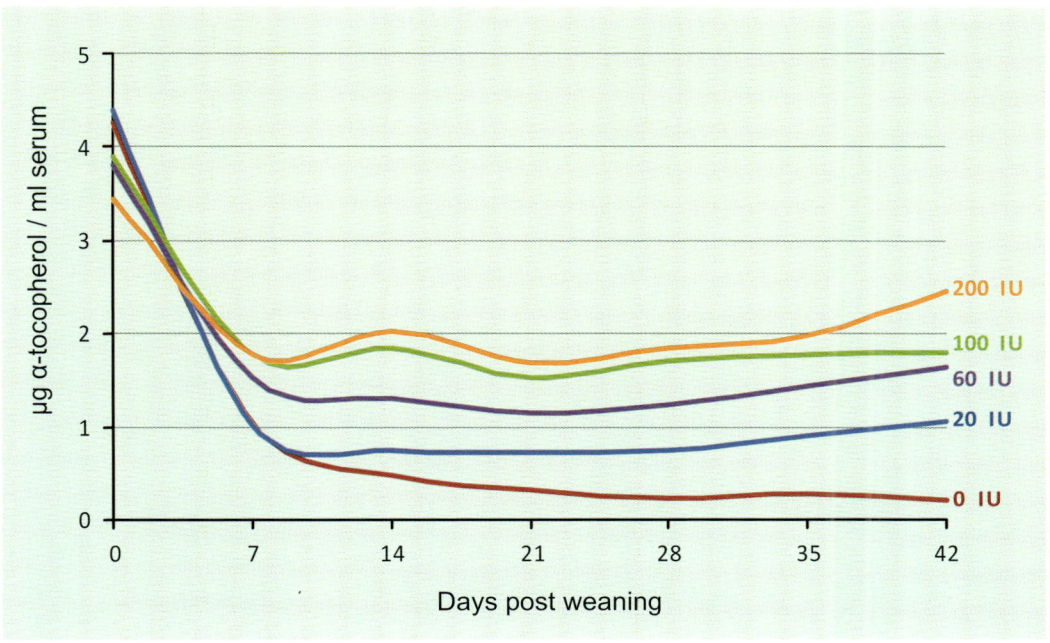

with other liposoluble compounds such as vitamin A (Ching *et al.*, 2002): it is therefore necessary to supply a concentration in the feed of 100 IU/kg or more. The same authors demonstrated that the inclusion of fat in the feed (around 5%) is effective in preventing a sharp fall in the concentration of α-tocopherol in recently weaned piglets, especially during the first few days after weaning, so that an intake of around 60 IU might be sufficient (**Figure 13**). On the other hand, Lauridsen and Jensen (2005) demonstrated the benefits of supplementing weaned piglet feed with vitamin C (500 mg/kg of feed), especially if the piglets are starting with a low/moderate level of α-tocopherol in the liver, while this is less effective if the hepatic concentration of α-tocopherol is already high at the time of weaning.

With regard to growing pigs productive results are varied. Although some authors have found an improvement in zootechnical parameters when fortifying feeds with vitamin E (Asghar *et al.*, 1991), most of the available literature indicates that there is no

effect. In a recent work a lesser epithelial desquamation of the mucous membrane of the small intestine was found in pigs receiving 200 mg α-tocopherol acetate per kg of feed, compared with those receiving feed with a content around 20 mg/kg (López Bote *et al.*, 2001). Bearing in mind the quantitative importance of desquamation of intestinal cells in pigs, the energy and amino acid saving could explain the possible zootechnical benefit found in some cases. The relationship between vitamin E intake and the phenomenon of apoptosis (cell death) could be the basis to explain this phenomenon (and possibly phenomena related to the decrease in the number of somatic cells in milk) and opens up an interesting field of research not just in pigs.

As for boars, little information is available on the effects of supplementing feed with vitamin E. Cerolini *et al.* (2000) have observed that when including α-tocopherol in the diluting medium of semen, this vitamin is incorporated in spermatozoid membranes, increasing the spermatozoa's resistance to

Figure 13. Effect of the concentration of vitamin E (20 vs. 60 IU/kg of feed) and the inclusion of added fat in the feed of weaned piglets on the α-tocopherol concentration in the blood serum (From Moreira and Mahan, 2002).

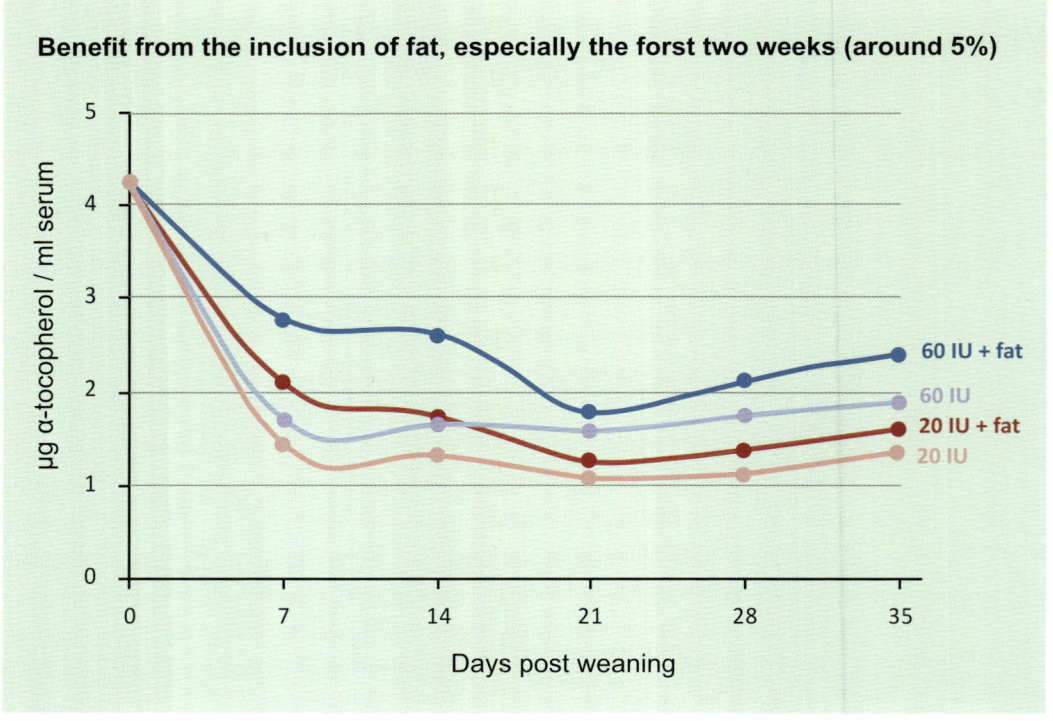

oxidative deterioration, maintaining a higher concentration of some polyunsaturated fatty acids in phospholipids and significantly reducing the loss of viability of the ejaculate during storage.

Vitamin E requirements have been estimated by the NRC (1998) on the basis of the minimum quantity required to avoid the appearance of biological problems and are given as 16 IU/kg feed up to 10 kg live weight and 11 IU/kg feed up to 120 kg live weight. For gestating and lactating sows and for boars the recommendation rises to 44 IU/kg (NRC, 1998).

Given the variability of swine production systems and the broad range of functions of vitamin E, practical recommendations can differ considerably. In their review, Fraga and Villamide (2000) found that the average level of added vitamin E supplied in the vitamin and mineral premix for feed for piglets was 31.4 IU/kg (with a range from 3.3 to 100 IU), for grower-fattener pigs 9.5 IU (range from 0 to 20 IU) and for breeders 23.6 IU (range from 5.4 to 53.6 IU). Coelho (2000) found much higher concentrations in the US, with average values for piglets, growers, fatteners and breeders of 52, 28, 20 and 54 IU/kg, respectively.

Vitamin E and meat quality

Many studies have demonstrated a positive relationship between the administration of large quantities of vitamin E in pig feed and some attributes of meat quality. Therefore it is essential first to find what the possible positive effects are and then to establish quantity and guidelines for appropriate administration in each case. Kerth *et al.* (2001) have recently demonstrated that the effect of vitamin E on the quality of meat depends on whether the genotype carries the halothane gene, meaning that in the non-carriers supplementation is more effective. The interaction of genotype with the action of vitamins (for both vitamin E and other vitamins) promises to be an interesting line of investigation in the coming years.

Vitamin E and oxidative stability

Once an animal has been slaughtered most of the mechanisms which control oxidative

processes become inactive and oxidative reactions occur. These cause marked alterations in meat properties within a few days. Oxidative deterioration is regarded as the main reason for these alterations in the meat after microbial activity, although this can be controlled with appropriate storage temperatures. Numerous experiments have shown that supplementation with α-tocopherol acetate produces a high tissue content of α-tocopherol, leading to an improvement in the oxidative stability of muscle in pigs (Monahan *et al.*, 1990; Asghar *et al.*, 1991; Morrissey *et al.*, 1996). The effectiveness of vitamin E has also been observed in cooked muscle (Monahan *et al.*, 1990) and in the presence of salt (Buckley *et al.*, 1989). Different studies have also been carried out to investigate the antioxidant effect of vitamin E in relation to the fat composition of the ration. Monahan *et al.* (1992) observed a positive antioxidant effect of vitamin E when supplemented at 200 ppm to pig rations fortified with 3% soy oil and tallow.

Leskanick *et al.* (1997) observed similar effects. They also suggested that the greater the addition of unsaturated fatty acids, the greater the amount of vitamin E to be administered, since when adding the same quantity to rations containing 2% rape seed oil and 1% fish oil and to control rations containing tallow and soy oil, the levels were lower in the former. This could be explained by an increase in the metabolic demand on the vitamin as a result of the higher level of polyunsaturated fatty acids. Vitamin E requirement increases, therefore, when there is an increase in the proportion of polyunsaturated fatty acids (Wang *et al.*, 1996).

There are studies which indicate that supplementing the ration with α-tocopherol inhibits the production of cholesterol oxides (COPs) in heated and refrigerated pork (Rey *et al.*, 2001). Monahan *et al.* (1992) observed a decrease in total COPs formed in pork from animals whose rations had been supplemented with 200 mg/kg α-tocopherol acetate compared with those consuming unsupplemented rations.

Vitamin E and meat color

Meat color is determined mainly by the content and chemical form of the hemin myoglobin pigment. The heme group of myoglobin contains a central atom of iron which can form 6 coordinate bonds, four of which occur with N-atoms of the porphyrin ring and a fifth with a hemin apoprotein. The sixth bond, together with hematic iron status, determines meat color. If the unifying molecule is O2, oxymyoglobin is formed, a bright red color which with storage tends to oxidize and form methemoglobin causing dark coloration.

Rhee and Ziprin (1987) found a correlation between the total pigment and myoglobin content and lipid peroxidation in raw beef. Supplementation of animal rations with different quantities of α-tocopherol acetate brought about better color stability and a lesser reduction in "a" values (directly linked to the color red) than were found in unsupplemented animals. This has also been observed in pigs (Monahan et al., 1994; Asghar et al., 1991; Lanari et al., 1995; Phillips et al., 2001), although data are less conclusive than with cattle (Faustman et al., 1989; Liu et al., 1996) and lambs (López Bote et al., 2001). It has generally been observed that the greater the supplementation, the less the color loss (Asghar, 1991; Monahan et al., 1994) although some authors have not found significant differences between the high supplementation levels. Faustman et al. (1989) observed that to stabilize the color in beef muscle a concentration of 3.0 to 3.7 µg of α-tocopherol/g of tissue was necessary. In pigs, Asghar et al. (1991) observed that when supplementing rations with 100 or 200 mg/kg, deposition in the longissimus dorsi muscle was 2.60 and 4.72 µg of α-tocopherol/kg, which was sufficient to stabilize color. The possible actuating mechanism of α-tocopherol could be related to the inactivation of free radicals which can oxidize myoglobin or the systems of reduction of metamyoglobin from skeletal muscle.

Vitamin E and water holding capacity

Tests have shown that it is possible to reduce drip losses through the incorporation of high levels of α-tocopherol acetate in the ration.

Asghar et al. (1991) observed that after 10 days of refrigeration (4°C) under fluorescent light, samples of frozen meat from pigs which had consumed rations supplemented with 200 IU of α-tocopherol acetate/kg of feed had lower drip losses than samples from pigs consuming feeds supplemented with 100 or 10 IU/kg. Monahan et al. (1994) obtained comparable results with fresh muscle. These authors suggested that this could be explained by the fact that changes in the α-tocopherol content could alter the passage of biomolecules through cell membranes and therefore the degree of muscle exudation, due to physiochemical interactions of α-tocopherol with molecules in the lipid membrane. Any other change in the lipid microenvironment could affect the ability of membranes to act as a semi-permeable barrier (Monahan et al., 1994). Furthermore, α-tocopherol could act to preserve the integrity of cellular membranes of the muscle by preventing oxidation of their phospholipids, thereby impeding the passage of sarcoplasmic liquid through them (Asghar et al., 1991; Monahan et al., 1994). As with color, the level of vitamin E supplementation affects this action, although the effect appears to be less pronounced (Cannon et al., 1996).

Vitamin E and quality of meat products

The administration of vitamin E in high concentrations to improve meat quality is of special interest in swine as it has been shown that vitamin E accumulated in tissues remains there during processing, improving the technological properties of the meat (transfer of water) as much as the qualitative attributes of the products (color stability, acceptability, dryness, presence of unpleasant smells and flavors, etc.). It has been possible to observe these effects even in cured products processed for over ten months (Isabel et al., 1999). In this respect, it is useful to remember that products from Iberian pigs (best example of the quality of meat production in swine) show a high α-tocopherol content which they acquire from their particular outdoor feeding system (Rey et al., 1997). However, some data indicate that it is possible to reduce the amount of certain additives included during processing if the meat contains a good quantity of antioxidants at the time of slaughter (Dineen *et al.*, 2000), which brings a benefit to public health and the positive commercial implications associated with it.

If the effects of the supply of fatty acids and antioxidants on the quality of these products are taken into account, as well as the production costs, interest in optimizing this supply appears to be justified. This means matching the cost of feed not to the carcass or to fresh meat, but to the end-product. This is a point of particular relevance in Spain, the world leader, where currently around 40 million cured hams are processed.

Recommendations and guidelines for administration

There are few studies which aim to establish in a systematic way the most appropriate intake and times of administration for each case. Additionally, the difficulty of analyzing tocopherols in feeds and in animal tissues means that the existing data in the literature are very heterogeneous and therefore make comparison difficult.

Roth and Kirchgessner (1975) added tocopherol acetate to the feed at amounts from 5 to 95 mg/kg and found a linear response to vitamin E incorporation in tissues depending on the amount given. Machlin and Gabriel (1982) however, working with rats, chickens, ducks and calves found a logarithmic response between the α-tocopherol supplied in the diet and that analyzed in plasma and various tissues. In a more recent study, Hoppe *et al.* (1993) administered 0, 20, 40, 80 and 160 IU of α-tocopherol acetate/kg of feed, respectively, to groups of six animals per treatment. The α-tocopherol analyses were conducted by means of saponification of the sample. A fluorescence detector was used in the analysis. According to these authors, there is a logarithmic relationship between the ingestion of vitamin E (expressed in mg of DL-α-tocopherol acetate/kg of feed) and the content of α-tocopherol in the various tissues (expressed as μg of α-tocopherol/g of fresh tissue). Several equations have been established:

Plasma

$$y = -(1.08\pm0.27) + (0.89\pm0.07) \ln x \ (R^2=0.61, \ p < 0.0001)$$

M. Longissimus dorsi

$$y = -3.2 + 2.09 \ln x \ (R^2 = 0.77, \ p < 0.0001)$$

Liver

$$y = -10.2 + 5.54 \ln x \ (R^2 = 0.62, \ p < 0.0001)$$

Adipose tissue

$$y = -13.9 + 7.63 \ln x \ (R^2 = 0.63, \ p < 0.0001)$$

y = α-tocopherol in the tissues (μg of α-tocopherol/g of fresh tissue)
ln = ingestion of vitamin E (mg of DL-α-tocopherol acetate/kg feed)

It can be seen that the greatest quantities of vitamin E are found in adipose tissue, followed by liver and longissimus dorsi muscle. Nevertheless, when the data from these authors are compared with most of the existing literature it is evident that their values are higher (almost double) than the majority. Recently a research project was carried out within the scope of the European Union (Diet-Ox, 1998) which includes a total of 14 laboratories which interchange data, so that data are perfectly comparable. If the data supplied by these 14 laboratories only is used (and only in experiments in which feed fortified with vitamin E is given for at least seven weeks) the dose response curve obtained is very similar to that of Hoppe et al. (1993), but with much lower tissue content. According to data from these 14 research groups, the α-tocopherol concentration in muscle tissue should be between 3.5 and 4 µg/g for it to have an antioxidant effect. Below this concentration the effect is marginal. The effective level is equivalent to the inclusion of 100-200 mg of α-tocopherol acetate per kg feed. These data

are in agreement with most of the existing literature and with the most widely used recommendations (Buckley et al., 1995).

Fortification of feed with vitamin E represents an additional cost. Therefore it is necessary to consider not only the optimum quantity but also the period of administration when trying to establish recommendations for vitamin E supplementation in pig feed.

In this case too the work of two research groups belonging to the group of 14 constituting the Diet-Ox project has been selected. Firstly, Morrissey et al. (1996) found that supplementation with 200 mg/kg feed for 7 weeks before slaughter produced a concentration of 4 µg/g tissue, only slightly less than in animals receiving feed supplemented with the same concentration throughout the growth phase. According to this investigation, feed fortified for the last 7 weeks increases the α-tocopherol concentration in muscle tissue much more efficiently (around 0.07 µg/g per day) than feed supplemented for a much longer period (0.03 µg/g per day) (**Figure 14**).

Figure 14. Effect of the period of administration on the concentration of α-tocopherol in the muscle tissue of the pig (●= 200 IU/kg during the entire fattening phase, ●= 10 IU during the same period, ●= 10 IU during the whole period, except during the last 7 weeks, where the supply becomes established at 200 IU/kg) (Morrissey et al., 1996).

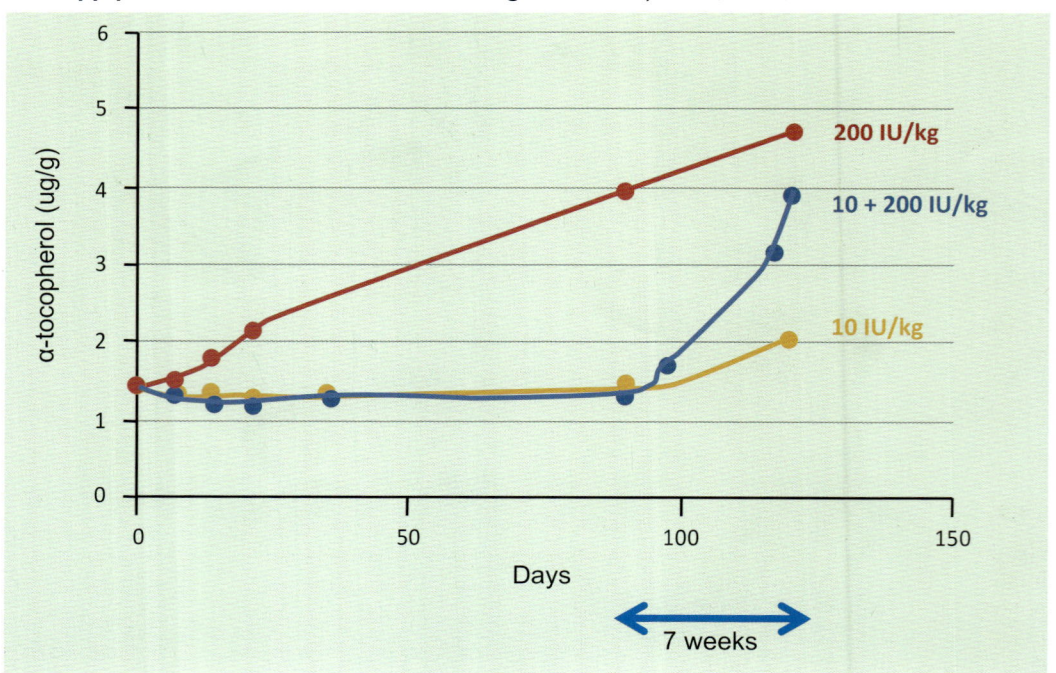

More recently Monahan (1999, personal communication) carried out a study which included various periods of administration and different quantities. Administering feed with 1000, 500 or 200 mg/kg vitamin E produces an average increase of 0.18, 0.10 and 0.04 µg/g of muscle per day. That is to say, approximately 0.20 µg per g tissue per day for each mg vitamin E above requirements supplied in the feed. This means that if 1000 mg/kg feed were supplied, in just one week the level would reach 3.8 µg/g of tissue. In the experiment by Monahan this concentration in muscle was not reached in the four weeks of the trial in which 200 mg/kg was supplied, although a theoretical calculation puts the necessary period at around six weeks. Similarly, in the work by Morrissey *et al.* (1996) it took five weeks to reach 3.9 µg/g of muscle tissue with a supply of 200 mg vitamin E/kg of feed.

According to these calculations the same concentration can be achieved in muscle by administering 1000 mg/kg for 1 week, 500 mg/kg for 2 weeks or 200 mg/kg for 5-6 weeks. In all cases the extra consumption is around 20-22 g per pig and the efficiency of tocopherol accumulation in tissues can be calculated as less than 5% of the total ingested.

VITAMIN K

Chemical structure and units

The term vitamin K is used to designate a series of compounds which are characterized by possession of a quinone group and which have antihemorrhagic properties in animals. Vitamin K is essential because it cannot be synthesized in mammal cells. The two most important natural compounds are vitamin K_1 (phylloquinone), found in green vegetables, and vitamin K_2 (menaquinone) which is produced in bacterial cultures (**Figure 15**). Vitamin K_3 (menadione) is a product of synthesis and has a quinone group without a lateral chain (2-methyl-1.4-naphthoquinone). It is yellowish and has a viscous oily appearance.

All vitamin K forms convert to menaquinone in the liver, which suggests that this is the active form of the vitamin.

The different forms of vitamin K are relatively stable at room temperature, although they are degraded when exposed to light (especially ultraviolet light).

Metabolism

As with the other fat-soluble vitamins, vitamin K must be incorporated into micelles in association with food lipids in order to be absorbed. It appears that absorption takes place mainly in the small intestine, although it has been shown that it can also occur in the colon. It seems that phylloquinone absorption is an active process and occurs mainly in the small intestine, while menaquinone is absorbed by a passive process in the small intestine and colon. Digestibility of menaquinone is much greater than that

Figure 15. Schematic representation of the different forms of vitamin K.

Phyilloquinone (K1)

Menaquinone 4 (K2)

Menadione (K3)

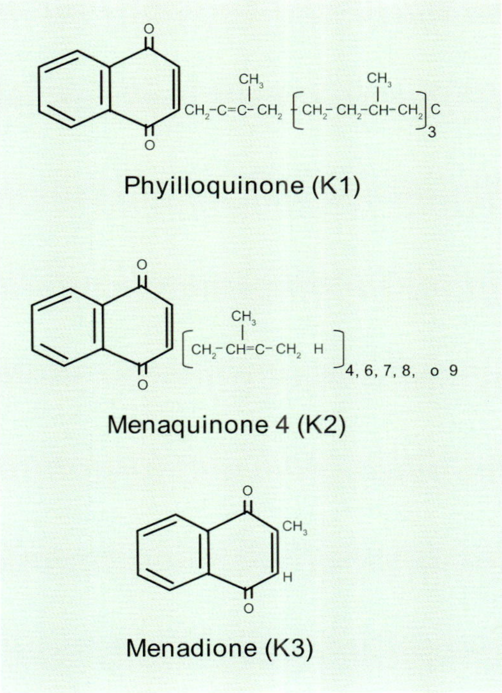

of phylloquinone. Griminger and Donis (1960) observed in rats that around 60% of the phylloquinone had been eliminated in feces 24 hours after ingestion, while in the case of menaquinone elimination was only 11%. Retention in the liver, however, is much higher in the first case (Griminger and Donis, 1960).

Vitamin K is necessary for synthesis of prothrombin, factor VII (proconvertin), factor IX, factor X and protein C in the liver and for the conversion of prothrombin to thrombin (**Figure 16**). Vitamin K acts as a coenzyme in the carboxylation process which gives rise to the formation of gamma-carboxyglutamic acid, to which calcium ions are linked prior to activation of prothrombin. Prothrombin is the inactive precursor of the enzyme thrombin which has the function of converting fibrinogen to fibrin, the principal compound responsible for blood clotting.

Some experimental data indicate that independently of its well-proven role in blood clotting, vitamin K could be linked to calcium metabolism (Kormann and Weiser, 1984).

Figure 16. Cascade of reactions involved in blood coagulation.

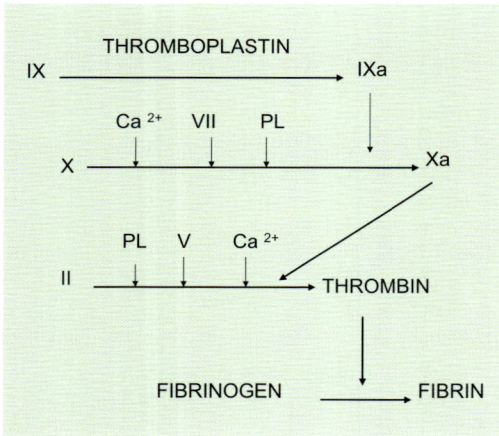

Deficiency symptoms

The main symptoms of vitamin K deficiency are the increase in blood coagulation time and anemia.

Under normal conditions, deficiency symptoms occur infrequently, although there are some compounds with antivitamin activity, such as dicumarol, present in some plants, which can provoke symptoms. However, the administration of some antimicrobial agents in pig feed can cause an inhibition of vitamin K production by microbial flora, also causing deficiency symptoms. Finally, some mycotoxins can produce antivitamin K factors, causing deficiency symptoms (Osweiler, 1970).

A characteristic symptom is the increase in coagulation time of the umbilical cord in piglets after birth. Other symptoms which occur are blood in the urine and subcutaneous hemorrhages.

Sources

Vitamin K_1 is found in most vegetables, especially green ones. Dried alfalfa contains 10 mg/kg vitamin K (phylloquinone) and cereals around 0.2-0.3 mg/kg (NRC, 1998). Foods of animal origin also contain vitamin K. Fish meal has a concentration of around 2 mg/kg. Vitamin K2 is synthesized by bacteria of the digestive system, although there is some disagreement on the real importance of this synthesis in swine, since most production takes place in the large intestine, where there is the greatest microbial activity. In any case, if animals are in contact with feces, coprophagy is a very concentrated source of vitamin K.

Recommendations

The NRC (1998) has established requirements as 0.5 mg menadione per kg feed for all ages and productive phases (Tables 1-3). No data have been published on vitamin K deficiency in pigs in good physiological condition and maintained in adequate production conditions. It is considered that microbial synthesis in the digestive system is sufficient to meet the needs of these animals. Nevertheless, when animals are produced in confined conditions, with little possibility of contact with feces, and particularly when animals are young and digestive flora are not well established, administration independent of the animal's own production is recommended. In fact, the recent review by Fraga and Villamide (2000)

on vitamin supply in vitamin and mineral premixes showed that most manufacturers choose to incorporate vitamin K in feed for pigs of all ages. Average concentration in piglet feed increases to 1.85 mg/kg feed, that is to say, some four times greater than the level recommended by the NRC. The range of variation between manufacturers of vitamin and mineral premixes for piglets fluctuates between 0 and 5 mg/kg. For growing pigs the average value is 0.67 mg/kg (range 0-4 mg/kg) and for breeders, 1.54 mg/kg (0-6 mg/kg). The coefficient of variation of this vitamin is among the highest. The situation in the US is different, since all manufacturers there always include vitamin K in the vitamin and mineral premix, average values being 3.58 mg/kg for piglets and 3.5 mg/kg for breeding animals.

WATER-SOLUBLE VITAMINS

As their name indicates, water-soluble vitamins are soluble in water, so they are present in the plasma, cytoplasm and cellular organelles. Within this broad group of vitamins, two large groups may be differentiated: the so-called B complex (which includes thiamine, riboflavin, niacin, pantothenic acid, pyridoxine, cyanocobalamin, folacin and biotin) and ascorbic acid or vitamin C. The study of the B complex is difficult because the enzymes with which they are involved take an active part in cell metabolism, and they are interrelated in many ways, to the extent that individual recommendations are hard to establish. The genetic improvement achieved in recent years may affect the vitamin requirements recommended by the NRC (1998). These recommendations were based on experimental trials with animals which presented indications of

growth less than those reached through current genetics and in accommodation very different from current housing. All this has caused nutritionists to decide on an increase in the supply of B group vitamins in feeds. A review carried out by McDowell, (2006) emphasizes the need to use higher vitamin levels due to diverse factors such as intensification of production, use of antimicrobials, the appearance of new diseases which compromize the animal's immune system and also to provide adequate body reserves. The consumption of food enriched with these and other nutrients is a demand of the 21st century consumer.

In this study we will first carry out a detailed review of each vitamin, and then present an overview of requirements, although little information is available.

THIAMINE (VITAMIN B₁)

Chemical structure and units

Thiamine is formed by one molecule of pyrimidine and one of thiazol linked by a methyl group. The presence of a hydroxyl (OH) group at one end allows it to form ester bonds with phosphoric acid, producing thiamine mono, di- or triphosphate. Most of the vitamin B_1 in animal tissues is in the form of thiamine diphosphate, also known as thiamine pyrophosphate (TPP) or cocarboxylase.

Concentration and requirements of vitamin B_1 are usually expressed in milligrams (mg).

This vitamin is highly soluble in water and sensitive to alkalis. Although it is quite stable in a dry state, thiamine tends to hydrate which, in practice, makes it deteriorate easily if not protected from contact with water.

Metabolism

The information available indicates that thiamine is highly bioavailable, being absorbed mainly in the duodenum. Although the mechanism of absorption is not known in detail, it is believed that it is by both active (mainly when it found in low concentrations) and passive diffusion. It has been shown that phosphorylation takes place in most tissues, although hepatic tissue seems to be the most important one.

In most species thiamine is not stored in tissues and reserves are depleted within a few days, so a continuous thiamine supply is required. For unknown reasons, however, tissue concentration in pigs is very high. Studies carried out more than five decades ago showed that as a result of this fact, pigs receiving feed lacking in thiamine can live for at least two months without showing signs of deficiency.

The main function of thiamine is to participate in the oxidative decarboxylation of α-keto acids. It participates, therefore, in the decarboxylation of pyruvate to acetate which then combines with coenzyme A and enters the tricarboxylic acid cycle to produce energy. It also participates in α-ketoglutaric decarboxylation to give place to succinyl coenzyme A, as well as in the pentose phosphate pathway (and therefore carries out an essential function in ribose synthesis, necessary in turn for formation of nucleotides) and in valine synthesis. Although a little-studied function, there is evidence of the intervention of thiamine in the physiology of the nervous system, probably through its involvement in the formation of neurotransmitters and transport of sodium, besides its well known involvement in the processes of obtaining energy by the neuron.

Deficiency symptoms

As in most cases, the symptoms of thiamine deficiency are quite unspecific and include loss of appetite (which can become extreme depending on the degree of deficiency involved), growth retardation, low body temperature, muscular weakness, progressive dysfunction of the nervous system and occasionally vomiting, breathing disorders and sudden death from heart failure. Inactivation of decarboxylise pyruvic acid leads to an accumulation of lactic acid and a drop in intracellular pH. As the acetyl coenzyme A is an important metabolite in fatty acid synthesis, deficiency reduces lipogenesis, or fat synthesis.

In **Table IV** we can see the principal clinical and subclinical symptoms of deficiencies of different vitamins (water-soluble and fat-soluble).

Sources

Brewer's yeast contains a large quantity of thiamine, as do cereals (usually between 3 and 6 mg/kg), soy (up to 7 mg/kg for whole soy and around 1.5 mg/kg for soy cake), peas (2 mg/kg), etc. As the vitamin is generally concentrated in the germ and the aleurone layer, thiamine concentrations are usually higher in the by-products of these feedstuffs (bran 7-20 mg/kg).

Table IV. Main clinical symptoms of vitamin deficiencies

	Principal Clinical Symptom	Principal Sub-Clinical Symptom
Thiamine	Epileptic convulsions	Iron in plasma high
		Analytic disturbance in urine
Vitamin B12	Retarded growth	Low levels of B12 in plasma
	Irritability	Low lymphatic count
	Born small and weak	Enlarged liver
Choline	Piglets born with spraddle legs	Fatty liver
	Splay Leg	Renal necrosis
Folic Acid	Retarded growth	Normocytic anemia
Biotin	Dermatitis	
	Foot lesions	

Requirements and recommendations

Since thiamine is found in almost all feedstuffs, especially in cereal grains, it is unlikely that pigs suffer thiamine deficiency under practical conditions. According to the NRC (1998) a piglet of between 3 and 5 kg requires 1.5 mg of vitamin B_1 per kg of feed. In other cases (including breeders), recommendations are set at 1 mg/kg (Tables 1-3). Bearing in mind the ready supply and availability of thiamine in almost all the primary materials used in pig nutrition, it may be thought unnecessary to include thiamine in feed for pigs. The NRC has however based these recommendations on studies geared exclusively to production parameters and carried out approximately half a century ago (Ellis and Madsen, 1944).

More recently, it has been suggested that measurement of the activity of certain enzymes linked to the process of oxidative decarboxylation be used to establish thiamine requirements more precisely and improve enzyme activity. One of the enzymes proposed was erythrocyte transketolase. According to Peng and Heitman (1973) a concentration of approximately 4 times more than the amount proposed by the NRC (1998) is needed to obtain the maximum response in the activity of this enzyme. It has also been shown that a rise in ambient temperature from 20°C to 35°C causes an increase in thiamine requirements.

A relationship has also been described between thiamine requirement in pigs and the proportion of energy provided by fat and carbohydrates in feed. The higher the fat content of the ration, the less need there is for thiamine (Ellis and Madsen, 1944).

In a recent experiment using different quantities of thiamine (between 200% and 720% of the level recommended by the NRC) in feed for piglets weighing between 10 and 27 kg, no significant effect was observed on production parameters or carcass composition (**Figure 17**) (Lutz et al., 1999). Nevertheless this figure seems to show a certain tendency towards a quadratic response, with a maximum response between 4 and 5 mg/kg, although the anomalous behavior of one of the groups did not allow any significant effects to be seen. Nor did Woodworth et al. (2000) find any effects when comparing groups of piglets fed without added thiamine to others which received feed including 2.8 and 5.5 mg/kg.

In a recent review which studied the actual situation in Spanish industry, Fraga and Villamide (2000) found that while some vitamin and mineral premixes did not include thiamine (in any of the phases), others included a quantity up to 3 times higher than that recommended by the NRC (1998). In accordance with the composition and inclusion level of the vitamin and mineral premix, the average value of thiamine supplied by the vitamin and mineral premix in feed for piglets, growers and breeders in Spain is 1.5, 0.8 and 0.7 mg/kg, respectively. In a review carried out in the USA a similar situation is described, where some vitamin and mineral premixes do not include thiamine and others (mainly for piglets and

Figure 17. Effect of the supply of thiamine at concentrations above those recommended by the NRC in piglets on weight gain (Lutz *et al.*, 1999).

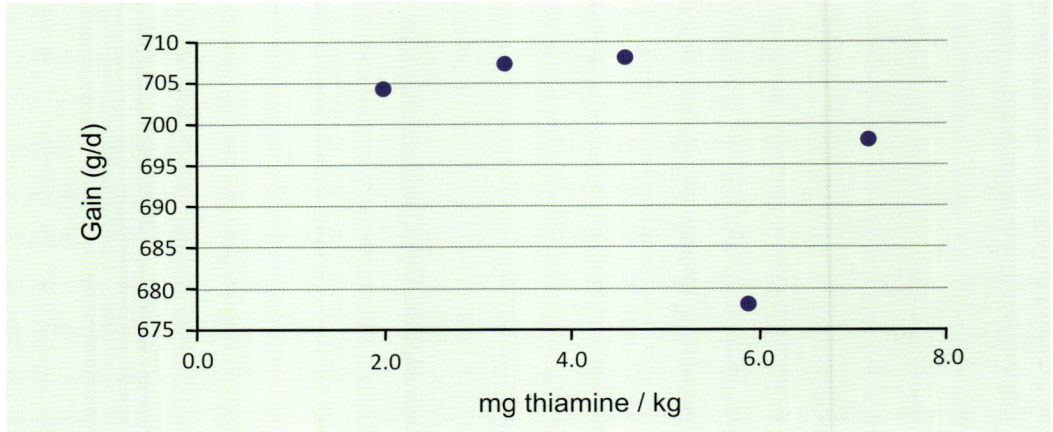

breeders) follow the recommendations by the NRC. Average values in this case for piglets, growers, finishers and breeders are 0.8, 0.4, 0.6 and 2.9 mg/kg of feed. There is an interesting difference between the situations described in the US and Spain, mainly regarding piglets and breeders. Audet *et al.* (2004) found a significant increase of motility in seminal cells and a positive tendency in sperm production in boars fed with 20 mg/kg of feed, coupled with higher levels of the remaining B group vitamins (biotin, B_{12}, B_6, folic acid, niacin, riboflavin, pantothenic acid and choline).

RIBOFLAVIN (VITAMIN B₂)

Chemical structure and units

Vitamin B_2, or riboflavin, is composed of a dimethylisoalloxazine nucleus combined with ribitol.

It is a water-soluble substance of a yellow color. It is stable to heat in a neutral or acid medium. In aqueous solution it is sensitive to visible and ultraviolet light. This can be an important factor when pigs are given liquid feed.

Metabolism

Vitamin B_2 or riboflavin combines with phosphoric acid to form two coenzymes, flavin mononucleotide (FMN) and flavin adenine dinucleotide (FAD). These coenzymes are part of a prosthetic group of denominated flavoproteins which are involved in metabolic utilization of carbohydrates, specifically in intermediate steps in which the involvement of electrons is necessary in biological oxidation-reduction reactions.

Riboflavin is absorbed in free form. For this reason, when found in a covalent bond with proteins in food, it must be released by digestive proteases, just as phosphorylated forms must be released by phosphatases. Free riboflavin is absorbed very efficiently throughout the small intestine of the pig. If it is found at a low concentration in feed, absorption takes place actively and involves energy consumption, while if the concentration in feed is high it is absorbed by passive diffusion. Inside the intestinal mucous membrane riboflavin phosphorylates to FMN, then passes to plasma where it is transported bound to albumin. In the liver it can be converted to FAD.

In animals there is very little accumulation of vitamin B_2, most of it being in the liver.

There is a close relationship between riboflavin and niacin, because flavoproteins can accept hydrogen ions from nicotinamide adenine dinucleotide (NAD) or nicotinamide adenine dinucleotide phosphate (NADP). Besides its essential function in the metabolic utilization of carbohydrates, riboflavin also participates in the processes of oxidation of amino acids and fatty acids.

It has been possible to observe that uterine flow during the first moments of gestation contains a high riboflavin concentration and that this concentration varies with the supply of this vitamin in the ration (Bazer and Zavy, 1988). The specific reasons for this high concentration remain to be identified. Pettigrew *et al.* (1996) observed that cyanocobalamin must perform an essential function in the initial moments of gestation, metabolically adapting the uterine tissue.

Deficiency symptoms

Signs of lack of vitamin B_2 in pigs are quite unspecific and usually involve the tissues and functions which are most dependent on energy from carbohydrates: epithelial and nervous tissue and functions related to reproduction. Signs usually include loss of appetite, growth retardation, poorer feed conversion, vomiting, dermatitis, alopecia, inflammation of anal mucosa, etc. A decrease in consumption of up to 30% has been described in sows consuming feeds which contained low levels of riboflavin (Frank *et al.*, 1988).

Riboflavin deficiency has a negative effect on reproduction with anoestrus, embryonic death and reabsorption, birth of weak piglets which die in the first 48 hours, edema in piglets, premature birth (up to 2 weeks), litters without hair, etc. (Esch *et al.*, 1981; Pettigrew *et al.*, 1996).

In the last few years, it has been observed that riboflavin deficiency can affect the reproductive system of young sows.

Sources

Vitamin B_2 is abundant in green vegetables (alfalfa 15 mg/kg), yeast, fungi and most bacteria (except lactobacilli) and products of animal origin (buttermilk 28 mg/kg, fishmeal between 5 and 10 mg/kg).

Riboflavin is present at a low concentration in cereals (between 1.0 and 1.4 mg/kg, except for sorghum and rice, which contain up to 4 mg/kg). For this reason special attention must be paid to this vitamin when large quantities of cereals are included in pig feed. Cereal by-products contain slightly higher amounts (for example, wheat bran contains approximately 3 mg/kg).

Concentrates of vegetable protein generally contain appreciable amounts (whole soy 2.6 mg/kg, soy cake 3.0-4.0 mg/kg, sunflower meal 7 mg/kg, peanut 6 mg/kg).

However, there is little information on the availability of riboflavin, although Chung and Baker (1990) have calculated that in chickens fed a conventional feed, based mainly on corn and soy, availability is less than 60%. It can be assumed that the situation is similar in swine (at least for young animals).

Riboflavin is one of the most stable vitamins, but, as previously shown, it is very sensitive to light (especially ultraviolet light). For this reason, conditions of processing and storage may represent important losses if exposure to sunlight is not limited. **Table V** shows a summary of the content of water-soluble vitamins in the raw materials most frequently used in pig feed.

Requirements and recommendations

According to the NRC (1998) the riboflavin requirement of pigs between 3 and 5 kg is 4 mg/kg; between 5 and 10 kg, 3.5 mg; between 10 and 20 kg, 3 mg; between 20 and 50 kg, 2.5 mg and from then just 2 mg/kg. In breeders, requirements are 3.75 mg/kg in all cases (Tables 1-3). As previously indicated, these recommendations were established years ago and recent work by Monahan *et al.* (2007) has demonstrated that using levels of riboflavin in conjunction with niacin, pantothenic acid and vitamin B_{12} which are 100% higher than those recommended by the NRC (1998) produces improvements in growth of pigs in the starter and growth phases but not in the final period (85-120 kg). In the study, carried out with 660 animals, a quadratic response was obtained on the inclusion of levels one, two or four times as high as those indicated by the NRC (**Figure 18**), although the use of three or four times NRC levels did not bring a significant response over an addition of double the

Table V. Levels of water-soluble vitamins in raw materials commonly used in pig diets (FEDNA, 2003).

Raw Materials	Thiamine mg/kg	Riboflavin mg/kg	Niacin mg/kg	Pantothenic Acid mg/kg	B6 mg/kg	B12 ug/g	Folic Acid mg/kg	Biotin mg/kg
Cereals	3–6	1–4	20–60	5–15	3.6		0.4	0.2
Cereal by-products	7–20		300	18–30			1.8	0.1
Whole soy	7	2.6	20–60		3.5			0.3
Soy cake	2	3–4		15	0.5			0.3
Sunflower meal		7	200	10				1.6
Peanut meal		6	150–220	47				0.4
Peas	2			5				0.2
Alfalfa		15		30			4.5	0.3
Animal proteins (blood, bloodmeal)		28				500	1	0.1
Fishmeal		5–10	50–150	10–20	4.0		0.2	0.3
Brewer's yeast	33							
Yeast, fungi and microorganisms		28				100–400		
Dairy by-products				20–45				0.4

recommendations estimated by the NRC (1998).

Considering the variability of both content and availability of riboflavin in most feed ingredients, it seems advisable to include a quantity of riboflavin in feed to complement the supply in the feed ingredients, especially for young animals and probably for breeder sows.

Some authors have found including higher quantities of riboflavin (between 60 and 160 mg/day) in the early stages of gestation to have a positive effect on the number of piglets born (Bazer and Zavy, 1988, Pettigrew et al., 1996), and this effect is most marked in farms with poor reproductive performance. Including higher levels of riboflavin (between 175% and 300% greater than NRC recommendations) in feed for piglets (between 10 and 27 kg) has also been observed to have a significant effect (Lutz and Stahly, 1998). Additional weight gain in this period may be calculated as around 6 g per piglet per day per mg riboflavin included in

feed, with a linear response being observed (p < 0.05) (**Figure 19**).

In the review by Fraga and Villamide (2000) on the composition of vitamin and mineral premixes used for swine in Spain, they found that riboflavin was included in all cases. The average inclusion for piglets (expressed as mg/kg of feed) was 5.9 mg/kg (with a range of variation between 1.0 and 10.1 mg/kg), for growers 3.35 mg/kg (range 0.5-8.0) and breeders 4.25 mg/kg (range 2.9-10). In the US Coelho (2000) found average values of 8.4 mg/kg for piglets, 5.4 and 3.8 mg/kg respectively, in growers and finishers and 7.8 mg/kg in gestation. The difference between inclusion levels of riboflavin in these two countries is surprising – the level in the USA is between 40% and 80% higher than that in Spain – since the difference in composition of feed ingredients used in feed does not appear to justify such a wide variation. The study by Mahan et al. (2007) places value on the possibility of reducing the inclusion levels of riboflavin in the period from 85 to 120 kg liveweight.

Figure 18. Average daily gain in a pig (25-120 kg) according to the level of incorporation of B group vitamins in feed (Mahan *et al.*, 2007).

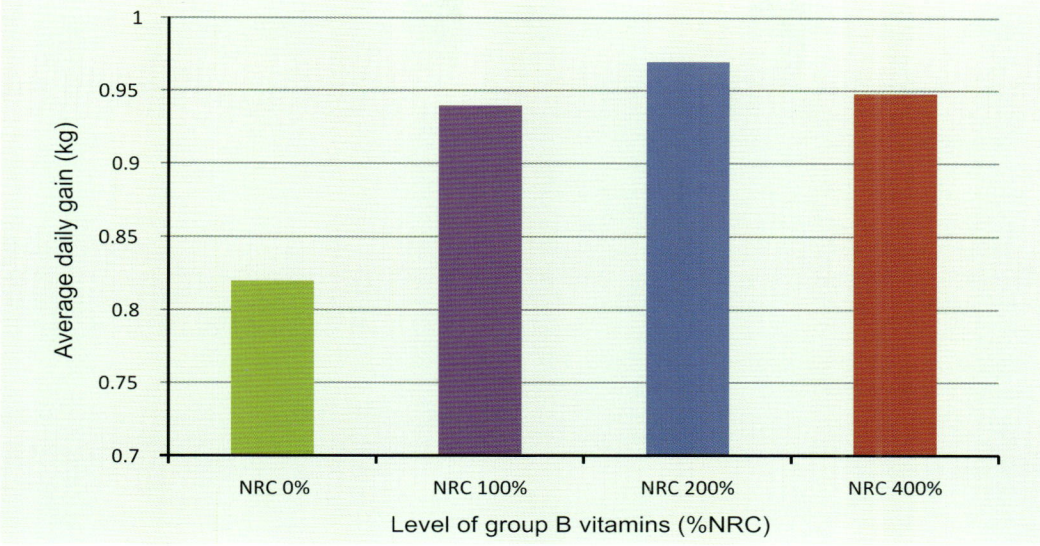

Figure 19. Effect of the supply of riboflavin at concentrations above those recommended by the NRC in piglets on protein and fat deposition, and on weight gain (Lutz and Stahly, 1998).

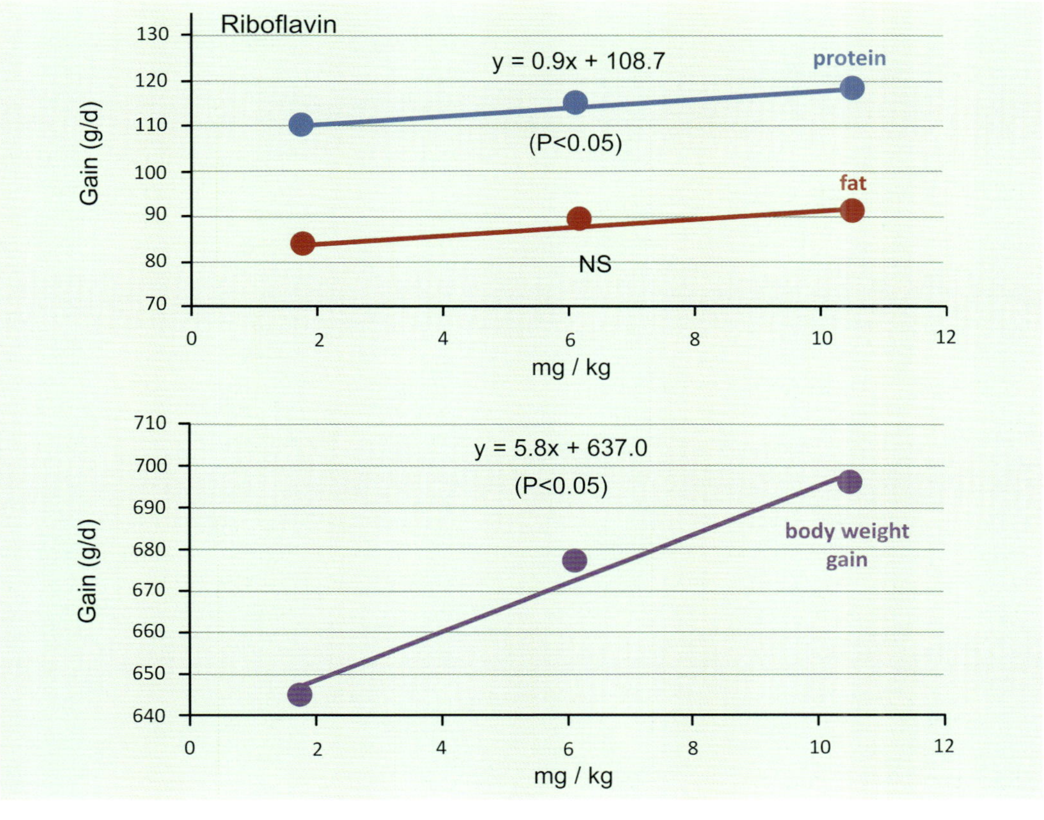

Chemical structure and units

Nicotinic acid (or pyridine-3-carboxylic acid) alters in the animal's body to an amide (nicotinamide), which is the active form of the vitamin. As conversion takes place easily and very efficiently, it is considered that both forms possess the same vitamin activity. Frequently, the term niacin is used for both the free acid form and the amide form. Niacin content in feed and niacin requirements is usually expressed in mg per kg feed. Niacin is also known as vitamin PP (pellagra preventive) or, less frequently, as vitamin B_3.

Metabolism

Nicotinic acid and nicotinamide are absorbed without difficulty in the stomach and small intestine. Absorption is deemed complete when they are not in the combined form. If nicotinic acid is absorbed it can convert to the amide form in intestinal mucosa. Nicotinamide is carried by red blood corpuscles, thus reaching various tissues where it is incorporated into the corresponding coenzymes. Its preferred target is hepatic tissue, although it is also found at high concentrations in the kidney and in adipose tissue. Niacin is not stored in the animal's body.

Niacin and its metabolites are excreted in urine, where nicotinic acid and nicotinamide can be found (principally when the animal receives large quantities which are excreted unabsorbed), as well as metabolites (methylated or oxidized derivatives).

Nicotinamide is found in the animal's body forming part of the active group of nicotinamide adenine dinucleotide (NAD) and nicotinamide adenine dinucleotide phosphate (NADP). These coenzymes are hydrogen donors and therefore carry out an essential function in oxidation-reduction reactions. They are involved in many biochemical processes, especially those linked to energy supply to the cell, the most important of these being glycolysis, the tricarboxylic acid (or Krebs) cycle, synthesis and catabolism of glycerol, synthesis and beta-oxidation of fatty acids, synthesis and oxidation of amino acids, etc.

Deficiency symptoms

Niacin deficiency produces a marked change in metabolism, and manifests itself particularly in the skin (dermatitis, hair loss) and in digestive organs (inflammation, necrotic ulcers, occasionally diarrhea, etc.). As in most cases, unspecific signs are also observed, such as growth retardation or loss of appetite.

Most rations for pigs have sufficient quantities of niacin to prevent deficiency signs.

Sources

It has been demonstrated experimentally that the pig can convert tryptophan to nicotinic acid, albeit inefficiently. The capacity to carry out this conversion depends mainly on the activity of a hepatic carboxyl which acts specifically on picolinic acid, such that the greater the activity of this enzyme the lower the capacity to obtain niacin from tryptophan. Its activity in pigs is markedly greater than in rats, humans or chickens, so the capacity to produce niacin is proportionally small. According to studies by Firth and Johnson (1956) around 50 mg of tryptophan is needed to produce 1 mg of niacin. As a result it is usually considered necessary to add niacin to feed for pigs.

Good sources of niacin are fishmeal (50-150 mg/kg), yeast and peanut meal (150-200 mg/kg), sunflower meal (>200 mg/kg) and soy meal (20-60 mg/kg), although around 40% of the niacin in oilseeds is in a combined form which cannot be utilized by pigs. Although cereals and their derivatives show an appreciable niacin content (for example wheat or corn, around 60 and 20 mg, respectively, wheat bran up to 300 mg/kg), less than 30% of this niacin can usually be obtained by pigs so it is common in practice to ignore its contribution.

Nicotinic acid and nicotinamide are both very resistant to heat, air, light, acids, alkalis and oxidation.

Requirements and recommendations

According to the NRC (1998) piglets weighing between 3 and 5 kg require 20 mg niacin per kg feed. Within the weight range of 5 to 10 kg the requirement is 15 mg, within 10 to 20 kg it is 12.5 mg, within 20 to 50 kg it is 10 mg and above that it is 7 mg. For breeders the recommendation is 10 mg/kg of feed in all cases (Tables 1-3). These requirements may be considered low in comparison with the supply usually provided by the ingredients used in feed formulation for pigs and the possibility of obtaining niacin from tryptophan, which could suggest that inclusion of niacin is not necessary. Nevertheless, the little niacin available in most feed materials, the low tryptophan content in feeds (an amino acid which may represent a high marginal cost), the fact that these requirements are calculated for low production genotypes with higher consumption than modern ones and the great variety of factors which can lead to a higher niacin requirement mean that in practice niacin is included in the vitamin and mineral premix.

In an experiment (Lutz et al., 1999) it was observed that the inclusion of niacin in feed for piglets (between 10 and 27 kg) at a concentration up to 3 times higher than levels recommended by the NRC (1998) has no positive effect on growth, the accumulation of protein or that of fat.

In the review by Fraga and Villamide (2000) all the pig vitamin and mineral premixes studied in Spain included niacin. The same authors found an average value in the vitamin and mineral premixes studied (expressed per kg of feed) for piglets of 33 mg (range between 8.3 and 75, with a coefficient of variation of 52%), for fatteners of 15.5 mg (range of 7.5 to 30 and a coefficient of variation of 30%) and for breeders of 21 mg (range 10-30, 21% CV), i.e. a value around 70% higher for piglets and fatteners and up to twice as high for breeders as the values recommended by the NRC (1998). Coelho (2000), using data obtained in the US, found an average value of niacin in feeds for piglets of 46 mg/kg (37% CV), and in feeds for fatteners and finishers of 29 (28% CV) and 22 (41% CV) mg/kg, respectively. In breeders the average value was 42 mg/kg (30% CV). The higher niacin concentration in feeds used in the US than those in Spain is striking. It is also significant that in both cases the niacin concentration in feed for piglets is approximately twice as much as that in feeds for growers and fatteners, which is partly explained by the inability of the piglet to convert tryptophan to niacin (Firth and Johnson, 1956).

The work of Real et al. (2002), with a range of 13-55 mg/kg, may optimize the relationship between weight gain and feed consumption. These investigators also observed a tendency to improvement in meat quality with lower drip loss, and better color and pH.

PANTOTHENIC ACID

Chemical structure and units

Chemically, pantothenic acid is the amide of pantoic acid with beta-alanine: 3-[(2,4-dihydroxy-3, 3-dimethyl-1-oxobutyl) amino]propanoic acid. It is sometimes identified as vitamin B_5.

The form in which is marketed for animal feed is calcium D-pantothenate which has an activity equivalent to 92% of the free form. The racemic form (dl) exhibits only 46% activity. Requirements and concentrations in feed are usually expressed in units of mass (mg).

Metabolism

Pantothenic acid is normally found in bound form in feed for pigs (mainly as CoA), so it must be released to be absorbed. Relatively little is known about this process, nor about the manner and site of absorption, although it is believed to be by diffusion. Some studies in humans indicate that availability of pantothenic acid is between 40 and 60%. In tissues it converts to CoA and other compounds.

As with the other vitamins of the B complex, accumulation of pantothenic acid is very limited and is found mainly in the liver.

Pantothenic acid is part of coenzyme A (CoA) and of acyl carrier protein groups (ACP). In both cases it plays an essential role in the transfer of acyl groups. CoA participates in many acylation reactions (choline formation, para-aminobenzoic acid, etc.), synthesis (fatty acids, cholesterol, sphingosine, porphyrins, sterols, etc.) and oxidation (fatty acids, pyruvate, etc.), and therefore has a key role in metabolic regulation. ACP participates in fatty acid synthesis. Chemically, CoA is 3-phospho-adenosine-5-diphospho-pantothene.

Deficiency symptoms

Owing to its involvement in multiple biochemical processes, inadequate intake of pantothenic acid causes a series of unspecific signs and symptoms which include growth retardation, reduced appetite, diarrhea, hair loss, dermatitis, loss of immune response capacity, etc. In gestating and lactating sows, fatty liver has been observed as well as enlargement of the adrenal glands, hemorrhages, rectal congestion, atrophy of ovaries and reduced estrogen and progesterone synthesis, leading to uterine atrophy. Even with moderate deficiency, fertility decreases and embryonic development is compromized. As has been pointed out for other B group vitamins involved in the process of obtaining energy (especially from glucose), deficiency also shows in nervous degeneration, the characteristic "goose step", as well as the effects on epithelial tissue and functions linked to reproduction.

Pantothenic acid deficiency is rare in practice although pigs bred in intensive conditions may occasionally present some of these symptoms.

Sources

This vitamin is very abundant as is suggested by its name, which derives from the Greek pantothen (from every side).

Concentration in cereals is around 10 mg/kg, ranging from 5-6 mg in corn to 15 mg in oats. According to Southern and Baker (1981), availability of pantothenic acid in barley, wheat and soy is high, but it is much lower in sorghum. By-products of cereals generally have a much higher concentration (rice bran 22 mg/kg, wheat bran 18-30 mg/kg, etc.), although it has not been possible to find information on its availability.

Amounts in vegetable protein concentrates vary. While peanut meal contains 47 mg/kg, soy and linseed contain around 15 mg and sunflower only 10 mg/kg. Legumes have a lower concentration (peas, 5 mg/kg). The concentration in milk by-products is between 20 and 45 mg/kg and in fishmeal between 10 and 20 mg/kg. Finally, the concentration in fibrous foods such as alfalfa is around 30 mg/kg.

Requirements and recommendations

That pantothenic acid is found "everywhere" (in nearly all feeds) is frequently equated with "being very abundant", even in some works on animal nutrition. This is incorrect because it is frequently found in concentrations which are inadequate to achieve high production or even to avoid deficiency symptoms.

According to the NRC (1998), the minimum requirement for a piglet of 3 to 5 kg is 12 mg/kg, and reduces progressively for weights up to 50 kg; the recommendation for this weight upwards is 7 mg/kg of feed. For breeders, the established recommendation is 12 mg/kg (Tables 1-3). Groesbeck et al. (2007) carried out a very interesting experiment intended to explain previous findings which pointed at a relationship between levels of pantothenic acid and meat quality (Stahly and Lutz, 2001); it also includes ractopamine-HCl showing that the improvements this compound produces in growth should be associated with higher levels of pantothenic acid in the ration.

The review by Fraga and Villamide (2000) shows that in Spain the average concentration of pantothenic acid provided in the vitamin and mineral premix is 15.6 mg/kg for piglets, 9 mg/kg for growers and finishers and 12 mg/kg for breeders. Pantothenic acid was included in all the vitamin and mineral premixes studied by these authors. Coelho (2000) found that in the US the average concentration provided in the vitamin and mineral premix in feed for piglets, growers, finishers and gestating pigs was 27, 18, 15 and 25 mg/kg, respectively. Once again, the

differences between the situation in the US and Spain are striking.

PYRIDOXINE (VITAMIN B$_6$)

Chemical structure and units

The term vitamin B$_6$ includes three compounds with vitamin activity that are characterized by a common structure: 3-hydroxy-2-methylpyridine. The three forms correspond to alcohol derivatives (pyridoxol or pyridoxine), aldehyde (pyridoxal) and amine (pyridoxamine). These three forms are inter-convertible in the animal's body, the main active form being pyridoxal phosphate, followed by pyridoxamine phosphate.

Vitamin B$_6$ is fairly stable to heat and resistant to acids and alkalis, but it is sensitive to exposure to light.

Metabolism

The three compounds with vitamin B$_6$ activity are absorbed in dephosphorylated form in the small intestine, being carried to the liver by enterohepatic circulation, where they convert mainly to pyridoxal phosphate. Both niacin and vitamin B$_2$ participate in this conversion.

Excretion is by way of urine, principally through its derivative acid.

Vitamin B$_6$ participates as a coenzyme in nearly all reactions related to amino acid metabolism, including absorption, transamination, decarboxylation, deamination and synthesis of amino acids. It plays a key role in the interconversion of amino acids from food and from protein catabolism in substrate necessary for protein synthesis. More than 50 enzymes have been identified which use vitamin B$_6$ as coenzyme and intensive work is being done to determine the mechanisms which relate this vitamin with the formation of imines (Sonnet et al., 2008).

As part of its role in amino acid metabolism, vitamin B$_6$ participates in conversion of tryptophan to niacin, which once again suggests the close relationship between different vitamins of the B complex, and probably an association in the requirements of some of them. Vitamin B$_6$ is also involved in the formation of adrenaline and noradrenaline from phenylalanine and tyrosine, in the transmethylation of methionine, and in the incorporation of iron into the heme group of hemoglobin and myoglobin. On the other hand, there is evidence to suggest a role of vitamin B$_6$ in the conversion of linoleic acid to arachidonic acid and in the formation of antibodies.

Deficiency symptoms

Vitamin B$_6$ deficiency gives rise to a series of unspecific signs including appetite loss, growth retardation, dermatitis, hair loss, convulsions and anemia. Given its leading role in amino acid metabolism, deficiency in this vitamin is associated with a decreased capacity to utilize protein, with a marked drop in the nitrogen balance.

In practice problems of vitamin B$_6$ deficiency are uncommon, due to its abundance in most ingredients used in swine nutrition.

Sources

Vitamin B$_6$ is found in most of the ingredients used in swine nutrition, especially in products derived from fish (around 4 mg/kg) and cereals (barley 3 mg/kg, corn around 6 mg/kg, sorghum 3 mg/kg, oats 1 mg/kg).

Requirements and recommendations

According to the NRC (1998) the minimum requirements for vitamin B$_6$ in pigs weighing between 3 and 5, 5 and 20, and over 20 kg (including breeders) are 2, 1.5 and 1 mg/kg, respectively (**Tables I - III**). If the concentration in most feed ingredients for pigs is taken into account, it might not be thought necessary to include additional supplies of vitamin B$_6$. Indeed, in studies carried out more than 50 years ago, Ritchie et al. (1960) did not find an improvement

281

in reproductive indicators or in the growth of suckling piglets as a consequence of including 10 mg/kg of vitamin B_6 in breeder sows. But nor did Easter et al. (1983) find appreciable benefits when they stopped including vitamin B_6 in feed based on soy and corn for piglets or growers and fatteners. All this has led to the suggestion that this is one of the vitamins for which in practice it is least probable that deficiency problems will arise.

Nevertheless, the fact that deficiency symptoms are infrequent does not necessarily mean that it is not useful to include quantities beyond those supplied in ingredients. On the one hand it should not be forgotten that losses of up to 70% in the concentration of this vitamin have been described as a consequence of the handling of feedstuffs during preparation and storage of feeds. On the other hand, information on the availability of this vitamin in different feed ingredients is incomplete, although there is evidence that it is not always equally available. According to a report by Hoffmann-La OVN (1979), availability of vitamin B_6 in corn and soy is between 45 and 65%.

However, the experiment by Easter et al. (1983) showed that the inclusion of 1 mg/kg pyridoxine in feeds for sows produces an improvement in litter size at birth and weaning. More recently, Russel et al. (1985) found significant differences in transaminase enzyme activity in red corpuscles and muscular tissue depending on the level of vitamin B_6 included in the feed, such that activity (and therefore transaminase capacity) increased considerably when higher levels were included. These experiments show that the capacity for amino acid interconversion can be modulated according to the level of vitamin B_6 included in the feed and that it might, therefore, be useful to include additional amounts depending on the total quantity of protein in feed and the amino acid imbalance. According to the results of these authors the minimum requirement for proper transaminase activity in gilts is achieved when feed provides at least 2.1 mg of vitamin B_6 per day.

In piglets, weaning brings an abrupt change

in the supply and balance of amino acids that they receive, as it is impossible to formulate feeds with an amino acid profile as perfectly balanced in essential and non-essential amino acids as milk. In humans, it has been shown that weaning involves a considerable increase in vitamin B_6 requirements due to the need to modify amino acids (Bender, 1999). However, the vitamin B_6 concentration in milk is so low (around 0.4 mg/l) (Benedikt et al., 1996) that it can barely meet half of the requirement (Matte et al., 2001). In consequence, the vitamin B_6 concentration in weaned piglets is reduced and the requirement is high. In a recent study, Matte et al. (2001) have described how administering 7.7 mg/kg vitamin B_6 to piglets weaned at 2 weeks (almost five times the amount recommended by the NRC) is sufficient to avoid the appearance of deficiency symptoms, but not to raise the pyridoxal-5-phosphate concentration in erythrocytes to within the optimum range, suggesting that an even higher supply is necessary (which they calculate as 20 times the recommendation of the NRC). Woodworth et al. (2000) also found a positive effect of fortifying feed for piglets with vitamin B_6 (3.9 and 7.7 mg/kg).

In practice, the inclusion of vitamin B_6 in feed reflects the discrepancies mentioned. The recent review by Fraga and Villamide (2000) on the composition of vitamin and mineral premixes in feed for pigs in Spain found that some manufacturers inclined towards not including vitamin B_6 at all in any of the commercial feeds for different ages and production types, while the great majority did do so, reaching an average concentration of 2.4, 1.0 and 1.7 mg/kg feed for piglets, growers and breeders, respectively. Coelho (2000) describes a similar situation in the US, where some vitamin and mineral premix manufacturers did not include vitamin B_6 either. The average values in this case are 1.2, 0.4, 0.9 and 1.2 mg/kg for piglets, growers, finishers and breeders, respectively.

In both reviews the coefficients of variation for this vitamin are among the highest, being between 54% and 82% in Spain and between 96% and 180% in the US, which indicates the great diversity of opinion. One possible explanation for the discrepancies in current information might be the different effects of vitamin B_6 depending on its quantity and availability in the different feed ingredients used in formulation, as well as possible different effects of supplementation depending on the level of protein included

in the feed – it is likely that the benefits of additional vitamin B_6 increase as the protein included increases above the required level – or the imbalance in amino acids (for example, methionine).

VITAMIN B_{12}

Chemical structure and units

Vitamin B_{12} has a very complex structure which includes a corrin nucleus (itself containing four rings) with a cobalt atom in the center, in a layout reminiscent of the heme group. When there is a cyanide group bound to cobalt it is referred to as cyanocobalamin. Nevertheless, there are other compounds with vitamin B_{12} activity such as hydroxycobalamin.

The reference product is cyanocobalamin, and requirements and concentrations are expressed in units of mass (usually μg per kg).

Metabolism

Vitamin B_{12} is absorbed in the ileum by a complex mechanism which first requires the release of the vitamin (which is frequently found in a protein matrix) by the action of digestive proteases (mainly trypsin). Also, although it has not been demonstrated in swine, it is believed that for released vitamin B_{12} to be absorbed, it has to be bound to a specific glycoprotein which is synthesized in the lining of the stomach, known as "intrinsic factor". It is also known that pyridoxine and iron deficiency, as well as the presence of tannins, have negative effects on vitamin B_{12} absorption.

In the animal's body two coenzymes are formed from vitamin B_{12}; methylcobalamin (which is a carrier enzyme of methyl groups) and adenosylcobalamin (which carries hydrogen). Vitamin B_{12} coenzymes catalyze in three types of reaction: 1) intramolecular reordination, by the exchange of two chemical groups bound to two contiguous atoms of carbon, 2) methylation (as in methionine synthesis) and 3) reduction of ribonucleotides to deoxyribonucleotides (Stryer, 1996). For this reason vitamin B_{12} is involved in many

functions that include purine and pyrimidine synthesis (therefore intervening actively in nucleic acid metabolism), transfer of methyl groups (intervening in the formation of methionine, folic acid, etc.), protein synthesis from amino acids and metabolism of fats and carbohydrates. The important role it plays in the transfer of methyl groups means that there is a close relationship between the metabolism and vitamin B_{12} and folacin requirements (Matte et al., 2006). Also for this reason it is linked to choline and methionine metabolism and requirements. Erythrocyte synthesis and maintenance of the integrity of the nervous system stand out among the many functions that are affected by, and regulate, this vitamin, since it is in these functions that deficiency symptoms first present themselves.

There have also been various studies in recent years which demonstrate the importance of vitamin B_{12} in reproduction (McDowell, 2000), its role as limiting factor for the effect of folic acid in the prevention of malformations (Guay et al., 2002) and the differences between gilts and sows with several litters, since sows with their first litters have lower levels of vitamin B_{12} in their tissues than other breeder sows (Matte et al., 2006).

Deficiency symptoms

The problems of vitamin B_{12} deficiency are much more frequent in young animals than in adults, whose intestinal flora can synthesize an important part of the requirements in the duodenum and jejunum, before absorption in the ileum. Nevertheless, the need for cobalt, which enables microorganisms to synthesize this vitamin, must be emphasized, as well as the possible effect of the design of the farm and the possibility of the pig having contact with feces.

The most frequent signs of deficiency are growth retardation, dermatitis, poor hair condition, anemia and high mortality. Growth retardation is attributed essentially to a difficulty in protein synthesis and not to a problem related to energy metabolism, as occurs with other B complex vitamins. Nervous signs are also frequently apparent, characterized by uncoordinated movement, which mainly affects the hind legs.

Sources

In practice, the only natural sources of vitamin B_{12} are feed ingredients of animal origin or microorganisms. In fact, it is considered that the small quantities of this vitamin which are found in some foods of vegetable origin are probably due to the presence of microorganisms.

The concentration in fishmeal can reach more than 500 µg/kg, but in by-products of the dairy industry it is much lower (for example, in whey it barely reaches 10 µg/kg). It is important to point out the high variability in the concentration of this vitamin in the feedstuffs indicated. In meat meal, the concentration is around 100 µg, while in bloodmeal it exceeds 400 µg/kg.

As has been pointed out, there is endogenous production of vitamin B_{12} by microorganisms in the digestive tract of pigs, although this is difficult to quantify.

Requirements and recommendations

According to the NRC (1998) pigs between 3 and 5 kg need at least 20 µg/kg of feed; between 5 and 10 kg, 17.5 µg; between 10 and 20, 15 µg; between 20 and 50 kg, 10 µg and from then on only 5 µg. In breeders requirements are 15 µg/kg in all cases (Tables 1-3). These concentrations are lower than those found by Fraga and Villamide in Spain (average values of 30, 20 and 22 µg/kg in piglets, growers and breeders, respectively) and Coelho (2000) (37, 24, 19 and 34 µg/kg in piglets, growers, finishers and gestating sows, respectively) (Tables 1-3). In both cases, all vitamin and mineral premixes incorporated vitamin B_{12}.

Although there is some evidence that the inclusion of vitamin B_{12} at much higher concentrations than the minimum recommended by the NRC (1998) may be useful, it is not substantial enough due to the complexity of the processes in which this vitamin is involved, endogenous production and accumulation in the liver. In this respect, the studies carried out by Teague and Griffo (1966) more than 40 years ago indicated that the inclusion of raised levels of vitamin B_{12} in feed for sows had a positive effect on the number and weight of weaned pigs, but that this effect was only appreciable from the third litter onwards if supplementation continued uninterrupted.

In indoor production conditions, in accommodation where contact with feces is limited, special attention should be paid to this vitamin because there are few ways of correcting an inadequate supply. Taking into account the improved sanitary conditions of operations, it seems advisable to ignore supplies of vitamin B_{12} from pig flora and feces in order to avoid deficiency. The problem arises precisely when trying to establish these requirements with accuracy. Simard et al. (2007), in a study with gilts, have related the optimization of the reproductive function in sows with concentrations of B_{12} and homocysteine. As can be seen (**Figure 20**), an optimum maximum of B_{12} is produced by administering 164 µg/kg of feed and a minimum of homocysteine with concentrations of 93 µg of cyanocobalamin/kg of feed.

Furthermore, any aspect that may affect intestinal flora (parasites, antimicrobial agents, etc.) can have a negative effect on endogenous production of vitamin B_{12}.

Health problems derived from the use of feed of animal origin and their legal and commercial implications mean that it is probably advisable to increase the vitamin B_{12} concentration in feeds in Europe, especially for young animals.

Figure 20. Levels of vitamin B$_{12}$ and homocysteine in plasma according to the level of cyanocobalamin in feed (Simard *et al.*, 2007).

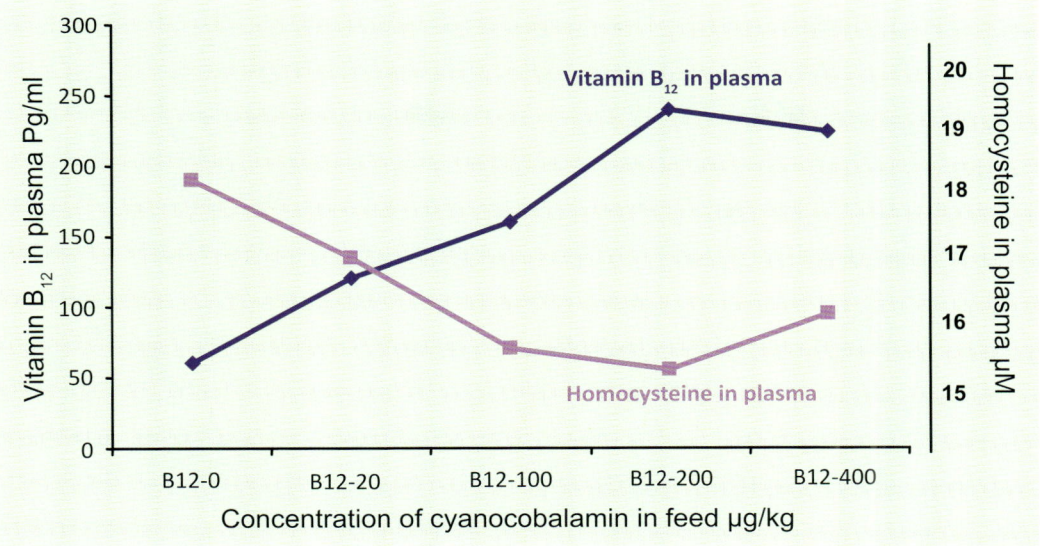

FOLACIN

Chemical structure and units

There is no agreement on naming a series of compounds with vitamin activity which is characterized as derivatives of folic acid (monopteroylglutamic acid). The most frequently used names are folacin, folic acid or folate. A molecule of folic acid is made up of a pteridine nucleus, a para-aminobenzoic acid molecule and one or several molecules of glutamic acid in a covalent bond.

Metabolism

When there is more than one molecule of glutamic acid in folacin, the action of intestinal peptidase is necessary to eliminate all but one of the residuals of this amino acid. Absorption is via active transport in the duodenum and jejunum. Most folacin is reduced to tetrahydrofolic acid (FH4) and can also be methylated (Nijhout *et al.*, 2004; **Figure 21**). Folacin also enters the target cells by active transport.

Folacin acts as a coenzyme in the transfer of single carbon groups. For this reason, it is very important in the process of interconversion of amino acids and in the synthesis of purine and pyrimidine, which are constituents of nucleic acids. Folacin has an especially important role in tissues active in protein synthesis and cell division. It participates in the increase of nuclei in the case of muscle cells.

Its function in metabolism is closely linked to that of vitamin B$_{12}$, choline and vitamin C, but also to vitamin B$_6$, because of its role in the process of reassembling the profile of amino acids circulating in plasma on explicit demand by ribosomes which regulate the process of protein synthesis.

Various studies have recently been done to determine exactly the metabolic functions of folic acid, using piglets as a model because of the similarity between their digestive and circulatory systems and those of humans (Nijhout *et al.*, 2004; Farhan *et al.*, 2005). These authors emphasize the importance the consumption of folic acid has in humans for the prevention of diseases such as megaloblastic anemia, Down's syndrome and various types of cancer, especially those related to the gastrointestinal tract and leukemia (Bailey, L.B., 1995;).

Figure 21. Description of the folic acid cycle (Nijhout *et al.*, 2004).

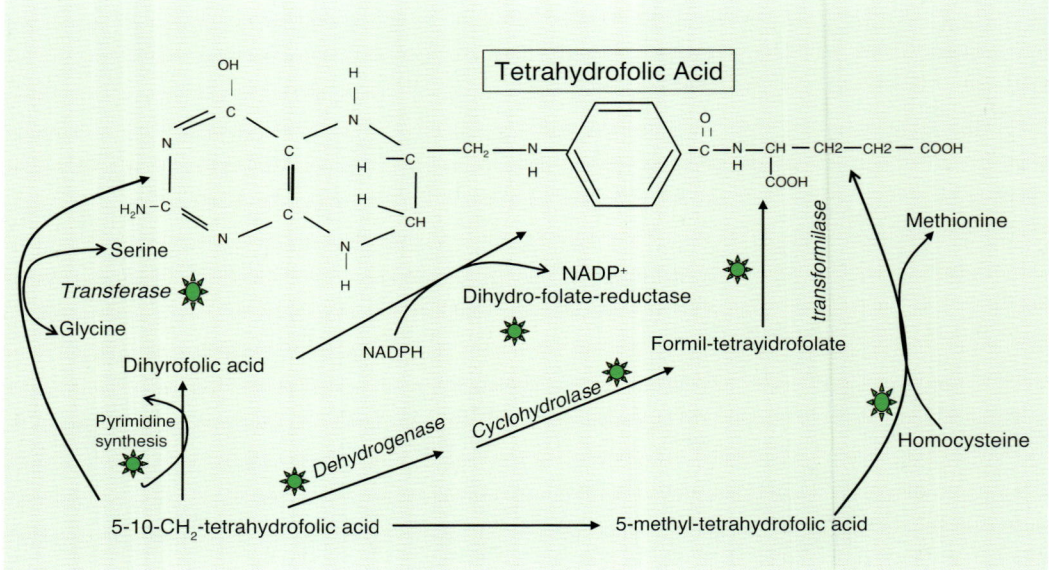

Deficiency symptoms

Folacin deficiency produces a series of unspecific symptoms, such as anemia and growth retardation. Deficiency symptoms are uncommon as this vitamin can be synthesized by microorganisms in the digestive tract of pigs, although special attention must be paid to young animals, in which intestinal flora are still insignificant, and when substances with antimicrobial action are administered in the feed.

Sources

Folacin is found in high concentrations in food containing lush green leaves (hence its name folic, which derives etymologically from *folium* or leaf). Alfalfa contains around 4.5 mg/kg. Nevertheless, folacin is present in most feed ingredients used in swine nutrition. In cereals it is found in moderate concentration (around 0.4 mg/kg), although in cereal by-products the concentration is higher (up to 1.8 mg/kg). It is also found in oilseeds (between 0.5 and 2.5 mg/kg), especially in whole seeds (soy bean 3.5 mg/kg compared with 0.5 mg/kg in soy meal). Products of animal origin also have moderate concentrations (blood meal 0.8 mg/kg, fishmeal between 0.2 and 1.0 mg/kg, whey 0.9 mg/kg, etc.).

Also, as has been pointed out, folacin is synthesized by intestinal microorganisms in the pig.

Availability of folacin in natural form is variable depending on the feedstuff in question, with a range of variation calculated as between 37% and 72% (Babu and Skrikantia, 1976).

Folacin is very sensitive to heat.

Requirements and recommendations

Although folacin was discovered in the 1930s, until very recently it has been considered a vitamin of little practical importance in pig nutrition. In part, this has been due to the fact that the first studies to evaluate requirements established a low value (Easter *et al.*, 1983). In fact, even in the 1988 report by the NRC the recommendation was still only of 0.3 mg/kg for all ages and production types. Also, there is evidence that synthesis by intestinal flora (and its frequent association with coprophagy) and the relatively high concentration in most pig feed ingredients is sufficient in almost all circumstances to meet these low requirements.

Research carried out more recently, however, indicates that none of these assumptions has a satisfactory scientific basis. On one hand, Matte *et al.* (1984) observed that periodic intramuscular administration of 15 mg of folacin to future breeding sows from weaning up to 60 days after insemination increased the number of piglets born. These same authors also observed an increase in weight gain of the litter when between 5 and 15 mg/kg folacin (Matte *et al.*, 1992) was included in the feed for gestating sows. It is hard to draw clear conclusions as to possible recommendations because of the difficulty of working with animals that have such a long productive cycle as breeders and are therefore subject to many variables. It is also difficult to quantify levels of folacin stored in tissues (and therefore levels in feed before the beginning of the breeding phase). Thus, while in the first experiment folacin was supplied mainly during the growth phase of the future breeder, in the second a higher level was given during gestation only.

Furthermore, the benefit produced by administration of high dosages of this vitamin was different (number of piglets born versus growth rate of the litter). It is essential to carry out systematic studies with more exhaustive experimental designs to draw clear conclusions. However, the information gathered suggests that the recommendation by the NRC in its 1988 report includes little more than the minimum concentration below which deficiency symptoms can arise, with the obvious result that supplementation improves production indicators, especially those of reproduction and those obtained in young animals.

Lindemman (1993) administered feed that included 1 mg/kg added folacin to sows during gestation, obtaining a mean size of litter of 10.79 piglets instead of 9.86, that is to say, almost one piglet more per litter. Furthermore, the effect was more marked in subsequent parities, reaching a difference of 1.8 piglets in the third litter. Harper *et al.* (1994), studied a range of between 1 and 4 mg/kg of folacin included in feed for sows during all the phases of their life of the breeder (including several litters), reaching the conclusion that there is no additional production benefit with highest levels of inclusion. These findings have led the NRC to recommend in their last report (1998) a level of 1.3 mg/kg in feed for sows during gestation and lactation, as well as in feed for boars. No specific recommendation has been indicated for gilts, in spite of the evidence described by Matte *et al.* (1984). However, Stanic *et al.* (1993) confirmed that the inclusion of up to 4 mg/kg folacin in feed results in an increase in embryo viability (88.5% in sows receiving feed with a high inclusion level versus 62.9% in control sows). In an experiment with boars, Audet *et al.* (2004) demonstrated an increase in sperm production when the quantity of B vitamins in feed was increased; in the case of folic acid the supplied dose was 40 mg/day. Due to practical difficulties, the effects of folacin on reproductive parameters has not been studied over multiple parities.

Matte and Girard (1999) calculated folacin requirements of gestating sows by an indirect procedure based on the metabolic utilization of this vitamin during different phases of gestation. In theory, metabolic utilization is an indicator of current requirements. According to their calculations, folacin requirements are 10 mg/kg feed during gestation (15 mg/kg during the early stages). These data have not been verified against production results.

Lutz *et al.* (1999) found no positive effects on growth and carcass composition in piglets weighing 8 to 23 kg as a consequence of folacin inclusion between 200% and 720% of the levels recommended by the NRC (1998), suggesting that the benefit is mainly limited to breeders. In fact the NRC, in its 1998 report, gave the same requirements for piglets and growers and fatteners as those in previous reports (0.3 mg/kg).

This great variation and lack of verifiable results has led to heterogeneity in the implementation of feeding programs for pigs. The review carried out by Fraga and Villamide (2000) on the situation in Spain shows that some vitamin and mineral premixes still do not include folacin, even for sows. However, most vitamin and mineral premixes do include it, in some cases reaching a concentration of up to 5 mg/kg in feed. The average value (taking into account vitamin and mineral premixes which do not include it) is 1.34 mg/kg. In growers the average value is only 0.04 mg/kg, while in piglets it reaches 0.44 mg/kg. The coefficient of variation of folacin supplied in feed by the vitamin and mineral premix is the highest of all vitamins in each of the phases studied, in all cases exceeding 100% (and in the case of growers reaching 317%), demonstrating the confusion in this sector.

The situation in the US is slightly different, with generally greater inclusion values. Coelho (2000) found an average folacin value (supplied by the vitamin and mineral premix) of 1.0 and 1.7 mg/kg in feed for piglets and gestating sows, respectively (Tables 1-3). This same study shows that 25% of vitamin and mineral premixes supplying a higher concentration have an average value of 2 and 3 mg/kg for piglets and gestating sows, respectively.

BIOTIN

Chemical nature and units

Biotin (5-[(3aS,4S,6aR)-2-oxohexahydro-1H-thienol[3,4-d]imidazol-4-yl]pentanoic acid) has a very characteristic structure which includes an atom of sulfur, a carboxyl group and three asymmetric carbons. Previously biotin has been known as vitamin H or coenzyme R. Requirements and concentrations are usually expressed in units of mass (mg or µg/kg).

Metabolism

Biotin is a cofactor of various enzymes which allow CO_2 to be fixed or eliminated in organic molecules (pyruvate carboxylate, propionyl coenzyme A carboxylase, acetyl coenzyme A carboxylase, among others). It plays an essential part in lipid, carbohydrate, protein and nucleic acid metabolism. It participates in the synthesis of non essential amino acids from carbohydrates, but also in the reverse (gluconeogenesis) and has a key role in fatty acid synthesis because it participates in the initial process of combining a carboxyl group to acetyl CoA, generating malonyl CoA, whence the elongation process takes place in the enzymatic fatty acid synthetase complex by successive additions of acetyl groups. Biotin is also linked to fatty acid metabolism, and participates in the elongation and desaturation of linoleic acid to arachidonic acid (but not of n-3 essential fatty acids). Deficiency produces a lower concentration of eicosanoids derived from this fatty acid (Watkins and Kratzer, 1987). Furthermore, biotin participates in the production of energy from carbohydrates due to its intervention in the Krebs cycle by participating in the conversion of malic acid to pyruvic acid and in the carboxylation of pyruvic acid, among others. All the enzymes with which biotin is involved require ATP and magnesium for activation.

For these reasons, biotin has very wide involvement in animal metabolism.

Deficiency symptoms

Owing to the multitude of metabolic processes in which biotin is involved, deficiency in this vitamin can express itself in various symptoms depending on which activity is most demanding in each swine production phase.

Deficiency is accompanied by a range of unspecific symptoms which include a reduction in growth rate, poor food conversion, reduction in reproductive efficiency, etc. Probably the most characteristic symptom in pigs is dermatitis (scaly and dry skin, exhibiting a drab color) which can be accompanied by alopecia and disorders of the hoof. Depending on the degree of deficiency and type of flooring, the claws may become deformed and soft (rubbery), or even cracked, which causes evident pain. In other animals such as dairy cattle, the relationship between biotin deficiency and the appearance of lesions in the extremities has been well documented in studies such as that by Fitzgerald *et al.* (2000). There is a compound (avidin) in raw egg white which binds to biotin and prevents its absorption. Some microorganisms produce anti-biotin factors, and can cause deficiency problems, although the factors are heat-sensitive.

Sources

Biotin is found in many feed ingredients. In cereals the concentration in most cases is around 0.1-0.2 mg/kg, although availability in the case of wheat, barley, sorghum and oats is very low. Although some studies carried out years ago on chickens showed availability of biotin from corn to be high, more recent studies have demonstrated it to be also very low, digestibility around 4%, (Kopinsky *et al.*, 1989). Something similar applies to products derived from meat and fish. The availability of biotin in oilseeds is proportionately high although digestibility is no greater than 50-60%, (Sauer *et al.*, 1988). Biotin can be synthesized by some microorganisms, reaching an especially high concentration in yeast.

Biotin concentration in feeds is very variable.

Requirements and recommendations

For years it was considered that the botin requirements of pigs could be met by feed ingredients and synthesis by intestinal flora. However, where antimicrobial agents are present in feed, or when the animal has little possibility of contact with feces, the likelihood of insufficient intake increases.

According to the NRC (1998), most of the literature agrees that inclusion of biotin at between 110 and 880 µg/kg does not produce an improvement in production parameters either in piglets weaned between 21 and 28 days or in growers and finishers (Hanke and Meade, 1971; Washam *et al.*, 1975; Simmins and Brooks, 1980; Easter *et al.*, 1983; Bryant *et al.*, 1985; Hamilton and Veum, 1986). The situation is disputed, however, because other authors have observed beneficial effects (Adams *et al.*, 1967, Peo *et al.*, 1970, Partridge and McDonald, 1990).

In sows, biotin inclusion in feed produces an improvement in hoof resistance and reduces the occurrence of toe lesions. An improvement has also been observed in hair and skin (Misir and Blair, 1986). Lewis *et al.* (1991), however, found that the inclusion of 330 µg/kg of biotin in feed for breeders improved the number of pigs weaned although surprisingly it did not have any effect on the hoof. Whitehead (1988) also added between 200 and 500 µg/kg to feed for sows and observed more piglets born and a higher weight at weaning. All of these points suggest that a biotin concentration within that range might be advisable. However, there is no agreement on the usefulness of including biotin in feed at above 200 µg/kg, since some authors did not find positive effects (Watkins *et al.*, 1991).

It is likely that the multiple interactions between different concentrations of vitamins and nutrients, the variability in the concentration and availability of biotin in feed ingredients (Brooks *et al.*, 1977; Simmins and Brooks 1988) (rations based on barley or wheat present a biotin deficiency as opposed to the typical American corn-soy), the possible effect of the genotype, and even the design of the accommodation (which governs contact with feces) may be responsible for the variability in results and in consequence the difficulty in establishing concrete recommendations. On the other hand, the effect of biotin on hoof lesions is difficult to quantify in small populations (as in most experimental situations), since they generally occur in a relatively small proportion of animals. In this context, using large scale field data obtained in Holland, a marked reduction in problems of limping in pigs was observed when biotin was added to feeds in a systematic way, reducing the number of sows culled for this reason to almost half. Knauer *et al.* (2007), in a study conducted with culled sows in the US, have related the lesions present in the reproductive system to low biotin provision in the feed.

Bearing all these inconsistencies in mind, and recognizing the difficulty of fixing a guide figure, the NRC (1998) chose to recommend only 80 µg/kg for piglets of up to 5 kg and 50 µg/kg for the remaining growth period. In breeders the recommendation is 200 µg/kg of feed in all cases (Tables 1-3).

The situation in practice reflects the confusion which exists. Thus, Fraga and Villamide (2000) observed that some manufacturers of vitamin and mineral premixes have chosen not to include biotin in any phase of pig production in Spain. Specifically, in the case of growers this appears to be the dominant tendency, unlike the case of piglets and breeders. Other manufacturers, however, include 200, 100 and 250 µg/kg for piglets, growers and breeders, respectively. In fact some manufacturers not included in that review, or who have recently altered the formulation of their vitamin and mineral premix, currently recommend up to 300 µg/kg. The average values found by Fraga and Villamide (2000) of 90, 7 and 150 µg/kg were for piglets, growers and breeding pigs, respectively. Once again the situation in

the US is slightly different and the inclusion level in general is higher than in Spain. Coelho (2000) found an average value in feed for piglets (supplied by the vitamin and mineral premix) of 261 µg/kg, while in growers it was 46 µg/kg. In gestating sows the average value reached 153 µg/kg, a figure much closer to that found in Spain. In both cases the coefficient of variation is amongst the highest for vitamins, indicating the wide variation of values found in the market.

B-COMPLEX VITAMINS: INDIVIDUAL OR COLLECTIVE RECOMMENDATIONS

The latest studies published on B-complex vitamins (Stahly et al., 2007, and Mahan et al., 2007) contemplate their joint use at levels higher than those recommended by the NRC (1998). These investigations found a higher average daily gain and improvement in production parameters in genotypes with a high growth potential.

Some members of the committee in charge of the review by the NRC point out that there is clear evidence that requirements of current genotypes are probably higher than those indicated in the 1998 report, although concrete information is lacking on the interrelation of requirements of different vitamins included within the B complex. For example, it is evident that thiamine, riboflavin, pantothenic acid and niacin are directly involved in the process of obtaining energy from carbohydrates via identical biochemical pathways and therefore their requirements are quite likely to be interrelated. It is thus impossible to establish concrete recommendations different from the ones previously indicated by the NRC itself (Lewis and Pettigrew, 1998). This situation gives rise to considerable uncertainty and, in practice, means that recommendations vary widely.

Figure 22 shows a schematic representation of the complex interrelations of different enzymes associated with B-complex vitamins.

A series of studies carried out at the universities of Iowa and Kentucky (USA) supplemented piglets weighing between 9 and 28 kg with a blend of B complex vitamins

(niacin, vitamin B_2, folacin, pantothenic acid and vitamin B_{12}). The piglets received 70%, 170%, 270%, 470% and 870% of the levels recommended by the NRC (1998). Results showed a linear and quadratic response which may be adjusted to give an exponential equation such as that shown in **Figure 23** (Stahly et al., 1995). Surprisingly the response was more pronounced in genotypes with greater productive capacity. In fact Lutz and Stahly (1998) proposed that the quantities of some vitamins (such as riboflavin) required for muscle tissue are up to five times higher than the quantities needed for adipose tissue.

In the case of growers, Lindemann et al. (1999) observed a quadratic response in the feed conversion rate (G:F) for the two age ranges studied and for the thickness of the loin and the lean meat content of the carcass (**Figure 24**). This shows that the best response is obtained by supplying approximately four times the NRC (1998) recommendation for each of these vitamins.

Studies which relate the ingestion of vitamin B with an improvement in chronic pathological situations are of great interest due to discoveries made in humans (Andres et al., 2004). Simard et al. (2007) have established the relation between the concentration of B_{12} in plasma and homocysteine as a possible predictor of reproductive status in primiparous sows and their dependence on a greater concentration (close to 200 mg/kg) of cyanocobalamin in the ration. Audet et al. (2004) used levels ten times higher than recommended by the NRC (1998) for boars, and obtained improved sperm production. Without doubt the relation of water-soluble vitamins with reproduction and prevention of aging will be one of the most exciting lines of study in the near future.

Figure 22. Schematic representation of some of the interrelations in the metabolism of carbohydrates, amino acids, nucleic acids and lipids and role of enzymes in the B complex.

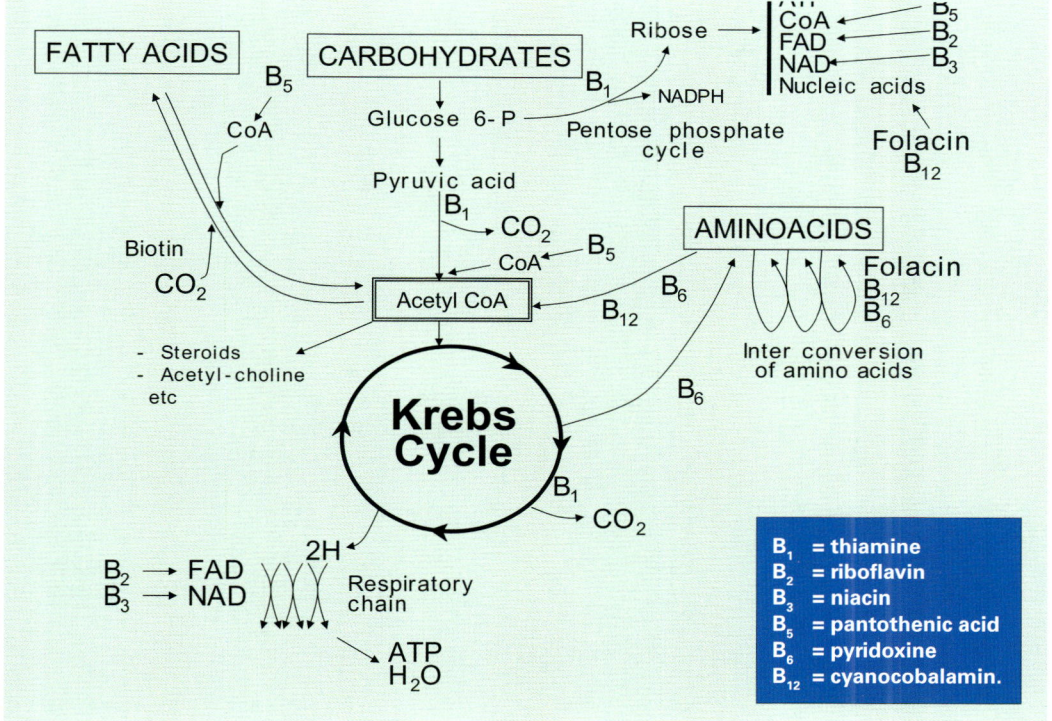

Figure 23. **Effect of the simultaneous supply of five vitamins of the B complex (niacin, riboflavin, folacin, pantothenic acid and vitamin B$_{12}$) in quantities equivalent to 70, 170, 270, 370 and 470% of those recommended by the NRC (1998) in each case on the productive response in piglets of moderate or high productive potential to concentrations** (Stahly *et al.*, 1995).

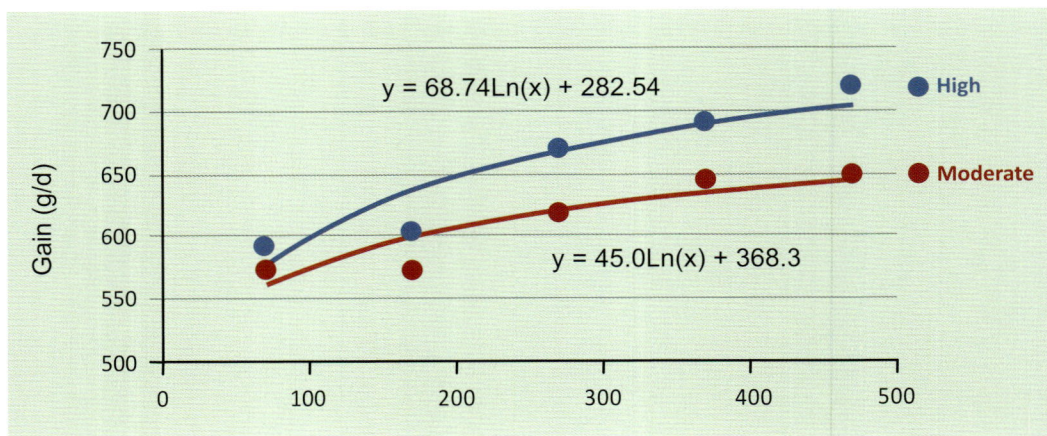

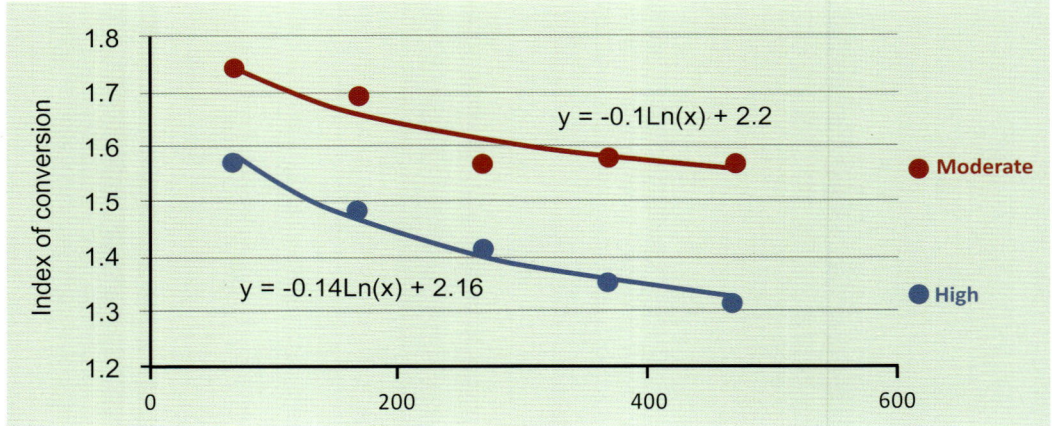

Figure 24. Effect of the simultaneous supply of five vitamins of the B complex (niacin, riboflavin, folacin, pantothenic acid and vitamin B12) in quantities equivalent to 70, 170, 270, 370 and 470% of those recommended by the NRC (1998) in each case on A.- the productive response in growing pigs in the period of 10-50 kg or 50-100 kg, B.- the thickness of the loin (mm) and % of lean meat content the carcass (Lindemann *et al.*, 1999).

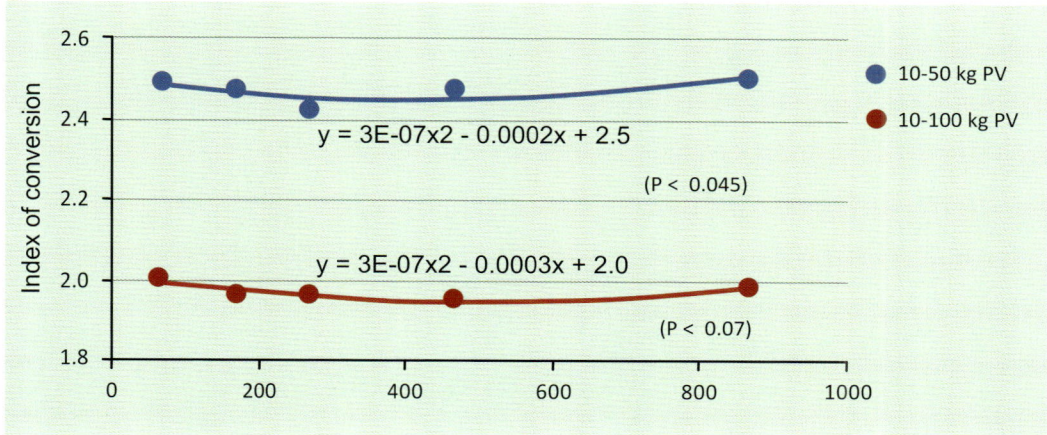

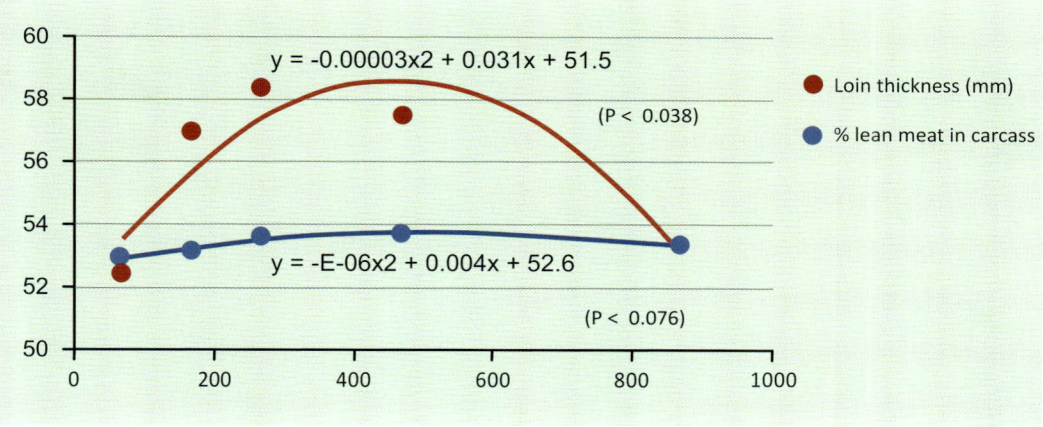

Chemical nature and units

Vitamin C (2-oxo-L-threo-hexono-1,4-lactone-2,3-enediol) exists in two forms: L-ascorbic acid (reduced form) and L-dehydroascorbic acid (oxidized form).

Vitamin C is very sensitive to oxidation.

The requirements and concentrations are expressed in units of mass (mg/kg).

Metabolism

Unlike other species, pigs are able to synthesize ascorbic acid from glucose in the liver (Wenk *et al.*, 1992) depending on the live weight of the animal (Rucker and Steinberg, 2001). Evidence suggests that in some circumstances this endogenous synthesis may be insufficient (Riker *et al.*, 1967). The capacity for vitamin C synthesis varies with age and hereditary predisposition. Palludan and Wegger (1985) studied plasma concentration at 11 to 14 weeks of life in pigs from different litters which were handled identically, and observed a considerable degree of homogeneity in the values among pigs of the same litter, but marked differences between litters, with average values between 0.18 and 0.56 mg/dl.

Vitamin C is absorbed efficiently in the small intestine – some estimates suggest availability is around 80%. From there it is distributed to all animal tissues, although experimentally a preference has been found for the brain, adrenal glands, corpus luteum of the ovary, testicle and leukocytes.

Ascorbic acid converts to dehydroascorbic acid and is subsequently reduced in cell cytoplasm, playing an essential part in the phenomenon of electron transfer (oxidation-reduction). Vitamin C acts as an antioxidant in the aqueous medium of the body (cytoplasm, plasma, etc.), eliminating hydroxyl and peroxyl radicals, hydrogen peroxide, etc. It also allows reduction of tocopherol radicals which are formed from stabilization of fatty acid peroxyl radicals, thus assisting in maintenance of the vitamin E concentration and its physiological role in the cell (in particular the cell membrane).

Furthermore, vitamin C participates in collagen synthesis, since it intervenes in the process of hydroxylation of proline and lysine, which constitutes the basis for the crossover of tropocollagen molecules, giving rise to structures of great size and consistency. Also, because of its hydroxylation capacity it is essential in carnitine synthesis, and may for that reason be involved indirectly in fatty acid metabolism. Because of its chelating properties, vitamin C can boost absorption of some metals, as well as their distribution through the body (and probably their mobilization). It has also been linked to the process of healing wounds, adrenaline and anti-inflammatory steroid synthesis, the phagocytic function of leukocytes and the production of antibodies, besides being a natural inhibitor of nitrosamines which are potent carcinogenic agents.

The high concentration of vitamin C in the testicle and ovarian corpus luteum suggests a physiological role linked to reproduction.

Deficiency symptoms

In pigs endogenous synthesis guarantees a minimum intake which prevents the occurrence of deficiency symptoms. In other species, vitamin C deficiency produces edema, blood loss, emaciation and diarrhea. The structure of collagen is seriously affected, thereby producing marked defects in the skeleton, skin, cartilage, teeth, etc.

Sources

Well known sources of this vitamin are citrus fruits and green, leafy vegetables. Synthetic ascorbic acid is available commercially.

Requirements and recommendations

For years it has been assumed that the pig syntheisizes an adequate supply of vitamin C. Grollman and Lehninger (1957) estimated a production in the liver of pigs of 13500 μmol of ascorbic acid per day. In fact, different versions of estimated requirements of nutrients for pigs by the NRC, including the last one published in 1998, have proposed no concrete recommendation. Nevertheless, there is evidence to suggest that, in some circumstances at least, it is necessary to supplement in order to achieve the maximum productive response. Pigs vary in their capacity for ascorbic acid synthesis, which could on occasion lead to a lack of response.

It has also been confirmed that vitamin C requirements are greater when the animal suffers some pathological processes (parasitic illnesses, infections, tumors, etc.) and in situations of stress (especially heat). In these circumstances, endogenous synthesis cannot meet the elevated demand for ascorbic acid and the plasma concentration diminishes. There is some evidence to indicate that calorie supply in the form of carbohydrates or fat could determine the endogenous production of vitamin C. Brown et al. (1970) observed a positive relationship between energy consumption (principally carbohydrates) and the vitamin C concentration in piglet serum, observing also that the addition of vitamin C produced an improvement in production indicators only when piglets received feed with a lower energy concentration (Brown et al., 1975). It appears that if feed with a limited supply of carbohydrates is given, capacity for synthesis may be reduced. This may be useful if we bear in mind the tendency to increase the level of fat included in feed to increase its energy concentration, given the high productive potential and the low consumption of modern pig genotypes.

On the other hand, it is possible that exogenous supply of vitamin C causes a negative stimulus on endogenous synthesis (Ching and Mahan, 1999).

For all these reasons, and some other non-controlled variation factors, the literature is complex with regard to the possible usefulness of including vitamin C in feeds for piglets or growers. For example, Jewel et al. (1981) observed an improvement in growth when supplementing feed for piglets with vitamin C in one experiment, but not in the following one. Yen and Pond

(1981) and Mahan et al. (1994) also observed a beneficial effect on weight gain of piglets of 3-4 weeks. An improvement was also observed by Cromwell et al. (1970) with pigs of up to 90 kg, although these same authors and some others did not find any effect in other experiments (Mahan et al., 1994).

The usefulness of including vitamin C in feeds for breeding pigs is even more evident than for piglets. In a trial with sows with a genetic defect in vitamin C production (Wegger and Palludan, 1994), it was verified that supplementation with this vitamin is necessary to avoid problems of edema, blood loss, calcification of the fetal skeleton, etc. Lauridsen and Jensen (2005) conducted a study which points to a close relationship between levels of vitamin E and C. They administered 150-250 ppm of vitamin C during gestation and then supplied 500 mg of vitamin C to the weaned piglets, finding higher levels of vitamin E in the tissues and of IgM in the plasma of the animals. Pinnelli-Saavedra et al. (2008), working with vitamin E and ascorbic acid, found improved immunity in piglets of sows which had received feed with vitamin C levels of 10 g/day and vitamin E of 500 mg/kg. There is much evidence from cattle and laboratory rodents indicating a role for ascorbic acid in reproductive females. Sandholm et al. (1979) observed that the umbilical cord ceased bleeding sooner if the mother received an additional supply of 1 g of vitamin C during the last 5 days of gestation, and also observed an improvement in the weight of the litter three weeks after birth. Other authors have been unable to confirm this response of increase in the weight of a litter of sows given feed enriched with vitamin C (Lynch and O'Grady, 1981).

The physiological role of vitamin C in the reproductive male is of great importance because it participates in the development, maturity and maintenance of semen production and in testosterone synthesis. There is evidence from work carried out with guinea pigs and from experiments on humans that deficient intake of ascorbic acid produces semen of poor quality, including a reduction in fertilization capacity of up to 50%, reduction of sperm motility, etc. In extreme cases the testicle, seminal vesicles and prostate may be structurally affected. However, supplementation with 500 mg ascorbic acid daily improves motility and sperm concentration and reduces susceptibility to oxidation (Whittington *et al.*, 1995). Lin *et al.* (1985) observed that administering 300 mg daily to boars during summer months – when thermal stress increases vitamin C requirements and it is more likely that the endogenous production is insufficient – produced an increase in sperm concentration and in motility, with a decrease in the proportion of malformations. Independent of stress, it is likely that situation in which a boar may be subjected frequently to semen collection, unrelated to physiology, could overload the capacity for endogenous synthesis in practice. Other authors have not found any positive effect of including vitamin C in feed for boars, probably due to all the previously indicated variable factors, such as inhibition of endogenous synthesis, energy intake from carbohydrates in the ration, etc. (Mateos *et al.*, 1997). In rabbits, Castellini *et al.* (2000) determined the need to formulate levels of vitamin C in reproductive males in conjunction with an increase of vitamin E and a balance with the rest of the vitamins in order to prevent adverse effects on the reproductive functions.

Finally, ascorbic acid can have some effect on the quality of pork, as Wenk *et al.* (2000) point out in their review. One possible explanation is its antioxidant role, although it has not been possible to demonstrate experimentally the existence of a relationship between vitamin C intake and oxidative stability of meat. However, ascorbic acid is a precursor of oxalic acid. The sodium salt of this acid (sodium oxalate) is a potent inhibitor of the enzyme, pyruvate quinase, essential in anaerobic metabolism of carbohydrates and therefore involved in the formation of lactic acid, the main cause of a drop in intramuscular pH after slaughter. Mourot *et al.* (1990) administered 0, 100, 250 and 500 mg/kg of L-ascorbic-acid to pig growers and finishers, observing a higher final pH and a slightly darker coloration of meat from groups with a higher inclusion level. Kremer *et al.* (1999) observed similar results, together with a greater capacity for water retention, which is to be expected bearing in mind the relationship between final pH of the meat and water retention. Although the usefulness of this observation in practice seems low in itself, the possibility of modifying the final pH and the pattern of falling pH in meat after slaughter by way of controlled feeding is an area of great interest, since it determines in great measure the use of technology in meat production.

Many attempts have been made to modify the pattern of the drop in pH after slaughter, some of them based on modifications in feeding, most have been ineffective or impracticable. Studies must be carried out to link this effect to other production and handling parameters, such as period of administration, interaction with other nutrients, importance of the timing of withdrawal from feed, and to quantify not only the existence of an effect but also the consequences on variability of the drop in pH. The measure of variation (standard deviation, coefficient of variation) is of great relevance, but it is difficult to investigate, given the involvement of other variables and the need to use a very broad experimental population.

The possibility of using the antioxidant activity of vitamin C and its possible synergetic use with vitamin E are of less interest because ascorbic acid reduces metallic ions such as iron or copper, causing them to convert from the Fe^{+++} or Cu^{++} forms to the Fe^{++} or Cu^{+} forms which, in practice, have much greater capacity to promote oxidative processes (Schaefer *et al.*, 1995). King *et al.* (1995) found vitamin C to have no effect on the oxidative stability of broiler meat. These authors did, however, observe a significant increase in the concentration of vitamin C when supplying feed with a high content of this vitamin. The possibility of increasing the concentration of ascorbic acid through natural means may be useful because vitamin C prevents the formation of nitrosamines, highly carcinogenic compounds which accumulate in cured products derived from pig meat. In our view, the potential of animal feed to reduce the concentration of compounds of this type in meat products should be studied in more depth.

In their review of 2000, Fraga and Villamide did not find vitamin C in any vitamin and mineral premix added to pig feed in Spain. More recent information, however, indicates that some manufacturers include up to 300 and 200 mg/kg in pre-weaner and starter feeds, respectively, 400 mg/kg for breeder sows and up to 900 mg/kg in feed for boars. Vitamin C has not been found in vitamin and mineral premixes for growing pigs.

REFERENCES

Adams, C.R., Richardson, C.E. and Cunha, T.J. (1967) Supplemental biotin and vitamin B6 for swine. J. Anim. Sci. 26: 903 (abstract)

Agricultural Research Council (1981) The Nutrient Requirements of Pigs. Commonwealth Agricultural Bureaux. Slough, Reino Unido.

Anderson, L.E., Myer, R.O., Brendemuhl, J.H. & McDowell, L.R. (1995) The effect of excessive dietary vitamin A on performance and vitamin-E status in swine fed diets varying in dietary vitamin E. J. Anim. Sci. 73: 1093-1098.

Andres, E., Loukili NH, Noel, E., Kaltenbach G, Maher BA, Perrin AE, et al. 2004. Vitamin B12 (cobalamin) deficiency in elderly patients. CMAJ; 171:251-9.

Asghar, A., Gray, J.I., Booren, A.M., Gomaa, E.A., Abouzied, M.M., Miller, E.R. and Buckley, D.J. (1991). Effects of supranutritional dietary vitamin E levels on subcellular deposition of α-tocopherol in the muscle and on pork quality. J. Sci. Food Agric. 57: 31-41.

Asghar, A., Gray, J.I., Miller, E.R., Ku, P.K. and Booren, A.M. (1991). Influence of supranutritional vitamin E supplementation in feed on swine growth performance and deposition in different tissues. J. Sci. Food Agric. 57: 19-29.

Audet, I., Laforest, J.P., Martineau, G.P. and Matte, J.J. (2004). Effect of vitamin supplements on some aspects of performance, vitamin status, and semen quality boars. J. Anim. Sci. 82:626-633.

Babinsky, L. (1992) Effect of vitamin E and fat source in sows diets on immune response of suckling and weaned piglets. J. Anim. Sci. 69: 1833-1842.

Babu, S. and Skrikantia, S.G. (1976) Availability of folates from some foods. Am. J. Clin. Nutr. 29: 376-380

Bailey, L.B. (1995). Folate in Heath and disease. Marcel Decker, New York.

Baker, H., Handelman, G.J., Short, S., Machlin, L.J., Bhagavan, H.N., Dratz, E.A. and Frank, O. (1986) Comparison of plasma alpha and gamma tocopherol levels following chronic oral administration of either all-rac-alpha-tocopheryl acetate or RRR-alpha-tocopheryl acetate in normal adult male subjects. Am J Clin Nutr 43: 3 382-387

Bar, A., Edelstein, S., Eisner, U., Ben-Gal, I. and Hurwitz, S. (1982) Cholecalciferol requirements of growing tukeys under normal conditions and during recovery from rickets. J. Nutr. 112: 1779.

Batra, T.R., Singh, K., Ho, S.K. and Hiridoglou, M. (1992) Concentration of plasma and milk vitamin E and plasma carotene of mastitic and healthy cows. Int. J. Vit. Nutr. Res. 62: 233-237.

Bazer, F.W. and Zavy, M.T. (1988) Supplemental riboflavin and reproductive performance of gilts. J. Anim. Sci. 66: 234 (abstract).

Bebravicious, H. and Medzevivious, A. (1987) The dynamics of vitamin A content in the serum of pigs during experimental trichurosis. Acta Parasitológica Lituanica 22: 102.

Bender, D.A. (1999) Non-nutritional uses of vitamin B6. Br. J. Nutr. 81: 7-20.

Benedikt, J., Roth-Maier, D.A. and Kirchgessner, M. (1996) Influence of dietary vitamin B6 supply during gravidity and lactation on total vitamin B6 concentration in blood and milk. Int. J. Vitamin Nutr. Res. 66: 146-150.

Bieri, J.G., Wu, A. and Tolliver, T.J. (1981). Reduced intestinal absorption of vitamin E by low dietary levels of retinoic acid in rats. J. Nutr. 111: 458-467.

Blair, R. and Newsome, F. (1986) Involvement of water-soluble Vitamin in Diseases of Swine. J. Anim. Sci. 60:1508-1517.

Brief, S. and B.P. Chew (1985). Effects of vitamin A and ß-carotene on reproductive performance in gilts. J. Anim. Sci. 60: 988-1004.

Brooks, P.H., Smith, D.A., Irwin, V.C.R. (1977). Biotin-supplementation of diets; the incidence of foot lesions, and the reproductive performance of sows. Vet. Rec. 101, 46-50.

Brown, R.G., Buchanan-Smith, J.G. and Sharma, V.D. (1975) Ascorbic acid metabolism in swine. The effects of frequency of feeding and level of supplementary ascorbic acid on swine fed various energy levels. Can. J. Anim. Sci. 55: 353-358.

Brown, R.G., Sharma, V.D., and Young, L.G. (1970) Ascorbic acid metabolism in swine. Interrelationship between level of energy intake and serum ascorbate levels. Can. J.

Anim. Sci. 50: 605-609.

Bryant, K.L., Kornegay, E.T., Knight, J.W., Webb, K.E. and Notter, D.R. (1985) Supplemental biotin for swine. Influence on feedlot performance, plasma biotin and toe lesions in developing gilts. J. Anim. Sci. 60: 136-144

Buckley, D.J., Gray, J.I., Asghar, A., Price, J.F., Crackel, R.L., Booren, A.M., Pearson, A.M. and Miller, E.R. (1989). Effects of dietary antioxidants and oxidized oil on membranal lipid stability and pork product quality. J. Food Sci. 54: 1193-1197.

Buckley, D.J., Morrissey, P.A. and Gray, J.I. (1995). Influence of dietary vitamin E on the oxidative stability and quality of pig meat. J. Anim. Sci. 73: 3122-3130.

Cannon, J.E., Morgan, J.B., Schmidt, G.R., Tatum, J.D., Sofos, J.N., Smith, G.C., Delmore, R.J. and Williams, S.N. (1996). Growth and fresh meat quality characteristics of pigs supplemented with vitamin E. J. Anim. Sci. 74: 98-105.

Castellini C., Dal Bosco A., Bernardini M. (2000) - Effect of dietary α-tocopheryl acetate and ascorbic acid: vitamin content and oxidation status of rabbit semen. 7th World Rabbit Congress - Valencia, Vol A, 105-110.

Cerolini, S., Maldjian, A., Surai, P. and Noble, R. (2000) Viability, susceptibility to peroxidation and fatty acid composition of boar semen during liquid storage. Anim. Repr. Sci. 58: 99-11.

Ching S., Mahan D. C., Wiseman T. G. and Fastinger N.D. (2002) Evaluating the antioxidant status of weanling pigs fed dietary vitamins A and E. J Anim Sci. 80:2396-2401.

Ching, S. and Mahan, D.C. (1999) Ascorbic acid synthesis in the fetal, nursing and weaned pig. J. Anim. Sci. 77: 58.

Ching, S., Mahan, D.C. & Wiseman, T.G. (2002) Evaluating the antioxidant status of weanling pigs fed dietary vitamins A and E. J. Anim. Sci. 80: 2396-2401

Chung, T.K. and Baker, D.H. (1990) Riboflavin requirement of chicks fed purified amino acid and conventional corn-soybean meal diets. Poult. Sci. 69: 1357-1363.

Coelho, M. (2000) Update on commercial poultry, swine and dairy vitamin supplementation. Scientific reviews. www.feedinfo.com

Coffey, M.T. and J.H. Britt (1983). Enhancement of sow reproductive performance by

ß-carotene or vitamin A. J. Anim. Sci. 71: 1198-1202.

Cromwell, G.L., Hays, V.W. and Overfield, J.R. (1970) Effect of dietary ascorbic acid on performance and plasma cholesterol levels of growing swine J. Anim. Sci. 31: 63-66

Davey, R.J. and Stevenson, J.W. (1963). Pantothenic acid requirement of swine for reproduction. J. Anim. Sci. 22:9-13.

De Jong, M.F. and Sitsema, J.R. (1983) Field experience with d-biotin supplementation to gilt and sow feeds. Vet. Quart. 5: 58.

Diet-Ox (1998) Dietary Treatment and quality characteristics of muscle and meat products. AIR CT94-1577

Dineen, N.M., Kerry, J.P., Lynch, P.B., Buckley, J.D., Morrissey, P.A: and Arendt, E.K. (2000) Reduced nitrite levels and dietary α-tocopheryl acetate supplementation: effects on the Color and oxidative stability of cooked hams. Meat Sci. 55: 475-482.

D.N.D. D'Souza, D.W. Pethick, F.R. Dunshea, J.R. Pluske and B.P. Mullan (2003) Nutritional manipulation increases intramuscular fat levels in the Longissimus muscle of female finisher pigs, Australian Journal of Agricultural Research 54 pp. 745–749.

Easter, R.A., Anderson, P.A:, Michel, E.J. and Corley, J.R. (1983) Response of gestating gilts and starter, grower and finisher swine to biotin, pyridoxine, folacin and thiamine additions to a corn-soybean meal diet. Nutr. Rep. Int. 28: 945-953.

Eicher, S.D., Mckee, C.A. and Caroll, J.A. (2006). Supplemental vitamin C and yeast cell wall ß-glucan as growth enhancers in newborn pigs and as immunomodulators after an endotoxin challenge after weaning. J. Anim. Sci. 84:2352-2360.

Ellis, N.R. and Madsen, L.L. (1944) The thiamine requirements of pigs as related to the fat content of the diet. J. Nutr. 27: 253-292

Enright, K.L., Anderson, B.K., Ellis, M., McKeith, F.K., Berger, L L. and Baker, D.H. (1998) The effect of feeding high levels of vitamin D_3 on pork quality. J. Anim. Sci. 76: 149 (abstract)

Esch, M.W., Easter, R.A. and Bahr, J.M. (1981) Effect of riboflavin deficiency on estrous cyclicity in pigs. Biol. Reprod. 25: 659-665.

Farhan, B., Asrar M., Deborah L. O'Connor (2005) Bacterially synthesized folate and supplemental folic acid are absorbed across the large intestine of piglets. J. Nutr. Bioch 16 587–593

Faustman, C., Cassens, R.G., Schaefer, D.M., Buege D.R., Willians, S.N. and Scheller, K.K. (1989). Improvement of pigment and lipid stability in Holstein Steer beef by dietary supplementation with vitamin E. J. Food Sci., 54: 858-862.

FEDNA. (2003). Fundación española para el desarrollo de la nutrición animal. Tablas de composición de alimentos 2ed.

Firth, J. and Johnson, B.C. (1956) Quantitative relationship of tryptophan and nicotinic acid in the baby pig. J. Nutr. 59: 223-234.

Fitzgerald, T., Norton, B.W., Elliot, R. et al. (2000). The influence of long-term supplementation with biotin on the prevention of lameness in pasture fed dairy cows. J. of Dairy Science 83-2: 338-344.

Fraga, M.J. and Villamide, M.J. (2000) The composition of vitamin supplements in Spanish pig diets. Pig News and Information 21: 67-72.

Frank, G.R., Bahr, J.M. and Easter, R.A. (1988) Riboflavin requirement of lactating swine. J. Anim. Sci. 66: 47-52.

Gallo Torres, H.E. and Miller, O. N. (1971). Tissue uptake and metabolism of d, 1-3, 4-H_2-α-tocopheryl nicotinate and d,1-α-tocopheryl-1,2-H_2-acetate following intravenous administration. Int. J. Vit. Nutr. Res. 41: 339-354.

Gallo-Torres, H.E. (1980). Absorption. En: Vitamin E: A Comprehensive Treatise, pp 170-192. Ed Machlin L.J. Marcel Dekker, New York.

Gonnerman, W.A., Toverud, S.V., Ramp, W.K. and Mechanic, G.L. (1976) Effects of dietary vitamin D and calcium on lysyl oxidase activity in chick bone metaphyses. Proc. Soc. Exp. Biol. Med. 151: 435

Gorocica-Buenfil, M.A., Fluharty, F.L., Reynols, C.K. and Loerch, S.C. (2007). Effect of dietary vitamin A restriction on marbling and conjugated linoleic acid content in Holstein steers. J. Anim. Sci. 85: 2243-2255.

Gregoire, F.M., Smas, C.M. and Sul, H.S. (1998). Understanding adipocyte differentiation. Physiology Review, 78: 778-809.

Griminger, P. and Donis, O. (1960) Potency of vitamin K and two analogues in counteracting the effects of dicumarol and sulfaquinoxalone on the chick. J, Nutr. 70: 361-364.

Groesbeck, C.N., Goodband, R.D., Tokach, M.D., Dritz, S.S., Nelsen, J.L. and Deroukey J.M. (2007). Effects of pantothenic acid on growth performance and carcass characteristicas of growing-finishing pigs fed diets with or without ractopamine hydrochloride. J. Anim. Sci 85: 2492-2497.

Grollman, A.P., and A.L. Lehninger. 1957. Enzymatic synthesis of L-ascorbic acid in different animal species. Arch. Biochem. Biophys. 69:458-464.

Guay, F., Matte, Girard, J.J., Palin, M.F., Giguère and I.P. Laforest. 2002. Effect of folic acid and glycine supplementation on embryo development and folate metabolism during early pregnancy in pigs. J. Anim. Sci. 80:2134-2143.

Guo Q., Richert B. T., J Burgess. R., Webel D. M., Orr D. E., Blair M., Grant A. L. and Gerrard D. E. (2006) Effect of dietary vitamin E supplementation and feeding period on pork quality. J Anim Sci 2006. 84:3071-3078.

Hamilton, C.R. and Veum, T.L. (1986) Effect of biotin and (or) lysine additions to corn-soybean meal diets on performance and nutrient balance of growing pigs. J. Anim. Sci. 62: 155-162.

Hanke, H.E. and Meade, R.J. (1971) Biotin and pyridoxine additions to diets for pigs weaned at an early age. Minnesota Swine Research Report H-120, St Paul. University Minnesota Press.

Harper, A.F., Lindemann, M.D., Chiba, L.I., Combs, G.E., Handlin, D.L., Kornegay, E.T. and Southern, L.L. (1994) An assessment of dietary folic acid levels during gestation and lactation on reproductive and lactational performance of sows: a cooperative study. J. Anim. Scie. 72: 2338-2344.

Hidiroglou, M., E. Farnworth and G. Bulter. 1993. Effects of vitamin E and fat supplementation on concentration of vitamin E in plasma and milk of sows and in plasma of piglets. Internat. J. Vitam. Nutr. Res. 63:180.

Hill, G.M., Link, J.E., Meyer, L. and Fritsche, K.L. (1999) Effect of vitamin E and selenium on iron utilization in neonatal pigs. J. Anim. Sci. 77: 1762-1768.

Hoffmann-La Roche (1979) Rationale for Roche Recommended Vitamin Fortification-Swine Rations. RCD 5159/979. Hoffmann-

La Roche Inc., Nutley, New Jersey.

Hollander, D. (1981). Intestinal absorption of vitamins A, E, D, and K. J. Lab. Clin. Med. 97: 449-462.

Hoppe, P. P., Schoner, F. J. & Frigg, M. (1992) Effects of dietary retinol on hepatic retinol storage and on plasma and tissue alpha-tocopherol in pigs. Int. J. Vitam. Nutr. Res. 62: 121-129.

Hoppe, P.P, Schöner, F-J., Wiesche, H., Stahler-Geyer, A., Kammer, J., and Hochadel, H. (1993). Effect of graded dietary α-tocopherol supplementation on concentrations in plasma and selected tissues of pigs from weaning to slaughter. J. Vet. Med. A 40:219-228

Hoskinson C.D., Chew B.P. and Wong T.S. (1992) Effects of injectable beta-carotene and vitamin-A on lymphocyte-proliferation and polymorphonuclear neutrophil function in piglets. Biol. Neonate 62: 325-336

Isabel, B., López-Bote, C.J., Rey, A.I. and Sanz, R. (1999). Influence of dietary α-tocopheryl acetate supplementation of pigs on oxidative deterioration and weight loss in dry cured ham. Meat Sci. 51: 227-232

Ivers, D.J., Rodhouse, S.L., Ellersiech, M.R. and Veum T.L. (1993). Effect of supplemental niacin on sow reproduction and sow and litter performance. J. Anim. Sci. 71:651-655.

Jensen, M., J. Hakkarainen, A. Lindholm and L. Jonsson. 1988a. Vitamin E requirement of growing swine. J. Anim. Sci. 66:3101.

Jewel, D.E., Siwecki, J.A. and Veum, T.L. (1981) The effect of dietary vitamin C on performance and tissue vitamin C levels in neonatal pigs. J. Anim. Sci. 53: 98 (abstract)

Kelly, K. and Easter, R. (1987) Nutritional factors can influence immune response of swine. Feedstuffs 59: 14.

Kerth C. R. Carr, M. A., Ramsey C. B., Brooks J. C., Johnson R. C., Cannon J. E. and Miller, M. F.(2001) Vitamin-mineral supplementation and accelerated chilling effects on quality of pork from pigs that are monomutant or noncarriers of the halothane gene. J Anim Sci. 79:2346-2355.

King, A.J., Uijttenboogaart, T.G. and de Vries, A.W. (1995) α-tocopherol, ß-carotene and ascorbic acid as antioxidants in stored poultry muscle. J. Food Sci. 60: 1009-1012.

Knauer, M., Stalder, K.J., Karriker, L., Bass, J.J., Johnson, C., Serenius, T., Layman, L and Mckean, J.D. (2007). A descriptive survey of lesion from cull sows harvested at two Midwestern U.S. facilities. Preventive Veterinary Medicine 82:198-212.

Kopinski, J.S; Leibholz, J. and Bryden, W.L. (1989) Biotin Studies In Pigs. 4. Biotin Availability In Feedstuffs For Pigs And Chickens. Brit J Nutr 62:773-780

Kormann, A.W. and Weiser, H. (1984) Protective functions of fat-soluble vitamins. Proc Nottingham Feed Manufacturer's Conference. Nottingham. Butterworth.

Kremer, B.T., Stahly, T.S. and Ewan, R.C. (1999) The effect of dietary vitamin C on meat quality of pork. J. Anim. Sci. 77: 46 (abstract).

Lanari, M.C., Schaefer, D.M. and Scheller, K.K. (1995). Dietary vitamin E supplementation and discoloration of pork bone and muscle following modified atmosphere packaging. Meat Sci. 41: 237-251.

Lauridsen C. and Jensen S. K. 2005 Influence of supplementation of all-rac-{alpha}-tocopheryl acetate preweaning and vitamin C postweaning on {alpha}-tocopherol and immune responses of piglets J Anim Sci. 83:1274-1286.

Lauridsen C., Engel H., Craig A. M. and Traber M. G. (2002) Relative bioactivity of dietary RRR- and all-rac-alpha-tocopheryl acetates in swine assessed with deuterium-labeled vitamin E. J Anim Sci 2002. 80:702-707.

Lauridsen, D., Hedemann, M.S., and Jensen, S.K. (2001). Hydrolysis of tocopheryl and retinyl esters by porcine carboxyls ester hydrolase is affected by their carboxylate moiety and bile acids. J. Nutr. Biochem. 12: 219-224.

Leskanick, C.O., Matthews, K.R., Warkup, C.C. Noble, R.C. and Hazzledine, M. (1997). The effect of dietary oil containing (n-3) fatty acids on the fatty acid, physicochemical, and organoleptic characteristics of pig meat and fat. J. Anim. Sci. 75: 673-683.

Lewis, A.J. and Pettigrew, J.E. (1998) A review of the 1998 NRC requirements of swine. Proceedings 1998 Cornell Nutrition Conference for Feed Manufacturers. Cornell University Agricultural Experiment Station.

Lewis, A.J., Cromwell, G.L. and Pettigrew, J.E. (1991) Effects of supplemental biotin during gestation and lactation on reproductive performance of sows: A cooperative study. J. Anim. Sci. 69: 207-214

Lilian B.M., Tijburg, Edward Haddeman, Gerard A.A. Kivits, Jan A. Weststrate and Elizabeth J. Brink. (1997). Dietary linoleic acid at high and reduced dietary fat level decreases the faecal excretion of vitamin E in young rats. Br. J. Nutr. 77: 327-336.

Lin, K.H., Chen, S.Y., Huang, C.Y. (1985) Studies on improving semen quality of boars fed diets with addition of vitamin C in summer season. Ann. Res. Rep., Anim. Ind. Res. Inst., Miaoli, Taiwan (citado por Kolb, E. The importance of vitamins for reproduction. Roche Vitamins Europe Ltd. Basel, Switzerland)

Lindeman, M.D. (1993) Supplemental folic acid: A requirement for optimizing swine reproduction. J. Anim. Sci. 71: 239-246.

Lindemann, M.D., Brendemuhl, J.H., Chiba, L.I., Darroch, C.S., Dove, C.R., Estienne, M.J. and Harper, A.F. (2008). A regional evaluation of injections of high levels of vitamin A on reproductive performance of sows. J. Anim. Sci. 86:333-338.

Lindemann, M.D., Cromwell, G.L., Van de Light, J.L.G. and Monegue, H.J. (1999) Higher levels of selected B vitamins improve performance and lean deposition in growing/finishing swine. J. Anim. Sci. 77: 58 (abstract)

Liu, Q., Scheller, K.K., Arp, S.C., Schaefer, D.M., and Frigg, M. (1996). Color coordinates for assessment of dietary vitamin E effects on beef color stability. J. Anim. Sci. 74: 106-116.

Lopez Bote, C.J. (2000) Dietary treatment and Quality characteristics of Mediterranean meat products. In Antioxidants in Muscle Foods: Nutritional Strategies to Improve Quality. Ed E. Decker, C. Faustman and C.J. Lopez Bote. Wiley Interscience, New York, pp 345

Lopez Bote, C.J., Isabel, B. and Flores, J.M. (2001) Effect of dietary linoleic acid concentration and vitamin E supplementation on cell desquamation and susceptibility to oxidative damage of pig jejunal mucosa. J. Anim. Physiol. Anim. Nutr. 85: 22-28

Lutz, T.R. and Stahly, T.S. (1998) Riboflavin needs for body maintenance, protein and fat accretion. J. Anim. Sci. 81: 190.

Lutz, T.R., Stahly, T.S., Cook, D.R. and Ewan, R.C. (1999) Effect of thiamin, folacin and niacin regimen on growth in high lean pigs. J. Anim. Sci. 81: 190 (abstract)

Lynch, P.B. and O'Grady, J.F. (1981) Effect of vitamin C (ascorbic acid) supplementation on sows in late pregnancy on piglet mortality. Irish J. Agric. Res. 20: 217-219.

Machlin, L.J. (1984). Vitamin E. In: Handbook of vitamins: Nutritional, Biochemical and Clinical Aspects, p. 99-145. Ed. L.J. Machlin, Marcel Dekker, Inc. New York.

Machlin, L.J. and Gabriel, E. (1982). Kinetics of tissue α-tocopherol uptake and depletion following administration of high level of vitamin E. Ann. New York Academ. Sci. 393: 48-60.

Mahan D.C., Carter, S.D., Cline, T.R., Cline, G.M., Kim, S.W., Miller, P.S., Nelssen, J.L., Stein, H.H. and Veum T.L. (2007) Evaluating the effects of supplemental B vitamins in practical swine diets during the starter and grower-finisher periods - A regional study J. Anim. Sci. 85:2190-2197.

Mahan, D. C., Kim, Y.Y. and Stuart R.L. (2000) Effect of vitamin E sources (RRR- or all-rac-alpha-tocopheryl acetate) and levels on sow reproductive performance, serum, tissue, and milk alpha-tocopherol contents over a five-parity period, and the effects on the progeny. J Anim Sci. 78:110-119.

Mahan, D.C. (1991) Vitamin E and selenium in swine nutrition. In: Swine Nutrition. E.R. Miller, D.E. Ullrey and A.J. Lewis. Butterworth. Boston.

Mahan, D.C., Kim, Y.Y. and Stuart, R.L. (2000) Effect of vitamin E sources and levels on sow reproductive performance, serum, tissue and milk α-tocopherol contents over a five-parity period, and the effects on the progeny. J. Anim. Sci. 78: 110-119.

Mahan, D.C., Lepine, A.J., and Dabrowski, K. (1994) Efficacy of magnesium-L-ascorbyl-2-phosphate as a vitamin C source for weaning and growing-finishing swine. J. Anim. Sci. 72: 2354-2361.

Mahan, D.C., Pickett, R.A:, Perry, T.W., Curtin, T.M., Featherston, W.R. and Beeson, W.N. (1966) Influence of various nutritional factors and physical form of feed on oesophagogastric ulcers in swine. J. Anim. Sci. 25: 1019-1023.

Mahan, D.C.; Lepine, A.J.; Dabrowski, K. (1994) Efficacy Of Magnesium-L-Ascorbyl-2-Phosphate As A Vitamin-C Source For Weaning And Growing-Finishing Swine. J Anim Sci 72: 2354-2361

Mateos, G.G., Medel, P. and Carrión, D. (1997)

Necesidades nutricionales del verraco de alta selección. Avances en Nutrición and Alimentación Animal. XIII Curso de especialización FEDNA. pp 233-253.

Mathias, P.M., Harries, J.T., Peters, T.J. and Muller, D.P.R. (1981). Studies on the in vivo absorption of micellar solutions of tocopherol and tocopheryl acetate in the rat. J. Lipid Res. 22: 829-837.

Matte, J.J. and Girard, C.L. (1999) The estimation of the requirement for folic acid in gestating sows: the metabolic utilization of folates as a criterion of measurement. J. Anim. Sci. 77: 159-165

Matte, J.J., Girard, C.L. and Brisson, G.J. (1984) Folic acid and reproductive performance of sows. J. Anim. Sci. 59: 1020-1025.

Matte, J.J., Girard, C.L. and Brisson, G.J. (1992) The role of folic acid in the nutrition of gestating and lactating primiparous sows. Liv. Prod. Sci. 32: 131-148.

Matte, J.J., Girard, C.L. and Seve, B. (2001) Effects of long-term parenteral administration of vitamin B6 on B6 status and some aspects of the glucose and protein metabolism of early-weaned piglets. Br. J. Nutr. 85: 11-21.

Matte, J.J., Guay, F; Girard, C.L. (2006). Folic acid and vitamin B12 in reproducing sows: new concepts. Can. J. Anim. Sci. Vol. 86, I:2, 197-205.

McCormick, E.C., Cornwell, D.G. and Brown, J.B. (1960). Studies of the distribution of tocopherol in human serum lipoproteins. J. Lipid Res. 1: 221-228.

McDonald, P., Edwards, R.A., Greenhalgh, J.F.D. and Morgan, C.A. (1995) Nutrición Animal. 5ª Edición. Ed. Acribia, Zaragoza.

McDowell, L.R.(2000).Vitamin B_{12} in vitamins in animal and human nutrition. 2nd rev. Ed. Iowa State University Press, Ames, IA.

McDowell, L.R.(2006) Vitamin nutrition of livestock animals: Overview from vitamin discovery to today. Can. J. Anim. Sci. 86:171-179.

McFarlane, B.J. and Unruh, J.A: (1996) Effects of blast chilling and post mortem calcium chloride injection on tenderness of longissimus muscle. J. Anim. Sci. 74: 1842-1845.

Miller, C.W., Waters, K.M. and Ntambi, J.M. (1997). Regulation of hepatic stearoyl-CoA desaturase gene 1 by vitamin A. Biochemical and Biophysical Research Communication 231: 206-210.

Misir, R. and Blair, R. (1986) Reproductive performance of gilts and sows as affected by induced biotin deficiency and subsequent dietary biotin supplementation. J. Anim. Physiol. Anim. Nutr. 55: 196-208.

Monahan, F.J., Asghar, A., Gray, J.I., Buckley, D.J. and Morrissey, P.A. (1994). Effect of Oxidized Dietary Lipid and Vitamin E on the Color Stability of Pork Chops. Meat Sci. 37: 205-215.

Monahan, F.J., Buckley, D.J., Gray, J.I., Morrissey, P.A., Asghar, A., Hanrahan, T.J. and Lynch, P.B. (1990). Effect of dietary vitamin E on the stability of raw and cooked pork. Meat Sci. 27: 99-108.

Monahan, F.J., Buckley D.J., Morrissey P.A., Lynch P.B. and Gray J.I. (1992). Influence of dietary fat and α-tocopherol supplementation on lipid oxidation in pork. Meat Science 31 (1992), pp. 229–241.

Moreira I. and Mahan D. C. (2002) Effect of dietary levels of vitamin E (all-rac-tocopheryl acetate) with or without added fat on weanling pig performance and tissue alpha-tocopherol concentration. J Anim Sci 2002. 80:663-669.

Morel P. C. H., Janz J. A. M., Zou M., Purchas R. W., Hendriks W. H. and B. H. Wilkinson (2008) The influence of diets supplemented with conjugated linoleic acid, selenium, and vitamin E, with or without animal protein, on the composition of pork from female pigs. J Anim Sci.86:1145-1155.

Morrissey, P.A., Buckley D.J., Sisk, H., Lynch, P.B. and Sheehy, P.J.A. (1996). Uptake of α-tocopherol in Porcine Plasma and Tissues. Meat Sci. 44: 275-283.

Morrissey, P.A. (1994). Overview of vitamin E. Symposium on vitamin E and meat quality. University College Cork. Ireland.

Mourot, J., Aumaitre, A, and Wallet, P. (1990 Effect of a dietary supplement of vitamin C on growth and pig meat quality. In: Ascorbic acid in domestic animals. Proceedings of the 2nd symposiumm Kartause, Ittingn, Switzerland.

National Research Council (NRC, 1998) Nutrient Requirements of Swine. 10th Ed. National Reserarch Council. National Academy Press. Washington DC.

Nijhout, F.H., Reed, M.C., Budu, P. and Ulrich, C.M. (2004). A mathematical model of the folate cycle. The J. Biol. Chemistry 279: 55008-55016.

Olivares, A., Daza, A., Rey, A.I. and López Bote, C. J. (2008). Dietary vitamin A concentration alters fatty acid composition in pigs. Meat Science (in press).

Osweiler, G.D. (1970) Porcine hemorrhagic disease. Proc. Pork Producers Day, Ames. Iowa State University Press

Palludan, B. and Wegger, I. (1985) Ascorbic acid in pig nutrition. 36th Meeting European Association of Animal Production, Kallithrea.

Parker, R.S. (1989). Dietary and biochemical aspects of vitamin E. Advances in Food and Nutrition Research, 33: 157-232.

Partridge, I.G. and McDonald, M.S. (1990) A note on the response of growing pigs to supplemental biotin. Anim. Prod. 50: 195-197.

Peeters E., Driessen B. and Geers R. 2006 Influence of supplemental magnesium, tryptophan, vitamin C, vitamin E, and herbs on stress responses and pork quality. J Anim Sci. 84:1827-1838.

Peng, C.L. and Heitman, H. (1973) Erythrocyte transketolase activity and the percentage stimulation by thiamin pyrophosphate as criteria of thiamin status in the pig. Br. J. Nutr. 30: 391-399.

Peo, E.R., Wehrebein, G.F., Moser, B., Cunningham, P.J. and Vipperman, P.E. (1970) Biotin supplementation of baby pig diets. J. Anim. Sci. 31: 209 (abstract)

Pettigrew, J.E., El-Kandelgi, S.M., Johnston, L.J. and Shurson, G.C. (1996) Riboflavin nutrition of sows. J. Anim. Sci. 74: 2226-2230.

Phillips, A.L., Faustman, C., Lynch, M.P., Govoni, K.E., Hoagan, T.A: and Zinn, S.A. (2001) Effect of dietary α-tocopherol supplementation on color and lipid stability in pork. Meat Sci. 58: 389-393.

Pinelli-Saavedra, A., Calderón de la Barca, A.M., Hernández, J., Valenzuela, R. and Caif, J.R. (2008). Effect of supplementating sow's feed with α-tocopherol acetate and vitamin C on transfer of α-tocopherol to piglet tissues, colostrum, and milk. Aspects of Immune Status of piglets. Research in Veterinary Science 85:92-100.

Pudelkiewicz, W.J., Webster, L. & Matterson, L.D.S. (1964) Effects of high levels of dietary vitamin A acetate on tissue tocopherol + some related analytical observations. J. Nutr. 84: 113-117.

Rea, J.C. and Trygve, L. V. (1993). Vitamin Requirements of Swine. University of Missouri. Http://extension.missouri.edu/explore/agguides/ansci/g02321.htm

Real, D.E., Nelssen, J.L., Unruh, J.A., Tokach, M.D., Goodband, R.D., Dritz, S.S., DeRouchey, J.M. and Alonso E. (2002) Effects of increasing dietary niacin on growth performance and meat quality in finishing pigs reared in two different environments J. Anim. Sci. 80:3203-3210

Rey, A.I., López Bote, C. and Sanz Arias, R. (1997) Effect of extensive feeding on α-tocopherol concentration and oxidative stability of muscle microsomes from Iberian pigs. Anim. Sci. 65: 515-520.

Rey, A.I:, Kerry, J.P., Lynch, P.B., López Bote, C.J., Buckley, D.J. and Morrissey, P.A. (2001) Effect of dietary oils and α-tocopheryl acetate supplementation on lipid (TBARS) and cholesterol oxidation in cooked pork. J. Anim. Sci. 79: 1201-1208

Rhee, K.S.; Ziprin, Y.A. (1987) Lipid oxidation in retail beef, pork and chicken muscles as affected by concentrations of heme pigments and nonheme iron and microsomal enzymatic lipid-peroxidation activity. J. Food Biochem. 11:1-15

Riker, J.T., Perry, T.W., Picket, R.A., and Heidenreich, C.J. (1967) Influence of controlled temperatures on growth rate and plasma ascorbic acid values in swine. J. Nutr. 92: 99-103.

Ritchie, H.D., Miller, E.R., Ullrey, D.E., Hoefer, J.A. and Luecke, R.W. (1960). Supplementation of the swine gestation diet with pyridoxine. J. Nutr 70: 491-496.

Robien K. and Ulrich, C.M. (2003). 5,10-Methylenetetrahydrofolate reductase polymorphisms and leukemia risk: a HuGE minireview. Am. J. Epidemiol. 157:571-582.

Roth, F.X., Kirchgessner. (1975). Blut- und Gewebe-Konzentrationen an Vitamin E von Wachsenden Schweinen bei unterschiedlichen DL-α-Tocopherylacetat-Zulagen. Int.. Z. Vit. Ern. Forschung 45, 333-341

Rucker, R.B. and Steinberg, F.M. (2001). Vitamin Requirements. Relationship to basal metabolic need and functions. Biochemistry and Molecular Biology Education 30:86-89.

Russel, L.E., Bechtel, P.J. and Easter, R.A. (1985) Effect of deficient or excess dietary vitamin B6 on amino transaminase and glycogen phosphorylase activity and pyridoxal phosphate content in two muscles from postpubertal gilts. J. Nutr. 115: 1124-1135.

Sandholm, M., Honkanen-Buzalski, T. and Rasi, V. (1979) Prevention of navel bleeding in piglets by preparturient administration of ascorbic acid. Vet. Rec. 104: 337-338.

Sauer, W.C., R. Mosenthin and L. Ozimek (1988) The digestibility of biotin in protein supplements and cereal grains for growing pigs. J. Anim. Sci. 66:2583.

Schaefer, D.M., Lui, Q., Faustman, C. And Yin, M.C. (1995) Supranutritional administration of vitamins E and C improves oxidative stability of beef. J. Nutr. 125: 1792S-1798S.

Schweigert, F.J., Rosival, I., Rambeck, V.A. and Gropp, J. (1995) Plasma transport and tissue distribution of [14C] ß-carotene and [3H] retinol administered orally to pigs. Int. J. Vit. Nutr. Res. 65: 95-100.

Shaw D. T., Rozeboom D. W., Hill G. M., Booren A. M. and Link J. E. (2002) Impact of vitamin and mineral supplement withdrawal and wheat middling inclusion on finishing pig growth performance, fecal mineral concentration, carcass characteristics, and the nutrient content and oxidative stability of pork. J Anim Sci 80:2920-2930.

Shaw D. T., Rozeboom D. W., Hill G. M., Orth M. W., Rosenstein D. S. and Link J. E. (2006) Impact of supplement withdrawal and wheat middling inclusion on bone metabolism, bone strength, and the incidence of bone fractures occurring at slaughter in pigs. J Anim Sci. 84:1138-1146.

Shin, D. and McGrane, M.M. (1997) Vitamin A regulates genes involved in hepatic gluconeogenesis in mice: phosphoenolpyruvate carboxykinase, fructose 1-6 biphosphatase and 6-phosphofructo-2-kinase/fructose 2-6 biphosphatase. J. Nutr 127: 1274

Siebert, B.D., Kruk,Z.A., Davis, J., Pitchford, W.S., Harper, G.S. and Bottema, C.D.K. (2006). Effect of low vitamin A status on fat deposition and fatty acid desaturation in beef cattle. Lipids, 41: 365-370.

Simard, F., Guay, F., Girar, C.L., Giguere, A., Laforest, J.P. and Matte J.J. (2007).Effects of concentrations of cyanocobalamin in the gestation diet on some criteria of vitamin B12 metabolism in first-parity sows. J. Anim.Sci. 85:3294-3302.

Simmins, P.H. and Brooks, P.H. (1980) The effect of dietary biotin level on the physical characteristics of pig hoof tissue. Anim. Prod. 30: 469 (abstract)

Simmins, P.H. and Brooks, P.H. (1988). Supplementary biotin for sows: effect on claw integrity. Vet. Rec. 122,43-435.

Soares, M. (1999) Utilización de distintas fuentes de grasas and del emulsionante lecitina de soja en piensos de primera edad para lechones. Tesis Docotral. Universidad Complutense de Madrid.

Sonnet P.E., Mascavage, L.M. and R.D. Dalton. (2008). The first steps. The attack on the carbonyl carbon of pyridoxal cofactor in pyridoxal-dependent enzymes. Bioorganic & Medicinal Chemistry Letters 18: 744-748.

Southern and Baker (1981) Bioavailable pantothenic-acid in cereal-grains and soybean-meal J. Anim Sci. 53: 403-408

Sparks, J.C., Wiegand, B.R., Parrish, F.C., Ewan, R.C., Horst, R.L., Trendle, A.H. and Beitz, D.C. (1999) Effects of short term feeding of vitamin D3 on pork quality. 1998 Swine Research Report, Iowa State University, pp 218-220.

Stahly, T.S. & Lutz, T.R. (2000). Biological role of pantothenic acid in the pig. J. Anim. Sci. 78 (Suppl. 2):60 (Abstr.).

Stahly, T.S. (1999) Dietary B vitamin needs of high lean pigs examined. Arkansas Nutrition Conference, Sept 1999.

Stahly, T.S., Williams, N.H., Swenson, S.G., and Ewan, R.C. (1995) Dietary B vitamin needs of high and moderate lean growth pigs fed from 9 to 28 kg bodyweight. J. Anim. Sci. 73: 193 (abstract)

Stahly, T.S., Willians, N.H., Lutz, T.T., Ewan, R.C., and Swenson, S.G. (2007). Dietary B vitamin needs of strains of pigs with high and moderate lean growth. J. Anim. Sci. 85:188-195.

Stanic, B., Pirko, J. and Grafenau, B. (1993) Early embryo survival after addition of folic acid to gilt diets. J. Farm. Anim. Sci. 26: 13-16.

Stender, D., Irvin, R. and Baas, T.J. (1999) Effect of beta-carotene on reproductive performance in swine. Swine Research Report. Iowa State University.

Stryer, L. (1996) Bioquímica 4ª Edición. Ed. Reverté. Barcelona

Swanek, S.S., J.B. Morgan, F.N. Owens, H.G. Dolezal and D.R. Gill. 1997. Effects of vitamin D3 supplementation on longissimus muscle tenderness. J. Anim.

Sci. (Suppl.1) 75:252

Talavera, F. and Chew, B.P. (1988) Comparative role of retinol, retinoic acid and beta-carotene on progesterone secretion by pig corpus luteum in vitro. Journal of Reproduction and Fertility 82: 611.

Teague, H.S. and Griffo, A.P. (1966) Vitamin B_{12} in sow rations. Swine Research. Research Research Summary 13. Ohio Agricultural Research Development Center. Ohio State University, Wooster.

Teige, J. (1982) Swine dysentery: the influence of dietary vitamin E and selenium on the clinical and pathological effects of Treponema hyodysenteriae infection in pigs. Res. Vet. Sci. 32: 95-100.

Terman, A., Kmiec, M., Polasik, D. and Pradziadowicz, K. (2007). Retinol binding protein 4 gene and reproductive traits in pigs. Archiv für Tierzucht. 50: 181-185.

Traber, M. G., Olivecrona, T., and Kaiden, H.J. (1985). Bovine milk lipoprotein lipase transfers tocopherol to human fibroblasts during triglyceride hydrolysis in vitro. J. Clin. Invest. 75: 1729-1734.

Van Heugten, E, Hasty, J.L., See, M.T., Larick, D.K. 2003 Storage stability of pork from Berkshire and Hampshire sired pigs following dietary supplementation with vitamin E. Journal of muscle foods, 14: 67-80

Wang, Y. H., Leibholz, J., Bryden, W.L. and Fraser, D.R. (1996). Lipid peroxidation status as an index to evaluate the influence of dietary fats on vitamin E requirements of young pigs. Br. J. Nutr. 75: 81-95.

Washam, R.D., Sowers, J.E. and DeGoey, L.W. (1975) Effect of zinc-proteinate or biotin in swine starter rations. J. Anim. Sci. 40: 179 (abstract)

Watkins, B.A. and Kratzer, F.H. (1987) Tissue lipid fatty acid composition of biotin-adequate and biotin-deficient chicks. Poultry Sci. 66: 306-310

Watkins, K.L., L.L. Southern and J.E. Miller (1991) Effect of dietary biotin supplementation on sow reproductive performance and soundness and pig growth and mortality. J. Anim. Sci. 69:201-206

Wegger, I. and Palludan, B. (1994) Vitamin C deficiency causes hematological and skeletal abnormalities during fetal development. J. Nutr. 124: 241-248.

Wenk, C., Fenster, R. and Volker, L. (1992) Ascorbic acid in domestic animals.

Proceeding 2nd symposium. Institute for Domestic Animal Science. ETH. Zurich

Wenk, C., Leonhardt, M. and Scheeder, R.L. (2000) Monogastric nutrition and potential for improving muscle quality. In Antioxidants in Muscle Foods: Nutritional Strategies to Improve Quality. Ed E. Decker, C. Faustman and C.J. Lopez Bote. Wiley Interscience, New York, pp 199

Whitehead, C.C. (1988) Biotin in animal nutrition. F. Hoffmann-La Roche, Basel, Switzerland, 58 pp.

Whittington, K., Ford, W.C. and Hull, M.G. (1995) The effect of antioxidant therapy on semen quality and reactive oxygen species production. J. Reprod. Fertil., 103, 15 (A): 3-9

Wilborn B. S., Kerth C. R., Owsley W. F., Jones W. R. and Frobish L. T. (2004) Improving pork quality by feeding supranutritional concentrations of vitamin D_3. J Anim Sci. 82:218-224.

Wilburn E. E., Mahan D. C., Hill D. A., Shipp T. E. and Yang H. (2007) An evaluation of natural (RRR-{alpha}-tocopheryl acetate) and synthetic (all-rac-{alpha}-tocopheryl acetate) vitamin E fortification in the diet or drinking water of weanling pigs. J Anim Sci 86:584-591.

Woodworth, J.C., Goodband, R.D., Nelssen, J.L., Tokach, M.D: and Musser, R.E. (2000) Added dietary pyridoxine, but not thiamin, improves weanling pig growth performance. J. Anim. Sci. 78: 88-93

Wuryastuti, H., Stowe, H.D., Bull, R.W. and Miller, E.R. (1993) Effects of vitamin E and selenium on immune responses of peripheral blood, clostrum and milk leukocytes in sows. J. Anim. Sci. 71: 2464-2472.

Yen, J.T. and Pond, W.G. (1981) Effect of dietary vitamin C addition on performance, plasma vitamin C and hematic iron status in weanling pigs. J. Anim. Sci. 53: 1292-1296.

OPTIMUM VITAMIN NUTRITION IN BEEF CATTLE

R. Casals and S. Calsamiglia
Department of Animal and Food Science
Autonomous University of Barcelona
08193-Bellaterra, Spain

INTRODUCTION

Vitamins are nutrients which animals cannot synthesize in amounts large enough to guarantee that the body will function properly. Quantitatively the supply in feed is of little significance because only small amounts of vitamins are required. The development of recommendations for beef production is highly complex owing to the diversity of production systems (extensive, semi-intensive, intensive), the different categories of animals (cows, weaner calves, feedlot calves, etc.) and the variety of breeds (native, imported). This diversity hinders the standardization of nutritional requirements in general and of vitamins in particular. Additionally, the availability of scientific literature is more limited for vitamins than for other nutrients.

The concept of vitamin supplementation has undergone an important change in the last few years and has moved from the minimum supplementation, which guarantees the functioning of the body and production, to necessary supplementation which also reduces the incidence of pathological problems and/or improves the quality of the product. Under the conditions of stress frequently associated with intensive production systems (weaning, transport, poor adaptation to the feeder, restricted voluntary intake, the presence of pathogenic agents in the environment, etc.), it may be advisable to increase vitamin supply to above the established requirements in order to improve the immune status of the animals.

Vitamins are either fat-soluble or water-soluble. Fat-soluble vitamins (A, D, E and K) are considered essential, and should be supplied in the ration. Water-soluble vitamins (B group vitamins, vitamin C and choline) have traditionally been considered non-essential for bovine livestock due to the important contribution from synthesis by rumen microorganisms. The availability of certain water-soluble vitamins may be limited in some situations, however, and their supplementation can improve the state of health or production of the herd.

In this chapter we aim to review and update the recommendations for vitamins in beef herds, with the purpose of supplying vitamin levels appropriate to this group of animals. When making recommendations on the necessary vitamin supply in the diet of fattening calves, we will also be considering the content of this in the final product for human consumption, which in this case is meat.

FAT-SOLUBLE VITAMINS

The recommended supplies of fat-soluble vitamins in the diet of beef cattle are shown in **Table I**. There is no consensus among investigators when establishing the minimum and maximum requirements recommended for beef cattle, so that very wide margins of use are established between the recommendations and habitual practice. There is no consensus on the vitamin content of meat, according to origin or cut (**Table II**).

VITAMIN A

Vitamin A is a family of molecules grouped under the name retinol. Vitamin A is measured in international units (IU), one IU being equivalent to 0.3 µg of all-trans retinol, its more active isomer of the same name. Retinol is obtained from the ß-carotene (or pro-vitamin A) in forage, which converts to vitamin A in intestinal mucous. Bovine livestock can store some ß-carotene in fat reserves. One milligram of ß-carotene has an activity equivalent to 400 IU of vitamin A.

Table I. Supplies of fat-soluble vitamins (IU/kg DM) recommended in beef cattle.
Source: Adapted from NRC (2000).

	Type of animal			Optimum level	Maximum tolerable
	Cows in gestation	Cows in lactation	Feedlot calves		
Vitamin A					
INRA (1988)	3,900	3,900	2,200	5,000-10,000	66,000
NRC (1996)	2,800	3,900	2,200	......	......
Vitamin D					
INRA (1988)	......	......	300	500-1,200	22,000
NRC (1996)	275	275	275	......	......
Vitamin E					
INRA (1988)	5 – 15	5 – 15	25	Anti-stress:	......
NRC (1996)	......	......	......	+ 500 IU/day	......

The concentration of ß-carotenes in plants diminishes as they mature and also due to the oxidation processes which take place during storage once plants have been cut, so the concentration in hay and silage is very much lower than that in fresh plants. However, industrial dehydration conserves ß-carotenes better than drying on the ground. Similarly, increased storage time reduces ß-carotene concentration (Brunh and Oliver, 1978). Retinol is very sensitive to oxidation, light and the presence of acids, humidity and microminerals (NRC, 2001). Prolonged storage of the vitamin in premixes containing minerals, raised temperature and humidity, pelleting, processing in blocks or by extrusion, or the presence of rancid fats in the ration all reduce the stability of vitamin A.

Of all the vitamins required in the feeding of beef cattle, vitamin A is of the most practical importance for production, since it is essential for normal growth and development, tissue maintenance and bone development (NRC, 1996, 2000). Vitamin A fulfils many functions in the body, and the most important of these are its involvement in vision, in embryo development, in reproduction, in immunity, in maintenance of homeostasis, as well as the differentiation of a wide range of mammary gland cells (Goodman, 1980). In productive herds, symptoms of deficiencies are infrequent. However, there are periods when the availability of vitamins is less than optimum, which may affect reproductive performance and/or immune competence. A vitamin A deficiency is most likely to occur during the winter, in rations with a high proportion of concentrates, and when the feed provided has been exposed to sunlight and high temperatures or stored for long periods of time. On the other hand, toxicity due to an excess of vitamin A is not very likely in ruminants, since its high degree of microbial degradability in the rumen limits the quantity available to the animal (NRC, 2000).

Recommendations

Suckler cows
According to the latest NRC report on beef cattle (1996) and its updated version (NRC, 2000), vitamin A requirements for gestating cows are 2,800 IU/kg of DM feed. This value is lower than that given by INRA (1988) for suckler cows in general (**Table I**), and is equivalent to approximately half the level indicated for dry cows in the latest

311

Table II. Nutritional composition of beef by country and principal cuts.

Content (per 100 g of DM meat)	Spain[1]					Australia[2]		Denmark[2]						United States[4]			France[5]		Mean[6]	
	Beef fillet	Lean veal	Half-fat veal	Veal fillet (Schnitzel)	Galician veal	Calf	Veal calf	A	B	C	D	E	Veal calf	A	B	C	Veal shuck, raw	Veal breast, raw	Intake	% of RDI
Water, g	78.3	73.9	62.3	62.5	NI	73.1	74.8	NI	NI	NI	NI	NI	NI	57.9	61.9	58.4	73.4	73.0	70	
Protein, g	18.2	20.7	16.7	17.0	20.5	23.2	24.8	19.4	18.2	19.5	21.5	16.1	21.6	32.8	28.3	27.0	19.0	19.5	22	
Lipids, g	3.5	5.4	21.0	20.5	20.5	2.8	1.5	15.3	21.3	17.3	6.5	30.1	2.2	11.9	9.6	14.2	6.5	6.5	12	
Energy, KJ	435	548	1072	1059	NI	498	477	896	1098	972	606	1387	449	1034	870	1017	564	572	800	
Cholesterol, mg	140	59	65	65	NI	50	51	NI	NI	NI	NI	NI	NI	76	62	75	81	90	75	
Vitamin A, (mg)	Tr	Tr	Tr	Tr	NI	Tr	Tr	14	25	19	3	38	–	–	–	–	–	–	6	1.4
B-carotenes, mg	Tr	Tr	Tr	Tr	NI	10	Tr	–	–	–	–	–	–	–	–	–	–	–	0.6	NI
Vitamin D, µg	–	Tr	Tr	Tr	NI	–	–	0.6	0.8	0.6	0.4	0.9	0.2	NI	NI	NI	–	–	0.3	3.6
Vitamin E, mg	0.45	0.15	0.19	0.19	NI	0.63	0.50	0.48	0.65	0.54	0.23	0.91	0.15	0.48	0.41	0.43	0.15	0.15	0.4	2.6
Vitamin K, mg	NI	NI	NI	NI	NI	–	–	–	–	–	–	–	–	1.65	1.41	1.65	NI	NI	0.4	0.4
Thiamine (B_1), µg	450	60	50	50	120	40	60	64	39	37	43	30	76	75	65	73	110	140	90	8.0
Riboflavin (B_2), µg	800	220	200	160	200	180	200	175	160	130	105	150	173	174	150	130	–	–	210	18.8
Niacin (B_3), mg	6.3	8.1	7.2	7.3	6.8	16.0		9.4	8.8	9.2	9.8	7.9	9.8	5.7	4.9	7.2	7.1	6.2	7.7	51.2
Vitamin B_6, mg	0.23	0.32	0.25	0.25	0.60	0.52	0.8	0.45	0.40	0.44	0.50	0.37	0.41	0.43	0.37	0.56	0.42	0.40	0.4	33.0
Vitamin B_{12}, µg	13	2	1	1	2.2	2.5	1.6	1.4	1.4	1.4	1.4	1.4	1.3	1.82	1.56	1.59	1.29	1.20	2.2	90.4
Pantothenic acid, mg	NI	NI	NI	NI	1.0	0.4	1.5	0.7	0.6	0.7	0.9	0.5	1.1	0.7	0.6	0.5	1.1	0.9	0.8	NI
Folic acid, µg	4	8	10	8	NI	NI	NI	6	5	6	7	4	7	10.6	9.41	8.23	10.0	5.0	7.2	1.8
Vitamin C, mg	7	–	–	–	–	NI	NI	–	–	–	–	–	–	–	–	–	NI	NI	0.5	1.2

– = no content; NI = not indicated; Tr = traces; Vit A = retinol equivalents; Vit E = α-tocopherol; Vit K = phylloquinone.
(1) Adapted from: Moreiras et al. (2006); *Ternera gallega, available at: http://www.terneragallega.com/caracteristicas.asp?idioma=0%20%20&sec=74.
(2) Adapted from: Williams (2007).Ternera; average value for diced, stir-fry, round, rump, topside, silverside, fillet, sirloin, scotch fillet, T-bone, blade and chuck steak:Ternera Blanca; mean values for stir-fry, diced, leg steak and cutlet.
(3) Adapted from: Danish Food Composition Databank (2006), available at: http://www.foodcomp.dk/fcdb_download.asp. A= rump, raw; B= entrecote "cap on", raw; C= strip loin "cap on", raw; D= eye of round, raw; E= flank, raw.
(4) Adapted from: USDA (2008), available at: http://www.ars.usda.gov/Services/docs.htm?docid=17477; A= bottom round, separable lean and fat, trimmed to 1/8" fat; B= eye of round, separable lean and fat, trimmed to 1/8" fat; C= top sirloin, separable lean and fat, trimmed to 1/8" fat.
(5) Adapted from AFSSA (2008), available at: http://www.afssa.fr/TableCIQUAL/index.htm.
(6) Approximate mean value, estimated from data available in the table; data appearing as – and Tr were computed as zero (0). RDI = recommended daily intake for an adult (19-65 years).

NRC report (2001) on dairy cattle. The NRC (2001) has considered it advisable to increase vitamin A levels in dry cows to boost immune competence and reduce mammary health and postpartum reproduction problems. However, it must be remembered that the vitamin A concentration in colostrum depends on the concentration of vitamin A received by cows during the dry period, and this has an effect on the quantity of vitamin A that weaner calves consume during the first days of life. If the cows calve following a long period of winter feeding during which they have ingested low quality hay, colostrum will have a low vitamin A content and it may prove useful to supplement calves with this vitamin. A special case where the same recommendation would apply is that of primiparous cows. These are prone to producing colostrum with lower levels of vitamin A (INRA, 1981), which may not be sufficient to meet requirements of the calves.

Both the NRC (1996, 2000) and INRA (1988) recommend a vitamin A supply of 3,900 IU/kg of DM feed for beef cows either lactating or suckling the calf. However, with the objective of maximizing productivity, promoting calf growth and taking possible stressful situations into account, INRA (1988) suggests that an optimum vitamin A intake should be around 200 IU/kg of LW, equivalent to 10,000 IU/kg of DM feed (**Table I**). These requirements are not always met in the case of suckler cows which calve indoors some time before being put out to pasture (e.g., in the middle of winter in the north of the Spanish peninsula, or in summer in the south). Under these circumstances, the ß-carotene reserves accumulated by the animal itself may be useful, but if feed has been based on low quality hay or corn silage for a prolonged period, there is a risk that these reserves may become practically exhausted, leading to a shortfall, especially if the feed has been stored for a long period. For this reason INRA (1988) recommends a regular supply of at least 30,000 to 40,000 IU of vitamin A/day for cows in lactation as well as for those in late gestation.

Weaner calves

The most recent recommendations on vitamin A supplies for suckling calves or those on artificial feed are 110 IU/kg of LW, and correspond to those established for dairy cattle (NRC, 2001), which represents an important increase compared with previous reports. This is equivalent to the incorporation of around 9,000 IU/kg of DM milk replacer and around 4,000 IU/kg of DM starter feed (**Table III**). Fortunately it is normal practice to give weaner calves milk replacer containing vitamin A concentrations (20,000-40,000 IU/kg of DM) above recommended levels (Erdman, 1992). A special case is the production of veal calves, for which INRA (1988) recommends 48,000 IU/kg of DM milk replacer (**Table III**). However, negative effects have been observed when giving an over-dosage of vitamin A to young calves supplemented with 30,000 IU/day during the first weeks of life (Franklin et al., 1998). These effects were attributed to interference by vitamin A with the vitamin E status of the animals, so that in this case the vitamin E level should be raised as well.

Feedlot calves

The NRC report on beef cattle (1996, 2000) established recommendations for feedlot calves of 2,200 IU/kg of DM feed (**Table I**). This figure agrees with that given by INRA (1988) and by the NRC itself in previous reports. Dosages higher than those given would be justifiable for animals under stress, for example after weaning, or on arrival at the feedlot after a long journey, when one of the more common symptoms is reduced intake. In these situations, the vitamin A supply may be increased up to levels of 4,000 to 6,000 IU/kg of DM (NRC, 1996). The results of a descriptive analysis, based on surveys carried out among United States nutritionists (Vasconcelos and Galyean, 2007), indicate that the average recommended for diets in the final stage of fattening is 5,215 IU/kg (range 2,205–11,023). This is far above the values recommended by the NRC for fattening beef cattle (NRC, 2000).

The specific feeding conditions in Spain must be taken into account, as most of the meat marketed there is produced through intensive feed, using rations containing around 90% concentrate. As indicated by Rode et al. (1990), ruminal degradability of vitamin A is much higher under these circumstances than with rations rich in forage, so it seems reasonable to suggest a need to increase vitamin A supply. This increase should never exceed 100% of normal recommendations. Considering the possibility of negative effects the recommendation should be applied with caution and requires confirmation in operating conditions, given that excessive supplementation with vitamin A can lead to a reduction in the quality of the meat in beef cattle (Pyatt and Berger, 2005). It must be pointed out that using excessive dosages of vitamin A, for example three times higher than levels recommended by the NRC, has resulted in a drop in the daily live weight gain and in a poorer conversion index for feedlot calves (Hill *et al.*, 1995), which could be linked to an interaction with the availability of vitamin E, restricting its oxidative capacity. One possible alternative would be the application of a normal dosage of vitamin A, but by way of intramuscular injection. In all cases maximum tolerance limits of each vitamin must be respected (**Table I**). However, recent data suggest that the vitamin A content in the ration may affect the location of fat deposition in beef cattle (Pyatt and Berger, 2005) and

Table III. Content in natural milk and recommended concentration of vitamins in milk replacer and concentrates for young calves (in mg/kg of DM, except vits. A, D and E in IU/kg of DM).

	Natural milk (whole) (INRA, 1988)	Milk replacer intensive fattening[1] (NRC, 2001)	Concentrate (Starter and/or weaning) (NRC, 2001)	Milk replacer Veal[2] (INRA, 1988)
Vitamin A	11,500	9,000	4,000	48,000
Vitamin D	307	600	600	2,800
Vitamin E	7.8	50	25	10 – 30
Vitamin K	0.64	......	......	2
Thiamine (B$_1$)	......	......	......	......
Riboflavin (B$_2$)	3.3	6.5	......	1.0 – 5.3
Niacin (B$_3$)	12.2	6.5	......	0.8 – 2.5
Pirodoxina (B$_6$)	9.5	10	......	10 – 14
Vitamin B$_{12}$	4.4	6.5	......	2.0
Biotin	0.05	0.07	......	0.02-0.06
Folic acid	0.30	0.1	......	0.11
Pantothenic acid	0.56	0.5	......	0.8
Choline	25.9	13	......	5 – 11
Vitamin C	1,080	2,600	......	1,440
	120	1-2	......	100

(1) Fed with reconstituted milk, feed and straw (pink meat or "baby beef")
(2) Fed with artificial milk (plus a minimum quantity of fiber granules).
...... Data not provided

that is therefore not advisable to supply it excessively at the end of the fattening stage. In fact, it is recommended that the supply of vitamin A in the diet be reduced during this period, as a mechanism to favor deposition of intramuscular fat (Siebert *et al.*, 2006, Gorocica-Buenfil *et al.*, 2007, 2008; Kruk *et al.*, *in press*), which in addition favors the longevity of the color and reduces the oxidative capacity of lipids in the meat (Daniel *et al.*, 2008). In view of this, it seems the recommendations of the NRC (1996) on the vitamin A requirements for calf diets in the final fattening phase are an over-estimate, and should therefore be reviewed.

VITAMIN D

Vitamin D, also known as an antirachitic vitamin, is involved in the regulation of calcium metabolism and in the maintenance of correct calcium levels in blood. This vitamin can be obtained from sterols converted by ultraviolet irradiation from the sun. A good amount of vitamin D is produced in the skin of animals through photoconversion of 7-dehydrocholesterol to vitamin D_3 (cholecalciferol). Similarly, vitamin D_2 (ergocalciferol) is obtained from sun-dried forage. The two forms (D_2 and D_3) have the same potential in ruminants (1g is equal to 40,000 IU). In order to become completely functional, these vitamins must be activated, first in the liver, where they accumulate as 25-hydroxycholecalciferol, and then in the kidneys, where they finally convert to 1,25-dihydroxycholecalciferol. To evaluate the status of vitamin D in the animal, the plasmatic concentration of 25-hydroxycholecalciferol (Horst *et al.*, 1994) is generally recommended as a parameter.

Recommendations

The NRC (1996, 2000) recommends a supply of 275 IU of vitamin D/kg of DM feed for beef cattle in general (gestating or lactating cows and grower or finisher calves), where one IU is defined as 0.025 mg of cholecalciferol (D_3) or its equivalent. And INRA (1989) gives a similar recommendation (300 IU/kg of DM) that would be valid for most growing and fattening cattle (**Table I**). Data recently obtained from a descriptive study (Vasconcelos and Galyean, 2007), indicate that in the US, supplies of vitamin D in the diet of fattening calves are higher than the NRC recommendations (averaging 329.9 IU/kg of DM), but with a wide range of variation (0.0 to 1.102 IU/kg of DM). In the case of suckling calves (**Table III**) a supply of 660 IU/kg of DM milk replacer (and also in concentrate) is recommended, and this should be increased to 2,800 IU/kg of DM in the case of calves fed exclusively with milk (veal calves).

Because vitamin D is synthesized easily in animals exposed to sunlight or given sun-dried feed, a high percentage of bovine livestock (e.g. cows and calves in the field or in open sheds with sunny yards) do not require additional supplementation of this vitamin (NRC 1996, 2000). Recently, differences have been observed in storage capacity, tissue concentration and supplementation requirements of vitamin D between *Bos indicus and Bos taurus* cattle, which may be associated with a greater capacity for adaptation in the former (Montgomery *et al.*, 2004). However, it is evident that systematic addition is needed for animals permanently housed indoors. According to INRA (1988), it would also be appropriate to increase vitamin D levels in animals receiving significant amounts of ß-carotene or suffering from metabolic acidosis, but these must always be within tolerance limits (**Table I**) to avoid the toxicity caused by an excess. However, recent data suggest that supplementation with raised quantities of vitamin D (between 0.5 and 7.5 x 10^6 IU) during the week prior to slaughter improves the tenderness of the meat (Swanek *et al.*, 1999; Montgomery *et al.*, 2002; Foote *et al.*, 2004). This improvement in the quality of the meat may be associated with increases in the calcium concentration, which would cause greater proteolysis in the days following slaughter (Montgomery *et al.*, 2000, 2002).

VITAMIN E

Vitamin E is a group of molecules of which α-tocopherol is the most potent and common form in vegetables. One IU vitamin E is equal to 1 mg of all-rac-α-tocopherol acetate. The vitamin E content of feed is very variable. Forage, depending on its state of maturity, contains between 80 and 200 IU of vitamin E per kg of DM (Tramontano et al., 1993; Jukola et al. 1996). The α-tocopherol concentration reduces rapidly once the plant is cut. Prolonged exposure to oxygen or sunlight increases the speed of degradation (Thafvelin and Oksanen, 1966). Silage and hay, frequently used in winter feed for beef cattle, have between 20 and 80% less tocopherol than fresh forage. Concentrate feeds are low in vitamin E, except for whole soy bean and cotton seed.

Vitamin E is a potent antioxidant agent which is very important in rations rich in unsaturated fatty acids. It stimulates the production of antibodies and enhances immune response (Craven and Williams, 1985; Hogan et al., 1993; Rivera et al., 2002). An optimum intake of vitamin E brings about a lower incidence of retained placentas and metritis, improvements in mammary gland health and the health of the reproductive system (Smith et al., 1985; Hogan et al., 1993; Harrison et al., 1984; Lacetera et al., 1996), and improvements in immune competence and meat quality (McDowell et al., 1996, 2000a; Rivera et al., 2002). It is difficult, however, to discuss vitamin E without considering the role of selenium, since the effects of both micronutrients are closely related in animal productivity (Patterson, 2002). Both elements are required by the animals and fulfill a metabolic role in the animal in addition to their antioxidant effect. In some cases, although not always, vitamin E can be substituted by selenium to a certain extent or vice versa. Although selenium cannot replace vitamin E completely as a nutrient, it does reduce the requirements for it and delays the appearance of symptoms of vitamin E deficiency in the animal (Spears, 2000; Hemingway, 2003).

Recommendations

Suckler cows

Neither INRA (1988) nor the NRC report on beef cattle (1996) give a specific value for the vitamin E requirements of suckler cows. INRA (1988) does, however, point out more generally that in ruminants these requirements would be around 5-10 IU (or mg) per kg of DM feed (**Table I**), recommending in the case of dairy cows (gestating and/or lactating) a supply of 15 IU/kg of DM feed. This value could probably be extrapolated and used directly for beef cows.

The NRC in its report on dairy cows (2001) increased vitamin E recommendations for lactating cows considerably, by 30%, to 20 IU/kg of DM, and increased its recommendation for dry cows even more markedly (1.6 IU/kg of LW, equivalent to 80 IU/kg of DM). The usefulness of applying these recommendations to beef cattle is debatable, since the increment recommended by the NRC (2001) for dairy cows is based on the improvement in immune competence in animals subjected to very demanding production conditions. However, the evidence of its effect on the health of the mammary gland and the reproductive function should be considered, given that the vitamin E reserves in a suckling calf are low. Some investigators recommend supplementation of prepartum gestating cows with vitamin E to increase the concentration of vitamin E in the colostrum (Weiss, 1994). The dose recommended for the supplementation of cows is 1000 IU/d of vitamin E (Zobell et al., 1995; Quigley and Bernard, 1995) and it has been proposed as an alternative for increasing blood levels of vitamin E in the cow and the colostrum, and minimizing the incidence of post-partum metabolic disorders. The adoption of this practice is also recommended as a mechanism for maximizing resistance to diseases in calves during the first weeks of life (Quigley and Drewry, 1998; Debier et al., 2005).

Weaner calves

According to the NRC (1996, 2000), vitamin E requirements have not been well established, although for young calves they are considered to be between 15 and 60 IU/kg of DM (**Table I**). The recommendation for weaner calves in the new NRC report on dairy cows (2001) is within this margin, at 50 IU/kg of DM, which has increased by 25% compared with the 40 IU/kg of DM in previous reports. In the particular case of veal calves (**Table III**), a supply of between 10 and 30 IU vitamin E/kg of DM is recommended (INRA, 1988).

The tendency to provide higher levels of vitamin E than those recommended is based on increased requirements of animals in the stress situations typical of current production systems, especially in feedlots which are becoming more and more intensive. Here an additional supplement of vitamin E can boost the immune system (Hidiroglou et al., 1995; Reddy et al., 1986 and 1987; Carter et al., 2005). However, the presence of unsaturated fatty acids in milk replacer can increase the risk of oxidation of the ration, increasing the need for antioxidants. Stobo (1983) suggested that vitamin E concentration in milk replacer should be formulated according to the unsaturated fatty acid content of the ration, and suggested a ratio of 1.5-2.5 IU of vitamin E per gram of linoleic acid. In normal milk replacer, this ratio is achieved with daily intake of between 25 and 63 IU/kg of DM.

Although there is no solid evidence to justify the need to use in practice levels above those recommended for vitamin E, there are two situations that merit special consideration. First, the frequent incidence of digestive disorders in young calves reduces vitamin E absorption. Second, as has been previously indicated, supplementation with high quantities of vitamin A interferes with vitamin E absorption. For these reasons, and because of the wide safety margin of vitamin E (**Table I**), it seems reasonable to consider a possible increase in the supply of this vitamin above recommended levels in certain situations.

Feedlot calves

The NRC (1996, 2000) recommends a vitamin E supply of between 15 and 60 IU/kg of DM in concentrate for feedlot calves, while INRA (1988) recommends 25 IU of vitamin E/kg of DM. These results should be increased in situations of stress, since vitamin E participates actively in the immune system and it is known that stress suffered as a result

of factors such as weaning, transport, mixing with animals from other farms and adapting to the feedlot leads to rapid depletion of reserves of this vitamin (Hill and Williams, 1995). Vitamin E supplementation (400 IU/animal per day) during the first 3-4 weeks in the feedlot can have positive effects on growth, conversion index and incidence of disease (Lee et al., 1985; Droke and Loerch, 1989; Galyean et al., 1999). For this reason, the NRC (1996) recommends a supplemental supply of 400-500 IU/d of vitamin E in these critical periods (**Table I**). More recent data demonstrate the favorable effect of supplementation with vitamin E in stress situations associated with transfer of animals to feedlots. Elam et al. (2006b) carried out an analysis of bibliographical data to evaluate the effect of the quantity of ingested vitamin E (range 0 – 2,000 IU/animal/day), in the productive response and health of calves just arrived at the feedlots. The results indicated that, although no positive effects were observed in daily weight gain or in the ingestion of food, the provision of vitamin E did produce a reduction in the incidence of respiratory diseases. The average reduction was 0.35% for each 100 UI of vitamin E ingested per day.

Supplementing with vitamin E during finishing with the aim of improving productive yield has had varied responses. In general, positive responses have been observed in animals which had previously suffered vitamin E deficiency (Hutcheson and Cole, 1985), but were not observed in those that had always been well fed (Carrica et al., 1986; Schaeffer et al., 1989; Arnold, 1992). Improvements in growth rates and/or in conversion indexes are generally found in young animals with good growth potential which have undergone conditions of stress (Hill and Williams, 1995).

Another possible reason for supplementing higher vitamin E levels in rations for beef calves in the finishing phase is to reduce the oxidation of lipids, improve the color of the meat, and in consequence of this to obtain a product with a longer shelf life (Descalzo and Sancho, 2008). The supply of high quantities of vitamin E in the final fattening period improves the color stability of refrigerated or frozen meat (McDowell et al., 1996). This allows the display period of the fresh meat to be lengthened from 1 to 3 days without loss of color and is important in meat destined for export. The loss of color in meat, which in the case of red meat production changes from bright to dark red, is due to the high potential for myoglobin oxidation. Oxidation of muscle pigments is one of the main causes of deterioration in meat quality (Faustman *et al.*, 1989). Supplementation with a high dosage of vitamin E improves color and also inhibits fat oxidation, reducing the risk of rancidity (Schaefer *et al.*, 1991, Arnold *et al.*, 1992; Hill and Williams, 1993 and 1995), and lengthening the shelf life of saleable meat (McDowell *et al.*, 1996). According to these latter authors, the α-tocopherol concentration in muscular tissue should reach 0.30-0.35 mg/100g of meat to obtain this kind of result, and this is possible by means of supplementation with 500 IU/d of vitamin E during a period of about 100-125 days prior to slaughter of the calves (Schaefer *et al.*, 1991; Stubbs *et al.*, 1999; Rowe, 2004). In some countries the use of a quick and cheap spectrophotometric method in slaughterhouses has been proposed, which allows identification of meat from animals supplemented with vitamin E (Smith, 1994), with the objective of paying a better price to the farmer according to the quality of meat produced. Recent data also suggest that supplementation with vitamin

E in a dose of 1,000 IU/day 125 days prior to slaughter improves the tenderness of the meat, given that it protects the calpain (the enzyme responsible for the softening of the meat) from oxidation (Rowe, 2004). It has also been suggested that supplementation with vitamin E during the final fattening phase of calves constitutes an effective method to increase the stability of lipids during cooking (Lanari et at., 1994), although this effect is not always evident (Robbins *et al.*, 2003). In an article recently reviewed, where the effect of the inclusion of antioxidants in diet on the characteristics and quality of the meat is analyzed (Descalzo and Sancho, 2008), the conclusion is that the magnitude of the beneficial effect of supplementing the fattening diet with vitamin E is very variable and dependent on the basic diet offered (forage vs. concentrate; silage, nature of the supplement, etc.).

In conclusion, the available data suggest that current recommendations for feedlot animals (15-60 IU/kg of DM) may be increased during the period of entry and adaptation to the feedlot (400-500 IU/d) with the objective of improving their immune competence, and in the finishing period (500-1,000 IU/d, for about 3 months) if an economic profit may be obtained from an improvement in the quality of the meat produced.

VITAMIN K

Vitamin K has antihaemorrhagic effects, as it is necessary for the synthesis of a series of blood coagulation factors (Combs, 1992). Vegetables (K_1) and ruminal bacteria (K_2) are important sources of this vitamin. K_2 is the principal source of vitamin K in ruminants and deficiencies in ruminants are almost never detected. They are only reported in

situations where anticoagulant substances have been consumed, such as when forage contaminated with fungal dicumarol is consumed. Therefore, recommendations are only given for veal calves, which require an intake of 2 mg vitamin K/kg of DM milk replacer (**Table II**; INRA, 1988).

WATER-SOLUBLE VITAMINS

THIAMINE (VITAMIN B₁)

Thiamine is a coenzyme which participates in many metabolic reactions. The quantity of thiamine synthesized in the rumen (between 28 and 72 mg/d) is the same as or higher than that ingested in the ration (Breves *et al.*, 1981). No requirements have been laid down for ruminants in good health and with a functional rumen. Supplies from microbial synthesis and the diet are sufficient to meet requirements of cows and calves, even considering ruminal degradation of dietary thiamine of 48% (Zinn *et al.*, 1987). For ruminants, thiamine is not toxic and the safety margins in monogastrics are 1,000 times the recommended dose (NRC, 1987), although no safety limits have been established for ruminants.

The requirements of thiamine for feedlot ruminants have not been determined, and it is assumed that ruminal micro-organisms provide a sufficient quantity (INRA 1988, NRC 1996). In the exceptional case of veal calves a supply of between 1 and 5.3 IU/kg of DM is recommended (INRA, 1988). However, the NRC (2001) recommends the incorporation of 6.5 mg/kg of DM thiamine in milk replacer. By extrapolating the requirements for pigs, Zinn (1992) estimated the requirements for feedlot calves as 0.14 mg/kg $LW^{0.75}$. Under normal conditions, intake from dietary thiamine and ruminal synthesis is sufficient. There are, however, situations in which the thiamine finally available to the animal can be a limiting factor (INRA, 1988, Zinn, 1992; NRC, 1996). For example, when rations contain high levels of concentrate or are rich in quickly fermentable carbohydrates, typical of intensive feed, abrupt drops in the ruminal pH can occur, leading to the release of thiaminases (exogenous enzymes) which destroy thiamine. Also, in situations of acidosis, destruction of thiamine by thiaminase has been linked to the appearance of polioencephalomalacia (PEM) or cerebro-cortical necrosis. A similar situation may occur in rations with excessive sulfur levels (Zinn, 1992; NRC, 1996; Patterson *et al.*, 2002; Pritchard, 2007). Conditions of low ruminal pH also favor reduction of sulfur to its gaseous form (H_2S), increasing its concentration in the rumen. H_2S, when eructed, can be inhaled by the animal and trigger PEM. This fact, coupled with the blood levels of thiamine, is considered responsible for the appearance of PEM in cattle (McAllister *et al.* 1997; Loneragan *et al.* 1998). The positive effect of supplementation by thiamine, independently of the clinical diagnosis of PEM syndrome, may be due to the fact that this precedes the sub-clinical apparition of PEM, or because supplementary thiamine may prevent the deficiency (Ward and Patterson, 2004). Under these conditions, thiamine supplementation may alleviate symptoms and improve animal performance (Ward and Paterson, 2004), although parenteral administration is more advisable.

Another important aspect to consider is also the meat's thiamine content, since this, together with the presence of the sulfurous components, principally cysteine, is involved in the production of certain intermediary compounds responsible for the development and boosting of certain aromas characteristic of meat while it is being cooked (Jooh *et al.*, 2002).

RIBOFLAVIN (VITAMIN B$_2$)

Riboflavin is a constituent of many enzymes which participate in intermediary metabolism. In dairy cattle no requirements have been established, since ruminal microorganisms synthesize abundant quantities of this vitamin. This synthesis and the flow of riboflavin in the rumen appear to be independent of the level of concentrate in the ration (Zinn *et al.*, 1987), and it is synthesized at a rate of 15.2 mg/kg organic matter digested. Furthermore, ruminal degradation is almost complete (Zinn *et al.*, 1987), and intestinal digestibility is approximately 25% (Miller *et al.*, 1986; Zinn *et al.*, 1987).

Neither the NRC (1996) nor INRA (1988) have established specific recommendations for riboflavin for beef cattle or feedlot calves, except in the case of veal calves, for which a supply of between 0.8 and 2.5 IU/kg of DM milk feed is recommended (INRA, 1988), or its inclusion in milk replacer (6.5 mg/kg of DM; NRC, 2001). Zinn (1992) calculated, using data collected from pigs (NRC, 1979), that the requirements for feedlot or finisher cattle were 0.32 mg/kg LW$^{0.75}$. Taking into account that ruminal degradation of riboflavin provided in the diet is almost complete, and that riboflavin synthesis by ruminal bacteria is 15.2 mg/kg of DOM (Zinn, 1987, 1992), it is very unlikely that riboflavin deficiencies occur in ruminants. Riboflavin deficiencies have only been observed in young preruminant animals (NRC, 1996). In any case, supplementation should only be considered in animals under stress and with a low feed intake, when bacterial supplies are diminished (Zinn, 1992).

NIACIN (VITAMIN B$_3$)

Niacin is an active component of two coenzymes (NAD and NADP) which play a fundamental role in carbohydrate, lipid and amino acid metabolism. Niacin is found in high concentrations in by-products of animal origin and in cereals.

Ruminal bacteria synthesize abundant quantities of niacin (Zinn *et al.*, 1987). Zinn (1992) calculated that niacin synthesis in the rumen was at a rate of 107.02 mg/kg of DOM. However, when it is added to the ration, the quantity of niacin which reaches the intestine may be even less than that provided in the ration, due to the inhibition of bacterial synthesis in the presence of exogenous niacin (Abdouli and Schaefer, 1986). Moreover, between 94 and 99% of niacin present in the diet is degraded in the rumen (Zinn, 1992), although other studies have estimated that between 17 and 30% of dietary niacin reaches the small intestine (Harmeyer and Kollenkirchen, 1989; Campbell *et al.*, 1994).

Niacin stimulates microbial protein synthesis (Mizwicki, 1976; Bartley *et al.*, 1979; Ridell, *et al.*, 1980; Arambell *et al.*, 1982), the production of propionic acid (Ridell *et al.*, 1980; Arambell *et al.*, 1982; Hannah and Stern, 1985), and digestion of cellulose (Hannah and Stern, 1985). On the metabolic level, niacin participates in lipid and energy metabolism. Supplementation with niacin leads to an increase in the concentration of glucose in blood, and a decrease in the concentration of ß-hydroxybutyric acid and free fatty acids in plasma, which are indicators of its activity as gluconeogenesis stimulator.

Niacin is required in rations for calves before weaning due to the scant microbial synthesis in the rumen. Hopper and Johnson (1955) observed that calves fed with synthetic milk deficient in niacin presented with diarrhea within 48 hours and that there was an immediate improvement the day after administering an oral dose of 6 mg/d or an intramuscular dose of 10 mg/d nicotinic acid. The NRC (2001) recommends the incorporation of 10 mg/kg DM of niacin in milk replacer.

There is no evidence that niacin supplementation improves the growth rate of calves. Ridell *et al.* (1981) supplemented calves between 110 and 370 kg with 1.3

g/d niacin and observed no benefit, which suggests that a functional rumen provides enough niacin for the growth and normal development of the calves.

Nor have recommendations been established for niacin in feedlot cattle (NRC, 1996; INRA, 1988) due to the abundant synthesis of this vitamin in the rumen. Only in the case of veal calf production is the inclusion of between 10 and 14 IU niacin/kg of DM in milk feed recommended (INRA, 1988).

By extrapolating the requirements for pigs (NRC 1979), Zinn (1992) calculated that the requirements for growing and/ or finishing calves were 1.75 mg/kg $LW^{0.75}$. Considering that microbial synthesis is 107.02 mg/kg DOM (Zinn, 1992), the supply by ruminal bacteria would be sufficient to meet these requirements. However, when animals are fed rations with an imbalance in amino acids, an inadequate supply of energy, or containing rancid ingredients, niacin requirements are altered (NRC, 1996). Specifically, an excess of leucine, arginine or glycine, an excess of energy or the incorrect use of antibiotics increase niacin requirements. In experiments on production, niacin supplementation at up to 10 times the theoretical requirements up to entry to the feedlot improved productive yield (Cole *et al.* 1982, Zinn *et al.* 1987). However, Overfield and Hatfield (1976) observed improvements in growth when supplementing with niacin (250-500 mg/ kg). Hutcheson (1990) also observed an improvement of 20% in weight gain when supplementing starter rations for healthy calves with 125 ppm niacin, although in sick calves a positive response was only observed with a higher dosage (250 ppm).

PYRIDOXINE (VITAMIN B$_6$)

As with other B group vitamins, neither INRA (1988) nor the NRC (1996; 2001) have established recommendations for adult bovines. In the case of veal calves, INRA (1988) recommends a supply of 2 IU pyridoxine/ kg of DM. The NRC (2001) recommends the incorporation of 6.5 mg/kg of DM in milk replacer. Zinn (1992), extrapolating the data collected from pigs, recommends a supply of 0.14 mg/kg $LW^{0.75}$ for feedlot and/or finishing calves. In the rumen, pyridoxine is not degraded but is synthesized abundantly, so a deficit is very unlikely (Zinn, 1992).

CYANOCOBALAMIN (VITAMIN B$_{12}$)

Vitamin B$_{12}$ is the cofactor of methylmalonyl-CoA mutase (necessary for the conversion from propionate to succinate) and tetrahydrofolate methyl transferase (which participates in methionine metabolism). Up to 90% of vitamin B$_{12}$ of dietary origin is degraded in the rumen (Zinn, 1992). Bacteria are the only natural source of vitamin B$_{12}$. The NRC (2001) considers that the requirements of milk cows are between 0.34 and 0.68 µg/ kg LW. However, using the requirements for fattening pigs (NRC 1979), Zinn (1992) calculated the requirements for growing and/or finishing cattle as 1.42 g/kg $LW^{0.75}$. Due to the high ruminal degradability of dietary vitamin B$_{12}$, the supply by the rumen is of fundamental importance. Microbial synthesis of B$_{12}$ depends on the presence of cobalt, and increases in a linear fashion when cobalt is administered (in chloride form) up to levels of 0.2 mg/kg (Tiffany and Spears, 2005). Under normal conditions, ruminal bacteria synthesize at a rate of 4.1 mg/kg of DOM, and synthesis increases in rations high in forage (Sutton and Elliot, 1972; Walker and Elliot, 1972). Considering the requirements and the capacity for ruminal synthesis of vitamin B$_{12}$, it is unlikely that a deficiency would occur in beef cattle, except when there is a cobalt deficiency (Zinn *et al.*, 1987).

Supplementation in suckling calves may be necessary under some conditions (Lassiter *et al.*, 1953). The NRC (2001) recommends supplementation of 0.07 mg/kg of DM in milk replacer, and INRA (1988) recommends a supply of between 0.02 to 0.06 IU/kg of DM in rations for calves destined for veal production. Other than this exception, there is no evidence in the literature to suggest a need for vitamin B_{12} supplementation of rations for beef cattle, provided that the ration contains a sufficient quantity of cobalt, which according to the NRC (2000) should be 0.10 ppm. More recent data, however, indicate that this value should be raised (Stangl et al., 2000, Tiffany et al., 2003).

BIOTIN (VITAMIN H OR B_8)

Biotin is a cofactor of enzymes which catalyze carboxylation reactions, and intervenes in the tricarboxylic acid cycle, that of gluconeogenesis and fat synthesis (Campbell et al., 2000). It is also involved in the control and production of keratin, which is why supplementation with biotin is recommended as a mechanism to reduce laminitis in beef cattle (Tomlinson et al., 2004; Schwab and Shaver, 2005). It has also been shown that supplementation with 10 mg of biotin/animal/day (Campbell et al., 2000), exerts a positive effect in the prevention of foot problems in beef cattle. However, Chiquette et al. (1993) observed no differences in the digestibility or ruminal fermentation of growing calves supplemented with 2 mg/kg LW of biotin in diets based or forage or concentrate.

Ruminal bacteria synthesize large quantities of biotin depending on the availability of energy (0.79 mg/kg of DOM) (Briggs et al., 1964) although this synthesis reduces with an increase in the amount of concentrate in the ration. In experimental conditions in vitro it has been observed that in rations rich in concentrate (> 50% of the ration) the synthesis of biotin is reduced (Da-Costa-Gómez et al., 1998). Mock (1996, cited by Tomlinson et al., 2004) pointed out that a biotin deficiency is associated with a lesser pyruvate carboxylase enzyme activity, which is related to the development of lactic acidosis. It is therefore possible that the calves which receive higher quantities of concentrate in their diet, as in the case of the intensive beef production in Spain, may not have enough biotin in the rumen to convert all the lactic acid to pyruvate acid, and that this condition may be a precondition for acidosis (Tomlinson et al., 2004). However, biotin does not degrade to any great extent in the rumen (Frigg et al. 1993; Midla et al., 1998). Zinn (1992) estimated the requirements of biotin for feedlot and/or finisher calves as 0.13 mg/kg of $LW^{0.75}$. The combination of microbial synthesis and the supply in the base ration are generally sufficient to meet the requirements of both dairy as well as beef cattle.

Neither INRA (1988) nor the NRC (1996, 2000) have established recommendations for beef cattle, with the exception of veal calves (0.11 IU/kg of DM) and in milk replacers (0.1 mg/kg of DM) (**Table III**; INRA, 1988; NRC, 0.2001).

FOLIC ACID

Folic acid participates in the metabolism as a methyl group donor. Methionine is also used as a methyl group donor, so supplementation with folic acid increases the availability of methionine for productive functions. Zinn (1992) used data collected from pigs (NRC, 1997) to extrapolate the requirements of folic acid for feedlot and/or finisher cattle, and concluded that the requirements were 0.75 mg/kg of $LW^{0.75}$. A significant amount of folic acid is synthesized in the rumen depending on the availability of energy (0.42 mg/kg of DOM; Zinn, 1992). By comparing the estimated requirements with microbial synthesis of folic acid, Zinn (1992) concluded that folic acid could be a vitamin of limited use in cattle.

In preruminant calves poor bacterial synthesis may lead to deficiency. Daily injection of 40 mg folic acid between weeks 1 and 16 of life increased average weight gain by 8% between weeks 7 and 12 (Demoulin et al., 1991). Recommendations have only been established for the production of veal calves and for milk replacer (**Table III**), for which a supply of 0.8 mg/kg of DM (INRA, 1988) and 0.5 mg/kg of DM (NRC, 2001) respectively is recommended. Due to the high level of ruminal degradation (97%, Zinn, 1992), oral supplementation in adult animals would only be justified if a protection system against ruminal degradation were developed.

INOSITOL

Inositol is an important nutrient in the transport and metabolism of fats. Inositol is a constituent of phytic acid, very common in plants, and a deficit is therefore unlikely in ruminants.

PANTOTHENIC ACID

Pantothenic acid is a constituent of coenzyme A, and it is essential in many reactions including fatty acid oxidation metabolism, amino acid catabolism and acetylcholine synthesis.

As with other B group vitamins, there are no recommendations on requirements of pantothenic acid in bovines (INRA, 1988; NRC, 1996; NRC, 2000; NRC, 2001), apart from some exceptions. INRA (1988) recommends a supply of between 5 and 11 IU/kg DM for veal calves, and the NRC (2001) recommends the incorporation of 130 mg/kg of DM milk replacer. Zinn (1992) estimated from the requirements of growing pigs that the requirements of fattening calves were 1.42 mg/kg of $LW^{0.75}$. Taking into account that synthesis by ruminal bacteria is 2.2 mg/kg of DOM and ruminal degradation of dietary pantothenic acid is 78%, it appears that supplementation may be necessary (Zinn et al., 1987; Zinn, 1992), especially in the case of animals under stress or with low feed intake. It is possible that the development of forms which are less degradable in the rumen may provide an opportunity to improve the alimentary supply and obtain possible production responses.

VITAMIN C (ASCORBIC ACID)

Vitamin C is synthesized fundamentally as ascorbic acid within the cells of adult ruminants, and it is provided depending on the synthesis of vitamin C in the liver, since most of the vitamin C delivered in the diet is degraded in the rumen. It is generally accepted that adult cattle synthesize sufficient ascorbic acid to cover their vitamin C requirement (Toutain et al. 1997). There are thus no data on the effects of oral supplementation of vitamin C in adult animals. However, ruminants are considered the domestic species least likely to present vitamin C deficiencies when in some cases the synthesis of ascorbic acid is insufficient. Calves cannot synthesize it until they are 3 weeks old, so it is considered an essential nutrient only for young calves.

Vitamin C is an antioxidant and it participates in the regulation of steroid synthesis. Roth and Kaeberle (1985) suggested that it is implicated in immune response. Under conditions of stress, the plasma concentration of vitamin C diminishes as much in young as in growing calves (Cummins and Brunner, 1991; Hidiroglou et al., 1977). Oral supplementation of 1-2g vitamin C in preruminant calves increased the plasma concentration of vitamin C (Hidiroglou et al., 1995), which might be related to an improvement in the immune response (Eicher-Pruiett et al., 1992). In sheep, supplementation of the ration with 4 g/d vitamin C resulted in a rise in the plasma concentration of vitamin C (Hidiroglou et al., 1995). In no cases has supplementation with vitamin C shown an improvement in production. However, parenteral administration of vitamin C is indeed recommended in cases of stress, since its provision in the diet for a prolonged period might cause adverse effects in the immune response, due to the potential of vitamin C for acting as pro-oxidant in high concentrations (Rose and Bode, 1993).

The content of vitamin C in the tissues also varies according to the nutritional system of the calves. For example, the concentration of ascorbic acid (μg/g of muscle) in the psoas major muscle (selected for its high susceptibility to deterioration during storage), ranged from 15.92 in grain-based diets to 25.30 in pastured calves (Descalzo et al., 2005), (**Table II**).

Although neither the NRC (1996) nor the INRA (1988) set recommendations for beef cattle, with the exception of the production of veal calves, where a supply of 100 mg/kg of DM is recommended (INRA, 1988), it is necessary to monitor the requirements and supplies of this vitamin, above all in fattening calves fed with diets which include high quantities of concentrate, because of its effects on the quality of the carcass and the meat, such as its capacity to reduce the oxidative capacity of lipids, and the improvement and persistence of its color when treated post mortem (Descalzo and Sancho, 2008).

CHOLINE

Choline is not a vitamin in the traditional sense as it is not part of an enzyme system, and it is required in grams and not in milligrams like true vitamins. Phosphatidylcholine is the main natural form of choline present in food, although a small quantity of free choline may also exist in vegetable matter. As a component of phospholipids and of acetyl choline, it fulfils an essential role in the metabolism, serving as a methyl group donor. Biologically active methyl groups may also be obtained from methionine, so one of the advantages of supplementing choline is an increase in the availability of methionine for protein synthesis.

It has been demonstrated that both choline naturally present in foodstuffs and synthetic supplements of choline degrade by between 80 and 99% in the rumen, depending on the source (Sharma and Erdman, 1989). The flow of choline of mircrobial origin to the duodenum is slight, and the little that is available comes from protozoal synthesis (Sharma and Erdman, 1988). Choline is an important nutrient in lipid transport and metabolism. Supplementation should therefore when necessary come from sources which can guarantee that it is protected from ruminal degradability.

Johnson et al. (1951) observed a choline deficiency in one week-old calves when milk replacers contained 15% casein. The choline requirements calculated in this experiment were 260 mg/l milk replacer (1,733 mg/kg of DM). The NRC (2001) recommends the incorporation in milk replacer of 1,000 mg/kg of DM. In calves, signs of deficiency include muscular weakness, fatty infiltration of the liver and renal hemorrhage, as is observed in other species. In beef cattle, the only recommendation is to incorporate 0.26% choline in milk replacer and 1,440 UI/kg DM for veal production (NRC, 2000; INRA, 1988, respectively). Rumsey (1985) showed that supplementing rations for calves fed with concentrates did not alter the productive yields, or characteristics of ruminal fermentation, or carcass quality. The use of protected choline has improved the productive behavior of fatted calves with no negative effects on the characteristics of the carcass (Bryant et al., 1999; Bindel et al., 2000). While Bindel et al. (2005), who carried out choline infusions in the abomasum (5 g/d), with and without supplementary fat supply in the fatting calf ration, did not observe changes in the digestion of nutrients nor in the concentrations of metabolites in plasma.

SUPPLY OF VITAMINS AND NUTRITIONAL VALUE OF BEEF CATTLE FOR HUMAN CONSUMPTION

Beef cattle are seen as an important source of nutrition, which ensure proper nutrition and diet for the human population (**Table II**). Our food supply in general, and its essential vitamins in particular, represent an important part of a human being's recommended daily needs (**Table IV**). Various factors such as breed, the manufacturing system and the ingredients used in the feeding of livestock, the kind of cut you might consider, the post mortem handling of the carcass and of the meat, etc., will have an important effect on its composition and nutritional value (William, 2007). The lean component of the red meats, beef for example, are well-known as an excellent source of human nourishment. They have a high protein content of great biological value with the makeup and proportion of amino acids they can provide, with vitamins like niacin, riboflavin iron, B_6, B_{12}, pantothenic acid, folic acid and sometimes even vitamin D, minerals like iron, zinc, phosphorus, selenium and copper, endogenous antioxidants and other bio-active substances (McRae et al., 2005; Williams, 2007). The content of these macro and micro nutrients, with their organoleptic properties of tenderness, texture, juiciness and savour, (McRae et al., 2005; Dhiman et al., 2006) make beef an essential ingredient in the human diet.

Table II shows that the contribution of beef to daily vitamin requirements (estimated on the basis of a daily consumption of 100 g of beef and average vitamin content) is very important as regards B_2 (18.8%), B_3 (51.2%), B_6 (33%) and B_{12} (90.4%). In this respect, and for certain vitamins, the consumption of beef constitutes a very important contribution to human nourishment.

The results of numerous studies indicate that supplementation with vitamins A, D, E, C, and those from the B complex or its precursors, can exert a positive effect on different parameters of beef quality. Thus, for example, some data indicate that vitamin D has a positive influence on improving the tenderness of meat and increasing the levels of calcium in muscle (Swanek et al., 1999; Montgomery et al., 2002; Foote et al., 2004), even though the positive effects have not always been evident (Wertz et al., 2004). Nevertheless, this management practice has found little acceptance as a commercial strategy due to the fact that it reduces voluntary ingestion and animal productivity (Dikeman, 2007). In addition, excessive supplementation of vitamin D (in doses of 2×10^6 IU/d of vitamin D_3) can cause toxicity in beef cattle, and its harmlessness to human health has not been demonstrated (Dikeman, 2007).

Vitamins A, C and E intervene in the metabolism of lipids and deposition of intramuscular fat, a characteristic which in turn is related to an improvement in the flavor of meat and a change in the profile and provision of mono and/or poly-unsaturated long chain fatty acids (Siebert et al., 2003; Kawachi, 2006; Dhiman et al., 2006; Dikeman, 2007; Gorocica-Buenfil et al., 2007, 2008; Kruk et al., in press). Another aspect related to the quality of meat is the longevity of color and resistance to oxidation in post mortem treatment, in the case of which this group of vitamins also plays an important role with its antioxidant effect.

Beef also provides an important part of other bioactive substances (e.g. ubiquinones, glutathione, carnosine, anserine, L-carnitine, taurine, creatinine, etc.) which act as endogenous antioxidants and contribute to an improvement in the human immune system (Arihara, 2006; Williams, 2007).

Table IV: Recommended daily supply of vitamins in the human diet, separated according to type and age group.

Type and age group	A (µg RE/d)[1]	D (µg/d)[2]	E (mg/d)[3]	K (µg/d)[4]	B1 (mg/d)	B2 (mg/d)	B3 (mg/d)[5]	B6 (mg/d)	B12 (µg/d)	Biotin (µg/d)	Folic acid (µg/d)	Pantothenic acid (mg/d)	Vitamin C (mg/d)[6]	Choline (mg/d)
Infants and children														
0–6 months	180–375	5	4	2	0.2	0.3	2	0.1	0.4	5	80	1.7	25	125
7–12 months	190–400	5	5	2.5	0.3	0.4	4	0.3	0.7	6	80	1.8	30*	150
1–3 years	200–400	5	6	30	0.5	0.5	6	0.5	0.9	8	150	2.0	30*	200
4–6 years	200–450	5	7	55	0.6	0.6	8	0.6	1.2	12	200	3.0	30*	250–350
7–9 years	250–500	5	8–11	55–60	0.9	0.9	12	1.0	1.8	20	300	4.0	35*	375
Adolescents														
10–18 years	365–600	5	11–15	60–75	1.1–1.2	1.0–1.3	16	1.2–1.3	2.4	25	400	5.0	40*	400–550
Adult Women														
19–65 years	270–500	5–10	15	90	1.1	1.1	14	1.3	2.4	30	400	5.0	45	425
> 65 years	300–600	15	15	90	1.1	1.1	14	1.5	2.4	30	400	5.0	45	425
Gestating women	370–800	5	15	75–90	1.4	1.4	18	1.9	2.6	30	600	6.0	55	450
Lactating women	450–850	5	19	75–90	1.5	1.6	17	2.0	2.8	35	500	7.0	70	550
Men														
19–65 years	300–600	5–10	15	120	1.1	1.3	16	1.3	2.4	30	400	5.0	45	550
> 65 years	300–600	15	15	120	1.1	1.3	16	1.7	2.4	30	400	5.0	45	550

Source: Adapted from FAO (2004); for vitamin E, K, choline (IOM, 2000)
(1) RE= retinol equivalent (Average value – value recommended as insurance);
(2) Recommended daily intake (1 µg= 40 IU vitamin D);
(3) Equivalent α-tocopherol; Recommended daily intake;
(4) filoquinones, recommended daily intake;
(5) Equivalents niacin; for infants between 0–6 months pre-formed niacin;
(6) Quantity required to saturate half the tissues with vitamin C in 97.5% of the population.
*arbitrary values.

CONCLUSIONS

Vitamins play a fundamental role in numerous vital functions. In productive conditions, vitamin deficiencies should not only be considered from the point of view of maintenance of physiological functions. Vitamins should also permit optimum production and reduction in the incidence of clinical or subclinical pathologies. In the last few years, vitamin recommendations established by ration formulation systems, as well as those applied in field conditions by the industry, have increased. This is true especially of intensive systems, where the aims are to improve productivity and reduce pathologies. The most important increases in recommended levels affect vitamins A and E. Other vitamins, especially of the B group, which have not until now been considered necessary in formulations for adult ruminants, are necessary in the case of pre-ruminants, and may be necessary in adults under conditions of stress or high production, in which case systems must be developed to protect vitamins in order to avoid or reduce their ruminal degradability.

The establishment of requirements and provision of vitamins for the nutrition and feeding of beef cattle should be seen not only from the animal's point of view but also for the implications on the final product in the production system, i.e. the meat, and the importance this has in the human diet.

REFERENCES

Abdouli, H. & D. M. Schaefer. 1986. Impact of niacin and length of incubation on protein synthesis, soluble to total protein ratio and fermentative activity of ruminal microorganisms. *J Anim Sci* 62: 244–262

Arambell, M. J., S. M. Dennis, D. O. Riddel, E. E. Bartley, J. L. Camac & A. D. Dayton. 1982. Effect of heat treated soybean meal with and without niacin on rumen fermentation. *J Anim Sci* 55, (suppl. 1): 405.

Arihara, K. 2006. Strategies for designing novel functional meat products. *Meat Sci* 74: 219–229.

Arnold, R. N., K. K. Scheller, S. C. Arp, S. N. Williams, D. R. Buege & D. M. Schaefer. 1992. Effect of long- or short-term feeding of α-Tocopheryl acetate to Holstein and Crossbred beef steers on performance, carcass characteristics, and beef color stability. *J Anim Sci* 70: 3055–3065.

Bartley, E. E., E. L. Herod, R. M. Bechtle, D. A. Sapienza, B. E. Brent, & A. Davidovich. 1979. Effect of monensin or lasalocid, with and without niacin or amicloral, on rumen fermentation and feed efficiency. *J Anim Sci* 49: 1066–1075.

Bindel, D. J., J. S. Drouillard, E. C. Titgemeyer, R. H. Wessels & C. A. Loest. 2000. Effects of ruminally protected choline and dietary fat on performance and blood metabolites of finishing heifers. *J Anim Sci* 78:2497–2503.

Bindel, D. J., E. C. Titgemeyer, J. S. Drouillard & S. E. Ives. 2005. Effects of choline on blood metabolites associated with lipid metabolism and digestion by steers fed corn-based diets. *J Anim Sci* 2005. 83:1625–1632.

Breves, G., M. Brandt, H. Hoeller & K. Rohr. 1981. Flow of thiamin to the duodenum in dairy cows fed different rations. *J Agric Sci Camb* 96: 587.

Briggs, M. H., T. W. Heard, A. Whiteroft, & M. L. Hogg. 1964. Studies of urea fed cattle: rumen levels of B vitamins and related coenzymes. *Life Sci* 3: 11.

Bruhn, J. C., & J. C. Oliver. 1978. Effect of storage on tocopherol and carotene concentration in alfalfa hay. *J Anim Sci* 61: 980.

Bryant, T. C., J. D. Rivera, M. L. Galyean, G. C. Duff, D. M. Hallford & T. H. Montgomery. 1999. Effects of dietary level of ruminally protected choline on performance and carcass characteristics of finishing beef steers and on growth and serum metabolites in lambs. *J Anim Sci* 77:2893–2903.

Campbell, J. M., M. R. Murphy, R. A. Christensen & T. R. Overton. 1994. Kinetics of niacin supplements in lactating dairy cows. *J Dairy Sci* 77: 566–575.

Campbell, J. R., P. R. Greenough & L. Petrie. 2000. The effects of dietary biotin supplementation on vertical fissures of the claw wall in beef cattle. *Can Vet J* 41:690–694.

Carrica J. M., R. T. Brandt & R. W. Lee. 1986. Influence of vitamin E on feedlot performance and carcass traits of beef steers fed either lasalocid or monensin. *J Anim Sci* 63(Suppl. 1): 432.

Carter, J. N., D. R. Gill, C. R. Krehbiel, A. W. Confer, R. A. Smith, D. L. Lalman, P. L. Claypool & L. R. McDowell. 2005. Vitamin E supplementation of newly arrived feedlot calves. *J Anim Sci* 83: 1924–1932.

Chiquette, J., C. L. Girard & J. J. Matte. 1993. Effect of diet and folic acid addition on digestibility and ruminal fermentation in growing steers. *J Anim Sci* 71: 2793–2798.

Cole N. A., J. B. McLaren & D. P. Hutcheson. 1982. Influence of preweaning and B-vitamin supplementation of the feedlot receiving diet on calves subjected to marketing and transit stress. *J Anim Sci* 54: 911–917.

Combs, G.F. Jr., 1992. The vitamins: fundamental aspects in nutrition and health. Academ. Press. Inc.

Craven, N. & M. R. Williams. 1985. Defenses of the bovine mammary gland against infection and prospects for their enhancement. *Vet Immunol Immunopathol* 10: 71.

Cummins, K. A. & C. J. Brunner. 1991. Effect of calf housing on plasma ascorbate and endocrine and immune function. *J Dairy Sci* 74: 1582.

DaCosta-Gomez, C. M., A. L. Masri, W. Steinberg & H. Abel. 1998. Effect of varying hay/barley proportions on microbial biotin metabolism in the rumen simulating fermenter RUSITEC. *Proc Soc Nutr Phys* 7:30. (Abstr.)

Daniel, M. J., M. E. Dikeman & A. M. Arnett.

2008. Vitamin A restriction during finishing benefits beef retail color display life. Kansas State Univ. *Beef Cattle Research 2008 Report of Progress* 95: 28–30.

Debier, C., J. Pottier, C. Goffe & Y. Larondelle. 2005. Present knowledge and unexpected behaviors of vitamins A and E in colostrum and milk. *Livest Prod Sci* 98: 135–147.

Descalzo, A.M., E. M. Insani, A. Biolatto, A. M. Sancho, P. T. García, N. A. Pensel & J.A. Josifovich. 2005. Influence of pasture or grain-based diets supplemented with vitamin E on antioxidant/oxidative balance of Argentine beef. *Meat Sci* 70: 35–44.

Descalzo, A. M. & A. M. Sancho. 2008. A review of natural antioxidants and their effects on oxidative status, odor and quality of fresh beef produced in Argentina. *Meat Sci* 79: 423–436.

Dikeman, M. E. 2007. Review: Effects of metabolic modifiers on carcass traits and meat quality. *Meat Sci.* 77: 121–135.

Dhiman, T. R., C. S. Poulson, D. Cornforth & D. R. ZoBell. 2006. *Conjugated Linoleic Acid (CLA) and Vitamin E Levels In Pasture Forages for Beef Cattle*. Utah State Univ. Cooperative Extension. AG/Beef/2006–03.

Droke E. A. & S. C. Loerch. 1989. Effect of parenteral selenium and vitamin E on performance, health, and humoral immune response of steers new to the feedlot environment. *J Anim Sci* 67: 1350–1359.

Dumoulin, P.G., Girard, C.L., Matte J.J. and St-Laurent G. J. (1991) Effects of a parenteral supplement of folic acid and its interaction with level of feed intake on hepatic tissues and growth performance of young dairy heifers. J. Anim. Sci., 69:1657-1666.

Eicher-Pruett, S. D., J. L. Morrill, F. Blecha, J. J. Higgins, N. V. Anderson & P. G. Reddy. 1992. Neutrophil and lymphocyte response to supplementation with vitamins C and E in young calves. *J Dairy Sci* 75:1635–1642.

Elam, N. A. 2006b. Impact of vitamin E supplementation on newly received calves. Proc. Colorado Nutr. Roundtable, Colorado State Univ., Ft. Collins

Erdman, R. A. 1992. Vitamins. pp. 297. In: van Horn, H. H. & C. J. Wilcox. (Eds.). *Large Dairy Herd Management*. Champaign, IL: ADSA.

Faustman C., R. G. Cassens, D. M Schaefer, D. R. Buege, S. N. Williams & K. K. Scheller. 1989. Improvement of pigment and lipid stability in Holstein steer beef by dietary supplementation with vitamin E. *J Food Sci* 54: 858.

Food and Agriculture Organization of the United Nations (FAO). 2004. *Vitamin and Mineral Requirements in Human Nutrition*. Available at: http://whqlibdoc.who.int/publications/2004/9241546123.pdf (Consultado: 04-12-2008).

Foote, M. R., R. L. Horst, E. J. Huff-Lonergan, A. H. Trenkle, F. C. Parrish Jr., & D. C. Beitz. 2004. The use of vitamin D3 and its metabolites to improve beef tenderness. *J Anim Sci* 82: 242–249.

Franklin S. T., C. E. Sorenson & D. C. Hammell. 1998. Influence of vitamin A supplementation in milk on growth, health, concentration of vitamins in plasma, and immune parameters of calves. *J Dairy Sci* 81: 2623–2632.

Frigg, M., O. C. Straub & D. Hartmann. 1993. The bioavailability of supplemental biotin in cattle. *Int J Vitam Nutr Res* 63: 122.

Galyean M. L., L. J. Perino & G. C. Duff. 1999. Interaction of cattle health/immunity and nutrition. *J Anim Sci* 77: 1120–1134.

Goodman, D.S. 1980. Vitamin A metabolism. Fed Proc. 39:2716-2722

Gorocica-Buenfil, M. A., F. L. Fluharty, C. K. Reynolds & S. C. Loerch. 2007. Effect of dietary vitamin A restriction on marbling and conjugated linoleic acid content in Holstein steers. *J Anim Sci* 85: 2243–2255.

Gorocica-Buenfil, M. A., F. L. Fluharty & S. C. Loerch. 2008. Effect of vitamin A restriction on carcass characteristics and immune status of beef steers. *J Anim Sci* 86: 1609–1616.

Gould, D. H., M. M. McAllister, J. C. Savage & D. W. Hamar. 1991. High sulfide concentrations in rumen fluid associated with nutritionally induced poliencephalomalacia in calves. *Am J Vet Res* 52: 1164.

Hannah, S. M. & M. D. Stern. 1985. Effect of supplemental niacin or niacinamide and soybean source on ruminal bacterial fermentation in continuous culture. *J Anim Sci.* 61: 1252–1263.

Harmeyer, J. & U. Kollenkirchen. 1989. Thiamin and niacin in ruminant tissues. *Nutr Res Rev* 2: 201.

Harrison, J. H., D. D. Hancock & H. R. Conrad. 1984. Vitamin E and selenium for reproduction of the dairy cow. *J Dairy Sci*

67: 123.

Hemingway, R. G. 2003. The influences of dietary intakes and supplementation with selenium and vitamin E on reproduction diseases and reproduction efficiency in cattle and sheep. A Review. *Veter Res Communic* 27: 157–174.

Hidiroglou M., T. R. Batra & M. Ivan. 1995. Effects of supplemental vitamins E and C on the immune responses of calves. *J Dairy Sci* 78: 1578–1583.

Hidiroglou M., T. R. Batra & X. Zhoa. 1977. Comparison of vitamin C bioavailability after multiple or single oral dosing of different formulations in sheep. *Reprod Nutr Dev* 37: 443.

Hill G. M. & S. E. Williams. 1993. Vitamin E in beef nutrition and meat quality. pp. 197–211. Proc. 1993 Minnesota Nutr. Conf., Bloomington.

Hill G. M., S. E. Williams, S. N. Williams, L. R. McDowell, N. Wilkinson & B. E. Mullinix. 1995. Vitamin A and vitamin E fed at high levels in steer feedlot diets: tissue alpha-tocopherol and performance. *University of Georgia (UGA) Animal & Dairy Science Annual Report*. pp. 7

Hill G. M. & S. E. Williams. 1995. Vitamin E effects on performance of growing-finishing beef cattle and meat quality. *University of Georgia (UGA) Animal & Dairy Science. Annual Report*. 11 p.

Hogan, J. S., W. P. Weiss & K. L. Smith. 1993. Role of vitamin E and selenium in host defense against mastitis. *J Dairy Sci* 76: 2795.

Hopper, J. H. & B. C. Johnson. 1955. The production and study of an acute nicotinic acid deficiency in the calf. *J Nutr* 56: 303–310.

Horst, R. L., J. P. Goff & T. A. Reinhardt. 1994. Calcium and vitamin D metabolism in the dairy cow. *J Dairy Sci* 77: 1936–1951.

Hutcheson D. P. 1990. Rations for receiving and starting new cattle. Scott County Beef Cattle Conference.

Hutcheson D. P. & N. A. Cole. 1985. Vitamin E and selenium for yearling feedlot cattle. *Fed. Proc* 44: 549.

Goodman, D. S. 1984. Vitamin A and retinoids in health and disease. *N Engl J Med* 310 (16), 1023–1031.

INRA. 1981. Alimentation de los rumiantes. Mundi Prensa. Madrid. pp. 697

INRA. 1988. Alimentation des bovins, ovins et caprins. Institut National de la Recherche Agronomique. Paris. P. 471.

Johnson, B. C., H. H. Mitchell & A. Pinkos. 1951. Choline deficiency in the calf . *J Nutr* 43: 37–48.

Jooh, J.W., M.C. Lin, S. Sang, X. Cheng, N. Zhu, R. E. Stark & C. T. Ho. 2002. Characterization of 2 methyl 4 amino 5(2 methyl 3 furyl thiomethyl) pyrimidine from thermal degradation of thiamin. *J Agric Food Chem* 50: 4055–4058.

Jukola, E., J. Hakkarainen, H. Saloniemi & S. Sankari. 1996. Blood selenium, vitamin E, vitamin A and carotene concentrations and udder health, fertility treatments, and fertility. J. Dairy Sci. 79: 838.

Kawachi, H. 2006. Review: Micronutrients affecting adipogenesis in beef cattle. *Anim Sci J* 77: 463–471.

Kruk, Z. A., C. D. K. Bottema, J. J. Davis, B. D. Siebert, G. S. Harper, J. Di & W. S. Pitchford. Effects of vitamin A on growth performance and carcass quality in steers. *Livestock Science*. In print.

Lacetera, N., U. Bernabucci, B. Ronchi & A. Nardone. 1996. Effects of selenium and vitamin E administration during a late stage of pregnancy on colostrum and milk production in dairy cows, and on passive immunity and growth of their offspring. *Am J Vet Res* 57: 1776.

Lanari, M. C., R. G. Cassens, D. M. Schaefer & K. K. Scheller. 1994. Effect of dietary vitamin E on pigment and lipid stability of frozen beef: a kinetic analysis. *Meat Science* 38: 3–15.

Lassiter, C.A., G.M. Ward, C.F. Huffman, C.W. Duncan, and H.D. Webster, 1953. Crystalline vitamin B12 requirement of the young dairy calf. J. Dairy Sci. 36:997.

Lee, R. W., R. L. Stuart, K. R. Perryman & K. W. Ridenour. 1985. Effect of vitamin supplementation on the performance of stressed beef calves. *J Anim Sci* 61(Suppl. 1): 425.

Loneragan, G. H., D. H. Gould, R. J. Callan, C. J. Sigurdson & D. W. Hamar. 1998. Association of excess sulfur intake and an increase in hydrogen sulfide concentrations in the ruminal cap of recently weaned beef calves with polioencephalomalacia. *J Am Vet Med Assoc* 213. 1599–1604.

McAllister, M. M., D. H. Gould, M. F. Raisbeck, B. A. Cummings & G. H. Loneragan. 1997. Evaluation of ruminal sulfide concentrations and seasonal outbreaks of polioencephalomalacia in beef cattle in the feedlot. *J Am Vet Med Assoc* 211:1275–1279.

McDowell L. R., S. N. Williams, N. Hidiroglou, C. A. Njeru, G. M. Hill, L. Ochoa & N. S. Wilkinson. 1996. Vitamin E supplementation for the ruminant. *Anim. Feed S. Tech* 60: 273–296.

McDowell, L.R. 2000a. Reevaluation of the metabolic essentiality of the vitamins. Asian-Aust. J. Anim. Sci. 13:115.

MacRae, J., L. O'Reilly & Peter Morgan. 2005. Desirable characteristics of animal products from a human health perspective. *Liv Prod Sci* 94: 95–103.

Midla, L. T., K. H. Hoblet, W. P. Weiss & M. L. Moeschberger. 1998. Supplemental dietary biotin for prevention of lesions associated with aseptic clinical laminitis (pododermatitis aseptica diffusa) in primiparous Holsteins. *Am J Vet Res* 59: 733.

Miller, B. L., J. C. Meiske, & R. D. Goodrich. 1986. Effects of grain source and concentrate level on B-vitamin production and absorption in steers. *J Anim Sci* 62: 473.

Mizwicki, K. L. 1976. Niacin and nitrogen metabolism in sheep. MSc Thesis, University of Illinois, Urbana, USA.

Montgomery, J. L., F. C. Parrish Jr., D. C. Beitz, R. L. Horst, E. J. Huff-Lonergan & A. H. Trenkle. 2000. The use of vitamin D_3 to improve beef tenderness. *J Anim Sci* 78: 2615–2621.

Montgomery, J. L., M. A. Carr, C. R. Kerth, G. G. Hilton, B. P. Price, M. L. Galyean, R. L. Horst & M. F. Miller. 2002. Effect of vitamin D3 supplementation level on the postmortem tenderization of beef from steers. *J Anim Sci* 80: 971–981.

Montgomery, J. L., J. R. Blanton, Jr., R. L. Horst, M. L. Galyean, K. J. Morrow, Jr., D. B. Wester & M. F. Miller. 2004. Effects of biological type of beef steers on vitamin D, calcium, and phosphorus status. *J Anim Sci* 82: 2043–2049.

Moreiras, O, Carbajal, A., Cabrera, L. & Cuadrado C. 2006. Tablas de composición de alimentos. *Ediciones Pirámide* (10th edition). p. 244. Madrid, Spain.

National Health and Medical Research Council of Autralia and New Zealand (NHMRC). 2006. *Nutrient Reference Values for Australia and New Zealand Including Recommended Dietary Intakes*. Available at: http://www.nrv.gov.au/_resources/n35-vitamine.pdf. (Referenced: 04-12-2008).

NRC. 1979. *Nutrient Requirements of Swine*. 8th Edition. pp. 157. National Academy of Science, National Research Council, Washington, DC.

NRC. 1996. *Nutrient Requirements of Beef Cattle*. 7th Rev. Ed. Natl. Academ. Press. Washington DC.

NRC. 2000. *Nutrient Requirements of Beef Cattle*. 7th Rev. Ed.: update 2000. Natl. Academ. Press. Washington DC.

NRC. 2001. *Nutrient Requirements of Dairy Cattle*. 7th Rev. Ed. Natl. Academ. Press. Washington DC.

Overfield, J. R. & E. E. Hatfield. 1976. Dietary niacin for steers fed corn silage diets. *J Anim Sci* 43: 329 (Abst).

Patterson, H. H., P. S. Johnson, T. R. Patterson, D. B. Young & R. Haigh. 2002. Effects of water quality on performance and health of growing steers. *Proc West Sec Amer Soc Anim Sci* 53:217–220.

Pritchard, R. H. 2007. Corn by-products: Considerations involving sulfur. pp. 43–48 In: Proceedings of the Plains Nutrition Council Spring Conference. Plains Nutrition Council, 6500 Amarillo Blvd. West Amarillo, TX.

Pyatt, N. A. & L. L. Berger. 2005. Review: Potential effects of vitamins A and D on marbling deposition in beef cattle. *Prof Anim Sci* 21: 174–181.

Quigley, J. D., III & J. K. Bernard. 1995. Effects of addition of vitamin E to colostrum on serum α-tocopherol and immunoglobulin concentrations in neonatal calves. *Food Agric Immunol* 7: 295–298.

Quigley, J.D., III, and Drewry, J.J. 1998. Nutrient and immunity transfer from cow to calf pre- and postcalving. J. Dairy Sci. 81:2779-2790.

Reddy, P. G., J. L. Morrill, H. C. Minocha, J. S. Stevenson. 1987. Vitamin E is stimulatory in calves. *J Dairy Sci* 70: 993.

Reddy, P. G., J. L. Morrill, H. C. Minocha, M. B. Morrill, A. D. Dayton & R. A. Frey. 1986. Effect of supplemental vitamin E on the immune system of calves. *J Dairy Sci* 69: 164.

Ridell, D. O., E. E. Bartley & A.D. Dayton. 1980. Effect of nicotinic acid on rumen fermentation in vitro and in vivo. *J Dairy Sci* 63: 1429–1436

Ridell, D. O., E. E. Bartley & A. D. Dayton. 1981. Effect of nicotinic acid on microbial protein synthesis in vitro and on dairy cattle growth and milk production. *J. Dairy Sci* 64: 782–791

Rivera, J. D., G. C. Duff, M. L. Galyean, D. A. Walker & G. A. Nunnery. 2002. Effects of supplemental vitamin E on performance, health, and humoral immune response of beef cattle. *J Anim Sci* 80: 933–941.

Robbins, K., J. Jensen, K. J. Ryan, C. Homco-Ryan, F. K. McKeith & M. S. Brewer. 2003. Effect of dietary vitamin E supplementation on textural and aroma attributes of enhanced beef clod roasts in a cook/hot-hold situation. *Meat Sci* 64: 317–322.

Rode L. M., T. A. McAllister & K. J. Cheng. 1990. Microbial degradation of vitamin A in rumen fluid from steers fed concentrate, hay or straw diets. Can. *J Anim Sci* 70: 227–233.

Rose, R. C. & A. M. Bode. 1993. Biology of free radical scavengers: an evaluation of ascorbate. FASEB 7:1135–1142.

Roth, J. A. & M. L. Kaeberle. 1985. In vivo effect of ascorbic acid on netrophil function in healthy and dexamethasone-treated cattle. *Am J Vet Res* 46: 2434.

Rowe, L. J., K. R. Maddock, S. M. Lonergan & E. Huff-Lonergan. 2004. Influence of early postmortem protein oxidation on beef quality. *J Anim Sci* 82: 785–793.

Rumsey T. S. 1985. Effect of choline in all concentrate diets of feedlot steers and on rumen acidosis. Can. *J Anim Sci* 65: 135–146.

Schaefer D. M., K. K. Scheller, S. C. Arp, D. R. Buege, & S. F. Lane. 1989. Growth of Holstein steers and beef color as affected by dietary vitamin E supplementation. *J Anim Sci* 68 (Suppl. 1): 190.

Schaefer D. M., R. N. Arnold, K. K. Scheller, S. C. Arp & S. N. Williams. 1991. Proc. Holstein Beef Prod. Symp. p. 175. Northeast Regional Agricultural Engineering Service, Harrisburg PA,

Schwab, E.C., and R.D. Shaver. 2005. B-Vitamin Nutrition in Dairy Cows. In Proc. Cornell Nutr. Conf., Syracuse, NY

Seifi H. A., M. R. Mokhber Dezfuly & M. Bolurchi. 1996. The effectiveness of ascorbic acid in the prevention of calf neonatal diarrhoea. *J Vet Med* B43:189–191.

Sharma, B. K. & R. A. Erdman. 1988. Effects of high amounts of dietary choline supplementation on duodenal choline flow and production responses of dairy cows. *J Dairy Sci* 71: 2670–2676

Sharma, B. K. & R. A. Erdman. 1989. In vitro degradation of choline from selected feedstuffs and choline supplements. *J Dairy Sci* 72: 2772–2776.

Siebert, B.D., Pitchford,W.S., Kruk, Z.A., Kuchel, H., Deland, M.P.B., Bottema, C. D.K., 2003. Differences in Δ_9 desaturase activity between Jersey and Limousin-sired cattle. Lipids 38, 539–543.

Smith R., 1994. Assay for vitamin E represents a major step to longer, redder beef color. *Feedstuffs* 66(16): 9

Smith, K. L., H. R. Conrad, B. A. Amiet & D. A. Todhunter. 1985. Incidence of environmental mastitis as influenced by vitamin E and selenium. Kiel. *Milchwirstsch. Forschungsber* 37: 482.

Spears, J. W. 2000. Micronutrients and immune function in cattle. *Proc Nut Soc* 59, 587–594.

Stangl, G. I., F. J. Schwarz, H. Müller & M. Kirchgessner. 2000. Evaluation of the cobalt requirement of beef cattle based on vitamin B_{12}, folate, homocysteine and methylmalonic acid. *British Journal of Nutrition* 84: 645–653.

Stobo, I. J. F. 1983. Milk replacers for calves. In: *Recent Advances in Animal Nutrition*. p. 113 London: Butterworths.

Stubbs R. L., J. B. Morgan, M. R. McGee, H. G. Dolezal & F. K. Ray. 1999. Effect of supplemental dietary vitamin E on the color and case-life of top loin steaks and ground chuck patties in various case-ready retail packaging systems. *Anim Sci Res Report* (Oklahoma State University).

Sutton, A. L. & J. M. Elliot. 1972. Effect of ration of roughage to concentrate and level of feed intake on ovine ruminal vitamin B_{12} production. *J Nutr* 102: 1341.

Swanek, S. S., J. B. Morgan, F. N. Owens, D. R. Gill, C. A. Strasia, H. G. Dolezal & F. K. Ray. 1999. Vitamin D_3 supplementation of beef steers increases longissimus tenderness. *J Anim Sci* 77: 874–881.

Thafvelin, B. & H. E. Oksanen. 1966. Vitamin E and linolenic acid content of hays as related to different drying conditions. *J Dairy Sci* 49: 282.

Tiffany, M. E., & J. W. Spears. 2005. Differential responses to dietary cobalt in finishing steers fed corn vs. barley-based diets. *J Anim Sci* 83: 2580–2589.

Tiffany, M. E., J. W. Spears, L. Xi & J. Horton.

2003. Influence of supplemental cobalt source and concentration on performance, vitamin B_{12} status, and ruminal and plasma metabolites in growing and finishing steers. *J Anim Sci* 81:3151–3159.

Tomlinson, D. J., C. H. Mülling & T. M. Fakler. 2004. Invited review: formation of keratins in the bovine claw: roles of hormones, minerals, and vitamins in functional claw integrity. *J Dairy Sci* 87:797–809.

Toutain P. L., D. Bechu & M. Hidiroglou. 1997. Ascorbic acid disposition kinetics in the plasma and tissues of calves. *Amer J Physiol* 273: R1585–R1597.

Tramontano, W. A., D. Ganci, M. Pennio & E. S. Dierenfeld. 1993. Distribution of α-tocopherol in early foliage samples in several forage crops. *Phytochem* 34: 389.

Vasconcelos, J. T. & M. L. Galyean. 2007. Nutritional recommendations of feedlot consulting nutritionists: The 2007 Texas Tech University survey *J Anim Sci* 85: 2772–2781.

Walker, C. K. & J. M. Elliot. 1972. Lactational trends in vitamin B_{12} status on conventional and restricted roughage rations. J. Dairy Sci. 55: 474.

Ward E. H. & H. H. Patterson. 2004. Effects of thiamin supplementation on performance and health of growing steers consuming high sulfate water. *Proc West Sec Amer Soc Anim Sci* 55: 375–378.

Weiss, W. P., J. S. Hogan, K. L. Smith & S. N. Williams. 1994. Effect of dietary fat and vitamin E on α-tocopherol and β-carotene in blood of peripartum cows. *J Dairy Sci* 77: 1422–1429.

Wertz, A. E., T. J. Knight, A. Trenkle, R. Sonon, R. L. Horst, E. J. Huff-Lonergan & D. C. Beitz. 2004. Feeding 25-hydroxyvitamin D_3 to improve beef tenderness. *J Anim Sci* 82: 1410–1418.

Williams, PG, (2007) Nutritional composition of red meat, Nutrition & Dietetics, , 64(Suppl 4), S113-S119.

Zinn R. A. 1992. B-Vitamins in Beef Cattle Nutrition. In: Takeda Technical Symposium. 53rd Minnesota Nutrition Conference. September 21, 1992.

Zinn R. A., F. N. Owens, R. L. Stuart, J. R. Dunbar & B. B. Norman. 1987. B-Vitamin supplementation of diets for feedlot calves. *J Anim Sci* 65: 267–277.

Zobell, D. R., A. L. Schaefer, P. L. LePage, L. Eddy, G. Briggs & R. Stanley. 1995. Gestational vitamin E supplementation in beef cows: Effect on calf immunological competence, growth and morbidity. *Proc West Sect Amer Soc Anim Sci* 46: 464–466.

OPTIMUM VITAMIN NUTRITION IN DAIRY CATTLE

S. Calsamiglia and M. Rodríguez
Dept. of Animal and Food Science
Animal Nutrition and Welfare Service
Universidad Autònoma de Barcelona
08193-Bellaterra, Spain
Tel.: 93-581-1495
Email Sergio.Calsamiglia@uab.es

INTRODUCTION

Vitamins are nutrients essential for the normal functioning of living beings. They are required in small amounts and are constituents of enzymes, coenzymes or factors in metabolic reactions. The development of the concepts of requirements and recommended amounts of vitamins has been limited by analytical difficulties and by the lack of response criteria sufficiently clear to allow recommendations to be established. However, the increase in productive yield of the dairy cow has revealed a series of production problems which, in recent years, have enabled deficiencies of some vitamins to be identified, and recommended amounts of these vitamins for commercial conditions should be modified.

Vitamins are generally classified as fat-soluble and water-soluble. Water-soluble vitamins have traditionally been considered non-essential for ruminants, due to microbial synthesis in the rumen. However, recent data suggest possible benefits from their supplementation. The National Research Council (NRC) in 2001 established new recommendations on optimum vitamin levels in dairy herds. In most cases, the recommended levels were increased considerably from previous reports. This chapter discusses these new recommendations and their justification, and provides a critical evaluation based on the available scientific literature.

FAT-SOLUBLE VITAMINS

VITAMIN A AND THE ß-CAROTENES

Introduction

Vitamin A activity is defined in retinol equivalent units. All-trans retinol is the isomer of greatest potency and activity, and the only important one for practical purposes (Ullrey, 1972). One international unit (IU) of vitamin A corresponds to 0.3 µg of all-trans retinol (equivalent to 0.344 µg all-trans retinyl acetate). Retinol is not found in plants, but it is obtained from the ß-carotenes (or provitamin A). One milligram of ß-carotene has an activity equivalent to 400 IU of vitamin A (equivalent to 120 µg of retinol). In plants, most of the ß-carotenes are found in the vegetative material, therefore forage is the main source of this vitamin. ß-carotenes are transferred from the plant to the animal and can modify the color of milk and its derivatives, as well as the fat deposited in tissues (Priolo *et al.*, 2002; Havemose *et al.*, 2004; Nozière *et al.*, 2006). Various factors affect the ß-carotene content of plants, and thus the supplies of vitamin A. Among the factors indicated are their physical state, the pH value (important in silage), the temperature, and the presence

of oxygen (**Table I**). These factors modify the availability for the animals which consume them. Their content diminishes with maturity, and they rapidly oxidize once the plant is cut, so that the concentration in hay and silage is much lower than that in fresh plants (Chauveau-Duriot *et al.*, 2005). Furthermore, there is a negative correlation between length of storage and concentration of ß-carotenes in forages (Chauveau-Duriot *et al.*, 2005). Retinol is very sensitive to oxidation, light and the presence of acids, humidity and microminerals (NRC, 2001; Nozière *et al.*, 2006). Williams *et al.* (1998) estimated that the average values of ß-carotenes in forages are 196, 159 and 81 mg/kg of DM for artificially dehydrated hay, silage and sun-dried hay, respectively.

Commercial forms of vitamin A – the most common ones are all-trans retinyl acetate, palmitate or propionate – are more stable, loosing around 1% per month under correct storage conditions. However, when they are stored with other minerals or feedstuffs, losses increase to 5-9% monthly (Coelho, 1991).

Table I. Factors affecting the stability of vitamins.

	Heat	Oxygen	Light	Humidity	pH < 7	pH 7	pH > 7
Vitamin A	–	–	–	–	–	+	+
Vitamin D	–	–	–	–	+	+	–
Vitamin E	–(+)	–(+)	–(+)	–(+)	+(+)	+(+)	+(+)
Vitamin K	+	+	–	–	–	+	
Vitamin B₁	–	–	+	–	+	–	–

+ = stable;   – = unstable;   ( ) = tocopheryl acetate

Bioavailability

In the context of animal diets, the prime factor determining the bioavailability of a vitamin from a feedstuff is its stability. Prolonged storage of the vitamin in premixes or in the final product, vitamin premixes containing minerals, raised temperature and humidity, pelleting, processing in blocks or by extrusion, or the presence of rancid fats in the ration all reduce the stability of vitamin A.

Bioavailability of vitamin A and ß-carotenes in the animal depends on the degree of ruminal degradability, on the absorption efficiency in the intestine and, for ß-carotenes, on the efficiency of conversion of ß-carotenes to vitamin A, a process that takes place in the intestinal mucosal cells. Dairy cattle can absorb and store a significant proportion of the ß-carotenes in a ration. Vitamin A can be stored in the liver and fatty tissue of ruminants in sufficient quantities to cover their requirements for a period of up to six months or more (McDowell, 2006).

Bioavailability of vitamin A
Several studies have observed that ruminal degradation of vitamin A varies between 40 and 70% (Ullrey, 1972). Warner *et al.* (1970) indicated that ruminal destruction of vitamin A was 55% in rations containing 50-75% forage, and increased to 65% when the percentage of forage was reduced from 40% to 20% of the ration. Rode *et al.* (1990) observed degradation of approximately 80% in animals fed with rations containing 30% forage, compared with 16 and 19% in animals fed hay or straw, respectively. Weiss *et al.* (1995) in their study also observed less ruminal degradation of vitamin A in rations containing 80% forage (20% degradability), compared with rations containing 50% forage (72% degradability). These results suggest that, in rations containing 50% or more concentrate, ruminal degradability of vitamin A is considerably greater than in those rations based on forage. In consequence, it seems reasonable to consider the possibility of using sources of protected vitamin A in rations rich in concentrate. Thus for example, Alosilla *et al.* (2007) evaluated the bioavailability of 5 commercial sources of vitamin A (80,000 IU/d) using a concentrate-rich diet in beef cattle, and they observed differences in the hepatic concentration of retinol – considered the best indicator for evaluating the status of vitamin A in the animal – between the different vitamin sources used. These differences were attributed to ruminal degradability and/or intestinal digestibility.

There are no data on vitamin A absorption in the small intestine of ruminants. Data collected from humans and rats indicate that intestinal absorption varies between 20 and 60% (Blomhoff *et al.*, 1991). Donoghue *et al.* (1983) observed that vitamin A absorption in lambs supplemented with 0, 100, and 12,000 µg of retinol/kg liveweight was 91, 58 and 14%, respectively, suggesting an inverse relation between intestinal concentration and vitamin A absorption.

Bioavailability of ß-carotenes
The ruminal degradability of ß-carotenes is lower than vitamin A, and varies between 0 and 30% (Potanski *et al.*, 1974; Mora *et al.*, 1999). Intestinal digestibility was calculated

337

to be 78% (Wing, 1969), and was affected by the type and physiological state of the plant, the processing method, the amount of dry material in the plant, and the month of harvest. However, Cohen-Fernandez et al. (1976) recovered 90% of marked ß-carotene administered to lambs in their feces, which suggests that it had a much lower level of absorption. Another study carried out in sheep, which evaluated the digestion and absorption of carotenoids from red clover (Cardinault et al., 2006), observed that apparent digestibility increased (>53%), although it varied according to the type of carotenoid considered. For ß-carotenes the values were over 100% in some cases, suggesting that the ruminal microorganisms are capable of synthesizing them. Furthermore, the efficiency of absorption of ß-carotenes and retinol depends on the quantity of fat and vitamin supplied in the diet (Blomhoff, 1994; Yeum et al., 2000). Yeum et al. (2000) indicated that in the presence of α-tocopherol, ß-carotene is converted exclusively into retinol, while if α-tocopherol is absent, it splits into apocarotenoids and retinol. Lastly, most domestic species convert ß-carotenes to vitamin A, but conversion in dairy cattle is low (24%), and their storage capacity varies according to breed, as some (e.g. Guernsey, Jersey) have a greater capacity than others (e.g. Holstein). In breeds such as Holsteins, supplementation may be beneficial.

Functions

Functions of vitamin A

Vitamin A fulfils various functions in the body, the most important being its involvement in vision, embryo development, reproduction, immunity, maintenance of homeostasis, and the differentiation of mammary gland cells (Goodman, 1984; Baldi et al., 2008). Vitamin A deficiency has been associated with loss of vision, reduced growth and development, changes in spermatogenesis and in the maintenance of skeletal and epithelial tissue and a reduction in reproductive and immune functions (Ikeda et al., 2005). In commercial herds, symptoms of deficiency are infrequent. However, marginal deficiencies lead to reduced reproduction and/or disruption of the immune system. In fact, the NRC (1989; 2001) uses reproductive performance

indicators as criteria to determine the needs of productive animals. Vitamin A deficiency in gestating cows leads to an increase in the incidence of abortions, retained placentas, and increased calf morbidity and mortality rates, as well as a reduction in fertility (Hurley and Doane, 1989).

Furthermore, although vitamin A is not considered an antioxidant as such, it plays an important role in the passive immunity of dairy cattle, since it intervenes directly in defense mechanisms through the maintenance of functional epithelial tissue and stimulation of the immune function (Chew, 1987; Bendich, 1993; NRC, 2001; Baldi, 2008). Stimulation of the immune function is complex, with intervention by elements of cellular, humoral and non-specific immunity (Chew, 1987). Studies carried out in cattle on the effect of vitamin A on the immune function are limited. Michal et al. (1994) indicated that vitamin A benefits the immune response by stimulating proliferation of lymphocytes and their killing capacity (**Figure 1**). Tjoelker et al. (1988) also observed stimulation of the polymorphonuclear neutrophil function in cattle, but the response depended on lactational status and on the presence of ß-carotene in the plasma. This stimulation of the immune function reduces mammary and reproductive problems, both in the dry period (Dahlquist and Chew, 1985) as during lactation (Chew and Johnson, 1985). It has been suggested that the minimum recommended level of retinol in plasma necessary to optimize immune action is 0.8 µg/ml (Weiss, 1998).

Recent studies bear out the importance of vitamin A in the immune biology of the mammary gland and its regeneration and in the activity of polymorphonuclear leukocytes peripartum. The results of an in vitro study (Meyer et al., 2005) indicate that retinoid compounds have a direct influence on oxidative capacity, in the potential for destruction of leukocytes and in apoptosis, but not in chemotaxis. Cheli et al. (2003) suggested that retinoids participate in the morphogenesis, differentiation and proliferation of the mammary gland cells. Although the way vitamin A acts at a cellular level is not known precisely, it may regulate effect normal growth of cells as it controls

Figure 1. Index of intracellular destruction of S. aureus by polymorphonuclear neutrophils of control cows (●) or cows supplemented with 120,000 IU of vitamin A (●) or 600 mg of β-carotenes (●) (Michal *et al.*, 1994).

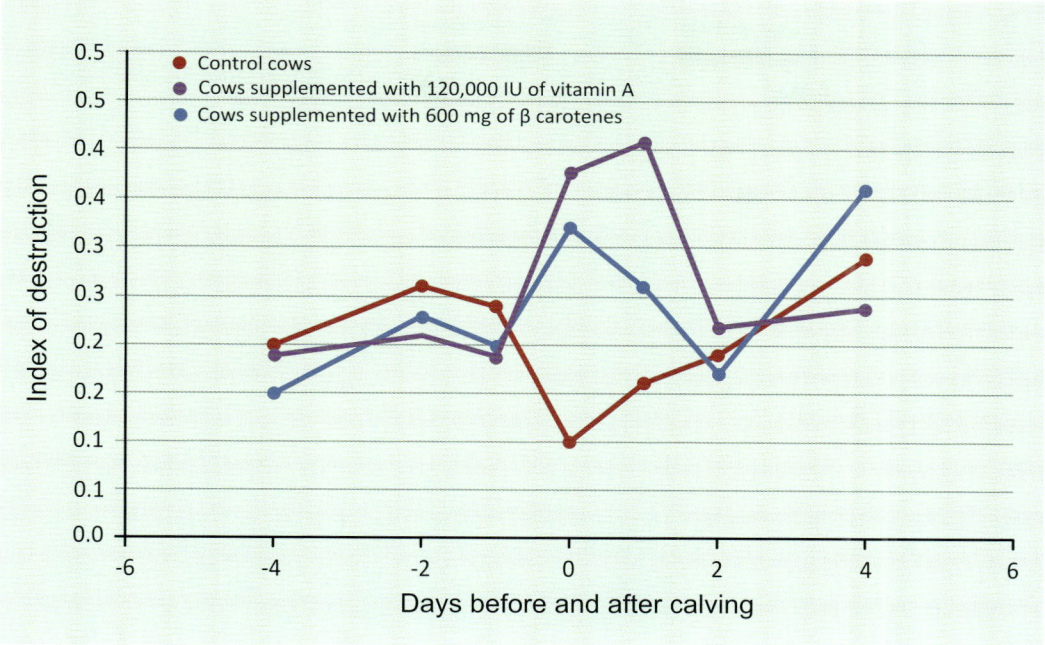

the genetic expression of various growth factors (Baldi, 2008).

Function of ß-carotenes

The ß-carotenes act as provitamin A. However, in addition to their function as vitamin A precursors, they have several other functions in dairy cows which are independent of the functions of vitamin A (Lotthammer, 1979; Bindas *et al.*, 1984a, b), and which affect the immune function and reproduction (Chew, 1993; Weiss, 1998; Chawla and Kaur, 2004; Akar and Gazioglu, 2006; Chew and Park, 2004), as well as the quality of milk (Cardinault *et al.*, 2006; Nozière *et al.*, 2006).

The involvement of ß-carotenes in the immune function was revised by Chew (1993), and Chew and Park (2004). ß-carotenes act as antioxidants (Mascio *et al.*, 1991; Zamora *et al.*, 1991), and stimulate the capacity for action of neutrophils (Chew, 1993; Chew and Park, 2004). Daniel *et al.* (1991) observed an increase in lymphocyte proliferation and in the bactericidal activity of milk lymphocytes against *S. aureus* peripartum. Furthermore, ß-carotenes boost

several aspects of the immune system during dry-off and peripartum in cows, depending on the physiological condition of the cows and on ß-carotene and vitamin A blood levels (Tjoelker *et al.*, 1988; Tjoelker *et al.*, 1990).

The effects on the reproductive function of supplementing rations with ß-carotenes have been variable. Hurley and Doane (1989) observed positive effects on the reproductive function in 12 of the 22 studies reviewed. When a positive result is obtained, the mechanism of action is not clear, because it is frequently difficult to separate the function of ß-carotenes from that of of vitamin A. The corpus luteum of cows is very rich in ß-carotenes, which suggests a possible function in the synthesis of progesterone (Arikan *et al.*, 2002; Haliloglu *et al.*, 2002). Lotthammer *et al.* (1979) observed an increase in fertility and a decrease in services per conception when rations with sufficient vitamin A were supplemented with 300 mg/d of ß-carotene (**Table II**).

Table II. Effect of the supplementation of ß-carotenes on the fertility rate and number of services per conception in cows supplemented with appropriate quantities of vitamin A (adapted from Lotthammer *et al.*, 1979).

Fertility:	Vitamin A (220 IU/kg LW)	ß-carotene (0.3 g) and vitamin A (100 IU/kg LW)	ß-carotene + vitamin A vs. vitamin A
1st service	40.0	68.4	+ 28.4%
2nd service	55.0	89.5	+34.5%
No. of services per conception	2.0 ± 0.91	1.42 ± 0.69	+29%

The supply of ß-carotenes in the diet of dairy cattle is also important from the perspective of human nutrition. The ß-carotene content of milk is highly variable, and depends on the type and quantity of carotenoids ingested by the animal (Havemose *et al.*, 2004; Nozière *et al.*, 2006; Calderón *et al.*, 2007). The relationship between the diet of cows and its ß-carotene content could have important implications from the perspective of product quality, because it can serve as an indicator in traceability studies for finding out the origin and systems of nutrition in cattle, particularly in the production of organic foods (Cardinault *et al.*, 2006).

Recommendations for Vitamin A

Suckling calves
According to recommendations the vitamin A requirement of suckling calves is 110 IU/kg of liveweight (NRC, 2001). In normal conditions, this means the incorporation of approximately 9,000 IU/kg of DM in milk replacer, and 4,000 IU/kg of DM in starter feeds. These recommendations exceed the 42 IU/kg liveweight recommended by the previous NRC report (1989). The recommended increase is based on studies by Eaton *et al.* (1972) who, using as a selection criterion the dose which permits maintenance of appropriate cerebrospinal fluid pressure, established a recommendation of 97 IU/kg liveweight. However, the build-up or loss of vitamin A in the liver is a more precise measure of the vitamin A status of the animal. Swanson *et al.* (2000) used this criterion and observed that supplementation with 134 IU/kg of LW led to the accumulation of vitamin A in the liver, while supplementation with 93

IU/kg led to reduction in hepatic reserves of vitamin A. These results suggest that appropriate supplementation is between 93 and 134 IU/kg.

The vitamin A status of calves depends greatly on the intake of vitamin A through the colostrum. Calves are born with very low levels of vitamin A because transfer through the placenta is very low. The transfer of vitamins from the colostrum to the calf is therefore vital to its health (Seymour, 2004). A delay in the supply from colostrum of more than 12 hours after parturition affects plasma levels of ß-carotenes, vitamin A and vitamin E during the first month of the calf's life (Zanker *et al.*, 2000; Debier *et al.*, 2005; Puvogel *et al.*, 2008). If the vitamin A levels remain low after parturition, the calf's health and its subsequent growth may be negatively affected (Debier and Larondelle, 2005). If the supply of appropriate quantities of a colostrum rich in vitamin A is insufficient, additional supplementation is needed.

Cows fed with rations rich in vitamin A during the dry period produce more colostrum with a greater vitamin A concentration. On the other hand, underfeeding with vitamin A during the dry period generates colostrum with a low vitamin A concentration, which has an effect on the vitamin status of the calf (Debier *et al.*, 2005). Supplementation to the cow should be achieved with sources of vitamin A and not with ß-carotenes, due to its reduced intestinal absorption (Yonekura and Nagao, 2007) or low capacity for converting ß-carotenes into retinol by the young calf (Nonnecke *et al.*, 2001). These considerations demand the administration of a minimum of 165 to 200 IU/kg liveweight

Table III. Recommendations (NRC, 2001), safety margins (NRC, 1987) and range of supplementations under commercial conditions (adapted from Erdman, 1992).

| | Type of Animal | | | |
	Lactating Cow	Dry cow	Heifers (12–24 months)	Calves (6–12 months)
Vitamin A				
NRC (2001)	63,800	39,600	22,000	11,000
Upper limit	1,320,000	660,000	660,000	330,000
Commercial dose	100–200,000	100–150,000	30–40,000	20–30,000
Vitamin D				
NRC (2001)	20,000	12,000	3,000	1,500
Upper limit	80–200,000	48–120,000	12–30,000	6–15,000
Commercial dose	20–30,000	12–15,000	3–4,000	1,500–2,000
Vitamin E				
NRC (2001)	308	154	242	121
Upper limit	20–40,000	10–20,000	10–20,000	5–10,000
Commercial dose	300–500	300–1000	200–300	100–150

for the first months of life to achieve normal hepatic reserves. Erdman (1992) observed that it is normal practice to supply vitamin A concentrations above recommended levels in milk replacers (**Table III**; 20,000-40,000 IU/kg of DM). Supplementation at much higher levels (87,000 IU/kg of milk replacer; 44,000 IU/kg of DM in milk replacer, Swanson *et al.*, 2000) had neither positive nor negative effects. Therefore an increase to such high dosages does not appear to be justified. On the other hand, Nonnecke *et al.* (1999) observed negative effects of overdosage of vitamin A in young calves. Franklin *et al.* (1998) observed a deterioration in the health of calves supplemented with 30,000 IU/d of vitamin A during the first 6 weeks of life. In both cases, the deterioration in health was attributed to the interference of vitamin A with the vitamin E status of the animals. Therefore, where large amounts of vitamin A are supplemented, the vitamin E levels in the milk replacer should also be raised.

Figures available indicate that the NRC (2001) recommendations for calves (110 IU/kg liveweight) are higher than those established by the NRC (1989) and INRA (1988), and are probably adequate. However,

where there are doubts about the intake or the quality of the colostrum administered to calves, or when stressful conditions are detected, often due to intensive production systems, the recommendation may be increased to 134-200 IU/kg of liveweight (**Table IV**) without risk of toxicosis.

Adult Lactating Cows

The currently available information on vitamin A requirements does not suggest a need to modify the recommendations for dairy cattle in the last NRC report (2001), which are 110 IU/d of vitamin A per kg liveweight, and which are approximately equivalent to 85,000-100,000 IU/d of vitamin A (Weiss, 2007). These recommendations are higher than the 76 IU/kg liveweight from the previous NRC report (1989). The NRC's 1989 recommendation was based on long-term reproduction studies of relatively low-yielding animals fed rations containing a high proportion of forage (Swanson *et al.*, 1968). However, in current production systems, animals are fed with rations containing a higher proportion of concentrate. Rode *et al.* (1990) and Weiss *et al.* (1995) demonstrated that the bioavailability of vitamin A was reduced by

30 to 60% in rations containing more than 50% of concentrate. From these figures, it would appear reasonable to consider an increase in the recommendations for vitamin A.

Some experimental studies suggest that increasing the vitamin supplement above these recommended levels may be beneficial. Oldham *et al.* (1991) observed an increase in milk production from 35 to 40 kg/d when the ration was supplemented with 250 IU of vitamin A per kg liveweight, compared with rations supplemented with 75 IU/kg liveweight. Michal *et al.* (1994) did not observe production responses when rations were supplemented with 200 IU of vitamin A per kg liveweight but the incidence of retained placentas and milk fever was reduced by 33% (**Figure 2**). Supplementing vitamin A in amounts much higher than those recommended (166 vs. 1,660 IU/kg liveweight) increased heat detection from 26 to 60%, and reduced the somatic cell count in postpartum weeks 2-8 (Chew and Johnson, 1985).

These results suggest that, under commercial conditions, in which animals are subjected to greater productive stress and in which rations contain a higher proportion of concentrate, the current recommendations (110 IU/kg liveweight) may be increased by 50 to 100 %. It must be remembered that the current recommendations were established for rations based on forage, and that ruminal degradability of vitamin A increases from 40 to 80% as the forage content of the ration decreases (Ullrey, 1972; Rode, 1990). Furthermore, the wide safety margin of vitamin A permits the increase without risk of toxicity (**Table III**). However, in some cases there have been indications that supplying very high concentrations of vitamin A in the diet (approximately 8 times the NRC's 2001 recommendations) can provoke reductions in the production of milk and its fat content (Puvogel *et al.*, 2005). These levels should serve as reference maximums.

Dry and Prepartum Cows

The NRC (2001) decided on the same recommendations for dry cows as for lactating cows (110 IU/kg liveweight). The

Figure 2. Incidence of retained placentas, metritis and milk fever in control cows or cows supplemented with 120,000 IU/d of vitamin A, or 300 or 600 mg/d of ß-carotenes (Michal *et al.*, 1994).

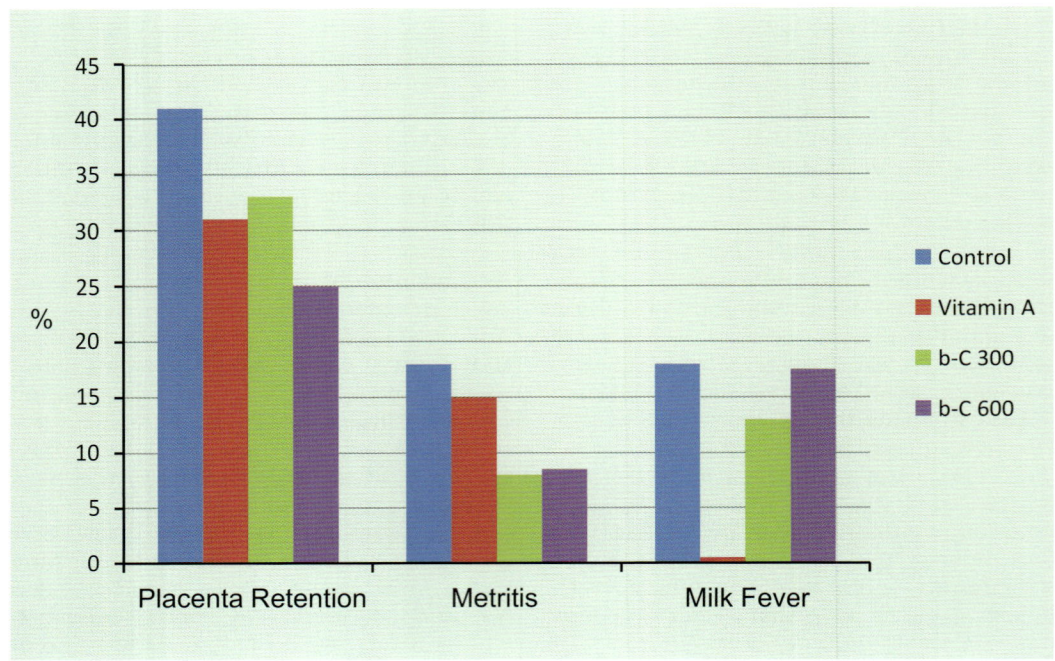

Figure 3. Normal plasma concentration of vitamin A (O) and ß-carotene (■) in cows during peripartum. (Akar Y., Gazioglu A. 2006)

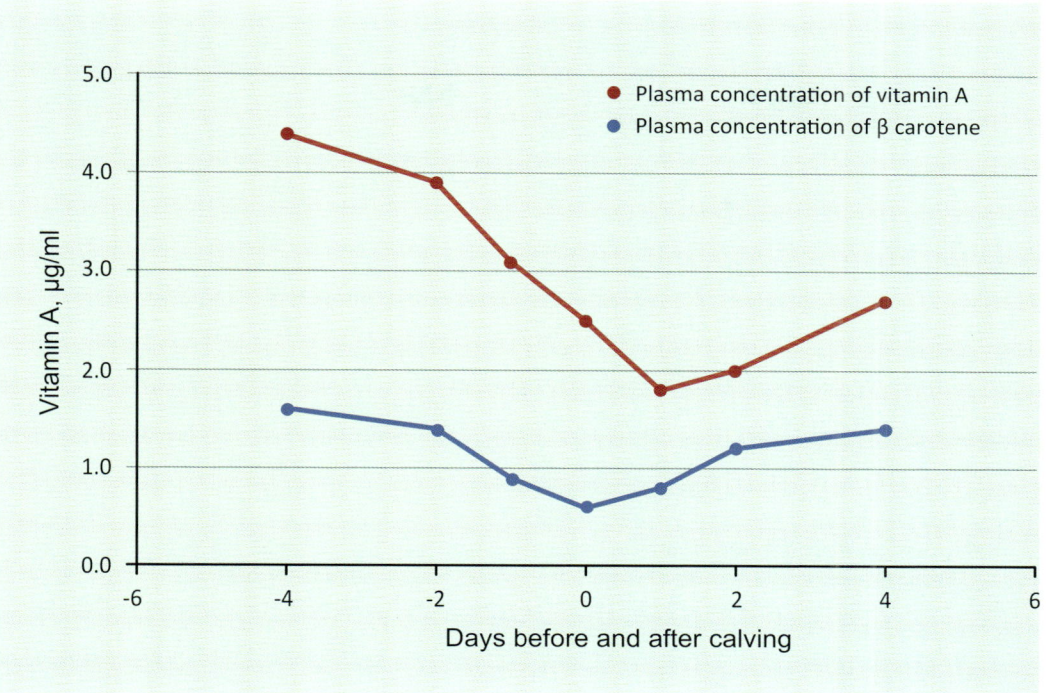

NRC (1989) previously recommended 76 IU/kg liveweight for dry cows. Weiss (1998) endorsed this recommendation on the basis of improved immune competence and fewer problems with mammary gland health and postpartum reproduction. Many reasearch studies have confirmed a reduction in vitamin A concentration peripartum (Tjoelker *et al.*, 1988; Michal *et al.*, 1994; Akar and Gazioglu, 2006; **Figure 3**). This reduction is at least partially due to the loss of vitamin A in colostrum.

Several studies show that supplementation during the dry period reduces the incidence of mastitis in the dry and productive periods (Dahlquist and Chew, 1985; Chew and Johnson, 1985; LeBlanc *et al.*, 2004). Weiss (1998) suggests that recommendations for vitamin A should also be applied to dry cows (150 IU/kg liveweight). Tjoelker *et al.* (1988) compared the supply of 80 vs. 350 IU/kg liveweight with 300-400 mg of ß-carotenes but did not observe improvements in the function of neutrophils and lymphocytes, which indicates that the current recommendations are appropriate. Michal *et*

al. (1994) also observed that supplementing prepartum rations with 120,000 IU/d of vitamin A led to an improvement in polymorphonuclear neutrophil function and a 28% reduction in retained placentas. Supplementation at levels 50% greater than current recommendations (NRC, 2001) may be advisable, given the reduction in problems peripartum, as well as to maintain retinol concentrations in plasma and in the colostrum post partum (Puvogel *et al.*, 2005).

Recommendations for ß-Carotenes

The NRC (2001) and INRA (1988) consider that there are not enough data to justify specific recommendations for ß-carotenes. However, the evidence that its concentration decreases peripartum (Tjoelker *et al.*, 1988; Michal *et al.*, 1994; Chawla and Kaur, 2004; Calderón *et al.*, 2007; Kawashima *et al.*, 2009b; F**igure 3**) and the benefits observed in some experimental studies suggest that, under some conditions, ß-carotene supplementation may be beneficial. The consumption of low-quality forage during the dry period and the increase in immunological requirements peripartum may explain the reduction in the plasma concentration of ß-carotenes peripartum, and the possible need for supplementation of the ration.

Several studies have shown that supplementing rations with between 300 to 600 mg/d of ß-carotene results in an increase in the proliferation of polymorphonuclear neutrophils and of their phagocytic capacity (Heriman *et al.*, 1990; Michal *et al.*, 1994; Tjoelker *et al.*, 1990; **Figure 1**), as well as an increase in the plasma concentration of both ß-carotenes and retinol (Michal *et al.*, 1994; Chawla and Kaur, 2004). The improved response capacity of the immune system may explain the improvements observed in mammary gland health – reduced somatic cell count, reduction in the number of new mammary infections, etc. – during the dry period (Dahlquist and Chew, 1985) as well as during lactation (Chew and Johnson, 1985). Chew *et al.* (1993) observed a negative correlation between the level of ß-carotenes in plasma and the somatic cells count, because ß-carotenes protect cells against oxidation, optimizing cellular function. However, the action of carotenoid compounds on the immune response is variable and depends not only on its type and concentration but also on the cell and species of animal (Chew and Park, 2004). Dietary supplements of 300 and 600 mg ß-carotene reduced the incidence of mastitis and intramammary infections both during the dry period and peripartum (Chew, 1987; Wang *et al.*, 1988; Chawla and Kaur, 2004; Akar and Gazioglu, 2006). Other authors did not observe effects on udder health (Oldham *et al.*, 1991; Jukola *et al.*, 1996), although it is possible that discrepancies are due to the presence of ß-carotenes in the basal ration.

Hurley and Doane (1989) observed an improvement in the reproductive function following the administration of ß-carotenes (300-400 mg/d). In their review, reproductive parameters improved in 12 of the 22 studies in which vitamin A was supplemented in quantities that met or exceeded those

recommended by the NRC (1989). Cows supplemented with ß-carotenes experienced more rapid uterine recovery (Wang *et al.*, 1988; Rakes *et al.*, 1985; Kawashima *et al.*, 2009b), a shorter interval from parturition to first estrus (Rakes *et al.*, 1985; Bremel *et al.*, 1982; Kawashima *et al.*, 2006), a more intense estrus, a shorter interval from parturition to conception (Lotthammer *et al.*, 1979), a higher conception rate, and lower incidence of follicular cysts (Bremel *et al.*, 1982; Larson *et al.*, 1983). Michal *et al.* (1994) observed that the incidence of retained placentas fell from 41% in unsupplemented cows to 31% in those supplemented with 300 mg/d of ß-carotenes, and to 25% with a supplementation of 600 mg/d of ß-carotenes, and the incidence of metritis was reduced by 25%. Although some authors observed no positive effects (Bremel *et al.*, 1982), these studies were carried out on Jersey cows which accumulate ß-carotenes (Bremel *et al.*, 1982) or ß-carotenes were only supplemented during lactation, and not during the dry period (Bindas *et al.*, 1984a).

The available figures suggest that supplementation with between 300 and 600 mg/d of ß-carotenes during the critical dry period and the 2 or 3 months postpartum may improve mammary gland health and reproductive function. Furthermore, Aréchiga *et al.* (1998) observed that supplementation with 400 mg/d 15 days prior to insemination increased milk production by 6-11%, and Chawla and Kaur (2004) observed a 28% increase in milk production when supplementing with 1,000 mg/d of ß-carotenes prepartum. These figures suggest that the benefits may be derived not only in the reduced incidence of pathologies and/or reproductive improvements, but also in an increase in milk production.

VITAMIN E

Introduction

Vitamin E is a generic term used for a group of compounds which have α-tocopherol biological activity (Bramley *et al.*, 2000), which is the most powerful and common form in plants. One IU vitamin E equals 1 mg of all-rac-α-tocopherol acetate. The vitamin E content of food is very variable. Forages, depending on its state of maturity, contains between 80 and 200 IU of vitamin E per kg DM (Tramontano *et al.*, 1993; Jukola *et al.*, 1996). As with other fat-soluble vitamins, the concentration in plants and the quantity available to the animal depend on various environmental and agricultural management factors (**Table I**). The α-tocopherol concentration decreases rapidly once the plant is cut. Prolonged exposure to oxygen or sunlight increases the rate of degradation (Thafvelin and Oksanen, 1966). Silage and hay contain between 20 and 80% less tocopherol than fresh forage. Concentrate feeds are low in vitamin E (except whole soy bean and cottonseed). The most common commercial form is all-rac-α-tocopherol acetate. DL-α-tocopherol has greater biological activity than DL-α-tocopherol acetate (Hidiroglou *et al.*, 1989). The esterified form of vitamin E is more stable, with a loss of less than 1% per month. When it is subjected to extrusion, losses increase to 6% per month (Coelho, 1991). In animal tissues, the most biologically active form of the vitamin is RRR-α-tocopherol (previously known as D-α-tocopherol), as it represents approximately 90% of the total (Bramley *et al.*, 2000).

The main focus of the studies undertaken to evaluate the role of vitamin E in ruminants arises from its potential as an antioxidant, as it can prevent the damage caused by free radicals at tissue level, and therefore prevent or retard the development of certain degenerative inflammatory diseases. Vitamin E also appears to play a fundamental role in the immune function (Baldi, 2005; Baldi *et al.*, 2008).

Bioavailability

In evaluating the bioavailability of vitamin E in dairy cattle the principal limiting factor is the efficiency of absorption, which is relatively low (approximately 30%). Factors such as the dose, the form of presentation (physical and/or chemical) and the method of administration will affect its availability. The results of various studies suggest that vitamin E is absorbed at a constant rate when increasing doses are applied. Part of the vitamin E which is absorbed de novo can at least partially replace the vitamin E present in the circulating lipoproteins (Baldi, 2005), which is an additional limiting factor if the plasma concentration of the vitamin is the parameter measured to evaluate the status of the animal (Bramley *et al.*, 2000). Furthermore, it is probable that intestinal absorption is limited when the transporting capacity is reached (Weiss and Wyatt, 2003).

There is no consensus in the literature on the potential causes of vitamin E deficiency, which include insufficient supply, ruminal degradability, lower intestinal absorption or higher post-absorption metabolism. Alderson *et al.* (1971) observed that an important proportion of vitamin E was degraded in the rumen, and degradability was greater the more concentrate the ration contained. However, Leedle *et al.* (1993) and Weiss *et al.* (1995) demonstrated that ruminal degradation of all-rac-α-tocopherol acetate *in vitro* was minimal. The discrepancy in results was attributed to the incomplete extraction of vitamin E from the digestive content in the methodology used by Alderson *et al.* (1971). Furthermore, as happens with vitamin A, the efficiency of α-tocopherol absorption depends on the quantity and type of fat present in the diet (Debier and Larondelle, 2005; Debier *et al.*, 2005).

Functions

In the course of inflammatory processes, leukocytes involved in phagocytosis generate reactive peroxides which are needed to kill pathogens, but which may at the same time cause lesions in the polyunsaturated fatty acids of the cellular membranes. Vitamin E is a powerful antioxidant agent integrated in the cellular membranes which protects them from attack by peroxides (Craven and Williams, 1985; Hogan *et al.*, 1993; Baldi,

2005), thus maintaining the integrity of the cellular membrane, and participating in the metabolism of arachidonic acid. Arachidonic acid is a membrane polyunsaturated fatty acid from which prostaglandins, thromboxanes and prostacyclins are synthesized, these being molecules which are particularly important in the immune response (Craven and Williams, 1985). Within the immune function, vitamin E stimulates antibody production, polymorphonuclear neutrophil migration, phagocytosis and its catabolic capacity (Gyang *et al.*, 1984; Reffett *et al.*, 1988; Erskine *et al.*, 1989; Hogan *et al.*, 1990; Grasso *et al.*, 1990; Baldi, 2005). These actions translate into a reduction in the incidence and severity of mastitis, retained placentas and metritis (Smith *et al.*, 1984 and 1985; Hogan *et al.*, 1993; Harrison *et al.*, 1984; Lacetera *et al.*, 1996), improving both mammary gland health and the reproductive function.

Although the best known function of vitamin E is its role as an antioxidant, it has other useful properties. It seems that α-tocopherol is involved in a series of processes mediated by a protein kinase which modulate genetic expression, and it plays an important role in the transmission of cellular information (Azzi *et al.*, 2000; Brigelius-Flohé *et al.*, 2002).

Recommendations for Vitamin E

Suckling calves

The NRC (2001) recommends 50 IU/kg of DM, which is higher than the previous level of 40 IU/kg of DM recommended by the NRC (1989) and INRA (1988). This change is based on the increased requirement by animals in the stressful situations typical of current production systems, where an extra vitamin E supplement may boost the immune system. However, the recommendations depend greatly on the intake of colostrum and its vitamin E content, since transfer of vitamin E through the placental membrane is low (Van Saun *et al.*, 1989). It is therefore essential to ensure the supply of colostrum in the first hours of the calf's life, since from 24 hours after parturition the efficiency of its intestinal absorption is reduced. Weiss *et al.* (1992) observed that the vitamin E concentration in colostrum increased by 40% when the ration for dry cows was supplemented with 70 IU/d during the dry period. Lacetera *et al.* (1996) observed an increase in colostrum

production and in its vitamin E content when dry cow rations were supplemented with 25 IU/d of vitamin E during the 3 weeks prepartum.

Hidiroglou *et al.* (1995) supplemented the ration of newborn calves with 1,000 IU/d vitamin E. They observed an increase in the plasma concentration in the first week, and this concentration remained constant afterwards. Immunoglobulin levels and average weight gain (0.34 kg/d vs. 0.42 kg/d) tended to increase in the group treated with vitamin E. Reddy *et al.* (1986 and 1987) observed that young calves supplemented with vitamin E had greater leukocyte activity, higher concentrations of immunoglobulins and serum cholesterol, and reduced indicators of cellular membrane lesions. In another study, Mohri *et al.* (2005) evaluated the effect of pre-weaning supplementation of suckling calves with vitamin E (300 IU/kg liveweight) and selenium (6 mg / 45 kg liveweight) administered parenterally at 24 and 48 hrs and 7, 14, 21 and 28 d after parturition. The supplementary supplies did not improve the immune response or post-weaning growth of the calves, except for a significant increase in the hematocrit and the concentration of ß-globulins. On the other hand, Stobo (1983) suggested that the vitamin E concentration in the milk replacer should depend on the ration's unsaturated fatty acid content, and suggested a ratio of 1.5-2.5 IU of vitamin E per gram of linoleic acid. In standard milk replacers, this ratio is achieved with daily intakes of between 25 and 63 IU/kg of DM.

Although there is no solid evidence to justify an increase in these recommendations, the NRC (2001) recognizes that it is necessary to undertake large-scale studies to determine the effects of additional vitamin E supplements on the health and production of suckling calves. In spite of the limited information available, there are two situations in which higher levels merit consideration. First, frequent digestive disorders in young calves reduce vitamin E absorption. Second, supplementation with high quantities of vitamin A interferes with vitamin E absorption. For these reasons, and because of the wide safety margin of vitamin E (**Table IV**), it may be justified to increase the recommendations, at least in some situations.

Lactating Cows

Because of the difficulty in determining the vitamin E content of feed ingredients, the NRC (2001) has made recommendations for supplemental vitamin E, and assumes that animals are fed on stored forage. The recommendations of the NRC (2001) for lactating cows are 0.8 IU/kg liveweight, approximately 20 IU/kg of DMI, or 500 IU/d. These recommendations are 30% higher than those established by INRA (1988) or previously by the NRC (1989; 15 IU/kg of DM, or 300 IU/d). This increase is based on the review by Weiss (1998), who established a clear inverse relationship between vitamin E intake and the incidence of mastitis. Many researchers have observed that the plasma concentration of vitamin E in herds with a high somatic cell count or with a high incidence of mastitis was lower than in those herds with a lower somatic cell count (Weiss et al. 1990), which suggests that low vitamin E plasma levels increase the risk of mastitis (Weiss, 1998). Weiss et al. (1994 and 1997) suggested that the plasma concentration of vitamin E should be greater than or equal to 3 µg/ml in order to reduce the risk of reproductive or mammary gland problems. Weiss et al. (1990) observed that supplementing vitamin E in the lactation ration tended to reduce the incidence of clinical mastitis. The cases of clinical mastitis increased in over half the herds when the supply was below 23 IU/kg of diet, which suggests that supplementation above the current recommended levels could have some benefit on mammary gland health.

Bourne et al. (2007a) evaluated the effect of the supplementation method in dairy cows at peak or mid-lactation (610, 1,864 and 737 mg of vitamin E per day for the control, oral and parenteral treatments, respectively). Oral supplementation above the recommendations (1,864 mg/d) did not translate into an increase in the concentration of vitamin E in plasma compared with the control dose (610 mg/d). The vitamin E level was higher in cows which received additional supplementation parenterally (737 mg/d in the food + 2,100 mg IM per week), which suggests that injection is more effective if the objective is a higher supplementation of this vitamin in lactating dairy cattle.

Stowe et al. (1988), after supplementing the lactation ration with vitamin E (500 IU/d) during two consecutive production cycles, observed an increase in the plasma concentration of vitamin E, and a tendency to fewer services per conception. Weiss et al. (1997) observed an increase in DM intake when vitamin E supplements increased from 100 to 1,000 IU/d.

It is difficult to discuss the requirements of vitamin E in dairy cattle without considering the requirements or supplies of selenium, because the effects of both micronutrients on animal health and productivity are closely related (Patterson, 2002). In some cases, although not always, vitamin E can be substituted to a certain extent by selenium or vice versa. Although selenium cannot replace vitamin E completely, it does reduce the requirements for it and delays the appearance of symptoms of vitamin E deficiency in the animal (Spears, 2000; Hemingway, 2003). The NRC (2001) has recommended a maximum of 0.3 ppm selenium, limited because of its toxicity. If the rations have a selenium content lower than the requirements, an additional supply of vitamin E is recommended.

Current vitamin E recommendations for lactating animals (500 IU/d) appear adequate for the majority of normal production situations (Weiss, 2005). In general, the quantity of ingested vitamin E is considered appropriate when the plasma levels of α-tocopherol are higher than 3.0–3.5 µg/ml, or higher than 2.0 when expressed in relation to the concentration of cholesterol in plasma. No additional benefits have been observed with values higher than these levels (Baldi, 2005). Some researchers suggest potential benefit for mammary gland health, but the evidence is limited. An increase in vitamin E supplies should only be considered in those situations where there is an excess of vitamin A, or where there is a deficit of selenium.

Another important aspect when evaluating the requirements and practical recommendations for vitamin E supplementation in dairy cattle relates to the quality of the milk and its vitamin E content (Haug et al., 2007). The concentration of vitamin E in milk depends on various factors, among them the type, quantity and method of administering the vitamin E to the animal. Bourne *et al.* (2007a) observed that the concentration of vitamin E in milk was higher in cows supplemented parenterally with vitamin E (4,200 mg IM per day for 3 weeks). The same authors showed a significant relationship between the content of vitamin E in the plasma and milk of cows, although the correlation was significant only when cows were supplemented parenterally (r=0.435; P<0.001). A similar tendency was observed by Calderón *et al.* (2007), who observed the effect of supplying, over six weeks, increasing levels of vitamin E (73.9; 510.2; 942.6 and 1384.9 mg/d) in the ration of dairy cattle in mid-lactation. The concentration of vitamin E in plasma increased in a similar way to the supply of vitamin E in the ration.

Cows in the dry period

The recommendations of the NRC (2001) for lactating cows are 1.6 IU/kg liveweight, approximately 80 IU/kg of DM, or 1,000 IU/d. These levels are much higher than the 15 IU/kg of DM (or 150 IU/d) established by INRA (1988) or the previous recommendation by the NRC (1989). This increase is based on the

improvements in the response of the immune system which translates into better mammary gland and reproductive health. Stowe *et al.* (1988) demonstrated that supplementing the lactation ration with vitamin E (500 IU/d) during two consecutive productive cycles did not allow the storage of enough vitamin E to maintain an unsupplemented dry period, indicating the need for specific supplementation during this period. In fact, the plasma concentration of vitamin E falls in the peripartum period (Smith *et al.*, 1985; Weiss *et al.*, 1990a, b; Weiss *et al.*, 1992; Goff *et al.*, 2002; Calderón *et al.*, 2007; **Figure 4**). The reduction in the plasma concentration of vitamin E in this period is at least partially due to a combination of the increase in activity of the immune system, reduced intake and the excretion of vitamin E in colostrum. This reduction coincides with the most critical time with respect to immunocompetence and with an increase in the incidence of diseases (Smith *et al.*, 1985; Weiss *et al.*, 1990b).

Oral or parenteral administration of vitamin E (1000 or 3000 IU/d) during the peripartum period improved macrophage and neutrophil function (Hogan *et al.*, 1990 and 1992; Politis

Figure 4. Evolution of plasma concentration of vitamin E in the peripartum. (Weiss *et al.*, 1990b)

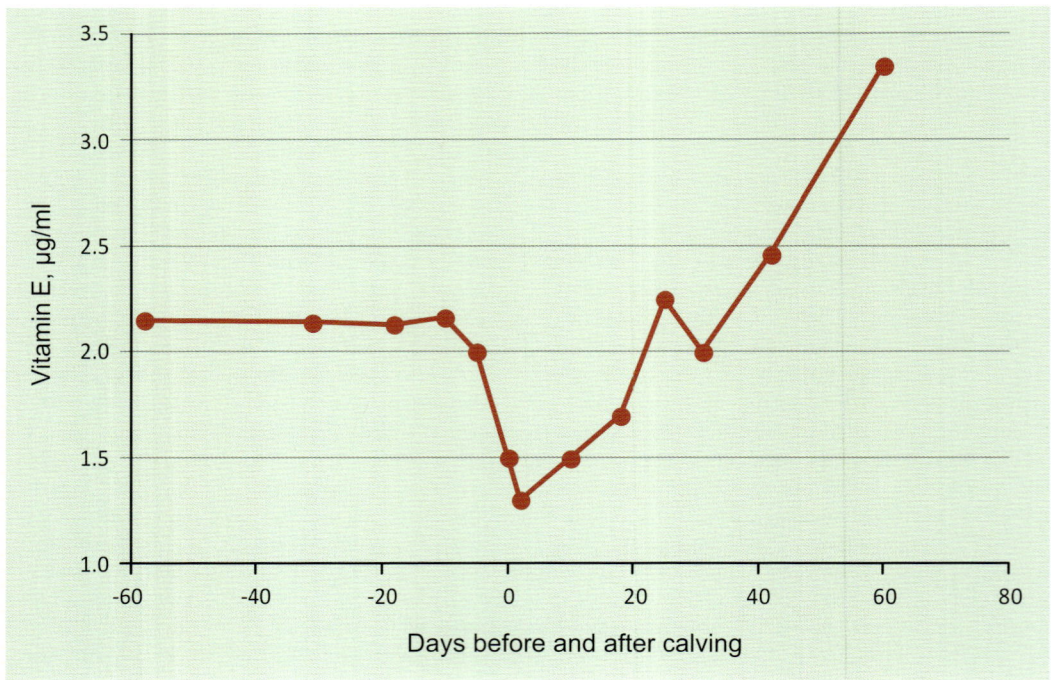

Vitamin E, µg/ml

Days before and after calving

et al., 1995 and 1996; Ndiweni and Finch, 1996). However, oral administration of up to 1,000 IU/d of vitamin E did not prevent a reduction in plasma concentration of vitamin E during the peripartum period. Only parenteral injection of 3,000 IU in days 10 and 5 prepartum was successful in increasing the plasma concentration of vitamin E during the critical peripartum days (Hogan et al., 1992; Weiss et al., 1992; **Figure 5**). Recent data confirm the importance of the parenteral supply of vitamin E (Bourne et al., 2007a). It has also been suggested that the supplementary supply of vitamin E by this method could help to reduce the risk of oxidative stress which occurs peripartum (Castillo et al., 2005) derived from a reduction in feed intake (Grummer et al., 2004).

Improved immune function translates into a greater capacity to fight mammary infections. Smith et al. (1984) reduced the incidence (-37%) and duration (-62%) of mammary infections and the number of cases of clinical mastitis by supplementing vitamin E at 1,000 IU/d during the 60 days of the dry period. Smith et al. (1985) also observed a reduction in the incidence of mastitis. Supplemental selenium and vitamin E during the prepartum period resulted in a reduction of 42% in the rate of mammary infections, of 32% in the cases of clinical mastitis and of 59% in the total number of infected days of lactation. Hogan et al. (1993) obtained similar results. Smith et al. (1985) observed that first lactation heifers, supplemented with 1,000 IU/d during the 60 days prepartum, had fewer mammary infections, other infections throughout lactation, and clinical cases and the duration of the infections and somatic cell counts were reduced. Batra and Hidiroglou (1992) also observed a reduction in the incidence of clinical cases and their duration after supplementing vitamin E during the dry period (1,000 IU/d). On the other hand, Bourne et al. (2008) did not observe any effect on the somatic cell count with a supplementary supply of vitamin E and selenium (2 injections: 2,100 mg vit. E + 7 mg of sodium selenite per injection, 2 weeks before parturition and 1 day after parturition) in three herds of dairy cattle (n=594 cows).

Figure 5. Changes in the concentration of vitamin E in blood leukocytes in control cows (●), or cows supplemented with 1000 IU/d of vitamin E orally (●), injected vitamin E (●) or the combination of 1000 IU/d of oral and injected vitamin E (●) (Weiss et al., 1992).

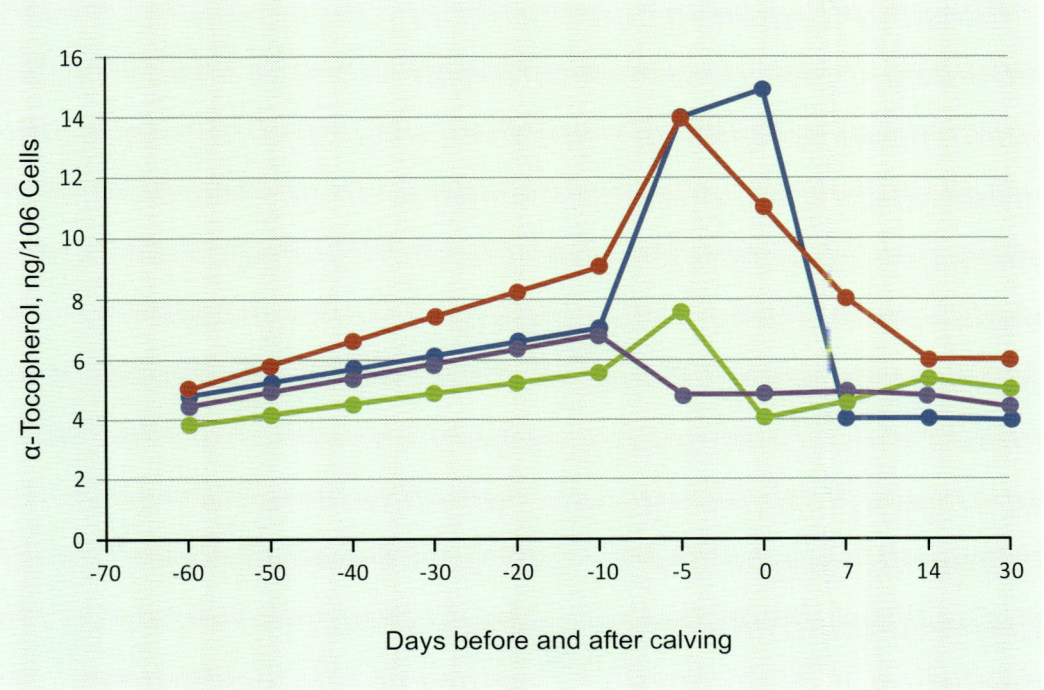

These results demonstrate that the increase in the vitamin E recommendations from 150 to 1,000 IU/d established in the NRC's 2001 report, while not resolving the reduction in the plasma concentration of vitamin E during the peripartum period, does improve immune competence and mammary gland health.

The summary presented by Weiss (2005) shows that, based on the data in the literature, the supply of high doses of vitamin E (above 1,000 IU/d) peripartum can be beneficial for a general improvement in the health of dairy cattle. Politis et al. (1995) observed that supplementation of 3,000 IU/d of vitamin E from 4 weeks prepartum to 8 weeks postpartum prevented the reduction in the immune response by polymorphonuclear neutrophils and macrophages typical of the peripartum period, suggesting that supplementation above current recommendations could be beneficial. The results obtained by Weiss et al. (1997) who supplemented 100, 1,000 and 4,000 IU/d of vitamin E during the 2 weeks prior to parturition, found that the highest level reduced the incidence of clinical mastitis by 80%, and intramammary infections by 60%, but supplementation of 100 and 1,000 IU/d did not prevent the reduction of plasma concentration of vitamin E peripartum. Supplementation with 4,000 IU/d of vitamin E maintained the plasma level throughout the peripartum period (**Figure 6**). Compared with supplementation with 100 and 1000 IU/d, supplementation with 4,000 IU/d of vitamin E increased the concentration of vitamin E in polymorphonuclear neutrophils by 200%. The incidence of intramammary infections was reduced compared with the control group by 11.8, 31.8 and 32.1% with 100, 1000 and 4000 IU/d, respectively. In staphylococcal infections, prevalence was 26, 14 and 9% with 100, 1000 and 4000 IU/d, respectively (**Figure 7**). The prevalence of clinical mastitis was 25, 17 and 3% of udders when supplemented with 100, 1,000 and 4,000 IU/d, respectively (**Figure 7**). The effect of supplementation with vitamin E on the prevalence of clinical mastitis was greatest in primiparous (37, 14 and 0% of udders when supplemented with 100, 1,000 and 4,000 IU/d, respectively). The results demonstrated, furthermore, that the reduction in the plasma concentration of vitamin E peripartum is an important mastitis risk factor, because if the plasma concentration was below 3 µg/ml, the risk of mastitis was 9.4 times higher.

Figure 6. Plasma concentration of vitamin E in cows supplemented with 100 IU/d of vitamin E (●), 1,000 IU/d of vitamin E prepartum and 500 IU/d of vitamin E postpartum (●) or 1,000 IU/d of vitamin E in dry period, 4,000 IU/d of vitamin E over 2 weeks prepartum, and 2,000 IU/d of vitamin E postpartum (●) (Weiss et al., 1997).

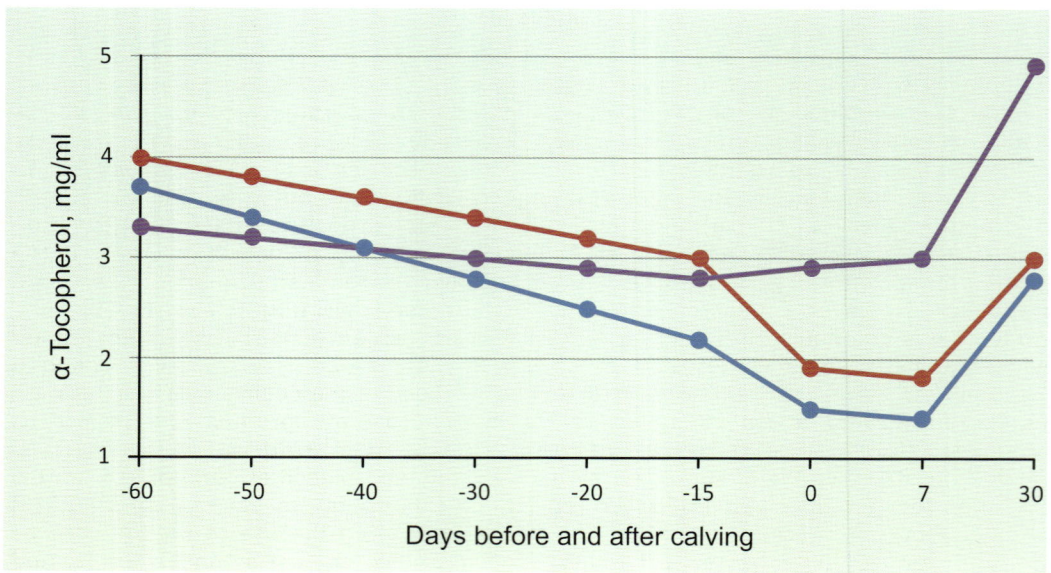

Figure 7. Prevalence of clinical mammary infections in adult cows and primiparous cows supplemented with 100, 1,000 and 4,000 IU/d of vitamin E (Weiss *et al.*, 1997).

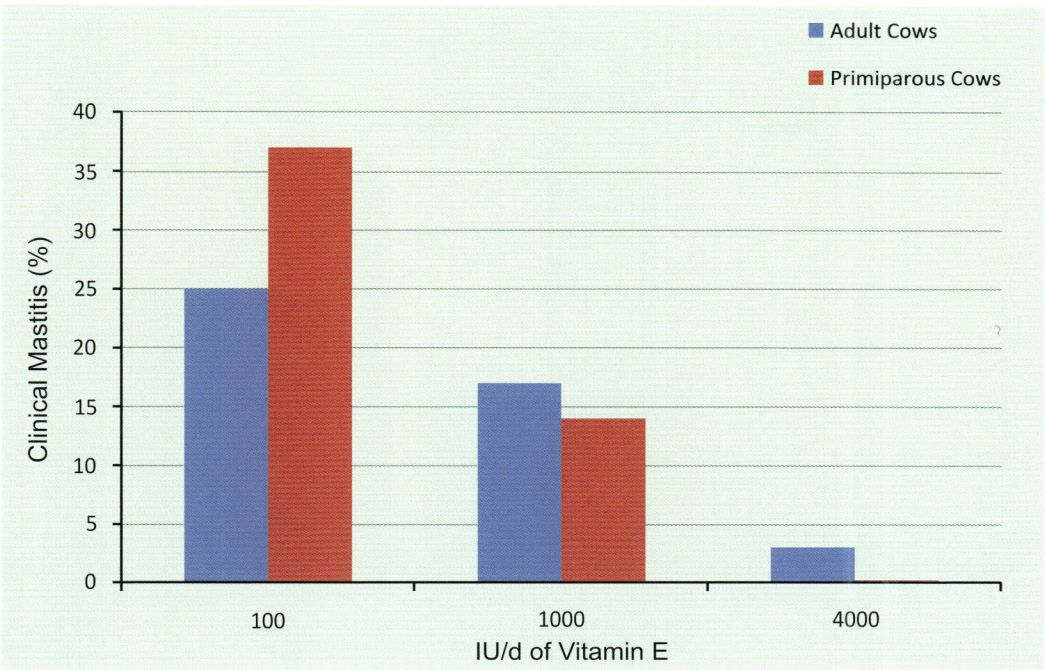

Vitamin E not only affects mammary gland health; there is considerable evidence of its effects on reproductive function. Harrison *et al.* (1984) demonstrated that supplementation, during the three prepartum weeks, of a combination of oral vitamin E (740 IU/d) and parenteral vitamin E (1 IU/kg liveweight), and selenium completely prevented the incidence of retained placenta in a herd with a previous incidence of 20%, and resulted in a quicker return to estrus, although the incidence of mastitis and ovarian cysts remained unchanged. Lacetera *et al.* (1996) also observed a reduction in the incidence of retained placenta from 33% to 8% following parenteral supplementation of selenium (5 mg per 100 kg) and vitamin E (25 IU per 100 kg) 3 and 1.5 weeks prepartum, and an increase of 10% in milk production. However, the increase in milk production is an effect which is not always evident (Kay *et al.*, 2005; Pottier *et al.*, 2006). Campbell and Miller (1998) reported a quicker return to estrus (from 60 to 42 days) and a reduction in the days to conception (from 71 to 62 days) when supplementing the ration for dry cows with 1,000 IU/d for 42 days (**Figure 8**). Because vitamin E was not supplemented in the postpartum ration,

the effects on reproduction were attributed to the residual effects of prepartum supplementation. Other authors (Harrison *et al.*, 1984; Miller *et al.*, 1993; Segerson *et al.*, 1981; Brzezinska-Slebodzinska *et al.*, 1994) obtained similar results which link supplementing the prepartum ration with vitamin E and improved reproductive activity.

In their review, Bourne *et al.* (2007b) concluded that supplementation with vitamin E during the dry period is associated with a reduction in the risks of the occurrence of retained placentas in dairy cattle, since out of 44 studies analyzed, 20 showed a positive effect, 21 showed no effect, and only in 3 was an increase in the incidence of retained placentas observed in the treated cows. Bourne *et al.* (2008) came to a similar conclusion, as supplementation with vitamin E and selenium was related to a decrease in the culling of cows from the herd because of reproductive problems, as well as a lower incidence of mastitis (8%) and retained placentas (dropping from 6.5 to 3%). Furthermore, Bourne *et al.* (2007b) also compared the use of natural sources of vitamin E against synthetic forms, and

Figure 8. Effect of supplementation of 1,000 IU/d of vitamin E on the occurrence of the first estrus and days to first insemination (Campbell and Miller, 1998).

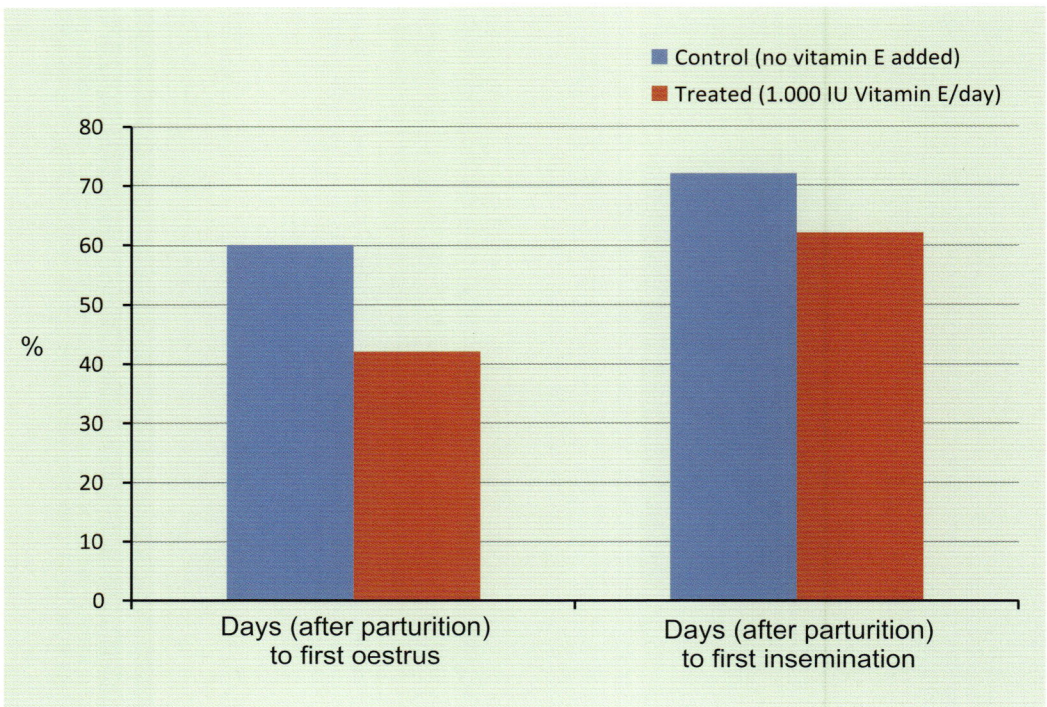

recommended the latter, as they were more effective than their natural equivalents.

Focant *et al.* (1998) studied the effect of supplementing vitamin E in rations rich in canola and flax seeds. Including these ingredients reduced the protein and fat concentrations in the milk, and increase the C:18 content as well as the proportion of unsaturated fatty acids (from 2.7 to 10.8%). This increase in the degree of unsaturation in milk fat increases the risk of its rancidity. Supplementing raised levels of vitamin E (9,600 IU/d) increased the vitamin E concentration in the milk by 45%, and prevented both the drop in milk fat and oxidation of the unsaturated fatty acids. These results are similar to those obtained by Charmley and Nicholson (1994), who supplemented the ration with 8,000 IU/d.

Kay *et al.* (2005) observed that the addition of 10,000 IU/d of α-tocopherol resulted in an increase of 6% in the fat content of the milk. The difference was even greater in the study conducted by Pottier *et al.* (2006), where the addition of 12,000 IU of α-tocopherol in the diet containing flax (extruded seed, 10% and oil, 1% of dry matter) increased the fat content in milk by 18% compared with the same diet without added vitamin E. These results suggest that the current recommendations for dry cows (1,000 IU/d) could be increased to 3,000-4,000 IU/d to boost the immune function, and to 9,000 IU/d for milk quality when selenium levels in the ration are marginal, the polyunsaturated fatty acid content of the ration is high, the incidence of mammary or reproductive disorders is high, or with the objective of reducing the risk of milk fat oxidation, without risk of reaching toxicity levels (**Table III**).

VITAMIN D

Introduction

Vitamin D, also known as antirachitic, is a prohormone required for the regulation of calcium metabolism and in the maintenance of correct calcium levels in blood. Much vitamin D is produced within the skin through photoconversion of 7-dehydrocholesterol to vitamin D_3. Vitamin D_3 accumulates in the liver, and its concentration in plasma is very low (1-2 ng/ml). To evaluate the status of vitamin D in the animal, the plasma concentration of 25-hydroxycholecalciferol (Horst et al., 1994) is generally recommended as the parameter.

Vitamin D is involved in the active transport of calcium and phosphorus across the intestinal epithelial cells and boosts the action of parathyroid hormone in reabsorbing bone calcium. It has also been demonstrated that vitamin D is involved in maintaining immune function by stimulating humoral immunity and by inhibiting cell-mediated immunity (Reinhardt and Hustmyer, 1987; Daynes et al., 1995). Plants generally contain vitamin D_2, while animals contain vitamin D_3. Horst and Littledike (1982) demonstrated that ruminants obtain little biological activity from vitamin D_2 due to its reduced ability to bind to the transport protein, which leads to faster metabolic degradation and a shorter average lifetime. However, the NRC (2001) does not look at these differences and considers that the two forms, D_2 and D_3, have the same potency in ruminants (1g is equal to 40,000 IU). There is little recent information with respect to the role of vitamin D in dairy cattle.

Recommendations for Vitamin D

Animals exposed to sunlight, or animals fed with sun-dried hay may not need supplementary vitamin D. However, the NRC (2001) does not look at the vitamin D content of feeds, and the recommendations refer to supplementation of the ration. The latest recommendation by the NRC (2001) upholds the previous recommendations by the NRC (1989) and INRA (1988) of 30 IU/kg liveweight (equivalent to 21,000 IU/d). As with other fat-soluble vitamins, oxidized fats in the ration can destroy the vitamin D present and limit its absorption (McDowell, 2006).

In recent years, interest in vitamin D has centered on its roles in anionic-cationic balance and the metabolism of calcium (Seymour, 2004). The normal concentration of 1,25 dihydroxy vitamin D_3 is between 20-80 pg/ml at the end of gestation and between 70-200 pg/ml at parturition. Levels can increase to 200-300 pg/ml in recurrent cases of milk fever (Horst et al., 1997, 2005). The increase in the plasma levels of 1,25 dihydroxy vitamin D_3 comes as a response to the fall in the concentration of ionized calcium in blood. That is to say, there is an inverse relationship between the plasma levels of 1,25 dihydroxy vitamin D_3 and the presence of hypocalcemia in dairy cattle (Joyce et al., 1997). However, the presence of sufficient levels of vitamin D or its precursors is not the only factor responsible for the maintenance of calcium homeostasis peripartum (Taylor et al., 2008).

Horst et al. (1994) found that blood concentrations below 5 ng/ml were indicative of vitamin D deficiency, and levels above 200-300 ng/ml were indicative of toxicosis. Vinet et al. (1985) observed that the plasma concentrations of vitamin D in housed dry cows fed on maize silage were 19 ng/ml 2 weeks prepartum, and only 10 ng/ml 35 days postpartum. Supplementing the ration with 7.5 or 15 IU of vitamin D per kg of live weight was sufficient to maintain the plasma concentration between 25 and 31 ng/ml. Ward et al. (1972) reduced the interval between calving and first estrus interval by 16 days by supplementing cows with 43,000 IU/d of vitamin D. In a review of several studies carried out at Ohio State University, Hibbs and Conrad (1983) concluded that cows supplemented with 50-70 IU of vitamin D per kg liveweight produced more milk and generally consumed more dry matter than those animals which were not supplemented or which were supplemented with 100-140 IU of vitamin D per kg liveweight. Astrup and Nedkvitne (1987) reported that supplementation with 10 IU/kg liveweight was sufficient to maintain the vitamin D status of the cow. These observations corresponded to studies carried out in conditions of low exposure to sunlight.

Based on this information the current recommendations by the NRC (2001) are sufficient, particularly where cows are exposed to sun as in Spain. Nevertheless, additional supplements of up to 50% may improve intake, production, and some reproductive parameters. However, an excess of vitamin D may be toxic (**Table IV**). The NRC (1987) suggests that toxic levels are reached with concentrations in the ration of 2,200 IU/kg DM over long periods or short-term at 25,000 IU/kg of DM in the ration.

VITAMIN K

Vitamin K includes a group of quinones that have anti-hemorrhagic effects. The most common isomers are polyquinones (K_1), menaquinones (K_2) and menadione (K_3). Plant chloroplasts are an important source of vitamin K_1, bacteria provide an important amount of vitamin K_2, and vitamin K_3 is a synthetic isomer used as a feed additive. Cows need vitamin K to synthesize a series of coagulation factors, and for the coagulation process by activating thrombin (Combs, 1992). Under normal conditions of production, good health and functional rumen, vitamin K deficiency almost never occurs, as the ruminal bacteria synthesize enough vitamin K to cover requirements (McDowell, 2006). Deficiency is only described in situations where anticoagulant substances have been consumed, as may occur with consumption of forage contaminated with dicumarol of fungal origin. The toxicity of vitamin K has not been studied in cattle.

There are no recommendations for vitamin K for dairy cattle (NRC, 2001; INRA, 1988), with the exception of the need to supplement veal calves with 2 mg vitamin K per kg DM (INRA, 1988). Lastly, it is important to remember that, as with other fat-soluble vitamins, ruminal synthesis, and consequently the intestinal availability of vitamin K, can be negatively affected by the presence of oxidized fats in the ration or when there are problems with fat absorption (McDowell, 2006).

WATER-SOLUBLE VITAMINS

Water-soluble vitamins have been traditionally considered non-essential for cattle, due to the contribution of synthesis by ruminal microorganisms. However, Erdman (1992) produced some estimates using published data which correlated animal requirements with live weight (estimated using data collected from pigs; NRC, 1987), milk production (according to the concentration of the vitamins in milk), vitamin synthesis in the rumen, and food supplements and their ruminal degradability (**Table IV**).

This information suggests that intake of most vitamins is sufficient to meet requirements. However, the calculations indicate that supplies of folic acid, pantothenic acid and choline may be insufficient to cover requirements, so that supplementation is recommended. On the other hand, when the rumen is not functioning fully, as in the case of preruminant calves and abnormal ruminal situations (acidosis, indigestion, reduced intake, etc.) the intake of water-soluble vitamins may be a limiting factor. There is a growing interest in knowing the real requirements, and how these vitamins affect the production and health of cows. There is also interest in the development of a method of improving the supply of these vitamins in milk and dairy products (Cooke *et al.*, 2007; Ferreira and Weiss, 2007; Enjalbert *et al.*, 2008; Girard and Matte, 2005a, b; Drackley *et al.*, 2006; Swensson *et al.*, 2007; Baldi, *et al.*, 2008).

BIOTIN (VITAMIN H OR B$_8$)

Biotin is a vitamin of the B complex considered essential for ruminants. Biotin acts as a cofactor of various enzymes which catalyze carboxylation reactions and other metabolic routes directly related to the synthesis of milk in the mammary gland, so that its supplementation can improve the productive response in high production dairy cattle (Weiss, 2005, 2007). Ruminal bacteria synthesize important amounts of biotin depending on the availability of energy (0.79 mg/kg digestible organic material; Zinn, 1992), although recent data suggests that this synthesis reduces when the amount of concentrate in the ration increases (De Costa-Gomez *et al.*, 1998), and it has been suggested

Table IV. Estimates of potentially limiting water-soluble vitamins in dairy cattle (mg/d)

	Feed[1]	Ruminal degradation	Ruminal production[2]	Small intestine absorption	Excreted in milk[3]	Potential requirements[4]
Thiamine (B$_1$)	90	47	100	147	18	25
Riboflavin (B$_2$)	120	8	197	205	70	95
Niacin (B$_3$)	700	210	1475	1685	38	250
Pyridoxine (B$_6$)	150	150	150	300	26	25
Vitamin B$_{12}$	0.10	0.01	49	49	0.17	0.38
Biotin (B$_8$)	10	10	9.5	19.5	1.2	5
Folic Acid (B$_9$)	40	1.2	5.0	6.2	2	75
Pantothenic Acid (B$_5$)	300	66	26	92	139	300
Choline	30	1	0	1	5	30–50

(1) Based on NRC (1989).
(2) Based on Zinn *et al.* (1987) and Miller *et al.* (1986).
(3) Based on a cow of 40 kg/d production.
(4) Extrapolated from swine requirements (NRC, 1988).

that this effect is associated with the fall in the cellulolytic microbial population which occurs when ruminal pH falls. Biotin does not degrade to a great extent in the rumen, and oral supplementation almost always results in an increase in the flow of biotin to the duodenum, and in its concentration in plasma and milk (Frigg *et al.*, 1993; Midla *et al.*, 1998). Estimates of requirements and supplies carried out by Erdman (1992) indicate that, under normal conditions, the supplies are sufficient to cover the requirements of cows in production (**Table IV**).

Some studies indicate that biotin deficiency is related to the development of laminitis in dairy cattle (Distl and Schmid, 1994), because there appears to be a relationship between high levels of biotin in the plasma and the hardness of hooves, and an increase in milk production (McDowell, 2004). Thus, many studies indicate that supplementing 20 mg/d of biotin improves hoof health (Midla *et al.*, 1998; Bergsten *et al.*, 1999; Fitzgerald *et al.*, 2000). Hedges *et al.* (2001) supplemented 20 mg/d of biotin for 18 months in 5 commercial herds in which the average incidence of laminitis was 69%. In two of the herds, biotin supplements reduced the incidence of laminitis by half. Pötzsch *et al.* (2003) also obtained similar results. These authors recommended supplementing cows over long periods (> 6 months) to achieve an effective reduction in the risk of the occurrence of these problems.

Some authors have observed that milk production increased by between 1.0 kg/d (Midla *et al.*, 1998) and 2.9 kg/d (Bergsten *et al.*, 1999) in response to supplementation.

Zimmerley and Weiss (2001) supplemented the rations of cows in production with biotin (10 or 20 mg/d) from two weeks prepartum to 100 days of lactation, and milk production increased from 36.9 in the control group to 37.8 and 39.7 kg/d, respectively, with supplements of biotin. Concentration in plasma, milk and colostrum also increased with the supplement. Several studies confirm the importance of the supplementary supply of biotin for dairy cattle (**Table V**). The production of milk or its main components is not always improved by supplementary biotin because the response may be affected by various factors such as the composition of the diet, the state of lactation and/or the status of biotin in the cow (Ferreira *et al.*, 2007).

Other results suggest that supplementation with biotin reduces the occurrence of fatty liver syndrome in high-producing dairy cattle. This effect has been associated with a reduction of non-esterified fatty acids in blood and of the concentration of lipids in the liver, and an increase of blood glucose levels (Rosendo *et al.*, 2004). This effect may be due to the fact that supplementation with biotin favors gluconeogenesis (Rosendo *et al.*, 2004) and lipolysis (Enjalbert *et al.*, 2008) in the liver.

Table V. Effect of supplementation with biotin on the incidence of hoof lesions and some productive parameters in dairy cattle

Treatment[1]	Hoof lesions	Production (kg/d)					Reference
		DMI	Milk	Fat	Protein	Lactose	
Control vs. biotin (20 mg/d), primiparous, P vs. multiparous, M	=/–	NA	NA	NA	NA	NA	Pötzsch et al. (2003)
Change compared to control, %	P:NS M:–45.2	NA	NA	NA	NA	NA	
Control vs. biotin, mg/d (A=20mg; B=20 mg+B-complex; C=40 mg+2xB-complex)	NE	+/=	=	=/–	+/=	+/–	Majee et al. (2003)
Change compared to control, %[2]	NA	A= +2.8	NS	C= –3.3	A= +5.5	A= +6.0	
Control vs. biotin (22 mg/d)	–	=	+	+	=	NI	Margerison et al. (2003)
Change compared to control[3]	(3.06 vs. 2.95)	NS	+5.3	+6.7	=	NA	
Control vs. biotin (20 mg/d) en peripartum	NE	+	NA	NA	NA	NA	Rosendo et al. (2004)
Change compared to control, %	NA	+18 (NS)	NA	NA	NA	NA	
Control vs. biotin (30 mg/d) en lactation	NE	=	=	=	=	NE	
Change compared to control, %	NA	NS	NS	NS	NS	NA	
Control vs. biotin (20 mg/d): Cows low(B); high production(A)	NE	=/(A=+)	=/(A=+)	=/(A=+)	=/(A=+)	(B/A)=+/+	Ferreira et al. (2007)
Change compared to control, %	NA	A=4.6	A=6.5	A=26.2	A=8.3	B=3.6/ A=12.3	

(1) Effect of treatment compared to control= +: increases; –: decreases; =: no change; NI: not indicated; NE: parameter not evaluated; NA= not applicable.
(2) Change in percentage terms from treatment compared to control.
(3) Refers to the score of incidences of hoof lesions.
DMI (Dry Matter Intake)

FOLIC ACID (VITAMIN M OR B$_9$)

Folic acid is essential in the synthesis of purines and pyrimidines, and forms part of the enzymes involved in the transfer of methyl groups (Girard and Matte, 2005b). Methionine may also act as a methyl group donor, so that folic acid reduces the need to use methionine for this purpose. Deficiency of folic acid can be critical for cell division and protein metabolism (Mason, 2003; Girard and Matte, 2005a). Some studies have been conducted to evaluate the effect of supplementation with folic acid on productive responses in dairy cattle. However, there is insufficient evidence to date to determine requirements and make recommendations for its use in practical conditions (Weiss and Ferreira, 2006a, b).

Most dietary folic acid is degraded in the rumen (approximately 97%; Zinn, 1992; Santschi et al., 2005a). On the other hand, a significant amount of folic acid is synthesized in the rumen depending on the availability of energy (0.42 mg/kg of digestible organic material; Zinn, 1992). The synthesis and degradation of folic acid in the rumen in turn determines the quantity available to be absorbed in the small intestine of the ruminant. Few studies to date have estimated the synthesis and degradation of this vitamin, so that there are no bioavailability values for the folic acid in feed ingredients for ruminants (Ragaller et al., 2008). The apparent intestinal absorption of folic acid seems to be very low, probably due to interaction with bile secretions (Santschi et al., 2005a).

Until recently, the published data indicated that the amount of folic acid provided in the basal ration and synthesized in the rumen were sufficient to prevent symptoms of deficiencies in cows (Girard et al., 1995). However, this estimate is different from that of Erdman (1992), which suggests that supplementation of this vitamin could increase productive efficiency (**Table V**). Other studies support this hypothesis (Girard and Matte, 2005b; Drackley et al., 2006; Graulet et al., 2007). However, due to the high ruminal degradation, oral supplementation would only be justified if a protection against ruminal degradation were developed.

In preruminant calves poor bacterial synthesis may lead to deficiency. Daily injection of 40 mg of folic acid between weeks 1 and 16 of life increased average weight gain by 8%. In adult cows, parenteral supplementation of 160 mg folic acid each week from 45 days of gestation to 6 weeks postpartum tended to increase milk yield and milk protein production during the second half of lactation in primiparous and in multiparous cows (Girard et al., 1995). In the postpartum period, the protein content of milk increased during the first 6 weeks in multiparous animals. Girard and Matte (1998) observed a linear increase in milk production when supplementing rations with 0.2 and 4 mg of folic acid/kg liveweight. The plasma concentration of folic acid also showed a linear increase, which suggests that at least a part of the folic acid escapes rumen degradation. The observed responses may be a direct effect of folic acid, or an indirect effect, due to the reduction in the use of methionine as a methyl donor.

Supplementation with folic acid (dose between 2 and 3 g/d) results in variable responses in production and composition of milk, and intake of dry matter. The positive response in dairy cattle has only been evident in cows with two or more calvings (Girard and Matte, 2005a). Graulet et al. (2007) evaluated the effect of folic acid (0 vs. 2.6 g/d) and/or vitamin B$_{12}$ (0 vs. 0.5 g/d) from the third prepartum week to 8 weeks postpartum. In this case, supplementation with folic acid increased the production of milk (+5.8%), fat (+16.2%) and protein (+3.3%).

There is insufficient information to establish practical recommendations (Girard et al., 2005; Santschi et al., 2005a, b; Girard and Matte, 2005a, b; Graulet et al., 2007). In a recent review, Ragaller et al. (2008) concluded that there are numerous questions regarding the effect of folic acid on dairy cattle, and that these should be addressed in future investigations before specific recommendations for dairy cattle can be made.

358

NIACIN (VITAMIN B₃)

Introduction

Niacin is an active component of two coenzymes (NAD and NADP) which play a fundamental role in carbohydrate, lipid and amino acid metabolism (Pires and Grummer, 2007). This water-soluble vitamin may be formed in the liver from tryptophan, and is found in two forms: nicotinic acid and nicotinamide. Both compounds have similar nutritional properties and can be used interchangeably to synthesize NAD, but are metabolized by different routes and have different properties when administered at supra-physiological levels (Carlson, 2005). As a vitamin from the B complex, niacin is widely available in products and byproducts of animal origin and in cereals.

Bioavailability

The flow of niacin to the duodenum is generally greater than intake of niacin when rations are not supplemented, which indicates that ruminal bacteria synthesize it abundantly (Zinn et al., 1987). Zinn (1992) estimated that niacin synthesis in the rumen was 107.02 mg/kg of digestible organic material. However, when niacin is added to the ration, the quantity which reaches the intestine may be even less than that provided in the ration, due to the inhibition of bacterial synthesis in the presence of exogenous niacin (Abdouli and Schaefer, 1986). While one review estimated that between 94 and 99% of niacin present in the diet is degraded in the rumen (Zinn, 1992), other studies have found that between 17 and 30% of dietary niacin reaches the small intestine (Harmeyer and Kollenkirchen, 1989; Campbell et al., 1994).

The study of the nutritional effects on the animal of supplying niacin is complicated, given the capacity of ruminants to synthesize niacin from tryptophan (with adequate levels of vitamin B₆ and riboflavin), and its high ruminal degradation which determines the necessity of using protected sources (Seymour, 2004).

Functions

Niacin functions in the rumen and in metabolic processes. In the rumen, niacin increases the efficiency of synthesis and production of microbial protein in vitro (Mizwicki, 1976; Bartley et al., 1979; Ridell, et al., 1980; Arambell et al., 1982), in a change in the molar proportion of VFAs towards the predominance of propionic acid (Ridell et al., 1980; Arambell et al., 1982; Hannah and Stern, 1985), and in an increase in the digestibility of cellulose in vitro (Hannah and Stern, 1985). Other studies have observed no effects on ruminal fermentation.

At the metabolic level, niacin participates in lipid and energy metabolism, reducing the risk of ketosis and fatty liver, and occasionally improving the production level and composition of milk. Zimmerman et al. (1992) observed that supplementation with niacin (12 g/day) interacted with the level of protein in the ration in multiparous cows, increasing blood glucose levels and reducing the concentrations of ß-hydroxy-butyrate and non-esterified fatty acids, only in rations with a higher protein level. Horner et al. (1986) also observed an improvement in milk and milk protein production. However, the data currently available indicate that productive responses are inconsistant.

Supplementation with niacin leads to an increase in the concentration of glucose in blood, and a decrease in the concentration of ß-hydroxybutyric acid and free fatty acids in plasma, which are indicators of niacin's activity as gluconeogenesis stimulator. This situation may be beneficial in cows in early lactation, since it helps to maintain energy levels and to meet intermediate needs in glucose metabolism. Furthermore, the presence of niacin spares tryptophan as a precursor. In these conditions, the greater availability of tryptophan for productive functions, especially in high-yielding cows in early lactation, may improve reproductive activity (Horner et al., 1986).

Recommendations for Niacin

Suckling calves

Niacin is required in calf rations prior to weaning because microbial synthesis in the rumen is limited. Hopper and Johnson (1955) observed that calves fed with milk replacer deficient in niacin presented with diarrhea within 48 hours and that there was an immediate improvement the day after administering an oral dose of 6 mg/d or an intramuscular dose of 10 mg/d of nicotinic acid. The NRC (2001) recommends the incorporation of 10 mg of niacin per kg of dry matter in milk replacer.

Dry cows and lactating cows

The NRC (1989; 2001) and INRA (1988) have not established recommendations for niacin. However, they recognize that supplementing adult cows with 6 to 12 g/d from prepartum to the peak of lactation has resulted in some positive effects. This supplementation results in increased milk production, often also raising the fat and protein content. It has also been found to prevent ketosis and fatty liver.

Horner *et al.* (1988) observed that including niacin (3, 6, or 12 g in 20.5 kg DM) accompanied by whole cottonseed in the ration of Holstein cows in lactation affected neither the ruminal pH nor the ammonia-N concentration. The content of fat and protein in milk tended to fall, although total production of both fat and milk was greater with the addition of 12 g of niacin.

Drackley (1992) summarized a set of 23 studies and concluded that supplementation of niacin resulted in a slight increase in average milk production (+0.62 kg/d), and in fat content (+0.033 g/l) and protein content (+0.002 g/l). Most of the negative responses occurred when the basal ration contained supplemental fat (Drackley, 1992). Erdman (1992) carried out another comparison with 29 published studies and calculated an average rise in milk production of 0.3 kg/d without effects on the composition of fat and protein. However, when the results were broken down according to lactational status, the average increase in production by animals in early lactation was 0.4 kg/d, a value close to that obtained by Drackley (1992). In three studies carried out on commercial farms in which supplements of 6 g/d of niacin were given, the responses were inconsistant, from an absence in improvements (Jaster *et al.*, 1983), to an increase in 1 kg/d during the first 70 days of lactation (Barttlet, 1983) or 0.9 kg/d during the first 90 days postpartum (Muller *et al.*, 1986). The response observed in high-yielding cows was greater than the production response in less productive animals.

More recently, Schwab *et al.* (2005) conducted an analysis of the published data from 27 studies related to the effect of supplementation with nicotinic acid in dairy cattle. The authors conclude that a response to the supplementation is achieved with levels of between 6-12 g/d, with small positive changes in milk production (0.4 kg/d), and moderate increases in the fat and protein content. However, it is not clear that the response justifies the cost entailed by supplementation throughout lactation, and in any case its use is recommended during the peripartum period. In other cases, the use of high doses of nicotinic acid (48 g/d) over 30 days prepartum reduced the levels of non-esterified fatty acids in plasma and the fall in the intake of dry matter in the week prior to parturition (French, 2004), although a subsequent study conducted by the same group of investigators was not able to replicate these effects (Chamberlain and French, 2006). Pires and Grummer (2007) infused nicotinic acid postruminally (between 0 and 60 mg/kg liveweight) and observed a fall in the concentration of non-esterified fatty acids in the blood which coincided with an increase in the concentration of insulin and a slight effect on the concentration of glucose in the blood. The authors concluded that supplementation with nicotinic acid can be beneficial in the regulation of non-esterified fatty acids and in the prevention of problems related to the lipid metabolism during the transition stage in high-yielding dairy cows.

Campbell *et al.* (1994) observed no benefits when supplementing rations with niacin or nicotinamide, although the apparent digestibility of most of the nutrients increased. Driver *et al.* (1990) observed with high-yielding cows in early lactation that the percentage of milk protein was greater when heat-treated soy was supplemented with niacin (6 g/d), suggesting that niacin ameliorated the drop in milk protein which is frequently associated with the supply of large quantities of fat in the ration. Furthermore, niacin tended to reduce the blood plasma concentration of non-esterified fatty acids.

Erickson *et al.* (1992) observed in cows in early lactation that supplementing with 12g of niacin per day increased the levels of methionine and phenylalanine produced in the mammary gland, and the content and total production of protein in milk. These results agree with Lanham *et al.* (1992), who observed an increase in casein synthesis following supplementation of the ration with niacin at the beginning of lactation. Kung *et al.* (1980) also obtained positive results when supplementing niacin (6 g/d) in early lactation. As well as the production responses, niacin has been used to prevent ketosis and fatty liver through its antilipolytic action (Fronk and Schultz, 1979; Waterman *et al.*, 1972; Jaster *et al.*, 1983). In a total of 14 experimental studies in which niacin was supplemented (NRC, 2001), non-esterified fatty acids in plasma were reduced in only one study, increased in two, and did not change in the others.

The results from these experiments are contradictory. While the NRC (2001) concludes that there is no evidence to support clear recommendations on niacin requirements, in some cases the production response has been important. In these cases, it appears that the best responses are produced by supplementing 6 g of niacin per animal per day from the period just before parturition and during early lactation (up to 12 weeks), on the basis of improved production and/or composition of milk, and a reduced risk of ketosis. When symptoms of ketosis are apparent, supplementation with between 20 and 50 g niacin per cow every 2 hours reduces the likelihood of a sudden fall in yield and improves normal plasma levels of free fatty acids, ß-hydroxy-butyrate, glucose and insulin.

PANTOTHENIC ACID (VITAMIN B$_5$)

Pantothenic acid is a constituent of coenzyme A, and it is essential in many reactions including fatty acid oxidation metabolism, amino acid catabolism and acetylcholine synthesis. Ruminal microorganisms synthesize between 20 and 30 times more pantothenic acid than is required by the cow, hence supplementation is unnecessary (NRC, 2001). The rumen degraded 78% of dietary pantothenic acid (Zinn *et al.*, 1987). Erdman (1992) determined on the basis of calculations of maintenance and production requirements, and microbial and dietary supplies, that pantothenic acid might be limiting under some conditions (**Table V**). Although the estimates of vitamin requirements made in the latest version of the NRC report for dairy cattle do not recommend its supplementation due to lack of supporting scientific data, it mentions that pantothenic acid could become a limiting factor in high-yielding cows (NRC, 2001).

There are no specific experimental studies that confirm the need to supplement dairy cows with pantothenic acid and, as with other B group vitamins, neither are there any recommendations on requirements of pantothenic acid in adult bovines (INRA, 1988; NRC, 1996; NRC, 2001). However, the NRC (2001) recommends the incorporation of 13.0 mg/kg of DM in milk replacer. In the study conducted by Majee *et al.* (2003) which compared the effect of supplementing dairy cattle with biotin (20 vs. 40 mg/d) and a mixture of B-complex vitamins (thiamine, riboflavin, pyridoxine, niacin, biotin, folic acid, B$_{12}$), which included 475 or 950 mg/d of pantothenic acid, they observed no additional benefit in response to the inclusion of the mixture of B-complex vitamins in the diet. As a final recommendation, they pointed out the need to use vitamin E sources which are resistant to ruminal degradation. Sacadura *et al.* (2008) conducted two experiments to evaluate the effect of a mixture of protected B-complex vitamins on the production of dairy cattle (at the start and mid-point of lactation). The mixture contained biotin, folic acid and pantothenic acid. The results indicated an improvement in the production of dairy cattle at the start of lactation, in that supplementation increased production (kg/d) of milk, fat and protein, and improved the general state of the herd (physical condition and locomotion problems), without effects on the intake of dry matter. The positive effects of the supplementation were less evident in the case of dairy cattle in mid-lactation. As the supplementation was done with a mixture of vitamins, the beneficial effect cannot be attributed to any one vitamin. The authors suggested that the active mechanism in the supplementation of the mixture of B-complex vitamins contributes to a greater efficiency in the metabolic function.

RIBOFLAVIN (VITAMIN B₂)

Riboflavin is one of numerous vitamins which participate in the intermediary metabolism, especially energy metabolism (Weiss, 2007), and oxidation-reduction reactions (Zempleni et al., 2007). In dairy cattle no requirements have been established, since it is presumed that ruminal microorganisms synthesize abundant quantities of this vitamin (15.2 mg/kg of digestible organic material; Zinn, 1992). Furthermore, ruminal degradation is almost total (Zinn et al., 1987; Santschi et al., 2005a), so that supplementary supplies should be resistant to ruminal degradation (Majee et al., 2003; Santschi et al., 2005a). On the other hand, it is estimated that intestinal digestibility is approximately 25% (Miller et al., 1986;

Zinn et al., 1987). The NRC (2001) only recommends inclusion of 6.5 mg/kg DM in milk replacers. Although the requirements and practical recommendations for the incorporation of riboflavin in the ration of adult cattle have not been established, the data provided by the analyses of Santschi et al. (2005a, b) and Schwab (2006) indicate that the average intake of riboflavin in dairy cattle fed with a normal diet was 123 mg/d (**Table VI**).

As with the other vitamins of the B complex, the increase in the production of dairy cattle indicates that the requirements for riboflavin have increased in the same proportion. Furthermore the only experimental work known to date (Majee et al., 2003) evaluated

Table VI. Concentration of B-complex vitamins in cattle diets and typical vitamin intake in dairy cattle[1]

Vitamin	Average concentration (mg/kg DM)	Range of variation in concentration (mg/kg MS)	Average intake (mg/d)[2]
Thiamine	2.0	1.5−2.6	45
Riboflavin	5.4	4.3−6.7	123
Niacina total	46.0	22.6−94.8	1045
Vitamin B₆	5.2	3.2−8.5	118
Total folates	0.5	0.4−0.7	11
Biotin	6.9	6.3−7.8	157
Biotin[3]	0.37	0.33−0.41	8

(1) Adapted from Weiss (2007), who in turn used data supplied by Santschi et al. (2005a, b) and Schwab et al. (2006).
(2) Based on an average ingestion of 22.7 kg/d.
(3) Data obtained from bibliographical sources, with analytical methods different to the rest (Zinn et al., 1987; Frigg et al., 1993; Midla et al., 1998).

the effect of the incorporation of biotin with or without a mixture of B-complex vitamins, which supplied 150 or 300 mg/d of riboflavin. Although the supplementation improved animal production in one of the experiments, the benefit cannot be attributed to any one vitamin. Given the limited number of studies and the inconsistency of the results, no practical recommendations for supplementation of this vitamin can be made.

THIAMINE (VITAMIN B_1)

Thiamine is a coenzyme which acts as cofactor in many reactions of oxidative metabolism of carbohydrates and proteins, and as intermediary in the synthesis of fatty acids (Harmeyer and Kollenkirchen, 1989; Weiss and Ferreira, 2006b; Zempleni et al., 2007). The quantity of thiamine synthesized in the rumen (between 28 and 72 mg/d) is the same as or higher than that ingested in the ration (Breves et al., 1981). No requirements have been established for ruminants in good health and with a functional rumen. Supplies from microbial synthesis and dietary thiamine are sufficient to meet requirements of cows, even considering a ruminal degradation of dietary thiamine of 48% (Zinn et al., 1987). Recent data indicate that 66% of dietary thiamine degrades in the rumen (Santschi et al., 2005a), although Weiss (2007) suggested a lower value (53.1%). For ruminants, thiamine is not toxic (NRC, 1987) and deficiencies only occur in abnormal situations, such as consumption of feed rich in thiaminases or high in sulfates or situations in which the ruminal pH drops suddenly (Zinn et al., 1987; Harmeyer and Kollenkirchen, 1989; Gould et al., 1991; Zempleni et al., 2007). The NRC (2001) recommends the incorporation of 6.5 mg of thiamine per kg of dry matter in milk replacers.

Even where no specific recommendations for cows have been established, under certain specific conditions, such as the case of animals subjected to stress situations and in high-yielding dairy cattle at the start of lactation, some investigators recommend increasing dietary supplies of thiamine (McDowell, 2006). Because a significant proportion is degraded in the rumen, supplementary sources should be resistant to ruminal degradation (Majee et al., 2003). The average supply of thiamine is considered less variable than other vitamins in the B complex, with an average intake of 45 mg/d in diets normally formulated for high-yielding dairy cattle (**Table VI**). As with the majority of vitamins in the B complex, the scant data available (Shaver and Bal, 2000; Majee et al., 2003) do not allow a clear conclusion on the benefits of a supplementary supply of thiamine for dairy cattle.

VITAMIN B_{12}

Vitamin B_{12} acts as cofactor in two important enzyme reactions in animal metabolism. The first is with methylmalonyl-CoA mutase, necessary for the conversion from propionate to succinate during the oxidation of branched chain fatty acids and the catabolism of ketogenic amino acids. The second is with tetrahydrofolate methyl transferase, which participates in methionine metabolism, and is therefore important for the synthesis of protein (NRC, 2001; Zempleni et al., 2007). The ruminal degradation of dietary vitamin B_{12} ranges between 90 and 100% (Zinn, 1992; Schwab et al., 2006). Bacteria are the only natural source of vitamin B_{12}, for which an adequate supply of cobalt is required (McDowell, 2000). The NRC (2001) considers that the requirements of dairy cows range between 0.34 and 0.68 µg/kg liveweight. Due to the high degradation of vitamin B_{12} in the rumen, the microbial synthesis of vitamin B_{12} is fundamental and depends on the presence of cobalt, the rate increasing linearly up to levels of 0.2 mg/kg. A supplementary supply of cobalt in the diet (0.17 vs. 0.29 mg of Co per kg of dry matter) higher than the NRC's 2001 recommendations stimulates the synthesis of vitamin B_{12}, which suggests that these recommendations should also be set higher (Stemme *et al.*, 2008).

Under normal conditions, ruminal bacteria synthesize at a rate of 4.1 mg of vitamin B_{12} per kg of digestible organic matter, and synthesis is higher in rations rich in forage (Sutton and Elliot, 1972; Walker and Elliot, 1972). However, these data contradict the results obtained in dairy cattle by Schwab *et al.* (2006), who estimated an average synthesis of 7.8 mg/kg of true digestible organic material (range: 6.4-9.4). The total dietary supply is estimated between 60-130 mg/d (Santschi *et al.*, 2005b; Schwab *et al.*, 2006; Weiss, 2007). Considering the requirements and the capacity for ruminal synthesis of vitamin B_{12}, a deficiency in dairy cattle is unlikely, except where there is a cobalt deficiency (Erdman, 1992), if the NRC's 2001 recommendations are taken as valid (Schwab *et al.*, 2006; **Table VII**).

Supplementing weaned calves may be necessary under some conditions (Lassiter *et al.*, 1953). The NRC (2001) recommends supplementation of 0.07 mg of vitamin B_{12} per kg of dry matter in milk replacers. In contrast, neither the NRC (2001) nor INRA (1989) establish recommendations for adult cattle. Nevertheless, the results of other recent studies (Girard and Matte, 2005b) suggest that supplementation with vitamin B_{12} in high-yielding dairy cattle in early lactation may interfere with other B-complex vitamins, such as folic acid, and become a limiting nutrient. Graulet *et al.* (2007) evaluated the effect of supplementation with folic acid and/or vitamin B_{12}, and only demonstrated an additive effect of both vitamins for the fat content of milk, while a supply of vitamin B_{12} alone had no effects. Nevertheless, Girard and Matte (2005b) suggested the need to evaluate the possible deficiencies of folic acid and vitamin B_{12} in dairy cattle, since supplementation with vitamin B_{12} considerably increased the content of the vitamin in milk, improving its nutritional quality for human consumption.

Table VII. Comparison of measured and estimated (NRC, 2001) values for the apparent synthesis of B-complex vitamins

Vitamin	Apparent synthesis of B-complex, (mg/kg of IDM)			
	NRC, mean[1]	Average values		
		Mean	Minimum	Maximum
Thiamine	127	51	44	61
Riboflavin	232	238	206	254
Niacin	1603	1025	446	1547
B_6	85	23	14	30
Biotin	12	-11	-16	-3
Folates	6.2	16	13	20
B_{12}	62	80	60	102

Adapted from Schwab *et al.*, 2006
(1) Ruminal synthesis adjusted to dry matter intake

PYRIDOXINE (VITAMIN B₆)

Pyridoxine or vitamin B_6 is a coenzyme which actively participates in the metabolism of amino acids, and requirements are therefore established according to the quantity of protein intake (Zempleni et al., 2007). The majority of published data indicate that the ruminal degradability of pyridoxine is very low and it is synthesized abundantly in the rumen, so a deficiency is unlikely (Zinn, 1992; Schwab et al., 2006). However, Santschi et al. (2005a, b) and Schwab et al. (2006, **Table VIII**) indicated that the intestinal flow of vitamin B_6 could be between 50-70 mg lower than the estimates of the NRC (2001). Although not much is known about the factors which affect the ruminal synthesis of vitamin B_6, it appears to be higher in

rations rich in non-fibrous carbohydrates (Schwab et al., 2006). Vitamin B_6 can also be important during the transition period, as it plays a strategic role as a donor of methyl groups (Mason, 2003). This role links it directly with the metabolism of lipids and the development of ketosis and fatty liver (Seymour, 2004; Zempleni et al., 2007). The importance of this productive period in cows should give rise to reflections on the need to revise the recommendations. As with other B group vitamins, neither INRA (1988) nor the NRC (2001) establishes recommendations for adult cattle. The NRC (2001) only considers the supplementary supply of 6.5 mg of pyridoxine per kg of dry matter in milk replacers.

VITAMIN C

Vitamin C plays a role as cofactor in many biochemical and oxidation-reduction reactions and processes (NRC, 2001; Zempleni et al., 2007). It acts as an antioxidant, protecting cells against damage from free radicals (McDowell, 2004), and in the regulation of steroid synthesis. Vitamin C is synthesized inside the cells of adult ruminants, principally in the liver and kidneys (Weiss, 2007), with the exception of young calves, which cannot synthesize it until three weeks of age (Cummins and Brunner, 1991), so that it is considered an essential nutrient only for this type of animal. Vitamin C requirements also increase in conditions of stress (Padilla et al., 2006; McDowell, 2006), when the plasma concentration falls

(Cummins and Brunner, 1991; Hidiroglou et al., 1977). Oral supplementation of 1-2g vitamin C in preruminant calves increased the plasma concentration of vitamin C (Hidiroglou et al., 1995). The positive effects attributed to vitamin C, refer to the immune response, as it stimulates the neutrophils and in some cases reduces mastitis indicators (Chaiyotwittayakun et al., 2002; Naresh et al., 2002; Weiss et al., 2004; Kleczkowski et al., 2005; Ranjan et al., 2005; Weiss and Hogan, 2007). Data on the effects of oral supplementation of vitamin C in adult animals show no solid evidence which would permit practical recommendations to be made (Weiss, 2007).

CHOLINE

Introduction

Choline is not a vitamin in the traditional sense as it is not part of an enzyme system, and it is required in grams and not in milligrams like true vitamins. Choline can be formed from serine and methionine (Zempleni, 2007). Phosphatidylcholine is the main natural form of choline present in food, although a small quantity of free choline may also exist in plant material. Choline is necessary for the biosynthesis of phospholipids and acetylcholine (Zempleni, 2007), and it plays a fundamental role in the metabolism as a methyl group donor. Biologically active methyl groups may also be obtained from methionine, so one of the advantages of supplementing choline is an increase in the availability of methionine for protein synthesis. Harper *et al.* (1977) considered that choline deficiencies only occur when the ration is deficient in protein. The majority of rations contain sufficient quantities of choline to cover the minimum requirements of ruminants.

Bioavailability

Both choline naturally present in feedstuffs and synthetic supplements degrade by between 80 and 99% in the rumen, depending on the source (Sharma and Erdman, 1989). The flow of choline of microbial origin to the duodenum is slight (Mathison, 1986), and the little that is available comes from protozoal synthesis (Sharma and Erdman, 1988). Due to the high degradation of dietary choline, it is probable that in high-producing dairy cattle methionine, betaine (derived from degradation of choline), and de novo synthesis of choline play an important role as methyl group donors (NRC, 2001). Choline is involved in the metabolism and transport of lipids, and its bioavailability is therefore associated with the fat digestion and absorption process (Zempleni, 2007; Weiss and Ferreira, 2006a).

Functions

Choline is involved in the transport and metabolism of lipids, so that its supplementation is associated with an increase in the percentage of fat in milk and the control of the development of ketosis and fatty liver (Pinotti *et al.*, 2002; Juslin, 1965; Zeisel, 1993).

Recommendations for Choline

Suckling calves

Johnson *et al.* (1951) found choline deficiency in one-week-old calves given milk replacer rations containing 15% casein. The choline requirements estimated in this experiment were 260 mg/l of milk replacer (1,733 mg/kg DM). The NRC (2001) recommends the incorporation in milk replacer of 1,000 mg/kg DM.

Adult lactating cows

Current sources for formulating rations have not established recommendations for choline for lactating cows (INRA, 1988; NRC, 2001). In spite of its important role in metabolism, the quantity of choline available for absorption in the small intestine is small, and the use of sources protected against ruminal degradation is recommended. Postruminal supplementation or supplementation in protected form of 15 to 90 g of choline per day resulted in an increase in milk production of between 0 and 3 kg/d. Grummer *et al.* (1987) obtained an increase in milk production (from 29.5 to 31.6 kg of milk per day) on infusing 22 g of choline per day. Erdman and Sharma (1991) supplemented 0.24% protected choline chloride between weeks 5 and 21 postpartum, and obtained an increase in milk yield of 2.6 kg/d compared with the control group.

Sharma *et al.* (1988) observed that while oral dosage of choline (0, 10 and 20 g/kg DM) resulted in low recovery of choline in the duodenum and brought no production response, abomasal infusion of 30 g/d resulted in an increase of 0.45% and 0.14% fat and protein, respectively, in milk. Atkins et al. (1988) also observed no positive results on administering an oral supplement of choline. The NRC (2001) indicates that to establish recommendations for the transition cow and/or production cow would require more experimental studies.

However, since the recommendations of the NRC (2001), interest in the supplementary supply of choline has increased, as demonstrated by the growing number of studies published subsequently (Pinotti et al., 2002, 2003; Piepenbrink and Overton, 2003; Brusemeister and Sudekum, 2006; Cooke et al., 2007; Elek et al., 2008). **Table VIII** shows a summary of the principal effects observed with the additional supply of choline in dairy cattle. Some of the data suggest that the supplementation of choline in a form protected from ruminal degradation may effectively improve the yield and composition of milk, especially in rations low in protein or with limited availability of methionine (Eastridge, 2006). Weiss (2007) summarized the results of 12 experimental studies and concluded that the median increase in milk production when rumen protected choline was fed was about 2,3 kg/d during the first 2 months of lactation. With this level of response the additional supply of protected choline in the diet is considered profitable. The effects on the incidence of fatty liver are less clear (Weiss, 2007). With regard to the recommended dose, Pinotti et al. (2005) concluded that, although the data are insufficient to establish the real requirements of choline in dairy cattle, supplementation of between 12 and 20 g/d would be appropriate for dairy cattle in transition.

Table VIII. Supplementary supply of choline resistant to ruminal degradation in dairy cattle Effects on some productive and metabolic parameters

Treatment / dose[1]	Lactation phase[2]	Metabolic parameters[3]				Productive parameters[4]				Reference
		NEFA	BHB	Glucogen	Lipolysis/ fatty liver	Ingestion	Milk	Fat	Protein	
45, 60 or 75 g/d CPR	21 d P-P – 63 d P-L	(=/=)	(=/=)	(+/NI)	(+/NI)	(=/=)	(NA/=)	(NA/=+)	(NA/=)	Piepenbrink and Overton (2003)
56 g/d CPR	21 d P-P – 28 d P-L	(=/=)	(=/=)	(NI/=)	(NI/=)	(=/=)	(NA/+)	(NA/=)	(NA/=)	Zahra et al. (2006)
20 g/d	14 d P-P – 30 d P-L	(–/NI)	NI	NI	NI	NI	(NA/+)	(NA/+)	(NA/=)	Pinotti et al. (2005)
14 g/d CPR	45-60 d P-P	(–/NA)	(=/NA)	NE	(+/NI)	NA	NA	NA		Cooke et al. (2007)
25 g/d CPR P-P; 50 g/d CPR P-L	21 d P-P – 60 d P-L		NE	NE	NE	(=/=)	(NA/+)	(NA/+)	(NA/+)	Elek et al. (2008)

(1) CPR= g/d choline protected against ruminal degradation.
(2) P-P= pre-partum; P-L= in lactation.
(3) NEFA= non-esterified fatty acids; BHB= beta-hydroxy-butyrate; Effect of treatment compared to control (/); (pre-partum/post-partum)= +: increases; –: decreases; =: no change; NI: not indicated; NE: parameter not evaluated; NA= not applicable.
(4) Effect of treatment compared to control (/); (pre-partum/post-partum)= +: increases; –: decreases; =: no change; NI: not indicated; NE: parameter not evaluated; NA= not applicable.

NUTRITIONAL VALUE OF COW'S MILK FOR HUMAN NUTRITION

The ultimate objective of the production of foodstuffs of animal origin is to obtain nutritional, quality products for human consumption (Zempleni *et al.*, 2007; Haug *et al.*, 2007, **Table XIII**). Milk makes an important, although variable, contribution to providing the daily requirement of vitamins for human nutrition (**Table XII**).

The composition and proportion of nutrients supplied by cow's milk depends on various factors intrinsic and extrinsic to the animal. Among the factors related to the animal are the lactation phase, age, breed, energy balance of the animal, health of the udder and the cow, etc. (Lucas *et al.*, 2006; Nozière *et al.*, 2006; Haug *et al.*, 2007; Swensson *et al.*, 2007). Even more important, the composition of the milk can be modified by means of different management and feeding strategies (forage to concentrate ratio, type and proportion of ingredients used, vitamin-

mineral supplementation, incorporation of specific food additives, etc.). Thus, for example, one can achieve considerable changes (> 100% of change) in the content of conjugated linoleic acid and vitamins A and E, moderate changes (between 25 and 100% of change) in the fat and unsaturated fatty acid content, and minor changes (< 25% of change) in the folate, riboflavin and vitamin B_{12} content (Haug *et al.*, 2007). A study conducted in Sweden (Lindmark-Månsson *et al.*, 2003), compared the changes in the composition of cow's milk between 1970 and 1996, and a significant increase in the content of total solids, fat, casein, calcium and phosphorous was observed, which is evidence that there is a real possibility of modifying the nutritional composition of milk. Another more recent study (Swensson *et al.*, 2007), compared the changes in the vitamin supply of milk products per capita between 1970 and 2000 (**Figure 9**). In general,

Figure 9. Contribution of milk and milk products to human daily vitamin requirements. (Swensson, 2007)

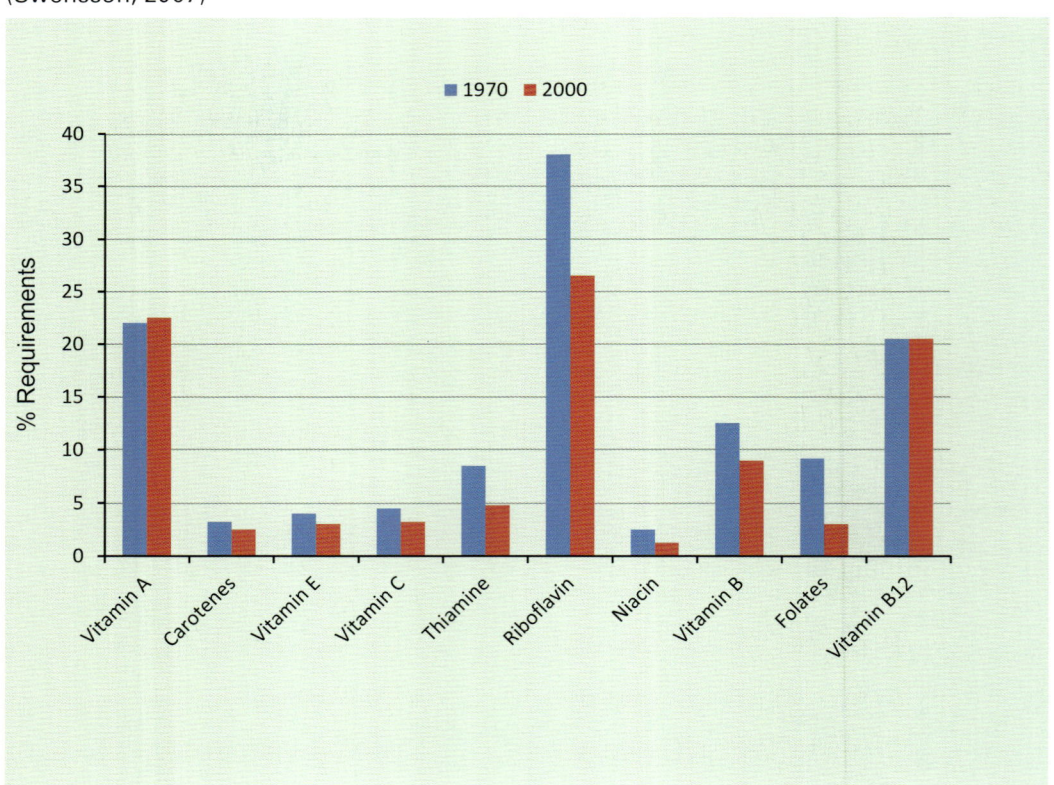

the supply has decreased for the majority of them, with the exception of vitamin A, which increased by 1.3%, and vitamin B$_{12}$, the supply of which remains constant. The most significant decreases have been in folic acid (71.4%), thiamine (47.2%), niacin (45.5%) and vitamin C (40.5%). Considering that the consumption of milk and dairy products is important in the human diet, it is necessary to reconsider some of the recommendations for the feeding of dairy cattle taking into account the contribution of milk in the human nutrition.

Table IX. Survey on the supplementation of vitamins A, D and E in commercial operations in the US[1] (adapted from Weiss. 1998)

| | Type of Cow[2] | | | |
	Dry	Peripartum	High Production	Low Production
Vitamin A				
NRC (2001)	40,000	40,000	80,000	51,600
Average	104,000	121,000	158,000	121,000
SD	42,000	55,000	48,000	37,000
Vitamin D				
NRC (2001)	10,000	10,000	25,000	16,000
Average	26,200	31,500	40,000	32,500
SD	10,000	12,500	10,700	8,200
Vitamin E				
NRC (2001)	150	150	375	240
Average	760	1080	590	450
SD	280	170	160	160

SD = Standard Devitation
(1) Survey conducted on 40 companies and nutrition consultants (Weiss, 1998).
(2) Average weight of cows=600 kg; Peripartum=21 d prepartum; High production=45 kg/d; Low production=22 kg/d.

Table X. Recommended vitamin supplementation levels for calves by different sources

| | | Source | | | | Source |
	Units	INRA (1988)	NRC (1989)	NRC (2001)	Units	DSM OVN (2011)
Vitamin A	IU/kg LW	42	42	42	IU/ head day	20000-32000
Vitamin D$_3$	-	-	-	-	IU/ head day	1400-1800
Vitamin E	IU/kg DM	40	40	50	IU/ head day	100-150
Vitamin K	-	-	-	-	mg/ head day	1.0-1.5
Vitamin B$_1$	mg/kg DM	-	-	6.5	mg/ head day	2.5-5.0
Vitamin B$_2$	mg/kg DM	-	-	-	mg/ head day	2.5-4.5
Vitamin B$_6$	mg/kg DM	-	-	6.5	mg/ head day	2.5-4.5
Vitamin B$_{12}$	mg/kg DM	-	-	0.07	mg/ head day	0.04-0.08
Niacin	mg/kg DM	-	-	10	mg/ head day	9.0-18
D-Panthothenic acid	mg/kg DM	-	-	13	mg/ head day	7.0-9.0
Folic acid	mg/kg DM	0.8	-	0.5	mg/ head day	0.2-0.3
Biotin	mg/kg DM	-	-	-	mg/ head day	0.05-0.10
Vitamin C	mg/kg DM	-	-	1.0-2.0	mg/ head day	250-500
Choline	mg/kg DM	-	-	1000	mg/ head day	500-750
ß-carotene	mg/kg DM	-	-	-	mg/ head day	100

Table XI Recommended vitamin supplementation levels for dairy cows by different sources

	Units	Source INRA (1988)	Source NRC (1989)	NRC (2001)	Units	Source DSM OVN (2011)	Maximum level in literature	Reference
Vitamin A								
Far-off & close-up	IU/kg LW	76	110	76	IU/head day	75000-100000		
Transition	IU/kg LW	76	110	76	IU/head day	75000-100000		
Lactation	IU/kg LW	76	110	76	IU/head day	100000-150000	200-250 IU/kgLW	Oldaham et al.,1991;Michel et al.,1994 - Acidosis
Vitamin D3								
Far-off & close-up	IU/kg LW	30	30	30	IU/head day	25000-35000		
Transition	IU/kg LW	30	30	30	IU/head day	25000-35000	50-70 IU/kg LW	Hibbs and Conrand, 1983
Lactation	IU/kg LW	30	30	30	IU/head day	30000-50000	50-70 IU/kg LW	Hibbs and Conrand, 1983
Vitamin E								
Far-off & close-up	IU/kg DM	15	15	50-80	mg/head day	1000-3000[1]	120-160 mg/kg DM	Politis et al., 1995; Weiss et al., 1997;Focant et al.,1998
Transition	IU/kg DM	15	15	50-80	mg/head day	1000-3000[1]		
Lactation	IU/kg DM	15	15	20	mg/head day	500-1000[2]	40-120 mg/kg DM	Weiss et al., 1997
Niacin								
Far-off & close-up	mg/day	-	-	-	mg/head day	-		
Transition	mg/day	-	-	-	mg/head day	5000-10000[3]		
Lactation	mg/day	-	-	-	mg/head day	5000-10000[3]	12000 mg/day	from 2 weeks pre-partum to 12 weeks post-partum
Biotin								
Far-off & close-up	mg/day	-	-	-	mg/head day	20[4]		
Transition	mg/day	-	-	-	mg/head day	20[4]		
Lactation	mg/day	-	-	-	mg/head day	20[4]	20 mg/day	Bergen et al.,1999;Fitzgerald et al.,2000;Midla et al.,1998
ß-carotene								
Far-off & close-up	mg/day	-	-	-	mg/head day	500-1000[5]	300-600 mg/day	Improved reproduction performances and reduced incidence of mastitis
Transition	mg/day	-	-	-	mg/head day	500-800[6]	300-600 mg/day	Improved reproduction performances and reduced incidence of mastitis
Lactation	mg/day	-	-	-	mg/head day	300-500[7]	300-600 mg/day	Improved reproduction performances and reduced incidence of mastitis

(1) Upper level from 21 days pre-partum through 28 days post-partum;
(2) Upper level for optimum udder health
(3) From 2 weeks before parturition until peak lactation;
(4) For optimum hoof health and milk yield
(5) Lower level during entire dry period (Far off and Close-up); upper level three to four weeks before calving (close-up only)
(6) 500-800 mg from 3 to 4 weeks before calving and 300-500 mg 4 to 6 week after calving
(7) Dry and fresh: beginning dry period until pregnancy is confirmed

Table XII. Variation in the vitamin content of milk and comparison with the recommended daily supplies in different countries.

Content[1] (per 100 g of milk)	Spain[2]	Sweden[2]	Denmark[4]	United States[5]	Australia/ New Zealand[6]	Averages[7] Intake	% of RDI
Water content, g	88.6	86.8	87.8	88.0	87.2	87.8	–
Protein, g	3.2	3.37	3.4	3.3	3.4	3.3	–
Lipids, g	3.6	4.34	3.5	3.3	4.0	3.7	–
Energy, KJ	260	NI	262	256	279	259.3	–
Cholesterol, mg	13.0	13.9	14.0	13.5	13.0	13.6	–
Vitamin A, (µg RE)	42	39.6	31	31	36	35.9	8.5
ß-carotenes, µg	22	20	16	NI	19	19.3	–
Vitamin D, µg	0.03	0.03	0.10	–	–	0.04	0.5
Vitamin E, µg	100	101	90	60	100	87.8	0.6
Vitamin K, µg	NI	0.41	–	0.20	–	0.2	0.2
Thiamine (B$_1$), µg	40	40	42	40	30	40.5	3.7
Riboflavin(B$_2$), µg	180	141	170	160	180	162.8	13.6
Niacin, µg	80	64	100	80	70	81.0	0.5
Vitamin B$_6$, µg	40	42	47	40	20	42.3	3.3
Vitamin B$_{12}$, µg	0.30	0.41	0.5	0.44	–	0.4	17.2
Pantothenic acid, µg	NI	340	340	NI	–	340.0	6.8
Folic acid, µg	5.0	5.6	11	NI	7.0	7.2	1.8
Vitamin C, mg	1.8	1.16	–	0.82	1.0	0.9	2.1

(1) – no content; NI= not indicated; Vitamin A: µg of retinol equivalents.
(2) Adapted from: La Industria alimentaria (http://www-ice.upc.edu/documents/eso/aliments/ HTML/ lacteo-3.html); Moreiras *et al.* (2006); whole pasteurized milk.
(3) Adapted from: Lindmark-Månsson *et al.* (2003); raw milk.
(4) Adapted from: in National Food Institute of Denmark (http://www.foodcomp.dk/fcdb_details. asp?FoodId=0156); whole milk, 3.5 % fat.
(5) Adapted from: in USDE, 2002. (http://www.nal.usda.gov/fnic/foodcomp/Data/SR21/nutrlist/sr21a318. pdf); whole milk, 3.25 % fat.
(6) Adapted from: Australian food composition tables, 2006 (www.foodstandards.gov.au/_srcfiles/ Final%20NUTTAB%202006%20Food%20Composition%20Tables%20-%20May%2020071.pdf); whole milk, 4% fat.
(7) % RDI= % of recommended daily intake. Approximate mean value, estimated from data available in the table; data appearing as – and Tr were computed as zero (0). RDI= recommended daily intake for an adult (19–65 years).

Table XIII. Recommended daily supply of vitamins in the human diet, according to age and physiological state.

Type and age group	Vitamin													
	A (µg RE/d)[1]	D (µg/d)[2]	E (mg/d)[3]	K (µg/d)[4]	B_1 (mg/d)	B_2 (mg/d)	B_3 (mg/d)[5]	B_6 (mg/d)	B_{12} (µg/d)	Biotin (µg/d)	Folic acid (µg/d)	Pantothenic acid (mg/d)	Vitamin C (mg/d)[6]	Choline (mg/d)
Infants and children														
0–6 months	180–375	5	4	2	0.2	0.3	2	0.1	0.4	5	80	1.7	25	125
7–12 months	190–400	5	5	2.5	0.3	0.4	4	0.3	0.7	6	80	1.8	30*	150
1–3 years	200–400	5	6	30	0.5	0.5	6	0.5	0.9	8	150	2.0	30*	200
4–6 years	200–450	5	7	55	0.6	0.6	8	0.6	1.2	12	200	3.0	30*	250–350
7–9 years	250–500	5	8–11	55–60	0.9	0.9	12	1.0	1.8	20	300	4.0	35*	375
Adolescents														
10–18 years	365–600	5	11–15	60–75	1.1–1.2	1.0–1.3	16	1.2–1.3	2.4	25	400	5.0	40*	400–550
Adult Women														
19–65 years	270–500	5–10	15	90	1.1	1.1	14	1.3	2.4	30	400	5.0	45	425
> 65 years	300–600	15	15	90	1.1	1.1	14	1.5	2.4	30	400	5.0	45	425
Gestating women	370–800	5	15	75–90	1.4	1.4	18	1.9	2.6	30	600	6.0	55	450
Lactating women	450–850	5	19	75–90	1.5	1.6	17	2.0	2.8	35	500	7.0	70	550
Men														
19–65 years	300–600	5–10	15	120	1.1	1.3	16	1.3	2.4	30	400	5.0	45	550
> 65 years	300–600	15	15	120	1.1	1.3	16	1.7	2.4	30	400	5.0	45	550

Source: Adapted from FAO (2004, available at: http://whqlibdoc.who.int/publications/2004/9241546123.pdf); for vitamin E, K, choline (IOM, 2000; Available at: http://www.iom.edu/Object.File/Master/7/296/0.pdf).
(1) RE= retinol equivalent (Average value – value recommended as insurance);
(2) Recommended daily intake (1 µg= 40 IU vitamin D);
(3) Equivalent α-tocopherol; Recommended daily intake;
(4) Filoquinones, recommended daily intake;
(5) Niacin equivalents; for infants between 0-6 months pre-formed niacin;
(6) Quantity required to saturate half the tissues with vitamin C in 97.5% of the population.
* arbitrary values.

CONCLUSIONS

Vitamins play a fundamental role in numerous vital functions. Under commercial conditions, vitamin deficiencies should not only be considered from the point of view of maintenance of physiological functions. They are also required to allow optimum production and to prevent clinical or subclinical pathologies. In the last decades, vitamin recommendations established by ration formulation systems, as well as those applied in field conditions by the industry, have substantially increased (**Table V**, **Table VIII** , **Table IX and Table X**), taking improved productivity health and welfare as evaluation criteria. The increases have been significant in vitamin E and moderate for vitamin A. Other vitamins previously considered unnecessary in the diet of adult ruminants, such as some of the water-soluble vitamins, may be beneficial under conditions of stress or high productivity (**Table VIII and Table XI**), although their use under commercial conditions might require the development of new forms less susceptable to degration in the rumen. Finally, the vitamin supply in dairy cattle is important not only from the perspective of animal production and its profitability. The ultimate objective is the production of quality milk that supplies all of the nutrients and vitamins in particular, to meet the requirements of consumers.

REFERENCES

Abdouli, H. & D. M. Schaefer. 1986. Impact of niacin and length of incubation on protein synthesis, soluble to total protein ratio and fermentative activity of ruminal micro-organisms. *J Anim Sci* 62: 244.

Akar, Y. & A. Gazioglu. 2006. Relationship between vitamin a and ß-carotene levels during the postpartum period and fertility parameters in cows with and without retained placenta. *Bull Vet Inst Pulawy* 50: 93–96.

Alderson, N. E., G. E. Mitchell, C. O. Little, R. E. Warner & R. E. Tucker. 1971. Preintestinal disappearance of vitamin E in ruminants. *J Nutr* 101: 655.

Aliev, A. A. & L. M. Burkova. 1987. Effect of choline chloride on the metabolism of nitrogen and choline in the stomach and intestines of lactating cows. *Skh Biol* 4: 80.

Alosilla, Jr., C. E., L. R. McDowell, N. S. Wilkinson, C. R. Staples, W. W. Thatcher, F. G. Martin & M. Blair. 2007. Bioavailability of vitamin A sources for cattle. *J Anim Sci*. 85:1235–1238.

Arambell, M. J., S. M. Dennis, D. O. Riddel, E. E. Bartley, J. L. Camac & A. D. Dayton. 1982. Effect of heat treated soybean meal with and without niacin on rumen fermentation. *J Anim Sci* 55(Suppl. 1): 405.

Arechiga, C. F., C. R. Staples, L. R. McDowell & P. J. Hansen. 1998. Effect of timed insemination and supplemental ß-carotene on reproduction and milk yield of dairy cows under heat stress. *J Dairy Sci* 81: 390–402.

Arikan, S. & R.G. Rodway. 2000. Effects of high density lipoprotein containing high or low beta-carotene concentrations on progesterone production and beta-carotene uptake and depletion by bovine luteal cells. *Anim Reprod Sci* 62: 253–263.

Arikan, S., H. S. Sands, R. G. Rodway, & D. N. Batchelder. 2002. Raman spectroscopy and imaging of ß-carotene in live corpus luteum cells. *Anim Reprod Sci* 71: 249–266.

Arnold, R. N., K. K. Scheller, S. C. Arp, S. N. Williams, D. R. Buege & D. M. Schaefer. 1992. Effect of long- or short-term feeding of α-tocopheryl acetate to Holstein and crossbred beef steers on performance, carcass characteristics, and beef color stability. *J Anim Sci* 70: 3055.

Astrup, H. N. & J. J. Nedkvitne. 1987. Effect of vitamin D supplement on cows and sheep. *Norw. J Agric Sci* 1: 87.

Atkins, K. B., R. A. Erdman & J. H. Vandersall. 1988. Dietary choline effects on milk and duodenal choline flow in dairy cattle. *J Dairy Sci* 71: 109.

Azzi, A., I. Breyer, M Feher, M. Pastori, R. Ricciarelli, S. Spycher, M. Staffieri, A. Stocker, S. Zimmer & J. M. Zingg. 2000. Specific cellular responses to α-tocopherol. *J Nutr* 130: 1649–1652.

Baldi, A. 2005. Vitamin E in dairy cows. *Livest Prod Sci* 98:117–122.

Baldi, A., F. Cheli, L. Pinotti & C. Pecorini. 2008. Nutrition in mammary gland health and lactation: Advances over eight Biology of Lactation in Farm Animals meetings. *J Anim Sci*. 86(Suppl. 1):3–9.

Baldi A, Pinotti L. (2008) Lipophilic microconstituents of milk Adv. Exp. Med. Biol.606:109-25.

Bartlett, C.A., C.G. Schwab, J.W. Smith, and J.B. Holter. 1983. Supplemental niacin for dairy cows under field conditions. II. Effects on production. J. Dairy. Sci. 66(Suppl. 1):176 (Abstr.).

Bartley, E. E., E. L. Herod, R. M. Bechtle, D. A. Sapienza, B. E. Brent & A. Davidovich. 1979. Effect of monensin or lasalocid, with and without niacin or amicloral, on rumen fermentation and feed efficiency. *J Anim Sci* 49: 1066.

Batra, T. R., M. Hidiroglou & M. W. Smith. 1992. Effect of vitamin E on incidence of mastitis in dairy cattle. Can *J Anim Sci* 72: 287.

Bendich, A. 1993. Physiological role of antioxidants in the immune system. *J Dairy Sci* 76: 2789.

Bergsten, C., P.R. Greenough, J.M. Gay, R.C. Dobson and C.C. Gay (1999) A controlled field trial of the effects of biotin supplementation on milk production and hoof lesions. J. Dairy Sci. 82 (Suppl.1):34.

Bindas, E. M., F. C. Gwazdauskas, R. J. Aiello, J. H. Herbein, M. L. McGilliard & C. E. Polan. 1984a. Reproductive and metabolic characteristics of dairy cattle supplemented with ß-carotene. *J Dairy Sci* 67: 1249.

Bindas, E. M., F. C. Gwazdauskas, M. L. McGilliard & C. E. Polan. 1984b. Progesterone responses to human chorionic gonadotropin in dairy cattle supplemented with ß-carotene. *J Dairy Sci* 67: 2978.

Blomhoff, R., M. H. Green, J. B. Green, T. Berg & K. Normun. 1991. Vitamin A metabolism: new perspectives on absorption, transport and storage. *Physiological Reviews.* 7: 951.

Bobe, G., J. W. Young & D. C. Beitz. 2004. Invited review: pathology, etiology, prevention, and treatment of fatty liver in dairy cows. *J Dairy Sci* 87: 3105–3124.

Bourne, N., D. C. Wathes, M. McGowan & R. A. Laven. 2007a. A comparison of the effects of parenteral and oral administration of supplementary vitamin E on plasma vitamin E concentrations in dairy cows at different stages of lactation. *Livest Sci* 106: 57–64.

Bourne, N., R. Laven, D. C. Wathes, T. Martinez & M. McGowan. 2007b. A meta-analysis of the effects of vitamin-E supplementation on the incidence of retained fetal membranes in dairy cows. *Theriogenology* 67: 494–501.

Bourne, N., D. C. Wathes, K. E. Lawrence, M. McGowan & R. A. Laven. 2008. The effect of parenteral supplementation of vitamin E with selenium on the health and productivity of dairy cattle in the UK. *Vet J* 177: 381–387 (Abstract).

Blomhoff, 1994. R. Blomhoff, Editor, Vitamin A in health and disease, Marcel Dekker Inc., New York.

Bramley, P. M., I. Elmadfa, A. Kafatos, F. J. Kelly, Y. Manios, H. E. Roxborough, W. Schuch, P. J. A. Sheehy & K. H. Wagner. 2000. Review, vitamin E. *J Sci Food Agric* 80: 913–938.

Bremel, D. H., R. W. Hemken, G. Heersche Jr., L. A. Edgerton & D. Olds. 1982. Effects of b-carotene on metabolic and reproductive parameters in lactating dairy cows. *J Dairy Sci* 65 (Suppl. 1): 178.

Breves, G., M. Brandt, H. Hoeller & K. Rohr. 1981. Flow of thiamin to the duodenum in dairy cows fed different rations. *J Agric Sci Camb.* 96: 587.

Brigelius-Flohé, R., F. J. Kelly, J. T. Salonen, J. Neuzil, J. M. Zingg & A. Azzi. 2002. The European perspective on vitamin E: current knowledge and future research. *Am J Clin Nutr* 76, 703– 716.

Brusemeister, F. & K. Sudekum. 2006. Rumen-protected choline for dairy cows: the *in situ* evaluation of a commercial source and literature evaluation of effects on performance and interactions between methionine and choline metabolism. *Anim Res* 55:93–104.

Brzezinska-Slebodzinska, E., J. K. Miller, J. D. Quigley & J. R. Moore. 1994. Antioxidant status of dairy cows supplemented prepartum with vitamin E and selenium. *J Dairy Sci* 77: 3087.

Calderón, F., B. Chauveau-Duriot, P. Pradel, B. Martin, B. Graulet, M. Doreau & P. Nozière. 2007. Variations in carotenoids, vitamins A and E, and color in cow's plasma and milk following a shift from hay diet to diets containing increasing levels of carotenoids and vitamin E. *J Dairy Sci* 90: 5651–5664.

Campbell, J. M., M. R. Murphy, R. A. Christensen & T. R. Overton. 1994. Kinetics of niacin supplements in lactating dairy cows. *J Dairy Sci* 77: 566.

Campbell, J. M. & J. Miller. 1998. Effect of supplemental dietary vitamin E and zinc on reproductive performance of dairy cows and heifers fed excess iron. *J Dairy Sci* 81: 2693.

Cardinault, N., M. Doreau, C. Poncet & P. Nozière. 2006. Digestion and absorption of carotenoids in sheep given fresh red clover. *Anim Sci* 82: 49–55.

Carlson, L. A. 2005. Nicotinic acid: The broad-spectrum lipid drug. A 50th anniversary review. *J Intern Med* 258:94–114.

Castillo, C., J. Hernandez, A. Bravo, M. Lopez-Alonso, V. Pereira & J. L. Benedito. 2005. Oxidative status during late pregnancy and early lactation in dairy cows. *Vet J* 169: 286–292.

Chaiyotwittayakun, A., R. J. Erskine, P. C. Bartlett, T. H. Herdt, P. M. Sears & R. J. Harmon. 2002. The effect of ascorbic acid and L-histidine therapy on acute mammary inflammation in dairy cattle. *J Dairy Sci* 85:60–67.

Chamberlain, J. L. & P. D. French. 2006. The effects of nicotinic acid supplementation during late gestation on lipolysis and feed intake during the transition period. *J Anim Sci* 89(Suppl): 232.

Charmley, E. & J. W. G. Nicholson. 1994. Influence of dietary fat source on oxidative stability and fatty acid composition of milk from cows receiving a low or high level of dietary vitamin E. *Can J Anim Sci* 74: 657.

Chauveau-Duriot, B., D. Thomas, J. Portelli & M. Doreau. 2005. Carotenoids content in forages: variation during conservation. *Renc Rech Ruminants* 12, 117.

Chawla, R. & H. Kaur. 2004. Plasma antioxidant vitamin status of periparturient cows supplemented with α-tocopherol and ß-carotene. Short communication. *Anim Feed Sci Technol* 114: 279–285.

Cheli, F., I. Politis, L. Rossi, E. Fusi & A. Baldi. 2003. Effects of retinoids on proliferation and plasminogen activator expression in a bovine mammary epithelial cell line. *J Dairy Res* 70: 367–372.

Chew, B. P. 1987. Vitamin A and carotene on host defense. *J Dairy Sci* 70: 2732.

Chew, B. P. 1993. Role of carotenoids in the immune response. *J Dairy Sci* 76: 2804.

Chew, B. P. & L. A. Johnson. 1985. Effects of supplemental vitamin A and ß-carotene on mastitis in dairy cows. *J Dairy Sci* 68(Suppl.1): 191.

Chew, B. P. & J. S. Park. 2004. Carotenoid action on the immune response. *J Nut* 134: 251–26l.

Coelho, M. B. 1991. Vitamin stability in premixes and feeds: a practical approach. BASF Tech, Symp. Bloomington, MN. Pp 56–71.

Cohen-Fernandez, S., P. Budowski, I. Ascarelli, H. Neumak & A. Bondi. 1976. Low utilization of carotene by sheep. *Int J Vit Nutr Res* 46: 446.

Combs, Jr., G. F. 1992. The vitamins: fundamental aspects in nutrition and health. Academ. Press. Inc.

Cooke, R. F., N. Silva del Río, D. Z. Caraviello, S. J. Bertics, M. H. Ramos & R. R. Grummer. 2007. Supplemental choline for prevention and alleviation of fatty liver in dairy cattle. *J Dairy Sci* 90:2413–2418.

Craven, N. & M. R. Williams. 1985. Defenses of the bovine mammary gland against infection and prospects for their enhancement. *Vet Immunol Immunopathol* 10: 71.

Croom, J. R.., A. H. Rakes, A. C. Linnerud, G. A. Ducharme & J. M. Elliot. 1981. Vitamin B_{12} administration for milk fat synthesis in lactating dairy cows fed a low fiber diet. *J Dairy Sci* 64: 1555.

Cummins, K. A. & C. J. Brunner. 1991. Effect of calf housing on plasma ascorbate and endocrine and immune function. *J Dairy Sci* 74: 1582.

Da Costa Gomez, C., M. Al Masri, W. Steinberg and Hj. Abel (1998) Effect of varying hay/barley proportions on microbial biotin metabolism in the rumen simulating fermenter (RUSITEC). Proc. Soc. Nutr. Physiol. 7(abstr.).

Dahlquist, S. P. & B. P. Chew. 1985. Effect of vitamin A and b-carotene on mastitis in dairy cows during the early dry period. *J Dairy Sci* 68 (Suppl. 1): 191.

Daniel, L. R., B. P. Chew, T. S. Tanaka & L. W. Tjoelker. 1991. ß-carotene and vitamin A effects on bovine phagocyte function in vitro during the peripartum period. *J Dairy Sci* 74: 124.

Daynes, R. A., B. A. Araneo, J. Hennebold, E. Enioutina & H. H. Mu. 1995. Steroids as regulators of the mammalian immune response. *J Invest Dermatol* 105: 14S.

Debier, C., J. Pottier, C. Goffe & Y. Larondelle. 2005. Present knowledge and unexpected behaviours of vitamins A and E in colostrum and milk. *Livest Prod Sci* 98: 135–147.

Debier, C. & Y. Larondelle. 2005. Vitamins A and E: metabolism, roles and transfer to offspring. *Br J Nut* 93: 153–174.

Deuchler, K. N., L. S. Piperova & R. A. Erdman. 1998. Milk choline secretion as an indirect indicator of post-ruminal choline supply. *J Dairy Sci* 81: 238.

Distl, O. & D. Schmid. 1994. Influence of biotin supplementation on the formation, hardness and health of claws in dairy cows. *Tierärztliche Umschau* 49: 581–584.

Donoghue, S., W. J. Donawick & D. S. Kronfeld. 1983. Transfer of vitamin A from intestine to plasma in lambs fed low and high intakes of vitamin A. *J Nutr* 113: 2197.

Drackley, J. K. 1992. Niacin and carnitine in the nutrition of dairy cows. Proc Pacific Northwest Nutr. Conf. Tech. Symp., October 20, Lonza Inc. Ed., Spokane, WA. 8.

Drackley, J. K., S. S. Donkin, & C. K. Reynolds. 2006. Major advances in fundamental dairy cattle nutrition. *J Dairy Sci* 89:1324–1336.

Driver, L. S., R. C. Grummer & L. H. Schultz. 1990. Effects of feeding heat-treated soybeans and niacin to high producing cows in early lactation. *J Dairy Sci* 73: 463.

Eastridge, M. L. 2006. Major advances in applied dairy cattle nutrition. *J Dairy Sci* 89:1311–1323.

Eaton, H. D., J. E. Rousseau, R. C. Hall, Jr., H. I. Frier & J. J. Lucas. 1972. Revaluation of the minimum vitamin A requirements of Holstein male calves based upon elevated cerebrospinal fluid pressure. *J Dairy Sci* 55: 232.

Elek, P., J. R. Newbold, T. Gaal, L. Wagner & F. Husveth. 2008. Effects of rumen-protected choline supplementation on milk production and choline supply of periparturient dairy cows. Animal: 1– 7.

Enjalbert, F., M. C. Nicot & A. J. Packington. 2008. Effects of peripartum biotin supplementation of dairy cows on milk production and milk composition with emphasis on fatty acids profile. *Livest Sci* 114: 287–295.

Erdman, R. A. 1992. Vitamins. In: Van Horn H. H. and C. J. Wilcox. (Eds.). Large Dairy Herd Management. American Dairy Science Association, Champaign, IL. 297–308.

Erdman, R. A. & B. K. Sharma. 1991. Effect of dietary rumen-protected choline in lactating dairy cows. *J Dairy Sci* 74: 1641.

Erdman, R. A., R. M. Shaver & J. H. Vandersall. 1984. Dietary choline for the lactating cow: possible effects on milk fat synthesis. *J Dairy Sci* 67: 410.

Erickson, P. S., M. R. Murphy & J. H. Clark. 1992. Supplementation of dairy cow diets with calcium salts of long-chain fatty acid in early lactation. *J Dairy Sci* 75: 1078.

Erskine, R. J., R. J. Eberhart, P. J. Grasso & R. W. Scholz. 1989. Introduction of *Escherichia coli* mastitis in cows fed selenium-deficient or selenium-supplemented diets. *Am J Vet Res* 50: 2093.

Ferreira, G. & W. P. Weiss. 2007. Effect of biotin on activity and gene expression of biotin-dependent carboxylases in the liver of dairy cows. *J Dairy Sci* 90:1460–1466.

Ferreira, G., W. P. Weiss & L. B. Willett. 2007. Changes in measures of biotin status do not reflect milk yield responses when dairy cows are fed supplemental biotin. *J Dairy Sci* 90:1452–1459.

Fitzgerald, T., B. W. Norton, R. Elliott, H. Podlich & O. L. Svendsen. 2000. The influence of long-term supplementation with biotin on the prevention of lameness in pasture fed dairy cows. *J Dairy Sci* 83: 338.

Focant, M. 1998. The effect of vitamin E supplementation of cow diets containing rapeseed and linseed on the prevention of milk fat oxidation. *J Dairy Sci* 81: 1095.

Franklin S. T., C. E. Sorenson & D. C. Hammell. 1998. Influence of vitamin A supplementation in milk on growth, health, concentration of vitamins in plasma, and immune parameters of calves. *J Dairy Sci* 81: 2623.

French, P. D. 2004. Nicotinic acid supplemented at a therapeutic level minimizes prepartum feed intake depression in dairy cows. *J Dairy Sci* 87(Suppl): 345 (Abstract).

Frigg, M., O. C. Straub & D. Hartmann. 1993. The bioavailability of supplemental biotin in cattle. *Int J Vitam Nutr Res* 63: 122.

Frobish, R. A. & C. L. Davis. 1977. Theory involving propionate and vitamin B_{12} in the low-milk fat syndrome. *J Dairy Sci* 60: 268.

Fronk, T. J. & L. H. Schultz. 1979. Oral nicotinic acid as a treatment for ketosis. *J Dairy Sci* 62: 1804.

Girard, C. L. & J. J. Matte. 1998. Dietary supplements of folic acid during lactation: Effects on the performance of dairy cows. *J Dairy Sci* 81: 1412.

Girard, C. L. & J. J. Matte. 2005b. Effects of intramuscular injections of vitamin B_{12} on lactation performance of dairy cows fed dietary supplements of folic acid and rumen-protected methionine. *J Dairy Sci* 88:671–676.

Girard, C. L. & J. J. Matte. 2005a. Folic acid and vitamin B_{12} requirements of dairy cows: A concept to be revised. *Livest Prod Sci* 98: 123–133.

Girard, C. L., J. J. Matte & G. F. Tremblay. 1995. Gestation and lactation of dairy cows: a role for folic acid? *J Dairy Sci* 78: 404.

Girard, C. L., H. Lapierre, J. J. Mattee, & G. E. Lobley. 2005. Effects of dietary supplements of folic acid and rumen-protected methionine on lactational performance and folate metabolism of dairy cows. *J Dairy Sci* 88:660–670.

Goff, J. P., K. Kimura & R. L. Horst. 2002. Effect of mastectomy on milk fever, energy, and vitamins A, E, and ß-carotene at parturition. *J Dairy Sci* 85:1427–1436.

Goodman, D. S. 1984. Vitamin A and retinoids in health and disease. *N Engl J Med* 310: 1023–1031.

Gould, D. H., M. M. McAllister, J. C. Savage & D. W. Hamar. 1991. High sulfide concentrations in rumen fluid associated with nutritionally induced poliencephalomalacia in calves. *Am J Vet Res* 52: 1164.

Grasso, P. J., R. W. Scholz, R. J. Erskine & R. J. Eberhart. 1990. Phagocytosis, bactericidal activity, and oxidative metabolism of milk neutrophils from dairy cows fed selenium-supplemented and selenium-deficient diets. *Am J Vet Res* 51: 2.

Graulet, B., J. J. Matte, A. Desrochers, L. Doepel, M. F. Palin & C. L. Girard. 2007. Effects of dietary supplements of folic acid and vitamin B_{12} on metabolism of dairy cows in early lactation. *J Dairy Sci* 90: 3442–3455.

Grummer, R. R., L. E. Armentano & M. S. Marcus. 1987. Lactation response to short-term abomasal infusion of choline, inositol, and lecithin. *J Dairy Sci* 70: 2518.

Grummer, R. R., D. G. Mashek & A. Hayırli. 2004. Dry matter intake and energy balance in the transition period. *Vet Clin North Amer Food Anim Pract* 20: 447–470.

Gyang, E. O., J. B. Stevens, W. G. Olson, S. D. Tsitsamis & E. A. Usenik. 1984. Effects of selenium-vitamin E injection on bovine polymorphonucleated leukocytes phagocytosis and killing of *Staphylococcus aureus*. *Am J Vet Res* 45: 175.

Haliloglu, S., N. Baspinar, B. Serpek, H. Erdem & Z. Bulut. 2002. Vitamin A and beta carotene levels in plasma, corpus luteum and follicular fluid of cyclic and pregnant cattle. *Reprod Dom Anim* 37:96–99.

Hannah, S. M. & M. D. Stern. 1985. Effect of supplemental niacin or niacinamide and soybean source on ruminal bacterial fermentation in continuous culture. *J Anim Sci* 61: 1252.

Harmeyer, J. & U. Kollenkirchen. 1989.Thiamin and niacin in ruminant nutrition. *Nut Res Reviews* 2: 201–225.

Harper, H. A., V. W. Rodwell & P. A. Mayes. 1977. *Review of Physiological Chemistry*. 16th edn. California: Lange Medical Publishers.

Harrison, J. H., D. D. Hancock & H. R. Conrad. 1984. Vitamin E and selenium for reproduction of the dairy cow. *J Dairy Sci* 67: 123.

Hartman D. & L. Dryden. 1974. The vitamins in milk and milk products. In: B. H. Webb, A. H. Johnson, and J. A. Alford (Eds.). *Fundamentals of Dairy Chemistry*. 2nd ed. AVI Publishing Co. Wesport, CT.

Haug, A., A.T. Høstmark & O. M. Harstad. 2007. Bovine milk in human nutrition – a review. *Lipids in Health and Disease* 6: 25–41.

Havemose, M. S., M. R. Weisbjerg, W. L. P. Bredie & J. H. Nielsen. 2004. Influence of feeding different types of roughage on the oxidative stability of milk. *International Dairy Journal* 14: 563–570.

Hedges, V., R. W. Blowey, A. J. Packington, C. J. O'Callaghan & L. E. Green. 2001. A longitudinal field trial of the effect of biotin supplementation on lameness in dairy cows. *J Dairy Sci* 84:1969–1975.

Heirman, L.R., *et al.*, (1990) Effects of Dietary Beta-Carotene on Lymphocyte Function in Peripartum Dairy Cows. J. Dairy Sci. 73 (Supp. 1): 166.

Hemingway, R. G. 2003. The influences of dietary intakes and supplementation with selenium and vitamin E on reproduction diseases and reproduction efficiency in cattle and sheep. A review. *Veter Res Communic* 27: 157–174.

Hibbs, J. W. & H. R. Conrad. 1983. The relation of calcium and phosphorus intake on digestion and the effects of vitamin D feeding on the utilization of calcium and phosphorus by lactating dairy cows. Rep No. 1150. Ohio State Univ.

Hidiroglou M., T. R. Batra & X. Zhoa. 1977. Comparison of vitamin C bioavailability after multiple or single oral dosing of different formulations in sheep. *Reprod Nutr Dev* 37: 443.

Hidiroglou, N., L. R. McDowell & O. Balbuena. 1989. Plasma tocopherol in sheep and cattle after ingesting free or acetylated tocopherol. *J Dairy Sci* 72: 1793.

Hidiroglou M., T. R. Batra & M. Ivan. 1995. Effects of supplemental vitamins E and C on the immune responses of calves. *J Dairy Sci* 78: 1578.

Hill G. M., S. E. Williams, S. N. Williams, L. R. McDowell, N. Wilkinson & B. E. Mullinix. 1995. Vitamin A and vitamin E fed at high levels in steer feedlot diets: tissue alpha-tocopherol and performance. University of Georgia (UGA) *Animal & Dairy Science Annual Report*. pp. 7.

Hogan, J. S., K. L. Smith, W. P. Weiss, D. A. Todhunter & W. L. Schockey. 1990. Relationships among vitamin E, selenium, and bovine blood neutrophils. *J Dairy Sci* 73: 2372.

Hogan, J. S., W. P. Weiss, D. A. Todhuner, K. L. Smith & P. S. Schoenberger. 1992. Bovine neutrophil response to parenteral vitamin E. *J Dairy Sci* 75.399.

Hogan, J. S., W. P. Weiss & K. L. Smith. 1993. Role of vitamin E and selenium in host defense against mastitis. *J Dairy Sci* 76: 2795.

Hopper, J. H. & B. C. Johnson. 1955. The production and study of an acute nicotinic acid deficiency in the calf. *J Nutr* 56: 303.

Horner, J. L., C. E. Coppock, J. M. Labore, J. K. Lanham & D. H. Nave. 1986. Influence of niacin and whole cottonseed on intake, milk yield and composition, and systemic responses of dairy cows. *J Dairy Sci* 69: 3087.

Horner, J. L., C. E. Coppock, J. M. Labore, J. K. Lanham & D. H. Nave.1988. Effects of whole cottonseed, niacin, and niacinamide on in vitro rumen fermentation and on lactating Holstein cows. *J Dairy Sci* 71: 3334.

Horst, R. L. & E.T. Littledike. 1982. Comparison of plasma concentration of vitamin D and its metabolites in young and aged domestic animals. *Comp Biochem Physiol* (B) 73: 485.

Horst, R. L., J. P. Goff & T. A. Reinhardt. 1994. Calcium and vitamin D metabolism in the dairy cow. *J Dairy Sci* 77: 1936.

Horst, R.L., J. P. Goff, T. A. Reinhardt & D. R. Buxton. 1997. Strategies for preventing milk fever in dairy cattle. *J Dairy Sci* 80:1269–1280.

Horst, R. L., J. P. Goff & T. A. Reinhardt. 2005. Adapting to the transition between gestation and lactation: differences between rat, human and dairy cow. *J Mammary Gland Biol Neoplasia* 10: 141–156.

Hurley, W. L. & L. M. Doane. 1989. Recent developments in the role of vitamins and minerals in reproduction. *J Dairy Sci* 72: 784.

Ikeda, Sh., M. Kitagawa, H. Imai & M.Yamada. 2005. Review: The roles of vitamin A for cytoplasmic maturation of bovine oocytes. *J Reprod Dev* 51: 23–35.

INRA. 1988. Alimentation des bovins, ovins et caprins. Institut National de la Recherche Agronomique. Paris. 471 pp.

Jaster, E. H., G. F. Hartnell & M. F. Hutjens. 1983. Feeding supplemental niacin for milk production in six dairy herds. *J Dairy Sci* 66: 1046.

Johnson, B. C., H. H. Mitchell & A. Pinkos. 1951. Choline deficiency in the calf. *J Nutr* 43: 37.

Joyce, P. W., W. K. Sanchez & J. P. Goff. 1997. Effect of anionic salts in prepartum diets based on alfalfa. *J Dairy Sci* 80: 2866–2875.

Jukola, E., J. Hakkarainen, H. Saloniemi & S. Sankari. 1996. Blood selenium, vitamin E, vitamin A and carotene concentrations and udder health, fertility treatments, and fertility. *J Dairy Sci* 79: 838.

Juslin, K. E. 1965. On the effect of choline chloride and cyanocobalamine on the livers of cows with parturient paresis. *Nord Veterinaermed* 17: 169.

Kawashima, C., E. Kaneko, C. Amaya Montoya, M. Matsui, N.Yamagishi, N. Matsunaga, M. Ishii, K. Kida, Y. I. Miyake & A. Miyamoto. 2006. Relationship between the first ovulation within three weeks postpartum and subsequent ovarian cycles and fertility in high producing dairy cows. *J Reprod Dev* 52: 479–486.

Kawashima, C., K. Kida, F. J. Schweigert & A. Miyamoto. 2009. Relationship between plasma ß-carotene concentrations during the peripartum period and ovulation in the first follicular wave postpartum in dairy cows. *Anim Reprod Sci.* 111:105–111

Kawashima, C., S. Nagashima, Y. Fujihara, F.J. Schweigert, K. Sawada, A. Miyamoto and K. Kida. 2009b. Effect of beta-carotene supply during the close-up dry period on ovulation at the first follicular wave postpartum in dairy cows. J. Dairy Sci. 92 E-Suppl. 1:106.

Kay, J. K., J. R. Roche, E. S. Kolver, N. A. Thomson & L. H. Baumgard. 2005. A comparison between feeding systems (pasture andTMR) and the effect of vitamin E supplementation on plasma and milk fatty acid profiles in dairy cows. *J Dairy Res* 72:322–332.

Kleczkowski, M., W. Klucinski, A. Shaktur &

J. Sikora. 2005. Concentration of ascorbic acid in the blood of cows with subclinical mastitis. *Pol J Vet Sci* 8: 121–125.

Kung, L., K. Gubert & J. T. Huber. 1980. Supplemental niacin for lactating cows fed diets of natural protein or nonprotein nitrogen. *J Dairy Sci* 63: 2020.

Lacetera, N., U. Bernabucci, B. Ronchi & A. Nardone. 1996. Effects of selenium and vitamin E administration during a late stage of pregnancy on colostrum and milk production in dairy cows, and on passive immunity and growth of their offspring. *Am J Vet Res* 57: 1776.

Lanham, J. K., C. E. Coppock, K. N. Brooks, D. L. Wilks & J. L. Horner. 1992. Effects of whole cottonseed or niacin or both on casein synthesis by lactating Holstein cows. *J Dairy Sci* 75: 184.

Larson, L. L., J. Y. Wang, F. G. Owen & J. E.. Meader. 1983. Effect of beta-carotene supplementation during early lactation on reproduction. *J Dairy Sci* 66(Suppl. 1): 240.

Lassiter, C. A., G. M.Ward, C. F. Huffman, C.W. Duncan & H. D. Welester. 1953. Crystalline vitamin B_{12} requirements of the young dairy calf. *J Dairy Sci* 36: 997.

LeBlanc, S. J., T. H. Herdt, W. M. Seymour, T. F. Duffield & K. E. Leslie. 2004. Peripartum serum vitamin E, retinol, and beta-carotene in dairy cattle and their association with disease. *J Dairy Sci* 87:609–619.

Leedle, R. A., J. A. Z. Leedle & M. D. Butine. 1993. Vitamin E is not degraded by ruminal microorganisms: assessment with ruminal contents from a steer fed a high-concentrate diet. *J Dairy Sci* 71: 3442.

Lindmark-Månsson, H., R. Fonden & H. E. Pettersson. 2003. Composition of Swedish milk. *Int Dairy J* 13, 409–425.

Lotthammer, K.H. 1979. Importance of beta-carotene for the fertility of dairy cattle. Feedstuffs 51(43):16.

Lotthammer, K. H., L. Ahlswede & H. Meyer. 1979. Untersuchungen uber eine spezifische, vitamin-A-unabhängige Wirkung des b-carotins auf die Fertilität des Rindes. 2. Mitt: Weitere klinische Befunde und Befruchtungsergebnisse. *Dtsch Tierärztl Wochenschr* 83: 353.

Lucas, A., C. Agabriel, B. Martin, A. Ferlay, I. Verdier-Metz, J. B. Coulon & E. Rock. 2006. Relationships between the conditions of cow's milk production and the contents of components of nutritional interest in raw milk farmhouse cheese. *Lait* 86: 177–202.

Majee, D. N., E. C. Schwab, S. J. Bertics,

W. M. Seymour & R. D. Shaver. 2003. Lactation performance by dairy cows fed supplemental biotin and a B-vitamin blend. *J Dairy Sci* 86:2106–2112.

Margerison, J. K., B. Winkler, G. Penny & A. Packington. 2003. The effect of biotin supplementation on milk yield, reproduction and lameness in dairy cattle. *J Dairy Sci* 86 (Suppl): 250.

Mascio, Di, P., M. E. Murphy & H. Sies. 1991. Antioxidant defense systems: the role of carotenoids, tocopherols, and thiols. *Am J Clin Nutr* 53:(Suppl): 194S.

Mason, J. B. 2003. Biomarkers of nutrient exposure and status in one-carbon (methyl) metabolism. *J Nutr* 133: 941S–947S.

Mathison. G. W. 1986. B-vitamins, choline, inositol and paraaminobenzoic acid for ruminants. In: 21th Annual Pacific Northwest Animal Nutrition Conference. Vancouver. 107-157.

McDowell, L.R. 2000. Reevaluation of the metabolic essentiality of the vitamins. Asian-Aust. J. Anim. Sci. 13:115

McDowell, L. R. 2004. Re-evaluation of the essentiality of the vitamins. In: California Animal Nutrition Conference, Fresno, Ca. 37–67.

McDowell, L. R. 2006. Vitamin nutrition of livestock animals: Overview from vitamin discovery to today. *Canadian Journal of Animal Science* 86, 171–179.

Meyer, E., I. La Mote & C. Burvenich. 2005. Retinoids and steroids in bovine mammary gland immunobiology. *Livest Prod Sci* 98:33–46.

Michal, J. J., L. R. Heirman, T. S. Wong & B. P. Chew. 1994. Modulatory effects of dietary carotene on blood and mammary leukocyte function in periparturient dairy cows. *J Dairy Sci* 77: 1408.

Midla, L. T., K. H. Hoblet, W. P. Weiss & M. L. Moeschberger. 1998. Supplemental dietary biotin for prevention of lesions associated with aseptic clinical laminitis (pododermatitis aseptica diffusa) in primiparous Holsteins. *Am J Vet Res* 59: 733.

Miller, B. L., J. C. Meiske & R. D. Goodrich. 1986. Effects of grain source and concentrate level on B-vitamin production and absorption in steers. JAS 62: 473.

Miller, J. K., E. Brzezinska-Slebodzinska & F. C. Madsen. 1993. Oxidative stress, antioxidants and animal function. *J Dairy Sci* 76: 2812.

Mizwicki, K. L. 1976. Niacin and nitrogen metabolism in sheep. MSc Thesis, University of Illinois, Urbana, USA.

Mohri, M., H. A. Seifi &. J. Khodadadi. 2005. Effects of preweaning parenteral supplementation of vitamin E and selenium on hematology, serum proteins, and weight gain in dairy calves. *Comp Clin Pathol* 14: 149–154.

Mora, O., J. L. Romano, E. González, F. J. Ruiz & A. Shimada. 1999. In vitro and in situ disappearance of beta-carotene and lutein from lucerne (*Medicago sativa*) hay in bovine and caprine ruminal fluids. *Journal of the Science of Food and Agriculture* 79: 273–276.

Moreiras, O, A. Carbajal, L. Cabrera & C. Cuadrado. 2006. Tablas de composición de alimentos. Ediciones Pirámide (10ª edición). Madrid, España. p. 244,

Muller, L. D., A. J. Heinrichs, J. B. Cooper & Y. H. Atkin. 1986. Supplemental niacin for lactating cows during summer feeding. *J Dairy Sci* 69: 1416.

Naresh, R., S. K. Dwivedi, D. Swarup, & R. C. Patra. 2002. Evaluation of ascorbic acid treatment in clinical and subclinical mastitis of Indian dairy cows. *Asian-Australas. J Anim Sci* 15: 905–911.

Ndiweni N. & J. M. Finch, 1996. Effects of in vitro supplementation with tocopherol and selenium on bovine neutrophil functions: implications for resistance to mastitis. *Vet Immunology and Immunopathology* 51: 67.

Nonnecke, B. J., R. L. Horst, W. R. Waters, P. Dubeski & J. A. Harp. 1999. Modulation of fat-soluble vitamin concentrations and blood mononuclear leukocyte populations in milk replacer-fed calves by dietary vitamin A and beta-carotene. *J Dairy Sci* 82: 2632.

Nonnecke, B. J., M. P. Roberts, J. D. Godkin, R. L. Horst, D. C. Hammell & S.T. Franklin. 2001. Influence of supplemental, dietary vitamin A on retinol-binding protein concentrations in the plasma of preruminant calves. *J Dairy Sci* 84: 641–648.

Nozière, P., B. Graulet, A. Lucas, B. Martin, P. Grolier & M. Doreau. 2006. Review: Carotenoids for ruminants: From forages to dairy products. *Anim Feed Sci Technol* 131: 418–450.

NRC. 1979. *Nutrient Requirements of Swine*. 8th Edition. National Academy of Science, National Research Council, Washington, DC. pp. 157

NRC. 1987. *Vitamin Tolerance of Domestic Animals*. Washington DC. Natl. Academ. Press.

NRC. 1989. *Nutrient Requirements of Dairy Cattle*. 6th Rev. Ed. Washington DC. Natl. Academ. Press.

NRC. 1996. *Nutrient Requirements of Beef Cattle*. 7th Rev. Ed. Washington DC. Natl. Academ. Press.

NRC. 2001. *Nutrient Requirements of Dairy Cattle*. 7th Rev. Ed. Washington DC. Natl. Academ. Press.

Oldham, E. R., R. J. Eberhart & L. D. Muller. 1991. Effects of supplemental vitamin A or carotene during the dry period and early lactation on udder health. *J Dairy Sci* 74: 3775.

Overfield, J. R. & E. E. Hatfield. 1976. Dietary niacin for steers fed corn silage diets. *J Anim Sci* 43: 329.

Padilla, L., T. Matsui, Y. Kamiya, M. Kamiya, M. Tanaka & H. Yano. 2006. Heat stress decreases plasma vitamin C concentration in lactating cows. *Livest Sci* 101: 300–304.

Patterson, H. H., P. S. Johnson, T. R. Patterson, D. B. Young & R. Haigh. 2002. Effects of water quality on performance and health of growing steers. *Proc West Sec Amer Soc Anim Sci* 53:217–220.

Piepenbrink, M. S. & T. R. Overton. 2003. Liver metabolism and production of cows fed increasing amounts of rumen-protected choline during the periparturient period. *J Dairy Sci* 86(1):1722–1733.

Pinotti, L., A. Baldi & V Dell'Orto. 2002. Comparative mammalian choline metabolism with emphasis on the high-yielding dairy cow. *Nutr Res Rev* 15:315–331.

Pinotti, L, A. Baldi, I. Politis, R. Rebucci, L. Sangalli & V. Dell'Orto. 2003. Rumen-protected choline administration to transition cows: effects on milk production and vitamin E status. *J Vet Med A Physiol Pathol Clin Med* 50:18–21.

Pinotti, L., A. Campagnoli, V. Dell'Orto & A. Baldi. 2005. Choline: Is there a need in the lactating dairy cow? *Livest Prod Sci* 98: 149–152.

Pires, J. A. A. & R. R. Grummer. 2007. The use of nicotinic acid to induce sustained low plasma nonesterified fatty acids in feed-restricted holstein cows. *J Dairy Sci* 90:3725–3732.

Politis, I., M. Hiridoglou, T. R. Batra, J. A. Gilmore, R. C. Gorewit & H. Scherf. 1995. Effects of vitamin E on immune function of dairy cows. *Vet Res* 56: 2

Politis, I., M. Hiridoglou, J. H. White, J. A. Gilmore, S. N. Williams, H. Scherf & M. Frigg. 1996. Effects of vitamin E on mammary and blood leukocyte function, with emphasis on chemotaxis, in periparturient dairy cows. *Am J Vet Res* 57: 468.

Potanski, A. A., R. E. Tucker, G. E. Mitchell Jr. & G. T. Schelling. 1974. Pre-intestinal losses of carotene in sheep fed high-starch or high-cellulose diets. *Int J Vit Nutr Res* 44.

Pottier, J., M. Focant, C. Debier, G. De Buysser, C. Goffe, E. Mignolet, E. Froidmont & Y. Larondelle. 2006. Effect of dietary vitamin E on rumen biohydrogenation pathways and milk fat depression in dairy cows fed high-fat diets. *J Dairy Sci* 89:685–692

Pötzsch, C. J., V. J. Hedges, R. W. Blowey, A. J. Packington & L. E. Green. 2003. The impact of parity and duration of biotin supplementation on white line disease lameness in dairy cattle. *J Dairy Sci* 86:2577–2582.

Priolo, A., D. Micol, J. Agabriel, S. Prache & E. Dransfield. 2002. Effect of grass or concentrate feeding systems on lamb carcass and meat quality. *Meat Science* 62: 179–185.

Puvogel, G., C. R. Baumrucker, H. Sauerwein, R. Rühl, E. Ontsouka, H. M. Hammon & J. W. Blum. 2005. Effects of an enhanced vitamin A intake during the dry period on retinoids, lactoferrin, IGF-system mammary gland epithelial cell apoptosis and subsequent lactation in dairy cows. *J Dairy Sci* 88: 1785–1800.

Puvogel, G., C. Baumrucker & J. W. Blum. 2008. Plasma vitamin A status in calves fed colostrum from cows that were fed vitamin A during late pregnancy. *J Anim Physiol Anim Nut* 92: 614–620.

Ragaller, V., L. Hüther & P. Lebzien. 2008. Folic acid in ruminant nutrition: a review. *Br J Nut* 1–12. doi: 10.1017/S0007114508051556

Rakes, A. H., M. P. Owens, J. H. Britt & L. W. Whitlow. 1985. Effects of adding beta-carotene to rations of lactating cows consuming different forages. *J Dairy Sci* 68: 1732.

Ranjan, R., D. Swarup, R. Naresh & R. C. Patra. 2005. Ameliorative potential of L-ascorbic acid in bovine clinical mastitis. *Indian J Anim Sci* 75:174–177.

Reddy, P.G., J.L. Morrill, H.C. Minocha, M.B. Morrill, A.D. Dayton, and R.A. Frey (1986) Effect of supplemental vitamin E on the immune system of calves. J. Dairy Sci. 69:164.

Reddy, P.G., J.L. Morrll, H.C. Minocha, and J.S. Stevenson (1987) Vitamin E is immunostimulatory in calves. J. Dairy Sci. 70:993.

Reffett, J. K., J. W. Spears & T. T. Brown. 1988. Effect of dietary selenium and vitamin E on the primary and secondary immune response in lambs challenged with parainfluenza3 virus. *J Anim Sci* 66: 1520.

Reinhardt, T. A. & F. G. Hustmyer. 1987. Role of vitamin D in the immune system. *J Dairy Sci* 70: 952.

Ridell, D. O., E. E. Bartley & A. D. Dayton.1980. Effect of nicotinic acid on rumen fermentation in vitro and in vivo. *J Dairy Sci* 63: 1429.

Rode L. M., T. A. McAllister & K. J. Cheng. 1990. Microbial degradation of vitamin A in rumen fluid from steers fed concentrate, hay or straw diets. *Can J Anim Sci* 70: 227.

Rosendo, O., D. B. Bates, L. R. McDowell, C. R. Staples, R. McMahon & N. S. Wilkinson. 2003. Availability and ability of biotin for promoting forage fiber in vitro ruminal digestibility. *J Anim Vet Adv* 2: 350–357.

Rosendo, O., C. R. Staples, L. R. McDowell, R. McMahon, L. Badinga, F. G. Martin, J. F. Shearer, W. M. Seymour & N. S. Wilkinson. 2004. Effects of biotin supplementation on peripartum performance and metabolites of Holstein cows. *J Dairy Sci* 87: 2535–2545.

Roth, J. A. & M. L. Kaeberle. 1985. In vivo effect of ascorbic acid on netrophil functions in healthy and dexamethasone-treated cattle. *Am J Vet Res* 46: 2434.

Rousseau, Jr, J. E., H. D. Eaton, C. F. Helmbolt, E. L. Hunghers, S. A. Robrish, G. Beall & L. A. Moore. 1954. Relative value of carotene and vitamin A from a dry carrier fed at minimum levels to Holstein calves. *J Dairy Sci* 37: 889.

Rumsey T. S. 1985. Effect of choline in all concentrate diets of feedlot steers and on rumen acidosis. Can. *J Anim Sci* 65: 135.

Sacadura, F. C., P. H. Robinson, E. Evans & M. Lordelo. 2008. Effects of a ruminally protected B-vitamin supplement on milk yield and composition of lactating dairy cows. *Anim Feed SciTechnol* 144: 111–124.

Santschi, D. E., J. Chiquette, R. Berthiaume, R. Martineau, J. J. Matte, A. F. Mustafa & C. L. Girard. 2005a. Effects of the forage to concentrate ratio on B-vitamin concentrations in different ruminal fractions of dairy cows. *Can J Anim Sci* 85:389–399.

Santschi, D. E., R. Berthiaume, J. J. Matte, A. F. Mustafa & C. L. Girard. 2005a. Fate of supplementary B-vitamins in the gastrointestinal tract of dairy cows. *J Dairy Sci* 8:2043–2054.

Schwab, E. C. & R. D. Shaver. 2005. B-vitamin nutrition in dairy cows. In Proc. Cornell Nutr. Conf., Syracuse, NY. Available at: http://www.wisc.edu/dysci/uwex/nutritn/pubs/ psubvitsfinalver805.pdf.

Schwab, E. C., C. G. Schwab, R. D. Shaver, C. L. Girard & D. E. Putnam. 2006. Dietary forage and nonfiber carbohydrate contents influence B-vitamin intake, duodenal flow, and apparent ruminal synthesis in lactating dairy cows. *J Dairy Sci* 89:174–187.

Segerson, E. C., G. J. Riviere, H. L. Dalton & M. D. Whitacre. 1981. Retained placenta of Holstein cows treated with selenium and vitamin E. *J Dairy Sci* 64: 1833.

Seymour, W. M. 2000. Biotin, hoof health and milk production in dairy cows. In: 12th Annual Florida Ruminant Nutrition Symposium, FL, USA. 70–78.

Seymour, W. M. 2004. In: Recent developments in vitamin nutrition of dairy cattle. Proc. Intermountain Nut. Conf. Available at: http://www.dsm.com/ enUS/downloads/dnpus/seymour_dairy1.pdf. 43–64.

Sharma, B. K. & R. A. Erdman. 1988. Effects of high amounts of dietary choline supplementation on duodenal choline flow and production responses of dairy cows. *J Dairy Sci* 71: 2670.

Sharma, B. K. & R. A. Erdman. 1989. In vitro degradation of choline from selected feedstuffs and choline supplements. *J Dairy Sci* 72: 2772.

Shaver, R. D. & M. A. Bal. 2000. Effect of dietary thiamin supplementation on milk production by dairy cows. *J Dairy Sci* 83: 2335–2340.

Smith, K. L., H. R. Conrad, B. A. Amiet & D. A. Todhunter. 1984. Incidence of environmental mastitis as influenced by vitamin E and selenium. *Kiel. Milchwirstsch. Forschungsber* 37: 482.

Smith, K. L., H. R. Conrad, A. Amiet, P. S. Schoenberger & D. A. Todhunter. 1985. Effect of vitamin E and selenium dietary supplementation on mastitis in first lactation dairy cows. *J Dairy Sci* 68(Suppl. 1): 190.

Spears, J. W. 2000. Micronutrients and immune function in cattle. *Proc Nut Soc* 59, 587–594.

Stemme, K., P. Lebzien, G. Flachowsky & H. Scholz. 2008. The influence of an increased cobalt supply on ruminal parameters and microbial vitamin B_{12} synthesis in the rumen of dairy cows. *Arch Anim Nut* 62: 207–218.

Stobo, I. J. F. 1983. Milk replacers for calves.

In Recent advances in animal nutrition. London: Butterworths. 113.

Stowe, H. D., J. W. Thomas, T. Johnson, J. V. Marteniuk, D. A. Morrow & D. E. Ullrey. 1988. Responses of dairy cattle to long term and short term supplementation with oral selenium and vitamin E. *J Dairy Sci* 71: 1830.

Sutton, A. L. & J. M. Elliot. 1972. Effect of ration of roughage to concentrate and level of feed intake on ovine ruminal vitamin B_{12} production. *J Nutr* 102: 1341.

Swanson, E. W., G. G. Martin, F. E. Pardue & G. M. Gorman. 1968. Milk production of cows fed diets deficient in vitamin A. *J Anim Sci* 57: 541.

Swanson, K. S., N. R. Merchen, J. W. Erdman Jr., J. K. Drackley, F. Orias, D. E. Morin & M. F. Haddad. 2000. Influence of vitamin A concentrations and health in preruminant Holstein calves fed milk replacer. *J Dairy Sci* 83: 2027.

Swensson, C. & H. Lindmark-Månsson. 2007. The prospect of obtaining beneficial mineral and vitamin contents in cow's milk through feed. *J Anim Feed Sci* 16(Suppl.): 21–41.

Taylor, M. S., K. F. Knowlton, M. L. McGilliard, W. M. Seymour & J. H. Herbein. 2008. Blood mineral, hormone, and osteocalcin responses of multiparous jersey cows to an oral dose of 25–hydroxyvitamin D_3 or vitamin D_3 before parturition. *J Dairy Sci* 91: 2408–2416.

Thafvelin, B. & H. E. Oksanen. 1966. Vitamin E and linolenic acid content of hays as related to different drying conditions. *J Dairy Sci* 49: 282.

Tjoelker, L. W., B. P. Chew, T. S. Tanaka & L. R. Daniel. 1988. Bovine vitamin A and beta-carotene intake and lactational status. 2. Responsiveness of mitogen stimulated peripheral blood lymphocytes to vitamin A and beta-carotene challenge in vitro. *J Dairy Sci* 71: 3120.

Tjoelker, L. W., B. P. Chew, T. S. Tanaka & L. R. Daniel. 1990. Effect of vitamin A and beta carotene on polymorphonuclear leukocyte and lymphocyte function in dairy cows during the early dry period. *J Dairy Sci* 73: 1017.

Tramontano, W. A., D. Ganci, M. Pennio & E. S. Dierenfeld. 1993. Distribution of α-tocopherol in early foliage samples in several forage crops. *Phytochem* 34: 389.

Ullrey, D. E. 1972. Biological availability of fat-soluble vitamins: vitamin A and carotene. *J Anim Sci* 35: 648.

Van Saun, R. J., T. H. Herdt & H. D. Stowe. 1989. Maternal and fetal vitamin E interrelationship in dairy cattle. *J Nutr* 119: 1156.

Vinet, C., H. R. Conrad, T. A. Reinhardt & R. L. Horst. 1985. Minimal requirements for vitamin D in lactating cows. *Fed Proc* 28: 549.

Walker, C. K. & J. M. Elliot. 1972. Lactational trends in vitamin B_{12} status on conventional and restricted roughage rations. *J Dairy Sci* 55: 474.

Wang, J. Y., F. G. Owen & L. L. Larson. 1988. Effect of beta-carotene supplementation on reproductive performance of lactating Holstein cows. *J Dairy Sci* 71: 181.

Ward, G., R. C. Dobson & J. R. Dunham. 1972. Influences of calcium and phosphorus intakes, vitamin D supplement, and lactation on calcium and phosphorus balances. *J Dairy Sci* 55: 768.

Warner, R. L., G. E. Mitchell Jr., C. O. Little & N. E. Alderson. 1970. Pre-intestinal disappearance of vitamin A in steers fed different levels of corn. *Int J Vit Res* 40: 585.

Waterman, R., J. W. Schwalm & L. H. Schultz. 1972. Nicotinic acid treatment of bovine ketosis. I. Effects on circulatory metabolites and interrelationships. *J Dairy Sci* 55: 1447.

Weiss, J. P. 2007. An update on vitamins for dairy cattle. In: Proc. Southeast Dairy Herd Management Conference. Available at: http://www.ads.uga.edu/extension/dairycattle/documents/MasterSEDHM2007.pdf. 17–29.

Weiss, W. P. & G. Fereira. 2006b. Are your cows getting the vitamins that they need? WCDS Advances in Dairy Technology. 18: 249–259. Available at: http://www.wcds.afns.ualberta.ca/Proceedings/2006/Manuscripts/Weiss2.pdf.

Weiss, W. P. 1998. Requirements of fat-soluble vitamins for dairy cows: a review. *J Dairy Sci* 81: 2493.

Weiss, W. P. 2005. Antioxidant nutrients, cow health, and milk quality. Penn State Dairy Cattle Nutrition Workshop. 11–18.

Weiss, W P. & G. Ferreira. 2006a. Water soluble vitamins for dairy cattle. Tri-State Dairy Nutrition Conference. Ohio, USA. 51–63. Available at: http://tristatedairy. osu.edu/Weiss.pdf.

Weiss, W. P. & J. S. Hogan. 2007. Effects of dietary vitamin C on neutrophil function and responses to intramammary infusion of lipopolysaccharide in periparturient dairy cows. *J Dairy Sci* 90: 731–739.

383

Weiss, W. P. & D. J. Wyatt. 2003. Effect of dietary fat and vitamin E on α-tocopherol in milk from dairy cows. *J Dairy Sci* 86:3582–3591.

Weiss, W. P., D. A. Todhunter, J. S. Hogan & K. L. Smith. 1990b. Effect of duration of supplementation of selenium and vitamin E on periparturient dairy cows. *J Dairy Sci* 73: 3187-3194.

Weiss, W.P., J.S. Hogan, K.L. Smith, and K.H. Hoblet 1990a. Relationships among selenium, vitamin E and mammary gland health in commercial dairy herds. J. Dairy Sci. 73:381-390.

Weiss, W.P., D.A. Todhunter, J.S. Hogan and K.L. Smith (1990b) Effect of duration of supplementation of selenium and vitamin E on periparturient dairy cows. J. Dairy Sci. 73:3187-3194.

Weiss, W. P., J. S. Hogan, K. L. Smith, D. A. Todhunter & S. N. Williams. 1992. Effect of supplementing parturient cows with vitamin E on distribution of α-tocopherol in blood. *J Dairy Sci* 75: 3479.

Weiss, W. P., J. S. Hogan, K. L. Smith & S. N. Williams. 1994. Effect of dietary fat and vitamin E on tocopherol and carotene in blood of peripartum cows. *J Dairy Sci* 77: 1422.

Weiss, W. P., K. L. Smith, J. S. Hogan & T. E. Steine. 1995. Effect of forage to concentrate ratio on disappearance of vitamins A and E during in vitro ruminal fermentation. *J Dairy Sci* 78: 1837.

Weiss, W. P., J. S. Hogan, D. A. Todhunter & K. L. Smith. 1997. Effect of vitamin E supplementation in diets with a low concentration of selenium on mammary gland health of dairy cows. *J Dairy Sci* 80: 1728.

Weiss, W. P., J. S. Hogan & K. L. Smith. 2004. Changes in vitamin C concentrations in plasma and milk from dairy cows after an intramammary infusion of *Escherichia coli*. *J Dairy Sci* 87: 32–37.

Williams, P. E. V., N. Ballet & J. C. Robert. 1998. A review of the provision of vitamins for ruminants. Proceedings of the Preconference Symposium of the Cornell Nutrition Conference 1998. Provision of Vitamins and Amino Acids for Ruminants, Rhône Poulenc Animal Nutrition, Antony, France. 7–37.

Wing, J. M. 1969. Effect of source and season on apparent digestibility of carotene in forage by cattle. *J Dairy Sci* 52: 479.

Yeum, K., A. L. Due, A. F. Smith, N. E. Krinoky & R. M. Russel. 2000. The effect of α-tocopherol on oxidative cleavage of beta carotene. *Free Radic Biol* 29: 105–114.

Yonekura, L. & A. Nagao. 2007. Intestinal absorption of dietary carotenoids. *Molecular Nutrition & Food Research* 51: 107–115.

Zahra, L. C., T. F. Duffield, K. E. Leslie, T. R. Overton, D. Putnam & S. J. LeBlanc. 2006. Effects of rumen-protected choline and monensin on milk production and metabolism of periparturient dairy cows. *J Dairy Sci* 89: 4808–4818.

Zamora, R., F. J. Hidalgo & A. L. Tappel. 1991. Comparative antioxidant effectiveness of dietary beta carotene, vitamin E, selenium and coenzyme Q10 in rat erythrocytes and plasma. *J Nutr* 121: 50.

Zanker, I. A., H. M. Hammon & J. W. Blum. 2000. Beta-carotene, retinol and alpha-tocopherol status in calves fed the first colostrum at 0–2, 6–7, 12–13 or 24–25 hours after birth. *Int J Vitam Nutr Res* 70:305–310.

Zeisel, S. H. 1993. Choline phospholipids: signal transduction and carcinogenesis. FASEB J. 7:551–557.

Zempleni, J., R. B. Rucker, D. B. McCormick, & J. W. Suttie. 2006. Handbook of vitamins ed. by Robert B. Rucker, John W. Suttie, Donald B. McCormick and Lawrence J. Machlin. 4th ed. CRC Press, Boca Ratón Fl. USA. p. 593.

Zempleni J. Handbook of vitamins (2007) Publisher: Boca Raton : Taylor & Francis.

Zimmerly, C.A., and W.P. Weiss. 2001. Effects of supplemental biotin on performance of Holstein cows in early lactation. J. Dairy Sci. 84: 498-506.

Zimmerman, C. A., A. H. Rakes, T. E. Daniel & B. A. Hopkins. 1992. Influence of dietary protein and supplemental niacin on lactational performance of cows fed normal and low fiber diets. *J Dairy Sci* 75: 1965.

Zinn R. A. 1992. B-Vitamins in beef cattle nutrition. In: Takeda Technical Symposium. 53rd Minnesota Nutrition Conference. September 21, 1992.

Zinn R. A., F. N. Owens, R. L. Stuart, J. R. Dunbar & B. B. Norman. 1987. B-Vitamin supplementation of diets for feedlot calves. *J Anim Sci* 65: 267–277.